D1703304

THE CODES
GUIDEBOOK FOR
INTERIORS

THE CODES GUIDEBOOK FOR INTERIORS

Eighth Edition

Katherine E. Kennon
Sharon K. Harmon

INTERNATIONAL CODE COUNCIL®

WILEY

This book is printed on acid-free paper.

Copyright © 2022 by John Wiley & Sons, Inc. All rights reserved

Published by John Wiley & Sons, Inc., Hoboken, New Jersey

Published simultaneously in Canada

No part of this publication may be reproduced, stored in a retrieval system, or transmitted in any form or by any means, electronic, mechanical, photocopying, recording, scanning, or otherwise, except as permitted under Section 107 or 108 of the 1976 United States Copyright Act, without either the prior written permission of the Publisher, or authorization through payment of the appropriate per-copy fee to the Copyright Clearance Center, 222 Rosewood Drive, Danvers, MA 01923, (978) 750-8400, fax (978) 646-8600, or on the web at www.copyright.com. Requests to the Publisher for permission should be addressed to the Permissions Department, John Wiley & Sons, Inc., 111 River Street, Hoboken, NJ 07030, (201) 748-6011, fax (201) 748-6008, or online at www.wiley.com/go/permissions.

Limit of Liability/Disclaimer of Warranty: While the publisher and author have used their best efforts in preparing this book, they make no representations or warranties with the respect to the accuracy or completeness of the contents of this book and specifically disclaim any implied warranties of merchantability or fitness for a particular purpose. No warranty may be created or extended by sales representatives or written sales materials. The advice and strategies contained herein may not be suitable for your situation. You should consult with a professional where appropriate. Neither the publisher nor the author shall be liable for damages arising herefrom.

For general information about our other products and services, please contact our Customer Care Department within the United States at (800) 762-2974, outside the United States at (317) 572-3993 or fax (317) 572-4002.

Wiley publishes in a variety of print and electronic formats and by print-on-demand. Some material included with standard print versions of this book may not be included in e-books or in print-on-demand. If this book refers to media such as a CD or DVD that is not included in the version you purchased, you may download this material at http://booksupport.wiley.com. For more information about Wiley products, visit www.wiley.com.

Library of Congress Cataloging-in-Publication Data

Names: Kennon, Katherine E., author. | John Wiley & Sons, publisher.
Title: Codes guidebook for interiors / Katherine E. Kennon.
Description: Eighth edition. | Hoboken, New Jersey : Wiley, [2022] |
  Includes index.
Identifiers: LCCN 2021021348 (print) | LCCN 2021021349 (ebook) | ISBN
  9781119720959 (cloth) | ISBN 9781119720973 (adobe pdf) | ISBN
  9781119720966 (epub)
Subjects: LCSH: Building laws—United States. |
  Buildings—Specifications—United States. | Interior
  architecture—Specifications—United States. | LCGFT: Model acts.
Classification: LCC KF5701 .H37 2021 (print) | LCC KF5701 (ebook) | DDC
  343.7307/8624—dc23
LC record available at https://lccn.loc.gov/2021021348
LC ebook record available at https://lccn.loc.gov/2021021349

Cover Design: Wiley
Cover Image: © Getty Images/E+/ExperienceInteriors
Printed and bound by CPI Group (UK) Ltd, Croydon, CR0 4YY

C110058_210222

This book is dedicated to the men in my life, James, Drake and Noel who continue to encourage me in my interests and endeavors. And a special thanks to Mr. Darcy for his constant companionship on my desk.

CONTENTS

INSET INDEX

PREFACE

Codes and standards continue to change and evolve. Even federal regulations are amended and updated. Why does this seem like a never-ending process? Because it *is* a never-ending process. The various organizations and individuals that develop the regulations continue to evaluate our interaction with buildings, the way we build them, and what we put in them; then, they propose and implement changes to the requirements to make buildings safer and better for us. Thus, we want codes, standards, and federal regulations to change to be consistent with what we, as a society, feel is a reasonable level of safety and health. So, you can view the regulations that we will discuss in this book as a codified form of expectations for the built environment to protect us and not harm us. That is why there is ongoing discussion and change.

Codes change for wide array of reasons and in response to a variety of events. Evaluations of recent building fires, natural disasters, and even acts of terrorism shed light on how building safety can be improved. Industry trends, new building products, and improved technology provide new options for addressing building safety. In addition to concerns about safety, changing ideals for the health, quality, and equitability of our environments drive changes in sustainability, energy efficiency, and accessibility requirements to name a few. In the future editions of the codes, we will most likely see evidence of what we have learned from a recent world pandemic that affects our desire for health and safety in our buildings. In many cases, each concern has a separate advocate group and results directly in code requirements. But the increase in collaboration between groups is helping to minimize redundant efforts that can create conflicts between requirements or redundant codes. Regardless, the ongoing changes challenge design professionals to stay up-to-date.

This book concentrates on the interior of a building because every building has an interior. As you will see, the majority of codes, regulations, and federal requirements will apply to all interior projects. Even if the building is being developed as a core and shell for future tenants, it must be designed to meet codes and with all the issues addressed in this book in mind. If the exterior and interior are being developed as single project, these codes, standards, and federal regulations apply in a more specific way. And, if the interior of an existing building (apart from the exterior) is being renovated, redesigned, or restored, both the key and detailed requirements must be revisited.

This book, however, does not take the place of the various code publications. The requirements are too detailed and complex. The goal of this book is to introduce the key code concepts and to make an identifiable path through the various codes, standards, and federal regulations.

What sets this book apart is that it does more than just repeat the code requirements; it explains how the requirements and concepts behind the requirements work together to produce a building that protects the health, safety, and welfare of its occupants. This book is also unique in that it considers the requirements from more than one code publication and organization. It discusses the relationship of these documents and indicates how different requirements may overlap in a single project. Understanding the terms and overall concepts behind the codes as well as the specific requirements make safer buildings. When the objectives are clear, the code research process can be more efficient and allow more time for the design process. This eighth edition of *The Codes Guidebook for Interiors* includes the most recent changes and updates to the codes, standards, and federal regulations. The following previews what is included.

❑ Focuses on the most current and widely used building code, the *International Building Code (IBC)* as well as other related International Code Council (ICC) codes, such as the *International Fire Code*, *International Plumbing Code* and *International Mechanical Code*. This edition of the book addresses the 2018 and 2021 cycles of these code publications.

❑ Discusses how to use the *NFPA 101*, also known as the *Life Safety Code (LSC)* in conjunction with the *IBC*. These documents overlap on various code topics including occupancy classifications, means of egress, fire resistant assemblies, and finish/furniture requirements. This edition of the book addresses the 2018 and 2021 cycles of the NFPA code publications.

❑ Incorporates information on standards referenced by the codes or used by the building and interior industry.

❑ Integrates the most up-to-date accessibility requirements including the *2010 ADA Standards* and *2017 ICC A117.1*. Each chapter highlights the similarities and differences in these guidelines based on the chapter topic.

❑ Addresses the influence of sustainability and green practices and the various green codes and standards, including the *International Green Construction Code (IgCC)* and the *ASHRAE/USGBC/IES 189.1, Standard for the Design of High-Performance Green Buildings Except Low-Rise Residential Buildings*.

❑ Describes the relationship between the energy codes, such as the *International Energy Conservation Code (IECC)*, sustainability codes, and federal energy regulations, and the *IBC*.

❑ Includes interior-related electrical code requirements based on the 2017 and the 2020 *National Electrical Code (NEC)*.

❑ Discusses current interior finish and furniture standards and testing required by the *IBC, IFC, NFPA 101*, and seen as industry best practices. Enhanced discussions on requirements for decorative and acoustic material applications.

❑ Explains the role of alternative materials and methods and performance codes to allow creative options for providing safety with innovative approaches and accommodating challenging existing conditions.

❑ Includes multiple examples and sample floor plans covering a wide variety of building types and occupancy classifications.

❑ Includes diagrams combining code and accessibility-related requirements for elements such as means of egress, toilet and bathing rooms, and finish- and furniture-related items.

❑ Discusses good practices and changing expectations for collaborating with code officials in the design process.

❑ Provides information that is applicable to a variety of interior project types, new construction, renovation, and tenant build out, both large and small.

❑ Appendixes provide information specifically for existing buildings, historic buildings, and single-family homes.

❑ New to this edition, the 'Research' section of each chapter, guides you to the specific codes, chapters and sections in the pertinent code publications for your research.

❑ To assist in documentation of your code research, digital code check lists are available with the purchase of this book. The individual checklists can be downloaded and used to document your code research and help you to apply the correct requirements to your projects. Instructions for the use of these interactive checklists are given at the end of each chapter.

❑ If you are an instructor and are using this as a textbook, there are PowerPoint presentations and suggestions for classroom activities available in the *Instructor's Manual*. These are available online as part of your purchase of this book. A companion *Study Guide* can be purchased separately. This contains word bank, application exercises, and short answer questions per chapter that can be used for class activities, work outside of the classroom, or as test applications.

❑ If you are a design student, recent graduate, pre-professional studying for your professional exam, flash cards and similar study materials are available online with the purchase of this book. You also may find the *Study Guide* to be a valuable resource to test your understanding of the terms, concepts, and requirements presented in this book.

Whatever your reason for opening this book, I hope that you find it helpful to you.

Katherine E. Kennon, AIA

ACKNOWLEDGMENTS

I am often asked how I became interested and subsequently so involved with building codes and accessibility issues. I always relate it back to an event early in my professional career. It began with a sign-up sheet circulating around the office with an offer to attend a code seminar compliments of the firm. At the time, not knowing a whole lot about codes from the brief introduction in design school and wanting to take advantage of the free education, I signed up. Days later, my boss, Richard Butcosk, called me into his office. He was wondering why I wanted to go to a code seminar, considering that I had been hired to be part of the design team, not particularly because of such pragmatic interests. My response was that if not being familiar with code requirements could negatively affect my designs, then I viewed them as critical design information. I was allowed to attend, the first of many. Shortly after that, the Americans with Disability Act was passed and again another series of seminars. And so began an interest intertwined in my design career.

Later, I taught a design studio class that integrated the teaching of codes and accessibility as related to a commercial project. This led to me meeting Sharon K. Harmon, who was the author of the assigned textbook. That book was the first edition of what was to become this book. Beginning with the second edition, Sharon and I became coauthors of the book. She has now moved onto a different emphasis in her career, and starting with the sixth edition, the book has been my opportunity to continue to present codes and accessibility issues to design students and designers (architects and interior designers). The common thread continues to be the importance of knowing code and accessibility requirements as we design buildings, particularly their interior layout and components.

For the book to continue to be relevant and accurate, having industry professionals give perspective on the content is essential. I luckily find people willing to take the time to read, comment, and make suggestions on sections and chapters within their professional purview. For this edition, I want to thank Lisa Ballard (electrical), Shaw Coleman (mechanical), Ricky Bost (plumbing/fire protection), and Joe Maddox (communication technology.)

I want to thank the International Code Council (ICC) and National Fire Protection Association (NFPA), who continue to allow the use of their source material and to clarify code requirements so that they can be accurately represented in this text.

I want to thank the building and associated industry representatives who continue to allow the use of their images and products such APCO Graphics, Steelcraft Manufacturing, Underwriters Laboratories, and ACT. They make it possible to give real examples and images of code-related elements.

Even though this book is on its eighth edition, the creation of the final product is continually redefined by new technologies, processes, and people. For perspective, the submission process for the second edition involved a large amount of paper and shipping time (and expense) for the physical delivery of the edited material: now, the process occurs instantaneously and completely through cyberspace. So, for this edition, I specifically appreciate Kalli Schultea, Amy Odem, and Todd Green at John Wiley & Sons, Inc., who helped me through nuances of the process for this edition. I thank Susan Geraghty, who after I had read the revision so many times, I couldn't see the words clearly, read the text with care and fine- tuned it to its present completeness. I appreciate all those at John Wiley who continue to be advocates for this book, to value its unique place in the industry, and who have been integral to its development, past and present.

I would particularly like to thank the readers, who continue to buy and recommend the book. Whether you use this book as a student, educator, or for your own personal professional development, your feedback and support of the book is what motivates me to keep this endeavor up-to-date and pertinent to the industry. I hope that this relationship continues to benefit the design community and safe building environments.

HOW TO USE THIS BOOK

Codes, standards, and federal regulations are an essential part of designing buildings. This book is intended to help whether you are an interior designer, architect, engineer, builder, building owner, or facility manager. Although most of the code publications address the entire building—exterior and interior—this book concentrates on the codes that pertain to the interior of a building. *The Codes Guidebook for Interiors* is designed help you understand the system of code requirements and to help determine which codes and regulations apply whether you are space planning the interior of a new building, designing a new tenant space in part of a building, or making some minor changes in an existing building. This will help you to minimize your research time. Incorporating these requirements into the design should become a natural part of every interior project. I hope that it will also make the many interior codes, standards, and federal regulations more user-friendly.

In this eighth edition of the *Codes Guidebook*, each section has been updated to inform you of the most current interior-related codes, standards, and federal regulations. Referencing both the 2018 and 2021 editions of the codes, this book concentrates on the requirements of the *International Building Code* and the *Life Safety Code*, two of the most widely used codes. However the parallel and prominent NFPA codes are also discussed. Most chapters also discuss interior-related information from the fire codes, the electrical and energy-related codes, and the plumbing and mechanical codes. The most current accessibility and sustainability requirements are discussed including the *2010 ADA Standards*.

It is suggested that you read through the book systematically at least once. In this way, you can get an overall understanding of how the various codes, standards, and regulations work during the progression of a design. Then you may refer to each individual chapter as needed to clarify or be reminded about the codes that address that part of the project. To help you understand the application of specific requirements, multiple examples, explanatory diagrams, and checklists are provided in each chapter.

Note

This book deals with interior codes only. Unless otherwise noted, it is assumed that the exterior walls—including doors and windows—and the existing shell of the building are either existing or already determined.

TERMS TO KNOW

Certain terms when used by the codes have specific meanings. Sometimes these meanings are different than how we may use them in our typical conversation. For example, although the terms *corridor, passageway,* and *hallway* may be somewhat interchangeable in our daily language, they are very different in code language. It is important to understand the specific definition of terms when using the codes. Each code typically has a chapter of terms used in the code to clarify how each term in defined. You may want to check the code specific definition of the terms used in this book. Many are defined in the glossary in the back of the book. Here are some common terms used throughout this book.

ACCESSIBLE: Unless otherwise noted, this term refers to areas, products, or devices usable by persons with disabilities, as required by the codes, federal legislation such as the Americans with Disabilities Act, and other accessibility standards.

AUTHORITY HAVING JURISDICTION (AHJ): Used by the code organizations to indicate organizations, offices, or individuals that administer and enforce the codes. In this book, we designate these as *code jurisdictions, code departments,* and *code officials,* respectively.

CODE OFFICIAL: Also known as a *building official*; an employee of a codes department who has the authority to interpret, administer, and enforce the codes, standards, and regulations within that jurisdiction. A code official can have several different titles, including plans examiner, building inspector, and, sometimes, fire marshal. Also generally referred to as the AHJ by the codes.

CODES DEPARTMENT: A local government agency that administers and enforces the codes within a jurisdiction. Some small jurisdictions may have a codes department that consists of only one person or code official, and some large jurisdictions may include many different agencies and departments. Also generally referred to as the AHJ by the codes.

GREEN DESIGN: Design of products, environments, and buildings that treats environmental attributes as an important design objective. It aims to minimize the potential harmful effects on human health and the environment by choosing eco-friendly building materials and construction practices. It may also include systems that increase the efficiency of a building so that it uses less materials, energy, and water. (See also Sustainable Design.)

JURISDICTION: A determined geographical area that uses the same codes, standards, and regulations. Each jurisdiction passes a law specifying which codes and standards are required and how they will be regulated. A jurisdiction can be as small as a township or as large as an entire state. The code jurisdiction of a project is determined by the location of the building. Also generally referred to as the AHJ by the codes.

PERFORMANCE CODE: A code that is more generally described and gives an objective but not specific instructions on how to achieve it. The focus is on the desired outcome, not a single solution, and compliance is based on meeting the criteria established by the performance code. (Engineering tools and methodologies are often used to substantiate the use of the code criteria.)

PRESCRIPTIVE CODE: A code providing a specific requirement that must be met for the design, construction, and maintenance of a building. The focus is on a specific solution to achieve an objective or outcome based on historical experience and established engineering. Historically, codes in the United States have been prescriptive in nature.

SUSTAINABLE DESIGN: More encompassing than green design, sustainability typically includes three main tenets: environmental responsibility, economic strength, and social responsibility. Buildings and spaces that incorporate sustainable design are designed to lessen their impact on the environment, stimulate the economy, and provide improvements to those involved in the development and the community.

> **✎ Note**
>
> Sustainable design and green design are not the same; sustainable design is more comprehensive.

USING CODES IN THE DESIGN PROCESS

The best time to research codes and use this book is in the early stages of a design project, preferably in the programming phase or schematic phase while the designs are still preliminary. It is especially advisable to review these requirements before construction documents are started and construction costs are estimated. Figure I.1 summarizes how the various phases of the typical design process relate to the steps taken during the suggested code review process. Refer to this chart as you work on a project to make sure you are covering the necessary code steps. (A more detailed flowchart of the code process is included in Chapter 11.) The *Codes Guidebook* is organized so that you can follow it while working on a design project from beginning to end, in the order in which you would typically research the codes.

ORGANIZATION OF THE BOOK

Chapter 1 in *The Codes Guidebook for Interiors* gives a brief history of codes and provides some background on each of the main code publications, federal regulations, and standards organizations. This edition concentrates

Design Process	Code Process	Description
Programming/Predesign	Preliminary Research	• Determine applicable codes, standards, and federal regulations. • Preliminary code research to determine important code issues such as occupancy type, occupancy load, etc. • Determine level of sustainability required: code, standard, rating system, and/or a green building program.
Schematic/Conceptual Design		• Incorporate code and sustainability compliance into design, keeping in mind means of egress, rated walls, etc.
Design Development	Preliminary Review	• Meet with code official to review conflicting code requirements (optional unless using performance codes, but could be helpful). • May also be done during Schematic Design Phase.
Construction Documents		• Check specific technical requirements such as aisle widths, stair dimensions, clearances, finish classifications. • Compare code, sustainability, and accessibility requirements. • Incorporate requirements into final design. • Specify and/or detail items as required to meet codes, standards, and federal requirements.
Bidding Process	Permitting Process	• Contractor applies for building permit.
Purchasing		• As items are ordered, confirm compliance with applicable codes and standards.
Construction Administration	Inspection Process	• Code officials review work by contractor to confirm that work complies with approved construction documents, including any incorporated performance and/or sustainability requirements.
Client Move-in	Final Inspection	• Final code approval of construction must occur before client can move in.
Post-Occupancy Evaluation		• Provide clients with documentation necessary for them to maintain building and/or contents as required for codes and standards (including performance and sustainability items).

Figure I.1 Comparison of design and code process.

on the International Codes® (I-Codes®) by the International Code Council (ICC) and a few NFPA codes including the *NFPA 101 Life Safety Code (LSC)* and the *National Electrical Code (NEC)*. Chapter 1 explains these individual codes. Chapter 1 is helpful in determining which codes and standards publications and which federal regulations apply to an interior project. Chapter 11, the last chapter in this book, discusses code officials and the code process. It describes how they work and how to work with them. If you are new to codes research, you may want to review Chapter 1 and Chapter 11 together to gain a basic understanding before reading the rest of the book.

Each of the remaining chapters pertains to a specific code concept and discusses the related code, standard, and federal requirements for that topic using the publications summarized in Chapter 1. The chapters have been organized in the order in which these issues are typically considered during an interior project. Once you have used Chapter 1 to determine which publications apply to your project, we suggest you research the codes the order presented by the book chapters.

Like the code publications, most of the chapters in this book build on and add to the preceding ones. For example, the occupancy classifications in Chapter 3 are important because many of the other codes are based on the occupancy of a building or space. Therefore, it is suggested that the first-time user read this book in the order in which it is written and use it as a guide while referencing the actual codes, standards, and federal publications. Each chapter in the book includes the most current code tables, realistic design examples, summary charts, helpful diagrams, and project checklists. Each chapter also includes relevant accessibility regulations, sustainability requirements, and performance code information.

An index is provided so that you can refer to specific topics of interest. As you become familiar with the codes, use the index and the table of contents to direct you to the section of the book that applies to a specific code issue. Then refer to the appropriate code, standard, and federal publication to get the specific details.

The appendixes in this book are intended to address additional code issues that may apply to your research or project. Appendix A addresses concepts pertaining to sustainability that are not currently required by the codes but may influence the development of a project. (See the section "Sustainability Requirements" later in this Introduction.)

Appendix B briefly describes the additional codes and regulations that may apply to existing and historic buildings. Most of this discussion concentrates on the requirements in the ICC *International Existing Building Code (IEBC)*, which, if adopted by the jurisdiction, may apply instead of the *IBC*. Special consideration is often given to historic buildings because they usually are subject to additional regulations on a local or even national level.

Appendix C briefly discusses codes relating to the interior of private residences. These residences (single-family or duplex structures) are regulated by a separate ICC code publication, the *International Residential Code (IRC)* instead of the *IBC*. Although the *Codes Guidebook* is primarily intended to cover codes and regulations that apply to commercial and public projects, some commercial residential occupancies are allowed to follow certain aspects of the *IRC*, so it is discussed briefly.

The bibliography for this book has been organized by topic to help you start or add to your personal reference library. The complete list can be found on the companion website, www.wiley.com/go/codesguide-book8e.

☑ Note

All codes can be divided into two types. In the past, most codes were considered *prescriptive-type* codes. These codes require specific compliance. The use of *performance-type* codes are increasing, which allows more than one solution to achieve acceptable results.

☑ Note

A project may be governed by more than one jurisdiction. For example, both a city and a state municipality may regulate a particular project.

☑ Note

When using the code tables, be sure to check all footnotes. They often specify extra conditions that may apply to a project.

AVAILABLE CODES AND STANDARDS

There are currently two main code organizations: the International Code Council (ICC), which publishes a comprehensive set of codes known as the International Codes, or I-Codes, and the National Fire Protection Association (NFPA), which publishes another set of codes known as the C3-Codes. The I-Codes continue to be the "family" of codes most widely used in the United States. At least one of the series has been adopted by a code jurisdiction in every US state. Often, several of the I-Codes are included in a jurisdiction's enforceable codes. In some cases, jurisdictions that had custom codes in the past have now adopted one of the I-Codes or modified it as their custom code. Although the *International Building Code* is more often chosen as the building code than the *NFPA 5000* (building) code, several of the NFPA codes are used as well. (See Chapter 1.)

Overall, this eighth edition of *The Codes Guidebook for Interiors* concentrates on the requirements and code tables from the 2018 and 2021 *International Building Code (IBC)*, as well as other current code publications from the ICC such as the *International Plumbing Code (IPC)* and the *International Energy Conservation Code (IECC)*. Because many jurisdictions also use NFPA's *Life Safety Code (LSC)* and *National Electrical Code (NEC)*, both of these codes are explained throughout this book in relation to the I-Codes. (See Chapter 1.)

Certain standards are referenced by the codes and, therefore, are required by a jurisdiction. Others have become standard practice to incorporate in a project, often for the health, safety, and/or welfare of the building occupants. Many of these standards are explained in this book. Some of them are explained in Chapter 1 as the various standards organizations are described; this includes standards by the ICC and the NFPA. Additional standards are discussed in other chapters based on the relevant topic.

PRESCRIPTIVE AND PERFORMANCE

Both the ICC and the NFPA now include performance criteria in addition to prescriptive requirements in their codes. (See preceding "Definitions" section.) The NFPA includes the performance-based requirements as a separate chapter within many of its publications. By contrast, the ICC produces a separate performance code publication that can be used in conjunction with its other codes when recognized by the code jurisdiction. Where a jurisdiction has not adopted the performance code, you have the option of using sections in the *International Building Code* that

☞ **Note**

Many jurisdictions throughout the United States are using the *International Building Code (IBC)* or a code based on the *IBC*.

☞ **Note**

When discussing prescriptive codes, the term *requirements* is often used. However, performance codes typically set *criteria*, *goals*, or *objectives*.

allow for some flexibility from the prescriptive code. The most common is titled *Section 104.11, Alternative Materials, Design and Methods of Construction and Equipment*. (See the subsection "Performance Codes" in Chapter 1.)

The performance codes are meant to be used in conjunction with the prescriptive codes. A project with an unusual design may require the use of a performance code. Most often performance-based criteria will be used for a particular part of the project and the standard prescriptive codes will be used for the rest. It would be unusual for an entire project to be designed using only performance codes. When a performance code requirement is used, there is more responsibility on the designer. Not only must the performance-related criteria be correctly documented but also it must be proven that these criteria are being met with the use of fire models, testing, and so on.

Various performance codes are mentioned in each chapter of this book as they relate to the corresponding prescriptive codes. Chapter 11 discusses how to document the use of performance codes for codes review. Ultimately, performance codes can be used to explore unique designs and allow for the use of new technology. Even if you do not typically use them, by becoming familiar with the various performance requirements you will gain more insight into the prescriptive codes. They will also give you insight into using *IBC Section 104.11*.

> **☑ Note**
>
> NFPA's *Life Safety Code* and *National Electrical Code* are widely used throughout the US.

ACCESSIBILITY REGULATIONS

Most interior projects are required to be designed to be accessible to persons with various disabilities. The building codes include accessibility requirements and reference the ICC accessibility standard *ICC A117.1*. In addition, federal laws require privately and federally owned buildings to be accessible based on individual standards. The ICC standard and the various federally required accessibility regulations are summarized in Chapter 1.

However, because accessibility affects all aspects of a design, accessibility standards and the ADA are also discussed throughout this book as they relate to each relevant topic. (The information focuses on the 2009 ICC standard and the *2010 ADA Standards*.) For example, accessible toilet facilities are discussed in the plumbing chapter (Chapter 8), and accessible ramps are discussed in the chapter on means of egress (Chapter 5). Like the codes discussed in this book, not every specific accessibility dimension and requirement has been mentioned. For specific requirements and additional information, you must still consult the ADA and its

> **☑ Note**
>
> Many of the diagrams in this book include code- and accessibility-related information.

> **☑ Note**
>
> With the adoption of the *2010 ADA Standards* by the Department of Justice (DOJ), the original *ADAAG* is now referred to as the *1991 ADA Standards*.

related guidelines or standards, specific chapters within the building codes, and any other accessibility regulations required by a jurisdiction. (When discrepancies are found between the ADA standards and ICC standard, the strictest requirements are typically discussed.)

SUSTAINABILITY REQUIREMENTS

> **✎ Note**
>
> *Universal design* is a term often used in relation to accessibility. However, universal design is more inclusive: It involves making sure a design considers the needs of different age groups as well as persons with disabilities.

Sustainability (and green) codes and standards add a whole new dimension to the code process, affecting design as well as material, equipment, and product selection. There have been code requirements, standards and federal regulations that promote or require sustainable practices such as energy efficiency, water usage (waterless urinals), and graywater recycling systems, and so on for several code cycles. Green and sustainable codes and standards are quickly increasing in development and use. The two most prominent are the *ASHRAE/USGBC/IES 189.1, Standard for the Design of High-Performance Green Buildings Except Low-Rise Residential Buildings* and the *International Green Construction Code (IGCC)*, both of which are discussed throughout this book. In addition, the federal government continues to raise the minimum requirements for energy efficiency, and various organizations have recently completed and continue to collaborate to create new sustainable standards.

> **✎ Note**
>
> Numerous jurisdictions have created customized green building programs, many of which incorporate a green rating system. (See Chapter 10 and Appendix B for more information.)

Chapter 1 summarizes these sustainability-related publications and federal laws. Actual sustainability requirements are discussed throughout this book (including the appendixes) as they pertain to the various code topics presented. In most cases, these requirements can already be found in the codes. In other cases, they exist only as industry standards that have become common practice. As the interest and commitment to sustainability increases, several code jurisdictions have adopted formal sustainable programs or created customized "green building programs" to fill the gap. Appendix A explains these sustainability topics that are used in the industry but are not necessarily part of the code process.

FIGURES IN THE BOOK

The figures in this book and the code tables are based on the 2018 and/or 2021 edition of the I-codes and the current 2010 *ADA Standards*, where applicable. In the diagrams, metric numbers are shown in parentheses, as in other code and accessibility documents, and represent millimeter measurements unless noted otherwise.

Many of the diagrams include both code and accessibility requirements. For example, the means of egress diagrams in Chapter 5 include clearances and minimum dimensions as required in the building codes, the *ADA Standards*, and the *ICC A117.1* standard. In each case, the most stringent requirements are used. In some instances, notes have been added to clarify conflicting requirements. When working on a project, however, be sure to consult the original document as required by the local jurisdiction.

GETTING STARTED

This book should be used as a guide to assist you in researching the codes and to help you organize your projects. It is not a substitute or replacement for the actual code publications. It would be impossible to discuss every specific code, standard, and federal regulation in one book. In addition, some jurisdictions may have modified some of the requirements. Therefore, this book must be used in conjunction with the appropriate code publications. A thorough investigation of the codes and standards may include working closely with code officials, engineers, and other professionals.

Before beginning a project, you need to know which codes, standards, and federal publications must be referenced. Use Chapter 1 to help you confirm which codes and standards are available. The local codes department can verify the publications that must be referenced and notify you of any required local codes or amendments. They should also be able to tell you if there are any state requirements you need to follow, and if there are any green building programs in place. Because federal publications are not typically regulated on a local level, you will need to keep abreast of the latest changes in the laws that may apply to a project. This book explains how to do this as well. It is important for you to have access to the actual publications during the project so that specific codes and regulations can be referenced and verified. Most code publications are available in hard copy and digital formats.

MINIMUM REQUIREMENTS

Always remember that codes, standards, and federal regulations have been developed as *minimum* requirements. There may be equivalent solutions, and often superior alternatives and solutions are available. By working with your client, the building requirements, and the budget for the project, you can make informed design decisions. By using the creative thinking process and working with the code officials and other professionals, the best design solutions can be developed.

◀ **Note**

The codes and accessibility publications do not always use the same metric conversion for a particular dimension. When there is a discrepancy, the most restrictive metric number is used.

◀ **Note**

This book is not intended to be a substitute for any code or standard required by a jurisdiction or any applicable federal publication. It should be used as a reference book to gain a better understanding of the codes and to guide you through the code process.

◀ **Note**

Rather than viewing codes as restrictive or as a burden, remember that they enable people to feel safe as they live and work in the buildings you design.

dardized and continuous differences as typified in the building codes, the ADA Standards, and the ICC A117.1 standard. In each case, the most stringent requirements are used. In some instances, notes have been added to clarify conflicting requirements. When working on a project, however, be sure to consult the original document as mandated by the local jurisdiction.

GETTING STARTED

This book should be used as a guide to assist you in researching the codes and to help you organize your project. It is not a substitute or replacement for the actual code publication. It would be impossible to discuss every specific code, standard, and federal regulation in one book. In addition, some jurisdictions may have modified some of the requirements. Therefore, this book must be used in conjunction with the appropriate code publications. A thorough investigation of the codes and standards may include working closely with code officials, engineers, and other professionals.

Before beginning a project, you need to know which codes, standards, and federal publications must be referenced. The chapters help you determine which codes and standards are available. The local codes department can clarify the publications that must be referenced. Especially, you are required legal codes or amendments that. They should also be able to tell you if there are any requirements you need to follow and if there are any grandfathering provisions in place. Because federal publications are not typically replicated on a local level, you will need to keep abreast of the latest changes in the laws that may apply to a project. This book explains how to do these as well. It is important for you to have access to the actual publications during the project so that specific codes and regulations can be referenced and verified. Most code publications are available in hard copy and digital formats.

MINIMUM REQUIREMENTS

Always remember that codes, standards, and federal regulations have been developed as minimum requirements. There may be equivalent tables, notes, and often superior alternatives and solutions are available. By working with your client, the building requirements, and the budget for the project, you can make informed design decisions. By using the creative thinking process and working with the code officials and other professionals, the best design solutions can be developed.

ABBREVIATIONS

There are many publications and organizations that are mentioned and discussed repetitively throughout this book. The ones that occur most frequently are listed here so that they do not have to be unnecessarily re-introduced but can be referenced quickly.

ABA	Architectural Barriers Act
ADA	Americans with Disabilities Act
IBC	International Building Code
ICC	International Code Council
ICCPC	ICC Performance Code
IEBC	International Existing Building Code
IECC	International Energy Conservation Code
IFC	International Fire Code
IGCC	International Green Construction Code
ICC A117.1	Accessible and Usable Buildings and Facilities
IGCC	International Green Construction Code
IMC	International Mechanical Code
IPC	International Plumbing Code
IRC	International Residential Code for One-and Two-Family Dwellings
LSC	NFPA 101, Life Safety Code
NEC	National Electrical Code, NFPA 70
NFPA	National Fire Protection Association
NFPA 1	Fire Code
NFPA 70	National Electrical Code

NFPA 900	Building Energy Code
NFPA 5000	Building Construction and Safety Code
UPC	Uniform Plumbing Code
UMC	Uniform Mechanical Code

CHAPTER 1

ABOUT THE CODES

The purpose of the codes that pertain to the built environment can be generally summed up to protect the *health, safety,* and *welfare* of its inhabitants. This seemingly simple objective results in a variety of codes that regulate the design and construction of buildings and building interiors. In addition, there are many standards and federal regulations that add to the requirements. The most nationally recognized codes, laws, and standards organizations are described in this chapter. Accessibility codes and regulations will be discussed in Chapter 2. Most of the codes and regulations presented in this chapter are referenced and discussed throughout this book as they pertain to the interior of a building.

While reading about each of these codes, standards, and regulations, keep in mind that not all of them may apply to your project. Each jurisdiction chooses which code publications and the specific edition of that publication that will apply to projects within their area. For example, a jurisdiction could decide to adopt the 2021 edition of the *International Building Code (IBC)* or continue to use the 2012 edition, or a jurisdiction could decide to adopt the *NFPA 101, Life Safety Code (LSC)* as a stand-alone document or to be used in conjunction with the building code. The jurisdiction could also make a variety of local amendments that add or delete clauses or sections from a code. Knowing which codes are being enforced is necessary to properly research the requirements for a project. (See Chapter 11.)

In addition, each code publication references specific standards as part of defining its requirements. The code will also indicate the specific edition of the standard that should be followed. Standards that are not referenced in a code may still apply to a project because they can be individually required by a jurisdiction or they may be accepted as industry-wide standards. For example, even though some finish and sustainability standards are not *required* by a local jurisdiction, designers may want to follow them for safety, health, and/or liability reasons. The only regulations that are consistent in every jurisdiction are the regulations that are made mandatory by federal law.

▨ **Note**

There are two main sets of codes: the ICC codes and the NFPA codes. Many of the ICC codes, such as the *International Building Code (IBC)*, have been widely adopted. Often adopted NFPA codes include the *LSC* and the *National Electrical Code (NEC)*.

A BRIEF HISTORY

We have been concerned about the safety of buildings for a long time. The use of regulatory codes can be traced back as far as the eighteenth-century BCE to the *Code of Hammurabi,* a collection of laws governing Babylonia. The *Code of Hammurabi* made the builder accountable for the houses he built. If a wall fell, the code required the builder to fix it at no cost to the owner. If one of his buildings fell and killed someone, the builder would be put to death. In the Old Testament, builders are instructed to build parapets around the roof of a house so they would not be guilty of the death of someone who fell from the roof. After the Great Fire of London in 1666, the Rebuilding of London Act was enacted to require fire-resistance qualities in the rebuilding.

In the United States, the first codes addressed fire prevention. The first building law on record was passed in 1625 in what was then called New Amsterdam (now New York). It governed the types and locations of roof coverings to protect the buildings from chimney sparks. Then, in the 1800s, there were several large building fires, including the famous Chicago fire of 1871, which caused many fatalities. As a result, some of the larger US cities developed their own municipal building codes. In the mid-1800s, the National Board of Fire Underwriters was set up to provide insurance companies with information on which to base their fire damage claims. One of the results was the publication of the 1905 *Recommended Building Code*—a code that helped spark the original three model building codes. Another group that originally represented the sprinkler and fire insurance interests also formed, and in 1896 this body published the first standard for automatic sprinklers. This group went on to become the National Fire Protection Association (NFPA).

> ✎ **Note**
>
> Federal agencies may reference ICC and NFPA codes or standards to establish safe building practices. But they are not considered "adopted" by the federal agency.

The increasing desire for building safety inspired the development of other organizations and additional codes. The first of the original three model code organizations, the Building Officials and Code Administrators International (BOCA), was formed in 1915. They produced the *BOCA National Building Code* and other codes. The BOCA codes were generally used in the eastern and mideastern regions of the United States. In 1922, 13 building officials created what eventually became the International Conference of Building Officials (ICBO), which published the *Uniform Building Code* and other related codes. These codes were used primarily in the western regions of the United States. A similar group of building officials met in 1940 to form the Southern Building Code Congress International (SBCCI), producing codes for the southern states. Initially known as the Southern Building Code, it eventually became the Standard Building Code (SBC). In 1994, these three legacy organizations (BOCA, ICBO, and SBCCI) consolidated as the International Code Council (ICC) putting their efforts into one set of codes. Each individual organization eventually stopped producing separate code publications.

Meanwhile, the federal government was also creating *regulations*. Initially, most of these laws pertained to government-built and -owned buildings. Today there are federal regulations that also affect private sector buildings. In 1972, Congress passed the Consumer Product Safety Act (CPSA) and formed the Consumer Product Safety Commission (CPSC). The initial goal of the CPSA and the CPSC were to protect the public from unreasonable risks of injury associated with the use of consumer products. They have the power to assist in the development of voluntary standards with industry representatives as well as to declare mandatory standards to be met for a specific industry. These initiatives helped to sponsor the development of several independent standards-writing organizations and trade associations. In many cases, industry representatives, various governmental agencies, and consumer groups work together to develop standards that address the safety of products and practices. Many of these affect the building industry. Additional legislation since then has been used to promote this process.

These code development organizations and federal departments continue to research best practices, analyze recent fire and emergency events, and identify innovations in the building and interior industry. These organizations each have a process to consider when changes to the requirements so that they promote the best regulations to result in healthy and safe buildings. Events within the past century or so that have particularly affected codes that pertain to the interior of buildings include the Triangle Shirtwaist fire (1911), the Rhythm Club fire (1940), the Cocoanut Grove Fire (1942), the Beverly Hills Supper Club fire (1977), and The Station nightclub fire (2003.) In addition, fire and emergency events such as the 9/11 attack and recent mass shooting also are evaluated and ultimately affect code requirements.

Today, there are various building-related codes in existence in the United States, a wide variety of federal and state regulations, and hundreds of standards organizations and regulatory and trade associations for almost every facet of the industry. Only the most widely recognized ones which apply to interior projects are described in this chapter. This will provide the groundwork for the codes, standards, and regulations discussed throughout this book.

> **◀ Note**
>
> Code requirements are not automatically retroactive: Existing buildings do not have to be updated when a new code is adopted. However, changes to the building may require updating to the new code.

> **◀ Note**
>
> The *code official* in the jurisdiction of your project is the responsible to administer, interpret, and enforce the provisions of the adopted and/or amended code. This is also referred to as the Authority Having Jurisdiction (AHJ) in some codes. See Chapter 11 for more information.

CODE PUBLICATIONS

Codes are collections of regulations, ordinances, and other statutory requirements put together by various organizations. A code publication is not applicable to a project unless it has been adopted by the governing jurisdiction. Each jurisdiction decides which codes it will follow and enforce. (See more on jurisdictions in Chapter 11.) Once certain codes are adopted, they become law within that jurisdiction.

The ICC produces a complete set of codes, known as the *International Codes*—or *I-Codes,* for short. Many of the I-Codes are used throughout the United States and in other countries including Jamaica, Honduras, and Afghanistan. Other countries use the I-Codes as a basis for their codes, including Haiti, Colombia, Mexico, Saudi Arabia, Abu Dhabi, and others. The interior-related ICC code publications are listed in Figure 1.1. These are the codes that will be discussed throughout this book.

NFPA is primarily known for developing standards; however, it also develops several codes including the *Life Safety Code* and the *National Electrical Code.* NFPA develops over 300 codes and standards, some of which were created in collaboration with other industry organizations. This series of codes is called the *Comprehensive Consensus Codes,* or *C3-Codes,* for short. Currently, the NFPA's collaboration partners include the Western Fire Chiefs Association (WFCA) and the American Society of Heating, Refrigeration, and Air-Conditioning Engineers (ASHRAE). Several of the NFPA codes are summarized in Figure 1.1.

ICC I-Codes®		NFPA C3-Codes	
IBC®	International Building Code®	**NFPA 5000®**	Building Construction and Safety Code®
ICC PC®	ICC Performance Code® for Buildings and Facilities		(performance requirements included in each code)
IFC®	International Fire Code®	**NFPA 1®**	Fire Code® (previously titled the Uniform Fire Code or UFC)
	(similar requirements found in IBC and IFC)	**NFPA 101®**	Life Safety Code® (LSC)
IPC®	International Plumbing Code®		
IMC®	International Mechanical Code®		
	(refers to NEC)	**NFPA 70®**	National Electrical Code® (NEC)
IECC®	International Energy Conservation Code®	**NFPA 900®**	Building Energy Code® (incorporating ASHRAE 90.1 and 90.2 and referenced by NFPA 500)
IRC®	International Residential Code® for One- and Two-Family Dwellings		(residential requirements included in other codes)
IEBC®	International Existing Building Code®		(existing building requirements included in each code)

Figure 1.1 Comparison of code publications. (This chart is a summary of 2018 and 2021 publications from the International Code Council® and the National Fire Protection Association that pertain to interior projects. Neither the ICC® nor the NFPA assumes responsibility for the accuracy or completeness of this chart.) NFPA 101®, Life Safety Code®, and NFPA 5000®, Building Construction and Safety Code® are registered trademarks of the National Fire Protection Association, Quincy, MA.

The ICC and NFPA codes are organized differently. Most of the I-Codes are organized using the *Common Code Format*. The code is arranged by chapters that address various aspects of a building and include specific requirements for each occupancy or building type. The C3-Codes use the *Manual of Style,* where there are several key chapters at the beginning and end of the code and the rest of the chapters are divided by occupancy type. The occupancy chapters allow the code review to start in the chapter that pertains to the project's occupancy type, which then indicates when to reference other chapters. It is important to learn how to navigate each code and be able to locate requirements.

HOW CODES CHANGE

Code and standard organizations have a membership that consists of a wide range of individuals. These often include code officials, design professionals, building users, academics, manufacturers, building owners, consumers, contractors, and others. When changes to an existing standard or new standards are needed, many standards organizations use a *consensus process* developed by the American National Standards Institute (ANSI) called the *ANS* process. This system attempts to ensure that the standard is developed by a qualified organization, that groups and individuals who may be directly, materially, or financially affected by the proposal including industry representatives and the public can have input on the proposals, and that there is appropriate due process. It is also intended to balance the process and avoid the dominance from any one group or industry. However, each code and standards organization, including the NFPA and the ICC, has its own specific variations to the process.

The basic process begins with a proposal for a modification to an existing requirement or the deletion or addition of a new requirement. The proposal is made public for comments. Typically, both members and nonmembers can propose and make comments. Once comments are received, a formal proposal is formulated by a technical committee. It is published again for another round of public comments. These comments are used to modify the proposal to its final form.

For NFPA standards, the proposal is then presented to their membership at their yearly conference. If supported, the proposal is then recommended to their Standards Council for approval. The council takes the membership votes into consideration but makes the final decision independently. Although members of the council can include industry representatives, a single industry cannot be heavily represented. Appeals can also be made at this point

The ICC uses what it calls a *governmental consensus process*, or *open process*. The main difference is that the final approval of proposals that were not decided on the consent agenda is made by the "governmental" members of the ICC rather than by a small council. These governmental members consist only of code officials and employees of the governmental agencies that administer and enforce the codes, not industry representatives.

Once a proposed code or standard change is voted on and approved, it is adopted by the organization. When the next full edition of the code or standard is published, it incorporates all the changes into one text.

Note

The *legacy* codes include the *National Building Code, Standard Building Code,* and the *Uniform Building Code.* These codes were used in the United States before the development of the I-Codes and C3-Codes.

In the past, the legacy codes catered to certain regions of the country. The current model codes by the ICC and NFPA now take into account the many regional differences found throughout the United States. For example, western states need more restrictive seismic building code provisions to account for the earthquake activity in those areas, and the northern states need codes to account for long periods of below-freezing temperatures. These various requirements are now in the current building codes. In some cases, a jurisdiction will make amendments to the code it adopts to remove or to add requirements appropriate for their area.

A few states and cities continue to develop their own independent set of codes. More often, jurisdictions that want a specialized code are working with the ICC to revise and amend the base requirements of the

KNOWING WHAT IS NEW IN THE CODE

When a new edition of a code publication is adopted by a jurisdiction, it is important to take some time to review the differences between the new edition and the previous edition. When a code is updated, the ICC and NFPA have a system to indicate changes that have been made in their documents.

In the ICC documents, a vertical line in the margin beside the paragraph or table indicates a change has occurred from the previous edition, such as revised text, relocated sections, or new information. An arrow in the margin indicates that information has been removed from the code. A single asterisk [*] indicates text or a table removed and relocated within the document. A double asterisk [**] indicates that the following text or table has been relocated there from elsewhere in the code.

In the NFPA documents, the system is different. Text revisions are shaded. A shaded triangle to the left of a section, table, or figure indicates a revision to that information. When a chapter is heavily revised the entire chapter is marked with the triangle. Where one of more sections were deleted a circle or dot is placed between the remaining sections. New chapters, annexes, sections, figures, or tables are indicated with a shaded N.

These systems allow for a quick overview of the changes that have been made from the last edition. Where substantial changes have occurred, it is a good idea to compare the affected sections to those in the previous code to become more familiar with the differences. In the front of each NFPA document, there is a summary of the development of each recent edition of that code. It will highlight the significant changes between editions. The ICC publishes a series of "Significant Changes" comparisons to show the most important changes that have taken place between code editions. These can be very useful. ICC also publishes a digital document, *Complete Revision History,* that documents all changes between editions of the I-Codes.

International Building Code (IBC) or other I-Code to meet their needs. The ICC then publishes the revised code specifically for that jurisdiction as a customized code and under a different title. For instance, the adopted set of codes in California is referred to as *California Title 24 Codes* or *2019 California Building Standards Codes* which are based on 2018 I-Code series. And the most recent New Jersey building codes are *2018 IBC, New Jersey Edition,* which is the *IBC* with the approved modifications included. This is also typical for use of the I-Codes in other countries including the Caribbean, Central America, Mexico, and the Middle East. The *Honduras Building Code* and the *Mexico Residential Building Code* are examples. Some jurisdictions have a complete set of unique codes, and others may have just one or two special code publications and use the standard I-Codes for everything else.

Most code publications are updated on a three-year cycle, but each jurisdiction has its own schedule for reviewing and adopting new codes. Jurisdictions may not be enforcing most recent edition of a code which is why it extremely important to not only know the code publication or standards that applies to your project, but also the year edition. (See the inset titled "Reviewing New Code Editions" in this chapter.) Each of the codes produced by the ICC and NFPA, as they pertain to interior projects, is described in this section. The various standards are described later in this chapter. Be sure you know which code publications will be enforced in the jurisdiction of your project and if there are other special requirements or addendums. The list of adopted codes can typically be found on the website of the building code department of the jurisdiction. (See Chapter 11.) Go to both the ICC website (www. iccsafe.org) and the NFPA website (www.nfpa.org) to learn about the latest code adoptions.

Building Codes

Building codes regulate the allowable physical aspects (size, height, manner of construction, etc.), building systems, and interior characteristics of a building. They may also place restrictions on hazardous materials or use of equipment within a building. The principal purpose is to ensure the health, safety, and welfare of the people using these buildings, so codes include requirements affecting structural, mechanical, electrical, plumbing, life safety (egress), fire safety (detection, alarm and suppression), natural light and air, accessibility standards, and energy conservation. Although other codes and standards may also be referenced, the building codes address each of these topics.

✄ Note

The IBC is in use or adopted in all 50 states: the NFPA 5000 is in used by reference in seven states.

✄ Note

A building code including the *IBC* is often used in conjunction with other NFPA codes or standards, including *NFPA 101* and *NEC.*

✎ Note

Because the *IBC* is the most widely adopted building code, this book concentrates on its requirements and its relationship to other code documents.

The most widely adopted building code is the *International Building Code (IBC)* published by ICC. It has been adopted at the state or local level in all 50 states, and most state-specific building codes are now based on the *IBC*. It is also used in several other countries. (See the inset titled "Codes and Standards in Other Countries" in this chapter.) The *IBC* was first published in 2000, with the most current editions published in 2018 and 2021. The NFPA first published the *Building Construction and Safety Code® (NFPA 5000®)* in 2003; however, it is not widely adopted. Its most current editions are 2018 and 2021.

Although there are more than 30 chapters and 13 appendixes in the *IBC* and even more chapters in the *NFPA 5000*, not all of them pertain to the interior of a building. The building interior–related chapters in both the *IBC* and the *NFPA 5000* are summarized in the comparative list in Figure 1.2. The chapters most commonly required for interior projects are listed as follows and are discussed throughout this book. Certain projects may require other sections of the building code to be referenced as well. For example, the information in the chapters on glass and glazing, plastic, or existing structures may also be required. (See Figure 1.2.)

IBC International Building Code		NFPA 5000 Building Construction & Safety Code		NFPA 101 Life Safety Code™	
Chapter 2	Definitions	**Chapter 3**	Definitions	**Chapter 3**	Definitions
Separate	References separate code: *ICC Performance Code for Buildings and Facilities (IC-CPC)* OR *IBC* Section 104.11	**Chapter 5**	Performance-Based Option	**Chapter 5**	Performance-Based Option
Chapter 3	Use and Occupancy Classification	**Chapter 6**	Classification of Occupancy, Classification of Hazard of Contents, and Special Operations	**Chapter 6**	Classification of Occupancy and Hazard of Contents
		Varies	Multiple chapters (16–30), each on a different occupancy classification	**Varies**	Multiple (even) chapters (12–42), each on a different new occupancy classification
Separate	References separate code: *International Residential Code (IRC)*	**Chapter 22**	One- and Two-Family Dwellings	**Chapter 24**	One- and Two-Family Dwellings

Figure 1.2 (Continued)

IBC International Building Code		NFPA 5000 Building Construction & Safety Code		NFPA 101 Life Safety Code™	
Chapter 4	Special Detailed Requirements Based on Use and Occupancy	**Chapter 31**	Occupancies in Special Structures	**Chapter 11**	Special Structures and High-Rise Buildings
		Chapter 32	Special Construction		
		Chapter 33	High-Rise Buildings		
Chapter 5	General Building Heights and Areas	**Chapter 7**	Construction Types and Height and Area Requirements		(none)
Chapter 6	Types of Construction				
Chapter 7	Fire and Smoke Protection Features	**Chapter 8**	Fire Resistive Materials and Construction	**Chapter 8**	Features of Fire Protection
Chapter 8	Interior Finishes	**Chapter 10**	Interior Finish	**Chapter 10**	Interior Finish, Contents, and Furnishings
Chapter 9	Fire Protection Systems	**Chapter 55**	Fire Protection Systems and Equipment	**Chapter 9**	Building Service and Fire Protection Equipment
Chapter 10	Means of Egress	**Chapter 11**	Means of Egress	**Chapter 7**	Means of Egress
Chapter 12	Interior Environment	**Chapter 49**	Interior Environment		(none)
Chapter 13	Energy Efficiency	**Chapter 51**	Energy Efficiency		(none)
Chapter 24	Glass and Glazing	**Chapter 46**	Glass and Glazing		(none)
Chapter 27	Electrical	**Chapter 52**	Electrical Systems		(none)
Chapter 28	Mechanical Systems	**Chapter 50**	Mechanical Systems		(none)
Chapter 29	Plumbing Systems	**Chapter 53**	Plumbing Systems		(none)
Chapter 34	Existing Structures OR separate code: *International Existing Building Code (IEBC)*	**Chapter 15**	Building Rehabilitation	**Chapter 43**	Building Rehabilitation **Varies** Multiple (odd) chapters (13–39), each on a different existing occupancy classification
Chapter 35	Referenced Standards	**Chapter 2**	Referenced Publications	**Chapter 2**	Referenced Publications

Figure 1.2 Comparison of building codes and Life Safety Code®. (This chart is a summary of information contained in the 2018 and 2021 editions of the International Building Code®, the NFPA 5000®, and the Life Safety Code®. Neither the ICC nor the NFPA assumes responsibility for the accuracy or completeness of this chart.)

Use or Occupancy Classifications
Special Use or Occupancy Requirements
Types of Construction
Fire and Smoke Protection Features
Interior Finishes
Fire Protection Systems
Means of Egress
Accessibility
Interior Environment
Plumbing Systems

◧ Note

Most codes contain appendixes or annexes. These provide clarifying information about the requirements in the code or are available for separate adoption by a jurisdiction.

To cover other aspects of a building, the building codes frequently reference additional codes and standards. These include a plumbing code, a mechanical code, a fire prevention code, an energy conservation code, and an existing building code, most of which are described later in this chapter. Although many of these topics are listed as chapters in the building codes, the chapters typically refer to another code or standard for complete information. (Refer to Figure 1.1 for a full list of interior-related code publications.) In addition, other nationally recognized standards organizations and publications are referenced by each of the codes. The *IBC* lists all the codes and standards it references in Chapter 35. (See also the section "Standards Organizations" later in this chapter.) Because the *IBC* is the most widely used building code, it is the one discussed throughout this book.

Performance Codes

Code requirements can be written in one of two ways: prescriptive or performance. A *prescriptive* code sets out a precise requirement, explaining exactly what must be done to be acceptable. A *performance* code, by contrast, provides an objective but not the specifics of how to achieve it. The purpose of performance codes is to allow unique solutions in design and engineering and in the use of materials and systems of construction, and to allow innovative solutions to provide appropriate level of health and safety in ways that can be appropriate to the project but not anticipated by the code. Historically, most code requirements have been written in a prescriptive manner, although performance concepts have been included in the codes for some time. In the *IBC*, an example of this can be found in *Section 104.11*, which is titled "*Alternative materials, design and methods of construction and equipment*" (referred to as "*IBC Section 104.11*" throughout this book). The NFPA codes also recognize an "equivalency," which would be similar to using *Section 104.11* in the *IBC*. In both cases, the final solution must be approved by the code official. (See also the inset titled "ICC Evaluation Service" in this chapter.)

The NFPA and the ICC codes provide additional performance-based options to the prescriptive requirements. The ICC developed a separate code, the *ICC Performance Code for Buildings and Facilities (ICCPC),* in 2001. The most recent editions include 2018 and 2021 and it is on a three-year revision cycle. The *ICCPC* is meant to be used in conjunction with the *IBC,* as well as most of the other I-Codes. It addresses the overall scope of each of the I-Codes in performance-based language and describes how to use them together. However, the *ICCPC* cannot be used with the other I-Codes unless it is adopted by the code jurisdiction. Currently, it has not been adopted as widely as the prescriptive-based *IBC.* If it has not been adopted, you must work with a code official using *IBC Section 104.11* to integrate performance criteria into the design solution.

The NFPA, by contrast, does not have a separate performance publication. Instead, the NFPA codes include both performance requirements and prescriptive requirements. For example, Chapter 5 of the *Life Safety Code* is titled "Performance-Based Option." In addition, the NFPA recommends referencing Chapter 4, which discusses some of the code's goals, assumptions, and objectives and provides additional insight in using prescriptive-type codes. A jurisdiction that adopts one of the NFPA codes does have the option to exclude Chapter 5, so confirm that the performance requirements are allowed before using them. *NFPA 5000* includes a separate chapter to provide a performance option. In both cases the performance-based requirements set an objective and provide an administrative process to follow for approval of the design solution. Many other countries use performance-based codes as well. Some examples include Australia, United Kingdom, Hong Kong, Japan, and others. (See the inset titled "Codes and Standards in Other Countries" in this chapter.)

A good example of the difference between a prescriptive requirement and a performance criterion can be found in the spacing of guardrail elements. In the *IBC,* the prescriptive requirement specifies that rail elements "shall not have openings which allow passage of a sphere 4 inches (102 mm) in diameter from the walking surface to the required guard height." This requirement was developed specifically with children in mind. The *ICC Performance Code* does not mandate this narrow spacing. Instead, it specifies "that the openings shall be of an appropriate size and configuration to keep people from falling through based on the anticipated age of the occupants." If it can be shown that children are not expected to frequent the building, then different spacing of the guardrail

✎ Note

A comprehensive list of code adoptions by location can be found on the ICC website (www. iccsafe.org) and the NFPA website (www.nfpa.org).

✎ Note

The use of performance codes started in other countries; the United States is one of the last major countries to use them. Australia was one of the first to use them.

elements may be allowed. An example might be a manufacturing facility. (See Chapter 10 and the inset titled "Performance Codes" for additional information.)

When using performance codes (or alternative methods and materials such as those allowed by *IBC Section 104.11*), it becomes even more important to work with the code official in the early stages of a project. Performance codes encourage and often require a team approach to the design solution. Additional documentation is often required. Ultimately, the code official must agree that the design and the supporting documentation meet the intent of the code based on the assumptions, parameters, and criteria that were set at the beginning of the project. (See the inset titled "Risk Factors and Hazards in Occupancies" in Chapter 3.)

The use of performance codes may be most effective in addressing unique situations, including the use of new technology, incorporation of sustainable design, and the reuse of existing and historic buildings, which may not easily meet the strict requirement of the prescriptive codes. In most cases, performance codes will apply only to a specific aspect of a project and will not totally replace the required prescriptive codes.

Fire Codes

The ICC and NFPA publish a fire code. The fire code produced by the ICC was first issued in 2000 and is called the *International Fire Code (IFC)*. Similar to the other I-Codes, it is on a three-year revision cycle, with newer editions in 2018 and 2021. Many of the requirements in the *IFC* are repeated in the *IBC*. To indicate that a particular requirement is also located in the *IFC*, a "F" is included in the section number.

Beginning in 2003, NFPA issued a fire code titled *Uniform Fire Code®* (*UFC*) or *NFPA 1®*. This code merged an original *NFPA 1* with a legacy code by the Western Fire Chief Association (WFCA). It was revised again in 2012 and is now simply known as the *Fire Code* (or *NFPA 1*). The new version is organized similarly to the other C3-Codes and includes a chapter for performance-based design. Much of *NFPA 1* is taken from various other codes and standards produced by the NFPA, such as the *Life Safety Code*. When a specific requirement comes from another publication, *NFPA 1* references the original document and section.

Note

Typically, only a certain aspect of a project will be based on a performance-based code or on the alternative materials, design, and methods section in the *IBC*. The rest of the project would then be designed using standard prescriptive code requirements.

Note

The *IFC* is in use or adopted by 41 states: the *NFPA 1: Fire Code* is adopted and enforceable in 19 states.

When adopted by a jurisdiction, a fire code is typically used in conjunction with a building code. The fire code addresses building conditions that are hazardous and could cause possible fire and explosions. This could be due to a number of reasons, such as the type of occupancy

ICC EVALUATION SERVICE

ICC Evaluation Service (ICC-ES) evaluates new materials, methods of construction, and testing to make sure they comply with the I-Codes, as well as other codes. The ICC-ES works closely with various accredited testing laboratories and approved inspection agencies to accomplish this. These laboratories and agencies are reviewed and approved by the International Accreditation Service (IAS), another independent subsidiary of the ICC.

The request to evaluate a product or system often comes from the manufacturer, but builders, code officials, engineers, architects, and designers, can do so as well. For example, a manufacturer might request an evaluation for a newly developed building product, or a designer might request a job-specific evaluation. The ICC-ES develops acceptance criteria for the installation of the product and the conditions of its use by which it would meet or exceed the requirements of the codes and standards. Once the product or system is tested and approved, an ICC-ES Evaluation Report is issued and made available to the industry. These reports of evaluated products can be accessed and downloaded for free at www.icc-es.org.

Another ICC-ES evaluation service, the ICC-ES Environmental Program, (formerly known as Sustainable Attributes Verification and Evaluation Program—SAVE®) verifies that a product has been independently tested to meet the sustainable attributes required by *International Green Construction Code (IgCC)*, *International Energy Conservation Code (IECC)*, *California Green Building Code (CALGreen)*, *ASHRAE 189.1*, or as part of green building rating systems such as LEED, Green Building Initiative GBI-01, ICC 700, etc. Also, ICC-ES PMG Listing and ICC-ES Building Products Listing Programs indicate product compliance with the codes specifically in the areas of plumbing, mechanical, and fuel gas and building products.

These evaluation reports and product listings can help designers to specify a wider range of innovative, sustainable, and code-compliant products. They are especially helpful as part of a performance-based design or when using the alternative materials, design, and methods sections in the *IBC*. When a designer specifies a product already approved by the ICC-ES, the report/listing provides a third-party validation that the product meets the minimum specified code or standard. This is helpful to the code official reviewing the project (although the code official still has to approve its use). This process also enables manufacturers to gain national recognition of a new product.

Other evaluation services are available as well. For example, some states, such as California and Florida, have developed their own uniform requirements to meet their statewide codes.

or use of the space, the type of materials used or stored, and/or the way certain materials are handled. The fire code becomes even more important with building types that may not be fully covered by the building code. For example, it includes specifics for a paint booth in a car body shop, a commercial kitchen in a restaurant, and a dry-cleaning facility. However, a fire code also has general requirements that must be met. For example, it includes information on fire extinguishers as well as interior elements not discussed in the building codes.

There are a few chapters or sections in the fire codes that will be referenced more frequently for interior projects. They include the following:

Means of Egress
Fire Resistance–Rated Construction
Fire Protection Systems
Interior Finishes
Furnishings and Decorative Materials

Again, some information may be included in both the fire code and another applicable code such as the *IBC* or *LSC*. In addition, the fire codes include a chapter on emergency planning and preparedness, which addresses such things as evacuation plans and fire drills for each type of occupancy. Although this chapter is geared more toward building owners and fire departments, there are certain occupancy provisions that may also affect an interior project, such as signage and keying requirements. Many of the various fire code requirements related to interiors and the chapters listed here are mentioned throughout this book.

Life Safety Code®

The *Life Safety Code (LSC)* was one of the first codes published by NFPA. It is also referred to as *NFPA 101®*. The *LSC* is revised every three years and the most current editions are 2018 and 2021. The *LSC* is not a building code. It is a life safety code that concentrates on problems involving safe evacuation of occupants from a building. It establishes minimum requirements for the design, construction, operation, and maintenance of buildings as required to protect building occupants from danger caused by fire, smoke, and toxic fumes. The difference between the *LSC* and the building codes can also be seen in Figure 1.2. Several *LSC* chapters correspond to those found in the building codes, but it does not address issues concerning the construction of a building to the same depth. For example, it does not include chapters on fire-stopping, glazing, or plumbing. Another unique aspect of the *LSC* is that it is used to measure the safety of a new building being constructed, an existing building in use and an existing building that is being renovated.

◀ Note

ICC-ES Evaluation Reports, ICC-ES Environmental Program, and Product Listings provide evidence that a product meets code requirements and are helpful when using performance codes or the alternative materials, design, and methods sections of the *IBC*.

◀ Note

The *Life Safety Code* has a corresponding document, *NFPA 101A, Alternative Approaches to Life Safety*. This document is intended to be used in conjunction with, but not in place of, the *LSC* when alternate solutions are needed.

The *LSC* uses the NFPA's *Manual of Style* format. The first part of the *LSC* concentrates on the broad topics of occupancies, means of egress, fire protection, and interior-related items setting the standard requirements. The remainder is divided into chapters by occupancy classification for both new and existing buildings. For example, there is a chapter on new apartment buildings and existing apartment buildings. (This is different from *NFPA 5000*, which has only one chapter per occupancy and puts all existing requirements into one separate chapter.) This distinction between new and existing is made to allow certain requirements (which may have been acceptable in a previous edition) to remain in place or indicate that a condition must meet the same standard as a new building. Once the occupancy classification and whether the occupancy will be considered new or existing is determined, most of the research will be concentrated in one chapter of the *LSC*. The occupancy chapter will then refer to other chapters as required. (See Chapter 2 for more detail.)

The *LSC* also includes a chapter on alternative performance-based options. This provides the ability to select the requirements that best suit a specific project. (See the section "Performance Codes" earlier in this chapter and the inset titled "Performance Codes" in Chapter 11.) Similar to other codes, the *LSC* also references additional code and standard publications. These are summarized in Chapter 2 of the *LSC*. (See also the section on the NFPA standards later in this chapter.)

The *LSC* is used throughout the United States and in several other countries. It is currently used in at least one jurisdiction in every state and has been adopted statewide by at least 43 states in the United States. (A map of the locations can be found on the NFPA website at www.nfpa. org.) It is not uncommon for a jurisdiction to adopt both the *IBC* and the *LSC*. When a jurisdiction requires both, the design must satisfy both sets of requirements. Sometimes a requirement in the *LSC* might conflict with one in the building code. When this occurs, the more restrictive requirement must be met. Or, if necessary, work with the local code official to determine the best way to satisfy the two codes. Throughout this book, many *LSC* requirements are discussed in relation to those found in the *IBC*.

> **◀ Note**
>
> The *Life Safety Code* is adopted in 43 states. Many other states use a portion of the requirements.

Plumbing Codes

The *International Plumbing Code (IPC)* was the first I-Code published by the ICC in 1995. The *IPC* is revised every three years. The *Uniform Plumbing Code (UPC)* became part of the NFPA's set of C3-Codes beginning in 2003. It is produced in conjunction with the International Association of Plumbing and Mechanical Officials (IAPMO). Currently, most code jurisdictions use the *IPC*. The most current versions of the *IPC* and the *UPC* are the 2018 and 2021. In addition, the Plumbing-Heating-Cooling Contractors Association has developed the *National Standard Plumbing Code (NSPC)* since 1933. Recently, it has become under the control of IAPMO. The newest edition is 2018 and 2021 and includes requirements to promote sustainable practices. Currently, New Jersey is the only state that uses this code. In addition to the *IPC*, *UPC* and the *NSPC*, some states such as Illinois, Kentucky, Louisiana, Maine, Minnesota, and Wisconsin developed their own plumbing code or have one that is based on the *IPC* or *UPC*.

☑ **Note**

The *IPC* is in use or adopted in 35 states.

The plumbing code defines acceptable materials, function, installation procedures, and inspection processes for plumbing systems. Therefore, most of the plumbing code is geared to the engineer and the licensed plumbing contractor. When designing interior projects, the plumbing code chapter that is used primarily by designers and architects contains a table that determines the minimum number and type of plumbing fixtures required for a project. Notice in Figure 1.2 that both building codes have a chapter on plumbing systems. These chapters refer you directly to the respective plumbing code. However, in the *IBC*, the plumbing chapter also includes the minimum plumbing facilities section of the *IPC* with the related table. The chapter also includes information on how to locate these fixtures in a building. This table and its related requirements found in the *IPC* are discussed in more detail in Chapter 8.

Mechanical Codes

A mechanical code is also published by both the ICC and NFPA. The *International Mechanical Code (IMC)* was first published by the ICC in 1996. The more current editions include the 2018 and 2021 versions. The *IMC* is widely adopted. The *Uniform Mechanical Code (UMC)* became part of the NFPA's set of C3-Codes starting in 2003. Its most current editions are 2018 and 2021. Jurisdictions may choose between the *IMC* and the *UMC*.

☑ **Note**

The *IMC* is adopted in 46 states.

Again, as shown in Figure 1.2, each building code has a chapter on mechanical systems. And like the plumbing chapters, these chapters refer to the respective mechanical code. The mechanical codes indicate requirements for the installation, inspection and maintenance of HVAC and are geared to mechanical engineers and professional installers. A designer may rarely have to refer to the mechanical codes. However, familiarity with some of the general requirements and terminology is useful when designing an interior project. These are discussed in more detail in Chapter 7.

Electrical Codes

The *National Electrical Code (NEC)*, published by the NFPA, is one of the oldest codes. Originally published in the late 1800s, it is now part of the NFPA C3-Code set. The most current edition is 2020. Also known as *NFPA 70*, the *NEC* is the most widely used electrical code and is the basis for electrical codes in most code jurisdictions. There is no separate electrical code developed by the ICC.

The electrical chapter in the *IBC* and *NFPA 5000* (see Figure 1.2) references the *NEC*. In the *IBC*, this chapter also includes a section on emergency and standby power systems. It is typically the responsibility of an engineer to design electrical systems using the *NEC*. Nevertheless, when designing an interior project, it is necessary to know certain basic electrical code requirements, especially when locating electrical outlets and fixtures and when specifying light fixtures and other equipment. The most common requirements and their relationship to energy codes are explained in Chapter 9.

Energy Codes

The ICC and the NFPA have an energy conservation code that establishes minimum requirements for energy-efficient buildings. The ICC has the *International Energy Conservation Code (IECC)*, which was first published in 1998; the most current editions include 2018 and 2021. It includes requirements for heating, air-conditioning, ventilation, and lighting systems for residential and commercial buildings. (See following.) Most states in the United States currently require use of the *IECC*. For commercial buildings, the *IECC* has three compliance options. The prescriptive path is to comply with *IECC* Chapter 5 or the *ANSI/ASHRAE Standard 90.1, Energy Standard for Buildings Except Low-Rise Residential Buildings* in its entirety. (You cannot mix and match compliance between the documents.) The trade-off approach allows a balance of enhanced energy efficiency in one area with less efficient areas or components to create an overall balance of energy efficiency. Another performance approach requires which requires a computer simulation analysis to compare the design baseline design to demonstrate the comparative performance.

In 2004, NFPA issued a stand-alone energy code, titled *NFPA 900, Building Energy Code (BEC)*. The most current edition is 2019. The *NFPA 900* establishes the provisions for administering and enforcing two existing ASHRAE energy standards: *ANSI/SHRAE Standard 90.1* (geared to

◀ Note

ASHRAE 90.1 is a standard geared to energy efficiency in commercial buildings. The DOE requires the use of the 2016 edition throughout the United States. (Newer editions might be required by a state or local code jurisdiction.)

commercial buildings), and *ANSI/ASHRAE Standard 90.2, Energy-Efficient Design of New Low-Rise Residential Buildings* (geared to residential homes). On a three-year cycle, both standards were most recently updated in 2019 and 2022. The same requirements are also included in *NFPA 5000*. buildings. There is also *ANSI/ASHRAE/IES/ASHRAE Standard 100 Energy Conservation in Existing Buildings*.

The building codes have a chapter on energy efficiency; however, the chapter simply references the respective energy code. Energy conservation codes address many sustainable aspects of a building, starting with the energy efficiency of the building envelope, which promotes adequate thermal resistance and low air leakage. For example, in an exterior wall the code will specify the quantity and type of glass that can be used, and the rating of the wall insulation required. When designing the interior, the energy codes will include requirements to maximize the amount of daylight entering the space, minimize the lighting densities, and require the use of occupant-sensing controls.

The energy codes also cover the design, selection, and installation of energy-efficient mechanical systems, water-heating systems, electrical distribution systems, and illumination systems. These requirements, as well as one of the codes tables in the *IECC*, are further explained in Chapters 8 and 9. Other energy requirements related to the interior of a building are mentioned throughout the book. (See also Appendix A for additional sustainability information.)

Sustainability Codes

Building codes and standards have historically concentrated on the safety of a building and its occupants; however, codes and standards to address the sustainability of the buildings is a fast-growing concept in the United States. Typical codes limit the potential physical hazards in the built environment and provide clear paths to escape dangerous conditions. Sustainability codes and standards, however, focus on how the building's environment and materials affect the occupants while occupying the building and how the construction and existence of the building affect the world around it.

Some of the codes and standards discussed earlier in this chapter incorporate sustainability requirements. The energy codes are a strong example (see preceding section). Other examples include the requirements for water-efficient fixtures and waterless urinals in the *IPC* and the various provisions for indoor air quality in several of the ICC codes. Some code jurisdictions have incorporated their own sustainability

Note

The *IECC* is adopted in 49 states.

Note

COMcheck (editor needs TM) is a free compliance software which automates the verification of compliance with the energy efficiency requirements. It is available at www.energycodes.gov/software.stm.

CODES AND STANDARDS IN OTHER COUNTRIES

Building codes and standards are used throughout the world to make buildings safe. Many countries develop their own unique sets of building codes. More recently, there has been a growing use of one or more of the I-Codes and/or the National Fire Protection Association codes or standards in other countries. For example, the *International Building Code,* as well as various other I-Codes, has been either adopted by a country or has been used as the base document for their own code publication. In some cases, these model codes are used in conjunction with locally developed requirements as well. For example, the *IBC* is used as the primary document or base document in the Caribbean, Central America, Mexico, Eastern Europe, and the Middle East. You can find a current list on the ICC website.

In Europe and many other countries many of the codes are considered performance-based, especially energy codes. To help foster communication between various countries and code organizations, the Interjurisdictional Regulatory Collaboration Committee (IRCC) was formed in 1997. The IRCC provides a forum for information concerning the support, development, implementation of codes especially as it relates to performance-based codes.

requirements as part of their requirements. Some states even require the use of a sustainability rating system, such as LEED or Green Globes (see Appendix A), as part of the design and code process. (See Chapter 11 for more information.) As more jurisdictions and clients require sustainability measures to be incorporated into design and construction, additional sustainability codes and standards will be developed.

The first comprehensive sustainability code was produced by the state of California. First adopted by the state in 2008, the most current edition of the *California Green Building Standards Code (CALGreen)* is 2019. In California, it applies to a variety of occupancies and building types, such as state buildings, housing, schools, hospitals, and correctional facilities. It applies to new construction as well as some additions and alterations to existing buildings. It establishes mandatory minimum requirements and provides two tiers of voluntary compliance levels. Local jurisdictions can choose the level to which they will require buildings to exceed the minimum requirements. The *CALGreen* addresses key sustainability elements of a building. Some characteristics such as water conservation and energy efficiency are similar to requirements found in the energy codes. Other requirements include the use of life cycle assessments (LCAs) when selecting building products and monitoring of volatile organic compounds (VOCs) of building materials and finishes define the interior environmental quality. And other sections of the code promote construction waste management, material conservation and site

✎ Note

The ICC *International Green Construction Code* is for use on commercial projects and the *ICC 700, National Green Building Standard*, is for residential occupancies.

plan effectiveness. (See Appendix A.) This code references private sources and recognized standards including sustainable product certifications to set benchmarks when selecting building materials and products. Application matrices and worksheets are provided to help implement and document sustainable aspects of the project while using the *CALGreen*. Although *CALGreen* was developed for buildings in California, it could be used as a source for the development of green codes by other jurisdictions.

The ICC initially collaborated with the National Association of Home Builders (NAHB) to develop the ICC *700, National Green Building Standard* released in 2008 for residential occupancies. The latest edition is 2020. In 2012, the ICC released the *International Green Construction Code (IgCC)* for new and existing commercial projects. The *IgCC* was originally based on the *CALGreen* so there are several similarities. However, in 2015, the ICC and ASHRAE began to share the development of the *IgCC*. Now, the ICC is responsible for defining the scope and administrative parameters and the technical provisions are developed by ASHRAE and are based on *ASHRAE/ICC/USGBC Standard 189.1, Standard for the Design of High-Performance, Green Buildings Except Low-Rise Residential Buildings (Standard 189.1)*. Now merged into a single document, the *IgCC* with the ASHRAE 189.1 establishes minimum green requirements for buildings with four voluntary levels of requirements. It is intended to be used with the other I-Codes, including the *IECC* and *ICC-700*, the *National Green Building Standard*. The latest editions are the 2018 and 2021.

The *IgCC* is comprehensive and covers a wide variety of occupancies and building types. The *IgCC* also covers a wide range of topics from conservation of materials, water, and energy to land use and environmental quality. It also includes a chapter on existing buildings as well as building operations and maintenance. Like the *CALGreen*, it uses performance benchmarks throughout the code to validate the outcome instead of specific design mandates. In each chapter, the *IgCC* provides "compliance electives" so that a jurisdiction can more easily customize the code to its needs, allowing for regional differences, variation in Site locations, and performance objectives. Checklists are provided within the code so that the project designer can also select compliance electives. (See the section "American Society of Heating, Refrigeration, and Air-Conditioning Engineers" later in this chapter.)

This book highlights the sustainability-related codes and standards as they relate to the various topics and code provisions discussed throughout this book. (See the section "Standards Organizations" later in this chapter for information on various sustainability standards.)

✎ Note

The *International Green Construction Code (IgCC)* was developed by ICC, ASTM International and the American Institute of Architects (AIA).

Residential Codes

The *International Residential Code (IRC)* was first published by the ICC in 1998. The more current editions include 2018 and 2021. Before that it had been developed and published the Council of American Building Officials as *CABO: One and Two Family Dwelling Code*. As the *IRC*, it is the main code used for the construction of single-family and duplex residences and townhouses. It covers the typical residential home that is not more than three stories in height and has a separate means of egress. All other types of residential uses would be regulated by a building code. For example, if working on a house that is more than three stories or an apartment building where there are more than two dwelling units, one would have to use a building code such as the *IBC* instead of the *IRC*. The *IRC* is a stand-alone code, meaning that it covers all construction aspects of the building without having to refer to other code documents. In addition to the typical building code chapters, it includes complete chapters on mechanical, electrical, plumbing, fuel gas, and energy requirements.

The NFPA does not have a separate residential code. Instead, it covers the building aspects of single-family homes in its other codes. For example, the *Life Safety Code* has an occupancy chapter titled "One- and Two-Family Dwellings." That chapter provides specific requirements and refers to other chapters that provide exceptions for single-family homes. This chapter also refers to other NFPA codes and multiple NFPA standards that are appropriate for one- and two-family dwellings. If a jurisdiction requires the *IRC* in addition to an NFPA code, the most restrictive requirements should be followed. (Although this book concentrates more on commercial projects, codes and standards specifically for residential homes are briefly discussed in Appendix C.)

Existing Building Codes

Codes are most easily applied to the design of new buildings or additions. Designing within existing building elements, systems and constraints can be more challenging to integrate new code requirements. Because of this, several codes give separate requirements for designing within an existing condition. For example, the *LSC* includes separate chapters to apply to a building when it is already occupied by a specific occupancy. For example, Chapter 38 is for New Business Occupancies and Chapter 39 applies to Existing Business Occupancies.

In 2003, the ICC published the first *International Existing Building Code (IEBC)*. This code is dedicated entirely to existing buildings and provides requirements for reasonable upgrades and improvements, depending on

☑ Note

The *IRC* is used or adopted by 49 states. Wisconsin is currently an exception.

☑ Note

You can find out what NFPA codes are in use all over the world by going to codefinder.nfpa.org.

☑ Note

Design and construction projects in existing buildings typically require the use of the building codes. However, a jurisdiction may also have the option of using the *IEBC*. See Appendix B for more information.

the type and extent of the work. In the *IEBC*, the extent of work (i.e., repair, alteration, or addition) will determine the level of code compliance required. The intent of the *IEBC* is to maintain appropriate level of safety including fire prevention, structural and life safety features within an existing building but may take into consideration what was allowed by previous codes. The *IEBC* includes prescriptive and performance-related provisions. Use of this code is explained in more detail in Appendix B. The most current editions are 2018 and 2021.

FEDERAL REGULATIONS

☑ Note

There are federal, state, and local governmental regulations that apply to buildings. However, most of the governmental regulations discussed in this book are federal regulations. These apply to project throughout the United States. Check for required state and local regulations as well.

A number of federal agencies and departments work with trade associations, private companies, and the general public to develop regulations for building construction. Proposed or updated requirements and policies are initially published in the *Federal Register (FR)*. The *FR* is published daily and includes the newest updates for each federal agency. However, not all rules published in the *FR* are enforceable laws. Typically, a federal agency must review the regulations published in the *FR* and make a formal ruling. Once the regulations are adopted and have become law, they are published in the *Code of Federal Regulations (CFR)*. The *CFR* is revised annually to include all permanent agency rules.

The federal government plays a part in the building process in several ways. First, it regulates the building of its own facilities. These include federal buildings, Veterans Administration (VA) hospitals, and military establishments, as well as other buildings built with federal funds. The construction of a federal building is technically not subject to state and local building codes and regulations. Instead, each federal agency can develop criteria and regulations for the construction or renovation of buildings used by their agency. However, since the passage of the National Technology Transfer and Advancement Act (NTTAA) of 1995, the federal agencies such as the OSHA, DOD, DoE, CMS, and others have begun to adopt more codes and standards from the private sector instead of creating its own. (NTTAA made federal agencies responsible for using national voluntary consensus standards instead of developing their own, wherever practical.) Many federal agencies have been working with the ICC and NFPA as well as standards organizations such as ASHRAE, using the ANSI process to adopt existing codes and standards. (See the section "Standards Organizations" later in this chapter.) For example, multiple federal agencies require the use of the *Life Safety Code* and the *International Building Code*. In some cases, federal agencies collaborate with other organizations to develop new documents. Some of these are discussed in this chapter. When working on a federally owned or funded building, contact the appropriate federal agency to determine which codes and standards apply. Keep in mind that more than one federal agency could be involved.

Another way the federal government plays a part in the building process is by passing legislation that supersedes all other state and local codes and standards. Each piece of legislation created by Congress is implemented by rules and regulations adopted by a specific federal agency. When a federal law is passed, it becomes mandatory nationwide; so do the agency rules and regulations. This is typically done to create a uniform level of standards throughout the country. The Americans with Disabilities Act (ADA) is one example. Although there is a wide variety of legislation covering everything from energy to transportation, only the pertinent laws that pertain to the design of interiors are discussed in this section and throughout this book.

Accessibility Legislation

In simple terms, discrimination laws are meant to prevent people from unfairly or unnecessarily being kept from an activity, service, or place. There are several federal discrimination laws that affect buildings and interiors because the built environment can be a significant barrier to these experiences for persons with a physical disability. These accessibility legislations each address a different project type based on the use and who owns or leases the building or space. Each law is supported by a set of guidelines that help architects and designers to design the space and specify interior elements in a way that someone with a disability can visit, occupy, and use the space. The goal is that the person can maneuver in the building independently.

There are three major accessibility legislations that affect the design of a building or space. Most projects will be required to be accessible under one of the laws. The Architectural Barrier Act enacted in 1968 addresses federally owned and operated buildings. The Americans with Disability Act of 1991 addresses privately owned and operated buildings. Originally established in 1967, The Fair Housing Act regulates the fair sale and rental of housing but was expanded in 1988 to include issues of accessibility. The development and applicable guidelines of these regulations are discussed in more depth in Chapter 2. The specific technical requirements are presented in the pertinent chapter and throughout the book.

Note

The Occupational Safety and Health Act (OSHA) is another federal regulation affecting building interiors. It stresses the safe installation of materials and equipment to ensure a safe work environment for construction workers and building occupants. It must be strictly observed by building contractors.

Energy Policy Act

 Note

The 2007 Energy Independence and Security Act required federal facilities to reduce energy use by 30 percent by 2015, eliminate use of fossil fuels by 2030, set a goal that new commercial buildings built after 2025 to be zero-net-energy and to retrofit all pre-2015 buildings to be zero-net-energy by 2050.

The Energy Policy Act (EPAct) was enacted by the federal government in 1992 and updated in 2005 to promote energy efficiency and conservation and establish regulatory standards. The Energy Conservation and Production Act (ECPA) had originally required the use of the 1989 edition of *ASHRAE/IES 90.1, Energy Standard for Buildings Except Low-Rise Residential Buildings,* as the minimum standard for new commercial and high-rise residential buildings and 1992 *Model Energy Code (MEC)* as the minimum standard for new residential buildings. The *MEC* was replaced by the *IECC* in 1998. The EPAct requires the US Department of Energy (DOE) to review each successive edition of the *ASHRAE/IES 90.1* and the *IECC* for consideration. If the DOE determines that the new edition of the standard will create greater energy efficiency, it must update to the new standard. The current benchmark standards are of the *ASHRAE 90.1–2016 and 2018 IECC.* The DOE must declare within 12 months whether the new standard will be used. After each update, states have two years to establish energy codes that are equivalent to the current standard. The EPAct also required federal buildings to meet or exceed the required standard.

The EPAct includes legislation that affects labeling requirements for electrical devices, tax deduction provisions for commercial buildings, and specific requirements for federally built and/or funded buildings. The goal of the standard is to make buildings more energy efficient, including lighting efficiency, use of day lighting, and energy efficiency of equipment and building systems and the building envelope. For example, every energy-efficient product purchased by a federal agency is required to be either an ENERGY STAR® product or one designated by DOE's Federal Energy Management Program (FEMP). (See Chapter 8.) It also now covers some residential uses such as low-rise hotels and prisons. (See the section "American Society of Heating, Refrigeration, and Air-Conditioning Engineers" later in this chapter.)

There are three allowable approaches for compliance under the EPAct: prescriptive, trade-off, or performance. A prescriptive approach implements the exact requirements as given within the IECC and the 90.1 for building systems and components. It is the most restrictive approach. For example, lighting would be chosen to meet the allowable watts per square foot and for mechanical systems and equipment would be designed using the prescribed minimum equipment efficiencies. A trade-off approach allows the use of enhanced energy efficiency in one component for the decreased energy efficiency in another component. These trade-offs typically occur between building systems including building envelope, lighting, or mechanical. For example, less efficient lighting fixtures may be specified if the exterior wall system exceeded the building envelop requirements. However, there are limited allowable trade-offs for mechanical systems and equipment. Use of compliance software tool or calculations may be necessary to confirm overall compliance. A performance approach (also known as a systems performance approach) allows use of baseline criteria to demonstrate that the proposed design is at least as efficient as what is required by the prescriptive requirements. A performance approach may be useful when the use of alternative energy sources are planned such as passive solar design, photovoltaic cells, thermal energy storage, and fuel cells.

Inspection and testing for building compliance are the responsibility of the US Secretary of the Treasury. However, compliance with the EPAct is mandated at the state level, which means that jurisdictions will be required to use the approved edition of *ASHRAE 90.1* (or an energy code that references the appropriate edition).

STANDARDS ORGANIZATIONS

A *standard* is a document that provides requirements, specifications, a recommended practice, a test method, or a desired characteristic that must be met. A standard can apply to a material, product, assembly of materials, or a procedure. Standards are developed by trade associations, government agencies, and standards-writing organizations, and members of these groups are often allowed to vote on specific issues. The size of these groups ranges from a worldwide organization to a small trade association that develops one or two industry-related standards.

By themselves, standards have no legal standing. Instead, they are typically referenced by the codes. The standards become law when the code is adopted by a jurisdiction. (In some cases, a jurisdiction will adopt an individual standard that then supplements the code. For example, some jurisdictions are adopting sustainability standards.) Typically, a code will establish the minimum quality and performance expectations for a material, product, assembly, or method by referring to a standard instead of including the detailed information in the code text. The standard then sets the detailed conditions or requirements for the material or method. For example, instead of setting specific fire extinguisher requirements, the *IBC* references *NFPA 10, Portable Fire Extinguishers. NFPA 10* thus becomes a part of the enforced building code. Using a standard, instead of defining unique requirements, creates consistency among the various codes as they apply to buildings.

When a standard is referenced, the acronym of the standard organization and a standard number are called out, followed by a title that describes the purpose of the standard. For example, *ASTM E84, Standard Test Method for Surface Burning Characteristics of Building Materials* is an

☑ Note

The Department of Homeland Security (DHS) develops standards relating to national security. These guidelines can be useful but not mandatory unless working on a project accepting DHS funds.

☑ Note

Each code publication has a chapter listing the standards mentioned in its text. The list will indicate which edition of the standard is applicable. This is referred to as the *active* standard.

American Society for Testing and Materials standard known as *E84*. As the title suggests, it is a standard method of testing the burning characteristics of building materials. The reference also typically includes the year of the required edition (e.g., *ASTM E84–07* is the 2007 edition of the standard). Although the year might not be used when mentioned within the text, each code publication includes a list of the referenced standards identifying the applicable edition or year. It is important that the correct edition of the standard is met.

The standards organizations that most commonly pertain to interior projects are described in this section. Each develops a wide variety of standards. Some standards may have to be examined in detail prior to designing an interior project. Others may only have to be mentioned in the specifications of the project. The standards that most commonly pertain to interior projects are discussed throughout this book. (See also the inset titled "Industry Standards" in Chapter 9.)

American National Standards Institute

✎ Note

Some standards-developing organizations are trade associations specific to an industry. For example, the Business and Institutional Furniture Manufacturers Association (BIFMA) and the Upholstered Furniture Action Council (UFAC) are specific to the finish and furnishings industry.

The *American National Standards Institute (ANSI)* is a private corporation that was founded in 1918 as the American Engineering Standards Committee. It is a coordinator of voluntary standards development. ANSI does not develop standards. Rather, it establishes a method by which standards can be developed and defined; this is known as the *American National Standard (ANS) consensus process*. (See also the inset titled "Code and Standards Changes" in this chapter.)

Presently, more than 220 organizations use the ANS consensus process, which results in over 10,000 standards. Accredited organizations include code and standards organizations, industry trade associations, and sustainability-related organizations. The ICC and NFPA, as well as most of the standards organizations described in this section, use this process to develop new standards. By representing virtually every facet of trade, commerce, organized labor, and the consumer, ANSI's approval procedures ensure a consensus of interests. They are widely accepted on an international level, and local jurisdictions often require compliance with ANSI standards. Although many standards organizations use the ANS consensus process, using the ANSI designation as part of the standard's title is optional.

In addition to maintaining a standardization process, ANSI acts as an overall monitor to the standards industry by establishing priorities and avoiding duplication between different standards. ANSI now also offers third-party certification, which is an important part of sustainability codes and standards. (See Appendix A.)

National Fire Protection Association

The National Fire Protection Association was originally founded in 1896 to develop standards for the early use of sprinklers. Today it is one of the largest standards organizations. It develops and publishes more than 300 different standards, many of which are referenced in the codes and used internationally. Each document is available from NFPA in printed or digital form. Many can be viewed on their website.

As mentioned earlier in this chapter, the NFPA also publishes a full set of codes. All of the NFPA codes, as well as those produced by the ICC, reference the NFPA standards in their text. Many of the NFPA standards are geared to fire protection. Generally, they are designed to reduce the extent of injury, loss of life, and destruction of property during a fire. Their testing requirements cover everything from textiles to fire-fighting equipment and means of egress design. The standards are developed by committees made up of NFPA members using the ANS consensus process. (See the inset titled "Code and Standards Changes" in this chapter.) They are reviewed and updated as needed. Many of the NFPA standards as they relate to building interiors are discussed throughout this book.

International Code Council

The *International Code Council (ICC)* is best known for its set of I-Codes. However, the ICC can be considered a standards organization as well. It currently has six standards available. Known as I-Standards, the ICC uses the ANS consensus process to create and update them. (See the inset titled "Code and Standards Changes" in this chapter.) The most widely used standard is *ICC A117.1, Accessible and Usable Buildings and Facilities* (also referred to as the *ICC A117.1*).

The *ICC A117.1* standard addresses the accessibility characteristics of buildings and their interiors. In addition to the many technical requirements included in the standard, the *ICC A117.1* standard refers to other industry standards for certain items such as power-operated doors, elevator/escalators, and signaling systems. (This standard will be discussed in Chapter 2.)

Other ICC standards are more building-type specific, such as the *ICC 300, Bleachers, Folding and Telescopic Seating, and Grandstands*, or are not interior-related. Originally published in 2008, *ICC 700, National Green Building Standard (NGBS)* was developed in conjunction with and published by the National Association of Home Builders. The *NGBS* was written to coordinate with the I-Codes and was created specifically for residential buildings, including single-family and multifamily homes,

> ☑ **Note**
>
> When a code requirement is different from that of a standard referenced by the code, the code requirement takes precedence over the standard.

> ☑ **Note**
>
> The accessibility chapter of the *IBC* provides the scoping parameters and references the *ICC A117.1* for technical requirements.

home remodeling/additions, and hotels/motels—as long as they are not classified as Institutional Occupancies (as explained in Chapter 2). Many regional and local green initiatives refer to the standard for energy-efficient homes. The standard is also referenced in the *International Green Construction Code (IgCC),* also developed by the ICC. The most recent edition is 2020. It is the only green residential building rating system approved by ANSI.

Beginning with the 2012 edition, the *ICC 700* is coordinated with the I-Codes including the *IECC.* The *NGBS* is unique in that, in addition to setting minimum requirements, it uses a point system to rate the environmental impact of the design and construction of a building. Similar to LEED or Green Globes green rating systems (see Appendix A), it allows a project to accumulate points as sustainability requirements are incorporated into the project. Points are acquired for lot preparation and design, resource efficiency, energy efficiency, water efficiency, indoor environmental quality, and operation and maintenance. Dedicated chapters are included to address renovations and remodeling projects, including small additions. The standard also allows the design to take two different paths, either a prescriptive path or a performance path. In each case, as more sustainable practices are used, more points are attained so that a building can be classified as one of the four threshold levels: Bronze, Silver, Gold, or Emerald. (See also the sections "Sustainability Considerations" in Appendix A and Appendix C for more information.)

Specific sections of the *NGBS* can be selected by a jurisdiction to establish a minimum level of compliance specific to its needs. For example, a jurisdiction may require all new residential buildings to meet the minimum threshold of Silver. Or, if water conservation is critical in that jurisdiction, the water conservation section of the standard might require a higher Gold rating, whereas the remaining sections require only a Silver rating. Because the thresholds are part of an enforceable standard, the requirements are reviewed by the code official as part of the code process.

ASTM International

The American Society for Testing and Materials (ASTM) is a standards-writing organization formed in 1898 as a nonprofit corporation. In 2002, it changed its name to ASTM International to reflect its global reach and participation. ASTM International primarily manages the development of standards and the promotion of related technical knowledge received from over 30,000 members around the world. Numerous ASTM committees and subcommittees review and manage this information.

There are more than 12,000 ASTM standards used to ensure quality and safety across a broad range of industries, materials, and consumer products. These standards are updated and/or published each year in a

✎ Note

When using the *NGBS*, the building must be designed to perform at the highest level in each section of the standard before the building as a whole can achieve the next level of recognition.

✎ Note

The largest international standards-setting organization is the International Organization for Standardization (ISO), with national standards bodies in more than 140 countries. The United States is represented in the ISO by ANSI.

multiple-volume *Annual Book of ASTM Standards*. These standards are divided into 15 different categories, two of which include construction and textiles. Many of the ASTM standards are referenced in the codes and other reference materials. These standards can be obtained from ASTM International both in print and digitally. In addition, they publish a special set of the ASTM standards that are used by the building industry including as referenced in the *IBC, IRC, and IFC*. This collection is updated every three years to coincide with the publication of the I-Codes. The NFPA codes reference some of these standards as well.

TESTING AGENCIES AND CERTIFICATION

Standards affect the way building materials and products are made. Many of these standards are required by the building codes. Others are required by the federal government or a local jurisdiction. For example, many jurisdictions adopt a standard that will require a certain level of sustainable practices but do not have a complete sustainability code. In addition, there are industry standards that can be used when specifying a product. These are typically considered "best practices" standards because they are not technically enforced by a jurisdiction.

The codes, standards, and federal regulations typically require that tested and/or certified building materials and products be specified. Manufacturers typically use outside testing agencies to obtain third-party certification of their products. Several independent testing agencies and certification organizations, in the United States and throughout the world, have been approved to perform these tests. A manufacturer will send the chosen organization either a component or a finished product, which is then tested and evaluated.

Tested products are given a permanent label or certificate to prove that they pass a required standard. Depending on the test and the specific standard, the manufacturer will either attach a label to the product or keep a certificate on file. For example, a fire-rated door typically has a label on the edge of the door; rated glazing is required to have details etched into the glass. Other materials, such as carpets or wallcoverings, might not be easily labeled. Instead, these labels may be located on samples or available from the manufacturer on request.

Often, these testing agencies and certification organizations have their own mark of approval. Some may have more than one mark. Each mark indicates a different level of approval or certification. It is important to know what each mark indicates on a product when specifying or approving the use of a specific product. It is also important to keep records of the specified products. Examples of common product marks include Underwriters Laboratories (UL), ENERGY STAR®, WaterSense®, Green Seal, GREENGUARD, and FSC Certified. Each standards organization will have descriptions and images of their marks on their websites.

ASTM International is taking an active role in coordinating the development of sustainable standards. The first two available standards, *E2114, Terminology for Sustainability Relative to the Performance of Buildings,* and *E2129, Practice for Data Collection for Sustainability Assessment of Building Products,* establish the basic vocabulary and methodology for the practice of sustainable design. The standard *ASTM E2432, Guide for General Principles of Sustainability Relative to Buildings* has been instrumental in setting basic principles from which other sustainable standards can be developed. (See also Appendix A.) Although not referenced by the codes, they are used by manufacturers to evaluate new sustainable products and by standards organizations to develop additional sustainable standards. ASTM has also developed the ASTM Product Certification Program to work with manufacturers, distributors, or private brand vendors to have their product tested by a third-party source and confirm that their products conform to one or more standards. It is a voluntary program but the *ASTM Directory of Certified Products* can help designers to determine if products contribute to the sustainability of a project.

ASTM E2921 Standard Practice for Minimum Criteria for Comparing Whole Building Life Cycle Assessments for Use with Building Codes, Standards, and Rating Systems is intended to assist with the evaluation of the environmental impact of a building including material selection, operating energy as part of a LCA required by a building code, other standard or sustainable rating system. The current edition is 2016.

NSF International

The National Sanitation Foundation (NSF), formed in 1944 and now known as NSF International, is a standards organization that focuses on food, water, indoor air, consumer products and the environment. Using the ANS consensus process, NSF International has developed more than 80 standards. NSF tests and certifies a wide variety of products, including electrical, fire safety, and plumbing elements. It also develops standards to provide third-party certification for several sustainability programs, including the Environmental Protection Agency's (EPA's) WaterSense® program. (See the inset titled "Federal Sustainability Certifications" in Appendix A.) Some of the standards created by NSF can be found in the ICC and NFPA codes.

NSF also creates sustainability standards. Their standards are life-cycle and multi-attribute based. The first interior finish standard, *NSF 140, Sustainability Assessment for Carpet* was initially published in 2007. The most current edition is 2019. The standards provide criteria for sustainable life cycle practices for products from raw material extraction, manufacturing, and use to end-of-life management. NSF has developed and continues to develop other sustainability standards as well, including ones for resilient flooring, wallcovering, and fabric for commercial furnishings: *NSF 332–2011, Sustainability Assessment for Resilient flooring, NSF 336–2018 Sustainability Assessment for Commercial Furnishings Fabric and NSF 342–2019 Sustainability Assessment for Wallcovering Products*. (See the section "Sustainability Considerations" in Chapter 10 for more information.)

American Society of Heating, Refrigeration, and Air-Conditioning Engineers

The American Society of Heating, Refrigeration, and Air-Conditioning Engineers (ASHRAE) came into existence in 1959 with the merger of two engineering groups. ASHRAE is a worldwide standards organization. It sponsors research projects and develops standards for performance levels of HVAC (heating, ventilating, and air conditioning) and refrigeration systems. ASHRAE standards, developed using the ANS consensus process, include uniform testing methods, design requirements, and recommended standard practices. ASHRAE also produces various guides and other special publications to assist with the implementation of its standards.

In the past, ASHRAE standards were typically used by mechanical engineers and refrigerant specialists and installers. More recently, ASHRAE started developing sustainability-related standards. These include *ASHRAE/IESNA 90.1, Energy Standard for Buildings Except Low-Rise Residential Buildings*, and *ASHRAE/IESNA 90.2, Energy-Efficient Design of New Low-Rise Residential Buildings*, which were developed in conjunction with the Illuminating Engineering Society of North America (IESNA). These standards, now updated on a three-year cycle, address building elements such as the building envelope, light fixtures and controls, HVAC systems, water heating, and energy management. They are referenced by the ICC and NFPA energy codes and are the basis for most of the energy provisions required in the United States. (See the sections "Energy Codes" and "Energy Policy Act" earlier in this chapter.)

ASHRAE also partnered with the U.S. Green Building Council (USGBC) and IESNA to develop another sustainability standard titled *ASHRAE/USGBC/IES 189.1, Standard for the Design of High-Performance Green Buildings Except Low-Rise Residential Buildings*. Completed in 2009, *ASHRAE 189.1* applies to new commercial buildings and major renovation projects, addressing sustainable sites, water use and energy efficiency, a building's impact on the atmosphere, materials and resources,

❖ Note

Two federally developed labeling systems include ENERGY STAR® for electrical devices and WaterSense® for plumbing fixtures.

❖ Note

ASHRAE publishes multiple guides, including the *Advanced Energy Design Guidelines (AEDGs)*. The *AEDGs* promote exceeding the established energy efficiency standards to achieve net-zero energy buildings. They are available on their website: ashrae.org.

◆ Note

USGBC, the creator of the LEED rating system was involved in the development of *ASHRAE 189.1*. The standard is structured similarly to LEED but was written with mandatory code language so that it could be enforced more like a code. A building built to the standard would be similar to a LEED Silver–certified building.

◆ Note

UL-labeled products may include country-specific identifiers such as US (United States), C (Canada), S (Japan), and D (Europe) to show that they comply with that country's product safety standards.

indoor environmental quality, and post-occupancy building commissioning and operations planning. It is also a resource for buildings that are intended to exceed the minimum requirement of the energy standard *ASHRAE/IESNA 90.1*. (See Chapter 7.) In 2018, ICC and ASHRAE merged the IgCC and 190.1 into one document. Because it is written more like a code than a rating system, *ASHRAE 189.1* can be used by a jurisdiction and/or a building owner that wants to incorporate sustainable practices. It can also assist in meeting the requirement of a green rating system (e.g., LEED, Green Globes). (See the section "Sustainability Codes" earlier in this chapter.)

Underwriters Laboratories

Underwriters Laboratories (UL) is both a standards developing organization and a testing agency that lists products. It is the largest and oldest nationally recognized testing laboratory in the United States and has over 170 testing laboratories and certification facilities around the world. It tests many products that could be used in an interior project including building materials, electrical/lighting elements, fire suppression, life safety equipment, security equipment, furniture, and bedding.

Typically, UL performs tests on products using an existing standard developed by another organization or by UL. If no standard exists, UL will create a new one based on the desired characteristics. More than 1,600 different UL safety standards, created using the ANS consensus process, are published in the UL *Catalog of Standards*. In addition, UL offers a comprehensive volume of standards referenced in the *IBC*. UL standards are referenced in the NFPA codes as well. More recently, UL created a sister company, UL Environment™, to provide third-party certification for a variety of sustainability programs. (See Appendix A.) These services include GREENGUARD, ECOLOGO Certifications, and Environmental Product Declarations (EPD), which help verify and highlight a products level of sustainability. (See Appendix A.)

UL's findings are recognized worldwide. When a product is listed, it receives a permanent label or classification marking that identifies Underwriters Laboratories, the word *classified*, a class rating, and a UL control number. UL has a database of products, components and assemblies called UL Product iQ™ available on their website.

UL LABELS

Underwriters Laboratories tests a wide variety of products all over the world. The UL label is the most widely recognized mark of compliance with safety requirements. These safety requirements are based on UL standards as well as standards from other organizations. Most federal, state and municipal authorities, as well as architects, designers, contractors, and building owners and users, accept and recognize the UL mark.

UL can test whole products, components, materials, and systems, depending on the standard required. Of the close to 20,000 different types of products tested, examples related to interior projects include building materials, finishes, upholstered furniture, electrical products, HVAC equipment, safety devices, and the like. Once the initial product passes a test, it is retested at random to make sure that it continues to function properly.

There are four common types of labels or UL marks a product sold in the United States (US) and/or Canada (C) can receive. (Other marks are more specific to other industries and/or other countries.) The UL website describes them as follows:

1. Listing Mark. The most popular, this mark indicates that samples of the product have been tested and evaluated and comply with UL requirements. It is found on a wide variety of appliances and equipment, including alarm systems, extinguishing systems, and light fixtures. The mark generally includes the UL registered name or symbol, the product name, a control number, and the word *listed*.

2. Classification Mark. This label may list a product's properties, limited hazards, and/or suitability for certain uses. It is found on building materials such as fire doors, as well as on industrial equipment. The label includes the UL name or symbol and a statement indicating the extent of the UL evaluation and a control number.

3. Recognized Component Mark. This covers the evaluation of a component only, such as electrical parts. The component is later factory-installed in a complete product or system. The label includes a manufacturer's identification and product model number.

4. Certificate. This is used when it is difficult to apply one label to a whole system. The certificate indicates the type of system and the extent of the evaluation. It accompanies the product and is issued to the end user on installation.

UL has other product-specific marks for plumbing fixtures and fittings, security-related products, and smoke detectors and fire alarms. UL also has marks specific to other countries. For example, the S Mark in Japan.

UL also has the Energy Mark for equipment and appliances that meet specific energy-efficiency requirements. A subsidiary, known as UL Environment™, validates environmental claims and certifies sustainable products as part of a third-party verification process.

Global Standards

In an effort to globalize standard development and use, many of the US standards organizations have facilities located in or agreements with other countries. Examples include Underwriters Laboratories, NSF International, and ASTM International. In addition, one of the largest global standards-setting organizations outside of the United States is the ISO, which has representation in more than 157 countries. For example, ISO standards are used extensively in Europe as well as Japan and China. Some ISO standards are referenced by codes in the United States. Unlike US-based standards, which are approved by a membership base made up of individuals, the ISO global standards are approved on a national level with each country getting one vote. (For more information see the insets titled "Code and Standards Changes" in this chapter and ISO Standards for Sustainability in Appendix A.)

The Canadian Engineering Standards Association was originally begun as a standard writing and certification agency for electrical and engineering standards. Reorganized and renamed as the CSA Group, it is now a standard writing, certification, and testing organization. CSA Group is recognized in Canada, the United States, and in many other countries. CSA Group provides certification marks, labels, and product listing to meet various standards, including sustainability and energy efficiency. For example, the DOE recognizes CSA Group for verification of energy efficiency, including testing for ENERGY STAR® requirements from the Environmental Protection Agency (EPA). Their marks are also recognized by OSHA for a wide variety of products including electrical, electronics, gas-fired, building, plumbing, and so on.

SPECIAL USE CODES

In addition to the typical codes, standards, and federal regulations already mentioned, there may be more specific codes within each jurisdiction. Some may be developed by the city, county or state local governments. Many state and local jurisdictions have created "green building programs" that mandate certain buildings to meet specific sustainability standards and/or LEED certification levels. Zoning regulations that control the use of land within a jurisdiction such as site setbacks, historic preservation rules, and neighborhood conservation restrictions may not typically affect an interior project.

Other regulations may only apply to specific types of projects, Examples include schools, day care centers, hotels and motels, restaurants, and health care facilities including hospitals. Although many of these regulations affect the management and policies of the user, some of the requirements can affect spaces that are required, the size of the space and the interior finishes that are required. For example, state health codes must typically be followed when working on projects that involve food preparation, such as restaurants. In addition, certain occupancies (e.g., hospitals) have regulations that must be incorporated into the design for the facility to obtain a license to operate. These regulations can control room sizes, adjacencies, amenities, and use of spaces with the building. (See Chapter 11 and Appendix A.)

This book does not cover these unique state and local codes or industry based regulations. It is important to consult the jurisdiction of a project for these specific regulations so that they can be appropriately researched and referenced. (See the section "Code Enforcement" in Chapter 11.)

✎ Note

State and local jurisdictions may have additional code requirements and government regulations that must be followed. Consult with the jurisdiction of the project.

RESEARCH: USING THE CODES

Depending on the type of interior project and the jurisdiction in which it is located, you could be using several codes, regulations, and standards described in this chapter. If you are uncertain which codes will be enforced, consult the code officials in the jurisdiction of the project or check the website of the jurisdiction for an adopted code list. The process of determining the applicable codes, standards and regulations is discussed in more detail in the section titled "Code Research and Design" in Chapter 11 of this book.

If you are not already familiar with the code requirements, it is important to do some research before you begin designing. The following chapters of this book can lead you through the research process appropriate for most projects. However, as you work on the project, continue to refer to the specific documents and compare the requirements in each of the applicable codes, standards, and regulations. The most stringent requirement must be incorporated in the design. You will find that as you research the codes, additional codes and standards may need to be referenced and researched.

It is important to document the codes and standards that you have used in your design. Typically, they are required to be identified as part of the documentation of the project. Use the online checklists provided with this book to help you document the appropriate information. (See also the "Documentation" section in Chapter 11.)

✎ Note

The National Institute of Building Sciences (NIBS) and the National Conference of States on Building Codes and Standards (NCSBCS) play a major role in supporting the use of codes or standards.

✎ Note

To document your research, you may want to keep copies or snapshots of specific sections of the codes that pertain to your project in your files.

CHAPTER 2

ACCESSIBILITY

Similar to the many code requirements that make it safe to occupy a building or space and exit in the event of a fire, accessibility requirements make it safe and *possible* for persons with disabilities to occupy buildings on a daily basis. Most buildings and their interiors are required to be accessible to persons with disabilities by several codes, standards, and federal regulations. The jurisdiction, the building type, the occupancy classification, and who owns and operates the building will determine which accessibility requirements apply to a project. More than one source may need to be used. The various sources are discussed in this chapter.

The objective of each accessibility guideline is to create an environment where the individual can approach and enter a building, perform the intended task (eat, work, shop, learn, receive care, etc.), and exit the building safely and independently. In a few cases when persons with disabilities are not expected to be able to leave the building safely or effectively, additional requirements are included in the codes to allow for their safety and assistance by firefighters. (Area of refuges and elevator evacuation are discussed in Chapter 5.) Also, the ability to perform personal care such as using the toilet facilities or bathing, if appropriate, must be possible. In most cases, every activity that can be accomplished by a person without a disability must be possible by someone with a disability, including mobility, sight, and hearing disabilities. To do this, accessibility requirements will affect exterior and interior building elements, beginning with the public access to the building. Interior elements that will be affected include room configurations and sizes, door locations, plumbing fixture types and locations, mounting heights of controls and accessories, floor finishes, and more. Because so many individual aspects of a building are required to be accessible, specific requirements have been discussed in the individual chapters of this book.

Accessibility requirements can be applicable to both new construction and renovations, and in many cases, existing spaces. Unlike most building codes, there is often no grandfathering from compliance. This means that even if the space was built before the accessibility requirements were applicable, the space may need to be modified to meet the current requirements. Building codes are generally not retroactive in this way. The conditions that must be met for each level of project are discussed in this chapter.

Some accessibility guidelines will set the *scope* of compliance that must be achieved—in other words, the number of each element (entrances, toilets, cabinets, etc.) that must be usable and to what extent. In some cases, it may be acceptable that a person could get into a room but not necessarily use everything in the room, whereas in other cases, the room and its contents must be accessible. This will vary by the guideline and specific use. Other accessibility guidelines set *technical* requirements. These describe how building elements should be specified, designed, and located so that they are usable by someone with a disability. This will include the size of a room, location of a toilet, mounting height of a control, configuration of grab bars, and so on. Discussion and diagrams of these specific requirements are addressed in the pertinent chapters of this book. Typically, the most restrictive requirements are presented. Any conflicting requirements are explained as well. This chapter will provide an overview of the various accessibility requirement sources and their application.

A BRIEF HISTORY

The built environment has caused difficulties for persons with disabilities for as long as there have been buildings. Stairs, level changes, narrow doorways, and so on have been obstacles as part of the typical design of buildings and spaces. For a long time, modifications or accommodations for persons with disabilities, especially mobile disabilities, were at the discretion or willingness of the building owner or occupants. This made access inconsistent and unreliable.

One of the events accredited to bringing attention to and inspiring change occurred in 1957. That year as part of President Eisenhower's Committee on the Employment of the Physically Handicapped, Hugo Deffner was to receive the annual "Handicapped American of the Year Award" because of his efforts advocating for accessibility in public buildings in his hometown of Oklahoma City, Oklahoma. While the president was waiting on the stage to present the award to him, Deffner, who used a wheelchair because of polio, was unable to get into the building because of stairs at the entrance. Ultimately, Marines had to lift and carry him and his wheelchair up the stairs, into the building, and onto the stage. The incident was said to have disturbed President Eisenhower and his committee. At their next meeting they began an effort to develop a standard to address architectural barriers. This led to the development of the first *ANSI A117.1 American Standard Specification for Making Buildings and Facilities Accessible to and Usable by the Physically Handicapped* released in 1961. This document eventually became the *ICC A117.1* document in use today, which is discussed throughout this book.

The federal government continued to implement legislation and develop guidelines to address accessibility in facilities built, altered, or leased using federal funds. Legislation that was passed includes the Architectural Barriers Act (ABA) in 1968, Rehabilitation Act in 1973, and the expansion of the 1968 Fair Housing Act in 1988. Each had accompanying guidelines and standards that gave direction how to design and arrange buildings so that they were usable by persons with various disabilities including mobility, sight, hearing, and other conditions. The specific impact of each of these legislations on the accessibility of federal buildings is discussed in this chapter.

One of the most far reaching legislations was signed into law in 1990 by President George Bush. The Americans With Disabilities Act (ADA) followed the concept of the 1964 Civil Rights Act that prohibited discrimination based on race, color, religion, sex, or national origin in employment, public accommodation, participation in federally funded programs, voting, and education. The ADA is a civil rights law that prohibits discrimination against persons with disabilities in the areas of employment, participation in state and local government programs, services and access to their facilities, access to buildings owned and operated by the public, and access and use of public transportation. This legislation applies to most building and interior projects that are not federal projects.

To develop guidelines and design criteria for accessibility, the United States Access Board Guidelines (also known as the Architectural and Transportation Barriers Compliance Board, or ATBCB or U.S. Access Board) was formed in 1973. This federal agency includes representatives from several federal departments and the public. It is dedicated to promoting and ensuring accessibility for people with disabilities. For example, the guidelines developed by the Access Board eventually became the technical and scoping guidelines for several of the federal regulations, including the ADA. Its requirements and applicability are discussed in more detail later in this chapter, as well.

The most prominently adopted and applicable codes, standards and federal legislations that affect buildings and their interiors are discussed in this chapter. The specific requirements, however, are introduced and explained in the individual chapters where they apply.

Knowing which accessibility requirements apply to your design is important. These federal accessibility guidelines, building codes, and adopted standards give designers specific design criteria for accessibility in all aspects of interior and architectural design. Most projects must comply with one or more of these documents. Although there has been collaboration between the organizations that develop the individual guidelines, the *ICC A117.1* and the *IBC*, for example, continue to be updated so some variations will continue. Using a rule of thumb to apply the most stringent requirement or provide a solution that satisfies both requirements may be necessary. In some cases, the building official can assist to clarify discrepancies. If there is conflict between federal and local guidelines or if a federal requirement is unclear for a specific condition, an opinion from the Access Board or federal agency can be requested. But in all cases, accessibility to the maximum extent possible should be the goal. (See the inset titled "Accessibility Requirements Compared" in Federal Regulations.)

☞ Note

The Access Board, ICC, and NFPA have created comparison documents of the accessibility requirements found in each of their respective publications. These documents can be found on their websites.

☞ Note

The Accessibility chapter in the IBC is Chapter 11. The Accessibility chapter in *NFPA 5000* is Chapter 12.

CODES AND STANDARDS

Accessibility is measured by the extent to which a building or space is usable by persons with disabilities and how that accessibility is accomplished. Although the ADA with the *ADA 2010 Standards* may be the most widespread accessibility requirement because of its applicability to almost all projects, it is not the responsibility of the local code official to review against that document because it is part of a federal law. Therefore, state and local jurisdictions often adopt or develop a document that they can use and enforce. The most prominent accessibility documents are discussed in the following sections.

To clarify, some accessibility guidelines set the scope and rely on another document to describe how it is to be achieved and vice versa. Some guidelines set the scope and the technical requirements. *Scope* determines the number of elements or types of areas that must meet the requirements. For example, the document may indicate that only one accessible toilet is required or half of all provided. *Technical* requirements will indicate by dimensions, diagrams, description, and physical details how to configure or design a space or element that is usable by persons with various disabilities. This means that more than one document and even a multiple of accessibility guidelines can apply to your project.

Building Codes

The *IBC* and the *NFPA 5000* have a chapter addressing accessibility. These chapters establish the *scope* of compliance for specific elements and areas of a project including accessible routes, entrances, dwelling units, sleeping units, special occupancies, signage, and so on. Each publication states that the intent is to meet or exceed the requirements established by the *2010 ADA Standards*. Because the building codes only contain scoping parameters, they both refer to the *ICC A117.1* for the technical requirements. This means that if a jurisdiction adopts the *IBC* or the *NFPA*, they by default include some applicable accessibility requirements.

However, some jurisdictions may want a different set of scoping or technical requirements so they will amend their adoption of the *IBC* or *NFPA 5000* to exclude the accessibility chapter. In place of the current accessibility chapter, they will reference a different document.

ICC A117.1

The *ICC A117.1 Accessible and Usable Buildings and Facilities* was the first standard written to address accessibility in buildings and continues to be the most widely known. As mentioned previously, this was originally developed by ANSI as the *ANSI A117.1*. It originally addressed walks, parking, entrances, doors, toilet rooms, drinking fountains, public telephones, and elevators. Over the years, it was expanded to cover other interior and exterior elements. In addition to being used for buildings developed by private entities and local and state governments, in 1974 the Department of Housing and Urban Development (HUD) joined the committee in charge of the standard. Beginning in 1998, it has been updated and published by the International Code Council (ICC), which also develops the I-Codes. (See Chapter 1.) This code is updated less often than the other codes. The most current editions of the *ICC A117.1* include 2009 and 2017. Older editions of this standard were used as the basis for the original guidelines for the ADA, ABA, and the FHA legislations (discussed later). It primarily contains

✍ Note

Accessible means of egress requirements are included in the Means of Egress chapters in the IBC and the *NFPA 5000*.

✍ Note

The accessibility chapter of the *IBC* requires that the work area and the residential area of a live/work unit be evaluated separately.

technical requirements for accessible routes, site and building elements, plumbing, communication elements, special rooms and spaces, built-in furniture, and equipment. It also contains special provisions for dwelling units, sleeping units, and recreational facilities. The *ICC A117.1* becomes applicable to a project when a local jurisdiction adopts a building code that references it or they adopt it as their accessibility standard separate from the building code. This may occur because the building codes reference a specific edition of the *ICC A117.1*. The jurisdiction may want to enforce a newer edition of the document. For example, the 2018 *IBC* references the 2009 *ICC A117.1* but the 2021 *IBC* references the 2017 *ICC A117.1*.

◤ **Note**

The 2018 *IBC* references the 2009 *ICC A117.1* but the 2021 *IBC* references the 2017 *ICC A117.1*.

State or Local Accessibility Codes

Most jurisdictions rely on a combination of the accessibility chapter in the building code and the *ICC A117.1* for their local accessibility requirements. However, there are few state and local governments that have their own unique accessibility codes. These may be based on the *ICC A117.1* or the *2010 ADA Standards* but vary in the organization, extent of accessibility required or the specific requirements, or they can be completely different. Regardless, the jurisdiction can use these documents to review proposed designs and evaluate existing conditions for accessibility like they do for building code compliance. If a jurisdiction has an accessibility code, they typically amend their adoption of the building code to exclude the use of the accessibility chapter to avoid conflict with their separate document. Local jurisdictions can also develop unique guidelines for specific use or occupancies, such as *Inclusive Design Guidelines Sports & Recreation: New York City*.

Certain state or local accessibility codes have been reviewed by the DOJ and are certified to be equivalent or to exceed the requirements of the ADA (this is discussed later in the chapter). Where differences occur between a locally enforced guideline and the ADA, it is important to remember the objective is always to provide the highest level of accessibility.

FEDERAL REGULATIONS

Architectural Barriers Act

The *Architectural Barriers Act (ABA)*, which became law in 1968, was the first *federal* legislation that addressed accessibility. The *ABA* requires access to facilities designed, built, altered, or leased with federal funds. It applies to a wide variety of federal buildings, such as post offices, Social Security offices, prisons, and national park facilities. It may also apply to nongovernment facilities such as schools, public housing, and mass transit facilities that receive certain types of federal funding.

The *ABA* also established the ATBCB (or U.S. Access Board) and charged it with development of a set of guidelines for the *ABA*. First issued in 1989, these guidelines were called the *Uniform Federal Accessibility Standards (UFAS)*. Recently, the *UFAS* has been replaced by a new document entitled *ABA Standards*, which are derived from the 2004 *ADA-ABA Accessibility Guidelines* developed by the Access Board. (See the inset titled "ADA-ABA Accessibility Guidelines Development.") The four agencies accountable for compliance under the *ABA* law and with the *ABA Standards* for the design of buildings and spaces under their departments are the General Services Administration (GSA), which is responsible for most federal buildings; the Department of Defense (DOD) for military facilities; HUD for government housing; and the US Postal Service (USPS) for postal facilities. The Department of Transportation (DOT) has also adopted similar guidelines for use in transportation facilities such as airports and train terminals. These standards are referred to as the *ADA Standards for Transportation Facilities*.

In some cases, the *ABA Standards* and the *2010 ADA Standards* will both apply to a building developed with private and federal funding. Although this would have been a challenge under the original *UFAS* and *ADA Accessibility Guidelines (ADAAG)* because requirements varied, the revised *ABA Standard* and the *2010 ADA Standards* use the same set of technical requirements and differ only in scoping requirement, making compliance with both easier.

Fair Housing Act

The Fair Housing Act (FHA) is a federal legislation enforced by HUD in partnership with the Department of Justice (DOJ). Established in 1968, the FHA originally was intended to regulate and protect consumers

---

☑ Note

Starting with the 2009 editions, the ICC and NFPA codes reference the *ICC A117.1* standard for technical requirements.

☑ Note

Federally funded buildings are covered by the ABA. These projects must follow the requirements of the *ABA Standards*.

☑ Note

Residential occupancies may have to meet the requirements of the *Federal Housing Accessibility Guidelines (FHAG)*, *UFAS*, or *ABA Standards*, if federally funded, and in some cases, the *ADA Standards* as well.

from discrimination because of race, color, national origin, religion, sex, or family status in housing when buying or renting. In 1988, the FHA was expanded to cover persons with disabilities and include accessibility requirements. The FHA regulations apply to private housing, private housing that receives federal financial assistance, and state and local government housing. The FHA typically pertains to multi-unit housing that has four or more dwelling units, such as apartments, condominiums, dormitories, and assisted living facilities. The accessible design requirements apply to new construction but do not apply to existing buildings renovated to serve as housing or housing built before 1991. Although the FHA is not specifically accessibility legislation, it does incorporate several provisions for people with disabilities and families with children.

In 1991, HUD developed the final *Fair Housing Accessibility Guidelines (FHAG)* to help clarify the requirements. Many of the interior aspects of a dwelling are regulated, such as the location of thermostats, electrical outlets, light switches, and maneuvering areas in hallways, bathrooms, and kitchens. In addition, at least the ground-floor units must be accessible and meet specific construction requirements. In some cases, "adaptable dwelling units" can be used and other cases certain accessible features must be incorporated in the dwelling, but it does not have to be completely accessible. The public elements of these facilities, such as the related sales and rental offices, are covered by the ADA. HUD also enforces Title II (public services) of the ADA when it relates to state and local public housing, housing assistance, and housing referrals; these types of projects may have to follow additional requirements based on the ADA requirements.

HUD endorses other documents as being equivalent to the most current version of the *FHAG*. These documents are considered to have "safe harbor" status, which means that it meets or exceeds the requirements in the *FHAG*. HUD recognizes 10 safe harbor documents, which include the use of specific versions of the *ICC/ANSI A117.1* (2009) and *IBC* (2009, 2012, 2015, 2018) when used in conjunction with other HUD documents. These are updated periodically, but the most current list can be found on their website.

⬛ Note

HUD recognizes 10 safe harbor documents, which include the use of current and past versions of the *ICC/ANSI A117.1* and *IBC* when used with their documents. See the complete list on the FHA website: www.fairhousingfirst.org/faq/safeharbors.html.

Americans with Disabilities Act

The Americans with Disabilities Act (ADA) is a federal civil law that prohibits discrimination against people with disabilities in buildings owned and operated by a private entity (not the federal government) and state and local governmental buildings. Although the ADA addresses more than just buildings, it is the most prominent and widely applicable accessibility standard that affects the design and renovation of buildings and interior spaces. Because it is a federal law, the ADA is enforceable throughout the United States and for most projects. It is applicable even if the local jurisdiction has a separate standard. Whether the project is new construction or a renovation to an existing building may affect how it applies.

Background

The ADA was enacted on July 26, 1990, and became enforceable beginning in 1992. Prior to this, only federal buildings and federally funded projects had to be made accessible under the *ABA* and its related *UFAS*. The ADA was developed by the DOJ and the DOT. The ADA is composed of five "titles." Each part protects individuals with disabilities in different environments and for different services. The titles cover the areas of employment (Title I), state and local government services and public transportation (Title II), public accommodations and commercial facilities (Title III), and telecommunication services (Title IV). The regulations that apply most often to interior projects are found in Title II and Title III. Title II applies to facilities and spaces where state and local governments provide services or hold events for the public. Title III of the ADA applies to facilities or spaces that would be considered a *place of public accommodations* or a *commercial facility*, which will be most projects. Title I could apply if changes such as adding a ramp or providing an adjustable desk is needed to accommodate employees because of their specific needs. And if public communication is provided, Title IV may also apply, as it requires the provision of relay services for those with hearing and speech impairments.

Places Requiring Accessibility

The ADA requires accessibility compliance in places of public accommodation and commercial facilities. The levels of compliance for public accommodations and commercial facilities are slightly different. A *place of public accommodation* is defined by the ADA as any facility that is owned, leased, leased to, or operated by a private entity whose operation affects commerce and falls within one of the 12 categories listed here. Some examples are provided in each category, although other types of facilities may be included as well.

> **◤ Note**
>
> The Access Board researches accessibility needs and is responsible for updating the ADA guidelines and providing other guidance materials. To review materials available from the Access Board, go to www. access-board.gov.

> **◤ Note**
>
> The ADA covers other aspects of accessibility that can affect a project, including employment, communication, and equipment.

❑ *Place of lodging.* A hotel, assisted living facility, or dormitory (except for owner-occupied establishments renting fewer than six rooms)

❑ *Establishment serving food.* A restaurant, bar, or cafeteria

❑ *Place of exhibition or entertainment.* A sports arena, theater, or concert hall

❑ *Place of public gathering.* An auditorium, convention center, or city hall

❑ *Sale or rental establishment.* A grocery store, clothing store, or shopping center

❑ *Service establishment.* A doctor's office, beauty shop, funeral parlor, pharmacy, or hospital

❑ *Station for public transportation.* An airport, train station, or bus stop/station

❑ *Place of public display.* A museum, library, or art gallery

❑ *Educational facility*: An elementary school, college classroom, or preschool

❑ *Recreation area*: An amusement park, nature park, or zoo

❑ *Place of exercise.* A gym, health spa, or bowling alley

❑ *Social service center.* A homeless shelter, adoption agency, or day care center

◧ Note

Places of public accommodation and commercial facilities are required to comply with the ADA.

A building or space whose use is considered a place of public accommodation assumes that employees, frequent occupants, and visitors will occupy the spaces. An accessible route between the public spaces and many individual elements is required to be usable by a person with disabilities without assistance. Certain spaces such as workrooms, storage areas, and certain raised areas may be allowed more limited access. Also, the services that are provided in the space and policies about the use of the space must also accommodate someone with a disability. This may include assisted hearing devices or alternative communication methods.

Commercial facilities include nonresidential facilities whose operations affect commerce but are not generally open to the public. Examples include factories, warehouses, as well as other businesses that do not typically receive clients or guests, such as a corporate office building or a telemarketing office. In general, commercial facilities must provide physical accessibility but not accommodation for procedures and policies that would affect the business operations. Commercial facilities must provide the strictest level of accessibility for their employees and are not allowed to use some of the alternative requirements permitted for alterations to places of public accommodation. Some facilities could be considered both a commercial facility and a place of public accommodation. For example, if a commercial facility such as a car factory offers public tours, the path of the tour would then be a place of public accommodation. This would require the path to be accessible but also the way in which the tour is given (by guided tour or written instructions, for example). The employee areas of the facility, however, would have to meet the requirements for commercial facilities. (The different levels of compliance are discussed later in this chapter.)

Although most places of public activity are included in the definition exempt from compliance with the ADA. These include facilities that are owned and operated by religious entities, one- and two-family dwellings, and private clubs. Those entities or facilities may not be completely exempt from compliance, however, if part of the facility is used as a place of public accommodation. For example, if a church rents part of its facility to a day care center during the week and the day care center is not operated by the church, the area that the day care center leases would be required to meet ADA requirements. (Although compliance is technically the day care center's responsibility, this assignment of responsibility may be modified in the landlord-tenant agreement.) Similarly, if part of a private residence is used for a business and it is usual for clients to come there for the operation of the business, the part of the residence that is used for the business would have to meet the requirements even though private residences are exempt from the ADA.

Conversely, an educational facility that is operated by a synagogue, for example, may not be required to conform to the ADA because of the exemption for religious entities. In some cases, it may be clear that a project has to comply with the ADA, whereas in other cases further discussion with the client may be needed to determine if the space would be considered a public accommodation or a commercial facility, or if it qualifies for any exemptions. It may be wise to seek an opinion from the Access Board if the nature of a project is not clear.

State and local government facilities are also required to be compliant with the ADA under Title II. The criteria of which facilities or spaces must be compliant is that persons with disabilities must be able to receive services, attend activities, and participate in programs offered by the city, county, or state. Spaces, interior elements, toilets that serve these areas, and so on must be compliant. For example, the counter where you renew car tags, a public school cafeteria, public library checkout counter, and courtroom jury box are examples.

ADAAG and 2010 ADA Standards

☙ **Note**

The original *ADAAG* is no longer the applicable document for compliance with the ADA.

☙ **Note**

The *2010 ADA Standards* and the *ABA Standards* are derived from the *ADA-ABA Accessibility Guidelines*. These guidelines include different scoping requirements for the ADA and the ABA but share the same technical requirements.

☙ **Note**

The *2010 ADA Standards* and the *ICC A117.1* provide alternate accessible requirements for children. If designing a space to be used primarily by children 12 years of age or younger, this information can be very useful.

The first guideline for the ADA was developed by the ATBCB (or U.S. Access Board). This document was originally referred to the *ADAAG*. First adopted by the DOJ in 1991, this document is now referred to as the *1991 ADA Standards*. This standard included scoping and technical requirements. It also included special occupancy sections including restaurants and cafeterias, medical care facilities, business and mercantile, libraries, transient lodging, and transportation facilities. Even after the *ADAAG* was published as the guideline for the ADA, the Access Board continued to research and develop revisions to the guidelines. In 2004, the Access Board released the *ADA-ABA Accessibility Guidelines* for consideration by federal agencies as a new guideline.

In 2010, the DOJ adopted components of the new *ADA-ABA Accessibility Guidelines* to replace the original *ADAAG*. (See the inset titled "ADA-ABA Accessibility Guidelines Development.") This new document for the ADA is referred to as the *2010 ADA Standards*. It is composed of an application chapter and a scoping chapter specifically developed for the ADA and eight technical chapters that were intended to be used by both the ADA and the ABA legislations.

In addition, the Access Board worked closely with the ICC to make the I-Codes and the *2010 ADA Standards* were usable together. As indicated previously, the *IBC* Chapter 11 only has scoping requirements and refers to the *ICC A117.1* for technical requirements; the *2010 ADA Standards* refers to the *IBC* for means of egress issues and the *2010 ADA Standards* is closely coordinated with the *ICC A117.1*. Figure 2.1 summarizes the organization of the *2010 ADA Standards* as compared to the 2017 *ICC A117.1*. When the new standard was adopted, a time line was developed for the transition from the *ADAAG* to the new *2010 ADA Standards*. However, as of March 15, 2012, the *2010 ADA Standards* is

ICC A117.1 (2009)	2010 ADA Standards	IBC Chapter 11: Accessibility
Chapter 1 Application and Administration	**Chapter** 1 Application and Administration	**Section 1101** General*
		Section 1102 Compliance
Chapter 2 Scoping	**Chapter** 2 Scoping Requirements	**Section 1103** Scoping Requirements
Chapter 3 Building Blocks	**Chapter** 3 Building Blocks	(references *ICC A117.1*)
Chapter 4 Accessible Routes	**Chapter** 4 Accessible Routes	**Section 1104** Accessible Route*
Chapter 5 General Site and Building Elements	**Chapter** 5 General Site and Building Elements	**Section 1105** Accessible Entrances
		Section 1106 Parking and Passenger Loading Facilities
Chapter 6 Plumbing Elements and Facilities	**Chapter** 6 Plumbing Elements and Facilities	**Section 1109** Other Features and Facilities*
Chapter 7 Communication Elements and Features	**Chapter** 7 Communication Elements and Features	**Section 1112** Signage*
Chapter 8 Special Rooms and Spaces	**Chapter** 8 Special Rooms, Spaces, and Elements	**Section 1109** Special Occupancies*
Chapter 9 Built-in Furnishings and Equipment	**Chapter** 9 Built-in Elements	**Section 1110** Other Features and Facilities*
Chapter 10 Dwelling Units and Sleeping Units	(Distributed throughout other chapters)	**Section 1108** Dwelling Units and Sleeping Units
Chapter 11 Recreational Facilities	**Chapter** 10 Recreation Facilities	**Section 1111** Recreational Facilities

* Additional advisory information is provided in Appendix E Supplementary Accessibility Requirements and may be helpful but not mandatory unless required by the local AHJ.

Figure 2.1 Comparison of accessibility publications. (This chart is a summary of information contained in the ICC A117.1 standard, the ADA Standards, and Chapter 11 of the IBC. The ICC and the Access Board do not assume responsibility for the accuracy or completeness of this chart.)

the only guideline to be used for ADA compliance. The original *ADAAG* should not be used as it is no longer the official guideline to the ADA and some requirements are different in the two documents, scoping and technical.

As mentioned, the Access Board continually works with other organizations to conduct research and create new documents. Some of the research is used to create proposed additions to the ADA guidelines; other research is used to create guidance materials, such as checklists and technical bulletins, which can be very helpful. In addition,

◄◄ Note

The *2010 ADA Standards* have commentary notes throughout the text. Although they are helpful, they are not binding.

ADA-ABA ACCESSIBILITY GUIDELINES DEVELOPMENT

After the publication of the *1991 ADAAG*, the Access Board worked with various organizations including the *International Code Council (ICC)* to create a new guideline that was coordinated with other accessibility documents including the *International Building Code (IBC)* and the ICC accessibility standard *ICC A117.1*. This document was also intended to be used under the ADA and ABA legislations. The objective was to minimize conflicts between the various documents and promote a consistent way to design an accessible building or space regardless of location or whether federally or privately owned or operated.

The Access Board released the new document called *ADA-ABA Accessibility Guidelines* in 2004. The *ADA-ABA Accessibility Guidelines* included a reorganized format, graphics, and numbering system from the original *ADAAG*. Two sets of the first two chapters, *Chapter 1: Application and Administration* and *Chapter 2: Scoping Requirements*, were developed. One set is intended to be used with the ADA legislation and apply to private sector buildings and the other is intended to be used with the ABA legislation and apply to federal buildings. The technical criteria in the following chapters are used for the ADA and ABA legislation. The *ICC A117.1* shares a similar organization, and the technical requirements are similar as well. This effort has made the scope and technical requirements for the *2010 ADA Standards*, the *ABA Guidelines*, *ICC A117.1* standard, and Chapter 11 of the *IBC* more consistent. Because the ADA and ABA documents are developed from a previous edition of the *ICC A117.1*, as the *ICC A117.1* document continues to be updated, some requirements may not stay consistent. The *ADA-ABA Accessibility Guidelines* also clarified dimensional tolerances and calculation rounding and added dimensions for spaces used primarily by children.

◀ Note

The Access Board, ICC, and NFPA have all created comparison documents of the accessibility requirements in each of their respective publications. These documents can be found on their websites.

updates, interpretations, or assistive information can be found on the websites of the Access Board (www.access-board.gov) and the DOJ (www.usdoj.gov). The Access Board also can send email updates, which include information about proposed changes to the *ADA Standards*.

LEVEL OF ACCESSIBILITY

Whether a project involves new construction, an alteration of an existing space, or minor cosmetic changes to an existing facility, accessibility must be considered in the design. Typically, the codes and ADA expect the highest level of accessibility to be provided in buildings and spaces. However, some areas such as workrooms may not require every aspect to be accessible even when newly built. In addition, spaces not intended to be used by the public, such as janitor closets or raised areas for security, may not be required to be accessible at all.

In alterations and renovations to existing space, it may be difficult or impossible to achieve the same level of accessibility as new construction. The codes and ADA provide for allowable variations. The level of accessibility that a project must meet should be established early in the design process. In some cases, it may be necessary to review and/or approval by the AHJ or the DOJ, if full accessibility is not planned or achievable. Additional considerations during design for the scope of the project are discussed next.

New Construction

For new construction projects, most aspects of the design must comply with the strictest accessibility requirements per the code or applicable federal law. A building built from the ground up or a completely new tenant space within an existing building, for example, would both be considered new construction. Typically, the ADA allows exceptions in new construction only when structural conditions and changes in level necessitated by site and other unchangeable constraints prohibit an area or element to be made accessible. But this is potentially rare in interior projects.

Generally, an accessible route must be provided from the point at which a person arrives on the site (whether by car, public transit, walking, etc.) to an accessible entrance to the building and/or space. From there, at least one continuous accessible route to most parts of the building must be maintained. In the codes, there are a few exceptions where it is not required to provide an accessible route to an interior space. This may include stories or mezzanines, areas with non-accessible fixed seating, some recreational facilities, and some areas not considered a public use space. However, each tenant space or dwelling unit must have an accessible entrance. (This is discussed in Chapter 5, "Means of Egress.") Exceptions may not be completely consistent between the codes and the ADA. You need to provide the highest level of accessibility possible. (See "Enforcement and Responsibility," later in this chapter.)

Alterations

In the case of an alteration or renovation to an existing building, compliance can be more complex. Although changes to an area or element must usually conform to the strictest accessibility requirements, there are acceptable reasons within the codes and ADA when a lesser level of accessibility is allowed. These include the scope of the project, feasibility, practicability, and cost. Many of these may overlap.

◀ Note

Differences in the technical requirements of the latest *ICC A117.1*, the *ICC A117.1* referenced in the current *IBC*, and the *ADA Standards* can occur as the ICC continues to update the standard; but the ADA Standards are not updated regularly.

◀ Note

The term *universal design* is not the same as *accessible design*. Universal design is intended to address needs not only of the disabled but of every person, regardless of age, ability, or status in life. It is not mandated by code or law and has a much broader scope than the ADA.

◀ Note

New construction must comply with the *new construction* requirements of the ADA almost without exception.

■ **Note**

An alteration to an existing building must comply with the *ADA Standards* to the *maximum extent possible*. In some cases, an alteration will not have to meet the guideline requirements (e.g., if the change is structurally unfeasible or would cause an unsafe condition).

The *International Existing Building Code (IEBC)* and the ADA require that complete accessibility to be achieved unless "technically infeasible." The ADA also requires that an attempt to meet the *ADA Standards* be made "to the maximum extent feasible." Modifications may be deemed infeasible because of spatial, structural, or cost issues. For example, there may be an adjacent area not included in the scope of the project or under the owner's control that will not allow a toilet to be enlarged. Likewise, existing structural elements may impede required clearances. However, if the modification or additional scope is determined not be "readily achievable" (meaning not possible without difficulty or considerable expense) or is determined to be an "undue burden" (meaning disproportionate to the financial situation of the owner or project), the regulations often allow for exceptions to strict compliance. Whether a modification is "readily achievable" or is an "undue burden" are complex legal issues that consider the scope of the modification and cost. Both categories are usually decided on a case-by-case basis by the regulating authority or the legal system and may be difficult and time consuming to determine.

The ADA generally uses a threshold of 20 percent to determine if an action is disproportionate in cost. If elements that would require renovation to be accessible exceed this ratio of the project cost, it could be considered disproportionate. Because the 20 percent rule is not intended to encourage or allow building owners to make a series of small alterations to an existing building to avoid a larger costlier accessibility update, the accumulative cost of alterations over a three-year period may be reviewed as well. Because the 20 percent rule is not included in the codes, a similar situation would have to be negotiated with the AHJ.

Sometimes an alteration could be considered an "undue burden" to the owner per the ADA. To do this, the cost of the modification, the financial resources of the facility, the number of employees, and the type of facility are considered. The decision to limit the scope of accessibility should be determined by the owner and should be primarily a financial decision, not a design decision. It is typically the owner's responsibility to approve and provide the legal documentation to support this decision.

■ **Note**

Modifications made to existing buildings to increase the accessibility of a space or building may qualify for tax credits or other financial benefits.

In addition, alterations to one area may require unplanned modifications in adjacent areas. For example, if a "primary function" space, such as a small auditorium in a high school, is altered and made more accessible, the ADA will typically require that the path to the primary function area and certain support areas, such as the corridors to the auditorium and to the bathrooms, drinking fountains, and telephones, be altered to provide a similar level of accessibility. This may increase the scope and cost of the project.

Existing Facilities

Although there have been accessible standards used for decades, incorrect implementation, lack of proper enforcement of the standards, and unpermitted changes to buildings allow noncompliant conditions in buildings and spaces to continue to exist and in some cases to be built to be not accessible. Because codes are not retroactive and periodic evaluations for accessibility are not performed for most occupancies, these conditions might remain in place for years. This continues to make daily and work life difficult for many disabled occupants. Because the ADA is a discrimination law, not a building code, persons with disabilities that encounter non-accessible spaces and elements can sue the owner or tenant for these conditions. This means that unlike the building codes, compliance with the ADA guidelines applies to existing buildings even if no alterations or renovations are planned.

Technically, an *existing building* is defined by the ADA as a building built before 1991 and the enactment of the ADA law. These buildings may not have been built under any accessible requirements. However, at the time of enactment of the law, a two-year period for the removal of "architectural barriers" from existing buildings was established. The intent was to allow building owners to make changes to their existing buildings, such as adding ramps, widening doors, adding power-assisted doors, and eliminating other existing barriers to bring their buildings into compliance with the law and make them accessible to the maximum extent possible. Because that was decades ago, owners are now expected to have evaluated their facilities and to have removed the architectural barriers that could keep persons with disabilities from using their buildings. And implemented renovations over the years to adjust non-accessible areas.

Because the ADA law came in effect in 1991, almost every building since that time should be accessible per the original *1991 ADAAG* requirements or the updated *2010 Standards*. So, a building built after 1991 that the *codes* would consider an "existing" building, would not be considered an "existing" building under the ADA. If non-accessible areas and elements within these buildings exist, they must be modified to meet the strictest level of accessibility possible like new construction. If these conditions are not modified, litigation can occur.

Because some requirements in the *1991 ADA Standards* and the *2010 ADA Standards* are different, technically buildings built to the original *ADAAG* may not be compliant with the ADA. However, the DOJ clarified that these buildings or spaces do not have to be renovated to meet the new requirements to be considered compliant with the ADA until alterations or renovations are done to the area. In other words, the *1991 ADAAG* is a "safe harbor" document to the *2010 ADA Standards*.

✎ Note

Existing facilities must be modified as *readily achievable* to meet the requirements of the ADA. Owners may seek the advice of a design professional concerning how the ADA applies to them.

✎ Note

Legal suits are typically filed by persons with disabilities who feel that the building conditions prevent them from gaining access or obtaining services.

Limited Accessibility

Even for new construction, there are certain spaces and some aspects of a space that may not have to meet all accessibility requirements. This includes areas used only by employees, special use rooms, and spaces used by individuals (such as private offices). As a rule of thumb, if the public would use or have access to the area or element, then it is required to be fully accessible. It is only used by employees; some areas may be allowed to provide a limited level of accessibility. For example, only a portion of shelves and storage cabinets in a teachers' workroom in an elementary school (used only by teachers) must be within the reach ranges described by the guidelines. However, per the employment sections of the ADA, if a disabled teacher were hired, their classroom, locker, or assigned work area would need to be fully accessible. When there are multiple components or individualized areas it is a best practice to make at least one of each element accessible. This would prevent the need for modifications for someone with a disability. In some occupancies, a percentage of the rooms, spaces, or elements will be required to be accessible. For example, only a specific number of hotel or hospital rooms must accommodate a disabled overnight guest or patient. Only a percentage of lockers in a locker room must be accessible. Other miscellaneous rooms, such as electrical closets, mechanical rooms, and data rooms, typically do not have to comply or have modified requirements. Many of these elements are clarified in the scoping requirements or special use requirements of each standard.

For areas accessible to the public, the minimum requirement is that everyone must be able to "approach, enter, and exit" each room. For example, even hotel rooms and offices that are not designated as accessible rooms should provide clearances at the door that allow a visitor in a wheelchair to open the door from the corridor and from inside the room. In areas that will be used by the public and employees, such as exhibits in a museum, full accessibility must be provided. In most projects, it is appropriate to make most spaces, even shared work areas, completely accessible.

There are other special use areas that may to be exempt from accessibility requirements as well. These include specific raised areas, limited access areas, maintenance areas, bed and breakfasts, and general use areas that serve non-accessible residential or detention areas and walk-in equipment. For example, areas that are on raised platforms such as a judge's bench, areas for religious ceremonies, and special employee work areas—where being raised is considered essential to the function of the space—are generally exempt. However, these areas may be required to be located on an accessible route so that a ramp, lift, or elevator can be installed in the future. These areas are also often limited in size to 300 sf (30 m²). Some raised areas are not required to be accessible or located on an accessible route. These include areas that are raised for security, life safety, or fire safety purposes such as observation galleries in prisons, fire towers, lifeguard stands, and similar uses. Areas that are limited in access such as catwalks and equipment spaces may also be exempt.

Accommodation

Sometimes, even if physical changes have been made "to the maximum extent feasible" (as described earlier in this chapter), the space or element may still not allow complete independent use. In this case, an accommodation or "reasonable modifications" of services or policies may need to be considered by the client. Most accommodations involve making minor adjustments to the normal way business is conducted to provide some assistance to a customer with a disability. For example, a salesperson may be allowed to retrieve an item for a disabled shopper that is stored in a manner that makes it not possible or unsafe for someone with a disability to retrieve it. Accommodation should not be used in place of providing physical accessibility to a space or activity if at all possible. This is where the legal intricacies begin.

If a complete accessibility is not possible or if there is phased effort to correct noncompliant conditions, the ADA suggests a hierarchy of priorities. These progress from an initial accessible exterior path to the building, an accessible entrance into the building, an accessible path within the building (to the goods and services), accessible toilet facilities, and then direct access to the actual goods and services. Commercial facilities and areas that are required to be accessible should meet a similar level of accessibility.

ENFORCEMENT AND RESPONSIBILITY

Often projects must meet accessibility requirements included in the local and state building codes, locally adopted accessibility standards, and a federal regulation such as the ADA. The review and approval for compliance is different for local, state, and federal guidelines. The penalty for non-compliance can differ as well.

Some jurisdictions adopt or create a standard that they can use to review for compliance like a building code. As discussed in Chapter 1 and Chapter 11, projects are reviewed for local code compliance including accessibility by the jurisdiction of the project. The code official can

◪ Note

Regulation and enforcement of the *ADA Standards* in design projects are different from the enforcement of code requirements. There is not a local official to verify your compliance.

help interpret or advise as whether a design or an element meets the accessibility code or standard that is enforced in their jurisdiction. They can also make the call if unique conditions are acceptable within their jurisdiction. But their responsibility does not include determining or confirming that a design satisfies the requirements of a federal guideline such as the ADA. It can be confusing, because it has become very common for people, even code officials, to say, "It is not ADA compliant," when they really mean to say it is not accessible to persons with disabilities. They are not actually making judgment for compliance with the ADA, but only their own locally adopted accessibility standard.

The challenge of federal accessibility standards such as the ADA is that there is typically no formal review process to verify compliance during the design, permitting, or construction phase. Federal agencies such as the DOJ provide technical assistance on its website and ADA Information Line and produces multiple publications to clarify the requirements but does not perform review of project designs or after construction. Litigation is the primary way noncompliant conditions are identified. Typically, an existing noncompliant element is discovered as the result of a complaint or a private lawsuit filed by a disabled individual who has encountered a non-accessible condition. In addition, legal action can be taken by a federal agency in support of a discrimination claim or on behalf of a group of persons who may have experienced discrimination because of an inaccessible design. The goal of the litigation is to bring awareness to the inaccessible condition and have the condition modified to be accessible, but the process can be costly because of attorney, court, and professional fees and renovation costs to resolve the issue.

However, local or state agencies can review projects for accessibility in a way that is recognized to be more consistent with the ADA by using a document that has been "certified" by the DOJ. Each state or jurisdiction may develop an accessibility standard and submit it for review by the DOJ. If it is found to be consistent with the *2010 ADA Standards*, the new standard may be deemed *certified*. For example, Florida has approved developed the *2012 Florida Accessibility Code for Building Construction* and Texas has the *2012 Texas Accessibility Standard*. Both documents are considered certified; others may currently be under review as well. This establishes a document recognized to be consistent with the federal standard and can be used for approval by a local entity. Despite this process, compliance with a certified guideline does not absolutely guarantee agreement with the ADA and the ADA standards. If legal action is taken, the certified document may be part of the defense but may not demonstrate complete compliance. Research, compare, and follow the most stringent requirements for a jurisdiction while maintaining the minimum federal requirements. (See the inset titled "Accessibility Requirements Compared" in this chapter.)

For several federal guidelines, there are also "safe harbor" documents identified. These documents are considered equal or to exceed the requirements of the federal guideline. In that case, either the original document can be used or the safe harbor document may be used under certain conditions. For example, the original *1991 ADA Guidelines* is considered a safe harbor to the *2010 ADA Standards* for existing buildings. Safe harbor documents apply on an "element-to-element" basis including the entire path of travel to an altered area.

In most cases, the requirements for an accessible interior will be clearly defined in the guidelines and can be easily implemented. There are multiple support and technical assistance documents developed by the Access Board to clarify many topics and typical applications. These are located on their website. Each state and many local governments also now has a central contact to assist with technical questions for the ADA.

For a building or space to be usable by persons with disabilities, accessibility must be considered during design, construction, maintenance, and use of the building. The design professionals must implement their knowledge of the design guidelines while designing the spaces; contractors must follow design criteria and ensure that what is built and installed in the building is consistent with the guidelines and within acceptable tolerances; and the owners and users must ensure that changes to the building do not interfere with the usability of the space—whether it is moving furniture or changing the configuration of a space. Although the issuing of a Certificate of Occupancy (discussed in Chapter 11) completes the code review process, it does not end liability for compliance with federal regulations such as the ADA, ABA, or FHA. Design, construction and maintaining the compliant condition after occupancy are equally important. In fact, recent legal cases between the DOJ and design firms suggest that the design professionals and potentially others involved in the construction process as well as owners may have specific legal responsibility for compliance with the ADA. Thus, the issue of responsibility is continuing to be defined through the courts.

Owners and tenants can be responsible for the compliance of specific elements within the buildings that they own or rent. It may depend on the location of the element or space. Typically, the owner of a building and a tenant within a building are responsible for the accessibility of the spaces that are under their control. For example, an accessible entrance into a building would be the owner's responsibility, but the accessibility of a work area within the tenant space would be the tenant's responsibility. The specific responsibilities between owner and tenant can sometimes be allocated by the lease. For example, the lease may state that the owner is responsible for using accessible hardware on tenant corridor doors. However, if a part of the facility is noncompliant, both may be held

◀ Note

The Access Board has an online guide to the standards for the ADA and the ABA. It includes illustrated technical guides that explain requirements, answer common questions, and recommend best practices. You can subscribe to email updates to changes or findings by the DOJ and the Access Board.

responsible by law. As the designer, it is important to recognize when the accessibility of your design could easily be altered by the client. For example, if you do not specify an recessed trash receptacle in a toilet room, and the owner provides a stand-alone trash, it may impede the required clear floor area and make the toilet noncompliant.

What is clear is that compliance is a joint effort among the client, designer, and contractor throughout the development of a design project. Documenting all decisions in drawings and other written documents is important.

RESEARCH: USING THE CODES

Because almost all buildings will have to provide some level of accessibility, each project will require knowledge or research of accessibility requirements. These regulations may come from local codes and federal laws and may require more than one document to be referenced. The extent of the research that is needed will be determined by who owns, leases, or is funding the project and its use. It is important to determine which accessibility regulations will apply to your project type and scope early in the process. It is recommended that you have an electronic or hard copy of any guidelines for reference during the development of the design and drawing documentation. For example, the ADA guidelines are available for free download at www.ada.gov.

Because federal regulations apply to projects in all jurisdictions, it makes sense to determine whether a federal accessibility law will apply to your project, first. For example, determine if the ABA, ADA, or FHA will apply to your project. And if so, which one. If the building is owned, operated, or funded by a federal agency, the ABA and the *ABA Standards* will provide the accessibility requirements (including scope and technical) for the building. However, if the building is owned or operated by a private entity, the ADA will require the building to comply with the *2010 ADA Standards*. (Remember there are some uses that are exempt. See the section on ADA earlier in this chapter.) Fortunately, because of recent efforts to coordinate the guidelines for these laws, and the ABA and the ADA will require different levels of compliance and application, the technical requirements will be the same. So, this may minimize research if your work includes federal and private projects. The scope and application requirements for these projects will be found in "Chapter 1: Application and Administration" and "Chapter 2: Scoping Requirements" of either document. The specific requirements (dimensions, locations, configurations) for each element are in the subsequent chapters. Again, in the ABA and ADA standards, the organization of the chapters and information is similar. If the project is residential and received federal funds, it may need to comply with the Fair Housing Authority legislation and conform to the *Fair Housing Accessibility Guidelines (FHAG)*.

In addition, you must identify local codes that contain accessibility requirements or if the jurisdiction has developed or adopted a separate accessibility code. The standard most often adopted by local jurisdictions is the *ICC A117.1*. The organization of this document parallels the organization of the ABA and ADA guidelines. To minimize conflicting requirements, the ICC has worked with the Access Board to create consistency between the *ICC A117.1*, the accessibility chapter in the *IBC*, and the 2004 *ADA-ABA Accessibility Guidelines*. (See the inset titled "ADA-ABA Accessibility Guidelines Development.") This effort made the four major accessibility documents, *ICC A117.1*, *ABA Standards*, *2010 ADA Standards*, and the accessibility chapter of the *IBC* more consistent. However, differences in the technical requirements can occur because while the *ABA Standards* and the *2010 Standards* are rarely updated, the *ICC A117.1* is updated regularly. Each new edition of the standard may contain changes in the specific requirements. In addition, the "Chapter 11: Accessibility" in the *IBC* references a specific edition of the *ICC A117.1*. Because the *IBC* reference edition of the *ICC A117.1* and the locally adopted edition of the *ICC A117.1* can be different, the requirements can be different as well. In addition, although the ADA and ABA guidelines were originally based on an older version of the *ICC A117.1*, updates to the standard will also cause slight or significant changes. You will at minimum have to compare the referenced and/or adopted *ICC A117.1* with the ADA and ABA guidelines. Some of these differences are highlighted in the individual chapters of this book.

A comparison of the various sections in the *ICC A117.1* standard, *2010 ADA Standards* and comparable sections of the *IBC* are shown in Figure 2.1.

DOCUMENTATION

Many of the specific accessibility requirements will be documented as part of the project documentation in your plans, details, and/or specifications. In addition, you may want to record any significant requirements that affected the design such percentage of the toilets that need to be accessible, number of lodging rooms, entrances, and so on.

◄ Note

Because the level of enforcement and responsibility for compliance with the ADA requirements continues to be developed through litigation, it is important to keep up-to-date by reading articles in professional journals and visiting the DOJ website.

Designers and architects often develop standard details that indicate how common elements in a project such as sinks, toilets, and workstations should be built or installed to be accessible. Specific items that are required to be accessible and to be documented are discussed in the "Documentation" section of each chapter of this book. You can also use the "Accessibility" section of the digital code checklist provided with this book to help you document your findings. They can also be used as a checklist for the project design.

CHAPTER 3

OCCUPANCY CLASSIFICATIONS AND LOADS

The occupancy classification of a building or space is generally determined by the way that building or space is to be used. In the same way that a building can have different activities occurring, a building can contain more than one occupancy classification. Occupancy classifications have been developed by the codes to address the different hazardous situations, often referred to as *risk factors,* associated with each type of use. These risk factors consider the typical characteristics of the environment, the activity that will occur in the space, and the occupants using the space. Risk factors may include spatial characteristics (low light levels, fixed seating, and high sound levels), fuel loads (amount of finish materials, upholstered furniture, and other flammable contents), concentration of occupants, characteristics of the occupants (mobility, age, alertness), and sometimes the familiarity of the occupants with the building. In some cases, these unique characteristics call for additional code requirements to ensure safety of the occupants. For example, more exits are required in auditoriums (Assembly) due to the large number of people using the space, and alternate exiting methods are required in hospitals (Institutional), where occupants often are not mobile due to age, health, or security reasons. The different occupancy classifications in the codes are based on these various characteristics. The codes address these conditions for each occupancy classification so that people can be considered equally safe at work, at a crowded concert, or with any other type of use.

In some cases, the projected occupant load (OL) will be a critical component in determining the occupancy classification. The occupant load is the number of people that is assumed to safely occupy a space or building. Because occupancy classifications and occupant loads are, in some cases, dependent on each other, both should be considered at the beginning of a project. The occupancy classification and the projected occupant load will be used to determine many other code requirements. The first part of this chapter concentrates on occupancy classifications and their relationships; occupant loads are discussed in the last part of the chapter.

UNDERSTANDING OCCUPANCY CLASSIFICATIONS

An occupancy classification must be assigned to every building or space within a building. Determining the occupancy classification should be the first task when designing the interior of a building, because almost every interior code and regulation is based on the assigned occupancy classification. The occupancy of a space must also be known to effectively use most of the remaining chapters in this book. Once the occupancy is known, it will guide the remaining code research.

For existing buildings that are occupied, the occupancy classification has already been established. However, the occupancy classification must be determined for new buildings and reexamined whenever changes are made in the use of an existing building or space. If the building is intended to have multiple tenants, the occupancy classification for each proposed tenant must be determined separately. If the intended use of an existing building is changing significantly, determining the new occupancy classification may be particularly important. Some of these changes are obvious, such as an old warehouse building being renovated into apartments. Other changes may be less noticeable but still require reclassification.

It may also be important to understand how the occupants will actually be using the space or plan to use it in the future. For example, if a space will be used temporarily as an open office plan but in the future will be used as a training room, both Assembly and Business requirements may have to be considered so that the design will address the most stringent code requirements. If not, significant renovations may be required when the change in use occurs.

The ICC codes and the NFPA codes assign the occupancy classifications slightly differently. However, generally the occupancy classifications used throughout the various building and life safety codes are listed here. Some of them also have subclassifications. The occupancy classifications and their subcategories are discussed in the first part of this chapter.

> Assembly
> Business
> Educational
> Factory or Industrial
> Hazardous
> Institutional
> Mercantile
> Residential
> Storage
> Utility or Miscellaneous

Many of these classifications seem self-explanatory, especially if a building type is straightforward, but remember that three things must be known before the occupancy classification can be accurately determined: (1) the type of activity occurring, (2) the expected number of occupants, and (3) whether any unusual hazards or risk factors are present. These factors can affect the appropriate classification of a building type or spaces within a building.

A boutique that sells clothing, for example, has an *activity* that is straightforward. It is a Mercantile occupancy. However, in some cases, small differences in use can change the occupancy classification. For example, a television studio is a Business occupancy, but if the studio allows audience viewing, it will typically be considered an Assembly occupancy. Knowing the specific type(s) of activities that are occurring is important.

Many of the classifications allow for a specific *number of people*. For example, a space may appear to be an Assembly use, but if a small number of people will be using the space, it may be allowed to be classified as Business. When using the *IBC*, if a day care center serves fewer than five children, it may be considered Residential, but if it has more than five attendees, it may be considered Institutional or Educational. So, if the number of occupants increase or decrease, the occupancy classification may have to be reexamined.

Hazardous conditions that could influence the assignment of occupancy classifications can be caused by the use or storage of flammable, explosive, or toxic materials within a building. However, other hazardous conditions can include certain settings within a building or the conditions of the occupants themselves. For example, low light levels, low awareness or mental capacity, restricted movement due to security, and similar characteristics can create potentially unsafe situations. (See the inset titled "Risk Factors and Hazards in Occupancies" in this chapter.) When any of these conditions are present, different requirements are necessary to offset the potentially unsafe situation. However, small quantities and limited occurrences of unsafe materials and situations are allowed in almost every occupancy classification. For example, a small amount of paint can be stored in any occupancy. However, in large amounts paint storage would be considered a Hazardous use. And similarly, a space where the lights might be dimmed for a presentation will not create the same hazard as a dark nightclub.

Consult the local code official early in a project whenever there is uncertainty as to the correct occupancy classification. It is always a good idea to have a code official confirm the choice of occupancy. If it is determined later that the choice is incorrect, or if the choice is not approved by the code official, the rest of the research may be incorrect, and the design may not meet the appropriate code requirements.

◄ Note

Most code jurisdictions require the use of a fire code in addition to a building code. Typically, the fire code will be either the *International Fire Code* or the *NFPA Fire Code (NFPA 1)*.

◄ Note

Occupancy classifications are defined in the *IBC* in Chapter 3. They are defined in the *NFPA 101* in the "Definition" chapter under "Occupancy."

RISK FACTORS AND HAZARDS IN OCCUPANCIES

The types of risk factors or hazards found in a building help to determine its occupancy classification. They can vary dramatically from one building type to the next. Each occupancy type was created to handle different types of hazards. Some of the risk factors that are typically considered when determining an occupancy classification are as follows:

❑ Number of occupants (a large group versus a small gathering)

❑ If occupants are at rest or sleeping

❑ Alertness of the occupants (considers mental capabilities and inherent distractions caused by the activities going on in the space)

❑ Mobility of the occupants (considers physical abilities, age, and security measures)

❑ Familiarity of occupants with the space or building

❑ Typical characteristics of the space used for a specific activity (includes fixed seating and aisles, light levels, noise levels, etc.)

❑ Potential for spread of fire (due to airborne flammable particles, storage of hazardous materials, combustible finishes, decoration or contents, etc.)

These risk factors were considered by the code organizations in the development of each occupancy classification, the various subcategories, and the appropriate code requirements. When assigning an occupancy classification for the design of a project, the occupants in the space, the use of the space and the environmental characteristics of the space must be considered in the same way.

DESCRIPTION OF OCCUPANCIES

The ICC and the NFPA codes designate occupancy classifications slightly differently. Both, the *I-Codes* and NFPA codes also subdivide certain occupancy classification into smaller, more specific categories which also may differ. For example, the *IBC* divides its Assembly occupancy into five subclassifications by types of use. The NFPA codes divide the Assembly occupancy by number of occupants. In the following sections, the ICC's designations (as used by the *IBC*) are used. A list of common building types that fall within that classification are provided as examples. Refer to Figure 3.1 for the comparative occupancy classifications as used by the NFPA codes.

☞ **Note**

Letters are often used to designate an occupancy classification. For example, "A" stands for Assembly and "E" stands for Educational.

Occupancy Classification	ICC International Building Code	NFPA Life Safety Code and NFPA 5000
ASSEMBLY	A-1 Assembly, Theaters (Fixed Seats) A-2 Assembly, Food and/or Drink Consumption A-3 Assembly, Worship, Recreation, Amusement A-4 Assembly, Indoor Sporting Events A-5 Assembly, Outdoor Activities	A Assembly (variations noted by occupant load)
BUSINESS	B Business Includes Ambulatory Health Care	B Business AHC Ambulatory Health Care
EDUCATIONAL	E Educational (includes some day care)	E Educational
FACTORY/INDUSTRIAL	F-1 Factory Industrial, Moderate Hazard F-2 Factory Industrial, Low Hazard	I Industrial, General Industrial, Special Purpose Industrial, High Hazard
HAZARDOUS	H-1 Hazardous, Detonation Hazard H-2 Hazardous, Deflagration Hazard or Accelerated Burning H-3 Hazardous, Physical or Combustible Hazard H-4 Hazardous, Health Hazard H-5 Hazardous, Hazardous Production Materials (HPM)	(included in Group I)
INSTITUTIONAL	I-1 Institutional, Custodial Care OL >16 separated in Condition 1 and 2 I-2 Institutional, Medical Care, separated in Condition 1 and 2 I-3 Institutional, Restrained (separated in to Conditions 1–5) I-4 Institutional, Day Care Facilities	D-I Detentional/Correctional (includes various subconditions IV) H Health Care DC Day Care
MERCANTILE	M Mercantile	M-A Mercantile, > 3 levels or > 30,000 SF (2800 SM) M-B Mercantile, ≤ 3 stories or > 3000 SF (280 SM) and ≤ 30,000 SF (2800 SM) M-C Mercantile, 1 story ≤ 3000 SF (280 SM)
RESIDENTIAL	R-1 Residential, Transient R-2 Residential, Multi-Dwelling Unit R-3 Residential, One and Two Dwelling Units R-4 Residential, Care and Assisted Living Facilities OL > 5 ≤16	R Residential, Hotels and Dormitories Residential, Apartment Buildings Residential, Lodging or Rooming Houses Residential, One- and Two-Family Dwellings Residential, Board and Care
STORAGE	S-1 Storage, Moderate Hazard S-2 Storage, Low Hazard	S Storage
UTILITY/ MISCELLANEOUS	U Utility and Miscellaneous	Special Structures and High-Rise Buildings

Figure 3.1 Comparison of occupancy classifications. (This chart is a summary of information contained in the 2018 and 2021 editions of the International Building Code®, the NFPA 5000®, and the Life Safety Code®. Neither the ICC nor the NFPA assumes responsibility for the accuracy or completeness of this chart.)

Assembly (A) Occupancy

A building or part of a building is classified as an Assembly occupancy if people gather for civic, social, or religious functions, recreation, entertainment, eating, drinking, or awaiting transportation. The most common characteristic of an Assembly occupancy is that it holds a large number of people (usually more than 50) who are unfamiliar with the space. Other common characteristics include such aspects as low light levels, the occupants' lack of awareness of surroundings, and the potential for panic because of the number of occupants. Because of these multiple risk factors, there are many requirements that apply strictly to Assembly occupancies.

The *IBC* bases its Assembly subclassifications on the specific type of activity which is occurring. The NFPA subclassification relies primarily on the number of people. As a result, NFPA codes have fewer Assembly subclassifications. (See Figure 3.1.) Both codes provide specific requirements for unique uses such as malls, theaters with stages, and other building types that may seem to fit the Assembly use. In the *IBC*, this information is in a separate special-use chapter; in the NFPA codes it is included in the Assembly occupancy chapters.

The *IBC* has five subclassifications of Assembly. They are designated as A-1 through A-5.

Note

A restaurant can be classified as a Business or Mercantile occupancy (if the number of occupants is small enough), an Assembly, or an accessory to a larger adjacent occupancy.

Note

If a space is intended to be used for different purposes at different times it will have to comply with all the applicable requirements for the different uses.

A-1

This category is for the viewing of performing arts or movies. The space often includes a stage. (There are many code requirements specifically for stages.) The common characteristics of these types of spaces are low light levels and above-normal sound levels. Seating usually consists of fixed seating with well-defined aisles. Occupants are alert but distracted and generally unfamiliar with the building.

Sample Building Types

Motion picture theaters	Symphony and concert halls
Radio and television studios with audiences	Theaters for stage production

A-2

This type is for the consumption of food and drink. Often these spaces have low light levels, loud music, late operating hours, and ill-defined aisles (e.g., movable tables and chairs). The serving of food and drink is the most defining characteristic.

Sample Building Types

Banquet halls

Casino (gaming areas)

Dance halls (serving food and drink)

Drinking establishments

Fast-food restaurants

Fellowship halls (serving food and drink)

Nightclubs

Restaurants (including kitchen; may also be classified as Business)

Taverns and bars (may also be classified as Business)

A-3

This type is for the gathering of people for worship, recreation, or amusement. Types of activities that are not classified by other types of Assembly are typically included in this subclassification. The common characteristics of this subclassification are clear or defined egress patterns and moderate to low fuel loads. For example, in a church or an auditorium, aisles used for egress are defined by the placement of pews or chairs. Occupants in an A-3 subclassification are also usually alert and are often more familiar with the space than in other assembly uses.

Sample Building Types

Amusement arcades

Armories

Art galleries

Assembly halls

Auditoriums

Bowling alleys

Churches and religious structures

Community halls

Courtrooms

Dance halls (not including food or drink consumption)

Exhibition halls

Pool and billiard rooms

Public assembly halls

Fellowship halls

Funeral parlors

Galleries

Gymnasiums (without spectator seating)

Lecture halls (may also be Business)

Libraries

Places of religious worship

Museums

Passenger stations, terminals, or depots (waiting areas)

Recreation or exercise areas (without spectator seating)

Tents for assembly

A-4

This type is for the viewing of indoor sporting events and other activities with spectator seating. The spectator seating can consist of a defined area for seating or fixed seats such as bleachers. Although A-3 and A-4 can have similar activities, if a defined area for viewing the activities is provided, then it is an A-4. For example, an indoor pool can be classified as an A-3 Assembly, but if the pool area also includes seating for viewing swim competitions, it is considered an A-4. (Similar activities can also occur in A-4 and A-5 Assemblies.)

Sample Building Types

Arenas

Gymnasiums (with spectator seating)

Indoor skating rinks

Indoor swimming pools

Indoor tennis courts

A-5

This type is for the participation in or viewing of outdoor activities. This subclassification is similar to A-4, except that it is outdoors or in a structure with no roof.

Sample Building Types

Amusement park structures

Bleachers

Grandstands

Stadiums

◄ Note

A good rule of thumb is that when the occupant load is 50 or more, the requirements for an Assembly occupancy should be researched.

Typically, in Assembly occupancies, there are a large number of occupants. Examples include a theater or large restaurant. However, when a space is used for a small group of people to gather—such as a college classroom, an office conference room, or a small restaurant—the codes often allow these uses to be classified under another occupancy type. The *IBC* and the NFPA codes use an occupancy of 50 people or more as a threshold. (Some jurisdictions may use a different limit.) For example, if the *IBC* is used, a small restaurant can be classified as a Business occupancy if its occupant load is less than 50. The NFPA codes would reclassify this as a Mercantile occupancy.

In many cases, the codes also allow an assembly-type use that is part of another occupancy classification to be considered the same occupancy that it serves. It may depend on the size or the occupant load. For example, the *IBC* allows rooms used for assembly purposes that are less than 750 square feet (70 sm) or have an occupancy less than 50 to be classified either as a Business occupancy or as part of the main occupancy classification. Assembly occupancies that are related to Educational or are accessory to a religious educational facility can also be classified with the occupancy that they serve, according to the *IBC*. These clarifications can have critical impact on the various code requirements that will apply.

Business (B) Occupancy

A building or part of a building is classified as a Business occupancy if it is used for the transaction of business such as office, professional, or service-type trades and other similar functions. Limited areas that are a natural part of a business setting, such as small storage, recordkeeping, supply areas, and break rooms, are included as well. The risk factors in a Business occupancy are considered to be relatively low. This is because there is typically a low concentration of occupants, and they are usually alert and generally familiar with their environment. It is considered one of the lowest-risk occupancies.

This classification can become very broad. For example, a smaller Assembly-like occupancy that has fewer occupants can sometimes be classified as a Business occupancy, such as a small restaurant. Conversely, when the function or size of spaces within a Business occupancy expands beyond a typical business use, they may be considered Assembly. For example, a conference room in an office would be part of the Business occupancy; but the courtrooms in a city hall or an auditorium classroom within a college facility would be considered Assembly. (This condition may result in a "mixed occupancy" building, which is discussed later in the chapter.) In addition, a doctor's office would be classified as a Business office; however, if procedures are performed that cause four or more patients to be under sedation or conditions that would prevent them from being able to exit the facility without assistance, the facility may have to be classified as an *ambulatory care facility*. Under the *IBC*, this type of use is still considered a Business occupancy. However, this use is assigned additional code requirements that differ from those for a typical Business occupancy. The NFPA codes have a separate occupancy classification of Ambulatory Health Care. However, in both cases additional requirements will apply.

> **◈ Note**
>
> A wide variety of building types can fall under the Business occupancy classification. For example, a small Assembly, such as a restaurant that has an occupant load fewer than 50 people, as well as college classrooms and outpatient clinics, can be classified as a Business occupancy.

Educational-type occupancies can also be confusing. Colleges and universities (educational facilities after the 12th grade) are considered Business occupancies. Yet, trade and vocational schools are often considered as the same occupancy as the trade that is being taught. For instance, general classrooms for a college would be classified as Business, but the areas for instruction in automotive repair may be considered Factory/ Industrial. In addition, places that offer various types of training or skill-development classes can be classified as Business instead of Educational, regardless of the age of the participants. Examples include places that offer music, dance, or tutoring.

Sample Building Types

Airport traffic control towers
Ambulatory care facilities
Animal hospitals, kennels, and
    pounds (part of the building
    could be considered Storage)
Automobile and other motor
    vehicle showrooms
Automobile service stations (can
    also be classified as Hazardous)
Banks
Barber shops

Beauty shops

Car washes
City halls
Civic administration buildings
Clinics (outpatient)
College and university classrooms
Dentist's offices
Doctor's offices

Fire stations
Florists and nurseries
Government offices

Greenhouses

Laboratories (testing
    and research)
Laundromats
Libraries (can also be
    classified as Assembly
    or Business)
Medical offices (separate from
    Institutional occupancies)
Motor vehicle showrooms
Office buildings
Outpatient clinics, ambulatory
Police stations
Post offices
Print shops
Professional offices (architect,
    attorney, dentist,
    physician, etc.)

Dry-cleaning facilities (can also be classified as Hazardous)

Educational facilities (above twelfth grade)

Electronic data processing facilities

Radio and television stations (without audiences)

Repair garages (small, nonhazardous)

Telecommunication equipment buildings

Travel agencies

Educational (E) Occupancy

A building or part of a building is classified as an Educational occupancy if it is used for educational purposes by a specified number of persons at any one time through the 12th grade. (For colleges and universities, see Assembly and Business occupancies.) Depending on the code publication, the specified number of persons range from four to the minimum number of people required for an Assembly occupancy. The NFPA codes also specify a minimum amount of time that a space is used for educational purposes. For example, if there are fewer than 12 hours of instruction per week, the building type could be governed by a different occupancy classification, according to the *LSC*.

It is common for a typical school to have spaces that might be considered a different occupancy, such as auditoriums, cafeterias, and gymnasiums. In most cases, these uses are not required to be classified separately as an Assembly occupancy but are allowed to be considered an Educational occupancy. Vocational shops, laboratories, and similar areas within a school will usually be considered Educational, even though they may require additional fire protection. As mentioned in a previous section, if the entire school is considered vocational, some codes may require that it fall into the same classification as the trade or vocation being taught.

If an Educational use also provides care and sleeping accommodations, those areas could be classified as another occupancy. For example, the sleeping area of a boarding school or an extended-stay rehabilitation program would be classified as Residential. Day care centers can also be classified as Institutional, depending on the number of children and their age.

◀ Note

Although it may be expected for college and university classrooms to fall under the Educational occupancy, these building types are classified as Business. However, they may also have spaces that are considered Assembly.

Sample Building Types

⬧ Note

Areas providing day care
during religious functions
can be considered part of
the primary occupancy;
this will affect many code
requirements.

Academies
Day care centers (can also be considered Institutional)
Elementary schools
High schools
Junior high schools
Kindergartens
Nursery schools
Preschools
Secondary schools

Factory (F) Occupancy

A building or part of a building is designated as a Factory or Industrial occupancy if it is used for assembling, disassembling, fabricating, finishing, manufacturing, packaging, processing, or repairing. This designation generally refers to a building in which a certain type of product is made. The product that is made or the materials used to make the product must typically be considered a low or moderate hazard. If it is a more hazardous material or product, the building or space where it is made may be considered a Hazardous occupancy. The sample product types listed here are typically considered low to moderate types of hazards by the building codes. However, each code groups them a little differently under the Factory/Industrial occupancy, and there may be different code requirements, depending on which hazardous group the product is in. For example, the *IBC* divides its Factory occupancy into F-1 and F-2. The NFPA uses the term *Industrial occupancy* and has three subclassifications of that category. (See Figure 3.1. Also see the section titled "Hazardous Occupancy" later in this chapter.) These subclassifications are made for the different levels of hazardous materials or activities that are part of the manufacturing process. Refer to the specific code to determine if a manufactured product is considered moderate or low hazard; if more hazardous materials are used or created in the space or building, it may have to be classified as a Hazardous occupancy.

Sample Building Types

Assembly plants   Mills
Factories   Processing plants
Manufacturing plants

Low and Moderate Hazardous Products

Aircrafts

Appliances

Athletic equipment

Automobiles and other
motor vehicles

Bakeries

Brooms or brushes

Business machines

Cameras and photo equipment

Canneries

Canvas or similar fabrics

Carpets and rugs (includes cleaning)

Ceramic products

Clothing

Condensed powdered milk
manufacturing

Construction and agricultural
machinery

Creameries

Disinfectants

Dry cleaning and dyeing

Electric light plants and power
houses

Electrolytic reducing works

Electronics

Engines (includes rebuilding)

Film (photographic)

Food processing and commercial
kitchens (not associated with a
restaurant, cafeteria, or similar
dining facility)

Foundries

Furniture

Glass products

Gypsum products

Hemp products

Ice

Beverages (alcoholic)

Beverages (nonalcoholic)

Bicycles

Boats (building)

Boiler works

Brick and masonry

Jute products

Laboratories (can also be
classified as Business)

Laundries

Leather products

Machinery

Metal products (fabrication
and assembly)

Millwork (sash and door)

Motion pictures and
television filming

Musical instruments

Optical goods

Paper mills or products

Printing or publishing

Recreational vehicles

Refineries

Refuse incineration

Shoes

Smokehouses

Soaps and detergents

Sugar refineries

Textiles

Tobacco

Trailers

Upholstering

Water pumping plants

Wood (distillation of)

Woodworking (cabinetry)

Hazardous (H) Occupancy

A building or part of a building that involves the generation, manufacturing, processing, storage, or other use of hazardous materials is typically classified as a Hazardous occupancy. These materials can include flammable dust, fibers or liquids, combustible liquids, poisonous gases, explosive agents, corrosive liquids, oxidizing materials, radioactive materials, and carcinogens, among others. In general, this classification is categorized by an unusually high degree of explosive, fire, physical, and/or health hazards.

Hazardous building types require additional precautions. Each code sets different standards and has special sections dedicated to hazardous uses, which list very specific materials. In most cases, a Hazardous occupancy can be subclassified as a low, medium, or high hazard. Each building code categorizes the hazards a little differently. Often the lower hazards are made part of the Factory/Industrial or Storage occupancy classification. Each code also has a different number of subclassifications. The *IBC* has five Hazardous classifications (H-1 through H-5). The NFPA codes, however, include high hazard building types as a subclassification under Industrial. (See Figure 3.1.) They do not have a separate Hazardous occupancy. When using the NFPA codes, be careful to identify how that specific code or standard defines the term *hazardous,* as they may vary slightly per code publication and the purpose of the regulation. For example, in the *LSC,* the term *hazardous* is used to describe the level of hazardous *content* of the space, whereas in the *NFPA 13, Installation of Sprinkler Systems,* the term is used to define the ability of the sprinkler system to control the fire.

An important factor to consider is the amount of hazardous materials. If the amount is small enough, the space or building may not be considered Hazardous by the codes. A common example is a chemistry lab in a high school. As more performance-type requirements are introduced into code publications, more emphasis will be placed on the types of products or materials used in a space rather than on the type of building.

If it is expected for a space to contain hazardous materials or conditions, consult the specific codes and work closely with the local code officials. Some buildings may require only part of the building to be classified as Hazardous. (Hazardous buildings and materials are beyond the scope of this book.)

▤ **Note**

The NFPA codes do not have a separate Hazardous occupancy. Instead, it is a subclassification under the Industrial occupancy and addresses hazardous uses in each occupancy type.

▤ **Note**

Sometimes two different buildings with the same building type may have different occupancy classifications if hazardous materials are present in one but not the other. For example, some auto repair shops are considered a Hazardous occupancy. Others are considered a Business occupancy.

Sample Building Types

Airport hangars or airport
  repair hangars

Dry cleaning plants

Explosives manufacturers

Laboratories with hazard-
  ous chemicals

Paint and solvent manufacturers

Paint shops and spray
  painting rooms

Pesticide warehouses

Film storage, combustible

Firearm/ammunition
  warehouses

Gas plants

Power plants

Pumping/service stations

Tank farms

Warehouses with
  hazardous materials

Institutional (I) Occupancy

A building or part of a building is classified as an Institutional occupancy if it includes care or supervision of the occupants, including medical care. The primary distinction of this classification is that the occupants are either limited in their mobility, immobile, or incapable of mobility due to physical or security restraints. In most cases, the occupants must depend on others to help them evacuate the building in case of an emergency. The *IBC* has four Institutional subclassifications (I-I through I-4). The NFPA, however, separates these uses into different occupancy classifications. The NFPA codes refer to them as Detentional/Correctional, Health Care, and Day Care occupancies. (See Figure 3.1.)

Using the *IBC* designations, each subclassification is described in the following subsections: the similar NFPA classification is given as well. Note, however, that the specific characteristics for each NFPA occupancy may vary from those in the *IBC*. The minimum and maximum number of occupants can vary as well. For example, the minimum number for an I-4 classification in the *IBC* is 6 and the minimum number for a Day Care occupancy in the *LSC* is 4. Refer to the applicable code to determine the correct occupancy classification. (Also see the inset titled "Rooms and Spaces" later in this chapter.)

☑ Note

The IBC has four Institutional subclassifications. The NFPA codes divide these into separate Health Care, Detentional/ Correctional, and Day Care occupancies.

Note

Custodial care describes when assistance with day-to-day living tasks is given but the occupant can evacuate independently at a slow rate. Depending on additional factors, these occupancies can be Institutional or Residential.

Because some uses can be determined by subtle differences, a discussion with a code official may be required to confirm whether the jurisdiction will consider the facility Institutional, Residential, or one of the other specific NFPA classifications. The applicable code requirements can vary significantly between these occupancies.

I-1

This type is for the housing and custodial care of a certain number of occupants on a 24-hour basis. The codes often use 16 occupants as the limit. (This number does not include staff.) These occupants, because of age or mental disability, require supervision. However, they can typically respond to an emergency without physical assistance from staff members. If fewer than 16 people with the same characteristics were being cared for, the occupancy would be reclassified as Residential. The NFPA considers this building type a Residential occupancy (Board and Care), which includes a section for larger and smaller types of facilities.

Sample Building Types

> Alcohol and drug centers
> Assisted living facilities (can also be classified as Residential)
> Congregate care facilities (16 or fewer occupants)
> Convalescent facilities
> Group homes
> Halfway houses
> Residential board and custodial care facilities
> Social rehabilitation facilities

I-2

This type is for medical, surgical, psychiatric, nursing, or other type of care on a 24-hour basis for more than five persons. These occupants are not capable of self-preservation. If fewer than five people are being cared for, the occupancy would typically be reclassified as Residential. There are additional designations of Condition 1 and Condition 2, which further separate the occupancy subclassifications into the levels of care provided. The similar NFPA category is under a separate occupancy classification called Health Care.

Sample Building Types

Day care centers (24-hour)
Detoxification facilities
Foster care
Hospitals
Infirmaries
Nursing homes (intermediate care and skilled nursing)
Psychiatric hospitals
Treatment or rehabilitation centers

I-3

This type is for the detention of more than five persons. These occupants are incapable of self-preservation due to security measures. There are five levels of "Conditions" based on the level of security provided and the amount of free movement allowed within the building. The similar NFPA category is the Detention/Correction occupancy classification, which is divided into five separate subclassifications (see Figure 3.1), depending on the level of security.

The *LSC* has special conditions for *lock-up areas* in facilities other than Detentional/Correctional. These areas are similar to those in typical I-3 facilities, because the occupants are incapable of self-preservation due to security measures. However, only one person has to be held in this condition for these requirements to apply. A lock-up area is most typically located in facilities such as immigration centers at border crossings; customs facilities in international airports; prisoner holding at police departments; or security areas at parks, sports stadia, and similar uses.

Sample Building Types

Correctional institutions
Detention centers
Jails
Prerelease centers
Prisons
Reformatories
Work camps

I-4

This type is for the care of more than five persons for less than 24 hours a day. This includes adults and children under two years of age. One typical exception is that if adults in this type of facility are capable of self-preservation without help from staff members, it would be reclassified as an R-3. (See Residential occupancy R-3.) Another is when the area where children are cared for opens directly to the exterior; it can then be reclassified as Educational. This is considered a Day Care occupancy in the NFPA codes.

Sample Building Types

Adult day cares
Day care centers—caring for infants (can also be classified as
   Educational)

Mercantile (M) Occupancy

✑ Note

According to the NFPA codes, a small use that would usually be classified as a type of Assembly occupancy, such as a small diner, can sometimes be classified as Mercantile. (In the *IBC*, this may be reclassified as Business.)

A building or part of a building is classified as a Mercantile occupancy if it is open to the public and used for the display, sale, or rental of merchandise. This classification includes most stores and showrooms. Mercantile in the NFPA codes has three subclassifications based on the type and size of the building. (See Figure 3.1.)

Retail stores grouped together may prompt additional code requirements. Each store would be considered a separate Mercantile occupancy. However, as a group, the stores may also be considered a *covered mall*. The codes have special requirements for malls because, in addition to the large anchor retail stores and the multiple smaller retail tenants, there can be other uses within the same building. Most typically, these include restaurants and entertainment areas. In some cases, the general Mercantile requirements apply; in other cases, the requirements for a covered mall may apply to the project. (Usually one or the other will be used.) These mall requirements can be found in the "Special Detailed Requirements Based on Occupancy and Use" chapter of the *IBC*. In the NFPA codes, special requirements for malls are called out within the Mercantile chapter.

Sample Building Types

Auction rooms	Rental stores
Automotive service stations	Retail stores
Bakeries	Salesrooms
Department stores	Shopping centers
Drug stores	Showrooms

Grocery stores

Markets

Paint stores (without
    bulk handling)

Specialty stores

Supermarkets

Wholesale stores (other than
    warehouses)

Residential (R) Occupancy

A building or part of a building that acts as a dwelling and provides sleeping accommodations for normal residential purposes is designated a Residential occupancy. Most of the codes further categorize this classification based on the probable number of occupants and how familiar they are with their surroundings. For example, a person in a hotel would probably not be familiar with the escape routes, making it more hazardous. Such an occupancy will be subject to stricter codes than an apartment complex, where tenants should be more familiar with their surroundings. In some cases, the number of units in the building may also make a difference. (For other occupancies that provide sleeping accommodations but with additional care, see Institutional occupancy.)

    The *IBC* has four Residential subclassifications: R-1 through R-4. These are differentiated by length of residence, number of residents and type of care, if any, being provided. The NFPA codes separate these into five separate classifications: Apartment Buildings, Hotels and Dormitories, Lodging or Rooming Houses, One- and Two-Family Dwellings, and Board and Care. (See Figure 3.1.) Refer to the applicable code to determine the correct occupancy or subclassification. (Also see the inset titled "Rooms and Spaces" later in this chapter.)

R-1

This type is for occupants who are transient—in other words, those who do not stay for an extended period of time. If occupants typically stay more than 30 days, a building type may be required to be reclassified as R-2 or another use. In the NFPA codes, transient residential building types are addressed separately as hotels in the Hotels and Dormitories subclassification or the Lodging or Rooming Houses subclassification.

Sample Building Types

Boarding houses (transient with more than 10 occupants)

Congregate living facilities (transient with more than 10 occupants)

Hotels

Inns

Motels

Rooming houses

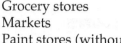
Note

Certain Residential building types may have to be reclassified as Institutional, depending on the number of occupants and their length of stay. Examples include day care centers and nursing homes.

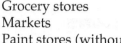
Note

The term *dwelling unit* is often associated with Residential and Institutional occupancies.

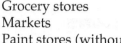
Note

Congregate living facilities are most often classified as an R-2. This building type contains sleeping units but shared bathroom and/or kitchen facilities (e.g., a small boarding house). If it is a large facility, it may be classified as R-1 or I-2.

CUSTODIAL CARE VERSUS MEDICAL CARE

Determining the correct occupancy classification when care is being provided for occupants often is determined by the number of persons receiving care. However, in some cases the type or level of care should be considered. The codes specify two basic types of care: custodial and medical.

❑ Custodial care includes assistance with typical daily tasks such as cooking, taking medications, bathing, and other personal care. This level of care assumes that the person receiving care can respond to an emergency situation but potentially at a slower rate. Their conditions may include physical or mental impairments.

❑ Medical care includes care or treatment involving medical or surgical procedures, nursing care, or psychiatric care. These occupants are often considered not to be able to respond in the event of an emergency because of their current physical or mental condition.

❑ Residential occupancies often assume that only custodial care is being provided. Institutional occupancies and ambulatory care facilities assume that some level of medical care is being provided.

R-2

This type is for buildings that contain more than two dwelling units with occupants who are somewhat permanent (less transient). The similar NFPA categories include Apartment Buildings, Lodging or Rooming Houses, and Hotels and Dormitories.

Sample Building Types

Apartments	Fraternities/sororities
Congregate care facilities (nontransient with more than 16 occupants)	Monasteries
Boarding houses (nontransient)	Hotels (nontransient)
Convents	Live/work units
Dormitories	Motels (nontransient)
	Vacation time-share properties

R-3

This type is for more permanent residences but, unlike R-2, is most often used for single or duplex units. The typical single-family home falls into this category. Some residential care facilities (see R-4) may also be allowed under this classification if the number of occupants is limited to less than 10 or the length of stay is less than 24 hours. Congregate living facilities for 16 persons or fewer are typically included in this subclassification as well. If the I-Codes are used, a jurisdiction will typically require the use of the *International Residential Code (IRC)* for the specific code requirements for single and duplex residences. Each NFPA code references its chapter on one- and two-family dwellings as well. (See Appendix C for more information on family residences.) Verify with the local code official which code is applicable to residential projects.

◀ Note

Single-family homes and duplex units are classified as an R-3 occupancy by the *IBC* and typically require use of the *IRC.* The NFPA designation is "One- and Two-Family Dwellings."

Sample Building Types

Buildings that do not contain more than two dwelling units
Care facilities (five or fewer persons receiving care)
Congregate living facilities (nontransient with 16 or fewer
   occupants)
Bed and Breakfast (10 or fewer occupants)
Boarding houses
Convents
Dormitories (16 or fewer residents)
Fraternities and sororities
Monasteries
Congregate living facilities (transient with 10 or fewer occupants)
Boarding houses (transient)
Lodging houses (owner occupied) with five or fewer guest rooms
   and 10 or fewer occupants

R-4

This type is for small to medium-sized residential care facilities. This occupancy is based on the number of persons receiving custodial care on a 24-hour basis and does not include staff members. The typical number of residents is between 6 and 16. If fewer people are receiving care, it may be considered an R-3. If a larger number of people are receiving care or if medical care is also being provided, then it may be considered Institutional. These occupants are capable of self-preservation. (See "I-1.") The similar NFPA category would be Residential Board and Care. It could also be considered a Health Care occupancy by the NFPA, depending on the number of occupants. If these types of facilities are protected by an automatic sprinkler system, they may be able to follow the requirements of the *IRC* instead of the *IBC*.

Sample Building Types

Alcohol and drug abuse centers
Assisted living facilities (can also be classified as Institutional)
Convalescent facilities (can also be classified as Institutional)
Group homes
Halfway houses
Retirement homes
Residential board and care facilities
Social rehabilitation facilities

Storage (S) Occupancy

A building or a predominant part of a building is classified as a Storage occupancy if it is used for storing or sheltering products, merchandise, vehicles, or animals. Minor storage spaces, such as smaller storage rooms and supply closets, are typically treated as part of the predominant occupancy.

As with Factory/Industrial occupancies, low- or moderate-hazard contents are typically allowed in the Storage occupancy, although the storage of high-hazard contents may cause the building or space to be classified as Hazardous. The classification depends on the type of hazard and the quantity of material being stored. It can also be affected by how the products are stored, that is, on pallets or in containers. It is important to check the code to determine the level of hazard of the material being stored. A list of low- and moderate-hazard items follows but remember that each code groups them differently and each level will have slightly different requirements. The *IBC* has two storage subclassifications, one for moderate hazards (S-1) and another for low hazards (S-2). The NFPA has only one main storage classification. If unsure about the types of hazardous materials being stored, check with the local code official.

In addition, within Storage building types, it is generally understood that relatively few people will occupy the space. If the number of occupants is large or increases substantially in the future, the building occupancy may have to be reclassified.

Sample Building Types

Aircraft hangars (nonhazardous)   Chalk and crayons
Cold storage facilities   Cold storage
Creameries   Dairy products in non-wax-
        coated paper containers

Freight terminals and depots
Grain elevators
Repair garages (nonhazardous)
Truck and marine terminals
Warehouses (nonhazardous)
Asbestos
Beer or wine
Cement in bags

Fresh fruits and vegetables in
    nonplastic trays or containers
Frozen foods
Glass
Glass bottles, empty or filled
    with noncombustible liquids
Gypsum board

Inert pigments
Ivory
Meats
Metal cabinets
Metal desks with plastic
    tops and trim

Dry cell batteries
Dry insecticides
Electrical coils
Electrical insulation
Electrical motors
Empty cans
Food products
Foods in noncombustible
    containers
Metal parts

Metals
Mirrors
New empty cans

Oil-filled and other types of
    distribution transformers
Open parking structures
Porcelain and pottery
Stoves
Talc and soapstone
Sample low- and moderate-
    hazard storage contents
Washers and dryers

Utility (U) Occupancy

A building or part of a building that is not typical and/or cannot be properly classified as any of the other occupancy groups is often classified as a Utility, Special, or Miscellaneous occupancy. The building codes and *LSC* list different items in this category, and they are usually covered as a group in a separate chapter or in multiple chapters within each of the codes. If unsure whether a building would be considered a Utility or Miscellaneous occupancy, check with the local code official in the early stages of a project. (Unusual structures are beyond the scope of this book.)

▤ **Note**

The *IBC* also includes requirements for children's playground structures. The requirements address size, materials, fire protection, and separation from other elements.

Sample Building Types

Agricultural buildings (including
    barns, stables, livestock shelters)
Carports

Parking garages (can also be
    classified as Storage)
Private garages

Grain silos	Retaining walls
Greenhouses (if not classified as another occupancy)	Sheds
Livestock shelters including stables	Tall fences (over six feet, or 1829 mm)
Open structures	Tanks
	Temporary structures
	Towers

For many projects, additional occupancy-related issues must be considered. The ICC and the NFPA have special requirements that address unusual conditions or uses that require additional regulation for safety. Unusual structures may include high-rise, underground, and windowless buildings. Special uses include malls, ambulatory care facilities, storm shelters, hospitals, live/work units, stages, play structures, animal housing units, detention areas, labs in colleges, and so on. The *IBC*, for example has a chapter titled, "Special Detailed Requirements Based on Use and Occupancy" where many of these issues are addressed. The NFPA codes address these in the individual occupancy chapters as needed.

OTHER OCCUPANCY CONSIDERATIONS

Occupancy classification must be determined at the start of every project whether it is for a new building or a new build-out in an existing space. However, changes to the space rarely end after the initial construction. Updates, renovations, and change-over in use can occur over the lifetime of a building. Sometimes these require additional consideration about occupancy classification and how the codes will apply. And certain uses, such as schools, hospitals, restaurants, and so on, are required to be reviewed for safety and compliance with the codes on a regular basis to continue in use.

New versus Existing

In some codes, the requirements depend on if the occupancy is considered *new* or *existing*. This concept becomes especially important when using the *Life Safety Code* because the *LSC* separates its regulations into *new* or *existing* categories for each occupancy classification. An occupancy is considered *new* if it falls into one of the following categories:

1. The occupancy is in a building or space constructed for that occupancy under the currently enforced code edition.
2. The occupancy is to be located in an existing building previously not used for that occupancy.
3. The occupancy is in an addition to an existing building previously not used for that occupancy.
4. The occupancy is remaining in the same building but changing its size or use that affects its subclassification.

This last category is important to consider because it is the least obvious. In some cases, a change in size or use will cause the occupancy classification to be considered new. However, in other cases, if the change does not result in an increase in hazards or risk factors, the code official may allow it to change subclassification but still be considered existing.

If the occupancy is considered new, then the renovations to the existing space or the design of the new space will have to meet the codes as if it were new construction. If the occupancy is considered existing, then certain conditions are allowed to remain. (See Appendix B for more information projects in existing buildings.)

The designation of new and existing occupancies in the *LSC* and other NFPA documents allows the code official to require existing facilities, not just new occupancies, to maintain safe environments for their occupants. The document that is most often used by the Fire Marshal for periodic reviews is the *LSC*. The determination of new or existing is important in this review. Under the typical building code, including the *IBC*, new code requirements do not become retroactively applicable to an existing occupancy. Only when the space is renovated or a major addition is made can existing space be required to meet the newer codes.

Change in Occupancy

A change in occupancy typically occurs with the introduction of a new use into an existing building. Even if no physical change to the space occurs, the new use within the space can cause a change in the occupancy classification. And, even if a space complies for its most recent use, it does not mean that it complies for the new use, even it was built recently. Changes in occupancy classification typically result in some change in code requirements.

In many cases, a project that changes the use and thus the occupancy classification of the space will be very evident. For example, renovating a space that was hospital into a medical office building. However, a change in occupancy classification or subclassification can also be subtle.

ROOMS AND SPACES

Each building or space must be assigned an occupancy classification so that it can be determined which codes apply. In addition, certain rooms within an occupancy can have specific requirements. This is especially true in Residential and Institutional occupancies. The codes have very distinct definitions for various types of spaces, depending on how those spaces are used. The following are commonly referenced in the codes:

Occupiable space. A room or enclosed space designed for human occupancy that is equipped with means of egress, light, and ventilation, as required by the codes. This can include the spaces and rooms in most occupancies. It excludes such areas as mechanical and electrical rooms, crawl spaces, and attics. If a space is not considered occupiable, it usually does not have to meet typical accessibility requirements as specified in the building codes, the ICC standard, or the ADA.

Dwelling unit. A single unit providing complete independent living facilities for one or more persons, including permanent provisions for living, sleeping, eating, cooking, and sanitation. Building types that fall into this category include single-family homes, apartment units, townhouses, and certain assisted living units. However, a hotel guest room or dorm room can also be considered a dwelling unit if it has a kitchenette, eating area (i.e., table or bar top), and living area (i.e., upholstered seating area) in addition to the typical sleeping area and bathroom. (The ICC standard and the *IBC* divide dwelling units into Type A and Type B types for accessibility reasons. Type B dwellings have requirements similar to those of the *FHA Accessibility Guidelines [FHAG]*. Type A dwellings have additional requirements for accessibility.)

Live/Work unit. A dwelling unit or sleeping unit where a significant portion (greater than 10 percent, but less than 50 percent) is used for nonresidential use by the tenant. It has a maximum area of 3000 square feet (279 sm) and must be located on the main floor of the unit. (A typical home office would not be considered a live/work unit.)

Sleeping unit. A sleeping unit or room is used primarily for sleeping and does not fit the definition of a dwelling unit. The space often includes a bathroom, but it would not include a cooking area (or it could include a kitchen area but no bathroom). Examples include typical guest rooms in hotels and boarding houses, jail cells, dorm rooms, and patient rooms in nursing homes or hospitals.

Guest room or suite. Used for living or sleeping in and may include sanitation and storage facilities within a compartment or a contiguous group of rooms. Examples include rooms and/or suites in hotels, motels, and dormitories.

Care suite. A special grouping of treatment rooms or sleeping rooms and their support rooms and the circulation space to the rooms. The arrangement usually occurs in Institutional or Health Care occupancies and typically must be under direct supervision by staff members. Examples include an emergency suite or a critical care suite in a hospital.

Living area or room. This is considered any occupiable space in a Residential occupancy, other than sleeping rooms or rooms that are intended for a combination of sleeping and living. It includes spaces such as bathrooms (or toilet compartments), kitchens, closets, halls, and storage/utility spaces, but it can also include other rooms such as living rooms, dining rooms, family rooms, and dens.

Habitable room. A room in a Residential occupancy that is used for living, sleeping, cooking, and eating, but excludes such things as bathrooms, storage/utility spaces, and hallways.

A change in the level of activity can be considered a change of occupancy. For example, if a restaurant changes the seating arrangements so that more people can occupy the space, the occupancy classification or sub-classification can be affected. Likewise, a music venue that begins to serve food would change the subcategory under the *IBC*. These are still considered a change of occupancy and can trigger code changes.

Because changes in tenants within a retail center are typical over time, the occupancy classifications can change as well. A space may be occupied by a use that would be classified as Business, Assembly, Mercantile, and in some cases, Institutional or Educational. Regardless, any change that results in a change in occupancy classification will shift the codes that will apply to the space. This often results in different requirements for sprinklering, fire detection, means of egress, finishes, and so on. A change in occupancy classification can affect requirements from several other code regulations, including the building codes, the *International Existing Building Code (IEBC), IFC* and the *LSC*.

> **☑ Note**
>
> When using the *LSC*, it makes a difference if the project is considered new or existing.

> **☑ Note**
>
> If working in an existing building, the *IEBC* may be required instead of the *IBC* in some jurisdictions.

MORE THAN ONE OCCUPANCY TYPE

Two or more occupancies can occur in the same building. In fact, it is more common to see several different occupancies in the same building than to see a single-occupancy building. A common example is a large hotel. Many large hotels have restaurants, indoor pools, shops, conference areas, and spas in addition to their guest rooms. The hotel itself would be classified as Residential, but the restaurants, pools, and conference areas would be considered Assembly occupancies, and the spa and shops would be classified as a Business occupancy.

> **☑ Note**
>
> When more than one occupancy exists in the same building or space, it will be considered an accessory, mixed, or multiple occupancy.

Additional examples are listed here so that different building types can be considered and differences between various uses can be distinguished. (There are many other possibilities.) Notice how often the Assembly and Business occupancies occur together. These are common occupancies in mixed building types.

1. Elementary, middle, and high schools (Educational) with gymnasiums, auditoriums, and cafeterias (Assembly)
2. Office buildings (Business) with day care centers (Educational or Institutional)
3. Hospitals (Institutional) with cafeterias (Assembly)
4. Factories (Industrial) combined with the office headquarters (Business)
5. Malls (Mercantile) with small restaurants (Business) or large food courts (Assembly)

It is important to determine if more than one occupancy is occurring in the same building. Different occupancies can be adjacent horizontally, as in the Plan in Figure 3.2, or vertically in the case of a multistory building, as shown in the Section in Figure 3.2. Because each occupancy type has different safety risks, special measures are necessary to make the

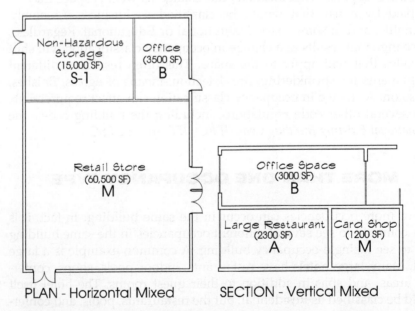

PLAN - Horizontal Mixed   SECTION - Vertical Mixed

Figure 3.2 Mixed occupancies: Horizontally and vertically (1 square foot = 0.0929 square meter).

building safe. In general, the codes require that either the occupancies be separated or all of them be treated as one, using the most stringent requirements. The codes use different terms for these relationships although they have common goals. The *International Building Code* refers to the relationship as accessory, separated mixed, or nonseparated mixed. In a similar way, the NFPA codes, including the *Life Safety Code*, define different occupancies as either accessory, mixed multiple, or separated multiple occupancies. The requirements for each type of "mixed" occupancy are described in the next sections. For all of these, the ultimate goal is to provide the safest building possible.

Incidental Use

Certain uses within a building are defined to be more hazardous regardless of the occupancy in which they occur. These are referred to as *incidental uses* in the *IBC*. They are referred to simply as *hazardous areas* in the NFPA codes. However, in both sets of codes, if their size is limited, they are not considered a separate occupancy. For example, the laundry room within the preschool facility (Educational) shown in Plan A of Figure 3.3 would be considered an incidental use within the other primary-use areas such as classrooms and office areas.

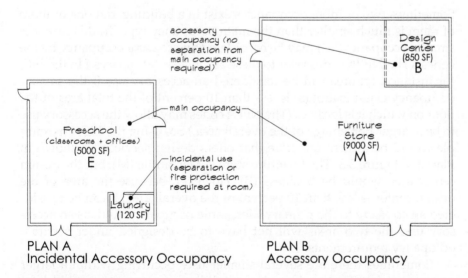

Figure 3.3 Incidental use versus accessory occupancy (1 square foot = 0.0929 square meter).

The types of spaces and rooms that are considered incidental use (hazardous) are indicated within the codes either in a table (*IBC*) or in the text (*NFPA*). These spaces include boiler rooms, large laundry rooms, waste and linen collection rooms, and other spaces containing hazardous items or machinery. In some cases, it will be specific to a certain occupancy classification. For example, laboratories in E occupancies can be considered incidental use. For some uses, the *IBC* and the NFPA codes provide minimum areas for when the space will be considered an incidental use. The *IBC* lists specific incidental uses in a table, as shown in Chapter 6 in Figure 6.8. As indicated in this table, additional fire and smoke protection is required for these areas. (This is discussed further in Chapter 6.) When this additional protection is provided, all other code requirements for the incidental use space follow the codes required for the main occupancy. If this protection is not provided, the building must be classified as a mixed occupancy. (See the section titled "Mixed Occupancies" later in this chapter.) The NFPA codes list these areas within the occupancy chapter in which they are most likely to occur. For example, the requirement for separation of soiled linen rooms can be found in the Health Care occupancy chapter.

Accessory Occupancies

Sometimes two or more occupancies exist in a building, but one or more of them is much smaller than the main occupancy type. In this case, the smaller occupancy(ies) may be considered an *accessory* occupancy by the codes. (The NFPA codes refer to these as "incidental" spaces.) In the *IBC*, for instance, an area can be considered an accessory use if the smaller occupancy classification(s) is less than 10 percent of the total area of the floor on which it is located. (The NFPA codes may allow the accessory use to be a larger percentage of the overall area.) So, using the *IBC*, an example would be a furniture store that offers design services, as shown in Plan B of Figure 3.3. The furniture store is Mercantile (M), but the design center area would be Business (B). However, because the area of the design center is less than 10 percent of the overall area, it can be considered an *accessory* to the primary Mercantile occupancy. And, as an accessory use, the two areas will not have to be designed under separate occupancy requirements.

Sometimes there are several smaller uses occurring within a larger occupancy classification in a single building. An example would be a large discount store, like the one shown in Plan A of Figure 3.4. The main use is the store, but it also includes a bakery, photo shop, hair salon, and snack bar. As long as the total area of the accessory spaces are not more

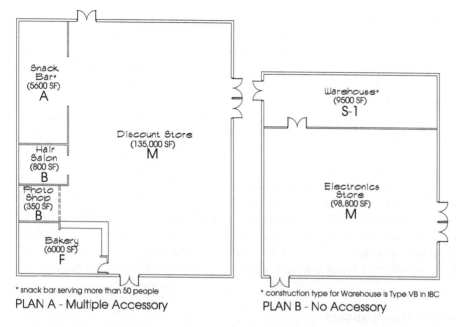

* snack bar serving more than 50 people
PLAN A - Multiple Accessory

* construction type for Warehouse is Type VB in IBC
PLAN B - No Accessory

Figure 3.4 Accessory versus occupancy examples (1 square foot = 0.0929 square meter).

than the allowable percentage of the total area, they can be considered accessory.

In addition to the proportionality requirement, an accessory occupancy cannot exceed the allowable area for that occupancy classification in relation to the construction type of the building. For example, Plan B in Figure 3.4 is an electronics store (Mercantile, or M) with its warehouse located in the same building. The warehouse is considered a Storage (S-1) occupancy. It could be considered an accessory occupancy by the *IBC* because it does not exceed 10 percent of the total area of the building. However, because the area of the S-1 occupancy exceeds the allowable area for this construction type, the S-1 occupancy cannot be considered an accessory to the Mercantile. In this case, the storage area would be considered a separate storage occupancy and would have to meet the code requirements for an S-1 occupancy classification instead of the requirements for a Mercantile occupancy.

In some cases, certain areas can be accessory regardless of the percentage of area. Starting with the 2018 *IBC*, storage areas of any size are do not have to be considered separately. Assembly areas with an occupant load less than 50 and an areas less than 750 square feet (69.7 sm) can also be considered accessory to a main occupancy. An example would be

 Note

The NFPA codes allow an accessory occupancy to be a larger percentage of the overall space or building than does the *IBC*.

a training room for a Business. However, in both the *IBC* and the NFPA codes, some occupancies cannot be considered accessory to any other classification. This includes Day Care occupancies (except for religious uses) and certain types of Residential and Educational building types. (Hazardous occupancies can never be considered as accessory to another occupancy.)

It is useful for design purposes to determine if an area can be considered accessory to the main area, because it simplifies the code requirements and allows areas to be more open. If the smaller occupancy(ies) cannot be considered accessory, the space or building would have to be designed as a separated or nonseparated mixed occupancy. (See the next section.) When there are approved accessory occupancies within a space or building, most of the code requirements (including the means of egress requirements) are based on the main occupancies. The fire protection requirements, however, are based on the most restrictive use (whether the accessory or main use) and apply to the entire building or space.

Mixed Occupancies

When two or more occupancies in a building or space are about the same size or do not meet the requirements to be considered an accessory use, it is a *mixed occupancy*. To address the specific situation, the *IBC* further divides mixed occupancies into separated mixed occupancies and nonseparated mixed occupancies. (The NFPA codes also use the term *separated* but only in relation to multiple occupancies. This is explained later in this chapter.)

When the different occupancies are divided by the required rated assemblies (e.g., walls, floor, and/or ceiling assemblies), these occupancies are considered by the *IBC* to be *separated mixed* occupancies. (The requirements for rated assemblies are discussed further in Chapter 5.) Once separated, each occupancy only needs to meet the requirements of its own occupancy classification. For example, in Plan A in Figure 3.5, the Business (B) occupancy and the Day Care/Institutional (I-4) occupancy are separated by a rated wall. Thus, the code requirements for the Business occupancy would apply to the post office and the Institutional requirements would apply to the day care. If certain conditions exist, the day care could be reclassified as an Educational (E) but the same separation would be required.

When there is no rated separation between the occupancies, it is considered by the *IBC* as a *nonseparated mixed* occupancy. (This term is not used by NFPA.) When the occupancies are considered nonseparated, the occupancies must both meet the requirements of the most stringent

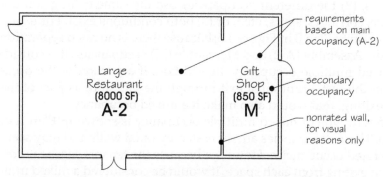

PLAN A - Separated Mixed Occupanices

PLAN B - Nonseparated Mixed Occupancies

Figure 3.5 Mixed occupancies in the IBC: Separated and nonseparated (1 square foot = 0.0929 square meter).

occupancy classification, including construction type, allowable area, finishes, fire protection, and exiting requirements. For example, in Plan B of Figure 3.5, the Mercantile (M) and Assembly (A-2) occupancies are separated by a partition only for visual reasons and so are considered nonseparated. In this case, the more stringent Assembly requirements for the restaurant would be applied to the entire area of the building, including the gift shop. In buildings where there are separated and nonseparated mixed occupancies, additional requirements apply. For instance, the most stringent fire protection requirements will apply to the entire building.

Many factors influence the decision to treat a mixed occupancy as separated or nonseparated. Constructing rated assemblies for separation can be expensive or undesirable for the design, but having to meet the most stringent exiting requirements, construction type, or area limitations

☑ **Note**

Both the *IBC* and the NFPA codes use the term *separated* for when two or more occupancies are divided by rated assemblies—called *separated mixed* by the ICC and *separated multiple* by NFPA.

for the whole building or space may limit the design unnecessarily. All these factors must be considered to determine the better choice for a project.

Multiple Occupancies

Multiple occupancies is a term used by the NFPA codes (not the I-Codes). It occurs when two or more occupancies exist in a building or space either horizontally or vertically. Multiple occupancies are designated more specifically as mixed or separated.

The NFPA codes consider a building or space to be a *mixed multiple occupancy* when two or more occupancies exist together and are "intermingled." This can occur if (1) there is no rated separation(s) between the occupancies, (2) the different occupancies use the same exiting components (aisle, corridors, stairs, etc.), or (3) both conditions exist. For example, refer again to Plan B in Figure 3.6; because there is no rated separation between the Assembly (A-2) and Mercantile (M) occupancies, it is considered a mixed multiple occupancy. In addition, if a portion of the occupants from the restaurant must exit through the gift store as part of the required exiting, that would also make it a mixed occupancy.

A different type of mixed multiple occupancy is shown in Plan A of Figure 3.6. These occupancies are separated by rated walls and may seem to be separated occupancies. However, because the tenants share the corridor when exiting from each space, it would be considered a mixed multiple occupancy by the NFPA codes. If a multiple occupancy is considered mixed, the construction type, fire protection, and means of egress, as well as other requirements, must follow the most restrictive occupancy requirements. (In this way, it is similar to nonseparated mixed occupancies in the *IBC*.)

However, if the occupancies are separated by rated walls but do not share exiting, then the NFPA considers the area a *separated multiple* occupancy. Like the separated mixed occupancy in the *IBC*, each space must only meet the code requirements for its occupancy classification. An example of a separated multiple occupancy can be seen in Plan B of Figure 3.6. Here the multiple occupancy classifications are separated from each other by a rated wall. In addition, each has its own separate means of egress, so they do not share a common corridor. These factors make it a separated multiple occupancy.

The NFPA codes designate how a mixed or separated multiple occupancy should be handled. More specific information on multiple occupancies may also be found within each occupancy chapter. These requirements supersede the general requirements for mixed or separated

◢ **Note**

The term *mixed multiple occupancy* is unique to the NFPA. Although similar to nonseparated mixed occupancies in the IBC, a mixed multiple occupancy includes a wider variety of building scenarios.

◢ **Note**

If they meet all the code requirements, incidental accessory use and accessory occupancies will not make a building a mixed-use occupancy.

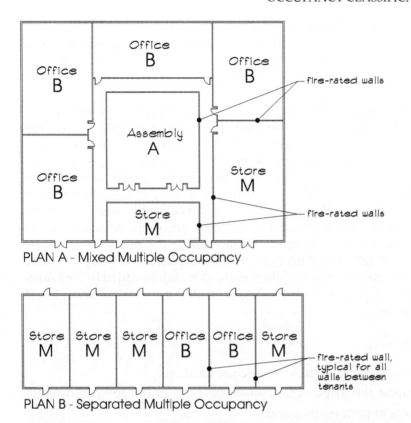

Figure 3.6 Multiple occupancies in the NFPA codes: Mixed and separated.

occupancy classifications in the general chapters. Because the *IBC* and the *LSC* defines the relationship of more than one occupancy in a building differently, a code official may need to be consulted to determine which requirements will apply to the different areas versus the whole building if both apply to your project.

ACCESSIBILITY REQUIREMENTS

Almost all uses and occupancies will be required to comply with an accessibility regulation whether it be local or federal. Most will be considered public accommodations and/or commercial facilities under the ADA. In addition to the accessibility requirements that apply generally to all uses, the *ADA Standards* include specific requirements for special rooms, spaces, elements, and facilities. These include medical care, long-term care, lodging guest rooms, courtrooms, dwelling units, transportation facilities, and

☑ Note

Both the *1991 ADA Standards* and the *2010 ADA Standards* include regulations specific to certain occupancies. Refer to these requirements for details.

various recreational facilities. Some of these may be associated with a specific occupancy; it is possible for some elements to occur in more than one occupancy classification. The building codes and the *ICC A117.1* accessibility standard include similar requirements, although these are not as extensive as those of the *ADA Standards*.

The following is a list of uses and building types that would have accessibility requirements. (The type of occupancy classification is indicated as well.) This list is based on the *2010 ADA Standards*. In addition, there are additional requirements for storage and dwelling units. When working within these occupancies, the code research should include reviewing the current *ADA Standards* as well as comparing them to the *ICC A117.1* standard, the accessibility chapter of the *IBC*, and other codes enforced by the local jurisdiction to see if there are contradictory or stricter requirements. Other federal accessibility regulations may also apply (e.g., *FHAG* and *ABA Standards*), as explained in Chapter 1, and additional regulations for certain occupancies may be added in the future. When necessary, consult the local code official or the ADA Access Board for clarification.

Assembly Areas

❑ Percentage of accessible wheelchair locations
❑ Location and dispersion of wheelchair spaces and companion seats
❑ Access to performance areas
❑ Types of floor surfaces
❑ Assistive listening systems requirements
❑ Types and availability of listening systems

Businesses and Mercantile

❑ Size and height of checkout counters and work surfaces
❑ Clearance and height of self-service shelves/display units
❑ Size and height of teller windows and information counters
❑ Width and quantity of checkout aisles
❑ Number, size, and types of dressing/fitting rooms
❑ Type and clearance of automatic teller machines

Medical and Long-Term Care Facilities (Institutional and Health Care)

❑ Size of covered entrances for unloading patients
❑ Percentage and dispersion of accessible patient bedrooms

❑ Dispersion of accessible patient bedrooms and toilets
❑ Size of maneuvering spaces in patient rooms
❑ Clearance area at patient beds
❑ Width of accessible doors and aisles

Restaurants and Cafeterias (Business or Assembly)

❑ Percentage of accessible fixed tables
❑ Access to sunken and raised platforms
❑ Width and height of food service lines
❑ Height of counters and self-service shelves
❑ Access to controls of vending machines
❑ Width of access aisles

Transient Lodgings (Residential)

❑ Percentage of accessible sleeping rooms
❑ Dispersion of accessible elements in types of rooms
❑ Specific requirements within accessible rooms
❑ Number and dispersion of rooms for hearing-impaired
❑ Dispersion of accessible rooms suitable for disabled with multiple disabilities (mobility, hearing, visual, etc.)
❑ Access to rooms and public and common areas
❑ Width of door openings
❑ Size of maneuvering spaces
❑ Percentage of accessible amenities (ice machines, washers and dryers, etc.)
❑ Clearance, height, and hardware of storage units

Housing at Places of Education (similar to Transient Lodging and Residential)

❑ Percentage of accessible units
❑ Dispersion of accessible elements among accessible rooms
❑ Specific requirements within accessible rooms
❑ Access to rooms and public and common areas
❑ Width of door openings
❑ Accessible circulation within units
❑ Access to kitchen units

Judicial, Legislative, and Regulatory Facilities (Business and Assembly)

- ❑ Access through secured entrances
- ❑ Access to courtroom elements (judge's bench, witness stand, jury assembly, and deliberation areas, etc.)
- ❑ Access to holding cells (and amenities)
- ❑ Dispersion of accessible cells
- ❑ Percentage of assistive listening systems
- ❑ Types and availability of listening systems

Detention and Correctional Facilities (Institutional)

- ❑ Percentage of holding and housing cells or rooms (and amenities)
- ❑ Dispersion of accessible cells
- ❑ Access to cells and visiting areas

Spaces for Children (Educational and certain Institutional)

- ❑ Access to drinking fountains
- ❑ Access to toilet facilities (including water closets, toilet stalls, lavatories)
- ❑ Access to dining and work surfaces
- ❑ Adjusted reach ranges
- ❑ Height of handrails at ramps and stairs
- ❑ Height of mirrors
- ❑ Height of controls
- ❑ Play areas

Transportation Facilities (Assembly or Business)

- ❑ Boarding areas
- ❑ Signs
- ❑ Accessible routes
- ❑ Communication elements

Recreational Facilities (Assembly)

- ❑ Percentage of accessible sauna and steam rooms
- ❑ Access to exercise machines and equipment

❑ Number of accessible means of entry to pool
❑ Number of accessible shooting facilities

Social Service Establishments (Residential)

❑ Access to beds
❑ Access to accessible toilet and roll-in showers

DETERMINING OCCUPANT LOADS

In addition to assigning the occupancy classification, the occupant load (OL) must also be determined at the beginning of a project. The *occupant load* sets the number of occupants for which adequate exiting must be provided from a space or building. Proper exiting allows people to evacuate

DESIGN LOADS

Occupant loads as described in this chapter are not to be confused with two other types of design loads required by the codes: dead loads and live loads. *Dead loads* include all permanent components of a building's structure, such as the walls, floors, and roof. *Live loads,* by contrast, include any loads that are not the actual weight of the structure itself. They include interior elements such as people, furniture, equipment, appliances, and books. Other loads that are sometimes considered live loads but are separate exterior elements include wind loads, rain and flood loads, snow loads, and earthquake loads. These types of load factors affect the design of the building's structure.

Dead load and live load calculations are typically done by engineers during the initial design and construction of a building. Most of the calculations take into consideration that some of the loads will change during the normal use of a building. For example, in an office building it is common for interior walls to change and be relocated as tenants move. The number of people will vary as well.

Some interior projects may require certain live loads to be researched when significant changes are proposed in a project. The most common situations include (1) adding a wall, such as brick or concrete, that is substantially heavier than a standard wall; (2) creating a filing area or library that concentrates the weight at one point; (3) adding a heavy piece of equipment; and (4) adding an assembly seating area in an existing space.

In most cases, a structural engineer is needed to determine if the existing structure will hold the added load/weight. If not, the structural engineer will determine how to add additional support, if possible.

safely and quickly in case of an emergency. And, therefore, the occupant load is the number of people that can safely be in a space or building. Generally, an occupant load is determined for each space and then added together to create the occupant load for the entire floor or building. The occupant load is determined by two basic methods: by using a load factor given by the code or by establishing a desired number of occupants—which requires additional approval by the code official. Although it may be interesting to know the total occupant load of a multistory building, the most important occupant loads for using the codes is the total occupant load for each floor and the occupant load in each individual space.

It is important to determine the occupant load early in the design process. In some cases, the occupant load may determine the occupancy classification. An example is a restaurant with an occupancy under 50 (Business) and a restaurant with an occupant load over 50 (Assembly). The occupant load is also needed to size the means of egress components, such as the number of exits and the width of corridors and aisles. (See Chapter 5.) The number of required plumbing fixtures and certain mechanical calculations also depend on the occupant load. (See Chapter 8.) The remainder of this chapter explains occupant loads.

Occupant Load by Load Factor

To provide for safe buildings, the codes have established a way to consistently calculate a reasonable number of people for typical uses within a building. To figure the occupant load, each code assigns a predetermined amount of area or square feet (or square meters) to each occupant based on the specific *use* of the space. This predetermined figure is called the occupant *load factor*. Basically, it establishes a relationship between the size of the room and the number of people allowed for any given activity or use. In most cases, this means that a larger space allows more occupants, and the need for more occupants requires a larger space.

Using the load factor to determine the occupant load generates the minimum number of occupants for which the space *must* be designed. In a few cases, the number of occupants can be increased without increasing the size of the space. However, the building codes, such as the *International Building Code* and the *Life Safety Code,* do set limits on the maximum concentration of occupants within a space or building. (See "Modifying the Occupant Load.")

◢ Note

Occupant loads are typically determined using the load factors given by the codes.

Using the Table

Each code provides occupant load requirements, including load factors and exiting requirements, within the means of egress chapter. The NFPA codes, including the *LSC*, have additional occupant load factors and requirements in each separate occupancy chapter as well. Figure 3.7 is the load factor table from the *IBC* titled Table 1004.5, "Maximum Floor Area Allowances per Occupant." The NFPA codes have similar load factor tables. The load factors for a specific use may be different between the codes. For example, the load factor for a commercial kitchen in the *IBC* is 200 square feet (18.58 sm); in the *LSC*, it is 100 square feet (9.3 sm). A code may also have specific load factors for unique uses that may not be included in the other code. For example, the NFPA codes have a load factor for Ambulatory health care but the *IBC* does not.

To use Table 1004.5 in Figure 3.7, you must first determine the specific function or use of the space. See the first column titled "Function of Space." This column lists the different uses for spaces within a building. Although some uses are similar to occupancy types, you must choose the specific *use* of the space. For example, if you were designing the classrooms for a college, you would still use the "Educational, Classroom area" occupant load factor to determine the occupant load of the space even though the space would be assigned to a Business occupancy. Again, the specific *use* of the space must be considered not the occupancy type. Another example, bowling alleys are considered an Assembly occupancy. But in this chart, bowling centers is a separate category of use and has a unique floor area factor.

The occupant load factors for each use are listed in the next column in square feet per person. (A metric conversion is shown at the bottom of the table.) For example, the load factor for "Educational, Classroom area" is 20 net square feet per occupant. The load factor indicates the amount of space or area it is assumed each person present will require. Although the square foot figures may seem high for one person, they allow for furniture and equipment and, in some cases, corridors, closets, and other miscellaneous areas.

The area for each load factor refers to the floor area *within* the exterior walls of a building. The load factors are designated as gross or net area. The *gross* area refers to the building as a whole and includes all miscellaneous

◄ Note

In some cases, it may be possible to design a space for an occupant load less than that calculated by the load factor. However, it usually requires additional design documentation and approval by a code official.

TABLE 1004.5 MAXIMUM FLOOR AREA ALLOWANCES PER OCCUPANT

FUNCTION OF SPACE	OCCUPANT LOAD FACTOR[a]
Accessory storage areas, mechanical equipment room	300 gross
Agricultural building	300 gross
Aircraft hangars	500 gross
Airport terminal	
Baggage claim	20 gross
Baggage handling	300 gross
Concourse	100 gross
Waiting areas	15 gross
Assembly	
Gaming floors (keno, slots, etc.)	11 gross
Exhibit gallery and museum	30 net
Assembly with fixed seats	See Section 1004.6
Assembly without fixed seats	
Concentrated (chairs only—not fixed)	7 net
Standing space	5 net
Unconcentrated (tables and chairs)	15 net
Bowling centers, allow 5 persons for each lane including 15 feet of runway, and for additional areas	7 net
Business areas	150 gross
Concentrated business use areas	See Section 1004.8
Courtrooms—other than fixed seating areas	40 net
Day care	35 net
Dormitories	50 gross
Educational	
Classroom area	20 net
Shops and other vocational room areas	50 net
Exercise rooms	50 gross
Group H-5 fabrication and manufacturing areas	200 gross
Industrial areas	100 gross
Institutional areas	
Inpatient treatment areas	240 gross
Outpatient areas	100 gross
Sleeping areas	120 gross

Figure 3.7 *(Continued)*

FUNCTION OF SPACE	OCCUPANT LOAD FACTOR[a]
Kitchens, commercial	200 gross
Library	
Reading rooms	50 net
Stack area	100 gross
Locker rooms	50 gross
Mall buildings—covered and open	See Section 402.8.2
Mercantile	60 gross
Storage, stock, shipping areas	300 gross
Parking garages	200 gross
Residential	200 gross
Skating rinks, swimming pools	
Rink and pool	50 gross
Decks	15 gross
Stages and platforms	15 net
Warehouses	500 gross

For SI: 1 foot = 304.8 mm, 1 square foot = 0.0929 m².
a   Floor area in square feet per occupant.

Figure 3.7 *International Building Code* Table 1004.5, Maximum Floor Area Allowances per Occupant (2015 International Building Code, copyright© 2021. Washington, DC: International Code Council. Reproduced with permission. All rights reserved. www.iccsafe.org).

spaces within the exterior walls. The *net* area refers to actual occupied spaces and does not include ancillary spaces such as corridors, restrooms, utility closets, or other unoccupied areas. The area these spaces including fixed items, such as interior walls, columns, and built-in counters and shelving (areas that are not habitable), should be deducted from the overall area before calculating the occupant load using a *net* load factor. When net figures are required, it is assumed that the occupants who are using an ancillary area would have left the occupied space to do so and, therefore, would already be taken into account. For example, a person in the corridor of a school would most likely be a student or teacher already accounted for in a classroom. However, you must consider the actual use of a space, even a corridor.

The Formula

The formula that is used with the load factor tables is

$$\text{Occupant Load} = \text{Floor area} (\text{sq ft or sq m}) / \text{Load factor}$$

To determine the occupant load for a building or space, take the area of the interior space and divide it by the load factor for the appropriate use. If the space or building has more than one type of use, the same is done for each area according to its use and added together. This provides the number of occupants that is allowed in the overall space. If the total results in a fraction over a half of an occupant, round up to the nearest whole number. Depending on the project, calculations for separate areas and separate occupancies may also need to be made and added together. The final occupant load indicates the number of occupants for which the space especially the means of egress must be designed.

Example 1

To further understand the difference between gross and net area and how to use the load factor table, refer to the floor plan for a library in Figure 3.8. "Library" is listed separately in the *IBC* table in Figure 3.7. This building type is further divided into two separate functions: reading rooms and stack area. A study room, corridor, and utility closet are also noted on the plan. These will have to be addressed as well. The occupant load for each separate function must be determined separately.

The load factor for the stack area of the library is indicated in the table in Figure 3.7 as 100 *gross* square feet (9.3 sm). So, the area measurement should include the entire stack area with aisles, reference area, checkout counter, and so forth. The occupant load factor for the reading rooms is indicated to be 50 *net* square feet (4.6 sm), meaning that the area should not include ancillary spaces. Although there is not a specific function listed in the table in Figure 3.7, a study room use is similar to a small conference room. A small conference room may be determined by using the Assembly-Unconcentrated (tables and chairs). The load factor for this use is 15 *net* square feet (1.39 sm). Both the reading room and the study room areas call for net load factors. Therefore, the corridor or the utility closet adjacent to the reading rooms on the floor plan should not be included when determining the area of the reading room or study room. These areas are essentially left out of the load factor calculation because they are not considered to contribute additional occupants to the library.

✎ Note

The NFPA codes give load factors in square feet and in metric dimensions. The *IBC* provides a metric conversion at the bottom of the load factor table.

✎ Note

Gross area includes all areas within the exterior walls. *Net area* consists of all areas within the exterior walls minus ancillary spaces such as corridors, restrooms, utility closets, and other unoccupied areas.

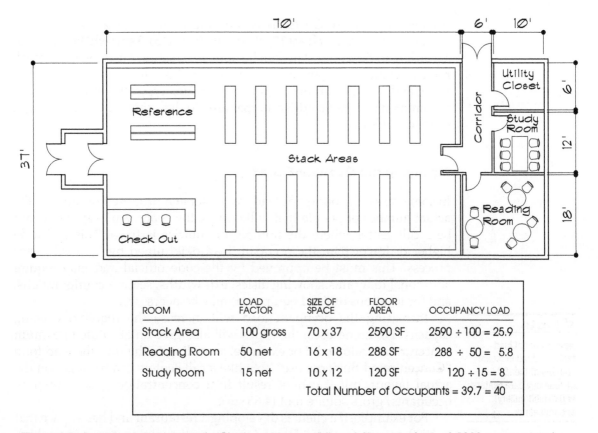

ROOM	LOAD FACTOR	SIZE OF SPACE	FLOOR AREA	OCCUPANCY LOAD
Stack Area	100 gross	70 x 37	2590 SF	2590 ÷ 100 = 25.9
Reading Room	50 net	16 x 18	288 SF	288 ÷ 50 = 5.8
Study Room	15 net	10 x 12	120 SF	120 ÷ 15 = 8
			Total Number of Occupants =	39.7 = 40

Figure 3.8 Occupancy load example: Single occupancy (Library) (1 square foot = 0.0929 square meter).

Using the dimensions of the floor plan and the occupant load formula to determine the area for each space, Figure 3.8 shows how to determine the occupant load for the entire library. Rounding up, the total occupant load is 40 people.

Example 2

Sometimes, load factors can be used in a slightly different way. If the area required for a particular occupancy or use needs to be determined, the load factors may help establish the space requirements. This may be helpful in the programming stage of a project. For example, if planning a new office space for a client with 125 employees, the table can be used to look up the occupant load factor under Business areas (100 gross square feet, or 9.3 sm). Multiply this factor by the number of people intended to occupy the space (125) to determine the minimum size of the space needed. In this case, at least 12,500 square feet (1161.3 sm) will be required, according to the codes. This can be done for a smaller use such as a break room or conference room as well. Although this will provide a good estimate and the minimum required by code, typically other program requirements must be added to that area to determine the final size of a space or building.

Modifying the Occupant Load

In some cases, the occupant load can be set at a proposed number or the actual number of people that will occupy the space. An example would be a call center where the number of cubicles is fixed. This might be higher or lower than the occupant load determined by the load factor process. This must be approved by the code official and may require additional diagrams showing aisles, exit widths, seating configurations, and/or locations of fixed equipment may be necessary.

Note

New occupant load factors added in recent editions of the *IBC* include day care centers and exhibit gallery and museums.

Increasing the occupant load will increase the required existing capacity. For some uses, the codes will also give an absolute maximum concentration allowed. For example, according to the *IBC*, the load for a "Concentrated Business use" area like a call centers can be based on the actual layout, but it cannot result in a concentration greater than 50 occupants/gross square foot (4.65 sm).

For example, if a client is developing a restaurant and has a space that is 5000 square feet (464.5 sm) for use as the dining area (Assembly). Referring to the load factor table in Figure 3.7, the load factor is 15 gross square feet (1.4 sm) for an "Assembly without fixed seats, Unconcentrated (tables and chairs)." By dividing 5000 square feet (464.5 sm) by 15 gross square feet (1.4 sm), the result is an occupant load of 333 occupants. However, if the client wanted to be able to seat 400, then 400 would be considered the desired occupant load—the modified number. The means of egress (i.e., exits, aisles, corridors, and number of doors) would then be designed for an occupant load of 400. That would also be the maximum number allowed within the space at any one time. Making sure that the space can be designed to handle the increased exiting requirements and other accessible clearances is also necessary. When designing for an increased occupant load, it is advisable or may be required to review it with the code official early in the design process.

There may be instances when it is desirable that a space is designed for a *reduced number* of occupants than the number determined by the load factor. For example, a workshop may not typically be occupied by the number of occupants determined by the load factor because of the size and amount of equipment used in the room. Generally, designing for a lower number is not allowed. A proposal to design to a reduced occupant number would require approval by the code official. In addition, to allow the lower occupant load, the code official can require special conditions and limitations for use of the space. Remember, designing the space for the lower occupant load can affect the future use of the space because of the lower means of egress capacity.

Occupant Load for Converging Spaces

In many cases, rooms will exit through an adjacent space before reaching the final exit. A simple example is the path through a waiting room in a dentist's office. When multiple spaces *converge*, the codes usually require that the occupant load of the final space includes the occupant loads of all the rooms that must exit through it. A different example is shown in Figure 3.9. Occupants in the business offices must walk through the open office area to exit the space. Occupants from the training room would also empty through the open office area to get to the exit. In this case, the occupant load for the large training room in Figure 3.9 should be calculated using an Assembly (A) factor, either "Concentrated" or "Unconcentrated," depending on its intended use. The open area, breakroom and the offices can then be grouped together, and the occupant load determined by using the "Business area" load factor. When these separate calculations are added together, they provide an occupant load that accurately represents the number of people that use and will have to exit this space. Similarly, when paths of travel to an exit using an aisle, corridor or stair converge, the number of occupants must be accumulative. This will be discussed further in Chapter 5.

An accessory use space sometimes creates a similar situation. For example, the occupant load for the design center (B) in Figure 3.3B should be added to the occupant load of the Mercantile (M) portion of the furniture store, because the occupants of the design center must walk through the store to exit the building. Each would be calculated separately according to the load factor for its use. This total would be used to determine the exiting from the overall space.

In some cases, spaces such as mezzanines, partial floors or whole floors above or below can be allowed to converge on to another floor. In these cases, the occupant load from those spaces must be added to the floor exiting floor level.

> ☑ **Note**
>
> If the allowable occupant load of a space needs to be increased, a maximum load factor of 7 square feet (0.65 sm) could be used. This is the maximum density allowed by the code.

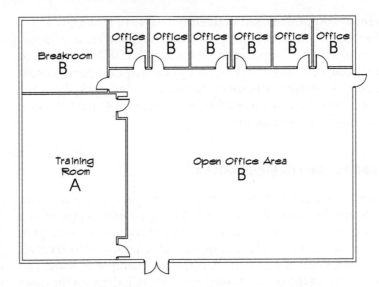

Figure 3.9 Occupant load example: Primary and secondary spaces.

Occupant Load for a Building Floor

The occupant load for a building floor will determine the exiting requirements (corridor widths, number of exits, etc.) from that floor. If it is occupied by a single tenant but has a variety of functional spaces such as offices, cafeteria, and locker rooms, the occupant load of each use area must be calculated. These will be added together to determine the total occupant load of the floor.

Whenever there is more than one use, tenant, or occupancy classification on the same building floor, additional calculations are required. If the floor has multiple tenants, it is often best to calculate the occupant load of each tenant separately. In some cases, the tenants might be different occupancies such as Business, Mercantile, and Assembly. In this case, it is important to calculate them separately because the occupant load may affect various requirements for each occupancy classification. The load factors for the separate functions within the individual tenants and occupancies should be used. Although the exiting for each tenant space must be designed for their separate occupant load, the combined occupant loads of all the tenants or occupancies will be used to establish the requirements for the common areas (including public toilet facilities) and the exiting requirements for the entire floor. (This is described more in Chapter 5.) This process is similar whether calculating the occupant load under the *IBC* (mixed occupancies) or the *NFPA 101* (mixed-multiple occupancies.)

A simplified example is shown in Figure 3.10. In this example, there is a mixture of Mercantile (M) and Business (B) spaces on the first floor and multiple Business (B) spaces on the second floor.

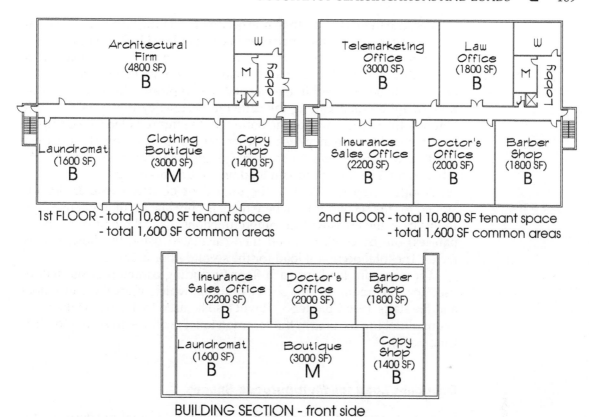

FIRST FLOOR	LOAD FACTOR	FLOOR AREA	OCCUPANCY LOAD
M (Mercantile) Tenants	30 gross	3000 SF	3000 ÷ 30 = 100
M Common Area*	30 gross	448 SF (1,600 x 28%)	448 ÷ 30 = 15
B (Business) Tenants	100 gross	7800 SF (10,800 - 3000)	7800 ÷ 100 = 78
B Common Areas*	100 gross	1152 SF (1,600 x 72%)	1152 ÷ 100 = 12
		Total Number of Occupants @ 1st FLOOR =	205
SECOND FLOOR			
B (Business) Tenants	100 gross	10,800 SF	10,800 ÷ 100 = 108
B Common Areas	100 gross	1600 SF	1,600 ÷ 100 = 16
		Total Number of Occupants @ 2nd FLOOR =	124
		TOTAL OCCUPANT LOAD FOR BUILDING =	329

*NOTE: Of the total tenant square footage for the 1st floor, the Business tenants occupy 72% of the space (7800 divided by 10,800) and the Mercantile tenant occupies the remaining 28%.

Figure 3.10 Occupant load example: Mixed/multiple occupancy building (1 square foot = 0.0929 square meter).

Because there is more than one occupancy on the first floor, the occupant load for each tenant space has been calculated based on the uses in each tenant space. In this case, because the occupancy a gross load factor is required, the public areas (i.e., lobby, restrooms, main corridor) will also have to be included in the calculations. Typically, this would be proportionally divided among the different occupancy types, as shown in Figure 3.10. (See the note at the bottom of the figure.) Once the occupant load for each occupancy/use or each tenant is determined, add them together with the common areas to get the total occupant load for the whole floor. The total occupant load on the first floor is 205.

Another way to calculate the total floor occupant load is demonstrated for the second floor where there is only one occupancy/use type. In this case, the areas with common functions (i.e., all the Business occupancies) can by combined and then calculated using the Business use factor. The total occupant load for the second floor is 124.

The occupant load for each floor (including common areas) will be used for code requirements such as exiting, which affect the entire floor and the stairs. (See Chapter 5.) It will also be used to determine the number of plumbing fixtures in the common toilet facilities on each floor. (See Chapter 8.)

Occupant Load for Multipurpose Spaces

Some buildings or building areas are used for different purposes at different times. For example, a church building might be used for a large gathering, celebration meal, or exercise on various days or at various times during a single day. In other words, any area of a building that has more than one function is considered to have multiple uses. The occupant load is determined by the use that indicates the largest concentration of people. Several calculations may be required to determine which occupancy will provide the largest number.

Occupant Load for Fixed Seats

 Note

When reading code tables, it is important to read all the footnotes at the bottom of the tables for additional information and possible exceptions.

Fixed seating arrangements are common in some building types, especially in Assembly occupancies. The seats are considered fixed if they are not easily moved and/or if they are used on a relatively permanent basis. Instead of using the standard formula for calculating the occupant load per area, the actual seats are counted. For example, the occupant load in a movie theater, as shown in Plan A of Figure 3.12, would be determined by the number of seats used in the space (including spaces specifically created for wheelchair users).

Counting seats with arms is self-explanatory. However, fixed seating may also consist of continuous seating such as benches, bleachers, and pews. Each of the codes provides a variable (either in the occupant load table or the text) to be used for continuous seating. The typical increment is 18 linear inches (457 mm) of seating for each occupant. If, for example, a church has 28 pews and each pew is 12 feet long, as shown in Plan B of Figure 3.11, the 18-inch (457 mm) variable would be used. A 12-foot pew equals 144 inches (3658 mm). Divide the 144 (3658 mm) by the 18-inch (457 mm) variable to get 8 people per pew. Because there is a total of 28 pews, this church has an occupant load of 224 people (28 pews × 8 people/pew).

Booth seating is another type of continuous fixed seating. Booth seating usually has a separate variable provided by the codes. The typical increment is 24 inches (609.6 mm). For example, Plan C in Figure 3.11 shows several types of booth seating. Each should be calculated separately. Measure the length of the bench along the *front* edge (especially at corners) and divide by 24 inches (609.6 mm). Add all the calculations together to determine the occupant load for the bench areas. This would be added to the occupant loads of the other seating areas within the space to determine the total occupant load of the restaurant.

✎ Note

The continuous seating variable will not always evenly divide into the length of the seating. For any remaining fraction, round down. Consult the local code official when there is uncertainty.

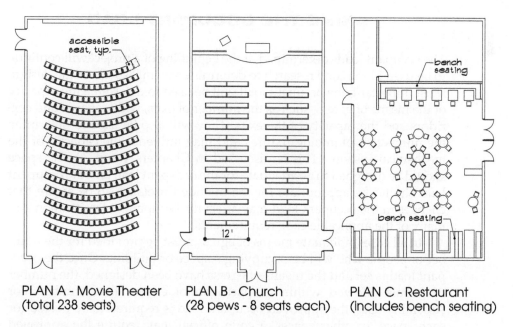

PLAN A - Movie Theater
(total 238 seats)

PLAN B - Church
(28 pews - 8 seats each)

PLAN C - Restaurant
(includes bench seating)

Figure 3.11 Occupant load example: Occupancies with fixed seats.

All areas of a building or space must be included in the occupant count. If the space has different types of seating and different types of activities occurring, each area would be assigned by its specific use. For example, a nightclub might have fixed seating in one area, tables and chairs in another, and a dance floor in another. In this case, calculate the occupant load for all the different areas separately and add them together to get the final count.

Occupant Load for Unusual Uses

There may also be occasions when the use of a space is not typical. The occupant load factors given in the code table represent the most common space uses. On other occasions, the use of a space may not clearly fit into one of the use categories, for example, a dog washing area. When this occurs, you should choose the closest use category. If it is still unclear, you may want to contact the code official for guidance. Typically, only the code official can approve a different or unique load factor. This decision should be clarified at the beginning of a project because the occupant load will affect many of the codes that apply to the project.

USING THE OCCUPANT LOAD

The occupant loads determined at the beginning of a project will continue to be used in the code research to determine several aspects of the design. Most important, the occupant load will be used to determine the capacity of the means of egress, such as the number of exits, width of aisle and corridors and the capacity of the exits. They will also be used to determine the number of plumbing fixtures and may influence the capacity of the mechanical system. (This is discussed in Chapters 4 and 7.) The space should be designed to be adequate for the occupant load and the occupant load should be appropriate for the intended use(s). Also be aware that changes in the occupant load may affect the occupancy classification and many of the applicable code requirements.

In all cases, adequate means of egress must be provided for the number of people who will be occupying a space or building. Once the occupant load is set and the means of egress have been designed, the number of people allowed within a space cannot exceed that number. For Assembly uses, the approved occupant load is required to be posted for each space. In other spaces, a code official may require the approved occupant load to be posted where a modified occupant load has been used to design the space. Exceeding the posted allowable occupant load is unsafe and unlawful.

RESEARCH: USING THE CODES

Assigning the occupancy classification and/or subclassification should be the initial step in researching a project. It is the most important step in understanding which code and standard requirements apply to a space or building. Most of the requirements and many of the exceptions are based on occupancy. For some projects, the occupancy classification may be straightforward or already determined. If you are having to determine an occupancy classification for a new or unusual use, compare the risk factors and the characteristics of the occupants to the definitions of each occupancy classification and/or subclassifications. If hazards are present, consider them as well. (Each of the code publications lists the types of hazards to look for and whether they are explosive, fire, physical, or health hazards.) If your proposed use clearly meets one of the established occupancy classifications, then the process may be simple. If the use does not clearly fall within one of the standard occupancy definitions or multiple types of activities or uses occur within the space, you may have to propose an occupancy classification and request agreement by the code official. However, if the use is more complex or unusual, then a performance approach may be necessary or helpful.

For typical projects, the building codes and the *Life Safety Code (LSC)* will be used to assign an occupancy classification and/or subclassifications for a typical project. The occupancy classifications are defined and described in Chapter 3 of the *IBC* and Chapter 6 of the *NFPA 5000*. The text of the *IBC* will then designate when an occupancy must follow or is exempt from the requirements within the code. The NFPA codes including the *LSC* are organized largely by individual occupancy chapters; therefore, the correct occupancy classification is essential to determine the appropriate chapter to apply to the project. Also, determine if the space will be considered new or existing according to the NFPA codes. (You may also be required to use the *International Existing Building Code*.) If there is any concern about the correct assignment of occupancy classifications, you should seek approval from the code official before extensive research as this can change the direction of much of the required research. You do not want to proceed with research or design if it is not clear.

The established occupancy classifications in the building codes and *LSC* make assumptions as to how people will react and move within a space or building in case of a fire or emergency. If the proposed use of your space or building is unique, additional research may be necessary to appropriately design a safe environment. By contrast, in the performance codes, only general parameters for what should be considered about the activities and the occupants. For example, the *ICC Performance Code (ICCPC)* has a section titled "Use and Occupancy Classification" within the "Design Performance Levels" chapter. Instead of grouping types of activities into occupancy classifications, it states that the objective is to identify the primary use of a space or building and the risk factors associated with that use. The risk factors that must be considered include the type of activity, hazards, number of occupants, length of occupancy, alertness (sleeping or awake), familiarity with the space, vulnerability (lack of mobility or cognitive awareness), and whether occupants are related. The NFPA codes discuss similar issues that should be considered by discussing occupant characteristics and assumptions within the "Performance-based Option" chapter in each code. The design must then consider the unique characteristics of the use and occupants. Remember, a performance code may not be accepted in the jurisdiction of your project. And the use of performance criteria must be reviewed and approved by the code official. Again, most projects will be easily assigned to one of the occupancy classifications in the building codes or *LSC*.

Other codes also use the occupancy classifications to call out specific code requirements. This includes the fire codes, such as the *International Fire Code (IFC)*, which provides specific fire-related requirements for each occupancy type. The fire codes provide additional requirements for unusual building conditions and uses that might not be covered in the building codes. For these conditions, special requirements are called out in separate chapters or sections within the fire codes. For example, the fire codes typically have chapters on airports, clean rooms in laboratories, and rooms used for dry cleaning. If a project includes a special use area, research both the building code and the fire code when it is required by a jurisdiction.

Accessibility requirements apply consistently to almost every occupancy classification or building use. However, in some cases, specific building types will be subject to additional requirements. For example, the *ADA Standards* have requirements that must be met for certain occupancies, such as Mercantile, Residential, and Health Care. Other building uses may be exempt. (See the section titled "Accessibility Requirements" earlier in this chapter and Chapter 2 for more information.)

☟ Note

Open areas adjacent to spaces with fixed seats may require additional occupant load calculations. The open area may be considered standing space and increase the occupant load.

☟ Note

Every assembly room or Assembly occupancy usually requires the approved occupant load to be permanently posted near the main exit from the space. A typical sign might read: "Occupancy by more than 100 persons is dangerous and unlawful."

DOCUMENTATION

It is important to indicate the occupancy classification and occupant load clearly on your drawings and documents. Usually both the occupancy classification and the occupant load are documented on the coversheet with a diagram or list. Because occupancy classification determines most code requirements, this information sets the stage for review by the code official and others. In some cases, it be necessary to get approval from your code official at this point in a project. The occupant load should also be clearly indicated. Sometimes, the code reviewer will want to see the calculation for the occupant load to verify their agreement. Occupant loads may need to be assigned per room or for overall portions of the building. You may need to verify with the code official their preferences. (See the section titled "Preliminary Review" in Chapter 11.)

Keep in mind that you may have more than one type of occupancy within the space or building, incidental uses, accessory uses, mixed occupancies (separated or nonseparated), or multiple uses (mixed or separated), as discussed in this chapter. If there are multiple occupancies within the building, you should indicate whether the occupancies are being separated or if they are non-separated per the requirements of the code as discussed earlier in this chapter. You need to document this as well because it may affect other aspects of the project such as location of rated walls, exit paths, locking systems, and mechanical systems (discussed in later chapters). It may be helpful to create a diagram of the different uses, occupancies, and occupant loads in the space or building.

You can use the "Occupancy Classification" section of the digital code checklists provided with this book. This will help you determine and document the occupancy classification(s) and occupant load(s) aspects of your project.

◪ Note

Not only can a building have more than one occupancy, but each occupancy can have more than one use for the purpose of determining the occupant load. Therefore, one building or a large tenant space could require several calculations.

CHAPTER 4

CONSTRUCTION TYPES AND BUILDING SIZES

Construction types determine the construction systems and materials that can be used throughout a building—both exterior and interior. The construction type will also affect the allowable size and height of a building. Structural engineers and architects consider the proposed building use, size and height, location, budget, and other design parameters to choose a structural system and construction type. If a specific level of sustainability is desired, that too may influence the final selection of construction type.

Understanding the considerations and the essential parts of a building's construction system can come into play on interior projects as well. When working on an interior project that requires the reconfiguring of building elements, such as relocating walls, making changes that affect the floor or ceiling conditions, or adding a ramp, it is important to be familiar with what changes can safely be made to the existing building. Some construction types are stricter than others as to what materials can be used and what modifications can be made.

This chapter includes a basic discussion of construction types, building floor areas, and building heights as regulated by the codes. It covers the purpose of construction types and when and why they need to be considered during an interior project. The first half of this chapter concentrates on what distinguishes each of the construction types. The second half of the chapter focuses on how the construction type affects the overall building, particularly in size and height.

UNDERSTANDING CONSTRUCTION TYPES

Every building is made up of a variety of parts that the codes define as *building elements*. Building elements may or may not be structural, in other words, they may or may not support the weight of the building and its contents. Building elements that are also structural elements include foundations, bearing walls, columns, beams, and certain floor and roof elements. They can be as simple as four exterior walls and a roof or as complicated as the many parts that make up a high-rise building. Many of the requirements for the structural elements are defined as part of the construction type and are explained in this chapter. Other building elements that are not structural to the building may also have rating and material requirements. Some of these are addressed in this chapter; others will be discussed in Chapter 5 and 6.

The construction types are typically referred to as Type I, Type II, Type III, Type IV, and Type V by the ICC and the NFPA codes. Primarily, the codes define the differences in construction types by governing the kinds of materials allowed in the building components, especially those that are structural, but also, by setting minimum hourly fire resistance ratings for each structural building element. Although in each code, Type I is the most fire resistant and Type V the least fire resistant, there are slight differences in the types between the codes.

Note

On interior projects, it is important not to affect the fire rating of existing structural or building elements. For example, removing the gypsum board from a structural column could reduce the rating of the column.

Materials in Construction Types

Building elements can be built of an array of different materials including but not limited to concrete, steel, and wood. (NFPA codes refer to them as *construction* elements.) Each has its own unique characteristics that make it a practical building material. The code separates building materials into noncombustible, limited combustible, and combustible according to their resistance to burning. These materials are categorized based on how easily they ignite, how long they burn once ignited, how quickly the flames spread, and how much heat the material generates.

Noncombustible materials are defined as materials that will not ignite, burn, support combustion, or release flammable vapors when subject to fire or heat. Most materials are required to pass *ASTM E136, Standard Test Method for Behavior of Materials in a Vertical Tube Furnace at 750 degrees C*. Materials that are inherently considered to be noncombustible are not required to be tested such as steel, concrete, masonry, and glass. Their actual performance in the event of a fire, however, depends on how they are used. Occasionally, they may require additional fire treatment or protection for extra strength and stability. For example, steel has a rapid loss of strength at high temperatures. To avoid this, steel is often encased in concrete or covered by a protective coating. Noncombustible materials are used in construction types to prevent substantial fire spread, because they do not contribute fuel to a fire.

On the other side of the spectrum are *combustible materials*. These are materials that will ignite and continue to burn even when the flame source is removed. Wood is a common combustible item. Combustible materials are usually allowed by the codes when low or no ratings are specified and in limited amounts in construction types considered to be noncombustible. However, wood and other construction materials can be chemically treated to achieve some fire resistance. For example, chemically treated wood is called "fire-retardant-treated wood" (also commonly known as *FRTW*). These are considered limited *fire resistant materials* and are typically tested using *NFPA 703, Standard for Fire-Retardant-Treated Wood and Fire-Retardant Coatings for Building Materials, ASTM E84, Standard Test Method of Surface Burning Characteristics of Building Materials or UL 723, Standard for Test for Surface Burning Characteristics of Building Materials*. Once treated, they will delay the spread of a fire for a designated amount of time and can prevent or retard the passage of heat, hot gases, and flames. The fire-retardant treatment allows the material to be used in more places throughout a building. It can even be substituted for materials required to be noncombustible where specified in the code. For example, fire-treated wood can sometimes be used in a rated wall. (See the inset titled "Combustible Materials" in this section.) It can also be used as finish materials and trim in even the most stringent construction types.

Wood components can naturally obtain a level of fire resistant if they are large enough in cross-section. For example, when a large dimension timber element burns, a char develops on the surface that creates a natural fire resistance. Wood structural elements that meet a certain dimensional requirement are referred to as *"mass timber"* or *"heavy timber."*

The NFPA uses an additional term, *limited combustible materials,* to define certain types of fire resistant materials. These materials do not meet the requirements of noncombustible material because they do have some capacity to burn. Although treated materials typically fall into this category, the material is considered limited combustible only if it passes a specific standard test. The test used to determine if a material or assembly is considered limited combustible is *NFPA 259, Standard Test Method for Potential Heat of Building Materials.* Some materials may also be required to be tested using *ASTM E84, Standard Test Method of Surface Burning Characteristics of Building Materials,* or *ANSI / UL 723, Standard for Test for Surface Burning Characteristics of Building Materials* to be considered limited combustible.

These fire resistant and limited combustible materials can also be used in conjunction with other materials to create rated assemblies. The materials work together as an assembly to create higher fire resistance. For example, wood studs used with gypsum board on both sides can create a 1-hour-rated wall. Other common fire resistant materials include gypsum concrete, gypsum board, plaster, and mineral fiber products.

The proper use of combustible, noncombustible, limited combustible (if allowed) is important on architectural and interior projects. For example, Type I and Type II are usually designated to be constructed of noncombustible materials, Type III is a combination of combustible and noncombustible materials, and Types IV and V are typically allowed to be constructed of fire-resistant and combustible materials. The introduction of combustible materials into a building can jeopardize the construction type classification.

Ratings of the Building Elements

The building codes and the standard *NFPA 220* each give a detailed description of the construction types within their text. These descriptions indicate the appropriate use of noncombustible, combustible, and limited combustible materials. In addition, each construction type is further defined by fire-resistance ratings assigned to each building or construction element. See Figure 4.1. Note that a fire resistance rating does not mean fireproof. Instead, it is an hourly *fire endurance rating*. These ratings are based on the number of hours the component will resist being adversely affected by flame, heat, or hot gases. (Other uses of these ratings will be discussed in Chapter 6.) A higher fire rating typically indicates that noncombustible materials are required, and lower ratings indicate that fire resistant materials or limited combustible materials are allowed. To be classified as a specific construction type, all the components of the building must use the appropriate materials and meet the assigned set of the fire resistant hourly requirements for that construction type.

The hourly ratings of each building element as shown in Figure 4.1 can be found in similar tables in the *IBC*, *NFPA 5000* and reprinted in the appendix of *LSC*. Because each code is slightly different and because the rating of the structural elements is one of the main ways that construction types are defined, this means that a building's structure could be considered a Type I for one code but a Type II under a different code. See Figure 4.2 for the alignment between the *IBC* and the NFPA construction types.

Construction assemblies and systems have natural fire resistant characteristics based on the materials used. This is usually referred to an assembly which is *unprotected*. When more fire resistance is desired, noncombustible, limited combustible or fireproofing materials can be used to enclose or cover the building elements to provide additional fire resistance. The building element or system is then said to be *protected*. Typically, when an element or construction type is "protected," this results in an additional hour of fire resistance to building element. In the

TABLE 601
FIRE RESISTANCE RATING REQUIREMENTS FOR BUILDING ELEMENTS (HOURS)

BUILDING ELEMENT	TYPE I		TYPE II		TYPE III		TYPE IV				TYPE V	
	A	B	A	B	A	B	A	B	C	HT	A	B
Primary structural frame[f] (see Section 202)	3[a, b]	2[a, b, c]	1[b, c]	0[c]	1[b, c]	0	3[a]	2[a]	2[a]	HT	1[b, c]	0
Bearing walls Exterior[e, f]	3	2	1	0	2	2	3	2	2	2	1	0
Interior	3[a]	2[a]	1	0	1	0	3	2	2	1/HT[g]	1	0
Nonbearing walls and partitions Exterior	See Table 705.5											
Nonbearing walls and partitions Interior[d]	0	0	0	0	0	0	0	0	0	See Section 2304.11.2	0	0
Floor construction and associated secondary structural members (see Section 202)	2	2	1	0	1	0	2	2	2	HT	1	0
Roof construction and associated secondary structural members (see Section 202)	$1^1/_2$[b]	1[b,]	1[b,c]	0[c]	1[b,c]	0	$1^1/_2$	1	1	HT	1[b,c]	0

For SI: 1 foot = 304.8 mm.
a Roof supports: Fire resistance ratings of primary structural frame and bearing walls are permitted to be reduced by 1 hour where supporting a roof only.
b Except in Group F-1, H, M, and S-1 occupancies, fire protection of structural members in roof construction shall not be required, including protection of primary structural frame members, roof framing, and decking where every part of the roof construction is 20 feet or more above any floor immediately below. Fire-retardant-treated wood members shall be allowed to be used for such unprotected members.
c In all occupancies, heavy timber complying with Section 2304.11 shall be allowed for roof construction, including primary structural frame members, where a 1-hour or less fire resistance rating is required.
d Not less than the fire resistance rating required by other sections of this code.
e Not less than the fire resistance rating based on fire separation distance (see Table 705.5).
f Not less than the fire resistance rating as referenced in Section 704.10.
g Heavy timber–bearing walls supporting more than two floors or more than a floor and a roof shall have a fire resistance rating of not less than 1 hour.

Figure 4.1 International Building Code Table 601, "Fire Resistance Rating Requirements for Building Elements (hours)" (2021 International Building Code, copyright © 2021. Washington, DC: International Code Council, Washington, DC: International Code Council.

IBC, an "unprotected" structural element is represented as a B subcategory and a protected element as an A subcategory. So, a construction type could be referred to a Type IIIB or Type IIIA. These would have different hourly rating requirements even though it is essentially the same system and material, but one has additional fire resistant materials applied to it.

ICC International Building Code	NFPA NFPA 220 Standard
(no equivalent)	I (442)
TYPE IA Highly Protected	I (332)
TYPE IB Protected	II (222)
TYPE IIA Protected	II (111)
TYPE IIB Unprotected	II (000)
TYPE IIIA Protected	III (211)
TYPE IIIB Unprotected	III (200)
TYPE IV-A Protected	
TYPE IV-B	
TYPE IV- C	
TYPE IV Heavy Timber	IV (2HH) Heavy Timber
TYPE VA Protected	V (111)
TYPE VB Unprotected	V (000)

Figure 4.2 Comparison of construction types. (This chart is a summary of information contained in the *International Building Code and the NFPA 220.* Neither the ICC nor the NFPA assumes responsibility for the accuracy or completeness of this chart.)

☑ **Note**

Nearly all materials are eventually affected by flame and heat. Even materials that have been treated to be fire retardant will still burn or char when exposed to a continuous flame.

☑ **Note**

After a fire occurs in a building, the exposed building elements may be affected. Many noncombustible materials may appear to have endured the fire unchanged, but flame and heat can change the strength and structural makeup of noncombustible materials.

The requirements for fire resistance rating of the building elements and the difference between a protected (A) and an unprotected (B) elements can be seen in Figure 4.1 *IBC Table 601, "Fire Resistance Rating Requirements for Building Elements (hours)."* In this table, the construction types are listed across the top of the table in descending order from the most fire resistive (Type I) to the least fire resistive (Type V). Each construction type is further separated into A and B subcategories. The various structural or building elements are listed down the side to the left. The required hourly fire endurance ratings are listed under the construction type and subcategory for each structural element in the body of the table. For example, interior bearing walls in a Type IIIA construction type are required to be rated 1 hour, but in a Type IIIB, no rating is required. In addition, A floor construction in a Type IA is required to be 2 hours but the same element in a Type IIIA is only required to be 1 hour. The NFPA documents use a different numbering system to indicate the various hourly ratings. (This can be seen in the comparison in Figure 4.2 and is discussed later in this section.)

Every building, whether new or existing, can be categorized as one of the construction types. To be assigned, it must meet the minimum requirements for every structure or building element in that type. If it fails to meet even one of the criteria, the construction type will then be based on its lowest component. For example, if a building meets all the requirements of a construction Type IA in Figure 4.1 except that the floor construction is rated only 1 hour, the whole building will be classified as a Type IIA.

This becomes important on interior projects. Modifications to a rated building element can be detrimental to maintaining the proper construction type. For example, if part of an existing concrete floor is chipped away to create a slope to the drain for a new tiled shower, reducing the depth of the concrete could reduce the fire resistance rating of the floor/ceiling assembly. If the floor is required to have a specific hourly rating, the whole building could be reassigned to a lower construction type. As will be presented in the following sections, this could make the building noncompliant for its use and size.

IDENTIFYING CONSTRUCTION TYPES

There may be interior projects when knowing the construction type of a building is important. For example, the scope of some interior projects may affect the building elements or structural elements of an existing building. Because these elements are essential to maintaining the integrity of the construction type of the building, it is important to identify the existing construction type and to research the fire-resistance rating requirements and the building materials that the code allows.

Sometimes, identifying the construction type becomes a process of elimination as well as identification. For example, there can be a combination of noncombustible and combustible components: the materials that have been used to construct the building, as well as the materials that have not been used, should be detected. Determining the rating of existing assemblies can be especially difficult. Remember, the building will be classified by the lowest-rated element or the use of the most combustible material. For example, if a building does not meet the bearing wall rating for Type I, even though the other structural elements meet the requirements, it will be considered a Type II. Or, if combustible materials are predominantly used, then it cannot be classified as a noncombustible construction type.

For an older building, it may be problematic to impossible to unquestionably classify the construction type of an existing building, but one must be assigned and agreed to by the code official. The original construction documents are the best source of information, although modifications and additions over the years may change the original condition. It may be necessary to consult an architect, structural engineer, or building official. Once the construction type is established, the information in the codes can help to determine what ratings and materials are critical to maintaining the construction type.

Note

Subcategory A, protected, does not refer to the use of an automatic sprinkler system within a building even though the phrase "protected by an automatic sprinkler system" is used in the codes.

Note

Noncombustible is different from *fire resistant*. Additional precautions should be taken when fire resistant material is used in place of noncombustible materials.

Note

Some fire-retardant chemicals may cause wood to absorb more moisture. This can cause loss of strength, rot, decay, corrosion of fasteners, poor paint adhesion, staining, and even loss of the fire-retardant chemical. Therefore, in high-moisture areas, the correct type of fire-treated wood must be specified.

COMBUSTIBLE MATERIALS

Combustible, limited combustible, or treated materials are allowed in all construction types, even in noncombustible Type I and Type II, in limited amounts and uses. The following are some of the allowable uses of combustible materials:

❑ Fire-retardant-treated wood (FRTW) in non-load-bearing walls less than 2 hours
❑ Interior walls of a single tenant (with additional conditions)
❑ Interior finishes, trim, and millwork for doors, door frames, and window sashes
❑ Blocking required for mounting handrails, millwork, and cabinets
❑ Interior floor finish and floor coverings
❑ Construction of certain stages or platforms for worship, music, and other entertainment
❑ Thermal or acoustical insulation with a flame spread not greater than 25
❑ Foam plastics and other plastics
❑ Plastic glazing and decorative veneers
❑ Nail strips and furring strips (fire blocking may be required)

In each case, there are requirements for the proper installation of these materials and exceptions for situations in which the materials may not be allowed. For example, if a hardwood floor is installed with sleepers (i.e., furring strips) on a noncombustible floor slab, the code specifies how to fire block the space created by the sleepers. Refer to the codes for more information.

Construction Types

The building codes and the standard *NFPA 220* each give a detailed description of the construction types including the use of noncombustible, combustible, and limited combustible within their text. As discussed, each construction type is further defined by fire resistance ratings assigned to each building element. Each code defines the construction types slightly differently. And can result in separate construction type assignments for each code. (See the comparison in Figure 4.2.) The conceptual summary and composition of the construction types diagrams in Figure 4.3 are based on the *IBC*.

Types I and II

Type I and Type II construction types provide the highest level of fire resistance. Generally, these construction types consist almost completely of noncombustible materials; combustible materials are allowed only in

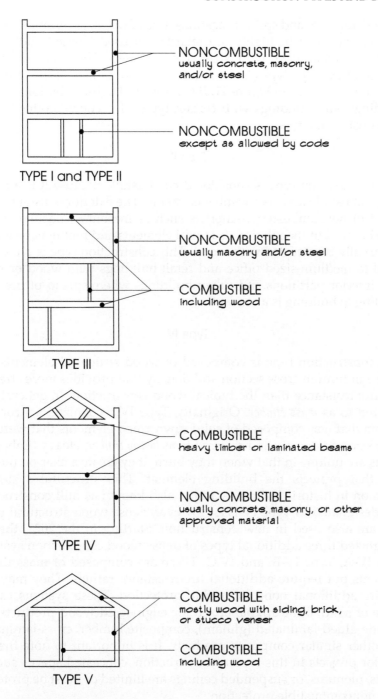

NONCOMBUSTIBLE
usually concrete, masonry, and/or steel

NONCOMBUSTIBLE
except as allowed by code

TYPE I and TYPE II

NONCOMBUSTIBLE
usually masonry and/or steel

COMBUSTIBLE
including wood

TYPE III

COMBUSTIBLE
heavy timber or laminated beams

NONCOMBUSTIBLE
usually concrete, masonry, or other approved material

TYPE IV

COMBUSTIBLE
mostly wood with siding, brick, or stucco veneer

COMBUSTIBLE
including wood

TYPE V

Figure 4.3 Typical construction type characteristics.

◀ Note

The main difference between Type I and Type II construction is the fire-resistance ratings of the structural members.

limited amounts and specific locations. Use of wood, for example, is very limited and must be highly fire retardant if used. These buildings are typically constructed with steel and concrete. The main difference between these two types is the required hourly ratings of the structural elements, as shown in Figure 41, *IBC Table 601*. High-rise buildings, large buildings, and buildings with certain types of occupants often require this construction type.

Type III

This construction type is considered combustible because it is a mix of noncombustible and combustible elements. The exterior is usually composed of noncombustible materials such as masonry (concrete or concrete block), but the interior structural elements and roof may be wholly or partially constructed with wood. This construction type is typical for small to medium-sized office and retail buildings with wood or metal stud interior partitions and urban buildings where spread of fire from building to building is a concern.

Type IV

This construction type is composed of wood structural elements that have a minimum cross section and density that provides more strength and fire resistance than the typical wood construction. In general, it is referred to as *mass timber*. Originally, Type IV recognized a structural system that was composed of solid sawn wood elements that were of a large size and density and referred to as *heavy timber*. Heavy timber elements are unique in that when they burn, they create a char on the surface that protects the building element. This structural system is common in historic buildings and is also known as mill construction. It is designated as Type IV-HT. However, dense wood structural products are also used in new construction. Starting in the 2021, the *IBC* recognized three additional types of dense wood construction systems: Type IV-A, Type IV-B, and IV-C. These are composed of mass timber elements but require additional fire-resistance ratings. They may also require additional noncombustible protection. These systems can be made of solid, built-up, panelized, or engineered wood products that include glued-laminated (glulam), composite lumber, cross-laminated, and other similar composite products. It is important to note that for interior projects in this type of construction, concealed spaces such as soffits, plenums, or suspended ceilings are limited or must be protected with noncombustible protection.

Type V

This is the most combustible construction type and is basically an all-wood structure. These buildings are usually characterized by wood-framed exterior walls and interior walls. The exterior may have a veneer of any exterior material such as brick, siding, metal panel, and so on. These buildings are typically small. Common examples include a residential house, a small dentist's office, and a convenience store.

Mixed Construction Types

According to the codes, a building can only be composed of a single construction type. However, it is possible for multiple construction types to coexist in a single building structure. Examples are a medical office building attached to a hospital or a factory connected to its business offices. For a single structure to be composed of two different construction types, they must be separated formally into two separate buildings according to the codes. This is accomplished by either a fire wall, which enables them to exist side by side, or a horizontal separation, which enables one construction type to occur above or below the other. (Fire walls are discussed in more detail in Chapter 6.) Whether the separation is vertical or horizontal, it creates, in effect, two or more separate buildings. Each separate building is then limited to the size and height allowed by the code for that occupancy classification and construction type.

Construction Type by Occupancy

The occupancy classification and the proposed size of the building are the two strongest determinants in the options of construction type by the codes. The allowable construction types for each occupancy classification consider the structural integrity in case of a fire, the use, and the risk factors of the occupants. For example, Type I is the strictest construction type and will result in the most fire resistant building and allow the most evacuation time. This evacuation time is important for all occupancy classifications but even more critical for larger buildings with more occupants or for occupants who will need additional time to exit. Examples would be a large arena for concerts or an assisted living facility for older adults. In a few cases, the code will not allow an occupancy to occur in a construction type. For example, in the *IBC*, a hospital (I-2) cannot exist in a Type VB construction type. And for other combustible construction types, the size will be extremely limited.

> ☑ **Note**
>
> A *party wall* is a similar separation wall to fire wall but is located on a shared lot line between two parcels of land.

SUSTAINABILITY CONSIDERATIONS

For new buildings and additions to existing buildings, the choice of a structural system must first meet the requirements in the building codes for the occupancy classification and the building size and height. However, if a jurisdiction enforces a sustainability code or standard such as the *International Green Construction Code (IgCC)*, which uses the *ASHRAE/USGBC/IES 189.1, Standard for the Design of High-Performance Green Buildings Except Low-Rise Residential Buildings* for certain technical requirements, these may influence the choice as well. These set standards for the construction process including how efficiently materials are obtained, managed during construction, and disposed of or recycled as construction waste. The recycled content and recyclable potential of materials also are regulated. With these requirements in mind, each construction type results in different levels of waste and has unique recycling characteristics.

In addition, because construction types are based largely on the materials used and sustainability is affected by using certain materials, the construction type can play a significant role in the overall sustainability of a project.

For example, the *IgCC* sets percentages for use of previously used, recycled, recyclable, regionally available, and bio-based materials. In most cases, wood and concrete are regionally available and are considered bio-based. Steel and concrete are considered good components for recyclable and or recycled content. For example, steel is often made of 100 percent recyclable content and easily recycled during deconstruction and from scraps. Concrete can be composed of recycled content, is easily recycled for various construction products, and is usually locally sourced.

The *IgCC* requires that a specific proportion of the materials be bio-based materials. The bio content of these materials must be evaluated based on *ASTM D6866 Standard Test Methods for Determining the Biobased Content of Solid, Liquid, and Gaseous Samples Using Radiocarbon Analysis.* Wood is bio-based and a renewable material; however, there are additional considerations. Sustainable wood products should come from sustainably managed forests. The Forestry Stewardship Council (FSC) is one organization that identifies forests that are managed, based on their standard FSC Principles and Criteria. FSC-Certified lumber has been certified to meet these criteria and is more sustainable than wood that has been harvested traditionally. The organizations that certify these products in the United States include the Smartwood Program and Scientific Certification Systems. (See the section "Sustainable Standards and Certification Programs" in Appendix A.) The *IgCC* requires that wood

☞ **Note**

The Rainforest Alliance has compiled a list of environmentally responsible wood products called *SmartGuide to Green Building Sources.*

☞ **Note**

Certified wood is considered sustainable. Certifications include FSC Certified and SFI Certified. (California has a separate certification as well.) These certification programs typically consist of fiber sourcing, chain of custody tracking, and certified product labels.

meeting these standards either be labeled or have a certificate of compliance. (LEED and GreenGlobes recognize these standards and certifications in their point systems as well.)

ASHRAE/USGBC/IES 189.1, Standard for the Design of High-Performance Green Buildings Except Low-Rise Residential Buildings has sustainable requirements for the materials used in a building, including the structural components. For example, *ASHRAE 189.1* can require that wood components, including the structural framing, sheathing, and subflooring found in certain construction types, be composed of predominately certified wood. This certified wood must meet the requirements of *ISO/ IEC Guide 59* or *WTO Technical Barriers to Trade guidelines*.

Both the *IgCC* and the *ASHRAE 189.1* allow a life cycle analysis (LCA) to be developed as an alternate way of meeting the specific requirements of these guidelines. The *IgCC* allows a performance analysis of materials, which is accomplished by developing an LCA of the various components of the building. (LCAs are described in more detail in Appendix A.) If an LCA is not developed, the *IgCC* provides specific sustainable quantities and characteristics that must be met, such as recycled content of specific materials (post-consumer and pre-consumer), recyclability of materials, use of bio-based materials, and use of indigenous or locally available material. The sustainable standard *ASHRAE/USGBC/IES 189.1, Standard for the Design of High-Performance Green Buildings Except Low-Rise Residential Buildings* may also independently applicable to a project even if the *IgCC* is not used.

Maintaining the Construction Type

Although many interior projects involve primarily non-load-bearing walls, modification to essential building elements such as existing load-bearing walls, structural frame, floor/ceiling assemblies, and ceiling/ roof assemblies can become part of an extensive renovation, new tenant build-out or similar interior projects. When an interior project requires reconfiguration or changes to these elements, it is critical that the requirements of the construction type are not compromised. Although the building codes also include a non-load-bearing wall category in the table, the rating of these walls are not typically determined by the construction type but by the need for compartmentation. This is discussed in more detail in Chapter 6.

When the construction type requires floor/ceiling, ceiling/roof, structural frame, and interior bearing walls to be rated, these must be maintained during interior renovations or remodeling. Penetrating them for any reason can be a problem if the required rating is not maintained.

> **☑ Note**
>
> Construction types of some existing buildings are difficult to differentiate. The original construction drawings are the best source, if available. Or consulting a structural engineer, architect, or codes official may be necessary.

ATRIUMS AND MEZZANINES

Atriums and mezzanines are common design elements used in the interior of a building. The codes set several additional requirements for them, some of which are described here. However, check the codes for the specifics and work closely with the local code officials. (Typically, coordination with engineers is required as well.)

Atriums

An atrium is a multistory open space contained within a building, often surrounded by glass or open balconies. It is commonly found in building lobbies, hotels, and shopping malls. Atriums are typically required to be separated from all adjacent spaces by fire resistance–rated walls. When glass is used as part of the enclosure, additional requirements may apply. The codes usually limit the number of floors that can open directly into the atrium to three floors, unless additional fire protection is included. Atriums typically require a building to be fully sprinklered, with a few exceptions. In addition, a mechanical smoke exhaust system is usually required at the ceiling and is typically tied into other fire protection systems that would activate the exhaust system should a fire occur.

Mezzanines

A mezzanine is an intermediate floor level placed between the floor and the ceiling of a room or space. It is usually allowed only if it does not exceed more than one-third of the room or area in which it is located. There can be more than one mezzanine in a space, and even some at different levels, but the one-third rule would still apply. (This can be greater in construction types with higher fire resistance and in sprinklered buildings.) The appropriate headroom must also be provided at each level. The construction of a mezzanine is required to be the same as the construction type of the building in which it is located, and it is usually not counted as a story when determining the building height. Typically, the mezzanine must be open to the room in which it is located and requires one or two exits to the room or space below.

Examples include penetrations for sprinkler pipes, ducts, conduit, and so on. The removal of building materials can reduce necessary depths of material or remove rated protective enclosures. It is equally important to replace material with appropriate noncombustible materials if required. When adding interior elements or materials, including finish floors, walls, ceilings, or other interior materials, appropriate materials and assemblies must also be specified. For example, you must determine if wood or metal framing is allowed. All these modifications can have a serious effect on the construction classification. Also, specific construction types do not allow concealed spaces or plenums.

UNDERSTANDING BUILDING HEIGHT AND AREA

Many factors are considered to design a building of a desired size and number of stories for its proposed use. For each construction type, there are limits to the allowable size and height according to the codes. Even when additions are made, the overall size of the building must remain within these height and area limitations. In some cases, a building structure may appear to be a single building, but the use of fire walls separates it into separate buildings, which allows a large continuous and connected structure.

Although code limitations on building size will not play a major role in most interior projects, it is important to be aware of them and understand their role. In some cases, when the occupancy of a building is changes, it may be necessary to confirm that the new occupancy, use, and size is within the allowable parameters set by the codes.

Allowable Height and Area Factors

Ultimately, the allowable height and area of a building are directly related to a variety and combination of factors. Each has a unique effect on the allowable height or area of the structure. The most significant are discussed next.

Construction type. Generally, the more noncombustible materials that are used and the higher the fire-resistance rating of the building elements for a construction type, the greater the allowable building area and height. For example, Type I construction, which is considered noncombustible and requires the highest ratings for building elements, has no height limitations and few area limitations in many cases.

Occupancy classification and the construction type. The combination of the occupancy classification and the construction type will set the initial allowable size and height of a building. In reverse, comparing the proposed size of a building and the occupancy classification can determine the options for acceptable construction types. If there are more than one occupancy classifications in the building, the allowable size of the structure will be limited by the occupancy classification that allows the smallest area or height. For example, because Assembly and Institutional occupancies represent a high concentration and specific type of occupants, they are uniquely limited in height and area based on the construction type. In addition, some occupancies must meet specific requirements to allow an increase in area and/or height. For example, if an Educational building has at least two exits per classroom with one opening directly outdoors it can be larger.

Use of a sprinkler system. The installation of an automatic sprinkler system throughout a building permits an increase in height, number of stories and area per floor for most construction types. For example, a restaurant (A-2) in a single-story building built in Type VB (combustible) construction would only be allowed to be 6,000 square feet (557 sm) if it were unsprinklered but would be allowed to be 24,000 square feet (2,230 sm) (sprinklered). In some cases, sprinklering a building can result in more allowable area than constructing in a more fire resistant construction type. For example, that same restaurant but would only be allowed to be 9,500 square feet (883 sm) in a Type II (unsprinklered). Some occupancies, such as I-2 (hospitals), require sprinklers in buildings of any size or construction type. Some combination of occupancies and construction types are limited to one story unless they are sprinklered. (See Chapter 7 for additional sprinkler trade-offs.)

Location. The location and distance from adjacent buildings, as well as the amount of street frontage, can affect the allowed area of a building. The additional exterior space prevents fire spread to or from adjacent buildings, so the codes allow a proportional increase in floor area from what is initially allowed. Calculations provided in the codes indicate how much additional area is allowed.

Fire walls and horizontal separations. Fire walls and similarly rated horizontal separations can be used to divide the total area within a single structure. Each area on either side of the fire wall or horizontal separation is then considered a separate building. The separate buildings can be the same construction type or different construction types. Although each separate building must stay within its own size limitation for that construction type, it allows an overall continuous structure to become larger. (See Chapter 6 for more information.)

Number of stories, height, and area. Buildings are limited by height and by number of stories. Each of the codes define what makes a building story or level. Single-story buildings can usually have larger floor areas. In some cases, they are unlimited. (Each code sets a limit on the height of the story.) Each building code also determines whether a mezzanine can be considered part of the story in which it is located. In some cases, because of its size, a mezzanine must be treated as a separate story. (See the inset titled "Atriums and Mezzanines" in this chapter.) In addition, the codes will also define when a basement is counted as a story or part of the height. Area and height requirements for basements are specific to each code. Whether a basement is counted as a story depends on how much of it is above ground level and the occupancy of the building.

Using the Charts

The building codes control the allowable number of stories, height, and area through a series of charts in each of their respective chapter(s) on construction types and allowable height and areas. In previous editions of the *IBC*, this information was included in a single chart. Starting with the *2015 IBC*, this information is given in three separate charts. Although the complete charts are too extensive to include in this book, excerpts from 2018 *IBC* charts are shown in Figures 4.4–4.6 to explain their use. Because these figures show an excerpt (not the whole chart) from the tables taken from the *IBC* you should always refer to the full chart located in the code publication when doing research. In the following sections we will look at the information provided in *Table 504.3, "Allowable Building Height in Feet Above Grade Plane"*; Table 504.4, *"Allowable Number of Stories Above Grade Plane"*; and *Table 506.2, "Allowable Area Factor (A1= NS, Si, S13R, or SM as applicable) in Square Feet."* These charts are all from the *IBC*. Charts included in the NFPA codes will present similar information in similar formats, but the details may differ. Be sure in your research to use the correct publication.

Allowable Height and Number of Stories

Although the number of stories and the height of the building are related, they are not the same thing according to the code. Basically, a story of a building is a single level or floor of building. Height is the vertical distance measured from the ground to the highest part of the roof. (See the definitions for Story and Building Height in the Glossary.) The codes also limit the height of a story and determine if an intermediate floors such as mezzanines will as a separate story. (See the inset titled "Atriums and Mezzanines" in this chapter.).

Information in Figure 4.4, *IBC Table 504.3 (excerpt), "Allowable Building Height in Feet Above Grade Plane,"* governs the size of a building by limiting the height in feet based on occupancy classification, construction type, and if the building is sprinklered. The Occupancy Classifications are listed in the first column of the chart. The second column designates

TABLE 504.3
ALLOWABLE BUILDING HEIGHT IN FEET ABOVE GRADE PLANE[a]

OCCUPANCY CLASSIFICATION	See Footnotes	Type I A	Type I B	Type II A	Type II B	Type III A	Type III B	Type IV A	Type IV B	Type IV C	Type IV HT	Type V A	Type V B
A, B, E, F, M, S, U	NS[b]	UL	160	65	55	65	55	65	65	65	65	50	40
	S	UL	180	85	75	85	75	270	180	85	85	70	60
H-1, H-2, H-3, H-5	NS[c, d]	UL	160	65	55	65	55	120	90	65	65	50	40
	S												
H-4	NS[c, d]	UL	160	65	55	65	55	65	65	65	65	50	40
	S	UL	180	85	75	85	75	140	100	85	85	70	60
I-1 Condition 1, I-3	NS[d, e]	UL	160	65	55	65	55	65	65	65	65	50	40
	S	UL	180	85	75	85	75	180	120	85	85	70	60
I-1 Condition 2, I-2	NS[d, e, f]	UL	160	65	55	65	55	65	65	65	65	50	40
	S	UL	180	85	55	65	55	65	65	65	65	50	40
I-4	NS[d, g]	UL	160	65	55	65	55	65	65	65	65	50	40
	S	UL	180	85	75	85	75	180	120	85	85	70	60
R[h]	NS[d]	UL	160	65	55	65	55	65	65	65	65	50	40
	S13D	60	60	60	60	60	60	60	60	60	60	50	40
	S13R	60	60	60	60	60	60	60	60	60	60	60	60
	S	UL	180	85	75	85	75	270	180	85	85	70	60

For SI: 1 foot = 304.8 mm.

UL = Unlimited; NS = Buildings not equipped throughout with an automatic sprinkler system; S = Buildings equipped throughout with an automatic sprinkler system installed in accordance with Section 903.3.1.1; S13R = Buildings equipped throughout with an automatic sprinkler system installed in accordance with Section 903.3.1.2; S13D = Buildings equipped throughout with an automatic sprinkler system installed in accordance with Section 903.3.1.3.

a See Chapters 4 and 5 for specific exceptions to the allowable height in this chapter.

b See Section 903.2 for the minimum thresholds for protection by an automatic sprinkler system for specific occupancies.

c New Group H occupancies are required to be protected by an automatic sprinkler system in accordance with Section 903.2.5.

d The NS value is only for use in evaluation of existing building height in accordance with the *International Existing Building Code*.

e New Group I-1 and I-3 occupancies are required to be protected by an automatic sprinkler system in accordance with Section 903.2.6. For new Group I-1 occupancies Condition 1, see Exception 1 of Section 903.2.6.

f New and existing Group I-2 occupancies are required to be protected by an automatic sprinkler system in accordance with Section 903.2.6 and Section 1103.5 of the *International Fire Code*.

g For new Group I-4 occupancies, see Exceptions 2 and 3 of Section 903.2.6.

h New Group R occupancies are required to be protected by an automatic sprinkler system in accordance with Section 903.2.8.

Figure 4.4 *International Building Code,* excerpt from Table 504.3, "Allowable Building Height in Feet Above Grade Plane" (2021), International Building Code, copyright © 2021. Washington, DC: International Code Council. Reproduced with permission. All rights reserved. www.iccsafe.org).

TABLE 504.4
ALLOWABLE NUMBER OF STORIES ABOVE GRADE PLANE[a, b]

OCCUPANCY CLASSIFICATION	See Footnotes	Type I		Type II		Type III		Type IV				Type V	
		A	B	A	B	A	B	A	B	C	HT	A	B
A-1	NS	UL	5	3	2	3	2	3	3	3	3	2	1
	S	UL	6	4	3	4	3	9	6	4	4	3	2
A-2	NS	UL	11	3	2	3	2	3	3	3	3	2	1
	S	UL	12	4	3	4	3	18	12	6	4	3	2
A-3	NS	UL	11	3	2	3	2	3	3	3	3	2	1
	S	UL	12	4	3	4	3	18	12	6	4	3	2
A-4	NS	UL	11	3	2	3	2	3	3	3	3	2	1
	S	UL	12	4	3	4	3	18	12	6	4	3	2
A-5	NS	UL	UL	UL	UL	UL	UL	1	1	1	UL	UL	UL
	S	UL	UL	UL	UL	UL	UL	UL	UL	UL	UL	UL	UL
B	NS	UL	11	5	3	5	3	5	5	5	5	3	2
	S	UL	12	6	4	6	4	18	12	9	6	4	3
E	NS	UL	5	3	2	3	2	3	3	3	3	1	1
	S	UL	6	4	3	4	3	9	6	4	4	2	2

UL = Unlimited; NP = Not Permitted; NS = Buildings not equipped throughout with an automatic sprinkler system;
S = Buildings equipped throughout with an automatic sprinkler system installed in accordance with Section 903.3.1.1;
S13R = Buildings equipped throughout with an automatic sprinkler system installed in accordance with Section 903.3.1.2; S13D = Buildings equipped throughout with an automatic sprinkler system installed in accordance with Section 903.3.1.3.

a See Chapters 4 and 5 for specific exceptions to the allowable height in this chapter.
b See Section 903.2 for the minimum thresholds for protection by an automatic sprinkler system for specific occupancies.
c New Group H occupancies are required to be protected by an automatic sprinkler system in accordance with Section 903.2.5.
d The NS value is only for use in evaluation of existing *building height* in accordance with the *International Existing Building Code*.
e New Group I-1 and I-3 occupancies are required to be protected by an automatic sprinkler system in accordance with Section 903.2.6. For new Group I-1 occupancies, Condition 1, see Exception 1 of Section 903.2.6.
f New and existing Group I-2 occupancies are required to be protected by an automatic sprinkler system in accordance with Section 903.2.6 and 1103.5 of the *International Fire Code*.
g For new Group I-4 occupancies, see Exceptions 2 and 3 of Section 903.2.6.
h New Group R occupancies are required to be protected by an automatic sprinkler system in accordance with Section 903.2.8.

Figure 4.5 *International Building Code,* excerpt from Table 504.4, "Allowable Number of Stories Above Grade Plane" (2021), International Building Code, copyright © 2021. Washington, DC: International Code Council. Reproduced with permission. All rights reserved. www.iccsafe.org).

TABLE 506.2

ALLOWABLE AREA FACTOR (A_t = NS, S1, S13R, S13D or SM, as applicable) IN SQUARE FEET[a], [b]

OCCUPANCY CLASSIFICATION	SEE FOOTNOTES	TYPE OF CONSTRUCTION											
		Type I		Type II		Type III		Type IV				Type V	
		A	B	A	B	A	B	A	B	C	HT	A	B
A-1	NS	UL	UL	15,500	8,500	14,000	8,500	45,000	30,000	18,750	15,000	11,500	5,500
	S1	UL	UL	62,000	34,000	56,000	34,000	180,000	120,000	75,000	60,000	46,000	22,000
	SM	UL	UL	46,500	25,500	42,000	25,500	135,000	90,000	56,250	45,000	34,500	16,500
A-2	NS	UL	UL	15,500	9,500	14,000	9,500	45,000	30,000	18,750	15,000	11,500	6,000
	S1	UL	UL	62,000	38,000	56,000	38,000	180,000	120,000	75,000	60,000	46,000	24,000
	SM	UL	UL	46,500	28,500	42,000	28,500	135,000	90,000	56,250	45,000	34,500	18,000
A-3	NS	UL	UL	15,500	9,500	14,000	9,500	45,000	30,000	18,750	15,000	11,500	6,000
	S1	UL	UL	62,000	38,000	56,000	38,000	180,000	120,000	75,000	60,000	46,000	24,000
	SM	UL	UL	46,500	28,500	42,000	28,500	135,000	90,000	56,250	45,000	34,500	18,000
A-4	NS	UL	UL	15,500	9,500	14,000	9,500	45,000	30,000	18,750	15,000	11,500	6,000
	S1	UL	UL	62,000	38,000	56,000	38,000	180,000	120,000	75,000	60,000	46,000	24,000
	SM	UL	UL	46,500	28,500	42,000	28,500	135,000	90,000	56,250	45,000	34,500	18,000
A-5	NS	UL	UL	UL	UL	UL	UL	UL	UL	UL	UL	UL	UL
	S1												
	SM												

OCCUPANCY CLASSIFICATION	SEE FOOTNOTES	Type I		Type II		Type III		Type IV			HT	Type V	
		A	B	A	B	A	B	A	B	C		A	B
B	NS	UL	UL	37,500	23,000	28,500	19,000	108,000	72,000	45,000	36,000	18,000	9,000
	S1	UL	UL	150,000	92,000	114,000	76,000	432,000	288,000	180,000	144,000	72,000	36,000
	SM	UL	UL	112,500	69,000	85,500	57,000	324,000	216,000	135,000	108,000	54,000	27,000
E	NS	UL	UL	26,500	14,500	23,500	14,500	76,500	51,000	31,875	25,500	18,500	9,500
	S1	UL	UL	106,000	58,000	94,000	58,000	306,000	204,000	127,500	102,000	74,000	38,000
	SM	UL	UL	79,500	43,500	70,500	43,500	229,500	153,000	95,625	76,500	55,500	28,500

TYPE OF CONSTRUCTION

For SI: 1 square foot = 0.0929 m².

UL = Unlimited; NP = Not Permitted; NS = Buildings not equipped throughout with an automatic sprinkler system; S1 = Buildings a maximum of one story above grade plane equipped throughout with an automatic sprinkler system installed in accordance with Section 903.3.1.1; SM = Buildings two or more stories above grade plane equipped throughout with an automatic sprinkler system installed in accordance with Section 903.3.1.1; S13R = Buildings equipped throughout with an automatic sprinkler system installed in accordance with Section 903.3.1.2; S13D = Buildings equipped throughout with an automatic sprinkler system installed in accordance with Section 903.3.1.3.

a See Chapters 4 and 5 for specific exceptions to the allowable area in this chapter.

b See Section 903.2 for the minimum thresholds for protection by an automatic sprinkler system for specific occupancies.

c New Group H occupancies are required to be protected by an automatic sprinkler system in accordance with Section 903.2.5. SEE 2021 IBC FOR ADDITIONAL NOTES.

Figure 4.6 *International Building Code*, excerpt from Table 506.2, "Allowable Area Factor (A1= NS, Si, S13R, or SM as applicable) in Square Feet" (2018), International Building Code, copyright © 2021. Washington, DC: International Code Council. Reproduced with permission. All rights reserved. www.iccsafe.org).

whether the occupancy classification is sprinklered (S) or nonsprinklered (NS). The remaining columns note the Types of Construction including protected (A) or unprotected (B). For example, an office building (B occupancy) that is Type IIIA construction type and sprinklered can be 85 feet in height, whereas the same building that is not sprinklered would only be allowed to be 65 feet in height. Likewise, if that same building were Type V construction, the height would be limited to 50–70 feet depending on whether it was sprinklered. (A meter conversion of 1 foot = 304.8 mm is given in the notes of the table.) UL indicates that the height is unlimited.

The building codes also limit the number stories. In Figure 4.5, *IBC Table 504.4, "Allowable Number of Stories Above Grade Plane"* is organized like the previous chart, considering occupancy classification, construction type, and sprinklering. There are some noticeable differences in this chart. First, the occupancy classifications are listed individually instead of grouped as in *Table 504.3*. (Remember, the excerpt does not show complete list.) To use the same example, an office building that is Type IIIA construction type and sprinklered can be six stories, but if it were not sprinklered it would be limited to five stories. When the information from *Table 504.3* and *Table 504.4* is combined, the allowable height and number of stories can be determined. This may affect decisions about floor-to-floor ceiling heights in the building. In addition, when using this chart to determine the maximum story height of certain Residential occupancies, the use of different automatic sprinkler systems will affect the total number of stories that are allowed. For example, if an R-3 occupancy were housed in a Type IB construction type, it would be limited to four stories if an *NFPA 13R* system was used but allowed to be 12 stories if an *NFPA 13* system was installed. (See Chapter 7 for more details.)

Allowable Area

The codes also limit the allowable area per floor of a building. When this is combined with the limiting the allowable number of stories and height, it will ultimately determine the allowable overall size of a building. However, determining the allowable area has many factors to be considered. To begin to set the area constraints, the building codes consider occupancy classification, construction type, use of automatic sprinkler systems, and if the building is a single or multiple story as seen in the *IBC Table 506.2, "Allowable Area Factor (A1 = NS, Si, S13R, or SM as applicable) in Square Feet,"* in Figure 4.6. The construction types are noted along the top, the occupancy classifications are noted along the left. (Remember, this is an excerpt, and all occupancy classifications are included in the actual table in the *IBC*.) Also at the left, are rows noted as NS, SI, and SM. NS stands for not sprinklered; SI stands for sprinklered, one story; and SM stands for sprinklered, multiple stories. For an example, a restaurant (A-2) in a Type IIIB construction type is allowed 9,500 square feet per floor (unsprinklered), 38,000 square feet per floor (sprinklered if only 1 story–S1), or 28,000 square feet per floor (sprinklered, but multiple vstories–SM). Although the table does not give metric areas, a conversion factor is given in the notes at the bottom of the chart (not shown in the excerpt).

These allowable areas are the beginning of determining potential size of the building. Increases to these initial allowable areas can be granted by the codes if the building is separated from other buildings or open to a public street. In some cases, buildings of certain occupancies and construction types can be unlimited in size. If a building has multiple occupancies, additional calculations may be required. Determining the allowable area of a building with all the considerations is beyond the scope of this book. However, it is helpful to understand the relationship of these components and how this information can affect an interior project.

◀ **Note**

Some local jurisdictions may use a shorter dimension to define the height of a high-rise building based on local conditions and fire department equipment.

RESEARCH: USING THE CODES

Determining construction types and allowable building sizes may not be a part of most interior projects. These variables are usually determined and set at the initial construction of the building; however, interior projects often involve changing uses and users in existing buildings. And because there is a direct relationship between occupancy classification, allowable area, height and number of stories, construction types and the use of sprinklers, when the user or use changes, the existing conditions and newest requirements may need to be researched. These parameters as set by the codes can determine if a project is compatible or feasible with an existing space or building. In some cases, it may reveal that significant modifications such as the addition of an automatic sprinkler are required or that the proposed space or building is not compatible with the project because it exceeds the allowable floor area and construction type.

This research is important particularly if the building was not originally built for the proposed use. An example is a large restaurant (A-2) moving into an existing building that was built for office use (B).

Note

Construction type are defined in *Chapter 6: Types of Construction* and *Table 601* in the *IBC*. In the NFPA codes, they are defined in *NFPA 220* and in the Appendix A, *Table A.8.2.1.2* of the *LSC*.

Note

The *NFPA 220* assigns a three-digit code to describe the fire-resistance rating of each construction type. The three digits represent the hourly fire ratings for three structure elements: exterior load-bearing walls; the frame, columns, and girders; and the floor construction.

Note

The US Congress added the protection of timber to the Lacey Act of 1900. Effective November 2008, timber harvested illegally outside the United States cannot be sold legally within the United States.

Note

Structural steel and reinforcing steel in many cases can be composed totally of recycled scrap steel.

In some cases, the size of the restaurant may exceed the allowable area for an Assembly use in the existing construction type. However, even if the new occupant is a similar use to a previous user, allowable areas may need to be checked. For example, suppose an Ambulatory Health Care use takes over a space that was previously a medical office. Both are considered Business occupancies in the *IBC*. However, the area limitations for the construction type may be have changed since the building was initially constructed. Approval by the code official may be necessary, as well.

This same research can be useful if you are assisting a client to find a space that is appropriate for their use or if you are assisting a building owner to determine the type of tenants or uses that would be allowable in a particular building. In either case, the occupancy classification, construction type restrictions and area restrictions for that occupancy must be researched. In all scenarios, checking the compatibility of the actual project parameters with these building limitations should be accomplished in the early stages of the design project.

The building codes including the *IBC* and the *NFPA 5000* refer to construction types as Type I through Type V although the specific requirements assigned to each type may differ. A written description of the construction types is provided in Chapter 6, *Types of Construction* of the *IBC*. The fire-resistance ratings for each building elements are provided in the *IBC Table 601* in Chapter 6 as well. Building height and size limitations are covered in Chapter 5, *General Building Heights and Areas* in the *IBC*. In the *NFPA 5000* this information is provided together in the single Chapter 7, *Construction Types and Height and Area Regulations*. In the NFPA codes, the construction types are based on *NFPA 220, Standard on Types of Building Construction*. The *LSC* assigns allowable construction types for each occupancy within the individual occupancy chapter text. Although the *LSC* does not regulate building size and is primarily concerned about exiting and life safety, a summary chart of building size and height limitations is also provided in the Appendix A.

In certain cases, the use of performance codes may also be used. Performance codes, such as the *ICCPC*, do not have explicit requirements for limiting the size of the building. Instead, they set goals for structural stability, fire safety, means of egress, and the acceptable level of damage or impact caused by a fire for the building's size and use. The *ICC Performance Code (ICCPC)* includes several chapters such as Chapter 4, *Reliability and Durability*; Chapter 5, *Stability*; and Chapter 3, *Design Performance Levels*, with a section on "Maximum Level of Damage to be Tolerated" to set performance criteria for building construction systems. Appendix B of the *ICCPC* includes a worksheet to assist in assigning specific structural systems to performance groups. The NFPA codes also provide alternate performance criteria that can be used when dealing with the construction elements of a building. Performance codes such as the *ICCPC* set criteria for fire resistance of structural members within a building but do not give exact hourly ratings. These goals direct the fire resistance to be "appropriate" for the particular use of the structural member, its potential exposure to fire, the height of the building, and the use of the building.

Construction types are not specifically referenced by sustainability codes and standards. However, as discussed in this chapter, sustainability goals may influence the choice of materials for certain building and structural elements to add to the overall sustainability of a project.

 Note

Concrete as a structural and interior element has many green qualities, including durability, thermal mass, resistant to both fire and environmental damage, and local availability. In addition, concrete does not offgas or negatively affect the indoor air quality when the building is occupied.

HIGH-RISE BUILDINGS

The most common definition of a high-rise building is any building that has an occupied floor exceeding 75 feet (23 m) above the lowest level of fire department vehicle access. This dimension is based on the limitations of fire department ladder trucks. Therefore, the building height is typically measured from the lowest ground level a fire truck can access outside the building to the floor of the highest occupiable story.

The codes apply stricter requirements to high-rise buildings because of additional dangers posed by the increased height and characteristics of a tall building in the event of a fire. One danger created by a tall building is that it is often impractical to evacuate all the occupants within a reasonable time. Also, because the fires are often beyond the reach of fire department equipment, they must be fought in place within the building. Compartmentation (including protected stairwells and areas of refuge), means of egress, and active fire protection systems (including detection and suppression) become very important. (See Chapters 5, 6, and 7.) Smoke control is also critical because tall buildings are affected by the stack effect of smoke during a fire. Additional safeguards include the mandatory use of automatic sprinkler systems and an overlapping of detection and suppression systems.

Since September 11, 2001, there has been much discussion as to whether high-rise buildings can be made safer in the event of fire or other emergencies. Some changes to the codes have been introduced, such as the use of elevators as part of occupant evacuation and the need for a dedicated stair for firefighters in the event of a major fire. Other changes are still being discussed and researched to determine their practicality and appropriateness.

DOCUMENTATION

If the project is for new construction, the construction type, area, height, and number of stories will most likely be specified as part of the architectural and structural documentation. However, the code official may want to see this information provided for interior projects because it tells part of the story of the compatibility of the project type with the existing building parameters. In this case, this information should be provided with the other essential code information.

As part of your research and documentation, you can use the digital "Building Characteristics" checklist provided with this book. It combines the documentation of the construction types, height, area, and story limitations set by the various codes. It will prompt you to research and document the findings that are pertinent to your project.

CHAPTER 5

MEANS OF EGRESS

A *means of egress* is technically defined as a continuous and unobstructed path of travel from any point in a building to a public way. More simply stated, it is the system of building components that provide a path to safety for an occupant in the event of a fire or other emergency. A means of egress consists of vertical and horizontal elements, including doorways, corridors, passageways, stairs, ramps, and intervening rooms. The design of these components is crucial to the safety of the building occupants in normal use of a building and especially during emergencies.

There are two main strategies for the means of egress: evacuation and "defend in place." *Evacuation* means that the occupants will be provided with a direct path out of the building. In a *defend in place* strategy, occupants will remain where they are; go to a specific area, often on the same floor, to wait for assistance; and/or be provided with an alternative method to exit the building. Every means of egress has various components. This chapter identifies these components and explains how they work together. The first half of the chapter concentrates on describing the components of the means of egress. The rest of the chapter discusses how to determine the required quantities, sizes, and locations of the parts of the means of egress. Accessibility requirements are also discussed throughout the chapter.

Although the codes usually separate means of egress codes and accessibility requirements, they should be considered together. In most cases, the means of egress will be required to be accessible or special conditions must be provided. This chapter has combined the discussion of these topics wherever possible. (The figures typically show the strictest requirements as well.)

Remember that not every type of means of egress mentioned in this chapter will be used in every interior project. In addition, many existing buildings will already have the correct number of exits. If working with just one occupant or tenant in the building, only the exiting within and from that tenant space may need to be considered. It may generally be safe to assume that the number and size of the exits and exit stairways

Note

There are two basic strategies for means of egress: evacuation of occupants and defend in place.

have been correctly designed for the building. However, some projects may require reevaluating the existing exit requirements and making alterations, especially if the occupant load has been significantly increased. (See Chapter 3.) In the end, every interior project must provide adequate means of egress within the space and to the appropriate exits.

This chapter discusses the wide variety of codes, standards, and federal regulations that pertain to the means of egress. Some of the requirements are based on occupant loads, as discussed in Chapter 3. Specific fire ratings are also required for each means of egress component. Chapter 5 explains these fire-rating requirements. Chapter 9 explains the different types of finishes allowed in each area of a means of egress.

MEANS OF EGRESS SYSTEM

Note

The 9/11 Commission Act of 2007 is a federal legislation that calls for the development of voluntary, private-sector standards for emergency preparedness. Some of these standards are included in the *LSC* appendixes to provide additional emergency evacuation requirements.

Almost every part of a building interior, as well as some exterior elements, play a part in the *means of egress*. Each component has a role within the exiting system to provide occupants a path to safety and protect them while they move toward a place of greater safety. Each of the codes divides the means of egress into three main categories: exit access, exit, and exit discharge. In all cases, a public way is the final destination of a means of egress. The means of egress components are defined as follows:

❑ **Exit access.** The portion of a means of egress that leads from any occupied area to the entrance of an exit. It includes any room or space occupied by a person and any doorway, aisle, corridor, stair, or ramp traveled on the way to the exit.

❑ **Exit.** The portion of a means of egress between the exit access and the exit discharge or public way. It is often required to be physically separated from other interior spaces. It can be as basic as an exterior exit door or it can include enclosed stairwells and ramps. In some special cases, it can include certain corridors or passageways. The enclosure for an exit is often distinguished from the exit accesses because they are required to be fire resistant rated. (See Chapter 6.)

❑ **Area of refuge.** A space or area where persons who are unable to use a stairway (or elevator) can remain temporarily to await instructions or assistance during an emergency evacuation.

❑ **Exit discharge.** The portion of a means of egress between the termination of an exit and the public way. It can be inside a building, such as the main lobby, or outside a building, such as an egress court, courtyard, patio, small alley, or other pathway to the public way.

Note

An exterior space can be either an exterior exit discharge or a public way. To be a public way, the space must be at least 10 feet (3048 mm) wide and 10 feet (3048 mm) high and be considered a public space.

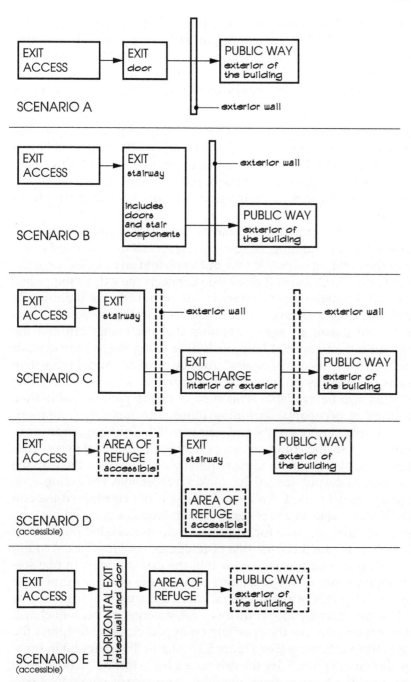

Figure 5.1 Means of egress components.

❏ **Public way.** The area outside a building that is legally considered public. Examples include a street, an alley, or a sidewalk. The area must have a minimum clear width and height of not less than 10 feet (3048 mm) to be considered a public way. The intent is to be a destination where occupants would be safe from exposure to a fire in the building.

It is important to understand the relationship of these components, when each exists and the role that it plays within the means of egress system. The simplest relationship is when the exit access leads directly to an exit that takes occupants out of the building. This is shown conceptually in Figures 5.1A and 5.1B. In the first diagram, the exit is simply an exterior door.

In the second diagram, the exit is an exit stair that opens at the bottom to the exterior of the building. In some cases, an exit does not end at the exterior of the building or public way but leads into an exit discharge. As shown in Figure 5.1C, the exit discharge connects the exit to the public way. The exit discharge can be either inside or outside the building. In either case, the code will have specific requirements for its use.

The typical means of egress assumes that occupants can exit the building without any special help, including using stairs. However, at least one "accessible means of egress" must be provided and if more than one means of egress is provided from a space, at least two accessible options must also be available. This type of egress path is usable by a greater range of occupants, including those with mobility limitations who, for example, cannot use the exit stair to exit the building. In an *accessible means of egress*, the common components of a means of egress (i.e., exit access, exit, etc.) meet the same requirements. It is often the way the occupant reaches the public way that makes it accessible. For example, an area of refuge may be used. An area of refuge is not considered the end point for the accessible means of egress, but instead is a place where people with disabilities can wait for additional help to reach the public way. As indicated in Figure 5.1D, an area of refuge can occur adjacent to but before entering an exit stairway or within the exit stairway. In one scenario, emergency personnel will assist or carry the occupant down the stairway to the public way. In special cases, an area of refuge can be included in the elevator lobby. In this case, emergency personnel will assist the occupant to use the specially equipped elevator to egress the building to the public way. (See Figure 5.13 later in this chapter.) In some cases, as shown in Figure 5.1E, the exit access leads through a horizontal exit to an area of refuge on the same floor. If necessary, emergency personnel will take disabled occupants down a stairway or elevator from the area of refuge side of the building. (See the sections titled "Areas of Refuge" and "Horizontal Exits" later in this chapter.)

To know which requirements, apply to a particular space, you need to determine whether that space is part of the exit access, exit, or exit discharge. For example, the finish classifications required for an area that is an exit access will differ from those for an area that is part of an exit. (See Chapter 9.) Some means of egress components within a space may be easy to identify. For example, exit stairs are always considered exits. For others, the path of the occupants may have to be considered to correctly identify the component and its role within the means of egress. For example, a corridor may be part of the exit access, exit or exit discharge. This is demonstrated on the floor plan in Figure 5.2.

Recognizing that a space can play more than one role in the means of egress is important. One way to determine which means of egress components need to be considered is to follow the path that an occupant might take from a point in the building to the exit. In the floor plan in Figure 5.2, different shading patterns indicate whether the space is considered an exit access, an exit, an exit discharge, or a public way. For example, if a person were standing in the lobby of this diagram, the distance from the person to the exterior door would be the exit access and the exterior door would be the exit. Once through the exterior door, the person would be in an exterior exit discharge (egress court), because, in this case, the sidewalk is the public way. However, for a person coming down the stairway at the left of the plan and emptying into the lobby, the stairway is the initial exit component, the lobby is then part of the exit discharge, and the exterior door is the end of the interior exit discharge because it leads to the exterior of the building. From that point, the egress court continues as an exterior exit discharge until it reaches the sidewalk, as previously discussed. When a space can be considered more than one part of the means of egress, it must meet the requirements of the most restrictive component.

Although the requirements for the individual parts of the means of egress may be slightly different between the various codes, they all assume that a means of egress must be continuous. This means that the path cannot become less safe, reduce in width, be disrupted by locked doors, or fail to lead the occupant safely all the way to the public way. To accomplish this there is an array of requirements for the means of egress components.

The following sections give a description of the typical means of egress components and their characteristics. Exit accesses are described first as they are the starting point of the means of egress. In addition, these components are elaborated in more detail since similar components of the means of egress have many of the same requirements. For example,

☑ **Note**

An area of refuge is a component of an "accessible means of egress."

☑ **Note**

If a building or space is only required to have one exit, it typically must be an accessible means of egress.

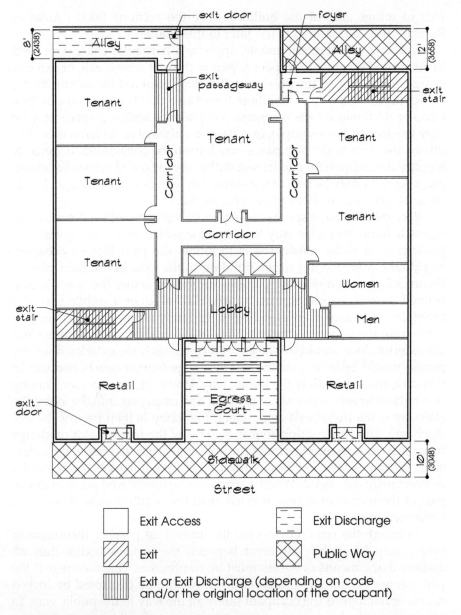

Figure 5.2 Means of egress in a typical building.

exit access stairs and exit stairs serve different purposes in the means of egress, but they both use the same tread and riser dimensions, landing widths, handrail requirements, and so on. When stairs are discussed in their role as an exit, only what is unique to that role will be discussed.

EXIT ACCESSES

An *exit access* is the portion of a means of egress that leads to an exit. It leads an occupant from anywhere in a room or space to an exit (including the exit from the room itself). Rooms, corridors, aisles, doors, unenclosed stairs and ramps, and intervening rooms can all be part of the exit access. Exit accesses do not necessarily have to be fully enclosed, such as an open office area with cubicles. Nor do they always require a fire resistance rating. For example, a corridor in a small tenant space usually does not have to be rated; however, a main building corridor connecting the tenants and the public spaces may be required to be rated. (See Chapter 6 for fire ratings.) The entire route through spaces, rooms, and corridors until an occupant reaches an exit is considered part of the exit access. (See Figure 5.2.)

Each component of an exit access is described in this section. The descriptions include the basic code requirements, as well as many of the necessary accessibility requirements. (The various diagrams typically include the most restrictive code and accessibility requirements.)

Doorways

Doors can be part of the exit access, exit, or exit discharge depending on where they are located. Doors that do not open to an exit but are within the path to an exit are called exit access doorways. The codes regulate each component of a doorway similarly, whether part of an exit or an exit access. First, the door itself must be of a particular type, size, and swing. In addition, the way that the door can be used by occupants while exiting is also regulated. The various components of a door as regulated by the codes is discussed in this section. (Fire ratings for doors are discussed in Chapter 6.)

> **⌧ Note**
>
> The path of the means of egress must maintain a minimum floor to ceiling height of 90 inches (2286 mm) except for doorways.

Doorway and Door Size

Any door that opens from a room or is used along a corridor and connects the adjacent rooms or spaces to the exit access corridor is an exit access doorway. In addition, all other doors encountered along the way to the exit are also considered exit access doors. The codes set minimum dimensions for doors within the means of egress. Most doors in the means of egress cannot be less than 80 inches (2032 mm) high. The codes specify the door components that can protrude into this height including door closers, overhead door stops, power door operators and electromagnetic door locks. The building codes, the *ICC A117.1* standard, and the *ADA Standards* specify that when in an open position, a door must provide 32 inches (813 mm) of clear width. Because this must be the clear inside dimension (with the door open), as shown in the plan in Figure 5.3, typically a door that is at least 36 inches (914 mm) in width must be specified. However, depending on the calculated number of occupants that will exit through a specific doorway, multiple doors and larger widths may be necessary. Determining the required size and number of doors is

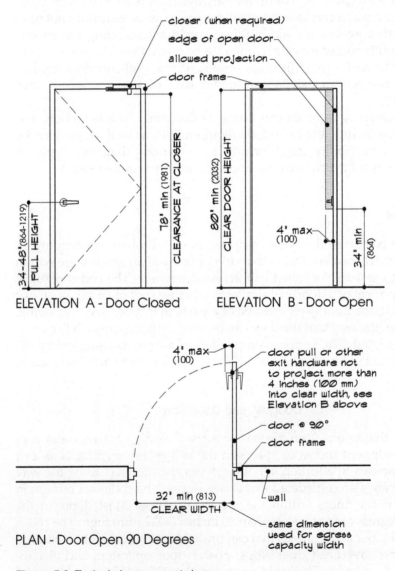

Figure 5.3 Typical clearances at doors.

described in the section "Exit Widths" later in this chapter. In addition, the codes may require larger doors and widths in certain occupancy classifications.

Door Type and Configuration

Most egress doors are required to be pivoted or the side-hinged swinging type. Doors within the means of egress path must typically swing in the direction of exit travel. (The actual rule is when the door serves a room or area with an occupant load of 50 or more, or a Hazardous occupancy.) Although most exit access doors will need to swing out of a space, this allows a door to swing into an office, exam room, or other small room. However, the door swing cannot impede on other means of egress clearances while opening or when it is completely open. For example, the door cannot reduce any required stair landing dimension or corridor width by more than 7 inches (178 mm) when the door is fully open. (This includes the door hardware, as shown in Plan B of Figure 5.4.) The door also cannot reduce the required corridor width by more than half in any open position.

At all doors, there are required maneuvering clearances for accessibility as well. If the approach to the door is perpendicular to the door from the push or pull side, a minimum clearance of 12 or 18 inches (305 or 445 mm) is required at the latch side. However, if the approach is parallel and from the hinge or latch side, a minimum clearance of 22, 36, or 42 inches (560, 915, or 1065 mm) is required at the latch side. (See Figure 5.4.) In some cases, additional clearance may be required at the hinge side as well. If an existing condition makes it virtually impossible to obtain the required accessible clearances, an automatic door may be an option. Furniture or other interior elements cannot impede on these dimensions.

If a door must swing out toward the path of exit travel, several options can be used to avoid conflicts with other required clearances. The most common ones are listed here. Figure 5.4 indicates these options and highlights the critical dimensions required by the codes and the ADA and *ICC A117.1* standards.

1. Increase swing of door. Use a 180-degree swing door instead of a 90-degree door to allow it to open fully against the wall. This can be done only if a corridor is wide enough, as shown in Plan B of Figure 5.4.

2. Create an alcove. Recess the door into the room, as shown in Plan E of Figure 5.4, so that the walls create an alcove that the door can swing into. (The alcove must allow maneuvering room.)

✎ Note

Everything within the pathway before an exit is considered exit access.

✎ Note

Most doors are side-hinged and swinging. However, certain occupancies can use other types of doors under certain conditions. These include sliding doors, overhead doors, revolving doors, security grills, and turnstiles.

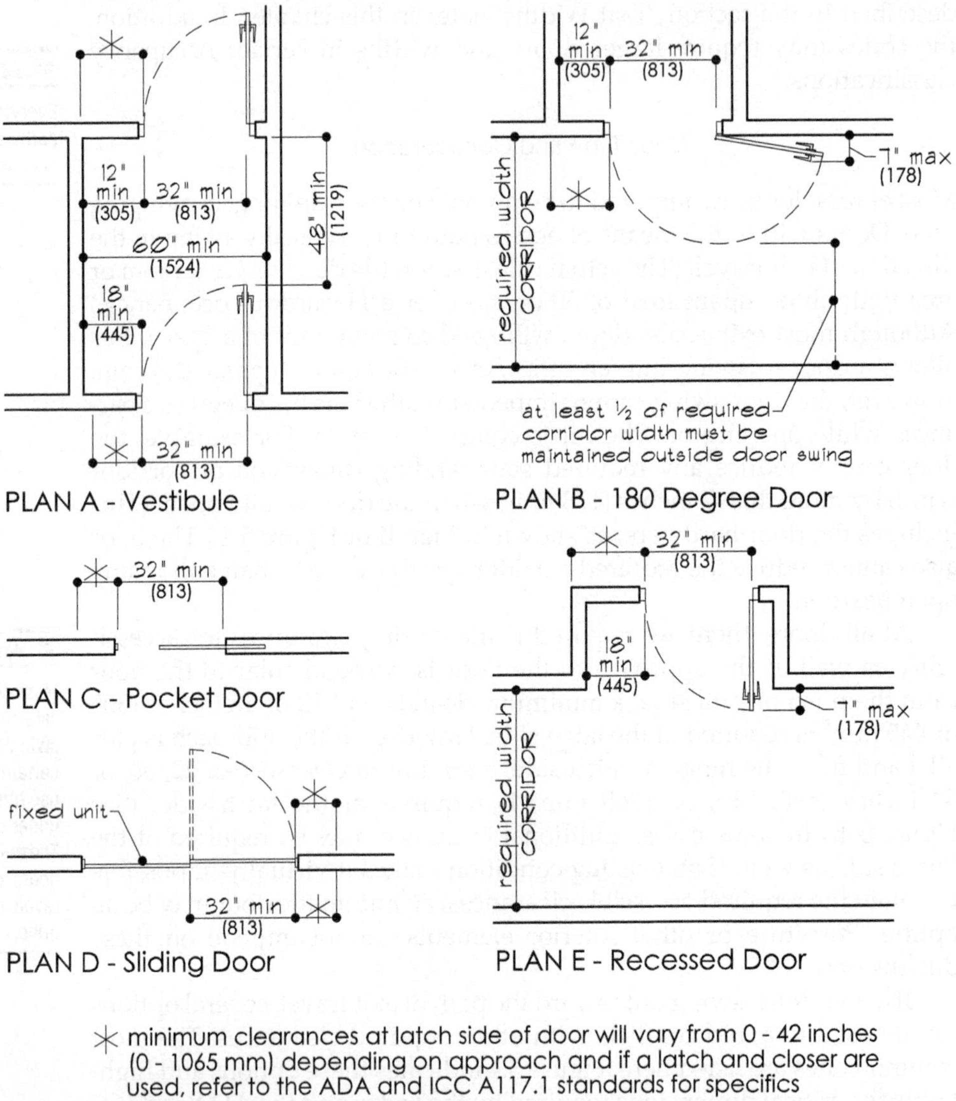

PLAN A - Vestibule

PLAN B - 180 Degree Door

PLAN C - Pocket Door

PLAN D - Sliding Door

PLAN E - Recessed Door

✳ minimum clearances at latch side of door will vary from 0 - 42 inches (0 - 1065 mm) depending on approach and if a latch and closer are used, refer to the ADA and ICC A117.1 standards for specifics

Figure 5.4 Typical clearances at doorways.

3. Enlarge the landing. Enlarge the landing at the door, such as by widening a corridor or lengthening a vestibule, to allow enough maneuvering space. Typical vestibule dimensions are shown in Plan A of Figure 5.4.

4. Use a sliding door. Use a sliding door in low-traffic areas and when allowed by the codes. (See Plans C and D in Figure 5.4.)

There are several exceptions and additional requirements for the use of sliding doors. In the interior, sliding doors are allowed for rooms with low occupant loads and for certain occupancies and uses including Institutional, Residential, offices, factories, and storage areas. For instance, sliding glass doors may be used in a hospital where visual monitoring of patients is critical. Automatic sliding doors (typically seen as exterior exit doors) can also be used, but when pushed with sufficient force they must be capable of swinging into the direction of exit travel.

Other types of doors are allowed in certain situations. These include revolving doors and power-operated swinging doors. Because they work differently than a typical swinging door type, the codes impose additional requirements for their use in an emergency. For example, revolving doors must be able to collapse when pushed with force in an emergency to provide the minimum clear exit width. In addition, revolving doors cannot be the only type of door provided for egress. Similarly, power-operated swinging doors must be capable of being opened manually in case of emergency or loss of electricity. The codes will also limit the number of these special door types in certain occupancies, including Institutional and Mercantile occupancies.

> **◀ Note**
>
> In the *IBC*, all doors located in rooms or space that are Assembly or Educational occupancies with an occupant load of 50 or more must use panic or fire hardware.

Door Hardware

The most common door hardware includes hinges, latches and locksets, operating mechanisms, and closers. The codes regulate the type, mounting height, and function of the hardware on doors. The type of hardware on a door affects the way that a door operates. It is important that exit access doors can be easily and readily used by occupants. This is so that occupants are not delayed in evacuating a building because of difficulty in opening a door in their path. Allowable operating devices on means of egress door can include door handles, pulls, latches, and locks. In most cases, the location of the door, the number of occupants using the door, and the occupancy classification will determine what type of hardware can or must be used. For example, in an elementary school (Educational occupancy), the classroom doors are required to have lever-type hardware, but the doors to the exterior must have exit hardware.

Most door hardware within an interior space will be doorknobs, levers, or pulls. Although used predominately in the past, doorknobs are not typically used in commercial buildings anymore because they do not meet accessible requirements of the building codes, ADA standards, or *ICC A117.1*. These regulations forbid the operating mechanism to require tight grasping or twisting to use. Lever hardware is predominately used because it can be made to operate with a closed fist or cupped hand as required by the accessibility guidelines. There are other types of latches including hospital latches that can also be used. If a door is not required to latch or close securely; a pull or push handle can be used.

However, for certain occupancies, including Assembly, Educational/Day Care, Hazardous, and others with an occupant load of 50, the code may require an exit hardware device. There are two basic types: panic hardware and fire exit hardware. Both simply require that a bar or panel to be pushed to release the door latch. Exit hardware has a function that will allow it to be left unlatched; fire hardware does not. Panic hardware must be listed to conform to *UL 305, Standard for Panic Hardware*. (Fire exit hardware is used on rated doors and is discussed in Chapter 6.)

Typically, doors within the means of egress path cannot be locked because locking would hinder egress, creating a dangerous situation. (The door can be locked in the non-egress direction, that is, an office door going into the office.) However, in some cases, it may be necessary to lock a door in the direction of egress for the protection and security of the occupants. For example, in some Institutional occupancies (hospital and detention) doors are locked to prevent occupants from freely leaving the area or they may be locked to prevent certain occupants from gaining access to specific areas. The codes regulate these conditions as either controlled egress/free egress, delayed egress, sensor release systems or locked egress doors. These conditions are typically controlled by a type of electric locking system including electromechanical and electromagnetic systems. Often an automatic sprinkler system is required. In most cases, these locking systems must be deactivated when the fire detections system is activated or there is a loss of power. Monitoring staff must also be able to unlock the system. However, whether an egress door can be locked will depend on several conditions. These include type of hardware, occupancy classification, location, whether the building is sprinklered, connection to a fire alarm, whether the door unlocks or remains locked in the case of loss of power, and if the area is monitored by staff members. It may need specific approval from the code official, as well. These specific requirements can vary between the building code and the *LSC*. In many cases, additional signage is required. It is important for the safety of the occupants that each requirement is met if a locking system is specified.

The most recent emergency condition to be addressed in the codes are guidelines for controlling an unwanted intruder. The *IFC* provides acceptable locking arrangements for educational occupancies, which include Educational, Business, and Institutional (day cares.) These allow the door to be locked from the outside the room but must allow occupants to leave the room. There are several conditions that must be met.

All operating hardware must also be installed between 34 and 48 inches (864 and 129 mm) And cannot project more than 4 inches

(100 mm) into egress or accessible route to meet the code and accessibility requirements. Door closers can project as long as they are 78 inches (980mm) above the floor.

Opening Force

Based on the type and location of each door, the building codes and the accessibility standards set a maximum allowable force to manually open the door. Separate allowable forces are given for unlatching and opening the door based on the type of door and hardware. For a typical door that is unlatched simply by a push or pull action, the maximum allowable force is 15 pounds (67 N). Where a door is unlatched by a downward rotational force (a lever handle), a maximum of 28 inch-pounds (315 N-cm) is allowed. Once unlatched, the allowable force for a typical swinging door within the exit access is usually between 5 and 15 pounds (22 to 67 N). However, for other special types of doors, such as revolving, automatic, sliding, or folding, the allowable force may vary from 30 to 180 pounds (133 to 801 N), depending on their use and location. (These maximum forces typically will not apply to fire-rated doors.) These requirements are consistent with the ADA-standard maximum force allowances for doors which are part of an accessible route or exit. To provide accessibility for public entrances at certain uses, the hardware and opening mechanism may have additional characteristics. For example, for large Assembly, Business, Mercantile, and Residential occupancies, automatic doors that eliminate the need for manual operation may be required.

Closers may also be required by the codes or accessibility standards so that the door is self-closing. For example, doors within rated walls are required to be self-closing to maintain the fire separation. In some cases, restroom doors are required to be self-closing for privacy and accessibility. Or, for convenience, it may be desirable to have a door to a particular room close after every use. In all cases, the maximum allowable force required to open the door still applies. The closer must also be located on the door and frame so that it does not interfere with head clearance requirements, as indicated in Figure 5.3. In some cases, the time it takes the door to close is also regulated by the codes and the accessibility standards. (For additional information, see the section titled "Security Systems" in Chapter 10.)

Stairways

Exit access stairs are different than exit stairs. An exit access stair is typically not required to be enclosed: An exit stair is always enclosed by fire resistant–rated partitions. Conditions that would allow exit access stair to be open include if does not connect more than a certain number of floors (varies by occupancy), serves a mezzanine or balcony, or the building is sprinklered. For example, a stairway that allows employees to move between the two levels of a business without leaving the tenant space would be an exit access stairway. Most of the technical requirements for an exit access stair are the same as those for exit stairs. (See also the section "Exit Stairs" later in this chapter.)

There are several different stair types in addition to the straight run stair. These include curved, winder, spiral, scissor, switchback, and alternating tread stairs. Most of these are allowed by the codes as part of the exit access but will depend on the occupancy classification, the number of occupants, the use of the stair, and the dimension of the treads. However, some of them may not be allowed as part of the means of egress. In addition, the materials used to build the stairway must be consistent with the construction type of the building. (See Chapter 4.)

Stairs are required to meet specific code and accessibility requirements. The most important are the tread and riser dimensions. The most common dimensions are shown in Figure 5.5, with a minimum tread depth of 11 inches (279 mm) and a range of 4 to 7 inches (100 to 178 mm)

⬛ **Note**

The *LSC* allows existing stairs to remain in use if they meet previous requirements when alterations are being made to a space. However, other codes may not.

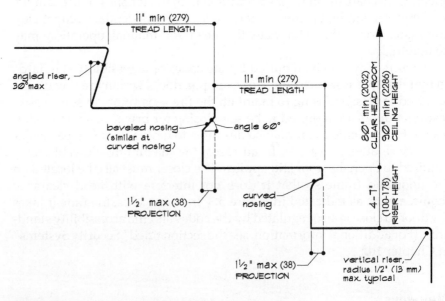

Figure 5.5 Typical stair requirements: Treads and risers.

for riser height. The actual height of the riser will be determined by the overall vertical height of the stairway. Once the riser size is determined, it is not allowed to fluctuate more than a small fraction from step to step. The shape and size of the nosings in relation to the riser are defined as well. Various stair nosing allowed by the codes and the accessibility standards as shown in Figure 5.5.

A *flight* of stairs is defined by the codes to be the run of stairs from one floor or landing to another. There must be a landing at the top and bottom of a flight of stairs. In addition, the codes do not usually allow a single flight to rise more than 12 feet (3658 mm). The width of the stair (as discussed later in this chapter) determines the minimum dimensions of these required landings or platforms. Other variables must also be considered. For example, when fully open, the door into the stair cannot project into the required clear egress width more than 7 inches (178 mm), and the door cannot reduce the required exit width by more than half at any open position, similar to the door shown in Plan B of Figure 5.4. Additional stair requirements are shown on the plan in Figure 5.6. Any required areas of refuge may also increase the size of a landing. (See the section titled "Areas of Refuge" later in this chapter.)

A minimum ceiling height and a minimum headroom above a stair and its landing are set by the codes. As shown in the elevation in Figure 5.6, the minimum ceiling height required by the code at any occupiable space is 90 inches (2 mm). Some projections below that height are allowed. These may include structural elements, light fixtures, exit signs, or similar ceiling-mounted items. However, the minimum headroom that must be provided along the run of the stair is 80 inches (2032 mm). It is measured vertically from the landing and the front edge of the tread of the stair to the ceiling directly above along the full length of the stair run. This headroom must be maintained along the full width of the stairway and landings as well. Spiral stairs are allowed a slightly lower headroom in some cases.

Handrails and guards are regulated as well. Most stairs require a handrail on both sides. (See the codes for exceptions.) When wide stairs are used, additional intermediate handrails may be required. The building codes and accessibility standards require handrails to be certain styles and sizes, to be installed at specific heights and distances from the wall, and to be continuous wherever possible. The *IBC* now indicates two types of handrails. Type I is the typical circular handrail as shown in Figure 5.7. (Type II, which includes additional shapes, is only allowed in certain Residential occupancies.) Figures 5.7 and 5.8 indicate some of these typical handrail dimensions and locations. Handrails must also typically extend a certain distance beyond the top and bottom of the stairway and

Note

When determining stair dimensions, it is important to know what floor covering will ultimately be used in the construction. Floor coverings may change the final dimension of the treads or risers and, therefore, the code compliance of the stair.

Note

Open risers are allowed for stairways that are not required to be part of the accessible means of egress as long as a 4-inch (102-mm) sphere cannot pass through. They are also allowed in I-3, F, H, and S occupancies for stairways not used by the public and in some spiral stairways.

Note

The requirements for the bottom handrail extension on stairs differ, depending on which accessibility document is used. If necessary, consult with a code official and/or another regulatory representative to determine how to satisfy these conflicting requirements.

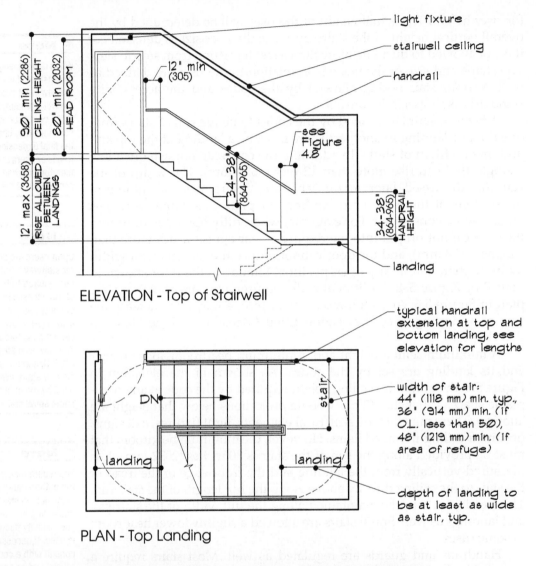

ELEVATION - Top of Stairwell

PLAN - Top Landing

NOTE: If an open stairway, guards at a minimum height of 42 inches (1067 mm) would be required in addition to handrails.

Figure 5.6 Typical stairway requirements: Clearances.

have an uninterrupted grip. (The bottom extension requirement may vary. See the note in Figure 5.8.)

Guards may also be required in certain locations. *Guards* are railings that the codes require to keep people from falling off when there are changes in elevation. They are typically necessary whenever there is a

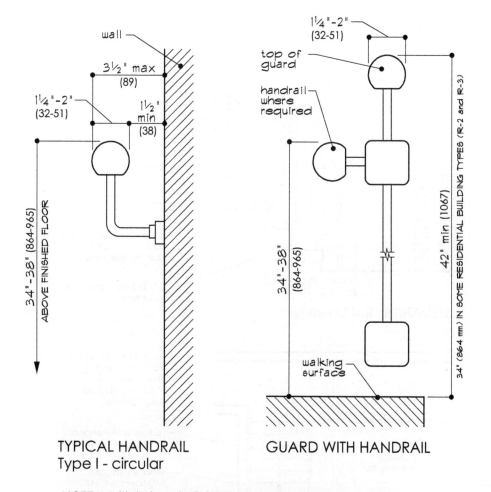

TYPICAL HANDRAIL
Type I - circular

GUARD WITH HANDRAIL

NOTE: Multiple handrail shapes are allowed. Refer to ADA
and ICC A117.1 standards for specific requirements. The
IBC also allows more than one type, allowing the newer
Type II handrials in certain Residential occupancies.

Figure 5.7 Typical handrail (Type I) and guard sections.

drop of more than 30 inches (760 mm) where occupants are walking and
there is no adjacent wall. The most common example of a guard is at a
balcony or a stair when a side of the stair is exposed and not enclosed by
a wall, as shown in Figure 5.8. In most instances, the guards must be at
least 42 inches (1067 mm) high. Lower heights are allowed in some

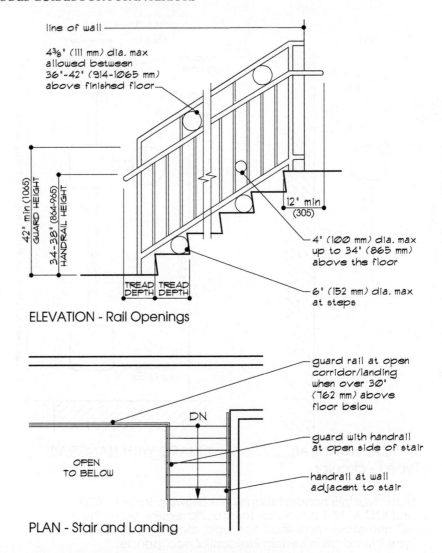

line of wall

4⅜' (111 mm) dia. max
allowed between
36"-42" (914-1065 mm)
above finished floor

42' min (1065)
GUARD HEIGHT

34-38' (864-965)
HANDRAIL HEIGHT

12" min
(305)

TREAD
DEPTH TREAD
DEPTH

4" (100 mm) dia. max
up to 34' (865 mm)
above the floor

6" (152 mm) dia. max
at steps

ELEVATION - Rail Openings

guard rail at open
corridor/landing
when over 30'
(762 mm) above
floor below

DN

OPEN
TO BELOW

guard with handrail
at open side of stair

handrail at wall
adjacent to stair

PLAN - Stair and Landing

NOTE: Older editions of the ICC/ANSI standard and the original ADAAG
require the bottom rail extension at stairs to equal the depth of one tread plus
12 inches (305 mm). You may need to consult a code official or other regulatory
representative when this conflicts with the new requirements as shown above.

Figure 5.8 Typical handrail and guard requirements.

residential occupancies. Guards at Assembly spaces are subject to special requirements. (Check the code for specifics.) If a handrail is also required, it must be mounted at the required height for a handrail along with the guard, as shown in Figures 5.7 and 5.8.

The guard must typically be designed so that nothing with a diameter of 4 inches (100 mm) can pass through any opening created by the rail configuration. This is shown at the top of Figure 5.8. In addition, 4⅜ inches (111 mm) is allowed above the handrail and 6 inches (152 mm) is allowed between the bottom rail and the steps. There are additional requirements and exceptions for certain occupancy types. Refer to the codes to determine if these apply. These requirements must be met whether a prefabricated rail system is specified or a custom rail is designed.

Escalators and Moving Walks

Escalators and moving walks are not typically allowed as a means of egress. However, there are some exceptions in existing buildings. Existing escalators may be allowed only if they are fully enclosed within fire-rated walls and doors. Some may also have specific sprinkler requirements.

Newer escalators and moving walks are usually installed as an additional path of travel or as a convenience to the occupants. Some of the more common occupancy classifications that use escalators and moving walks are Assemblies, large Mercantile, and certain Residential occupancies. According to the *LSC*, new escalators must comply with *ASME A17.1/CSA B44, Safety Code for Elevators and Escalators,* and existing escalators must comply with *ASME A17.3, Safety Code for Existing Elevators and Escalators,* for safety. In most cases, each space or building must still have the required number of enclosed stairs as specified by the codes.

Ramps

Ramps are used wherever there is a change in elevation and accessibility is required. Although changes in elevation should be avoided on a single floor, if steps are provided, then a ramp must be provided as well. In certain building types such as hospitals (I-2), ramps are required for any change in elevation; stairs are not allowed. The most important requirement of a ramp is the slope ratio. Most codes and accessibility standards set the *maximum* ratio at 1 unit vertical to 12 units horizontal. That means that for every vertical rise of 1 inch, the horizontal run of the ramp must extend 12 inches. The same proportion would be required

✎ Note

The width of a *stair* is measured to the outside edges of the steps. The width of a *ramp* is measured to the inside face of the handrails.

✎ Note

The *IBC* allows additional shapes for handrails used in some Residential occupancies. These are referred to as Type II handrails. The standard shape required by the codes is referred to as Type I.

✎ Note

Escalators, and moving walks are *not* considered part of the means of egress because the codes do not allow them to be used as an exit during an emergency. However, specially equipped elevators can be used as part of the accessible means of egress.

✎ Note

A ramp with a lower slope ratio should be used whenever possible. For example, a 1 to 16 ratio is more manageable and safer for persons with disabilities than the 1 to 12 slope allowed by the codes.

✎ Note

Handrails are critical during an emergency. When stairs are full of smoke, handrails often are the only guide to an exit.

Note

If glass is used as part of a handrail or guard, it must pass safety glass requirements as required by the codes. (See Chapter 6.)

in centimeters: 1 centimeter to 12 centimeters. This is shown at the top of Figure 5.9.

Typically, a ramp must be at least 36 inches (914 mm) wide (measured to the inside of the handrail). The other important requirement is the use of landings. The codes and the ADA and *ICC A117.1* standards require landings at certain intervals and of certain dimensions. In most cases, the

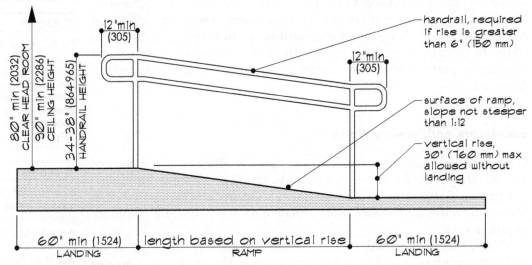

ELEVATION – Ramp with Handrail

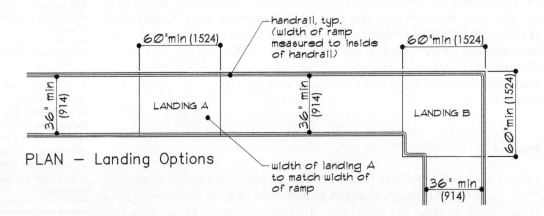

PLAN – Landing Options

NOTE: Ramps and landings not adjacent to a wall, must have curb, edge protection, and/or rail to prevent people from slipping off the ramp. See the ADA and ICC A117.1 standards and the building codes for specifics.

Figure 5.9 Typical ramp requirements.

width of the landing must be the same as the width of the ramp, although a minimum length of 60 inches (1524 mm) is usually required, as shown in Landing A on the Plan in Figure 5.9. When changes in direction are required, the landing must allow a 60-inch (1524-mm) turnaround, as shown in Landing B in Figure 5.9. To limit the amount of distance that has to be traveled on the incline in one run, a landing is usually required for every rise of 30 inches (760 mm) or a run of 30 feet (9144 mm). Landings are also required at the top and bottom of every ramp and must take into account any adjacent doors. Both the landings and the ramps may require specific edge details and a nonslip surface. (Refer to the ADA and *ICC A117.1* standards for specifics.)

The configuration of a handrail at a ramp is similar to that of stairs. Handrails are typically required when the ramp exceeds a certain length or rise. Similar to at a stair, the handrails are required to extend a certain distance beyond the landing. (See the elevation in Figure 5.9.) Guards are also required when there is no adjacent wall and the overall rise of the ramp is greater than 30 inches (760 mm). Width and clearance requirements for ramps are the same as exit with requirements at corridors.

Corridors

As part of a means of egress, a corridor is required by the codes to be enclosed. (This makes it different from an aisle, as discussed next.) A corridor can be part of an exit access or an exit. An exit access corridor leads to the exit in a building. Typically, these corridors are either nonrated or have a 1-hour fire rating, depending on their location, the occupant load they are serving, and whether the building is sprinklered. For example, the corridor in a small tenant space leading to a door that empties into the main exit access corridor for the building is not typically required to be rated. By contrast, the main exit access corridor that connects each of these tenant spaces and leads to the exit stairs may be required to be rated 1 hour. (If the building is sprinklered, a rating may not be required.) If the corridor is rated, the doors in the corridor will also be required to be rated. (See the section titled "Means of Egress Components" and Figure 6.11 in Chapter 6.)

The codes set minimum requirements for the width of a corridor. The occupancy, occupancy load, and typical use affect the required width of a corridor. In the *IBC*, these requirements are noted in Table 1020.3, "Minimum Corridor Width," as shown in Figure 5.10. The typical required minimum width of a corridor is 44 inches (1118 mm.) However, the type of use, occupancy, and the occupant load can require a different minimum corridor width. For example, as seen in *IBC* Table 1020.2, in

☑ Note

There is a distinction between ramps and curb ramps. Curb ramps are exterior ramps cut through or leading to a curb. Other ramps can be interior or exterior.

☑ Note

Ramps not intended for use by the disabled can sometimes have a slightly steeper slope.

TABLE 1020.3   MINIMUM CORRIDOR WIDTH

OCCUPANCY	MINIMUM WIDTH (inches)
Any facility not listed in this table	44
Access to and utilization of mechanical, plumbing or electrical systems or equipment	24
With an *occupant load* of less than 50	36
Within a dwelling unit	36
In Group E with a *corridor* having an *occupant load* of 100 or more	72
In *corridors* and areas serving stretcher traffic in ambulatory care facilities	72
Group I-2 in areas where required for bed movement	96

For SI: 1 inch = 25.4 mm.

Figure 5.10 International Building Code Table 1020.3, "Minimum Corridor" (2021 *International Building Code*, copyright © 2021. Washington, DC: International Code Council. Reproduced with permission. All rights reserved. www.iccsafe.org).

some occupancies a wider corridor may be required for moving gurneys or hospital beds or and a smaller corridor width may be allowed for smaller occupant load. Other configurations may require at least a portion of the corridor to be larger as indicated in Figure 5.11A–F. The codes also set maximum distances that an occupant will have to travel to an exit including the length of a corridor. (Travel distances are described later in this chapter.)

Specific accessibility requirements and clearances can affect the size of a corridor as shown in Figures 5.11B through 5.11F. These include (B) passing room for two wheelchairs in extra-long corridors, (C) minimum clearances for corridors that change direction, (D) turning space in narrow corridors, (E) maximum depth of objects protruding into the corridor, and (F) maneuvering space in a switchback configuration. Although a 60-inch (1524-mm) wide corridor so that two wheelchairs can pass as shown in Figure 5.11B is not specifically required by the codes or the accessibility standards, an area of the same size that allows a wheelchair to turn around is required. Typically, at least one turning space, as shown in Figure 5.11D, is required if the corridor is not 60 inches (1524 mm) wide along its length. (To accommodate this, the width of the corridor is often set at 60 inches (1524 mm) even when only 44 inches (1118 mm.) is required by code.) When doors are recessed or used at the end of a corridor, additional required clearances at the door may cause the required width of the corridor to exceed the minimum width required by code. (See the clearances in Figure 5.4 and the example given in the section "Exit Widths" later in this chapter.)

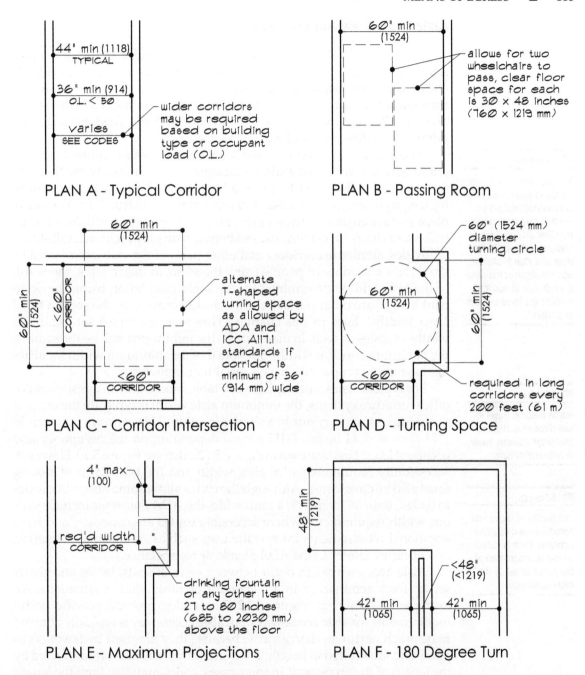

Figure 5.11 Typical corridor requirements.

Aisles and Aisle Accessways

An exit access *aisle* is similar to an exit access corridor in that it is a passageway required to reach an exit. The difference is that a corridor is enclosed by full-height walls, whereas an aisle is a pathway created by furniture or equipment. A short portion of an aisle that leads to another aisle is called an *aisle accessway*. The codes and the *ADA Standards* set minimum widths for aisles and/or aisle accessways.

Aisles can be created by fixed seats or movable furniture. Common building types with fixed seats are theaters and stadiums. When there are no fixed seats, aisles can be created by chairs, tables, counters, furnishings, equipment, merchandise, and other similar obstructions. For example, aisles are created between movable panel systems in offices, between tables and chairs in restaurants, and between display racks in retail stores.

Aisles, similar to corridors and other parts of the exit access, must be sized for the number of people using them. So, in many cases, the width of the aisle will be determined by the same calculation using the occupant load as are other parts of the means of egress. (See the section titled "Exit Widths" later in this chapter.) However, the codes set minimum widths of aisles as well. In many cases, the minimums will be the same as the minimum corridor widths but note that the minimum width for aisles for Assembly occupancies have special requirements.

For typical aisles, such as between tables and chairs in a restaurant or office furniture systems, the minimum aisle width is typically the same as the required for a corridor in a similar location. This can vary between 36 (914 mm) and 44 inches (1117.6 mm) depending on the occupancy and occupant load. This is shown in Figure 5.12. Also see Figure 5.10. However, accessibility requirements for aisle width and the placement of seating must also be considered. Although the codes allow some nonpublic aisles to be less than 36 inches (914 mm) wide, the *ADA Standards* include various width requirements where accessible routes are necessary and have additional requirements for specific uses such as restaurants, cafeterias, and libraries. (Refer to the *ADA Standards* for specifics.)

Aisle accessways can occur between rows of seats, tables and chairs set up for a seminar, or in a restaurant or other similar situations. An example is shown in Figure 5.12. The codes provide specific width requirements for aisle accessways. An aisle accessway is typically allowed to be much narrower than an aisle because they are used by fewer occupants and are limited in length. Their minimum width is often affected by the length of the accessway. In some cases, codes may also limit the length of the aisle accessway, depending on the occupant load. The length of the aisle accessway is measured to the centerline of the farthest seat. If an aisle accessway at a row of tables or chairs is less than 6 feet (1829 mm)

✎ Note

The required dimensions for stairs and ramps used in Assembly aisleways are different from those for other standard ramps and stairs. Typically, the riser of a stair is shorter and the slope of the ramp is shallower to accommodate the large number of people.

✎ Note

Aisles assume travel in two directions. Aisle accessways assume travel in only one direction.

✎ Note

The widths of aisles and corridors are calculated similarly. Each is based on the occupant load of the space or set by the code minimums.

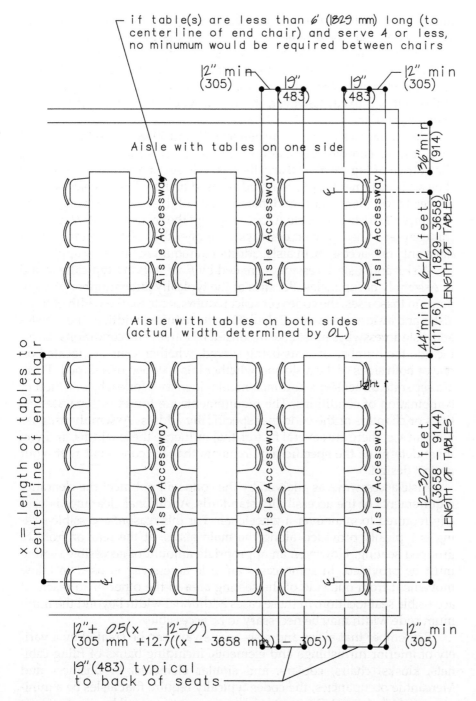

Figure 5.12 Typical aisle and aisle accessway requirements: Tables and chairs.

and is used by four or fewer people, the codes do not set a minimum width. However, for an aisle accessway that is between 6 and 12 feet (1829 to 3658 mm) in length, the accessway must be at least 12 inches (305 mm) wide. This width is measured from a point 19 inches (483 mm) from the edge of the table to allow for the chair, as indicated in Figure 5.12. If the seat is a fixed, however, the width would be measured from the actual back of the seat.

For a longer aisle accessway between 12 and 30 feet (3658 to 9144 mm) long, a more complex calculation is required. This formula is shown at the bottom of Figure 5.12. Basically, the code sets a minimum width and then adds incrementally to that width based on how long the accessways is over 12 feet (3658mm.) An demonstration of this calculation is given in "Example 2: Aisle and Aisle Accessways" in the section "Exit Widths" in this chapter. When aisle accessways are longer than 30 feet (9144 mm) or have only one access to an aisle, additional requirements may apply.

Aisles and aisle accessways created by *fixed seats* are typically found in Assembly occupancies. Because of the typically large number of occupants in these uses, the codes set strict requirements for the width of these aisles and aisle accessways. Calculating the required width of these aisles and aisle accessways must take in consideration several conditions. These include the number of seats being served, whether seats are located on one or both sides of the aisle and whether it is a sloped or stepped. There are separate dimensions and incremental increases for each condition or combination of conditions. The requirements are found in separate sections or chapters of the code that specifically address Assembly uses. As you can see, there are several factors that influence these widths, and you must determine the specific requirements that are consistent with your project design.

Aisle accessways as allowed by the code will not meet the clearance requirements of the accessibility standards. Additional clearance is usually required to maneuver a wheelchair. For this reason, accessible seating is typically provided along the main aisles, at the rear or front of grouped seating. However, an appropriate amount of accessible seating must be provided. In some cases an aisle accessway is used to allow movement from one side of the seating area to the other or to reach an accessible seat location, in those cases additional width beyond the minimum code width may be necessary to be accessible.

Remember that aisles and aisle accessways can be created by a variety of interior furnishings and elements, including banks of filing cabinets, kiosks, chairs, copiers, and similar elements. In Business and Mercantile occupancies, the codes typically require that aisles be a minimum of 44 inches (1117.6 mm). Aisle accessways created by display units in Mercantile occupancies, however, can be a minimum of 30 inches

☑ Note

Aisle accessways have special width requirements and can usually be less than the width of an aisle.

(760 mm). However, these minimums are not wide enough to provide an accessible path. Where an accessible path is required, the aisles and aisle accessways may need to be wider.

Adjoining or Intervening Rooms

Although an exit access should be as direct as possible, some projects may require an egress path to pass through an adjoining room or space before reaching a corridor or exit. Most of the codes will allow this if the path provides a direct, unobstructed, and obvious means of travel toward an exit. Such a path may be as simple as a route within a medical clinic that requires passing through the waiting room to reach the building corridor.

It is this requirement that allows smaller rooms adjoining larger spaces to exit through the large room to access a corridor. For example, several private offices might surround an open office area. Some other common adjoining or intervening rooms that are not restricted by the codes include reception areas, lobbies, and foyers. To be allowed to pass through an adjoining room or area, the areas must be accessory to one another, as well. (Exit access cannot pass through Hazardous occupancies, regardless.)

There are some rooms or spaces through which the codes will not allow or will limit exit access. Exit access cannot rely on passage through rooms that tend to be locked some or all of the time, such as storage rooms, private offices, secured rooms, restrooms, closets, bedrooms, and other similar spaces subject to locking. Exit access in dwelling units cannot lead through other sleeping areas or toilet/bathrooms. Rooms that are more susceptible to fire hazards, such as kitchens and file rooms, are also restricted. Exit Access passage through the storeroom or a Mercantile occupancy and through adjacent tenants is limited, as well. (See the inset titled "Rooms and Spaces" in Chapter 3.)

> **❖ Note**
>
> Elements that create aisles or aisle accessways may be movable or fixed. However, the furniture layout must provide the required egress and accessible path without requiring moving any elements.

EXITS

At the end of the exit access is an *exit*. There are four main types of exits typical to an interior project: exterior exit doors, enclosed exit stairways, horizontal exits, and exit passageways. Some are more common than others. In addition, an exit may include an area of refuge. These are explained throughout this section.

Except for exterior exit doors, exit components are typically separated from other parts of the building with rated construction. A typical example of an enclosed and rated exit is a stairway. The typical fire rating for an exit component is 1 or 2 hours. Some stairwells and other exits must be smoke protected as well. (See Chapter 7 for additional fire rating and smoke protection information.)

An exit must lead an occupant into an exit discharge or directly into a public way. The codes direct the quantity, location, and size requirements for exits. These are explained later in this chapter. Other basic code requirements and accessibility standards are similar to those for exit accesses, as described in the previous section.

Exterior Exit Doors

An exterior exit door is the most common type of exit and simply consists of a doorway. It is located in the exterior wall of the building and typically leads from the ground floor of the building to the open air of an exit discharge or a public way. For example, it might be a door at the bottom of an exit stair, at the end of an exit access corridor, or out of a building lobby on the ground floor. In older buildings, there may be an exterior door on each floor that leads to a fire escape attached to the exterior of the building. An exterior door is not typically required to be rated unless the exterior wall is rated because of the potential exposure to fire from an adjacent building. (All the code requirements for exit access doors as described earlier in "Doorways" in the section "Exit Accesses" apply to this door as well.) Depending on the occupancy type and occupant load, this door may be operated by lever hardware, panic, or fire exit hardware.

Exit Stairs

An exit stair is the most common type of enclosed exit. It includes the stair enclosure, any doors opening into or exiting out of the stairway enclosure, and the stairs and landings inside the enclosure. What makes an exit stair different from other stairs is that its enclosure must be constructed of rated assemblies. (See Chapter 6.)

Exit stair widths are determined in the same manner as the widths of other exits, as explained later in this chapter. The doors of an exit stair must swing in the direction of the exit discharge. In other words, all the doors swing into the stairway except at the ground level, where the door swings toward the exit discharge or public way. (The basic stair requirements are described earlier under "Stairways" in the section "Exit Accesses." See also, Figures 5.5–5.7 and 5.8.) Exit stairs may also include an area of refuge if required by the codes. This is explained in the next subsection.

Note

Although the means of egress is typically not allowed to pass through a storage areas, it is allowed under certain conditions in a Mercantile occupancy.

Note

The required minimum width of an exit stair can vary between 36 inches (914 mm) and 56 inches (1420 mm), depending on the occupancy, occupant load, and accessibility requirements.

Note

When exit stairs continue past the level of exit discharge at grade level, an approved barrier must be used. Typically, a gate (e.g., a metal gate) is installed at the grade-level landing of the stair to prevent occupants from continuing to the basement or sublevels during an emergency.

SPECIAL EGRESS STRATEGIES

Most of the time when a fire or emergency occurs, the code provides for a safe evacuation of building occupants. However, in some occupancies and for some occupants it is unsafe or impractical to leave or be removed from where they are. In these cases, the code requirements are based on a defend in place strategy. In that case, an occupant may not be expected to leave the space, building floor, or building but can go to or stay in a protected compartment of the building. A typical example is an area of refuge for disabled persons in any multistory occupancy. (See the section titled "Areas of Refuge.")

However, the most common use of a defend in place strategy is in health care occupancies, such as hospitals and ambulatory care facilities, or occupancies with high security needs such as correctional/detention facilities. Horizontal exits can be used for hospitals and ambulatory care and correctional/detention occupancies as part of the means of egress (See the section titled "Horizontal Exits.") However, for hospitals and ambulatory care facilities where patients may be unconscious or sedated, moving patients may not be feasible. To limit the exposure of patients to fire or smoke, the codes require most hospital and ambulatory care floors to be separated into more than one smoke compartment. These smoke compartments are used like a horizontal exit, in that patients can be moved from one compartment to the other for safety. Because the walls are required to be smoke partitions or rated, additional protection is provided. Smoke compartments must be sized to accommodate patients from the adjacent smoke compartment.

In addition, the codes also recognize different types of care suites within a typical hospital. For each type of care suite, the codes provide requirements that affect the configuration, travel distances, allowable number of intervening rooms, and so on. In addition, evacuation plans and additional training of staff to initiate and carry out the defend in place strategy is required. If special mean of egress must be provided, additional research will be required.

Horizontal Exits

A horizontal exit is different from the other exits because it does not lead a person to the exterior of a building. Instead, it provides a protected path to a safe refuge area. This refuge area may be another part of the same building or an adjoining building. As the name implies, there is no change in level. This allows the occupants to move into a safe zone where they can either wait for help or use another exit to safely leave the building. A horizontal exit can also be a part of a defend in place means of egress strategy for a building.

The components of a horizontal exit consist of the walls that create the enclosure around the areas of refuge and the doors through these walls. Plan A of Figure 5.13 shows an example of a horizontal exit in a one-story building. In this case, a horizontal exit is used for one of the

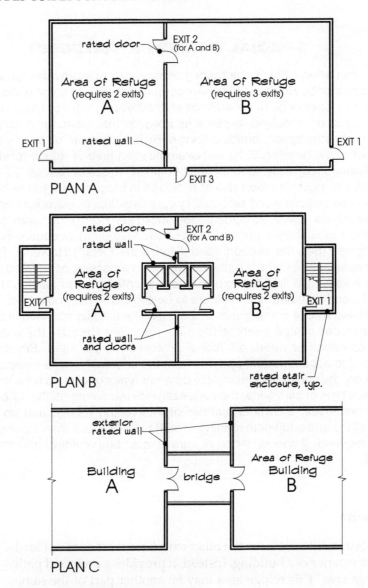

Figure 5.13 Horizontal exit examples.

☝ Note

The codes place certain limitations on a horizontal exit, such as the number of exit locations, size, and the number of occupants it can serve.

two required exits from Area A and one of the three required exits from Area B. Plan B of Figure 5.13 indicates the horizontal exits between the rated walls of a building core and the exterior wall. In this example, occupants from Area A can exit into Area B, and vice versa, because there are doors that swing in both directions of travel. Thus, each area serves as the area of refuge for the other area. When the horizontal exit leads to another building, such as in Plan C of Figure 5.13, structural features such as balconies and bridges can also be used. In this example, a horizontal exit is used for Building A into Building B, but Building B is not using the horizontal exit into Building A. This can be determined because the doors swing only in the direction of Building B. (Building B, therefore, must have the required number of exits without using the horizontal exit.)

The codes specify how to determine the additional area that must be provided in the refuge area to hold the occupants who come through the horizontal exit. This may vary based on occupancy classification and use. For example, the typical factor is 3 square feet (0.28 sm) per person for most occupancies, but for occupancies where occupants are confined to beds, 30 square feet (2.8 sm) may be required. It is assumed that this additional area is required for people to wait or to travel through to the next exit.

Because they are part of an exit, the codes place strict requirements on the components of a horizontal exit. The walls and doors used to make the separation must be fire rated. (See the section "Horizontal Exits" in Chapter 6 for more information.) As an exit, the doors must swing in the direction of exit travel toward the refuge area. If the horizontal exit has a refuge area on both sides of the horizontal exit, two doors must be used together, each swinging in the opposite direction, to serve the occupants on either side. (See Figure 5.13A and 5.13B in Plan B.) In most cases, horizontal exits can be used for only a portion of the total number of required exits. The number allowed varies according to the occupancy classification. A horizontal exit cannot serve as the only exit in any case.

Horizontal exits can be used in any occupancy classification. They can be considered part of an accessible means of egress required by the codes. The most common use is in Institutional occupancies. Hospitals use horizontal exits to divide a floor into two or more refuge areas. This allows the employees to roll patients' beds into safe areas should a fire occur. Prisons also use horizontal exits so that a fire can be contained, and the entire prison will not have to be evacuated in an emergency. Other types of buildings that commonly use horizontal exits are large factories, storage facilities, and high-rise buildings.

Exit Passageways

An *exit passageway* is a type of horizontal route or corridor that provides the same level of protection as an exit stair. An exit passageway must be a fully enclosed, fire-rated corridor that consists of the surrounding walls, the floor, the ceiling, and the doors leading into the passageway. It is most commonly used to extend an exit and must typically be the same width as the adjacent exit as well as have the same level of fire protection.

> ✎ **Note**
>
> Doors within the exit access typically must swing in the direction of travel to the exit.

> ✎ **Note**
>
> The length of an exit passageway cannot exceed the maximum dead-end corridor length.

> ✎ **Note**
>
> Exit access doors at rooms with limited occupant loads such as offices do not have to swing in the direction of exit travel.

For example, an exit passageway can be used to extend an exit to the exterior of the building, as indicated in Plan A of Figure 5.14. In this example, the exit stair empties into a corridor instead of directly to the exterior of the building. Because it has the same rating as the stair, occupants leaving the exit stair are still in a protected enclosure until they reach the exterior of the building. In this case, the exit passageway may be considered an exit discharge component of the means of egress. (See the section titled "Exit Discharges" later in this chapter.)

☑ **Note**

In some cases, an exit passageway can have an occupied room or rooms exit directly into it; however, because it is a rated corridor, the codes limit the types of rooms and require rated doors. Refer to the codes for specific requirements.

Another way to use an exit passageway is to bring an exit closer to the occupants in the building, as shown in Plans B and C of Figure 5.14. This is especially useful when needing to shorten a travel distance. (Travel distance is explained later in this chapter.) For example, if the travel distance to the door of an exit stair is 10 feet (3048 mm) longer than allowed, instead of relocating the exit stair an exit passageway can be added leading to the door of the exit stair, as shown in Plan B. The door of this newly created exit passageway is now the endpoint for measuring the travel distance. This can also be used to bring an exterior exit door closer to the interior of the building, as shown in Plan C of Figure 5.14. In both cases, the travel distance to the exit is reduced. This strategy may be useful in older existing buildings being renovated for new uses.

An exit access such as a door leading out of a tenant space can also exit into an exit passageway, as indicated in Plan D of Figure 5.14. This typically occurs on the ground floor of a building when secondary exits are required. In addition, when the tenants occupy the perimeter of the building, an exit passageway may be created between two of the tenants so that an exterior door can be reached off the common corridor. This is often seen in malls and office buildings with center building cores.

Emergency Escape and Rescue Opening

An emergency escape and rescue opening is often required in residential occupancies in addition to the means of egress system as explained so far in this chapter. Their intent is to provide a way directly out of the room to the exterior incase the egress path has become blocked or is already dangerous. It may also be used by emergency personnel to rescue someone from that space. Under the I-Codes, emergency escape and rescue openings are typically required for Residential occupancies covered by the *IBC* and single- and two-family dwellings covered by the *IRC*. (The NFPA codes have similar requirements.) If an R-2 occupancy is located on a floor with only one exit, then an emergency escape and rescue opening is required. They are also required for R-3 and R-4 occupancies. Although at least one is required in these occupancies, they are also specifically

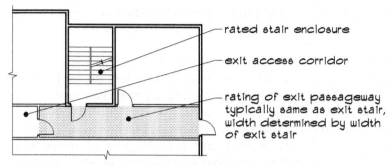

rated stair enclosure

exit access corridor

rating of exit passageway
typically same as exit stair,
width determined by width
of exit stair

PLAN A - Connecting Exit Stair to Exterior Exit

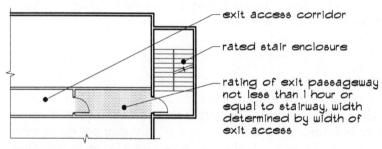

exit access corridor

rated stair enclosure

rating of exit passageway
not less than 1 hour or
equal to stairway, width
determined by width of
exit access

PLAN B - Extending Exit Stair

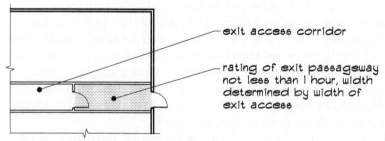

exit access corridor

rating of exit passageway
not less than 1 hour, width
determined by width of
exit access

PLAN C - Extending Exterior Exit

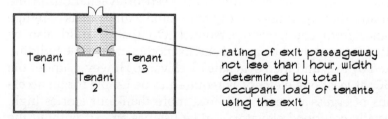

Tenant
1

Tenant
3

Tenant
2

rating of exit passageway
not less than 1 hour, width
determined by total
occupant load of tenants
using the exit

PLAN D - Connecting Tenants to Exterior Exit

Figure 5.14 Exit passageway examples.

required in basements and sleeping rooms below the fourth story. They may not be required for small unhabitable basements, storm shelters, or if the building is sprinklered.

Emergency escape and rescue opening can be either an operable window or a door to the outside. The bottom of the window cannot be more than 44 inches (1118 mm) above the floor so that a person can easily reach it. The window must also have a clear opening of a certain area and minimum height and width dimensions that allows a person to exit through the window in case of a fire or other emergency. Egress windows from floors above the grade level are required to be slightly larger than those from the ground floor. If a door is provided instead of a window, the code requires it to meet the same dimension as a window, although a typical door would exceed these requirements.

Elevators

There are two basic types of elevators: freight and passenger elevators. In most cases, elevators are not used as part of the required means of egress for a space or building. That means that typically *they are not counted* when determining the total number of exits provided in a building. Instead, elevators are typically used for convenience by occupants of the building. However, elevators are linked to a building's smoke alarm system and when a smoke or fire detector is activated during a fire, the elevators automatically are recalled to an approved location (usually the ground floor). Firefighters can then use the elevators to access the upper floors to fight the fire and assist in the evacuation of disabled occupants. Because they are not used for typical occupant evacuation, directional signage is required in the elevator lobby as well as a diagram that identifies the direction to the nearest exit for occupants.

In certain situations, however, elevators can be used to evacuate occupants. There are two reasons that elevators would be used as part of the means of egress: accessibility and speed of evacuation. In the past, occupants that could not exit by stair would wait in areas of refuge for assistance from emergency personnel. Occupants could also be required to exit through a horizontal exit to another area of the building (not affected by fire) and then evacuate by elevator. However, under the current *IBC*, at least one elevator is required to be usable for an accessible means of egress in most buildings more than four stories high. These specially equipped elevators can be used as an exit without the use of an area of refuge or horizontal exit if the building is sprinklered.

For an elevator to be considered part of the means of egress, additional code provisions must be met. These requirements affect its location

☑ **Note**

Accessible elevator requirements differ for private dwelling units and commercial buildings. Check the *ADA Standards*, the *FHAG*, and the *ICC A117.1* standard for specifics.

ELEVATORS

Although new code requirements allow an increased use of elevators as a means of egress, especially in high-rise buildings, they are typically not used as part of the means of egress during an emergency. However, because they are used on a daily basis during normal operation, elevators must meet specific accessibility requirements as defined in the codes, the *ADA Standards,* and the *ICC A117.1* standard. The following list includes some of the more common requirements. (Diagrams are available in the ADA and *ICC A117.1* standards.)

❏ Automatic operation with self-leveling within a certain range

❏ Power-operated sliding doors that open to a minimum width

❏ Door delay and automatic reopening device effective for a specific time period

❏ Certain size car, depending on the location and size of the sliding door (longer cabs allow for the transport of beds and gurneys should it be required)

❏ Hall call buttons and car controls with a specific arrangement, location, and height (including Braille and raised lettering)

❏ Minimum distances from hall call button to elevator door

❏ Hall lanterns and car position indicators that are visual and audible

❏ Specific two-way emergency communication system

❏ Handrail on at least one wall of the car

❏ Floor surfaces that are firm, stable, and slip resistant buildings, but many additional code requirements must be met

within the building, the construction of the elevator shaft, the type of elevator cab, and the controls of the elevator. The elevator itself must comply with emergency operation and signaling device requirements, as specified in *ANSI/ASME A17.1, Safety Code for Elevators and Escalators,* and be provided with standby power. Other special mechanical and electrical requirements apply as well. The elevator may require an adjacent area of refuge, an enclosed fire-rated lobby (as shown in Plan C of Figure 5.15), and two-way communication.

Because of all the specific requirements, the decision to include an elevator as an exit is typically made during the initial design of the building and is usually not part of an interior project or renovation. Retrofitting an existing elevator and shaft in most cases would be costly. Currently, using elevators as exits even in new buildings is not as common as providing areas of refuge in stairways and at elevator lobbies. However, more consideration is being given to the way elevators can be used for evacuation of occupants. This will become an

◁ Note

Elevators can be an efficient option to evacuate occupants from the multiple floors of high-rise buildings. This became especially apparent during review of the events of September 11, 2001. However, additional requirements must be met to make them safe for this use.

☑ Note

Platform lifts are a form
of elevator. They are
usually used in existing
buildings when short
vertical distances must
be covered for accessi-
bility reasons and a ramp
is not feasible. Most are
not allowed as a means
of egress.

increasingly important option as high-rise buildings are built to extreme heights.

Even if elevators are not to be used as exits, when they are included in a building, typically at least one is required to be accessible for use by persons with disabilities. (There is an exception in the ADA for some two-story buildings.) Many new buildings are required to make all passenger elevators accessible. If the elevators are existing, they must be made as accessible as possible. (See the inset titled "Elevators" in this chapter.) New or replacement elevators are usually designed in conjunction with an engineer or an elevator consultant.

AREAS OF REFUGE

Sometimes the codes determine that the characteristics or condition of the occupants in a building or space should not or are not capable of immediately exiting the building in the event of a fire or emergency. In this case, a defend in place strategy may be enforced by the codes. Typically, this requires that the building or space be separated by fire-rated and/or smoke partitions into at least two areas. The secondary space that is created is referred to as the *area of refuge*, or *refuge area*. The codes require areas of refuge to be provided in buildings of many occupancies and uses. Area of refuges can be part of a smoke compartment, storm shelter, horizontal exit, and an accessible means of egress.

Although they are similar in that they provide temporary protection for occupants, each type has different requirements and different space allocations. Smoke compartments are required in correctional and health care facilities including ambulatory care facilities. A smoke compartment is formed when the building area is separate into at least two compartments; they are not dedicated spaces. Storm shelters are required but the codes where severe weather like hurricanes and tornados are prevalent and in all Educational occupancies with a few exceptions. They do not have to be dedicated areas, that is, not used for any other purpose, but they must have the required free floor area to accommodate the required number of occupants. Storm shelters must be constructed to comply with *ICC 500, Standard for the Design and Construction of Storm Shelters*. Likewise, the area of refuge for a horizontal exit typically is corridor space and open areas in the general layout of the adjacent space. However, this needs to be planned for in the initial design.

Areas of refuge as part of an accessible means of egress is one type of area of refuge that is typically dedicated clear space. They are usually provided adjacent to exit stairwells, in exit stairwells, or at elevator lobbies as indicated in Figure 5.15.

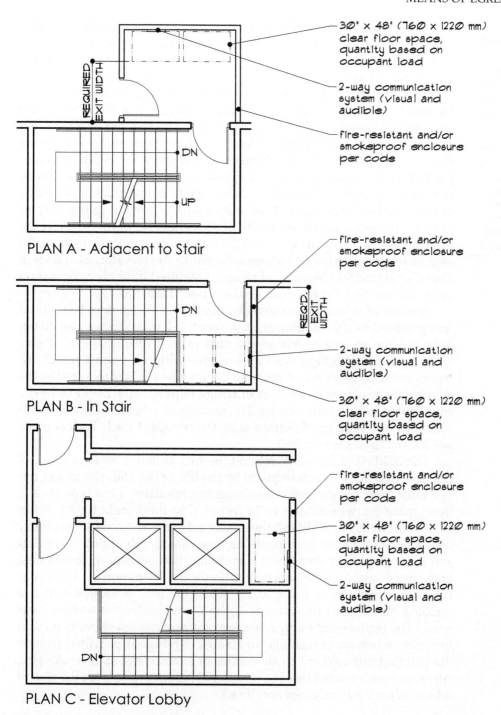

30" x 48" (760 x 1220 mm)
clear floor space,
quantity based on
occupant load

2-way communication
system (visual and
audible)

fire-resistant and/or
smokeproof enclosure
per code

REQUIRED EXIT WIDTH

DN

UP

PLAN A - Adjacent to Stair

fire-resistant and/or
smokeproof enclosure
per code

DN

REQD. EXIT WIDTH

2-way communication
system (visual and
audible)

30" x 48" (760 x 1220 mm)
clear floor space,
quantity based on
occupant load

PLAN B - In Stair

fire-resistant and/or
smokeproof enclosure
per code

30" x 48" (760 x 1220 mm)
clear floor space,
quantity based on
occupant load

2-way communication
system (visual and
audible)

DN

PLAN C - Elevator Lobby

Figure 5.15 Area of refuge examples.

Note

The most current edition of the *IBC* does not require areas of refuge in a sprinklered building.

 Note

When an area of refuge is used in conjunction with an exit stair, the minimum stair width required by the codes will usually increase.

An area of refuge located adjacent to an exit stair provides room for wheelchairs while maintaining the required exit width to the exit stairway, as shown in Plan A of Figure 5.15. When an area of refuge is located within an exit stairwell, the landings at the doors entering the stair are enlarged so that one or more occupants in a wheelchair can safely wait for assistance without blocking the means of egress at the landing and stair. This is shown in Plan B of Figure 5.15. The number of wheelchair spaces that must be provided is determined by the occupant load of the floor. The most common requirement is one space for every 200 occupants. (Other accessible means of egress on the same floor level can be considered as well.) Although the egress width of an exit stair is usually determined by the occupant load, a stair with an area of refuge may be required to have a minimum width of 48 inches (1219 mm) to allow the disabled person to be carried down the stair by emergency personnel. An area of refuge can also be located adjacent to the elevator, as shown in Plan C of Figure 5.15. An area of refuge is required if the elevator is serving as an exit. (See the previous section titled "Elevators.")

An area of refuge is required at exit stairs and elevators being used for egress unless the building is sprinklered. R-2 occupancies also do not have to have an area of refuge at a stair even if unsprinklered. If provided, the area of refuge must be available within the same travel distance limitation as an exit. If both the *IBC* and the *LSC* are required by the jurisdiction of a project, the area of refuge requirements may need to be coordinated with a code official. The number of wheelchair locations in each area of refuge are determined by the occupant load. Typically one per 200 occupants is required.

The *2010 ADA Standards* rely on the *IBC* to define when an area of refuge is necessary. When required by the *IBC* or the *LSC*, the area of refuge must meet the general accessibility requirements. (The typical clear floor space for wheelchairs is 30 inches (760 mm) wide by 48 inches (1219 mm) long.) In addition, the area of refuge is required to be clearly identified with visual and tactile signage directing building occupants and have a two-way emergency communication system. In some cases, both visual and audible communication must be provided. The codes typically use the term *area of refuge* when the area is located within a building. (In the 1991 ADA standard, the term *area of rescue assistance* was used.) The term *area of rescue assistance* or *area of assisted rescue* is used in the codes when an area similar to an area of refuge is provided outside the building but adjacent to an interior or exterior exit stair or elevator. An area of rescue assistance has additional requirements from the area of refuge. (Check the codes for specifics.)

EXIT DISCHARGES

An *exit discharge* is the part of a means of egress that connects an exit with a public way. It is typically found on the ground floor of a building; however, in older buildings, a fire escape is sometimes described as an exit discharge—connecting the exterior exit door(s) on each level to the sidewalk or alley. The required fire rating of an exit discharge will vary, depending on the type and where it is located. In some types of exit discharge, the enclosure may be allowed to have a lower rating than the exit it serves.

The first three exit discharges described in this section are used on the interior of a building. Others are exterior exit discharges. The width of an exit discharge is typically dictated by the width of the exit it is supporting, but accessibility requirements must be taken into consideration as well. Usually, when more than one exit leads into the exit discharge, the width of the exit discharge is a sum of these exit widths. In existing buildings, an existing exit discharge may dictate the maximum size of an interior means of egress. The key to determining if an exit discharge exists is that it occurs after a protected exit. A few common examples are explained next. Many of these are also shown in Figure 5.2.

Exit Lobby

One of the most common interior exit discharges occurs when an exit stair empties into the main lobby of a building. The distance between the door of the exit stair and the exterior exit door is then an exit discharge. An example is shown in Figure 5.2. Although furniture, decorations, and other rooms opening into an exit stair are not allowed, they are allowed in the exit discharge. In most cases, the lobby is required continue the separation from other areas of the building by fire-rated walls equal to the stairway. Every lobby is not considered an exit discharge. For example, the lobby shown in Figure 5.13D is not an exit discharge because it connects exit accesses, not exits. An exit discharge occurs only after a protected exit.

> **☞ Note**
>
> According to the *IBC* and the *LSC*, exit lobbies must have access to at least one exit without going through a locked door. This exit will typically be one of the exit stairways for the building floor.

Exit Foyer or Vestibule

An interior exit discharge can include an enclosed foyer or vestibule. These are small enclosures on the ground floor of a building between the end of a corridor or exit stair and an exterior exit door. An example is labeled and shown in Figure 5.2. These spaces cannot be used for any other purpose other than for egress from the exit—not even for vending machines. In addition, the energy codes (see Chapter 9) often require these to separate conditioned interior spaces from the outside air.

Depending on whether the building is sprinklered, the foyer or vestibule may be required to have the same rating as the corridor or stair. The distance of the foyer or vestibule is limited as well. However, the *ADA Standards* and *ICC A117.1* will require the space to be large enough to allow adequate maneuvering clearance within the vestibule or foyer and the swing of the doors. (See Plan A in Figure 5.4.)

Discharge Corridor

 Note

The codes have some exceptions for interior exit discharges in certain occupancies, especially Detentional/Correctional. Check the specific occupancies in the codes for details.

Occasionally, a corridor is considered an exit discharge. Usually, this occurs in older buildings where an exit stair empties into a ground floor corridor. The corridor connecting the exit stairs to the exterior exit door becomes an exit discharge corridor. Usually this is not recommended and is allowed only if the entire exit corridor is rated and protected by automatic sprinklers. (See the codes for specifics.)

Egress Court

An *egress court* is an exterior exit discharge, as shown in Figure 5.2. It can be a courtyard, patio, or other type of partially enclosed exterior area. It is the portion of the exit that connects the exterior exit door to the public way.

Small Alley or Sidewalk

If the width of an alley or sidewalk is less than 10 feet (3048 mm), it cannot be considered a public way. Instead, it becomes an exterior exit discharge that continues the means of egress path until it comes to a larger alley, sidewalk, or street that meets the requirements of a public way. An example is the alley shown in Figure 5.2. The sidewalk in this figure would also be considered an exit discharge if it were less than 10 feet (3048 mm) wide.

MEANS OF EGRESS CAPACITY

The capacity of the means of egress reflects the number of people who can safely exit a building in an emergency. This part of the chapter concentrates on determining means of egress capacities. It answers the questions: How many? How large? In what locations? The main factors to be determined include the required number of exits, width of exits, arrangement of exits, and allowable travel distance to an exit. These means of egress issues must be considered on any interior project, whether changing a room, a tenant space, one floor, or an entire building. Dead-end corridors and common paths of travel must also be considered. Each is explained in the next few subsections.

In most cases, an interior project will not change the exiting capacity of the building itself. Exits for an entire building are determined during the initial building design, and they usually allow for future changes within the building. However, there may be instances when redesigning an entire floor increases the occupant load, requiring additional exits or enlarged exits. For example, a new occupant may trigger the updating of the exits to meet a more current code, or a different occupant type or greater occupant load may require additional exits.

Each aspect of exit capacity is dependent on the others. So, in many cases, it may be necessary to work back and forth in the calculations to determine the final number and widths of exits. For example, the required exit width at a particular exit location will depend on the total number of exits provided from the space or building. But the number and location of required exits depend on the occupant load and maximum travel distances. If any of these changes or exceed the maximum requirements, the calculations have to be adjusted. The requirements must be determined using the building codes and the *LSC* as well as any accessibility requirements, such as those found in the ADA and *ICC A117.1* standards. Because the means of egress affects the layout of the space, it may be advisable to review with the code official review early in the design of the project. (See Chapter 11.)

> ☑ **Note**
>
> When determining means of egress, two things are important: egress capacity (number and width) and egress *arrangement* (locations and travel distances).

Number of Exits

The number of exits from a space or building floor is not simply the total number of doors from the space but the number of distinct locations from which to exit the space. A single exit location for a large space could be

Note

When an interior project involves only part of a building or floor, the exit capacity for the project area must be checked. However, it is also important to make sure that changes caused by the project do not affect the requirements of the other existing building exits. In some cases, the existing exits may have to be increased or the occupant load may need to be limited to fit the existing exit capacity.

Note

Occupant load and travel distance can affect the required number of exits.

composed of multiple doors. Typically, the required number of exit locations should be established before determining the total width required for each exit. Most of the codes require a minimum of two exits, whether they are for an entire building, a building floor, or an individual space within the building. However, there are exceptions that will be discussed.

The number of exits required for a specific building floor level is determined by the occupant load of that floor level and the number of exits required for a specific space is based on the occupant load of the space. When a floor has multiple occupancies, uses, or more than one tenant, the occupant load of each occupant, use, or tenant must be calculated and added together to get the total occupant load for the floor. If determining the number of exits for a particular room, space, or tenant within the building, only the occupant load for that area need be calculated. (Refer to Chapter 3 for a more detailed explanation of occupant loads and how to calculate them.)

Once the occupant load for the space or entire floor is established, refer to the building codes and/or the *LSC* to determine the required number of exit locations. The requirements are summarized in the *IBC* chart, Table 1006.3.1: Minimum Number of Exits or Access to Exits per Story, shown in Figure 5.16.

As you can see from the Table 1006.3.3 the lowest number of exits allowed from a room, floor, or building is two exits. However, each of the codes allows exceptions for a single exit. The allowance for a single exit from a space is based on occupant classification, occupant load, and whether the building is sprinklered. See Figure 5.17, *IBC* Table 1006.2.1, "Spaces with One Exit or Exit Access Doorway." This indicates when a single exit is allowed from a room or area such as a large training room or tenant space. The allowance for a single exit from a building story is

TABLE 1006.3.3 MINIMUM NUMBER OF EXITS OR ACCESS TO EXITS PER STORY

OCCUPANT LOAD PER STORY	MINIMUM NUMBER OF EXITS OR ACCESS TO EXITS FROM STORY
1–500	2
501–1,000	3
More than 1,000	4

Figure 5.16 International Building Code Table 1006.3.3, "Minimum Number of Exits or Access to Exits per Story" (2021 *International Building Code*, copyright © 2021. Washington, DC: International Code Council, Washington, DC: International Code Council. Reproduced with permission. All rights reserved. www.iccsafe.org).

TABLE 1006.2.1 SPACES WITH ONE EXIT OR EXIT ACCESS DOORWAY

OCCUPANCY	MAXIMUM OCCUPANT LOAD OF SPACE	MAXIMUM COMMON PATH OF EGRESS TRAVEL DISTANCE (feet)		
		Without Sprinkler System (feet)		With Sprinkler System (feet)
		Occupant Load		
		OL ≤ 30	OL > 30	
A^c, E, M	49	75	75	75^a
B	49	100	75	100^a
F	49	75	75	100^a
H-1, H-2, H-3	3	NP	NP	25^b
H-4, H-5	10	NP	NP	75^b
I-1, I-2^d, I-4	10	NP	NP	75^a
I-3	10	NP	NP	100^a
R-1	10	NP	NP	75^a
R-2	20	NP	NP	125^a
R-3^e	20	NP	NP	125^a, g
R-4^e	20	NP	NP	125^a, g
S^f	29	100	75	100^a
U	49	100	75	75^a

For SI: 1 foot = 304.8 mm.

NP = Not Permitted.

a Buildings equipped throughout with an automatic sprinkler system in accordance with Section 903.3.1.1 or 903.3.1.2. See Section 903 for occupancies where automatic sprinkler systems are permitted in accordance with Section 903.3.1.2.

b Group H occupancies equipped throughout with an automatic sprinkler system in accordance with Section 903.2.5.

c For a room or space used for assembly purposes having fixed seating, see Section 1030.8.

d For the travel distance limitations in Group I-2, see Section 407.4.

e The common path of egress travel distance shall only apply in a Group R-3 occupancy located in a mixed occupancy building.

f The length of common path of egress travel distance in a Group S-2 open parking garage shall be not more than 100 feet.

g For the travel distance limitations in Groups R-3 and R-4 equipped throughout with an automatic sprinkler system in accordance with Section 903.3.1.3, see Section 1006.2.2.6.

Figure 5.17 *International Building Code,* Table 1006.2.1, "Spaces with One Exit or Exit Access Doorway," copyright © 2021. Washington, DC: International Code Council. Reproduced with permission. All rights reserved. www.iccsafe.org).

indicated in Figure 5.18: *IBC* Table 1006.3.4(2), "Stories with One Exit or Access to One Exit for Other Occupancies" As shown in Table 1006.3.4(2) a single exit is allowed from a story or floor level based on distance above grade, the occupancy, occupant load, and the exit access travel distance. The floor or space must meet all of these requirements to be allowed a

TABLE 1006.3.4(2) STORIES WITH ONE EXIT OR ACCESS TO ONE EXIT FOR OTHER OCCUPANCIES

STORY	OCCUPANCY	MAXIMUM OCCUPANT LOAD PER STORY	MAXIMUM *EXIT ACCESS* TRAVEL DISTANCE (feet)
First story above or below *grade plane*	A, Bᵇ, E, Fᵇ, M, U	49	75
	H-2, H-3	3	25
	H-4, H-5, I, R-1, R-2ᵃ, ᶜ	10	75
	Sᵇ, ᵈ	29	75
Second *story above grade plane*	B, F, M, Sᵈ	29	75
Third *story above grade plane* and higher	NP	NA	NA

For SI: 1 foot = 304.8 mm.

NP = Not Permitted.

NA = Not Applicable.

a Buildings classified as Group R-2 equipped throughout with an automatic sprinkler system in accordance with Section 903.3.1.1 or 903.3.1.2 and provided with emergency escape and rescue openings in accordance with Section 1031.

b Group B, F and S occupancies in buildings equipped throughout with an automatic sprinkler system in accordance with Section 903.3.1.1 shall have a maximum exit access travel distance of 100 feet.

c This table is used for R-2 occupancies consisting of sleeping units. For R-2 occupancies consisting of dwelling units, use Table 1006.3.4(1).

d The length of exit access travel distance in a Group S-2 open parking garage shall be not more than 100 feet.

Figure 5.18 Table 1006.3.4(2), "Stories with One Exit or Access to One Exit for Other Occupancies" (2021 International Building Code, copyright © 2021. Washington, DC: International Code Council. Reproduced with permission. All rights reserved. www.iccsafe.org).

> **☑ Note**
>
> None of the codes specifically requires more than four exits in a building because of occupant load. Yet additional exits may be required to meet the exit distance requirements in larger spaces or buildings.

> **☑ Note**
>
> In some projects, the occupant load may be able to be increased by providing additional exits. This usually means increasing the provisions of every exit requirement.

single exit. The NFPA codes provide similar information within their texts. Each code has additional exceptions to using a single exit or the number of exits in general. For example, in the *IBC* rooms or spaces in day care facilities with only one exit are limited to the care of 10 infants or toddlers. Or, for example, when multiple occupancies want to use the single exit rules, additional requirements must be met. If it is necessary to design the space with a single exit, check the specific occupancy section of the code publications to determine the exceptions.

It is important to remember when verifying the required number of exits for a multistory building that the number of exits cannot decrease as occupants proceed along the egress path toward the public way. Therefore, the floor with the largest occupant load determines the number of required exits for all lower floors. For example, if the floor with the highest occupant load is in the middle of the building, all the floors below it must have the same number of exits. This is easily accomplished by additional exit stairwells starting on the floor with the highest occupant load and continuing down. (See the Example that follows.)

Several occupancy classifications have specific requirements that can affect the number of exits that must be integrated into your design. The occupancy classifications with the most exceptions and special requirements are Assembly, Institutional, and Residential occupancies. The following Example, which describes how to determine the number of exits for an entire building, provides an overall concept for determining exit quantities.

Example

Figure 5.19 is the outlined section of a multistory building. It indicates the occupant load for each floor and the number of exits based on these occupant loads (using the table shown in Figure 5.16). The fourth floor has the largest occupant load, with a total of 1020, and therefore requires the largest number of exits. The code specifies four exits for any occupant load

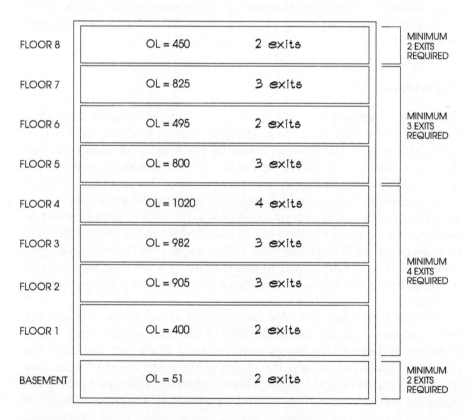

Figure 5.19 Number of exits: Example (multistory building).

over 1000. As a result, every floor below it must also have four exits, even though their occupant loads specify fewer exits. Four separate exit stairs that are continuous from the fourth to the first floor would meet the requirement. The first floor would require the exit doors to be located in four separate locations.

Each of the floors above the fourth floor has a lower occupant load than the fourth floor. Because these floors are above the fourth floor, fewer exits can be used. The seventh floor has the largest occupant load (above the fourth floor), so it controls the exit quantity for the seventh, sixth, and fifth floors. Three exits must be provided for these floors. However, the eighth floor has an even lower occupant load, requiring only two exits. So, in this example, at the eighth floor, only two exit stairs are required; at the seventh floor, a third stair is required; and beginning at the fourth floor, a fourth exit stair is required.

In most cases, these decisions will be made in the initial design and construction of a building. However, in some cases, when the use of an existing building changes significantly, an additional exit stairway may be required.

Exit Widths

☑ **Note**

It is not uncommon for a multistory building to have a large Assembly occupancy on the top floor. If it has the largest occupant load, it can dictate the exit requirements for the exit stairs for the entire building.

☑ **Note**

Exit widths for small spaces such as offices, apartments, and dwelling units will be dictated by the minimum requirements.

The codes determine how many exits are required based on the occupancy load of the space or floor. Then, the size or width of each exit or egress component can be determined by the number of occupants that the codes assume will use the particular egress component on their way to the public way, for example, a door or corridor. For large occupancies, calculations may be necessary. For smaller projects, the minimum widths set by the codes will apply. However, the exit width required cannot be reduced anywhere along the path of travel as it moves toward the exit, exit discharge, and/or public way. (The exception is at some door locations, which is explained later in this chapter.) Therefore, it is important to compare the exit width of each exit component along the exit path to verify that the exit width is maintained.

Similar to the number of exits, required width of the exit components are based on the occupant load of the area or floor they serve. However if determining the exit widths for a multistory building, the number of exits (stairs) and the width of the stairs are determined by the floor with the largest occupant load. Usually, that means figuring the occupant load of every floor to find the one with the largest occupant load. That floor will require the largest exit widths and dictate the exit widths of every floor below it. For example, in Figure 5.19, the fourth floor would determine the width of the exit stairs from the fourth floor down to the first floor.

The total required exit width must be determined for every floor, separate tenant space, or enclosed area. This exit width will ultimately determine the width of each component of the means of egress including the exit doors. To determine the required exit width for a single floor (including multiple tenants), use the occupant load of the entire floor. This will set the size of the doors that lead into the stairway or out of a single-story building. And, if it is a tenant space, use only the occupant load for that tenant space. This will set the size of the doors from the tenant into the corridor. And, if it is a room, use the occupant load of that space. This will set the size of doors that lead from the room or space. Similarly, determining the width of the shared exit access corridor leading from multiple tenant spaces to the exit stairs is based on the total occupant load for that floor.

The codes including the *IBC* and the *LSC* provide separate capacity factors for vertical egress components such as stairs and level components (including ramps). To begin, multiply the occupant load is by the specific width variables base on the width you are trying to determine. This results in the total exit width that is required. If determining the required width of a stairway, the occupant load is multiplied by 0.3 inches (7.62 mm). If the building is sprinklered and provides an emergency/voice alarm system, the occupant load is multiplied by 0.2 inches (5.08 mm) for the width of a stairway. If determining the width of other egress components, such as exit access corridors, aisles, ramps, and exit door widths, multiply the number of occupants using the component by 0.2 inches (5.08 mm). However, if the building is sprinklered and provides an emergency/voice alarm system, in this case you can multiply the occupant load by 0.15 inches (3.8 mm). The difference in the width variables for exit stairs and level exit components is because people travel on stairs at a slower pace and, therefore, could result in more people using the stairwell at one time during an emergency. The larger stair variable requires stairs to be wider than level exits such as corridors and ramps. Therefore, if calculating exit widths for an exit stair that empties into an exit passageway, the stair should be calculated first, because that width may be required to be maintained once occupants leave the stairway.

☑ **Note**

For larger rooms or spaces such as open offices, factories, malls, and assembly spaces, calculating the exit widths will be required to correctly size aisles, corridors, and doorways. The minimum required widths will not be sufficient for the occupant load.

TABLE 7.3.3.1 CAPACITY FACTORS

Area	Stairways (width/person)		Level Components and Ramps (width/person)	
	in.	mm	in.	mm
Board and care	0.4	10	0.2	5
Health care, sprinklered	0.3	7.6	0.2	5
Health care, nonsprinklered	0.6	15	0.5	13
High hazard contents	0.7	18	0.4	10
All others	0.3	7.6	0.2	5

Figure 5.20 Life Safety Code Table 7.3.3.1, "Capacity Factors" Reproduced with permission of NFPA from NFPA 101®, *Life Safety Code*®, 2021 edition. Copyright© 2020, National Fire Protection Association. For a full copy of NFPA 101®, please go to www.nfpa.org.

✍ Note

Handrails on ramps and stairs, trim and decorative features, and other projections may be allowed to project into the required exit width by a specified distance. Check the code for the exact allowable dimension.

The NFPA codes such as the *LSC* have similar requirements. However, the NFPA codes assign different variables for specific occupancy classifications, as shown in Table 7.3.3.1: Capacity Factors in Figure 5.20. These additional variables allow for the difference in occupancy classifications where wider exit widths are needed for faster egress times in more hazardous occupancies. Although in the past the *LSC* assigned a smaller factor for a building equipped with an approved automatic sprinkler system (as did the *IBC*), this is no longer allowed in the *LSC*.

The total exit width must typically be distributed equally among the total number of exits serving the area. For example, the total exit width for an entire floor must be divided among all exits leaving the floor. If the determined width is for a room or tenant space, it is divided among the exits leaving that area. If it is a space that contains aisles or aisle accessways, additional calculations may be required. (See Examples 1 and 2 that follow.) There are exceptions to the distribution for large Assembly occupancies and unique configurations.

When determining exit widths, make note of the following additional requirements. All of them can affect the final width. (Additional requirements may apply for specific occupancies.)

1. **Minimum door widths.** Building codes and accessibility standards require all means of egress doors to provide a minimum clear width of 32 inches (813 mm). In practical terms, a standard 36-inch (914-mm) wide door, when open, will provide 32 inches (813 mm) of clear width. (See Figure 5.3 for a diagram of clear width dimension.) Therefore, if an exit width of 30 inches (760 mm) is calculated, a 36-inch (914-mm) door will still have to be specified. In areas that are not required to be accessible, such as non-accessible showers, toilet stalls or dressing, fitting and changing rooms a minimum clear opening width of 20 inches (508 mm) may be allowed.

2. **Maximum door widths.** Although the codes use to limit the width of a single door in the means of egress to maximum of 4 feet (1220 mm) wide, wider widths are now allowed. However, the use of a 36-inch (914-mm) or 48-inch (1220 mm) wide door is still most common. These can also be used in pairs when wider widths are needed. For example, if 60 inches (1524 mm) of exit width is needed, typically a pair of doors will have to be provided instead of one large door. If two separate 36-inch (914-mm) doors are used, this will provide 64 inches (1630 mm) of clear width. This exceeds the required width but is the closest increment using a typically available door width. (Remember, each single 36-inch (914-mm) wide door must be considered in increments of 32 inches (813 mm) of clear width, which is the minimum for the codes and the accessibility requirements.) If 40 inches (1015 mm) of exit width are required, a 48-inch (1219-mm) door would provide adequate width, whereas a 36-inch (914-mm) door would not and the use of two 36-inch (914-mm) doors might seem excessive.

3. **More than one exit.** The required width of an exit access (e.g., a corridor) can be affected if it leads to more than one exit on the floor that it serves. The codes typically assume that occupants use the exits in an equally distributed manner. So, the total required exit width is distributed equally among the number of exits. Likewise, a corridor that connects two exits can assume that it must only accommodate one half of the total corridor width in each direction. (See Example 1, explained next.)

4. **Minimum exit discharge width.** When an exit discharge, such as a corridor, leads from an exit enclosure, its width cannot be less than that of the exit.

5. **Minimum corridor and stair widths.** In no case can a corridor width or stair width be less than 36 inches (914 mm); however, the typical code minimum is 44 inches (1118 mm), and some codes require accessible stairs to be a minimum of 48 inches (1219 mm) wide. The building codes set additional minimums for certain occupancy classifications. The ADA and *ICC A117.1* standards also specify certain accessibility and clearance requirements that may affect the width of a means of egress. (See Figures 5.4, 5.6, 5.9, and 5.10, as well as Example 1 that follows.)

6. **Exiting from basement.** If a building has a basement that is occupied, some codes require the occupant load of the level of discharge to be increased. The exit discharge on the ground floor would have to allow for the exiting of the basement level(s) in addition to the upper floors. (Not all of the codes require this cumulative effect.)

7. **Minimum horizontal exit sizes.** Horizontal exits are allowed only if the area of refuge created is large enough to accommodate its own occupants and those from the "fire side." For most occupancies, the codes allow 3 square feet (0.28 sm) of floor space per occupant. Increased area for the area of refuge is required for Institutional occupancies. (See the section titled "Horizontal Exits" earlier in this chapter.)

8. **Unobstructed paths.** The exit path must be clear and unobstructed. Unless the codes or accessibility requirements specifically state that a projection is permitted, nothing may reduce the determined exit width. The most common exceptions include a handrail that meets accessibility requirements, a nonstructural trim or wall application less than ½ inch (13 mm) thick, a wall sconce or other device not deeper than 4 inches (100 mm), or a door that does not project more than 7 inches (178 mm) when open. (See Figures 5.4 and 5.11E.)

9. **50 percent rule.** In some occupancies, the expected loss of any one exit location cannot reduce the total capacity of the exit width by more than 50 percent. For example, in a large Assembly occupancy, if multiple exit doors are required at the main entrance/exit and that location becomes blocked by a fire, the total exit width may be reduced significantly. If additional exit locations do not provide for at least 50 percent of the total exit width required, more exit locations or doors at the other exits must be added.

10. **Aisles and aisle accessways.** The codes set additional requirements for aisles and aisle accessways. Different aisle widths are required, depending on whether the aisles are created by fixed seats or movable furniture. The typical minimum width for an aisle between tables and chairs is 44 inches (1118 mm), although the occupant

📝 **Note**

Aisle accessways and horizontal exits have additional variables and specific requirements that must be met. Refer to the codes.

📝 **Note**

A 36-inch [914-mm] wide door will actually only provide 32 inches [813 mm] of clear width when open because of the width of the door and the hinge. The minimum for the codes and the accessibility requirements is 32".

load determines the actual width. Aisle accessways have additional code requirements. (See the section titled "Aisles and Aisle Accessways" earlier in the chapter and Example 2 following.)

The goal of these and other exit requirements is to balance the flow of occupants during an emergency. The goal is to make sure that an occupant can reach an exit and then get through it without any delay.

Example 1: Corridor and Doors

Figure 5.21 is the floor plan of the second floor in a two-story, mixed-use building that is nonsprinklered. Because the building is unsprinklered, the corridor walls are required to be rated and the tenant doors must be

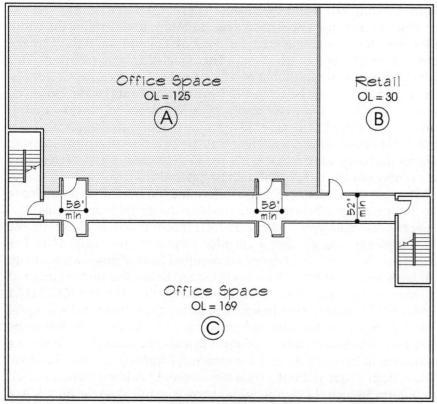

NOTE: Although typical minimum corridor width is 44 inches (1118 mm), additional width is often needed for accessibility clearances. A 60-inch (1524-mm) turning space is usually also required.

Total Occupant Load (OL) = 125 + 30 + 169 = 324

Figure 5.21 Egress width for a mixed occupancy building (nonsprinklered building).

on a closer. The client has requested three tenant spaces to be designed in this vacant floor. The final layout must have the correct number and width of exits. Spaces A and C (Business) are typical tenant office spaces, and Space B is a wholesale retail store (Mercantile). The following process would be used.

Space A

Based on the occupant load, two means of egress leading out of Space A are required. (Referring to the chart shown in Figure 5.16, in the section "Number of Exits," the occupant load of 125 is under 500.) The required width of the exits for Space A must now be determined to confirm that two 36-inch (914-mm) doors are sufficient.

This space is considered a Business occupancy. Using the *LSC* table in Figure 5.20, the exit width variable for "Level Components and Ramps" is 0.2 inch (5 mm) for a nonsprinklered building. To determine the width of the exit doors, take the occupant load of 125 and multiply it by the level exit variable of 0.2 inch (5 mm). This equals 25 inches (635 mm). This is the total required width that must be divided between the two doors. Hence, each door must be at least 12.5 inches (317.5 mm) wide. However, because the code requires all means of egress doors to provide a minimum clear width of 32 inches (813 mm), each door must be specified as a 36-inch (914-mm) wide door. (Note that the 25 inches [635 mm] seems to indicate that only one door or exit is required instead of two. That is why the number of exits required should be determined first.)

The size of the doors will also determine the minimum door alcove into the space and the corridor width within the tenant space. In this case, the corridors must work with a 36-inch (914-mm) door. However, the codes typically specify that a corridor cannot be less than 44 inches (1118 mm). Because tenant doors are required have a closer, accessibility standards require at least 18 inches (445 mm) to be clear on the latch and pull side of the door. (Refer to Figure 5.4 and the ADA and *ICC A117.1* standards.) Therefore, a minimum of 54 inches (36 + 18) (or 1319 mm [914 + 445]) is needed for the door and pull clearance. On the hinge side of the door, a minimum of 4 inches (100 mm) will also be needed to allow for a hollow metal door frame and the structural framing around the door. (This is from a practical not a code requirement.) Adding these together, a minimum 58-inch (1459-mm) wide alcove is required on the pull side of the door.

Inside the tenant space on the push side of the door, accessibility standards require a clearance of 12 inches (305 mm) if a latch and closer are provided (instead of 18 inches [445 mm]). Therefore, the required width on the tenant side can be 52 inches (1319 mm).

◢ Note

The accessibility clearance required at the latch side of a door is measured to the door opening not the door frame.

Floor

This is a mixed occupancy floor. Thus, before determining the exit widths for the entire floor, it is necessary to make sure that the egress width variables are the same for both Group B and Group M occupancies. Referring to the *LSC* table in Figure 5.20, both fall within the category of "all others" and require 0.3 inch (7.5 mm) for stairs and 0.2 inch (5 mm) for level components. (If they were different for the different occupancies, the higher of the two variables would be used.) The occupant loads for each tenant must also be added together to obtain the total for the floor. This total is 324 occupants.

Because the width variable for the stairs will result in a larger width, it should be determined first. The occupant load of 324 multiplied by the 0.3-inch (7.5-mm) stair variable equals 97.2, or 97 inches (2464 mm). (Typically, if it is less than 0.5, round down; if it is 0.5 or more, round up.) This total is divided between the two exit stairs, leaving 48.5 inches, or 49 inches (1245 mm). Therefore, each run of both stairs must be at least 49 inches (1245 mm) wide to meet the code requirements. (Note that this 49-inch [1245-mm] width cannot be reduced as the exit moves toward the public way. If the exit stairs empty into a corridor or exit passageway at the ground level, they must be at least 49 inches [1245 mm] wide as well.)

To determine the width of the corridor leading to the exit stairs, the layout of the floor must first be examined. Because the code assumes that the total occupant load exits equally among the two exits, it also assumes that half of the occupants travel in each direction in the corridor. So, you take the total occupant load of 324 and divide it in half to obtain 162 occupants. Then multiply 162 by the level variable of 0.2 inch (5 mm) to obtain a minimum corridor width of 32.4, or 33 inches (838 mm). That means that the doors entering the exit stairs can each be the minimum 36-inch (914-mm) width. However, most codes specify a 44-inch (1118-mm) minimum for the corridor. If using the same 36-inch (914-mm) door, allow 4 inches (100 mm) on the hinge side of the door (for door frame and wall construction), and allow the 12-inch (305-mm) accessibility requirement on the push side of the door (exit stairway doors and doors in corridors are typically on closers). The total exit width of the corridor for the floor is 52 inches (1319 mm). An additional consideration is that it takes 60 inches (1524 mm) for a person in a wheelchair to turn around. If the corridor is not 60 inches (1524 mm) wide, there are two options: either provide alcoves with sufficient turnaround space or add a turnaround space like the one shown in Plan D in Figure 5.11.

Example 2: Aisles and Aisle Accessways

Figure 5.22 shows the floor plan of a restaurant in a sprinklered building. It has an occupant load of 100. In this example, there are aisles and aisle accessways of different lengths and capacities. Each aisle and aisle accessway width must be determined separately. Some widths will be determined by the minimums set by the codes; others will require calculations. To determine the main aisle widths (indicated by W in the figure), the occupant load of the space and the number of exits must be calculated. Then, the calculated exit width should be compared to the minimum width required by the codes. The larger width should be used in the design. Refer back to the *LSC* table in Figure 5.20 and use the process described in Example 1 to calculate the required exit access width. First, multiply the occupant load of 100 by 0.2 inch (5 mm) to get a total exit width of 20 inches (510 mm). Then, because there are two exits, divide the total exit access width between the two exits. So, the calculated exit width is 10 inches (254 mm). However, the codes set a minimum width of 44 inches (914 mm) for aisles in this Assembly occupancy situation. (This was changed from a minimum of 36″ to 44″ in the 2015 *IBC*.) The main aisles (W) are therefore required to be at least 44 inches (1117.6 mm) wide.

If the occupant load is much greater, however, the calculated aisle width may be larger than the required minimum aisle width. For example, if the occupant load was 500, the calculated width would be 100 inches (2540 mm). The width would be split between the two exits, suggesting an aisle width of 50 inches. The main aisles (W) would then be 50 inches (1270 mm) wide instead of the minimum 44 inches (1117.6 mm) because the required calculated width exceeds the minimum required width.

Next, the widths of the aisle accessways must be determined. Some are determined by standard widths given by the codes, as discussed earlier in this chapter. (See Figure 5.12.) For example, the codes do not require a minimum width for the aisle accessway A at the lower right of the plan because of its limited length and capacity. The minimum width at the aisle accessway B at the left of the plan is 12 inches (305 mm). This is added to the 19 inches (483 mm) required for the chair (D) to obtain the overall distance between tables. (See the section titled "Aisles and Aisle Accessways" earlier in this chapter.) However, because aisle accessway C is longer than 12 feet (3658 mm), the required width must be calculated. The building codes and the *LSC* use a similar formula to obtain this calculation. The formula is 12 inches + 0.5 (x −12 feet); when using metrics, the formula is 305 mm + 12.7 ([x − 3658 mm] x 305). When using this formula, the calculated width of an aisle accessway will be wider for longer aisle accessways. As shown in Figure 5.22, the variable x is the length of the aisle, measured from the end of the last table to the centerline

◢ Note

The formula for calculating the width of accessways translates slightly differently when the formula is converted to metric values.

◢ Note

The *half-diagonal rule* is intended to cause at least two exits to be located a safe distance apart so that they cannot both be blocked by a single fire.

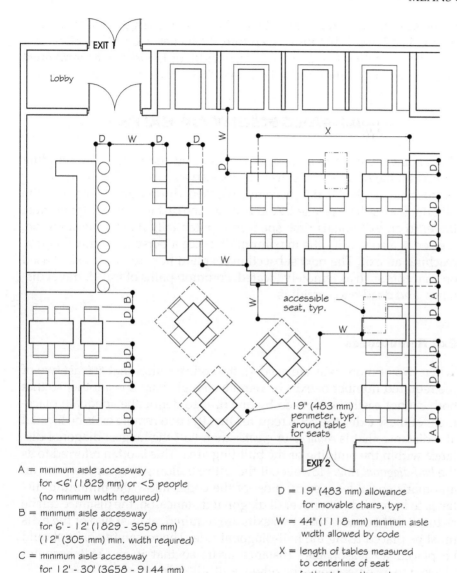

A = minimum aisle accessway
for <6' (1829 mm) or <5 people
(no minimum width required)

B = minimum aisle accessway
for 6' - 12' (1829 - 3658 mm)
(12" (305 mm) min. width required)

C = minimum aisle accessway
for 12' - 30' (3658 - 9144 mm)
(use width formula 12" + 0.5(x - 12'-0")
or 305 mm + 12.7((x - 3658 mm) - 305))

D = 19" (483 mm) allowance
for movable chairs, typ.

W = 44" (1118 mm) minimum aisle
width allowed by code

X = length of tables measured
to centerline of seat
farthest from the aisle

Figure 5.22 Egress and aisle widths for movable tables and chairs (sprinklered building, occupant load [OL] = 100).

of the seat farthest from the aisle. In this case, the length of aisle access-way C is 17 feet (5182 mm); therefore, 12 inches + 0.5 (17 − 12 feet) = 12 inches + 0.5(5) = 12 + 2.5 = 14.5. So, a width of 15 inches (381 mm) must be provided in addition to the 19 inches (483 mm) required for the chairs.

ARRANGEMENT OF EXITS

Note

The objective of the codes is to place exits as far apart as possible and always to provide two choices in exit paths.

The arrangement of exits is also specified by the codes. The building codes and the *LSC* require exits to be located as remotely from each other as possible so that if one becomes blocked during an emergency, the other(s) may still be reached. And because the distance an occupant must travel to an exit equals time spent in a potentially dangerous situation, the codes also specify the maximum distance a person can travel before reaching an exit. The next subsections explain how to locate exits based on concepts such as remotely located, common paths of travel, travel distance, and dead-end corridors.

Note

For Assembly occupancies, the required minimum aisle width varies if the aisle is level, stepped, or sloped, and if it has seats on one or both sides. Consult the codes for specific requirements.

Exit Remoteness

When two or more exits are needed, the code requires that at least two of the required number of exits be remote enough from one another so that both cannot easily be blocked by one fire. To define the adequate placement of these exits, the code requires that the two remote exits be located at a distance that is *equal to or greater* than half the longest diagonal distance within the building or the building area. This is often referred to as the *half-diagonal rule*. However, if the entire building is equipped with an automatic sprinkler system, most of the codes allow the minimum distance to be a third of the overall diagonal distance. So, the distance can be reduced. When more than two exits are required, at least two of the exits must be placed using the half-diagonal rule. The remaining exits should be placed a "reasonable" distance apart so that if one exit becomes blocked in an emergency, the others will still be usable.

The easiest way to understand this half-diagonal concept is to review Figure 5.23. These diagrams are representative of open building plans or separate tenant spaces within a building. In a tenant space, the measurement is unaffected by the presence of other surrounding spaces. The shape or size of the area or the building does not matter. The longest possible diagonal in that space must be found. Measure the length of that diagonal in a straight line from one corner of the floor plan to the other corner (as represented by D in each case). Then take one-half of that length (or one-third if the building is sprinklered). The result indicates

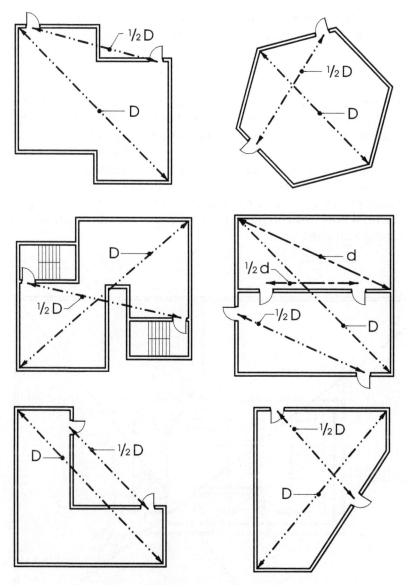

D = Diagonal or Maximum Distance

½ D = Half of Diagonal or Minimum Distance

NOTE: Some codes allow the minimum distance to be 1/3 the overall diagonal in lieu of 1/2 if the building has an automatic sprinkler system.

Figure 5.23 Half-diagonal rule example: Building.

✍ Note

When a building is sprinklered, the two exits can typically be located at a distance equal to at least one-third of the overall diagonal of the space or building.

how far apart the exits must be. This is the *minimum* distance allowed between the two remote exits: the exits can be located further apart. The *IBC* allows the distance to be measured to any point along the width of the doorway; the NFPA codes allow it to be measured to the edge of the door.

When a building has exit enclosures, such as exit stairs that are interconnected by a fire-rated corridor, some of the codes, including the *IBC*, require the exit distance to be measured differently. Figure 5.24 illustrates this point for an entire floor in relation to a tenant space. The overall diagonal length (D2) is also measured using a straight line across the top of the floor plan. By contrast, when placing the two exits at the stairwells, the half-diagonal distance between the exits is measured along the path of travel within the rated corridor. (The tenant space exit access doors are located using a straight line.)

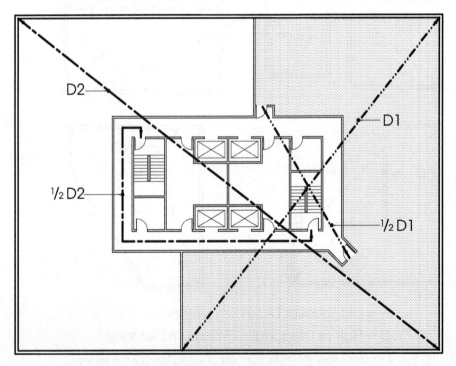

D1 = Diagonal Distance for Tenant Space

D2 = Diagonal Distance for Entire Floor

NOTE: Some codes allow the minimum distance to be 1/3 the overall diagonal in lieu of 1/2 if the building has an automatic sprinkler system.

Figure 5.24 Half-diagonal rule example: Tenant and floor

Common Path of Travel

When exiting a building in an emergency, it is important to have choices of direction and limited distance to travel. The first distance the codes limit is known as *common path of travel*, which is when a person can travel in only *one direction* before there is a choice of two directions to exits or exit access doorways. For example, in a tenant space with a single exit, the common path of travel would be the distance from any point in the space to the exit access doorway of that tenant space; it is assumed that the corridor then leads to two separate exits for the building. In Figure 5.25, paths A1 and A2 are common paths of travel (as described in the following

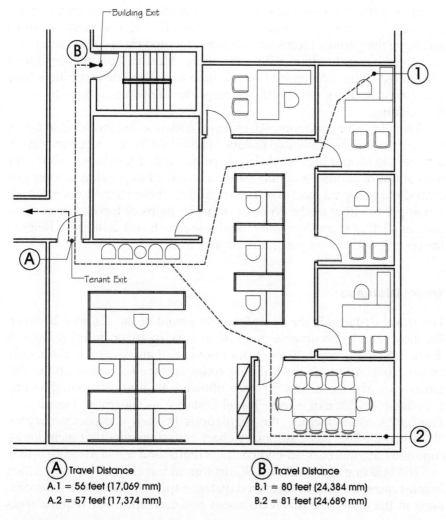

Ⓐ Travel Distance
A.1 = 56 feet (17,069 mm)
A.2 = 57 feet (17,374 mm)

Ⓑ Travel Distance
B.1 = 80 feet (24,384 mm)
B.2 = 81 feet (24,689 mm)

Figure 5.25 Common path of travel diagram

example). Similarly, any room that has only one exit access door also has a common path of travel, as indicated at A in Figure 5.18. In a larger tenant space or building floor with multiple exit locations, the common path of travel would be the distance from any point in the space to the point where an occupant can go in two different directions to reach separate exit access doorways from the tenant space or exits from the floor.

The common path is typically measured starting one foot from the wall at the most remote location. The distance continues along the natural path of travel to the point (most often the centerline of a door, corridor, or aisle) that provides a choice of two paths of travel to remote exits.

The second application of a common path of travel is an exit access where two paths merge to become one. The *merged* path becomes the common path of travel. For example, a reception area in a tenant space typically becomes a common path of travel. Two corridors or aisles accessing the various rooms and/or offices would merge at the reception area to arrive at the door exiting the space. Most exit discharges can be considered a common path of travel, such as a lobby or vestibule where other means of egress must converge to allow occupants to leave the building.

The allowable common path of travel distances are included in tables in Figure 5.18. The allowable distance is affected by the occupancy type, occupant load, and if the building is sprinklered. If the distance is longer than allowed, another exit may have to be added to provide a closer exit even if the occupant load does not require it. These restrictions in length can apply to either of the types of common paths of travel. Other occupancies such as Hazardous may require shorter travel distances. (Refer to the specific codes for more information.)

Travel Distance

The travel distance is the overall measurement of the distance between the most remote, occupiable point of an area, room, or building floor to the nearest exit. Travel distance does not end at an exit access door, only an exit door. Although the building codes and the *LSC* measure the distance similarly, the actual distance allowed may be different. The *IBC* uses Table 1017.2: Exit Access Travel Distance, as shown in Figure 5.26. The NFPA codes include the regulations in each occupancy chapter. However, the *LSC* has a summary chart in its appendix that includes all common path limits, dead-end corridor limits, and travel distance limits.

The building code and the *LSC* maximum travel distances may differ. In most cases, the shortest required distance applies. Also check for exceptions to the allowable travel distances based on sprinkler requirements

---

✔ Note

In hospitals (I-2), the use of suites allow unique arrangement of rooms and intervening rooms that provide better patient supervision. Special travel distances and exit location requirements apply to this situation.

✔ Note

If an occupant does not have two distinctly separate directions to travel to exits or exit access doorways they are in a common path of travel, which is limited by the codes.

TABLE 1017.2 EXIT ACCESS TRAVEL DISTANCE[a]

OCCUPANCY	WITHOUT SPRINKLER SYSTEM (feet)	WITH SPRINKLER SYSTEM (feet)
A, E, F-1, M, R, S-1	200[e]	250[b]
I-1	Not Permitted	250[b]
B	200	300[c]
F-2, S-2, U	300	400[c]
H-1	Not Permitted	75[d]
H-2	Not Permitted	100[d]
H-3	Not Permitted	150[d]
H-4	Not Permitted	175[d]
H-5	Not Permitted	200[c]
I-2, I-3	Not Permitted	200[c]
I-4	150	200[c]

For SI: 1 foot = 304.8 mm.

a See the following sections for modifications to *exit access* travel distance requirements:
  Section 402.8: For the distance limitation in malls.
  Section 407.4: For the distance limitation in Group I-2.
  Sections 408.6.1 and 408.8.1: For the distance limitations in Group I-3.
  Section 411.2: For the distance limitation in special amusement areas.
  Section 412.6: For the distance limitations in aircraft manufacturing facilities.
  Section 1006.2.2.2: For the distance limitation in refrigeration machinery rooms.
  Section 1006.2.2.3: For the distance limitation in refrigerated rooms and spaces.
  Section 1006.3.4: For buildings with one exit.
  Section 1017.2.2: For increased distance limitation in Groups F-1 and S-1.
  Section 1030.7: For increased limitation in assembly seating.
  Section 3103.4: For temporary structures.
  Section 3104.9: For *pedestrian walkways*.
b Buildings equipped throughout with an *automatic sprinkler system* in accordance with
  Section 903.3.1.1 or 903.3.1.2. See Section 903 for occupancies where *automatic sprinkler systems* are permitted in accordance with Section 903.3.1.2.
c Buildings equipped throughout with an *automatic sprinkler system* in accordance with
  Section 903.3.1.1.
d Group H occupancies equipped throughout with an *automatic sprinkler system* in accordance with Section 903.2.5.1.
e Group R-3 and R-4 buildings equipped throughout with an *automatic sprinkler system* in accordance with Section 903.3.1.3. See Section 903.2.8 for occupancies where automatic sprinkler systems are permitted in accordance with Section 903.3.1.3.

Figure 5.26 International Building Code Table 1017.2, "Exit Access Travel Distance[a]" (2015 *International Building Code*, copyright © 2015. Washington, DC: International Code Council. Reproduced with permission. All rights reserved. www.iccsafe.org).

⬧ Note

If an occupancy has an open stairway within its space that is part of an exit access, it must be included in the travel distance. It is measured up to the centerline of the nosing of the top tread. Then take the measurement of the stair on the angle of the stairway in the plane of the tread nosing. Measure from the top tread nosing to the bottom tread nosing to get the stair travel length. To continue the overall travel distance, start at the bottom edge of the last riser to the exit.

and occupancy. Travel distance is measured from the most remote point (usually the corner of a room) to the nearest exit. The measurement starts 1 foot (305 mm) from the nearest wall and moves in a direct but natural path curving around any obstructions such as walls, furniture and equipment, or corners with a clearance of 1 foot (305 mm). If there is an open stairway within the path of exit access, it must be included in the travel distance. (It is measured beginning at the centerline of the nosing of the top tread, down the angle of the stairway at the tread nosing to the bottom tread). The horizontal measurement continues from that point. The measurement ends anywhere along the exit door location. Common examples include the following:

1. The exterior exit door
2. The door to an enclosed exit stair
3. The door of a horizontal exit
4. The door to an enclosed exit passageway
5. The door to an enclosed area of refuge

Maximum travel distances for an individual floor can increase in length in certain occupancies when additional requirements are met. (Refer to the specific codes.) This can be seen in the *IBC* table in 6. For example, in a Business occupancy in a nonsprinklered building, the 200-foot (60,960-mm) travel distance can be increased to 300 feet (91,440 mm) if sprinklers are added.

Example

The floor plan in Figure 5.27 gives an example of measuring common path and travel distances in a space with only one exit. The floor plan is that of an accounting firm occupying part of the second floor in a four-story sprinklered building. It is considered a Business occupancy. Because it is a new occupancy and separate from the other tenants in the building, it must have a travel distance acceptable to the current code requirements.

The dashed lines on the floor plan indicate the path of travel distances. The travel distance measurement starts at the most remote point—in other words, the farthest point from the exit. It is indicated by the X on the floor plan. In this case, the common path of travel must be measured from the X to the exit access door leading from the tenant space to the exit access corridor, as indicated by A. Because the tenant has two points that seem to be about the same distance from the exit, both must

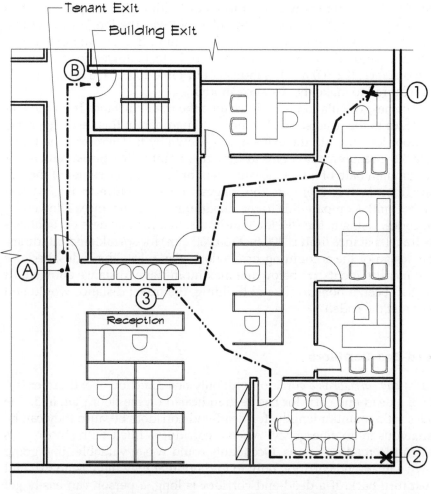

A1 = 56 feet (17,069 mm)   B1 = 80 feet (24,384 mm)
A2 = 57 feet (17,374 mm)   B2 = 81 feet (24,689 mm)

Figure 5.27 Travel distance example: Tenant space (sprinklered building).

be measured—from Point 1 and Point 2 to Door A. The measurement starts 1 foot (305 mm) from the wall at the farthest corner and moves toward the exit using the most direct path and staying 1 foot (305 mm) away from any obstacles. Obstacles can include walls, corners, furniture, fixtures, equipment, and machinery. The measurement ends at the tenant doorway at the corridor, Point A, because once in the corridor an occupant

◀ Note

Typically, if the longest
travel distance
within a space to the
entry door exceeds
75 feet (22,680 mm),
an additional exit
is required.

◀ Note

If designing a few
different tenant spaces
in the same building,
the travel distance
must be measured for
each tenant.

◀ Note

In some jurisdictions, the
placement of freestand-
ing furniture and movable
panel systems does
not create dead-end
corridors.

can go two different ways to get to an exit although Exit Doorway B is obviously closer. As shown on the plan, A2 was the longest travel distance to A at a distance of 57 feet (17.069 mm). Because the distance is does not exceed the maximum distance of 75 feet allowed for a common path distance, (22,860 mm) as indicated in Table 1006.2.1, a second exit is not required to make the distance shorter.

The next calculation is to determine the travel distance from the tenant space to the nearest exit for the building floor. In this case, the exit is the door leading into the exit stair, as shown by B. Therefore, the travel distance measurement begins at the same point as the measurement for the common path of travel measurement but ends at the center of the exit stair door. In this example, the longest travel distance to B is 81 feet (24,689 mm). Compare this to the maximum travel distances allowed by the codes. Using 6, the *IBC* table indicates that for Business occupancies the travel distance limit is 300 feet (60,960 mm) for sprinklered buildings. The design of the accounting firm's floor plan meets the codes, because both measurements are below the maximum travel distance allowed. (If this had been a nonsprinklered building, the travel distance would still have met the code.)

Dead-End Corridors

A *dead-end corridor* is a corridor with only one direction of exit. An example of a dead-end corridor has been indicated on the floor plan in 5. The codes set maximum lengths for dead-end corridors because they can be dangerous in an emergency. When a corridor is filled with smoke, it is difficult to read exit signs. Occupants could waste valuable time going down a dead-end corridor, only to find out that they there is no exit and must turn back. If a dead-end corridor is long, a person can easily get trapped by fire and/or smoke.

The building codes and the *LSC* describe the limits of a dead end within the text. (In the *LSC*, they are also listed in a table within its appendix.) The most common dead-end length is a maximum of 20 feet (6096 mm). It is measured 1 foot (305 mm) from the end of a corridor, following the natural path of travel, to the centerline of the corridor that provides the choice of two means of egress. In some codes, when an automatic sprinkler system is installed, a dead-end corridor can be longer. For example, in the *IBC*, a dead-end corridor in a sprinklered building in Business, Factory, Storage, and in some Educational, Institutional, Mercantile, and Residential occupancies it can be up to 50 feet (15,240 mm)

TRAVEL DISTANCE FACTORS

Travel distance measurement is not based on a code formula. Rather, it is based on the space or building as a whole. *The Life Safety Code Handbook* (2003) lists the factors on which the required code travel distances are based:

❑ The estimated number, age, and physical condition of building occupants and the rate at which they can be expected to move

❑ The type and number of expected obstructions, such as display cases, seating, and heavy machinery, that must be negotiated

❑ The estimated number of people in any room or space and the distance from the farthest point in that room to the door

❑ The amount and nature of combustibles expected in a particular occupancy

❑ The rapidity with which a fire might spread, which is a function of the type of construction, the materials used, the degree of compartmentation, and the presence or absence of automatic fire-detection and extinguishing systems

in length. There may be other conditions that would allow longer dead-end corridors. (Refer to the codes for specifics.)

Taking these variables in consideration, the safe travel distance will vary with the type and size of an occupancy and the degree of hazards present.

Although it would be best to eliminate dead-end corridors altogether, it is not always possible—especially in older existing buildings. Providing egress through adjacent rooms may be helpful. If the existing building configuration makes avoiding a dead-end corridor difficult, contact the code official for clarification for options that may be acceptable.

Note

A dead-end corridor longer than 20 feet (6096 mm) may be allowed if a building is sprinklered and for specific occupancies.

Note

For most occupancies, one exit is allowed if the occupant load is less than 50 and the travel distance to the exit is less than 75 feet (22,860 mm). Check the codes for specific requirements.

Example

A second travel distance example is an entire third floor of a hotel in a sprinklered building. The floor plan in Figure 5.28 indicates that there are two exits. Both are enclosed stairways. (In this example, it is assumed that the elevators do not constitute an exit in an emergency.) Refer to the *IBC* table in 6. Under the Residential (R) occupancy for hotels, the maximum travel distance allowed is 250 feet (76,200 mm) for a sprinklered building. (The bottom of the table gives the metric conversion unit.) This means that an occupant located anywhere on the floor of this hotel cannot travel more than 250 feet (76,200 mm) to reach the closest exit.

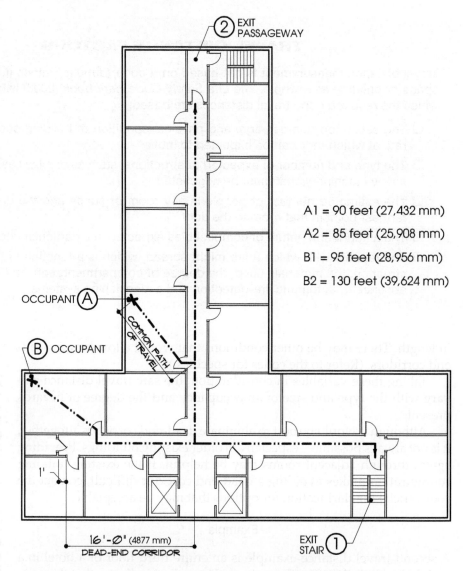

A1 = 90 feet (27,432 mm)

A2 = 85 feet (25,908 mm)

B1 = 95 feet (28,956 mm)

B2 = 130 feet (39,624 mm)

Figure 5.28 Travel distance example: Building (hotel) (sprinklered building).

In this example, several measurements must be made. Point A, as indicated on the floor plan, is midway between the two exits. An occupant in this location must be able to reach at least one exit within 250 feet (76,200 mm). In both cases (A1 and A2), the total distance is less than this.

Point B must also be within 250 feet (76,200 mm) from an enclosed exit stairs. Note, however, that the point is located in a dead-end corridor.

The length of the dead end cannot be longer than 20 feet (6096 mm). As the dead-end length is 16 feet (4877 mm), proceed to measure the travel distance. As shown in Figure 5.28, the travel distance to both exits (B1 and B2) is less than the 250-foot (76,200-mm) maximum distance.

SIGNAGE

A variety of signs are required by the codes for the means of egress. Some signs will be required by the codes; others may be requested by the client. Various types of signs are discussed next. It is important to specify signage products that meet the requirements of the jurisdiction as well as accessibility standards. The common code and accessibility requirements for signage including the ADA standards and the *ICC A117.1* requirements are discussed in Chapter 10.

Exit Signs

Exit signs are typically required whenever a space or a floor of a building has two or more exits. They must be installed at the doors of exits including exterior exit doors, stair enclosures, exit passageways, and horizontal exits on every floor. In some cases, if the main exterior exit/entrance is obvious, an exit sign is not required. Although they are typically mounted above the door, the requirement is that they be easily seen from any direction within the exit access.

The purpose of exit signs is to identify exits and to lead occupants to the nearest exit, identifying exiting options, if necessary. Exit signs must be installed within the exit access, including doors exiting a space or area, in large open areas and in corridors. When placing exit signs, consider the path and view of the occupant along the mean of egress. The codes require that exits signs be located where the way to reach the exit is "not readily apparent" to the occupant. The exit signs direct occupants to the exits so that no time is wasted going in the wrong direction. In some cases, exit signs should also be placed so that occupants are reassured that they are headed toward an exit. For example, both the *IBC* and the *LSC* require that no point within a corridor can be more than 100 feet (30,480 mm) from the nearest visible sign. Longer distances may be allowed if the sign is rated for longer viewing distances. Figure 5.29 indicates typical locations of exit signs within a building and within a tenant space.

✎ Note

If a travel distance exceeds the maximum length, the layout must be changed to meet the requirements.

✎ Note

Some exterior exit doors, such as those found in main lobbies or vestibules, may not require an exit sign if they are clearly identifiable. However, this must be approved by a code official.

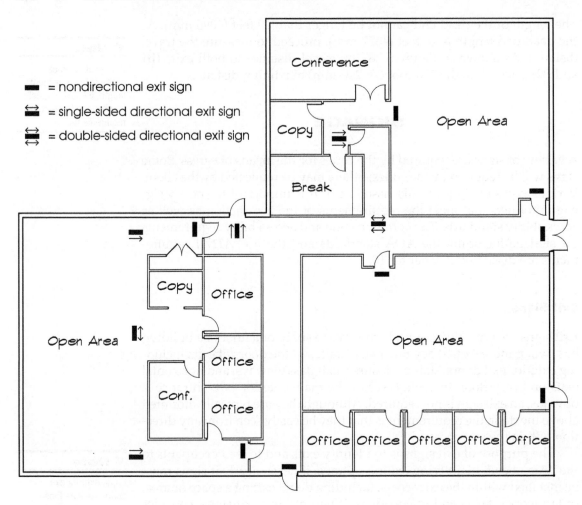

Figure 5.29 Exit sign location example.

Exit signs located directly over an exit door or exit access door are usually required to say only *EXIT*. Signs that lead occupants through corridors or open areas particularly at locations where a corridor changes direction or at an intersection which provides an option to travel in more than one direction are required to have directional arrows in addition to the word *EXIT*. Some jurisdictions may allow the use of other languages where many of the occupants may speak a language other than English. And in some cases, graphic signs without words may be used. Confirm the specific requirements with the jurisdiction.

The building codes and the *LSC* specify the location, size, graphics, and illumination of exit signs so that they will be seen and understood by occupants. Although exit signs are often provided in green and red with contrast letters, the code also requires that exit signs be a distinctive color from the decorations, interior finish, and other signs so they stand out visually. Other illuminated signs should not be placed near an exit sign that might distract an occupant from seeing the exit sign. The *IBC* refers to the *ICC A117.1* for accessibility elements for exit signage. The *IBC* requires certain exit signs at exits and areas of refuge to be tactile as well. Coordination between the *IBC* and the ADA Standards for graphic and tactile requirements is important.

Exit signs can be externally or internally lit. Internally illuminated signs can be electrically powered, self-luminous, or photoluminescent. However, according to the *IBC*, all types of internally illuminated exit signs are required to be listed and labeled according to *UL 924, Standard for Safety of Emergency Lighting and Power Equipment*. The codes may also refer to *NFPA 170, Standard for Fire Safety Symbols*.

Most exit signs are ceiling mounted or wall mounted. The *IBC* and *LSC* allow exit signs in some occupancies including R-1 (hotels) to be located at a low-level near the floor. The allowable height varies between the codes. They can be located on the wall or on the door. This location allows the exit signs to be seen even when smoke gathers at the ceiling. These systems are required to be internally lit.

Instructional Signs

In addition to signs that identify the exit access paths and exit locations as discussed above, other exit-related signs may be required. These signs may be needed or required when additional information is needed for safety. This can include unusual exit conditions or when a means of egress is confusing. For example, if a regular door or stairway can be mistaken for an exit, the codes typically require that a *NO EXIT* sign be posted on the door. (Supplemental lettering such as STOREROOM or *TO BASEMENT* can be used to indicate the use of the area as well.) If there are two doors out of an exit stairway, if one reenters the building to an elevator lobby it must be clearly marked *Elevator Lobby*. This will help the occupant to choose where to safely exit to the exterior.

In some cases, other components of the means of egress may need to be labeled or additional information given. This is particularly true if unique exiting systems or locking at exits has been incorporated. If exiting is on a delay, if an alarm will sound if the door is opened, or similar precautions, it should be clearly marked. Another example would include a sign mounted on a stairwell door that says, *KEEP DOOR CLOSED*. (Other signs may be requested by the client, such as room names and/or room numbers.)

> **◁ Note**
>
> Some code jurisdictions require *floor-level exit signs* in addition to regular exit signs in certain occupancies. These are typically placed 10–12 inches (254–305 mm) above the floor near the exit door so that they are easy to read in emergencies with heavy smoke.

> **◁ Note**
>
> The requirements for signage are found in the *ADA Standards* and the *ICC A117.1* standard for exit signs and other required signage. The *IBC* also refers to the *ICC A117.1* for accessibility aspects of exit signage.

If an exit stairway connects more than three stories, signs are also required at each landing within the stairwell. Stairway signage can be critical in the event of a fire in a multistory or high-rise building. The sign must indicate the story, direction to the exit discharge, and the availability of roof access for the fire department. These signs have very specific size, location, and graphic requirements. Also, as part of this sign or an adjacent sign, the floor level must be indicated in visual, raised, and Braille to meet accessible requirements. These signs orient the occupants to their location in the building including being able to identify floor levels, stair numbers, and elevator banks.

Accessible Exit Signs

The typical exit signs leads occupants visually to the required exits. To assist the visually impaired, exit stairways must also have a room identification sign that is a tactile sign located at the door to the stairwell indicating it as an exit. In addition, some occupants need to be able to identify an exit that is accessible and/or provides an area of refuge. (Area of refuge was discussed earlier in this chapter.) If the stairwell is not considered accessible (or does not provide an area of refuge), directional signage indicating the nearest accessible means of egress must be provided. (See the section titled "Signage" in Chapter 10.)

◄ **Note**

If an area of refuge sign is located near an illuminated exit sign, it may need to be illuminated as well. An International Symbol of Accessibility must also be included.

An area of refuge requires sign at the door to identify it as an *AREA OF REFUGE*. This sign must meet the visual and tactile requirements for a room identification signs of the ADA Standards and the *ICC A117.1* (as presented in Chapter 10.) The codes also require signage at the area of refuge that give directions how to use the two-way communication system as well as specific location information. (See codes for specifics.) Similar signage is required in the elevator lobby when an elevator is used as part of the means of egress. This sign should give instructions including the conditions and restrictions of its use as an exit. This sign is not required to be illuminated.

Another type of sign that is required by the codes for some occupancies and uses is an emergency evacuation diagram. This diagram indicates the emergency egress or escape routes for the space. They are sometimes referred to as a fire or life safety plan. As part of the emergency preparedness requirements, the *IFC* requires that an emergency evacuation process be developed for Assembly, Educational, Hazard, Institutional (hospitals and nurseries), certain Residential (hotels, motels, dormitories, etc.), Mercantile, and high-rise buildings. Although the diagram is just a part of the information developed to train staff, some jurisdictions will require the emergency evacuation diagrams to be posted in and/or throughout the space. They may also be required if the configuration of the building is confusing or complex. If posted, these signs help occupants that may not be familiar with the organization of the building orient themselves to the egress path to the exits. The plan of the building should be simple and only indicate the major features of the building while identifying exits, evacuation routes, areas of refuge, locations of manual fire alarms, portable fire extinguishers, and other fire protections components as required by the jurisdiction. It is most useful to occupants not accustomed to reading a plan if it is oriented in the way that the occupant is in the space. If required, these signs should be located so that occupants will notice them, for example, in hotels they are typically located on the inside the room on the entry door. These signs do not typically have to meet accessibility requirements.

Note

When double doors are used as an entry into a space, the sign is required on the wall to the right of the door opening.

EMERGENCY LIGHTING AND COMMUNICATION

Generally, the means of egress must be lit whenever a room or area is occupied. There are only a few exceptions including uses where a dark space is necessary or where people are sleeping. Similar to exit signage, emergency lighting is typically required whenever two or more exits are present. Sometimes referred to as exit lighting, emergency lighting must be connected to a backup system in case of power failure during an emergency. This could mean connection to a backup generator in the building or battery packs located within the light fixture. Generally, the codes require emergency lighting to be provided at all exits and aisles, corridors, passageways, stairways, ramps, and lobbies leading to an exit. Along with exit lighting, exit and area of refuge signs must always be lit when a building is in use. The codes specify minimum lighting illumination levels. Lower levels might be allowed for certain building types, such as theaters, concert halls, and auditoriums. (Chapter 9 describes emergency lighting in more detail.)

Beginning in 2009, the *IBC* and *IFC* require that the path within the exit stair, exit enclosures, and exit passageways in Assembly, Business, Educational, Institutional (assisted living), Mercantile, and Residential (hotels) high-rise buildings to have luminous markings that define the egress path. (The *LSC* includes similar requirements.) These exit path markings can be photoluminescent or self-illuminating. The codes require that the steps, landings, handrails, perimeters, doors, door frames, and door hardware be marked. In addition, obstacles along that path that project more than 4 inches (102 mm) must be marked as well. The codes have specific requirements how to properly mark each element. (Check the codes for specifics.)

Note

The *IBC* and the *LSC* include requirements for photoluminescent marking devices such as signage and tape in exit corridors and stairs to provide additional direction.

✎ Note

Other ways to notify and direct occupants continue to be developed. An example is the use of directional sound. These devices produce pulses of sound that can be localized by occupants' hearing. By following the source of the sound, they can locate the exit or area of refuge more easily.

It is important to design the space to meet the code requirements for a safe means of egress. The codes also have requirements for making the occupants aware of the systems that are in place of evacuation procedures. These requirements are found in the "Emergency Planning and Preparedness" chapter of the *IFC*. This typically includes announcing the location of exits at assembly events and practicing fire drills in schools. In addition, staff must be instructed and review procedures for evacuation for certain occupancies. The fire code often requires egress patterns in the form of life safety plans to be posted in certain locations so occupants can know before an emergency what options are available. Although these requirements may not directly affect the design of a space, in some cases development of these diagrams is part of the project.

Occupant safety is enhanced by not relying on one aspect, device or building system. For example, thick smoke can make exit signs difficult to see, or an occupant who is hearing impaired may not hear an audible alarm. A comprehensive exiting system will use a mix of clear organization, visual indicators, audible sounds, and voice communication to communicate to the occupants. The codes will specify when each of these is required by the occupancy or size of the space. However, as part of designing the means of egress system additional layers of communication and egress support may be appropriate for a particular project. (Several of these systems including communications systems and alarms are discussed further in Chapter 7.)

RESEARCH: USING THE CODES

The means of egress includes multiple components that need to be properly sized and arranged in your design. Many of these will become quickly familiar to you and others will require research with each project. Although the various codes define the parts of the means of egress in similar ways, the specific requirements can be different. For instance, the codes agree that the means of egress include exit accesses, exits, and exit discharges. However, the actual minimum width of exits, maximum travel distances, allowable length of dead-end corridors and other aspects may differ between codes. You may have to compare the requirements of several codes to determine which is the definitive requirement.

✎ Note

According to the 2021 *IBC*, 60 percent of the public entrances are required to be accessible. This excludes loading and service entrances.

The building codes and the *Life Safety Code (LSC)* set most of the requirements for the parts of the means of egress. You may often have to research and compare one building code with the *LSC*. These codes are frequently enforced together. (See Chapter 1.) Each of these code publications has a chapter dedicated to means of egress. In the *IBC,* the means of egress chapter is Chapter 10: in the *LSC,* Chapter 7; and in the *NFPA 5000,*

Chapter 11. Each chapter is titled, "Means of Egress." Most of the means of egress requirements for the *IBC* will be in this chapter. If your project is in a high-rise building, includes an atrium, is an Institutional occupancy, ambulatory care facility, live/work use or includes a special use like a stage, you may also have to refer to Chapter 4, "Special Detailed Requirements Based on Use and Occupancy." It is always good to check this chapter, if in doubt. A dedicated section, "Accessible Means of Egress," is located in the *IBC* Chapter 10, as well. Remember, accessible routes and means of egress must be provided for all projects. In addition, you may also want to review the sections within *IBC* Chapter 11, "Accessibility" for requirements for accessible route and accessible entrances. These may affect the layout and detailing of the doorways and corridors.

In the NFPA codes, requirements will be organized differently. In the *LSC*, the basic means of egress requirements are located in Chapter 7. However, specific requirements for an occupancy type will be in the individual occupancy chapter. Remember, that the designation of a use is sometimes different in the NFPA codes as in the I-codes. For example, a day care is a Day Care Occupancy in the *LSC* (and *NFPA 5000*) but it is either a Institutional, Educational or Residential in the *IBC* (and other I-Codes.) (This was explained in more detail in Chapter 3 of this book.) In addition, the *LSC* separates occupancies into New and Existing. The means of egress requirements can be different between these categories even within the same occupancy classification. So, if you are researching for a renovation of an existing elementary school, you would go first to the "Existing Educational" chapter in the *LSC* and look for the means of egress sections. If no specific requirements are indicated in that occupancy chapter, then the requirements in Chapter 7 apply. If the jurisdiction enforces the *IBC* and the *LSC*, you will have to compare the requirements of *IBC* and the *LSC*. They can differ. There is usually more coordination between the *LSC* and the *NFPA 5000*. If the *NFPA 5000* is being enforced as the building code, basic means of egress requirements will be found in Chapter 11 of that code. This will include the default finish requirements for the means of egress components. However, like the *LSC*, specific requirements will be in the individual occupancy chapters and override the general requirements. This is why it is more affective to start in the occupancy chapter for your research in the NFPA codes.

The means of egress requirements in Chapter 10, "Means of Egress" of the *IFC* are the same as found in Chapter 10 of the *IBC*. However, the *IFC* includes an additional section on the "Maintenance of the Means of Egress." Although these requirements focus on maintaining the conditions so that it continues to be usable after the building or space is occupied, it should be reviewed. This section includes limitations on the use of decorations, mirrors, and other objects that may obstruct or confuse the egress path. In addition, the *IFC* includes separate requirements for existing buildings that may allow exceptions to the constraints for new buildings. (See Appendix B.)

If the design calls for an alternative approach to the means of egress that does not conform to the prescriptive constraints of the building codes or *LSC*, the use of performance codes such as the *ICC Performance Code (ICCPC)* may need to be explored. Remember, when using performance codes, the criteria and the design response must be reviewed and accepted by the code official from the beginning of the project. And a design solution using performance criteria usually involves coordination between other design team members including engineers. To begin the research, an acceptable level of design performance based on the building use, identified risk factors and an assumed level of emergency must be established using Chapter 3, "Design Performance Levels" in the *ICCPC*. You must consider the characteristics of the occupants, the features of the design, and the hazards that may exist. This will identify the unique challenges to providing safe egress for your project. For example, consider if the occupants can move to an exit independently, if they can exit at a normal rate or a slower rate, or should not exit a building for safety or security reasons.

Then, Chapter 19, "Means of Egress" can be used to develop an egress strategy and configuration. Although this chapter does not set specific requirements for means of egress (like prescriptive requirements of the *IBC*), it does require that a building and its design allow occupants sufficient time to evacuate, relocate, or have a defend in place location. The same elements of a means of egress discussed by the prescriptive codes—such as area of refuge, travel distance, and unobstructed path—can be considered as part of a performance design; however, those specific terms are usually not used by performance codes. Instead, the phrases are more generic, like "safe place," "appropriate to the travel distance," and "adequate lighting." Therefore, it may not matter if a particular area is a corridor or a passageway according to the definition of the prescriptive code. Instead, what matters is how it works within the path to safety.

The *ICCPC* also has Chapter 7, "Pedestrian Circulation." This chapter can guide the development of many of means of egress components. The intent of this chapter is to ensure that the circulation components (like aisles, corridors, stairs, etc.) adequately protect the occupant during egress and rescue operations. This chapter includes accessibility criteria as well. Using a performance code may allow the means of egress objectives to be achieved in innovative ways.

If using the *ICCPC* is not allowed by the jurisdiction, the NFPA codes also recognize the use of performance design. In both the *LSC* and the

NFPA 5000, Chapter 5, "Performance-Based Option" will allow the use of alternative approaches to the means of egress. These chapters similarly have sections that guide and allow a performance-based response, fire scenarios and safety criteria, balance the use of performance and prescriptive requirements and set parameters to define the evaluation and documentation methods.

In addition, the *NFPA 101A, Guide on Alternative Approaches to Life Safety* provides a set of systems which can be used to request an equivalency to the prescriptive requirements in the *LSC*. (The *LSC* is also known as *NFPA 101*.) These systems include a numerically-based evaluation system, documentation forms, and tools to formally request an equivalency for different occupancy types. Separate chapters set a rating system for specific occupancies including Health Care, Residential, Detentions and Correction, Business, and Educational.

Having the option to address the special conditions within a building using performance criteria may allow a unique and appropriate system of evacuation to be developed. Prescriptive codes may then be used to define other specific elements of the means of egress, such as the location of exit signs and emergency lighting. Remember, it is rare that a whole building or all aspects of the means of egress to be designed using performance criteria. It is typically a balance of prescriptive and performance criteria. (See the discussion of performance codes in Chapter 1.)

Because the means of egress is required to be accessible, the code requirements must be reviewed in conjunction with the appropriate federal or local accessibility regulations or standards. (See Chapter 2.) In the *IBC*, the accessible requirements for the means of egress can be found in a section called "Accessible Means of Egress" within the means of egress chapter (*IBC* Chapter 10). Additional requirements that may affect rooms, aisles and corridors may also be found in *IBC* Chapter 11, "Accessibility." When considering the federal accessibility requirements, you should first determine which federal standard applies, how it applies, and which guideline is to be used. (See Chapter 1 of this book.) The requirements of the *2010 ADA Standards* (or other federal guideline) and the *ICC A117.1* should be carefully reviewed and compared. These documents contain many requirements that will apply to the accessible route (including aisles, corridors, stairs, ramps, doors, etc.) and many of the elements that have been indicated in this chapter that are essential to a complete means of egress, including signage. To understand the extent of the means of egress that must be accessible, you should start in "Chapter 2: Scoping Requirements" under the "Section 207 Accessible Means of Egress." Once the scope is known, the individual elements can be researched. The accessibility guidelines do not use the same terms as the codes, so you will have to look for similar elements. For example, the "accessible route" would include any area along the means of egress including a room, corridor or lobby. The primary chapters that must be reviewed in the *2010 ADA Standards* include "Chapter 3: Building Blocks" (changes in floor surfaces, operable parts, etc.), "Chapter 4: Accessible Routes" (doors, ramps, elevators, etc.), "Chapter 5: General Site and Building Elements" (stairs and handrails), "Chapter 7: Communication Elements and Features" (signs and two way communications systems). Information is located in the same chapter organization in the *ICC A117.1* and the *ABA Guidelines*. However, remember, specific requirements in the can different than the *2010 ADA Standards* (and other federal standards) based on the edition of the *ICC A117.1*. Accessibility requirements will affect the size of many of the means of egress components, as well as the shapes and mounting heights of the various elements that occupants must use as part of the means of egress.

DOCUMENTATION

☝ **Note**

Determining the occupancy classification correctly is very important and can often affect means of egress requirements, because the codes may allow exceptions or require more stringent regulations, depending on the occupancy.

☝ **Note**

When in the exiting process, once an occupant moves into a protected portion of the means of egress system, the level of protection that they encounter cannot be reduced or eliminated.

Incorporating your research into your design will result in a safe and proper layout for your project. The use, size, and scope of the project will affect what needs to be documented. For example, does your project involve a series of rooms, a complete tenant space, or an entire floor of a building? This will affect which exit and exit width calculations (including aisles and corridors) and distances should be calculated and documented. If you are working with an existing space, you may need to evaluate the location and capacity of the existing exits.

Use the "Means of Egress" section of the digital code checklists provided with this book. This will help you to determine the means of egress components to be researched, remind you of the required calculations, and provide a method and form for documentation of your research. This can be helpful in case questions come up during design development or code review. Some documentation may be more easily noted on a floor plan of the space. For example, you may want to measure and indicate the exits locations are within the common path of travel and the travel distances. Because some distances are measured along the natural path an occupant would travel, it may be appropriate to show these distances on a floor plan that includes furniture.

In your documentation, several of the code requirements for the means of egress components should be stated. For example, it is typical for the required number of exits, maximum travel distances, common path of travel distances, and dead-end corridor lengths to be indicated as part of the code requirements in the drawings. For many projects, a "life safety plan" may be required for a permit. Often this plan must be reviewed by both the code officials and the fire marshal. (See Chapter 11 for additional considerations.) The plan or diagram should demonstrate that the design provides the correct number, size, and location of exits. In some cases, the code official may require the calculations for exit widths be shown. It is helpful for actual dimensions for travel distances, dead-end corridor lengths, common path of travel length be indicated on the drawings. In some cases, code officials will require locations of manual fire alarms, portable fire extinguishers, and other fire protections components be indicated, as well. If a life safety plan will be required, you should confirm the specific information that should be included.

CHAPTER 6

FIRE AND SMOKE RESISTANT ASSEMBLIES

Most building-related codes deal with fire and life safety. Their enforcement affects practically every part of a building, focusing first on prevention and then on early detection, control, and suppression to make a building safe. Interior fire related codes focus on confining a fire to the room of origin and limiting the growth of the fire to prevent flashover. The ultimate goal is the protection of the occupants of the building by giving them time to exit the building safely and firefighters time to address the control and suppression of the fire.

The codes include provisions for *fire protection* and *smoke protection*. Originally, most regulations were directed toward controlling fire within a building. Yet, because smoke can travel swiftly through a building and is toxic, it can be just as deadly as fire, if not more so. Whether a fire is full-blown or just smoldering, the smoke it produces can travel quickly and cause harm to the occupants of the building before the fire ever reaches them. The smoke causes asphyxiation, obstruction of sight, and disorientation, making evacuation difficult.

Because the control of fire and smoke is such a serious life safety issue, the prevention of fire and smoke spread is addressed in the codes in several ways. The construction type of a building, as discussed in Chapter 4, determines the types of materials that can be used and assigns an hourly fire resistance rating to almost every structural element in a building. Other parts of the codes place restrictions on materials used inside the building. These materials include everything from interior walls, windows, and doors to ductwork, wiring, and plumbing pipes. Interior finishes and furniture, as discussed in Chapter 10, are also regulated by codes and standards. When composed of combustible materials, these components can feed and sustain a fire within a building. Also known as *fuel loads*, they are restricted and managed by the codes.

◰ Note

More people die from asphyxiation due to smoke than from burns due to fire. Toxic fumes from burning or smoldering items also cause many deaths.

In addition to regulating the materials that go into a building or space, the codes require various *systems* that are intended to promote fire safety. Generally, the systems can be defined as passive fire protection systems, active fire protection systems, and exiting systems. The specific issues in each category are listed next.

PASSIVE SYSTEMS

☑ **Note**

A balance of active and passive fire protection systems is necessary for a safe building.

☑ **Note**

Passive fire protection systems may also be referred to as *prevention systems*.

Passive systems focus on prohibiting and containing fires. They are sometimes referred to as *prevention systems*. These elements are considered *passive* because, once in place, nothing else has to occur for them to be part of the control of a fire. Most parts of a passive or prevention system are discussed in this chapter:

❑ Fire and smoke barriers and partitions (e.g., walls)
❑ Horizontal assemblies (e.g., floors, ceilings)
❑ Opening protectives (e.g., windows, doors)
❑ Through-penetration protectives (e.g., fire-stops, draftstops, dampers)
❑ Finishes and furniture (e.g., wall coverings, finish floor materials, upholstered pieces, mattresses, and similar elements; these are discussed in Chapter 10)

ACTIVE SYSTEMS

These systems are considered *active* because they must be *activated* in order to work against the fire:

❑ Detection systems (e.g., detectors, fire alarms, communication systems; these systems are discussed in Chapter 7)
❑ Extinguishing and suppression systems (e.g., fire extinguishers, fire hoses, sprinkler systems; these systems are discussed in Chapter 7)
❑ Emergency lighting (these systems are discussed in Chapters 5 and 9)

EXITING SYSTEMS

Exiting systems are the elements of a space or building that assist and direct occupants to a place of safety:

❑ Means of egress (e.g., corridors, exits, stairs, ramps, and similar components; these components are discussed in Chapter 5)

❑ Exit communication systems (e.g., signage, audible, visual communication; these are discussed in Chapters 5 and 7)

Each system plays an important part in making a building safe. In recent code development, emphasis on the use of active systems such as automatic sprinkler systems has affected many requirements. However, most experts agree that a balance of active and passive systems is necessary for the safest building. In other words, components of each system should be included in the overall fire protection design.

This chapter discusses how compartmentation in a building works as part of the passive fire protection system by using assemblies that resist the spread of fire or smoke. These assemblies include fire walls, fire barriers and partitions, horizontal assemblies, smoke barriers and partitions, opening protectives, and through-penetration protectives. Each type is explained in this chapter. The codes also reference a range of industry standards. Many of these standards are listed in Figure 6.1 and introduced in this chapter. (Detection and suppression systems are discussed in Chapter 7.)

NFPA 80	Standard for Fire Doors and Other Opening Protectives
NFPA 92	Standard for Smoke Control Systems
NFPA 105	Standard for Installation of Smoke Door Assemblies and Other Opening Protectives
NFPA 204	Standard for Smoke and Heat Venting
NFPA 221	Standard for High Challenge Fire Walls, Fire Walls, and Fire Barrier Walls
NFPA 252	Standard Methods of Fire Tests of Door Assemblies
NFPA 257	Standard on Fire Test for Window and Glass Block Assemblies
NFPA 259	Standard Test Method for Potential Heat of Building Materials
NFPA 270	Standard Test Method for Measurement of Smoke Obscuration Using a Conical Radiant Source in a Single Closed Chamber
NFPA 288	Standard Method of Fire Tests of Floor Fire Door Assemblies Installed Horizontally in Fire Resistance–Rated Floor Systems
NFPA 555	Guide on Methods for Evaluating Potential for Room Flashover
NFPA 703	Standard for Fire-Retardant-Treated Wood and Fire-Retardant Coatings for Building Materials

Figure 6.1 Common NFPA standards for building materials and assemblies.

COMPARTMENTATION IN A BUILDING

The overall concept of a passive fire -protection system is *compartmentation*. Compartmentation is the separation of areas in a building to control fire and smoke by the use of wall, floor, and ceiling assemblies. The building code, fire code, and/or *Life Safety Code (LSC)* will determine when rated assemblies are required. Each code specifies when certain areas must be separated from another area and when the spread of fire or smoke must be limited. Some of these assemblies will be required to be fire-rated; others will have to be smoke rated or a combination of both. (These are discussed later in this chapter.)

Fire compartments are created by fire resistance–rated assemblies, which include fire walls, fire barriers, horizontal assemblies, and fire partitions. These assemblies create defined and separate areas within a building and sometimes separate "buildings" in a single structure. As a result, the fire can spread to only a limited area before meeting resistance from the rated assemblies. These areas are required by the code at certain intervals, between different uses, and where different levels of hazard may exist. Fire resistance–rated assemblies can also be used to create separate *fire areas* for better fire protection and to limit the need for an automatic sprinkler system. (Fire areas are discussed later in this chapter.)

The control of smoke can be just as important as or even more important than the control of fire. And because assemblies that have fire resistance ratings do not necessarily resist the spread of smoke, the codes require the use of smoke barriers and smoke partitions in some cases. When required, these assemblies become part of the compartmentation of the space or building and referred to *smoke compartments*. When assemblies are required to be both fire resistant and smoke resistant, they are referred to as fire and smoke barriers (as discussed later in this chapter).

The use of an automatic sprinkler system within a building will affect the requirements for compartmentation as well. For example, if a building is equipped with a fully automatic sprinkler system, some fire rating requirements may be reduced or eliminated. This is discussed in more detail in the section "Sprinkler Systems" in Chapter 7. However, during a project, it is important to know if an automatic sprinkler system will be provided or if an approved one exists within the building so that the appropriate compartmentation requirements can be researched.

Each type of separation wall or assembly used to create a rated compartment has specific requirements, depending on its use and location. The various uses of fire resistance–rated walls and smoke-tight walls as part of compartmentation are discussed in the next several sections.

FIRE WALLS

Fire walls can be located within a building structure to create two or more separate buildings as defined by the code. The main purpose of a fire wall is to provide complete vertical separation between areas in a building. A fire wall must extend continuously from its foundation to or through the roof. Within a building, it must extend at least from exterior wall to exterior wall. In some cases, the wall is required to extend beyond the exterior walls and project through the roof (i.e., a parapet wall).

Fire walls can be used to subdivide a building structure that is composed of two separate types of construction or to create building divisions within the same construction type for the purpose of allowing larger building areas. (See Chapter 4.) For example, if a medical office building and a hospital were built of different construction types but were built so that they were connected, a fire wall would be necessary to separate construction types, and it would also serve to separate the different occupancies. Another example would be the design for a factory that exceeded its allowable area; fire walls could be used to divide the total area into two or more smaller areas that fall within the allowable area limitations.

Sometimes rated walls are used to separate ownership of a building not necessarily separate buildings per the code. When a rated wall is located on a lot line and shared between two structures, it is referred to as a *party wall*. In some cases, a party wall is required to be constructed as a fire wall. However, if the areas of the two sides are within the allowable area per the construction type and use, it can be simply a rated wall.

Fire walls are built so that if the construction on one side of the wall fell during a fire or emergency, the fire wall and the construction on the other side would remain standing. They are typically tested using *NFPA 221, Standard for High Challenge Fire Walls, Fire Walls, and Fire Barrier Walls.* A fire wall can be rated a minimum of 2 hours, but the most common required rating is 3 or 4 hours. The level of rating required is usually determined by the occupancy classification within the building, as shown in the *IBC* Table 706.4, "Fire Wall Fire Resistance Ratings" in Figure 6.2. The ratings of the fire walls are listed by the occupancy classification. If the two areas of the building are different occupancies, the highest rating is required. Although the NFPA codes set a minimum rating of 2 hours for a fire wall, higher ratings and other specific requirements are listed within the text and in the occupancy chapters. Within a fire wall, openings and penetrations are very limited. In some cases, certain penetrations are not allowed. Check the codes for the specific requirements for each fire wall location.

> **🖺 Note**
>
> Fire walls are not usually added to existing buildings. A fire wall must extend continuously from the foundation of the building up to or through the roof.

TABLE 706.4 FIRE WALL FIRE RESISTANCE RATINGS

GROUP	FIRE RESISTANCE RATING (hours)
A, B, E, H-4, I, R-1, R-2, U	3[a]
F-1, H-3b, H-5, M, S-1	3
H-1, H-2	4[b]
F-2, S-2, R-3, R-4	2

a In Type II or V construction, walls shall be permitted to have a 2-hour fire resistance rating.
b For Group H-1, H-2, or H-3 buildings, also see Sections 415.7 and 415.8.

Figure 6.2 International Building Code Table 706.4, "Fire Wall Fire Resistance Ratings" (2021 *International Building Code*, copyright © 2021. Washington, DC: International Code Council. Reproduced with permission. All rights reserved. www.iccsafe.org).

Because fire walls are usually planned and built during the initial construction of the building, they are not part of a typical interior project. However, if the fire wall must be penetrated for any reason (e.g., adding a door), additional research is necessary to make sure that the fire resistance rating is maintained and the opening is allowable. To determine the fire resistance rating of an existing fire wall, it may be necessary to refer to the original construction documents or contact the original architect to obtain the actual rating.

FIRE BARRIERS, HORIZONTAL ASSEMBLIES, AND FIRE PARTITIONS

☞ **Note**

For certain occupancies, the codes allow horizontal separations (between floors) that work like fire walls to separate a single structure into different construction types or buildings. (See Chapter 3.)

☞ **Note**

A fire barrier provides more protection than a fire partition.

Fire-rated assemblies are used by the codes to create compartments within a building or space. By separating the different areas of a building (either horizontally or vertically), the spread of a single fire and transfer of the heat generated by that fire can be limited. There are three basic types of rated assemblies: fire barriers, fire partitions, and horizontal assemblies. In the *IBC*, the terms *fire barrier* and *fire partition* are used to indicate vertical rated walls that separate certain areas or uses within a building. (The NFPA does not use the term *fire partition*. They refer to all rated walls as fire barriers but modify the requirements, as necessary.) In the *IBC* and the NFPA codes, *horizontal assemblies* are floor/ceiling or ceiling/roof assemblies that have a fire resistance rating. The codes determine when each type is required to provide the appropriate level of compartmentation within the building or space.

Fire barriers are walls that have a fire resistance rating. In most cases, they must be continuous and extend vertically from the top of a floor assembly to the bottom of a floor/ceiling assembly. For example, a fire barrier would extend through a suspended ceiling to the slab above. When a fire barrier is required, it is typically required to sit between floor and ceiling assemblies of the same rating, making a box-like enclosure. Also, when a fire barrier intersects another fire resistance–rated assembly—either another wall or a horizontal assembly (i.e., floor/ceiling assembly)—additional protection is required at the joint. The doors, windows, and other penetrations in the rated assemblies must be rated as well. (Referred to as opening protectives and through-protectives, these are discussed later in this chapter.) In addition, the number of openings in a fire barrier, including doors and windows, is limited.

In the *IBC*, a *fire partition* is similar to fire barrier in that it is a fire-rated wall, but it has slightly different requirements. In most cases, fire partitions have less restrictive requirements than fire barriers. For example, a fire partition can extend from structure to structure in a building, but it is also allowed to stop at a rated ceiling system; fire barriers cannot. This difference is shown in Figure 6.3.

Although a fire partition separates one area from another, it is not always required to create a full enclosure like is typical for a fire barrier. Fire partitions are most often used to separate corridors, tenant spaces in malls, dwelling units, sleeping units, areas of refuge and elevator lobbies from the rest of the floor. (Refer to the inset titled "Rooms and Spaces" in Chapter 3.) A fire partition usually has a rating of at least 1 hour. In certain situations, corridor walls and walls between dwelling and sleeping units can have a lower rating. Often an automatic sprinkler system is required for the lower rating to be allowed. Openings in a fire partition are required to be protected, although the number of openings is not limited. And unlike fire barriers, some fire partitions are not required to be supported by horizontal assemblies of the same rating. (Check the codes for specifics.)

The NFPA codes do not differentiate between fire barriers and fire partitions. However, by allowing exceptions to the requirements for fire barriers (in cases where the *IBC* calls for the use of fire partitions) and by adding requirements where a higher level of separation is necessary, the fire rating requirements of the codes become similar.

Horizontal assemblies are floor/ceiling, ceiling/roof assemblies, or other horizontal building components that are required by the codes to be rated. They serve the same function as fire barriers but are horizontal instead of vertical building elements. Horizontal assemblies must meet requirements like those of fire barriers. Horizontal assemblies extend horizontally from one rated wall or exterior wall to another. Where fire

◀ **Note**

Fire and smoke barriers are often important components of the means of egress. A safe means of egress is a combination of the requirements discussed in Chapters 5, 6, 7, and 10 of this book.

◀ **Note**

Fire barriers and partitions are given fire *resistance* ratings and opening and through penetrations are given fire *protection* ratings.

◀ **Note**

Fire and smoke barriers and horizontal assemblies are typically used to create full enclosures with wall, ceiling, and floor assemblies. Fire and smoke partitions are used to separate spaces on the same floor rather than to create compartments.

◀ **Note**

The *IBC* requires the hourly rating for rated wall assemblies to be indicated on the wall above the finished ceiling at specific intervals.

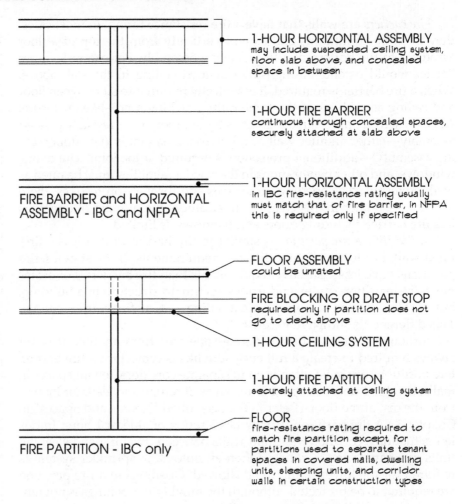

Figure 6.3 Fire barriers, horizontal assemblies, and fire partitions.

barriers and horizontal assemblies meet, the joints must be sealed. Openings and penetrations are limited and must be protected as well.

In most cases, when the codes require the separation of a specific area, fire barriers and horizontal assemblies are required. When the horizontal assemblies (floors and ceilings) and vertical assemblies (walls) surrounding an area have the same fire resistance rating, it creates a complete compartment or enclosure—like a four-sided box with a top and bottom. An example is the enclosure of an exit stairway where all four walls, the floor, and the ceiling/roof have a 2-hour rating. Depending on the codes, fire barriers and horizontal assemblies are tested using *ASTM E119, Standard Test Methods for Fire Tests of Building Construction and Materials; NFPA 251, Standard Methods of Tests of Fire Resistance of Building Construction and Materials;* or *UL 263, Standard for Fire Tests of Building Construction and Materials.* They may also be required to pass *NFPA 221, Standard for High Challenge Fire Walls, Fire Walls, and Fire Barrier Walls.*

The codes require that fire walls, fire barriers, and partitions be marked. The marking must indicate the type of use (i.e., fire barrier or fire partition) and the hourly rating it provides. This mark can be above the finish ceiling, but it must be accessible. The information must be repeated at specified intervals along the length of the wall and be in legible-size lettering. This is not required in certain Residential uses with drywall ceilings. However, this is very useful when working on a project in an existing building because it is a quick way to determine the location of existing rated walls.

It is very common for a rated wall to be added or modified during an interior project. Whether the project includes a new layout, new finishes, or the addition of wiring and cabling, modifications may affect a rated wall or assembly. Therefore, determining the purpose and rating of the assembly is critical to maintaining the compartmentation of the building. Also, keep in mind that the presence of an automatic sprinkler system may allow lower fire resistance ratings. Therefore, the rating depends on the purpose of the fire barrier, fire partition, or horizontal fire partition; the occupancy classification; and the existence of sprinklers in the space or building. (The sprinkler system must meet the current code requirements.)

The most common uses of fire barriers, horizontal assemblies, and fire partitions for compartmentation are described next. (Smoke assemblies are explained in the following section.) Keep in mind that an assembly may have to be rated for more than one reason. This is especially true for structural components such as a floor/ceiling assembly that must meet construction type requirements as well as provide compartmentation of an area. For example, if a space or room requires a 1-hour rated floor horizontal assembly, but the construction type requires the floor assembly to be rated 2 hours for that construction type, the floor assembly must provide the 2-hour rating. The highest required rating must be provided. If a horizontal separation is required and the existing floor/ ceiling assembly does not provide an adequate fire resistance rating, then a rated ceiling assembly may have to be installed below the existing ceiling structure to reach the required fire resistance rating.

Fire Areas

Fire barriers and exterior walls are used in a building to separate one area from another, creating two or more *fire areas*. Fire areas are most often required to provide compartmentation and to stay below the area limitations requiring an automatic sprinkler system according to the fire code. The building codes and fire codes determine the allowable size of a fire area and if multiple fire areas are required for each occupancy classification. For example, a large factory building can be divided into separate fire areas to manage the need for an automatic sprinkler system. The separate fire areas may allow one area of a building to be sprinklered and another to remain nonsprinklered, as shown in the plan in Figure 6.4. (When a fire wall is used to create separate buildings, the buildings are considered separate fire areas as well.)

Some occupancies require separate fire areas within a building regardless of size. For example, a fire area is almost always required to separate a Hazardous use from another occupancy type. An example is a small area of hazardous materials being stored within a large Storage occupancy. (This is different from incidental use or accessory occupancies, as described later.)

A horizontal assembly can also be used to create individual fire areas between floors of a multistory building. For example, in the building shown in the section in Figure 6.4, the Business and Factory uses are separate fire areas. As in the previous example, this may allow one floor to

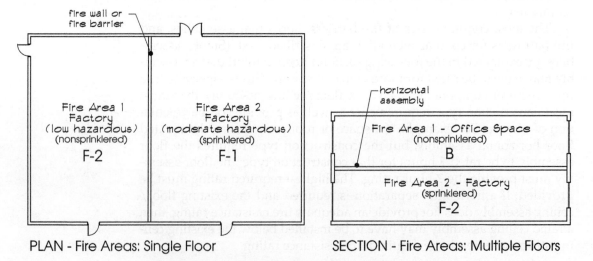

PLAN - Fire Areas: Single Floor   SECTION - Fire Areas: Multiple Floors

Figure 6.4 Fire areas: Single floor and multiple floors.

TABLE 707.3.10 FIRE RESISTANCE-RATING REQUIREMENTS FOR FIRE BARRIERS, FIRE WALLS OR HORIZONTAL ASSEMBLIES BETWEEN FIRE AREAS

OCCUPANCY GROUP	FIRE RESISTANCE RATING (hours)
H-1, H-2	4
F-1, H-3, S-1	3
A, B, E, F-2, H-4, H-5, I, M, R, S-2	2
U	1

Figure 6.5 International Building Code Table 707.3.10, "Fire Resistance Rating Requirements for Fire Barrier Assemblies, Fire Walls or Horizontal Assemblies Between Fire Areas" (2021*International Building Code*, copyright © 2021. Washington, DC: International Code Council. Reproduced with permission. All rights reserved. www.iccsafe.org).

be sprinklered and another to be nonsprinklered. A fire area can also include more than one floor. This is determined by the codes. For example, high-rise buildings are usually divided into separate fire areas every couple of floor levels.

The required fire resistance rating of the fire barrier or horizontal assembly separating each fire area is then determined by the code. Each building code has a table similar to *IBC* Table 707.3.10, "Fire Resistance Rating Requirements for Fire Barrier Assemblies or Horizontal Assemblies Between Fire Areas," shown in Figure 6.5. The plan in Figure 6.4 is an example of separate fire areas being created within a Factory occupancy. One area of the factory is considered F-2 because it contains materials that are considered low hazard. The other part of the factory contains more hazardous materials and is considered F-1. Knowing this and using the *IBC* table in Figure 6.5, the rating of the fire barrier between the fire areas can be determined: It is 3 hours. (The strictest requirement applies.) This may allow one area to be sprinklered and the other to be nonsprinklered. It can also be seen from the table that certain occupancies, such as Hazardous ones, can require ratings as high as 4 hours.

> **✔ Note**
>
> Fire ratings for floor/ceiling assemblies are first controlled by the construction type of the building. Other code requirements can require a higher rating but cannot allow a lower rating than required by the construction type.

Occupancy Separation

When more than one type of occupancy exists within a building or space, it is considered a mixed occupancy or a multiple occupancy, depending on which code is being used. It can be further defined as a separated or

✍ Note

Compartmentation is an important concept in the fire codes. It is used to prevent the spread of fire and is especially important in high-rise and Institutional buildings.

nonseparated mixed occupancy or as a separated or mixed multiple occupancy. (See the discussion of mixed and multiple occupancies in Chapter 3.) For it to be considered separated, each occupancy must be separated from the other by a fire barrier or horizontal assembly.

Occupancy separation may be required in various situations. The most obvious one is when multiple tenants of different occupancy types exist in a building. An example might be a building that has a restaurant, retail stores, and offices, each operated by different tenants. Another case is when a single user or owner operates more than one use (e.g., occupancy) within a single structure—for example, a sports center that includes a gymnasium (Assembly) and an exercise apparel store (Mercantile) in the same building. (The store might also be considered an accessory. See the section "Accessory Occupancies" in Chapter 3.)

In the past, all occupancies were typically required to be separated by at least a 1-hour fire rating. However, currently, the *IBC* code requires only occupancies that have dissimilar risk factors to be separated by a fire barrier or horizontal assembly. This allows many occupancies to have unrated walls separating them. (These unrated walls typically still have to be smoke-tight, however, as described later.)

Each building code and the *LSC* use a table similar to *IBC* Table 508.4, "Required Separation of Occupancies (Hours)," shown in Figure 6.6, to indicate when separation is required. In this table, the occupancies that are considered to have similar risk factors have been grouped together along the top of the chart and similarly down the left side. For example, B, F-1, M, and S-1 occupancies are grouped together. To determine if a rated separation is required, cross-reference the occupancy classifications along the top and the left side of the table. For example, in Plan A of Figure 6.7 there is an Assembly occupancy adjacent to a Business occupancy. Using the table in Figure 6.6, locate the group including Business (B) along the top and then locate Assembly (A) at the left side. Where the (B) column and the (A) row meet, a rating of 1 hour for a sprinklered (S) building and a rating of 2 hours for a nonsprinklered (NS) building are indicated. Because the building in this example is nonsprinklered, the wall that separates the two occupancy classifications must have a fire resistance rating of 2 hours. (Notes at the bottom of the table clarify the abbreviations used in the table and offer exceptions based on specific circumstances.) If the same table was used to determine the fire rating between the Business (B) and Mercantile (M) occupancies in Figure 6.7, no rated separation would be required because they are grouped together in the table.

✍ Note

A fire barrier typically must extend from the top of the floor/ceiling assembly to the underside of the floor slab, or roof deck above. It must pass through concealed spaces such as the plenum space above a suspended ceiling.

TABLE 508.4 REQUIRED SEPARATION OF OCCUPANCIES (HOURS)[f]

OCCUPANCY	A, E		I-1a, I-3, I-4		I-2		Ra		F-2, S-2b, U		Be, F-1, M, S-1		H-1		H-2		H-3, H-4		H-5	
	S	NS	S	NS	S	NS	S	NS	S	NS	S	NS	S	NS	S	NS	S	NS	S	NS
A, E	N	N	1	2	2	NP	1	2	N	1	1	2	NP	NP	3	4	2	3	2	NP
I-1a, I-3, I-4	1	2	N	N	2	NP	1	NP	1	2	1	2	NP	NP	3	NP	2	NP	2	NP
I-2	2	NP	2	NP	N	N	2	NP	2	NP	2	NP	NP	NP	3	NP	2	NP	2	NP
Ra	1	2	1	NP	2	N	N	N	1c	2c	1	2	NP	NP	3	NP	2	NP	2	NP
F-2, S-2b, U	N	1	1	2	2	NP	1c	2c	N	N	1	2	NP	NP	3	4	2	3	2	NP
Be, F-1, M, S-1	1	2	1	2	2	NP	1	2	N	N	N	N	NP	NP	2	3	1	2	1	NP
H-1	NP	NP	NP	NP	NP	NP	NP	NP	NP	NP	NP	NP	N	NP	NP	NP	NP	NP	NP	NP
H-2	3	4	3	NP	3	NP	3	NP	3	4	2	3	NP	NP	N	NP	1	NP	1	NP
H-3, H-4	2	3	2	NP	2	NP	2	NP	2	3	1	2	NP	NP	1	NP	1d	NP	1	NP
H-5	2	NP	2	NP	2	NP	2	NP	2	NP	1	NP	NP	NP	1	NP	1	NP	N	NP

S = Buildings equipped throughout with an automatic sprinkler system installed in accordance with Section 903.3.1.1.

NS = Buildings not equipped throughout with an automatic sprinkler system installed in accordance with Section 903.3.1.1.

N = No separation requirement.

NP = Not permitted.

a See Section 420.

b The required separation from areas used only for private or pleasure vehicles shall be reduced by 1 hour but not to less than 1 hour.

c See Sections 406.3.2 and 406.6.4.

d Separation is not required between occupancies of the same classification.

e See Section 422.2 for *ambulatory care facilities*.

f Occupancy separations that serve to define fire area limits established in Chapter 9 for requiring fire protection systems shall also comply with Section 707.3.10 and Table 707.3.10 in accordance with Section 901.7.

Figure 6.6 International Building Code Table 508.4, "Required Separation of Occupancies (Hours)" (2021 *International Building Code*, copyright © 2021. Washington, DC: International Code Council. Reproduced with permission. All rights reserved. www.iccsafe.org).

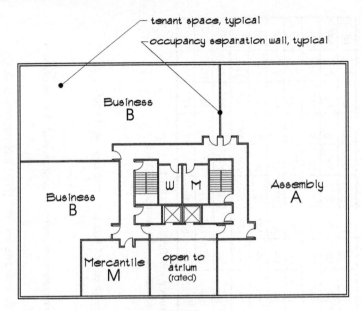

PLAN A - Multi-Tenant Building

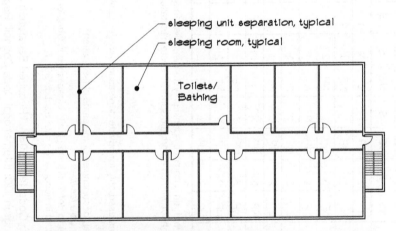

PLAN B - Multiple Residential Units (Dormitory - 2nd Floor)

Figure 6.7 Occupancy and dwelling unit separation (nonsprinklered building).

Occupancy separation can be required vertically as well. For example, if a Storage (S-2) use was located on the floor below the Business (B) occupancies in Figure 6.7, the table would be used again to determine that a 2-hour fire resistance separation is required between these occupancies in a nonsprinklered building. A horizontal assembly would then have to provide the required rating. Because floor/ceiling assemblies can also be regulated by construction types, this rating should be checked as well, and the strictest requirement should be used. For example, if working on a project in an existing building requiring a 3-hour rated floor assembly between occupancies, the rating of the floor assembly would need to be checked based on the construction type of the building. If the existing floor assembly provides only a 1-hour rating, for example, additional rated materials would be necessary to increase the fire resistance to 3 hours, as required by the codes. If the floor assembly meets or exceeds the required occupancy separation requirement, no additional materials are necessary. In addition, a rated wall may serve both to separate the different occupancies and create separate fire areas (as discussed in the previous section). If so, then the highest rating given from Table 707.3.10 in Figure 6.5 and Table 508.4 in Figure 6.6 must be specified.

> **☑ Note**
>
> Even though walls separating tenants may not be required to be rated, they are usually required to resist the passage of smoke.

Tenant Separation

In the past, codes required all tenants in a multi-tenant building were required to be separated by some level of fire resistance–rated construction. This was typically referred to as a *tenant separation* wall (also known as a *demising* wall). However, most recent building codes treat adjacent tenants as an occupancy separation issue. In other words, the codes no longer require a rated separation between tenants of the same occupancy, such as a law office next to an accounting office, which are both Business occupancies. In addition, because of recent changes in the way that the *IBC* determines the need for rated partitions between different occupancies, in some cases even tenants that are different occupancy classifications may not be required to be rated. (See the preceding section titled "Occupancy Separation.")

However, there is an exception. Tenant separation still applies to tenants within a covered mall. In most cases, tenants within a mall (e.g., stores, restaurants) are required to be separated by a fire partition. The walls open to the mall are not required to be rated. A covered mall has many specific code requirements because of its unique organization and use. If designing a covered mall, additional research would need to be done on these unique code requirements.

Dwelling and Sleeping Unit Separation

Dwelling units and sleeping units within most Residential occupancies are required by the codes to be separated by fire partitions. Examples

✎ Note

Walls that divide living units, such as sleeping units in hotels and dormitories and dwelling units in apartment buildings, must also meet sound transmission code requirements.

include different units in a hotel, dormitory, or apartment building. (See also the inset titled "Rooms and Spaces" in Chapter 3.) These must also be separated from other adjacent occupancy classifications by a fire partition. However, a dwelling or sleeping unit adjacent to another use but of the same occupancy classification, such as the lobby of a hotel, would not have to be separated by a fire partition.

Fire partitions separating dwelling and sleeping units are typically rated 1 hour. For example, a 1-hour separation is required between sleeping units in a dormitory, as shown in Plan B of Figure 6.7, but the floor/ ceiling assembly between the first and second floors would only require a rating of 1 hour if there were additional sleeping or dwelling units on the floor below. In some cases, the walls in a sprinklered building will be allowed a lower rating. These walls often must meet sound transmission requirements as well.

Incidental Use

✎ Note

The number and cost of fire resistance–rated walls are reduced by designing rooms with like fire ratings adjacent to each other—for example, a linen collection room and a laundry room.

The codes require that certain rooms within a building, such as machine rooms, laboratories, and laundry rooms, be separated from the other parts of the building. These are called *incidental use*. (See the discussion in the section titled "Incidental Use" in Chapter 3.) The codes require these rooms to be enclosed by fire barriers. The required ratings are given in the text and by tables within the codes. *IBC* Table 509, "Incidental Uses," shown in Figure 6.8, lists the types of rooms or areas that are considered incidental within the *IBC*.

For incidental use areas, passive and active fire protection might be required. In some cases, the requirement is specific to an occupancy classification. For example, the waste collection room shown in the nonsprinklered building in Figure 6.9 is 180 square feet (16.7 sm). The *IBC* table in Figure 6.8 indicates that waste and linen collection rooms over "100 square feet" (9.3 sm) and not in an ambulatory care or I-2 occupancy are required to be separated by a fire barrier with a rating of 1 hour or to be sprinklered. Because this building is nonsprinklered, this room would require fire protection to keep it separate from the rest of the space. For many of the incidental uses listed in the table, an automatic sprinkler system can be provided instead of the fire barrier, though in some cases a fire barrier and an automatic sprinkler system are required. If an incidental use is not surrounded by a fire barrier, the walls still must resist the passage of smoke. The NFPA codes identify similar areas that are considered "hazardous" and require separation by fire barriers, smoke partitions, and/or sprinklering within each occupancy chapter.

✎ Note

Shafts used for refuse and laundry chutes are subject to additional requirements. Refer to the building codes.

[F]TABLE 509.1 INCIDENTAL USES

ROOM OR AREA	SEPARATION AND/OR PROTECTION
Furnace room where any piece of equipment is over 400,000 Btu per hour input	1 hour or provide automatic sprinkler system
Rooms with boilers where the largest piece of equipment is over 15 psi and 10 horsepower	1 hour or provide automatic sprinkler system
Refrigerant machinery room	1 hour or provide automatic sprinkler system
Hydrogen fuel gas rooms, not classified as Group H	1 hour in Group B, F, M, S, and U occupancies; 2 hours in Group A, E, I, and R occupancies.
Incinerator rooms	2 hours and provide automatic sprinkler system
Paint shops, not classified as Group H, located in occupancies other than Group F	2 hours; or 1 hour and provide automatic sprinkler system
In Group E occupancies, laboratories and vocational shops not classified as Group H	1 hour or provide automatic sprinkler system
In Group I-2 occupancies, laboratories not classified as Group H	1 hour and provide automatic sprinkler system
In *ambulatory care facilities,* laboratories not classified as Group H	1 hour or provide automatic sprinkler system
Laundry rooms over 100 square feet	1 hour or provide automatic sprinkler system
In Group I-2, laundry rooms over 100 square feet	1 hour
Group I-3 cells and Group I-2 patient rooms equipped with padded surfaces	1 hour
In Group I-2, physical plant maintenance shops	1 hour
In ambulatory care facilities or Group I-2 occupancies, waste and linen collection rooms with containers that have an aggregate volume of 10 cubic feet or greater	1 hour
In other than ambulatory care facilities and Group I-2 occupancies, waste and linen collection rooms over 100 square feet	1 hour or provide automatic sprinkler system
In ambulatory care facilities or Group I-2 occupancies, storage rooms greater than 100 square feet	1 hour
Electrical installations and transformers	See Sections 110.26 through 110.34 and Sections 450.8 through 450.48 of NFPA 70 for protection and separation requirements.

For SI: 1 square foot = 0.0929 m², 1 pound per square inch (psi) = 6.9 kPa, 1 British thermal unit (Btu) per hour = 0.293 watts, 1 horsepower = 746 watts, 1 gallon = 3.785 L, 1 cubic foot = 0.0283 m³.

Figure 6.8 International Building Code Table 509.1, "Incidental Uses" (2021 *International Building Code*, copyright © 2021. Washington, DC: International Code Council. Reproduced with permission. All rights reserved. www.iccsafe.org).

Vertical Shaft Enclosures

There are various vertical openings that may occur in a building. These can be small or large and extend the whole height of the building or through several floors. Because these are opportunities for fire and smoke to move to multiple floors, the codes regulate their use and when they need to be enclosed. These protective enclosures are considered a type of shaft. Typically, the code allows vertical openings without enclosures in most occupancies when they are limited to certain uses and number of floors. However, fire barriers are required to enclose elevators, dumbwaiters, atriums, exit stairways, and shafts for building systems. Examples of these are shown in Figure 6.9. The fire ratings for vertical shaft enclosures are primarily determined by the number of floors that they penetrate. Typically, a 1-hour or 2-hour separation is required. An exit stairwell can be considered a vertical shaft, for instance. (Some openings for exit access stairs may not require enclosures.) Enclosure walls are usually continuous from the bottom of the building to the underside of the roof deck. When a shaft terminates at a floor level, the top and bottom of the shaft may also require a horizontal assembly.

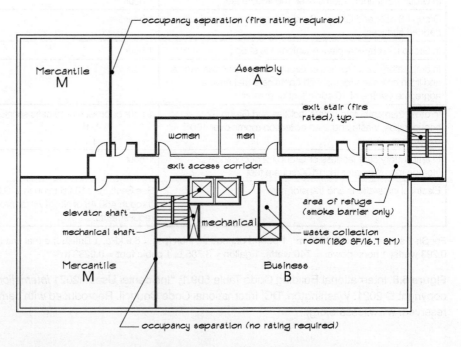

Figure 6.9 Rated building components (nonsprinklered building).

For elevators, the codes limit the number of elevator cars in a single shaft or hoistway enclosure to usually no more than two to four. If more elevators are used, additional rated walls will be required to separate them. In addition, each shaft often requires specific venting, smoke detection, and standby power. (See the section titled "Elevators" in Chapter 5.) The rating of an elevator shaft is also determined by the number of floors that it penetrates. (See the sections titled "Smokeproof Vertical Shafts" and "Stairways" later in this chapter.)

Means of Egress Components

In many cases, parts of the means of egress, as discussed in Chapter 5, are required to be separated by fire barriers. (Smoke barriers, as explained in the next section, may also be required.) These can include stairwells, exit passageways, horizontal exits, and other exit enclosures. In most cases, the fire resistance rating must be provided vertically and horizontally. The ratings typically get stricter as an occupant moves toward the exit. For example, an exit access may require a 1-hour rating, and the exit may require a 2-hour rating. As the different means of egress are discussed, refer to Figure 6.10 for examples of the components that require fire resistance ratings. Within the building codes and the *LSC*, these requirements are given in tables and within the chapters that discuss fire resistance ratings and occupancy requirements.

> ◪ **Note**
>
> Atriums also have additional fire protection requirements. See the inset titled "Atriums and Mezzanines" in Chapter 4 and the codes for specifics.

Stairways

Typically, the walls that enclose *exit stairs* must meet the same requirements as a vertical shaft. Usually stairway walls must have a 1-hour rating if the stairs are three stories or less and a 2-hour rating if they are four or more stories. Protection from smoke may also be required. (See Chapter 5 for additional information on stairs.) An *exit access stair* may also require a fire-rated enclosure if it connects more than two floors.

The walls surrounding a rated stairwell would be considered fire barriers and must be vertically continuous through each floor and fully enclose the stair. In most cases, the floor and ceiling of an exit access stair must also consist of rated horizontal assemblies. To protect the fire ratings of these assemblies, only limited penetrations are allowed. In addition, in a high-rise building the stairwells are required to be smokeproof to serve as an area of refuge. (See the section "Areas of Refuge" later in this chapter.)

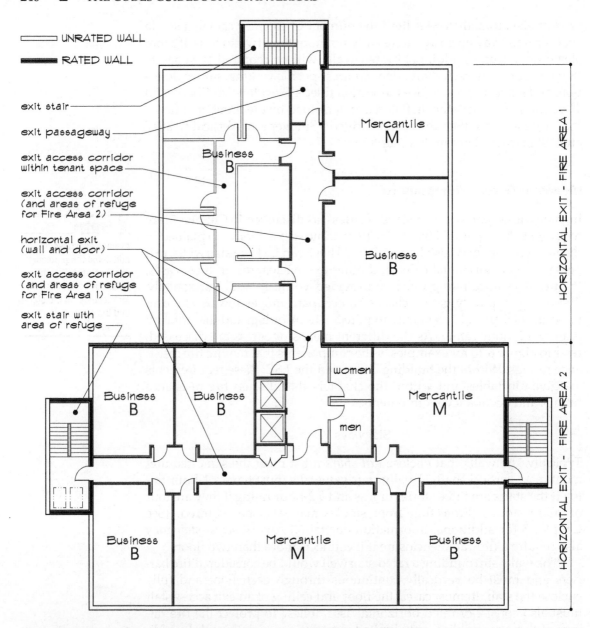

▭▭▭ UNRATED WALL

▬▬▬ RATED WALL

exit stair

exit passageway

exit access corridor
within tenant space

exit access corridor
(and areas of refuge
for Fire Area 2)

horizontal exit
(wall and door)

exit access corridor
(and areas of refuge
for Fire Area 1)

exit stair with
area of refuge

Mercantile
M

Business
B

Business
B

HORIZONTAL EXIT - FIRE AREA 1

Business
B

Business
B

women

men

Mercantile
M

HORIZONTAL EXIT - FIRE AREA 2

Business
B

Mercantile
M

Business
B

Figure 6.10 Rated means of egress components (nonsprinklered building).

Horizontal Exits

A horizontal exit is used to provide an alternate means of egress within a building. It uses a fire barrier to provide a protected exit from one space into another on the same floor of a building or to an adjacent building. (This is discussed in more detail in Chapter 5.) The walls must either be continuous through every floor to the ground or be surrounded by a floor and ceiling that are equally rated. This rated wall usually has a rating of 2 hours. The doors must also be rated (usually 2 hours) and swing in the direction of the refuge area. Although a horizontal exit in effect creates separate areas within a building in a manner similar to that of fire areas, the intent of the separation is different. A fire area is created to limit the spread of fire. A horizontal exit, by contrast, provides protected path to a refuge area away from the fire to protect occupants. A horizontal exit also usually includes smoke protection. Typically, the wall requires a rating of 2 hours and must extend to the exterior walls.

Areas of Refuge

Areas of refuge are an integral part of a "defend in place" means of egress strategy as defined in the codes. They can also be part of an accessible means of egress. Because these areas are most often meant to provide a place for people who cannot exit the building because of health or disability, the codes require that such areas be separated by a smoke barrier. Smoke barriers provide a minimum fire resistance rating of 1 hour and prevent the intrusion of smoke. (Smoke barriers are explained in more detail next.) Sometimes an area of refuge can be located within other parts of the means of egress, including an exit stair, an elevator lobby, or on the other side of a horizontal exit. The separation requirements of the other means of egress components will often be higher than just a smoke barrier. In these cases, the separation of the area of refuge must meet the more restrictive requirements.

Corridors

Exit access corridors are corridors that lead to an exit or an exit stairwell. The rating of exit access corridors ranges from ½ hour to 1 hour. Each of the codes provides this information differently. The *IBC* uses Table 1020.2, "Corridor Fire Resistance Rating," shown in Figure 6.11. To determine the rating of the corridor using this table, three things are required: the occupancy classification, the occupant load served by the corridor, and whether the building is sprinklered. (See Chapter 3 for occupant load information.) For example, for an exit access corridor in a Business (B)

TABLE 1020.2 CORRIDOR FIRE RESISTANCE RATING

OCCUPANCY	OCCUPANT LOAD SERVED BY CORRIDOR	REQUIRED FIRE RESISTANCE RATING (hours)	
		Without sprinkler system	With sprinkler system
H-1, H-2, H-3	All	Not Permitted	1[c]
H-4, H-5	Greater than 30	Not Permitted	1[c]
A, B, E, F, M, S, U	Greater than 30	1	0
R	Greater than 10	Not Permitted	0.5[c]/1[d]
I-2[a]	All	Not Permitted	0
I-1, I-3	All	Not Permitted	1[b, c]
I-4	All	1	0

a For requirements for occupancies in Group I-2, see Sections 407.2 and 407.3.
b For a reduction in the *fire resistance rating* for occupancies in Group I-3, see Section 408.8.
c Buildings equipped throughout with an *automatic sprinkler system* in accordance with Section 903.3.1.1 or 903.3.1.2 where allowed.
d Group R-3 and R-4 buildings equipped throughout with an *automatic sprinkler system* in accordance with Section 903.3.1.3. See Section 903.2.8 for occupancies where automatic sprinkler systems are permitted in accordance with Section 903.3.1.3.

Figure 6.11 International Building Code Table 1020.2, "Corridor Fire Resistance Rating" (2021 *International Building Code*, copyright © 2021. Washington, DC: International Code Council. Reproduced with permission. All rights reserved. www.iccsafe.org)

☑ **Note**

Within a single tenant space, rated corridors are often not required. The rating of a corridor within a building depends on whether the building is sprinklered.

☑ **Note**

Suspended acoustical ceilings alone do not typically possess a fire resistance rating, but they could possibly be used as part of a rated floor/ceiling assembly.

occupancy that has an occupant load greater than 30 and is nonsprinklered, the table indicates that a rating of 1 hour is required. If the building were sprinklered, then the corridor would not be required to be rated. If the same Business occupancy had an occupant load less than 30, the exit access corridor would not be required to be rated. Typically, corridors within a small tenant space do not require a rating. However, exit access corridors that serve an entire floor are usually required to be rated, especially in nonsprinklered buildings.

The codes also limit the types of uses that can be open to the corridor without any separation. For example, care provider stations in health care facilities and living areas, group meeting areas, therapeutic spaces, and cooking areas in assisted living facilities are sometimes allowed to be open to the corridor. There are typically additional conditions such as additional fire detection and protection or direct supervision by staff required.

The *IBC* requires the walls for an exit access corridor to meet the requirements of a fire partition. The rating of the floor/ceiling assembly may be required to have the same fire resistance rating as the partition in certain construction types and uses. Refer to the codes for the specific requirements.

Corridors used as exits, however, such as *exit passageways*, usually must have a 2-hour fire rating. In this case, both the *IBC* and the NFPA codes require that a fire barrier be used and that the horizontal assembly at the floor and ceiling provide the same fire resistance rating as the walls. For example, if a stairwell with a rating of 2 hours emptied into a lobby, then the lobby would be considered an exit discharge component and would have to maintain the 2-hour rating. Refer to the specific requirements of each exit component to determine the required rating.

SMOKE BARRIERS AND SMOKE PARTITIONS

Smoke barriers and smoke partitions are another part of the passive fire protection system. Smoke barriers typically provide a higher level of protection than smoke partitions. Smoke barriers *restrict* the movement or passage of smoke and fire gases and are often required to have a fire resistance rating. Smoke partitions only *limit* the passage of smoke and fire gases and are typically not required to have a fire resistance rating.

Smoke barriers can consist of either a configuration of vertical wall assemblies or a full enclosure; in either case, they must be continuous. For example, they must extend from exterior wall to exterior wall and from the floor below to the floor/ceiling assembly above. A full enclosure consists of vertical walls and horizontal ceiling and floor assemblies made of smoke barriers that create a continuous smokeproof compartment. Where smoke barriers have joints or intersect with other smoke barriers, smoke/fire barriers, and exterior walls, they must be sealed completely. When used horizontally as a floor/ceiling assembly, they must extend to a smoke barrier wall or an exterior wall.

Although a smoke barrier is similar to a fire barrier, additional precautions have been made to make the assembly resistant to the passage and leakage of smoke to or from adjacent areas. The *IBC* requires smoke barriers to have a minimum 1-hour fire resistance rating. To make them smoke resistant, only limited openings are allowed. When fire barriers are used, additional mechanical functions are required for ventilation and air circulation. For example, a smoke detector typically activates the ventilation system and automatically closes all doors with a closing device. In addition, smoke dampers are often required at mechanical

ducts. Similar requirements are in the *LSC*. Penetrations in smoke barriers are limited and require additional constraints. For example, the building codes provide conditions for doors in smoke barriers, including the type and operation of the door.

◄ **Note**

Smoke barriers typically provide a higher level of protection than smoke partitions.

A *smoke partition*, however, may be allowed by the codes when a lesser degree of protection from smoke is acceptable for life safety. Example uses include separation of dwelling and sleeping units in assisted living and other residential uses and elevator lobbies in sprinklered buildings) and hoistways. Unlike smoke barriers, smoke partitions can terminate at suspended ceiling systems and some solid ceilings, as described by the codes (similar to fire partitions, as shown in Figure 6.3). The ceilings are also allowed to be penetrated by certain items, such as speakers, recessed lighting, diffusers, and similar ceiling elements not typically allowed in smoke barriers. Other requirements also tend to be less restrictive. For example, neither smoke partitions nor doors in smoke partitions are required to be rated, but must be self-closing. Another example is that in most cases a duct passing through a smoke partition will not require a smoke damper. Smoke partitions are often allowed for incidental use areas (as discussed in Chapter 3) where sprinklering is part of the protection of that area.

Additional requirements for smoke barriers and smoke partitions depend on their specific use. Many of these requirements are specified in the building codes, the fire codes, and the *LSC*. The mechanical codes include requirements as well. (See Chapter 8.) Additional requirements are specified in standards such as *NFPA 92, Standard for Smoke Control Systems* and *NFPA 105, Standard for the Installation of Smoke Door Assemblies and Other Opening Protectives*. The various uses of smoke barriers and smoke partitions, as walls and full enclosures, are discussed next. Some enclosures required by the codes are referred to as "smokeproof," and this usually requires the use of smoke barriers as well as pressurization of the space so that smoke cannot get into the room.

Smoke Compartments

Smoke compartments are required within a building where protection from smoke is particularly important. They are typically used in Institutional (health care and detention) occupancies to subdivide areas within a floor of a building used by occupants for sleeping or treatment. Large ambulatory health care facilities are also required to be separated into multiple smoke compartments.

Smoke compartments are created by smoke barriers. A smoke compartment must be created by a full enclosure (walls, ceiling, and floor assemblies). Smoke barrier walls that create a smoke compartment typi-

SMOKE AND HOW IT TRAVELS

To gain a better understanding of smoke control systems and how they work, it is important to know how smoke moves. The Council on Tall Buildings and Urban Habitat, in the book *Fire Safety in Tall Buildings,* describes five major driving forces that cause smoke movement:

Buoyancy. As the temperature of smoke increases during a fire, it becomes buoyant due to its reduced density. As the buoyancy increases, pressure builds and the smoke is forced up through any available leakage paths to the floor above and to adjacent areas.

Expansion. As a fire develops, it emits gases. These gases expand and create pressure, causing smoke to be forced out of an enclosed fire compartment.

HVAC. As a fire progresses, the HVAC system can transport smoke to every area it serves. The system can also supply air to a fire, increasing its intensity.

Stack effect. The stack effect is a result of exterior air temperature. Generally, if it is cold outside, there is usually an upward movement of air within the building shafts, such as stairwells, elevators, and mechanical shafts. When the outside air is warmer than the building air, the airflow moves downward. This air movement can move smoke a considerable distance from a fire.

Wind. Windows frequently break during a fire, causing outside wind to force smoke through doors into adjacent spaces and other floors.

In a fire situation, smoke movement can be caused by one or more of these driving forces. That is why the correct use and placement of smoke barriers can be critical. (The three stages of a fire are explained in the inset titled "Fire Development Stages" in Chapter 10.)

cally extend from outside wall to outside wall and from floor to floor. Each compartment created by the smoke barrier provides a temporary area of refuge from the adjacent compartment. These compartments are limited in area, dimension, and travel distance for each occupancy type. Smoke barriers and their area of refuge are different from horizontal exits and are not technically considered exits. (See the section titled "Horizontal Exits" in this chapter and Chapter 5.) In most cases, occupancies that call for smoke compartments are required to be sprinklered.

Smokeproof Vertical Shafts

As mentioned previously, the walls and openings of all vertical shaft enclosures must be fire-rated. In some cases, they must be smokeproof as well. This is usually required for stairs, elevators, and waste and linen chutes when the shaft extends through a certain number of stories or the building is a certain height. To make them smokeproof, the walls must meet the requirements for smoke barriers and all openings into the shaft must automatically close on detection of smoke. A *smoke stop* or *smoke door* is usually required. This door is typically connected to the smoke detection and standby power systems in the building. And, this is a door specially designed to close tightly and inhibit the passage of smoke.

To create the necessary smoke protection, smokeproof shafts also typically must be pressurized. The mechanical system creates a positive air pressure out of the shaft so that should a fire occur, the smoke does not get sucked into the vertical shaft, which would potentially spread the smoke to other floors.

Lobbies and Vestibules

Certain lobbies and vestibules are required to be smokeproof. For example, an elevator lobby adjacent to an elevator hoistway or a vestibule that is located between the stair shaft and the exterior exit door must be smokeproof. Another example is an area of refuge located adjacent to an exit stairway. The walls typically are required to be smoke barriers and sometimes the floor/ceiling assemblies do as well. The doors must also be fire-rated, have self-closing devices, and have a drop sill to minimize air leakage.

The ceiling of the vestibule must be high enough so that it serves as a smoke and heat trap and allows an upward-moving airflow. Ventilation is required as well. It might be as simple as an opening in an exterior wall for *natural* ventilation. The most common is *mechanical* ventilation with vents opening to the outside air. The codes regulate several items, such as the type of system used, the amount of supply and exhaust air, and the location of duct openings. (See Chapter 8.)

OPENING PROTECTIVES

The codes regulate when an opening can occur in a rated assembly. In certain situations, an opening may not be allowed at all. In others, there may be size limitations. The sizes are typically limited to a percentage of the total size or area of a wall. In many cases, additional and/or larger openings are allowed in a sprinklered building. When an opening is allowed in a rated assembly, an opening protective is usually required. An *opening protective* is a rated assembly that prevents the spread of fire or smoke through an opening in a rated wall. An opening protective is

✒ Note

When sprinklering a building allows certain walls to be unrated, they are often still required to resist the passage of smoke.

✒ Note

The presence of an automatic sprinkler system can affect the codes required for smokeproof enclosures.

RATED DOORS	RATED WINDOWS	RATED GLAZING
Access doors	Casement windows	Clear ceramics
Accordion/folding doors	Double-hung windows	Glass block
Bi-parting doors	Hinged windows	Insulated glass
Conveying system doors	Pivot windows	Laminated glass
Chute doors	Service counter windows	Light-diffusing plastic
Floor fire door	Sidelights	Light-transmitting plastic
Hoistway doors	Stationary windows	Fire-rated glazing
Horizontal doors	Tilting windows	Tempered glass
Overhead doors	Transom windows	Transparent ceramics
Swinging doors	View panels	

Figure 6.12 Types of regulated opening protectives.

usually a door or a view window. Unlike wall and floor/ceiling assemblies that are assigned a fire resistance rating, door assemblies are assigned a *fire protection* rating.

The required rating of the opening protective component is determined by the rating of the wall in which it is located. Not only are the ratings important during a fire to stop the spread of fire and smoke and maintain the integrity of the entire wall but also they are crucial for the evacuation of the occupants during a fire. Opening protectives can also be considered a type of through-penetration system (discussed later in this chapter). Through-penetration components control openings required by wiring, ducts, pipes, and similar penetrations in a building. Both component types are intended to maintain the integrity of a rated wall or floor/ceiling assembly. The fire protection ratings for opening protectives are determined by the building codes and the *LSC*. The intent of the codes and other standards is to regulate openings in rated walls, floors, and ceilings so that the required rated construction does not lose its effectiveness. The most common opening protectives are described in Figure 6.12.

Rated Door Assemblies

A typical door assembly, according to the codes, consists of three main components: door, frame, and hardware. The doorway (or wall opening) can also be considered part of the door assembly—including the lintel above and the threshold below. Other doors, such as the rated doors listed in Figure 6.13, may consist of even more parts. If the door is a fire door, the whole assembly must be tested and rated as one unit. Each of

� Note

The *IBC* allows fire protection ratings for opening protectives to be determined using alternate methods or performance code criteria when approved by a code official. However, this may require additional documentation and/or engineering analysis of the opening protective.

the following door components has certain characteristics that make it fire-rated.

Doors and Frames

✎ Note

Fire-rated doors and windows are designed to protect the opening under normal conditions with clear space on both sides. When combustible materials are stored against them, the protection is not guaranteed.

If the wall is fire-rated, the door and frame must be rated as well. Because a protection rating is assigned to the entire door assembly, fire doors are typically specified and sold by the manufacturer as a unit. To obtain a rating, the door and frame must undergo a fire test as specified in *NFPA 252, Standard Methods of Fire Tests of Door Assemblies*. Alternate tests include *UL 10B, Standard for Fire Tests of Door Assemblies,* and *UL 10C, Standard for Positive Pressure Fire Tests of Door Assemblies*. Rated doors used horizontally in fire-resistance-rated floor/ceiling assemblies may also have to pass *NFPA 288, Standard Methods of Fire Tests of Floor Fire Door Assemblies Installed Horizontally in Fire-Resistance-Rated Floor Systems*. The *IBC* and the NFPA codes require fire-rated doors to be tested by a positive-pressure test that better resembles actual fire conditions than previous tests.

Depending on the code, the rating information is found in tables or within the text. For example, the *IBC* has separate tables indicating the requirements for the fire ratings for the different types of opening protectives including door assemblies (with and without glazing) and window assemblies (discussed in the next section.) These tables determine the required rating, glazing allowances, and other characteristics based on the type and rating of the wall in which it is located. *IBC* Table 716.1(2), "Opening Fire Protection Assemblies, Ratings and Markings," is shown in Figure 6.13. This table gives the requirements for door assemblies that can include a transom and/or sidelight. Based on the type and rating of the wall (fire barrier, shaft, fire partition, etc.), the fire protection rating of the fire door assembly or fire window assembly for the opening can be determined. For example, if a door is being added in an existing 2-hour fire barrier, the table indicates that it would require a 1½-hour rated fire door assembly. In addition, if glazing is to be installed in the wall, adjacent to the door, or in the door, the fire protection rating of those elements can also be determined by this chart. Note from this chart that in some cases, a door vision panel or sidelight/transom even if it is rated glazing with a fire *protection* rating is still not permitted. Nevertheless, if the glazing has been tested as a wall assembly and received a fire *resistance* rating, then it would be allowed. This chart also indicates the required marking of the allowable glazing. For example, glazing that has a fire resistance rating appropriate for a 2-hour fire barrier would be marked W-120 (wall assembly that is rated 120 minutes). The building codes and the *LSC* also reference several standards for additional information. For example,

TABLE 716.1(2) OPENING FIRE PROTECTION ASSEMBLIES, RATINGS, AND MARKINGS

TYPE OF ASSEMBLY	REQUIRED WALL ASSEMBLY RATING (hours)	MINIMUM FIRE DOOR AND FIRE SHUTTER ASSEMBLY RATING (hours)	DOOR VISION PANEL SIZE[a]	FIRE-RATED GLAZING MARKING DOOR VISION PANEL[b,c]	MINIMUM SIDELIGHT/TRANSOM ASSEMBLY RATING (hours) Fire protection	MINIMUM SIDELIGHT/TRANSOM ASSEMBLY RATING (hours) Fire resistance	FIRE-RATED GLAZING MARKING SIDELIGHT/TRANSOM PANEL Fire protection	FIRE-RATED GLAZING MARKING SIDELIGHT/TRANSOM PANEL Fire resistance
Fire walls and fire barriers having a required fire resistance rating greater than 1 hour	4	3	See Note a	D-H-W-240	Not Permitted	4	Not Permitted	W-240
	3	3[d]	See Note a		Not Permitted	3	Not Permitted	W-180
	2	1½	100 sq. in.	≤100 sq. in. = D-H-90 / >100 sq. in.=D-H-W-90	Not Permitted	2	Not Permitted	W-120
	1½	1½	100 sq. in.	≤100 sq. in. = D-H-90 / >100 sq. in. = D-H-W-90	Not Permitted	1½	Not Permitted	W-90
	Single-wall assembly rating (hours)[e] / Each wall of the double-wall assembly (hours)[f]			—				
Double fire walls constructed in accordance with NFPA 221	4 / 3	3	See Note a	D-H-W-180	Not Permitted	3	Not Permitted	W-180
	3 / 2	1½	100 sq. in.	≤ 100 sq. in. = D-H-90 / >100 sq. in.= D-H-W-90	Not Permitted	2	Not Permitted	W-120
	2 / 1	1	100 sq. in.	≤ 100 sq. in. = D-H-60 / > 100 sq. in. = D-H-W-60	Not Permitted	1	Not Permitted	W-60
Enclosures for shafts, interior exit stairways and interior exit ramps.	2	1½	100 sq. in.[b]	≤100 sq. in. = D-H-90 / >100 sq. in.= D-H-T-W-90	Not Permitted	2	Not Permitted	W-120

(Continued)

TABLE 716.1(2) (Continued)

TYPE OF ASSEMBLY	REQUIRED WALL ASSEMBLY RATING (hours)	MINIMUM FIRE DOOR AND FIRE SHUTTER ASSEMBLY RATING (hours)	DOOR VISION PANEL SIZE[a]	FIRE-RATED GLAZING MARKING DOOR VISION PANEL[b,c]	MINIMUM SIDELIGHT/TRANSOM ASSEMBLY RATING (hours)		FIRE-RATED GLAZING MARKING SIDELIGHT/TRANSOM PANEL	
					Fire protection	Fire resistance	Fire protection	Fire resistance
Horizontal exits in fire walls[g]	4	3	100 sq. in.	≤100 sq. in. = D-H-180; > 100 sq. in.=D-H-W-240	Not Permitted	4	Not Permitted	W-240
	3	3[d]	100 sq. in.	≤100 sq. in. = D-H-180; > 100 sq. in.=D-H-W-180	Not Permitted	3	Not Permitted	W-180
Fire barriers having a required fire resistance rating of 1 hour: Enclosures for shafts, exit access stairways, exit access ramps, interior exit stairways and interior exit ramps; and exit passageway walls	1	1	100 sq. in.	≤100 sq. in. = D-H-60; >100 sq. in. = D-H-T-W-60	Not Permitted	1	Not Permitted	W-60
					Fire protection			
Other fire barriers	1	3/4	Maximum size tested	D-H	3/4[h]		D-H[h]	
Fire partitions: Corridor walls	1	1/3[a]	Maximum size tested	D-20	3/4[a]		D-H-OH-45	
	0.5	1/3[a]	Maximum size tested	D-20	1/3		D-H-OH-20	

Type of assembly	Required wall assembly rating (hours)	Minimum fire door and fire shutter assembly rating (hours)	Door vision panel size[c]	Fire-rated glazing marking door vision panel	Minimum sidelight/transom assembly rating (hours) — Fire protection	Minimum sidelight/transom assembly rating (hours) — Fire resistance	Fire-rated glazing marking sidelight/transom panel — Fire protection	Fire-rated glazing marking sidelight/transom panel — Fire resistance
Other fire partitions	1	3/4[i]	Maximum size tested	D-H-45	3/4		D-H-45	
	0.5	1/3	Maximum size tested	D-H-20	1/3		D-H-20	
Exterior walls	3	1 1/2	100 sq. in.[a]	≤100 sq. in. = D-H-90; >100 sq. in. = D-H-W-90	Not Permitted	3	Not Permitted	W-180
	2	1 1/2	100 sq. in.	D-H 90 or D-H-W-90	1 1/2[h]	2	D-H-OH-90[h]	W-120
	1	3/4	Maximum size tested	D-H-45	3/4[h]		D-H-45[h]	
Smoke barriers	1	1/3	Maximum size tested	D-20	3/4		D-H-OH-45	

For SI: 1 square inch = 645.2 mm.

a Fire-resistance-rated glazing tested to ASTM E119 in accordance with Section 716.1.2.3 shall be permitted, in the maximum size tested.

b Under the column heading "Fire-rated glazing marking door vision panel," W refers to the fire-resistance rating of the glazing, not the frame.

c See Section 716.1.2.2.1 and Table 716.1(1) for additional permitted markings.

d Two doors, each with a fire protection rating of 1 1/2 hours, installed on opposite sides of the same opening in a fire wall, shall be deemed equivalent in fire protection rating to one 3-hour fire door.

e As required in Section 706.4.

f As allowed in Section 4.6 of NFPA 221.

g See Section 716.2.5.1.2.

h Fire-protection-rated glazing is not permitted for fire barriers required by Section 1207 of the International Fire Code to enclose energy storage systems. Fire-resistance-rated glazing assemblies tested to ASTM E119 or UL 263, as specified in Section 716.1.2.3, shall be permitted.

i Two doors, each with a fire rating of 20 minutes, installed on opposite sides of the same opening in a fire partition, shall be deemed equivalent in fire protection rating to one 45-minute fire door.

Figure 6.13 International Building Code Table 716.6(2), "Opening Fire Protection Assemblies, Ratings and Markings" (2021 *International Building Code*, copyright © 2021. Washington, DC: International Code Council. Reproduced with permission. All rights reserved. www.iccsafe.org).

Figure 6.14 Typical label for a fire-rated door assembly. Reprinted with permission from Ceco Door Products.

NFPA 80, Standard for Fire Doors and Other Opening Protectives, is specified for the installation of fire doors and windows. Others, as explained later, are specifically for fire and smoke testing.

When smoke stop doors are used in smoke barriers, they must undergo additional testing as required in *NFPA 105, Standard for the Installation of Smoke Door Assemblies and Other Opening Protectives,* or *UL 1784, Standard for Air Leakage Tests of Door Assemblies.* Any door that passes the required tests is assigned a fire protection rating, varying from 3 hours to 1/3 hour (20 minutes), and receives a permanent label indicating the manufacturer's name and/or logo, the name of the testing agency, and the rating it received. An example of such a label is shown in Figure 6.14.

Certain doors may also require a rated sill as part of the frame. For example, smoke stop doors usually require a sill to maintain a continuous seal around the door. The construction of the sill can vary, depending on the type of door and the construction of the floor on either side of the door. If a door requires a sill, the profile of the threshold will need to be considered. In most cases, it must meet accessibility requirements based on the *ADA Standards* and the *ICC A117.1* standard. (See Figure 10.17 in Chapter 10.)

Because doors usually undergo more stringent testing, make up only a portion of an entire wall, and are not generally exposed to the same level of fire as walls, their ratings are not as strict as those of the walls in which they are located. However, properly specified door assemblies maintain the integrity of the fire barrier. Doors that have a fire protection rating are available in a variety configurations, styles, and material including glazing. Fire-rated frames can be wood, steel (i.e., hollow metal), or aluminum, depending on the rating required. The most specified rated frame is hollow metal. The glazing used in fire-rated doors must also meet certain requirements. (This is discussed later in this chapter.)

▣ Note

Typically, no openings except for a limited number of doors are allowed in fire walls that require a 3-hour to 4-hour rating.

▣ Note

Most codes currently require positive-pressure testing of fire-rated doors. This test better represents the conditions of a fire that would cause flames to penetrate through cracks and openings in a fire door.

Door Hardware

The hardware components on fire-rated doors are stringently regulated. (See the general discussion in the section titled "Door Hardware" in Chapter 5.) For example, fire-rated hinges must be steel or stainless steel, and a specific number are required for each door. Both the hinges and the latch set are important to hold a fire door securely closed during a fire. To be effective, they must be able to withstand the pressure and heat generated during a fire.

The codes also regulate the type of latch and operating mechanism for fire-rated doors. In many cases, approved lever handle latchsets can be used on exit doors. However, if rated doors in Assembly, Educational/Day Care, Hazardous and in some occupancies with an occupant load of 50 or more, fire exit hardware must be used. Although fire exit hardware looks like panic hardware, fire exit hardware is tested and rated according to *NFPA 80, Standard for Fire Doors and Other Opening Protectives* and *UL10C, Standard for Positive Pressure Fire Test of Door Assemblies.* Both consist of a panel or bar that must be pushed to release the door latch.

The codes also require that most fire-rated doors be *self-closing* or *automatic closing.* To be self-closing, the door must have a device called a *closer* that closes the door after each use. Closers, in general, can be surface mounted or concealed within the door, frame, or floor. Verify that the closer application does not violate the rating of the door assembly in each case. A closer can be tested as part of the door assembly by one of the numerous test standards for fire door assemblies listed above. There are also specific standards that apply to closers, including *UL 228, Standard for Door Closers-Holders, With or Without Integral Smoke Detectors.* Another standard, *ANSI/BHMA A156.4, Door Controls-Closers,* tests the door closer for adjustable closing speed, closing force, cycle time, pivot performance, and finish grade. In some cases, doors that are required to be automatic closing can also have hold open devices when they meet additional criteria. Refer to the codes for these specific conditions. The closing speed and operating force of the door is specified by the *ADA Standard* and the *ICC A117.1* however, the codes exempt fire-rated doors from meeting these requirements in some cases. The 2018 *IBC* clarified that a delayed-action closer which will hold the door open for a limited amount of time before closing was allowable on rated doors not required to be automatic closing by the code.

If it is desirable that certain rated doors be open all the time, an electromagnetic or pneumatic hold-open device can be used. This device holds the door in an open position until an emergency occurs. Doors are released by the activation of the fire alarm system, loss of power, or activation of the sprinkler system that causes the door to close. This type of

> **✎ Note**
>
> When selecting fire-rated door hardware, it is important to meet the additional requirements set in the ADA and *ICC A117.1*, such as the shape of the item and the height of installation. (See Chapter 4.)

> **✎ Note**
>
> If a building is fully sprinklered, the codes may allow an exit door to have an automatic closure with a longer-than-standard time delay.

> **✎ Note**
>
> One reason the allowed door rating is usually lower than the wall rating is that it is expected that walls will typically have combustible material such as furniture and paperwork against them. This material would contribute to the fuel should a fire occur, requiring the wall to have a higher rating. Doors are usually kept clear of such fire loads.

door is considered *automatic closing* and is allowed in many occupancies. Doors on electromagnetic or pneumatic hold-open devices are tested using standard *UL 228*. (For additional hardware standards, see the section titled "Security Systems" in Chapter 9.)

In other cases, locking for security requirements may affect the choice of hardware on rated doors. (See the section titled "Security Systems" in Chapter 9.) The requirements of the *ADA Standards* and other accessibility standards should also be considered in the final selection of hardware. *NFPA 80* regulates aspects of rated doors, including installation, maintenance, and installation of protection devices. However, providing an uninterrupted means of egress and maintaining the fire rating of the doors are most important for occupant safety.

Fire Window Assemblies

A fire window assembly is considered an opening protective. A fire window assembly typically consists of a frame and an approved rated glazing material. It can be part of a door assembly, such as a transom, sidelight, or vision panel, or can be a separate element. The most common interior applications for a fire-rated window assembly are view panels within corridor walls, room partitions, and smoke barriers.

Fire window assemblies are given a fire protection rating similar to doors and are usually classified by hourly designations. Similar to doors, they must be tested as a complete assembly. The established testing requirements are typically specified in *NFPA 257, Standard on Fire Test for Window and Glass Block Assemblies* or *UL 9*. The required rating of a window depends on its use within the compartmentation system of the building. Generally, such fire protection ratings are not greater than 1 hour.

If the rated window is part of a door assembly, the requirements are typically given as part of the door assembly as exemplified in *IBC*, Table 716.6(2) in Figure 6.13. If the window occurs in a rated wall, the information may be provided differently. For example, in the *IBC*, a separate table is provided for window assemblies in fire-rated walls. This table is shown in Figure 6.15, *IBC* Table 716.6(3), "Fire Window Assembly Fire Protection Ratings." Using this table, if a window assembly was placed in a corridor wall (typically a fire partition) that had a 1-hour rating, the window assembly would have to be rated ¾ hour. The table also indicates how the glazing should be marked based whether it was tested as a wall assembly or an opening protective. In addition, fire windows are not permitted at all (as indicated by *NP*) as indicated in this table.

When the codes require a rated window assembly, the assembly must have a permanent label applied by the manufacturer guaranteeing its fire

✎ **Note**

If an interior window is operable and is in an accessible area, the operable parts should be within accessible reach ranges and have controls that are easy to operate.

TABLE 716.1(3) FIRE WINDOW ASSEMBLY FIRE PROTECTION RATINGS

TYPE OF WALL ASSEMBLY	REQUIRED WALL ASSEMBLY RATING (hours)	MINIMUM FIRE WINDOW ASSEMBLY RATING (hours)	FIRE-RATED GLAZING MARKING
Interior walls			
Fire walls	All	NP[a]	W-XXX[b]
Fire barriers	>1	NP[a]	W-XXX[b]
	1	NP[a]	W-XXX[b]
Atrium separations (Section 707.3.6) Incidental use areas (Section 707.3.7)[c] Mixed occupancy separations (Section 707.3.9)	1	$3/_4$	OH-45 or W-60
Fire partitions	1	$3/_4$	OH-45 or W-60
	0.5	$1/_3$	OH-20 or W-30
Smoke barriers	1	$3/_4$	OH-45 or W-60
Exterior walls	>1	$1^1/_2$	OH-90 or W-XXX[b]
	1	3/4	OH-45 or W-60
	0.5	1/3	OH-20 or W-30
Party wall	All	NP	Not Applicable

NP = Not Permitted.

a Not permitted except fire-resistance-rated glazing assemblies tested to ASTM E119 or UL 263, as specified in Section 716.1.2.3.

b XXX = The fire rating duration period in minutes, which shall be equal to the fire resistance rating required for the wall assembly.

c Fire-protection-rated glazing is not permitted for fire barriers required by Section 1207 of the *International Fire Code* to enclose energy storage systems. Fire-resistance-rated glazing assemblies tested to ASTM E119 or UL 263, as specified in Section 716.1.2.3, shall be permitted.

Figure 6.15 International Building Code Table 716.6 (3), "Fire Window Assembly Fire Protection Ratings" (2021 *International Building Code*, copyright © 2021. Washington, DC: International Code Council. Reproduced with permission. All rights reserved. www.iccsafe.org).

protection rating. By contrast, when a window is used in a smoke partition that is not fire-rated, the codes do not typically require the window to have a fire protection rating. Instead, it must be sealed to prevent the passage of smoke.

Rated Glazing and Frames

Similar to rated walls, rated glazing helps to protect occupants from various aspects of a fire, including flame, smoke, and radiant heat. The codes

✔ **Note**

A *fail safe* lock unlocks when there is a loss of power. A *fail secure* locks when there is a loss of power. In either case, the door should remain latched.

set specific requirements for the size, thickness, location, and types of glazing materials that can be used in opening protectives such as fire doors and fire windows. This information is found in the building codes and the *LSC* in tables or within the text. Size limitations may be given as a maximum height and width or a maximum area. Typically, the rated glazing can be any shape or configuration if it does not exceed the maximum sizes.

Glazing products used in fire-rated assemblies are assessed by their ability to stay in place in the event of a fire, resistance to thermal shock in a hose-stream test, strength against human contact, and resistance to heat transfer to the unexposed side. As part of an opening protective, most glazing is given a *fire protection* rating. In some cases, glazing can also meet the standards to receive a *fire resistance* rating similar to that of a rated wall. (This is described later in this section.) When glazing is used in a rated window, it must meet the requirements of *NFPA 257, Standard on Fire Test for Window and Glass Block Assemblies* or *UL 9, Standard for Fire Test of Window Assemblies*. When it is used in a rated door or fire barrier, it must meet the requirements of *NFPA 252, Standard Methods of Fire Tests of Door Assemblies*. The required markings to indicate the fire test standard are indicated in Figure 6.16, in *IBC* Table 716.1(1), "Marking Fire-Rated Glazing Assemblies."

Based on the results of these tests, the glazing assembly is given a fire protection rating. In most cases, the glazing in a rated assembly must also be tested by *NFPA 80, Standard for Fire Doors and Other Opening Protectives*. Check the codes for the tests necessary based on the specific use of the glazing in the rated assembly.

The codes require all new fire protection–rated glazing to marked in a way that indicates the manufacturer, the test standard used, and the results of the test. See Figure 6.16, *IBC* Table 716.1(1), "Marking Fire-Rated Glazing Assemblies" to show the specific marking that indicate the test the glazing has passed. They will also indicate if the glazing has passed the hose-stream test and provide the fire resistance or fire protection rating duration in minutes. These permanent markings become important during the life of the building so that, in the future, designers, owners, and code officials know what rating exists and must be maintained.

When used in certain locations, rated and unrated glazing products must also meet safety requirements. These safety tests are used to determine the resistance to impact. For example, all glazing in locations that could be subject to impact are required to pass the federal standard *16 CFR 1201, Safety Standard for Architectural Glazing Materials*. The glazing receives a rating of Category I or II. Category I represents glazing that will resist the equivalent impact of a small child or young teenager. Category II represents glazing that will resist the equivalent impact of a full-grown adult. Therefore, a Category II glazing is more impact-resistant. Glazing not

◀ Note

Labels required on rated glazing are added by a third-party agency during the manufacturing process to ensure reliability.

TABLE 716.1(1) MARKING FIRE-RATED GLAZING ASSEMBLIES

FIRE TEST STANDARD	MARKING	DEFINITION OF MARKING
ASTM E119 or UL 263	W	Meets wall assembly criteria
ASTM E119 or UL 263	FC	Meets floor/ceiling criteria[a]
NFPA 257 or UL 9	OH	Meets fire window assembly criteria including the hose stream test
NFPA 252 or UL 10B or UL 10C	D	Meets fire door assembly criteria
	H	Meets fire door assembly hose stream test
	T	Meets 450°F temperature rise criteria for 30 minutes
—	XXX	The time in minutes of the fire resistance or fire protection rating of the glazing assembly

For SI: °C = [(°F) − 32]/1.8.
a See Section 2409.1

Figure 6.16 International Building Code Table 716.6 (1), "Marking Fire-Rated Glazing Assemblies" (2021 *International Building Code*, copyright © 2021. Washington, DC: International Code Council. Reproduced with permission. All rights reserved. www.iccsafe.org).

located in doors or saunas, showers, and other bathing elements may be tested under *ANSI Z97.1, Safety Glazing Materials Used in Buildings—Safety Performance Specifications and Method of Test.* In this test, the glazing is given a rating of A, B, or C. Glazing material that is rated as Class A is equivalent to Category II glazing material; Class B is comparable to Category I. A Class C is given to fire resistant materials that are not required to be impact resistant. In addition, the most recent editions of the *IBC* require a higher level of impact resistance for glazing in certain locations such as gymnasiums and in "areas subject to human impact load." These are required to meet the Category II CPSC impact standard.

In the past, there were very few options for glazing products that could obtain a fire protection rating, fire resistance rating, or resist impact rating. Now there are several options, and new products continue to be developed. Each has unique characteristics to consider when selecting materials for a project. This section briefly discusses each of the general types of glazing that are currently available.

Wired Glass

Wired glass is the original standard for fire-rated glazing. Now, there are two types of wired glass: nonsafety and safety. The traditional type of wired glass, *nonsafety wired glass*, consists of wire mesh sandwiched between two layers of glass. The steel wire helps to distribute heat and

> ☑ **Note**
>
> Labels on glazing assemblies indicate the approved location, test standard used, and hourly rating.

> ☑ **Note**
>
> Tempered glass is approximately four times stronger than typical glazing products.

> ☑ **Note**
>
> The hose-stream test is required in the United States for glazing with fire rating over 20 minutes. All fire-rated glazing in Canada must meet the hose-stream test.

increase the strength of the glass when exposed to a fire. Although non-safety wired glass can obtain a fire protection rating of up to 45 minutes, this type of wired glass does not meet impact criteria determined by *CFR 1201* for Category I or II. Most recently, the building codes have begun to limit the allowable use nonsafety wire glass because of its lack of impact strength. Although nonsafety wired glass can still be used in some locations, as of the 2012 *IBC*, it cannot be used in hazardous locations in any occupancy. It is also limited in size and percentage of the overall wall area.

Safety wired glass can be used where fire resistance and impact resistance are required and in hazardous locations. It looks like traditional wired glass but is either laminated or uses a film to give it a higher level of impact resistance. Laminated wired glass can achieve a Category I impact resistance standard; however, filmed wired glass can meet the Category I and II standards. As a result, laminated wired glass may not be suitable or allowed in high-traffic locations in certain occupancy classifications, such as Educational, but filmed wired glass may be used in larger openings and in doors. Safety wired glass is required to meet the CPSC safety glazing requirements like other glazing products.

Specialty Tempered Glass

Specially tempered glass is glass that has been thermally treated to alter the way it breaks in case of exposure to extreme heat or impact. Not all tempered glass can be used in a rated wall. If the glass has been specially tempered, it can receive a 20- or 30-minute fire protection rating. However, because it cannot pass the hose-stream test, it can only be used in 1-hour rated walls or where only a 20-minute rating is required. It also should not be used near sprinkler heads. Water from an activated sprinkler system may cause this type of glazing to fail and thus not maintain the required fire resistance. This may limit the use of specially tempered glass in certain locations. Tempered glass can be used in fairly large sizes. Because it is typically six times stronger than wire glazing, it also meets the requirements for a Category II for impact loads.

Glass Block

Glass block is typically given a fire protection rating of 45 minutes or less and is usually allowed in a wall with a maximum 1-hour rating. There are new types of glass block that have ratings of 60 to 90 minutes, but glass block with this type of fire resistance rating may not be allowed by the current codes. Where glass block is allowed, there are often restrictions on the area of glass block, use in a rated wall, and installation methods. In addition, rated glass block cannot be used in the fire barriers that surround exit stairways, exit ramps, or exit passageways.

☑ Note

In addition to fire resistance, heat transfer must be considered when using large amounts of glass.

☑ Note

If a glazing product has a fire protection rating, it is intended to be used as glazing in a door or as a window unit. If it has a resistance rating it has been tested as a wall.

☑ Note

Most glazing that is rated more than 45 minutes is also required to protect against radiant heat transfer.

Clear Ceramics

Clear ceramics, also known as transparent ceramics, have very high resistance to heat and can resist the thermal shock of the hose-stream test. Because of this, they can be rated from 20 minutes to 3 hours and can typically be used in much larger sizes than wired glass, sometimes up to 23 square feet (2.1 sm) if approved by a code official. In addition, they can have up to four times the impact resistance of safety wired glass, usually achieving a Category II classification.

Although clear ceramics are considered transparent, they may have slightly more distortion and tint than some other glazing products. Clear ceramics can also be installed as insulated glass units (IGUs). These units are made of two layers of glass with an air space between them. In this configuration, they not only provide fire protection, but also help to reduce sound transmission. For use in interior applications, ceramic glazing can be sandblasted with decorative designs to enhance the aesthetics of the design. As part of an IGU, the ceramic layers can be tinted, mirrored, or clear to provide additional design elements. These characteristics make the use of clear ceramic products desirable in areas such as lobbies and offices, where aesthetics and safety are key.

Laminated Glass

Laminated glass typically consists of two pieces of glass laminated together, which can have various types of material sandwiched between them. Laminated glazing has traditionally been desirable for its impact resistance. Sometimes called *insulated* or *multilayered*, laminated glazing can have a Category I or II rating, so it can be used in multiple locations where safety is a concern. Although it typically has a limited rating of 20 minutes when used in a door, laminated glazing can obtain a rating of 45 to 90 minutes as an interior window. This allows its use as a window in a rated wall in sizes larger than typical wired glass. In addition, laminated glass can be sandblasted to make it opaque or create a decorative pattern.

Transparent Wall Units

As previously mentioned, openings in walls are typically assigned fire protection ratings and walls are given fire resistance ratings. So, when glazing is used in a wall, it typically is only required to have a fire protection rating. However, newer products have made it possible for some glazing assemblies to meet requirements like those of a wall and be given a fire resistance rating. These "wall units" are an assembly of different materials, including glazing products, that creates a unit that is transparent, fire resistant, and, in some cases, self-supporting. Often, these products use an inert material between two glazing components that, when exposed to heat, turns into foam and creates the fire resistant quality. These transparent wall units can be used for larger or unlimited openings or even in place of a conventional solid rated wall.

Because of the possibility of someone walking toward or adjacent to these walls, these transparent walls must pass high-impact safety tests for Category I and Category II glazing. They must also be tested according to *ASTM E119, Standard Test Methods for Fire Tests of Building Construction and Materials*. They can be rated up to 2 hours and must pass the fire hose–stream test. A unique characteristic of these units is that they do not allow the transfer of heat from the fire side of the "wall" to the opposite side, as typical glazing does. This allows them to be used as a "full-glass" barrier wall, such as at a stairwell, when approved by a code official. Similar to other rated glazing, these units are required by the codes to have a label. This label indicates the manufacturer and whether the glazing meets the fire resistance, hose-stream, and temperature-rise requirements of *ASTM E119*. The fire resistance rating of the glazing unit in minutes is also given.

Frames for Rated Glazing

Rated glazing materials such as typical glazing must be fixed within a frame. Similar to door frames, fire window frames must be rated to create the required fire protection rating. Most rated glazing is installed in hollow steel frames. The rating of the frame typically matches the rating of the glazing. Rated frames are also used around the windows installed in fire-rated doors and other fire window assemblies. Even glass block is required to be installed in a steel frame in certain applications.

Similar to the newer glazing products, new framing products are becoming available. These framing systems are much thinner than traditional rated frames. Although some systems can be rated for only 20 to 45 minutes, others may reach a rating of 1 to 2 hours. Some products also resist the transfer of heat. The design and performance requirements of a specific installation will need to be determined to correctly choose a framing system.

THROUGH-PENETRATION PROTECTIVES

A *through penetration* is defined as an opening that pierces the entire thickness of a construction assembly, such as a wall or floor/ceiling assembly.

When these construction assemblies are fire-rated, the codes require the penetrations to be protected with rated assemblies such as fire-stops, draft stops, fireblocking, and fire dampers. (The codes also include shutters as a common opening protective.) These rated assemblies act as prevention systems and are referred to as *through-penetration protection systems*, which are required to have a *fire protection* rating. Not only are the ratings important to the integrity of the entire fire barrier or horizontal assembly during a fire (to stop the spread of fire and smoke) but also they are crucial for the evacuation of the occupants. The most common through-penetration protectives are described in this section.

◿ Note

Membrane penetrations are not the same as through penetrations. Instead of piercing the entire thickness of the assembly, membrane penetrations penetrate only one side, or *membrane*. Examples include electrical outlets in drywall and HVAC ducts that pierce suspended ceilings. (See Chapter 8.)

Fire-Stops and Smoke Stops

Fire-stops are a type of through-penetration protection system that is required in fire and smoke barriers and horizontal assemblies. Their purpose is to restrict the movement of fire and hot gases through openings made in the fire resistance–rated walls and floor/ceiling or roof/ceiling assemblies. In some cases, they are required to limit the transfer of heat as well. They seal and protect any opening created by penetrations, such as plumbing pipes, electrical conduit and wire, HVAC ducts, communication cables, and similar types of building service equipment that pass through walls, floors, and ceilings. They may also be required at the intersection of walls and ceilings and at seams in gypsum board in rated walls.

The building codes, the *Life Safety Code*, and the *National Electrical Code (NEC)* require the use of listed and approved fire-stops in fire and smoke barriers and horizontal assemblies. They are rated under *ASTM E814, Standard Test Method for Fire Tests of Through-Penetration Fire Stops*, or *UL 1479, Standard for Fire Tests of Through-Penetration Fire-stops*. When the fire-stop is required at the intersection of two rated walls, it must be rated under *UL 2079, Tests for Fire Resistance of Building Joint Systems*. These tests established two basic ratings. An *F-rating* is based on the number of hours the fire-stop resists flame and hot gases, its hose-stream performance, and whether it remains in the opening. The *T-rating* is based on the number of hours until the fire-stop allows a specified temperature rise on the opposite side of the wall from the fire. When specifying a fire-stop, either the rating or the specific listed device needs to be identified. Although typically the fire-stop should have a rating equal to the rating of the wall, each code has slightly different criteria.

Fire-stops can be divided into two groups: systems and devices. A variety of noncombustible materials can be used in a fire-stop system. These include fire-rated caulk, silicone foam, mortar, mineral wool, wire

⬛ Note

The codes often limit the size of an opening made for a through penetration or a membrane penetration. This keeps the space around the penetrating item to a minimum so that a fire-stop and/or smoke stop can be more effective.

mesh, and various intumescent materials. (Intumescent materials swell when exposed to heat.) A *fire-stop system* is typically constructed in the field and added after the through penetration has been installed. The most common way to create a fire-stop is to fill the open space between the penetrating item and the fire barrier with fire-rated material and finish it with an approved sealant. However, when the openings are close to the size of the item penetrating the assembly, only the rated caulk or other sealant may be required. This can be seen in Figure 9.2 in Chapter 9. The amount of damming materials and/or noncombustible sealant is specific to the location of the penetration, the dimension of the opening, the type of smoke or fire barrier, and the type and size of the penetrating item.

A *fire-stop device* is factory built and is typically installed as part of the through penetration. Systems can include collars, sleeves, plugs, and clamp bands. For example, it may be a sleeve installed within the wall or floor assembly to allow a pipe to pass through, such as the one shown at the plumbing pipe in Figure 8.13 in Chapter 8. There are two types of devices that prevent the spread of flame and smoke while retarding the rise in temperature, as required by a T-rating. Endothermic fire-stops release water when exposed to heat and cause a cooling effect that enables the installation to meet the fire rating required by the code. An intumescent fire-stop expands in volume under fire conditions, forming a strong char. This expansive caulk seals the gaps created as the penetrating items melt away.

When a fire-stop is used in a smoke barrier, it must act as a *smoke stop* as well. However, not all fire-stops are rated to stop smoke. To be used in a smoke barrier, a fire-stop must pass an additional test for air leakage using *UL 1479*. This portion of the test provides the fire-stop with another rating, called an *L-rating*. The L-rating established criteria for the allowable amount of air and smoke leakage. Typically, if the L-rating is 5 or less, the fire-stop can be used as a smoke stop.

Some devices and construction elements, such as an electrical outlet or sprinkler head, penetrate only one side of a wall. These are called *membrane penetrations*. (Refer again to Figure 9.2 in Chapter 9.) Although similar, they are not technically a through penetration. However, in a rated wall, these too must be protected. The codes define the allowable placement and size of these items within a rated wall. For example, the codes limit the size of an opening cut for an outlet box. They also require adequate filling of the area around the penetration and may require additional fireblocking, depending on the location. (See the section titled "Electrical Boxes" in Chapter 9 for more information.)

Fireblocks and Draft Stops

Fireblocks (or fireblocking) and draft stops are used to restrict the spread of smoke and fire through concealed spaces. *Fireblocking* uses building materials to prevent the movement of air, flame, and gases through *small* concealed areas. In interior projects these could occur in several conditions:

❑ **Dropped or coved ceilings.** If a wall stops at the underside edge of a dropped or coved ceiling, fireblocking may be required at the top of the wall to break the continuous air space.

❑ **Double stud walls.** When a deeper wall assembly is necessary to accommodate large pipes and mechanical ducts or for acoustical separation, a double stud wall system may be used. In a long double stud wall, fireblocking may be required at certain intervals to limit the continuous air space.

❑ **Fire partitions.** When fire partitions in certain construction types do not extend to the underside of the floor/ceiling or roof deck above unless the area or building is sprinklered.

❑ **Stairs.** Blocking may be required at the openings at the top and bottom of a run of stairs to block the open space created between the steps and the ceiling below.

❑ **Concealed floor spaces.** When hardwood floors or other finishes are installed on furring strips (i.e., sleepers), fireblocking may be required at certain intervals to limit the continuous space between the sleepers.

Draft stops use building materials to prevent the movement of air, smoke, gases, and flame through *large* concealed spaces. Typically, these spaces include certain floor/ceiling spaces, attics, and concealed roof spaces in Residential type uses. The codes specify where draft stops are required and the allowable size of the spaces they divide. For example, the attic space in a row of townhouses might require a draft stop to be constructed above each tenant separation wall. Typically required in combustible construction types, draft stops may be required in noncombustible construction as well. However, in either type of construction, draft stopping may not be required if the building has an automatic sprinkler system.

Although there are no specific tests for materials that can be used as fireblocks and draft stops, each code lists acceptable materials within its text. They tend to be noncombustible types of materials. Some examples include gypsum board and certain sheathing and plywood materials.

> **✎ Note**
>
> There are two types of fire-stops: fire-stop systems and fire-stop devices.

> **✎ Note**
>
> Smoke stops are similar to fire-stops; however, smoke stops must pass an additional test for air leakage.

> **✎ Note**
>
> Fireblocks and draft stops are similar but not the same. Fireblocks are used in all types of buildings to close off small spaces. Draft stops are required in buildings with combustible construction to close off large concealed spaces.

The material must be properly supported so that it remains in place during an initial fire.

Damper Systems

A *damper* is another type of opening protective. It is used specifically in HVAC systems, either where a duct passes through a rated assembly or where an air transfer opening is cut into a rated assembly. It is typically specified by the mechanical engineer. It is a device arranged to automatically interrupt the flow of air during an emergency so that it restricts the passage of smoke, fire, and heat.

There are two kinds of fire or smoke damper systems: static and dynamic. A *static damper system* automatically shuts down during a fire, whereas a *dynamic damper system* remains in operation even during a fire. Dynamic dampers can be used in either static or dynamic HVAC systems, but static dampers can be used only in static systems. Depending on their installation, fire and smoke dampers may also be used to control the volume of air for the heating and cooling system during normal use. The energy codes also require dampers to control outside air.

When a fire occurs, the dampers stop or regulate the flow of heated air, smoke, or flame through the duct system. Three main types of dampers are used in HVAC systems: fire dampers, smoke dampers, and ceiling dampers. If required, combination fire and smoke dampers also are available. Each type of damper must meet a specific test standard. These are mentioned as the various dampers are explained in the following subsections.

Fire Dampers

Fire dampers are required by the codes in several locations. They are typically required in ducts that penetrate rated wall assemblies, at air transfer openings in rated partitions, and similar penetrations in rated horizontal assemblies. A damper can be installed within the duct or on the outside as a collar fastened to the wall or ceiling. The most common fire damper includes a fusible link on either side of the assembly the duct is penetrating. This fusible link melts during a fire when the area reaches a certain temperature, causing the fire damper to close and seal the duct. A similar system would be used on either side of an air transfer opening.

The rating of a fire damper can range from 1½ to 3 hours. The length of the rating is determined by the codes and depends on the rating of the fire-rated construction assembly that the duct passes through. Each building code has a table similar to *IBC* Table 717.3.2.1, "Fire Damper Rating,"

TABLE 717.3.2.1 FIRE DAMPER RATING

TYPE OF PENETRATION	MINIMUM DAMPER RATING (hours)
Less than 3-hour fire-resistance-rated assemblies	1.5
3-hour or greater fire-resistance-rated assemblies	3

Figure 6.17 International Building Code Table 717.3.2.1, "Fire Damper Rating" (2021 *International Building Code*, copyright © 2021. Washington, DC: International Code Council. Reproduced with permission. All rights reserved. www.iccsafe.org).

shown in Figure 6.17. This table indicates the required damper ratings based on the type of penetration. Once the rating of the assembly is known, it is easy to determine the required fire damper rating. The required fire test for fire dampers is *UL 555, Standard for Fire Dampers*. It is used to determine the hourly fire rating of a fire damper.

Smoke Dampers

Smoke dampers are similar to fire dampers, but they are activated by smoke rather than heat. They are typically required when ducts penetrate a smoke barrier. Because smoke barriers are not required by the codes as often as fire-rated partitions and assemblies, smoke dampers are not used as often as fire dampers. When a smoke damper is required, it is installed with a smoke detector. The smoke detector is typically located inside the duct, so that when it detects smoke it causes the smoke damper to close off the duct. Sometimes a smoke damper will be part of a smoke evacuation system. In the event of a fire, the action of the smoke dampers would be controlled by the system. *UL 555S, Standard for Smoke Dampers*, is the test standard for smoke dampers. The test assigns a smoke damper one of four classes (Class I, Class II, Class III, and Class IV), with Class I being the most effective. Combination fire/smoke dampers must comply with *UL 555* and *UL 555S*.

 Note

In addition to fire dampers, smoke dampers, and ceiling dampers, some jurisdictions may require the use of a corridor damper.

Ceiling Dampers

Ceiling dampers, referred to in the codes as *ceiling radiation dampers*, are used in suspended ceilings that are part of the rated horizontal assembly, such as a floor/ceiling or roof/ceiling assembly. The damper can be located in the duct or can be part of the air diffuser that supplies air to the space. In case of fire, ceiling dampers prevent heat from entering the space between the ceiling and the floor or roof above. They also prevent the heat from traveling through the duct system. The ceiling damper closes when the heated air tries to move up through the damper. Ceiling dampers are regulated by *UL 555C, Standard for Ceiling Dampers*. If the ceiling damper is located in a rated horizontal assembly, it may also be required to meet *ASTM E119* or *UL 263, Standard Test Methods for Fire Tests of Building Construction and Materials.*

TEST RATINGS

Various standard tests have been mentioned throughout this chapter. The National Fire Protection Association (NFPA), ASTM International, and Underwriters Laboratories (UL), in conjunction with the American National Standards Institute (ANSI), have established a wide variety of standard fire tests. These tests are performed by third-party testing agencies. Manufacturers use these agencies to ensure reliability and confirm that their products meet specific requirements.

Different tests are used for wall, ceiling, and floor assemblies and the items that penetrate these assemblies. These are explained here and are summarized in Figure 6.18.

Tests for Wall and Floor/Ceiling Assemblies

◄ Note

ISO 834, the standard used by European countries, is similar to *NFPA 251*.

Standardized tests are developed to determine the reaction of materials and assemblies to fire in specific uses within a building. There are two basic groups of tests for wall and floor/ceiling assemblies. One group of tests evaluates the fire resistance of a material or assembly; the other evaluates how a material reacts to fire. These tests apply to rated wall, floor, and ceiling assemblies required by the codes, as well as the building and structural elements used in the various construction types by the codes as discussed in Chapter 4.

The fire resistance tests generally evaluate how long an assembly will contain a fire, retain its own structural integrity, or both. The tests measure three aspects of the performance of construction assemblies: (1) the temperature rise on the non-fire-exposed side of the assembly; (2) the smoke, gas, or flames that pass through the assembly; and (3) the structural performance during exposure to the fire. If the assembly being tested is a load-bearing assembly, the test measures the load-carrying ability during exposure to fire. In addition, if a wall or partition obtains a rating of 1 hour or more, it is subjected to a hose-stream test to see if it will resist disintegration when subjected to water during the firefighting process. (Other components, such as certain doors, may have to pass a pressure test as well.)

RATED ASSEMBLIES AND MATERIALS	REQUIRED TESTS[a]
FIRE WALLS	NFPA 221
RATED WALL AND FLOOR/CEILING ASSEMBLIES (fire-rated) (smoke control)	ASTM E119 UL 263 (or NFPA 221) NFPA 92
RATED DOOR CLOSERS	UL 228 UL 10B UL 10C ANSI/BHMA A156.4
RATED DOOR ASSEMBLIES[b] (fire doors) (smoke doors)	NFPA 252 UL 10B and UL 10C NFPA 105 UL 1784
FLOOR FIRE DOORS CEILING ACCESS DOORS	NFPA 288 (or ASTM E119)
FIRE WINDOWS AND SHUTTERS WIRED GLASS GLASS BLOCK[c]	UL 9 NFPA 257
FIRE-RATED GLAZING[c]	NFPA 257 (or ASTM E119)
FIRE-STOPS	ASTM E814 UL 1479
RATED DAMPERS (fire damper) (smoke damper) (ceiling damper)	UL 555 UL 555S UL 555C

a NFPA 80 is not a fire test but should also be referenced since it regulates the installation of an assembly and therefore can affect the final rating.

b A 20-minute (1/3-hour) door does not require a hose-stream test.

c If large amounts of glass are used, it could be considered a fire barrier rather than a window and the radiant heat should be tested using ASTM E119 or NFPA 251.

Figure 6.18 Summary of tests for rated assemblies and materials.

Based on their performance in these tests, the assemblies are assigned fire resistance ratings according to the time elapsed when the test is terminated, in hourly increments. Some tests are used to determine how the assembly will restrict or limit smoke. All of these tests were mentioned earlier in the chapter for the applicable assembly and are summarized in Figure 6.17.

The other group of tests evaluate how a material or product reacts to fire. These tests specifically measure the extent to which a material contributes to the dangerous elements of a fire, including heat, smoke and combustion products, and flame spread. Whether a material is considered combustible, limited combustible, or noncombustible is also determined by these types of tests. Some of these tests were discussed in Chapter 4. Others, by NFPA, are shown in Figure 6.1. (ASTM has several comparable tests.) The codes will specify when each test is required. Others may be required or allowed by a jurisdiction.

Tests for Opening and Through-Penetration Protectives

Opening protectives and through-penetration protective systems must also pass specific tests. These tests were mentioned previously as each system was explained. For example, fire doors must conform to the test requirements of *NFPA 252*, and fire windows and shutters must meet the requirements of *NFPA 257*. The various fire tests are summarized in Figure 6.17. *NFPA 80, Standard for Fire Doors and Other Opening Protectives,* is also important for opening protective requirements and is listed as a note on the bottom of the summary chart. Although not technically a fire test, it regulates the installation of fire door and fire window assemblies. The installation can be just as critical as the fire test. For example, if a proper seal is not made between the perimeter of a rated door frame and the adjacent wall, it will not matter how resistant or strong the assemblies are—fire and smoke can still penetrate.

Any assembly that passes the required tests shown in 8 must have a permanent label attached to it to prove it is fire-rated, such as the label in Figure 6.14. When a required assembly such as a fire door is not sold as an assembly, it is critical for each of the additional required components to have the proper rating and for each to be appropriately labeled.

USING RATED MATERIALS AND ASSEMBLIES

✂ **Note**

Fire-rated labels are either permanently affixed to the product or directly etched into the opening protective or through-penetration protective.

Several organizations in the United States publish lists of tested assemblies. These organizations recognize a wide variety of assemblies that have been tested and assigned an appropriate hourly fire rating. Included assemblies are walls and partitions, floor/ceiling systems, roof/ceiling systems, beams, girders, truss protection systems, column protection systems, door and window assemblies, and various opening protectives. The following are three of the most widely used publications:

❏ Underwriters Laboratories (UL): *Fire Resistance Directory*, *Vol. 1* for beams, columns, floors, roofs, and partitions; *Vols. 2A and 2B* for joint systems, through-penetration fire-stop systems, electrical circuit protective systems, and duct assemblies; and *Vol. 3* for dampers, fire doors, hardware and frames, and glazing materials

Design No. U328
Nonbearing Wall Rating — 3/4 or 1 HR.
(See Item 2)

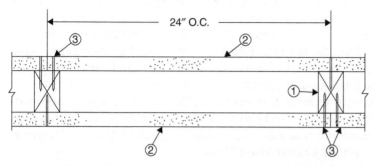

1. **Wood Studs** — Nom 2 by 3 in., spaced 24 in. OC effectively firestopped.
2. **Mineral and Fiber Board*** — 3/4 in. min thickness, 4 ft wide boards, for 3/4 hr rating. 1 in. min thickness, 4 ft wide boards for 1 hr rating.
   INDUSTRIAL INSULATION GROUP L L C — Type Super Firetemp — Boards investiagted for exierior use are marked "for exterior use". Pabco Dricote II silicone emulsion to be applied at a rate of approx 150 sq ft per gal in accordance with manufacturer's instructions which accompany the product.
3. **Nails** — 8 d box nails. 2-1/2 in. long, 0.114 in. shank diam, 1.4 in. diam heads, spaced 8 in. OC.
4. **Adhesive*** — (Not shown) — Mineral and fiber board joints and nailheads covered with adhesive.
   INDUSTRIAL INSULATION GROUP L L C — Type Calsilite CALBOND.
*Bearing the UL Classification Mark

Figure 6.19 UL fire resistant assembly example (Reprinted from the 2013 *Fire Resistance Directory*, Volume 1, with permission from Underwriters Laboratories Inc. Copyright © 2013 Underwriters Laboratories Inc.®).

❏ Gypsum Association (GA): Fire Resistance Design Manual
❏ Factory Mutual (FM): *Approval Guide*

These publications provide drawings and detailed descriptions of the rated assemblies. They indicate specific materials, workmanship, and detailed sizes and dimensions. An example of a common rated assembly from the *UL Fire Resistance Directory* is shown in Figure 6.19. Each rated assembly is assigned a file or design number specific to that assembly and an hourly rating. For example, Figure 6.19 is "UL Design No U328" for a nonbearing wall. Because this can be either a 3/4-hour wall or a 1-hour wall, depending on which materials are used, the desired rating must be specified as well.

When the codes require a fire-rated assembly (e.g., a rated wall) in an interior project, one of the publications listed previously can be used to

☑ **Note**

More current editions of the *UL Fire Resistance Directory* include specific manufacturer product information within each designed assembly.

Note

Performance-based criteria can be helpful when designing the passive fire protection system for a new or existing building.

find a detail of an acceptable assembly. For example, if existing steps in an exit access corridor are being replaced with a ramp and the ramp is required to be part of the existing floor/ceiling assembly, the construction of the ramp must maintain the rating of the existing construction type. Once this rating is determined, the *UL Fire Resistance Directory* can be used to find the detail of the rated assembly most similar to the existing construction conditions. The actual file number can be used to specify the exact way the assembly should be constructed.

It is important to note, however, that the test results and ratings of materials and assemblies can become invalid if the materials and assemblies are not used and maintained properly. Keep the following factors in mind when specifying rated assemblies:

❑ If a product is not used the way a manufacturer specifies, or if the contractor does not use the correct materials, the desired rating may not be achieved. The product must be retested the way it is built or have fire protection added to achieve the rating.

❑ If the construction of the joints between the assemblies, such as wall-to-wall, wall-to-ceiling, or wall-to-floor, is substandard, fire and smoke can penetrate and defeat the purpose of the rated assembly. Specifying the correct installation standard is just as important as specifying the right assembly.

❑ Conventional openings, such as electrical switches and outlets in wall assemblies and electrical raceways and floor boxes in floor/ceiling assemblies, can affect the fire endurance of an assembly if not properly located and spaced. Some assemblies are tested with these penetrations; others are not. (See more in Chapter 9.)

❑ Exposure to fire including flame and heat can impair the stability of a structural assembly or building element. After a fire, the original fire rating may no longer be valid.

When a rated assembly is required, the codes will often reference one or more of the three publications mentioned in this section. The codes may also allow other ways to determine the appropriate construction assembly. For example, some codes specify construction assemblies and their ratings in their texts. The *IBC* includes a table that lists and describes the installation of various structural elements, walls and partitions, floors, and roofs and their ratings. In addition, the *IBC* includes a section that allows "alternative methods for determining fire protection ratings" that may be used when standard testing methods do not work well for a specific design. Depending on the jurisdiction, it may be possible to reference these *IBC* details or to use the alternate method rather than using one of the three publications.

The codes already have provisions for allowing calculations or an engineering analysis of a proposed or existing construction assembly to determine the rating of the assembly. These calculations may be based on information given by the codes concerning the fire resistance of certain materials, or they may be performance based. For most projects, referring to the tested assemblies represented by the publications listed previously will be appropriate. For existing construction or for innovative design elements that are required to be rated, calculated or performance criteria may be required. If using special calculations or criteria in the performance codes, it is necessary to meet with the code official to discuss the design early in the process and then be prepared to provide the requested documentation to support the design. In many cases, this will require the assistance of other design professionals and engineers.

In either case, it is important to accurately document the rated assemblies and the compartmentation created by these assemblies. Construction drawings should indicate which walls or partitions are required to be rated and their required fire resistance rating. In addition, when providing details for their construction, reference the required testing and installation standards and the assigned number of the tested assembly if possible. All rated opening protectives and through-penetration protectives must be properly noted as well. In addition, everything should be verified during construction to confirm that they are installed correctly. If they are not, they will not provide the required compartmentation and may fail in the event of a fire. (See the section titled "Documentation and Liability" in Chapter 11.)

SUSTAINABILITY CONSIDERATIONS

The most critical task of the rated assemblies within a building is providing the separation and compartmentation required by code. However, because rated assemblies can be made from various combinations of materials, some more sustainable than others, with proper consideration, the rated assemblies can also contribute to the sustainability of the overall building. For example, a rated assembly could be composed of wood or metal studs with gypsum board, concrete, or concrete block; these materials have significant but different recycled content and recyclable characteristics. So, in many cases, the desired level of sustainability must be considered when specifying rated walls. If a jurisdiction requires the use of the *International Green Construction Code* with *ASHRAE/USGBC/IES 189.1, Standard for the Design of High-Performance Green Buildings Except Low-Rise Residential Buildings* or has level objectives for the project, all components, even rated walls may need to contribute to the goals. (See Appendix A for additional information.)

The individual materials and components within the rated assemblies must be considered both for its contribution to sustainability and how it potentially affects the rating of the wall. This can include materials used in the wall assembly, insulation, sound attenuation, caulking, finishes, and so forth. A sustainability standard commonly referenced includes the state of California's *Section 01350, Standard Method for the Testing and Evaluation of Volatile Organic Chemical Emissions from Indoor Sources Using Environmental Chambers.* It includes procedures to measure the volatile organic compound (VOC) emissions of building products, among other things. *Section 01350* is required by the state of California and is referenced in the *IgCC* and *ASHRAE 189.1* regarding testing of building products such as gypsum board, wood structural panels, particle board, insulation products, and other products. Certain building products, such as wood subflooring, may also need to meet specific urea-formaldehyde requirements. (See the section titled "Sustainability Considerations" in Chapter 10.)

Other industry sustainability standards are more comprehensive. For example, The Institute for Market Transformation to Sustainability (MTS) developed the standard known as *MTS 2006:4, SMaRT Sustainable Building Product Standard,* which can be used to test any building product except carpet and textiles. This standard evaluates a product over its entire supply chain for multiple environmental benefits and impacts, not just for VOC emissions. Another available standard is Green Seal's *Standard GS-36, Environmental Standard for Commercial Adhesives.* This and other standards may be required for adhesives and sealants used in building interiors.

Sound transmission and attenuation levels are addressed in the building codes and sustainability codes and standards. For example, both the building codes and the *IgCC* with *ASHRAE 189.1* set acceptable sound transmission levels for wall and floor/ceiling assemblies. In both cases, sound attenuation requirements are intended mostly to prevent the negative effects of long-term exposure to noise. For additional sustainability, the green aspects of materials that are used to achieve sound attenuation are also important. For example, specifying batt insulation made from recycled cotton fibers instead of fiberglass would be more desirable. However, the products that are used in the assembly to achieve the desired sound transmission characteristics cannot reduce or compromise the require rating of the assembly.

✎ Note

The *California Green Building Standards Code* (see Chapter 1) has many requirements similar to the *IgCC*.

✎ Note

SMaRT standards rate the products tested like a green rating system. Products are tested and classified in three categories based on the number of points received: Silver, Gold, and Platinum. SMaRT standards include the use of a life cycle assessment (LCA), as explained in Appendix A.

RESEARCH: USING THE CODES

Understanding the existing compartmentation of a building and as required by a new internal layout is important. It can affect many design choices particularly the inclusion of openings in walls and material choices. The building codes address integration of fire and smoke resistant assemblies in several places within their text. Each building code has a chapter that gives the requirements for fire resistance rating of wall assemblies, floor/ceiling assemblies, and ceiling roof assemblies. In the *International Building Code* (*IBC*) the chapter is titled, "Fire and Smoke Protection Features." In the NFPA 5000 and the *Life Safety Code* (*LSC*), the chapter is titled, "Features of Fire Protection." This chapter gives general requirements and then more specific requirements are provided in the individual occupancy-related chapters. You must refer to both chapters to know the complete requirements for a project. Requirements for rated assemblies for the structural components can be found in the code chapters defining each construction type. (See the section titled "Using the Codes" in Chapter 3.) For some projects, both a building code and the *LSC* will apply.

> **☞ Note**
>
> The chapter in the *IBC* on fire-rated assemblies is Chapter 7. In the *NFPA 5000*, it is Chapter 8. And in the *LSC*, they are covered in Chapter 8 with additional requirements in each occupancy chapter.

To determine the materials that are acceptable in the project and as part of any rated elements, the chapters in the building codes on construction types (combustible, noncombustible, fire treated, etc.) and fire protection in each applicable code must be compared. In many cases, the building codes and the *LSC* refer to various standards to define products that are allowed and when specific testing and installation methods are required. Many of these are NFPA standards. The NFPA standards that are more interior-related are listed in Figure 6.1.

The fire codes also give requirements for the different types of fire resistance–rated assemblies. For example, the *International Fire Code* (*IFC*) has separate chapters titled "Fire Resistance Rated Construction." However, this *IFC* chapter concentrates on the maintenance required once the assemblies are installed so that their integrity is maintained. (Similarly, *LSC* has a section titled "Inspection and Testing of Door Assemblies.") In some cases, the requirements of the fire code are repeated within the building codes so that the related documents are consistent. When multiple codes addressing fire-rated assemblies are required by a jurisdiction, they need to be compared. In some cases, there may be conflicting or overlapping requirements. The strictest or highest rating must be provided.

Sometimes the design of the passive fire protection system for a project, especially in an existing building, may require innovative solutions not represented in the prescriptive codes. And, because even new buildings or spaces do not always fit the configurations assumed by the codes, broader ideas about compartmentation sometimes need to be explored. In these situations, the use of a performance code, such as the *ICC Performance Code (ICCPC)*, may be helpful if allowed by a jurisdiction. Although the *ICCPC* does not have a specific section or chapter on the use of rated walls, it does include sections that set criteria for preventing a fire similar to the role of rated assemblies including sections on limiting the impact of a fire, exposure to hazards because of burning materials, and the overall fuel load. These criteria can assist the development of a unique solution if needed for a project.

Even if you are not allowed to use the *ICCPC*, the *IBC* allows for alternative methods and materials. For fire and smoke protection, the *IBC* includes Section 703.3, "Methods for Determining Fire Resistance," and Section 716.4, "Alternative Methods for Determining Fire Protection Ratings," which provide performance criteria to establish the fire resistance and fire protection ratings of an untested assembly. Likewise, in the *LSC*, the "Performance-Based Option" chapter also includes sections for design criteria and fire scenario requirements to guide the development a design the provides comparable safe conditions as defined in the prescriptive requirements with the *LSC*. These performance-based chapters and sections can allow the use of new materials, unique configurations, or innovative assembly solutions but will require additional documentation and approval. These methods must be reviewed and approved by a code official, similar to other provisions of the performance codes.

If the project has sustainability requirements or goals, appropriate codes such as the *International Green Construction Code (IgCC)* may need to be consulted. Although they do not include information specifically on fire-rated construction, they will provide information to influence the choice of materials. As discussed previously, certain construction materials are more sustainable than others, but careful attention must be given to the materials used in rated walls and other assemblies.

The Americans with Disabilities Act (ADA) standards and other accessibility standards such as *ICC A117.1* do not play a major role in passive fire prevention requirements. However, many components within the passive fire protection system, such as fire doors and enclosed stairwells, are still required to meet the accessibility requirements.

☑ **Note**

When choosing a product to minimize sound transmission for environmental quality and for sustainability, the effect on the fire protection rating of a rated wall must be considered.

DOCUMENTATION

There are several types of rated components and assemblies that may be required in a project including fire-rated walls, horizontal assemblies, smoke-rated assemblies, opening protectives, and through-penetration protectives. Not every type of fire resistant component is included in every project. You should indicate the location of existing and proposed rated walls within your project in your drawings. (Often this done graphically by inserting or overlaying a unique line type over each type of rated wall on the floor plan or on a separate plan so that it can be easily identified when looking at the drawings.) This is important for coordination with other disciplines, especially electrical and mechanical, and for review by the code official. In some cases, it may be important to indicate the appropriate tests and standards that should be met by the materials or construction. An example would be identifying a wall type as UL Design U419. Whether located on the drawings or specifications, documenting this information will make sure the correct products are provided and remind you to discuss these requirements with other project members.

As part of your research and documentation, you can use the "Fire and Smoke Resistant Assemblies" section of the digital code checklist provided with this book. This will prompt you to thoroughly research the parts of the passive fire protection system within your project and provide a comprehensive organization for your documentation.

CHAPTER 7

FIRE PROTECTION SYSTEMS

Fire and smoke are the primary threats to the safety of the occupants in a building. Fire and smoke can travel quickly horizontally and vertically unless special efforts are made to prevent this from happening. The use of rated assemblies in the *passive* fire protection system as discussed in Chapter 6 is considered the first step in controlling the spread of smoke and fire. In addition to this system of compartmentation, an *active* system that reacts when a fire is detected within a building or space can be used to provide another level of fire protection. This chapter discusses the active fire protection system and its basic components, which include detection, alarm, and extinguishing systems.

◀ Note

Fire extinguishers and sprinkler systems are sometimes referred to as *suppression systems*. However, the codes refer to them as *extinguishing systems*.

The overall aim of the active fire protection system is to detect a fire in a building or space, warn the occupants, and suppress the fire until the fire department arrives. (In some cases, the system will extinguish the fire.) If that fire can be detected quickly, occupants have more time to exit the building safely and with less panic. Also, if the fire can be suppressed or extinguished early in its development, less damage to the building and its contents may occur. Although the primary objective of the codes is occupant safety and not necessarily the contents of the building, a fire that is allowed to develop uncontrolled can cause severe structural damage to the building. This can lead to loss of life of the occupants who have not yet exited the building or the firefighters who are attempting to deal with the fire.

A building that has a comprehensive active fire protection system provides the best defense against fire. However, in some cases, such as a mixed occupancy or a building with separate fire areas, a detection and fire alarm system may be only required in one part of the building. In other cases, the owner's concerns for the contents of a building or space may make fire protection desirable even when not required by the codes. For example, it may be important for a small museum that contains valuable historic letters to protect that area even if the codes do not require the building to be protected. Building owners may add redundant fire protection systems if additional threats are a concern or if a higher level of protection is desired. In most cases, these systems should be installed using the same standards required by the code.

Depending on the system and the specific code requirements, the fire protection system may be automatic, manual, or a combination of both. The codes determine which aspects of the system must be automatic and which can be under the control of the occupants. For example, some occupancies do not require automatic detection and notification of fire and instead rely the occupants to signal that a fire has been detected. In a fully automatic system, however, once a detector indicates that there is a fire, it sets off an alarm to warn the occupants to evacuate and then initiates the extinguishing system.

The systems discussed in this chapter are directly tied to the plumbing, mechanical, or electrical system of a building. The design of these systems require a detailed knowledge of the building systems, what the code requires, and the impact of the many industry standards that are references. For this reason, an engineer is typically involved in this portion of a project. However, the designer must collaborate with the engineer(s) in designating preferred locations of devices, coordinating the locations of various design elements, and being involved in other decisions that may affect a design project. Some examples include locating fire extinguishers and fire alarms, selecting the type of sprinkler heads in decorative ceilings, and coordinating the location of sprinkler heads with the location of the light fixtures. Many of the specific code requirements and standards that are discussed in the following sections and indicated in Figure 7.1. The "Research and Documentation" sections at the end of the chapter will help you review the various fire protection requirements for the project.

✐ Note

Fire protection systems can be combined with other building systems designed to protect the occupants from emergencies other than fire. See the inset titled "Integrated Alarms."

DETECTION SYSTEMS

The best way to protect the occupants in a building from the dangers of a fire is to know that there is a fire as early as possible. This, of course, allows more time to contain the fire and remove the occupants, if necessary, before the danger escalates. For this reason, detectors are also known as *initiating devices,* because their activation initiates the rest of the fire protection system. According to the *IBC* and the *IFC*, some type of a detection system is required in all new buildings unless specifically exempted. The type and extent of the fire detection system required by the codes is based on the several factors including: the exiting needs and risk factors of the occupants, if the building type includes sleeping accommodations, and the anticipated characteristics of a fire that might occur.

NFPA 10	Standard for Portable Fire Extinguishers
NFPA 11	Standard for Low-, Medium-, and High-Expansion Foam
NFPA 11A	Standard for Medium- and High-Expansion Foam Systems
NFPA 11C	Standard for Mobile Foam Apparatus
NFPA 12	Standard for Carbon Dioxide Extinguishing Systems
NFPA 12A	Standard on Halon 1301 Fire Extinguishing Systems
NFPA 13	Standard for the Installation of Sprinkler Systems
NFPA 13D	Standard for the Installation of Sprinkler Systems in One- and Two-Family Dwellings and Manufactured Homes
NFPA 13R	Standard for the Installation of Sprinkler Systems in Residential Occupancies up to and Including Four Stories in Height
NFPA 14	Standard for the Installation of Standpipes and Hose Systems
NFPA 15	Standard for Water Spray Fixed Systems for Fire Protection
NFPA 17	Standard for Dry Chemical Extinguishing Systems
NFPA 17A	Standard for Wet Chemical Extinguishing Systems
NFPA 20	Standard for the Installation of Stationary Pumps for Fire Protection
NFPA 70	National Electrical Code
NFPA 70A	National Electrical Code Requirements for One- and Two-Family Dwellings
NFPA 72	National Fire Alarm and Signaling Code
NFPA 110	Standard for Emergency and Standby Power Systems
NFPA 111	Standard on Stored Electrical Energy Emergency and Standby Power Systems
NFPA 170	Standard for Fire Safety and Emergency Symbols
NFPA 750	Standard on Water Mist Fire Protection Systems
NFPA 2001	Standard on Clean Agent Fire Extinguishing Systems

Note: There may be other NFPA standards, not listed in this figure, that are specific to an occupancy, especially certain hazardous occupancies. Other standards, such as *NFPA 25*, may pertain to the inspection and maintenance of a system.

Figure 7.1 Common NFPA standards for fire protection systems.

In some cases, the building owner may ask that the fire protection of certain areas be supplemented for earlier detection.

The most typical sign of fire is smoke, although detection systems can be initiated by other fire signals or fire *signatures*, such as heat, gases released by combustion, changes in temperature, and other signatures. Different types of fires have different signatures. The fire source or characteristic of the fire can dictate the most affective choice of indicator. For example, a liquid fire causes a drop in temperature instead of a raise in temperature like a typical fire. In addition, smoke detectors are better for

☜ **Note**

Some detectors can recognize various fire *signatures*. Examples include the amount of smoke and a change in temperature.

a smoldering fire, but heat detectors are better for large flaming fires in large spaces. Some detectors will require a combination of indicators to confirm a fire is occurring.

Fire detection systems have changed dramatically over the past several decades due to technological advances. Today, these systems can employ everything from programmable computers to video detection and remote controls. Detectors can be programmed to require that more than one aspect of a fire be detected before signaling the alarm system and manage the sensitivity of the detector to prevent unnecessary false alarms. The codes will specify the use and type of detectors in for certain building uses. (See the inset titled "Fire Technology" in this chapter.)

These advances in detection systems have resulted in better-protected buildings. Although the building codes, fire codes, and the *LSC* will indicate when a detection system is required, they reference the *NFPA 72, National Fire Alarm Code and Signaling Code,* for more specific information. The *NFPA 72* provides the minimum performance, location, installation, and maintenance requirements for detection systems. These detectors, as well as fire alarm pull boxes, are discussed next.

Most of the time, collaboration with an electrical engineer or fire protection designer is necessary to coordinate these systems with the rest of the design. Detection systems must also be integrated into other systems within the building, including the electrical system. Detection systems rely on electricity as their main power source, and in most cases, require an emergency source of power as well. (See Chapter 9.)

Smoke Detection

Because smoke and toxic gases are the main killers in a building fire, smoke detection systems can be critical. Smoke detectors are especially effective in detecting smoldering fires that do not produce enough heat for sprinkler activation. For this reason, smoke detectors are the most widely used initiating device. Although often used interchangeably, there is a difference between a smoke *detector* and a smoke *alarm*. Both are regulated by the codes. Smoke detectors and smoke alarms are required to comply with *NFPA 72*. Single- and multiple-station smoke alarms are also required to comply with *UL 217 Standard for Smoke Alarms*. Smoke detectors are required in many commercial occupancies; smoke alarms are more common in residential occupancies and occupancies where occupants are sleeping or receiving care.

A smoke *detector* senses the presence of smoke and issues a signal to a fire alarm control panel which initiates an alarm. The alarm may sound in the specific area (or zone) or throughout the building depending on the

✎ Note

Never paint over smoke detectors, sprinkler heads, or other fire safety equipment. It can hamper their effectiveness. Many detectors operate by fusible links. Paint may keep the fusible links from melting.

✎ Note

A smoke detector and a smoke alarm are different. A smoke detector can sense the presence of smoke and send a signal to a remote alarm to be activated. A smoke alarm is self-contained and detects the smoke and releases an alarm.

design of the system. (Smoke alarms are discussed later.) Other *smoke detectors* may initiate the recall of elevators or activate the release of a door hold-open device so that doors close to complete the compartmentation. Smoke detectors must be tied into the building's power source. Smoke alarms can be tied to the building power source or work from internal batteries in some cases.

The type and extent of the fire detection system is based on the evacuation needs of the occupants and/or if the building type includes sleeping accommodations. Smoke detection is specifically required for Institutional, Educational, High Hazard, and most Residential occupancies, as well as high-rise buildings and ambulatory health care facilities. The building codes and the fire code indicate the general locations such as public corridors, elevator lobbies, waiting areas open to the corridors, group activity spaces, and kitchens. Smoke alarms are often required in addition to building smoke detection where sleeping occurs. *NFPA 72* set the specific requirements for the installation, locations, maintenance, and so on of the detection system.

The placement of smoke detectors is typically based on the layout of the space, ceiling type, and configuration. In addition, the locations should minimize the chance of false alarms. For example, in a cooking area, the smoke detector should not be placed where standard cooking procedures may activate the alarm. Instead, they are typically required in an exhaust hood. *NFPA 90* specifies the location of smoke detectors in the ductwork of air distribution systems. (See the section titled "Damper Systems" in Chapter 6.) When unusual design situations occur or include unique elements, such as coffered ceilings, work with the system designer, manufacturer, and the local code officials to locate the detectors.

Heat Detection

Next to a smoke detector, the heat detector is the most common type of detection system. Heat detectors are sensitive to any change in temperature. This can be especially important in liquid fires, where a drop in temperature occurs. Heat detectors can monitor temperatures at a specific spot or monitor the temperature range within a designated area. For example, they might be placed along an assembly line in a factory. Often, heat detectors are used with smoke detectors to avoid false alarms. In these systems, more than one sign of fire is needed before an alarm is signaled. A combination may also be used in highly sensitive areas so that the detection of either smoke or heat will activate the fire protection system.

> ### ◤ Note
>
> As more flame-resistant finishes are used in commercial and residential projects, smoke detectors become more important. These materials may smolder for longer periods without causing a fire that would activate a sprinkler system.

Alternative Detection

Continued developments in technology are creating additional ways to recognize the presence of fire. Fire produces more changes in the atmosphere than smoke and heat including molecular gases (smoke that includes carbon dioxide), aerosols, heat conduction, radiant energy, and acoustic waves. The use of alternative detection devices including radiant energy detectors or gas detectors alone or in combination with smoke or heat detectors provides for more accurate detection. New technology allows combination, multicriteria, and multisensor detectors to be used. This can require the detection of multiple fire signatures before initiation of an alarm or response. This can reduce the number of false alarms. For example, the presence of smoke does not necessarily mean that there is a fire. Someone with a cigarette or a smoking pan standing directly below a smoke detector could cause it to alarm. A change in temperature may not mean a fire, either. More sophisticated detection systems will then compare an initial detected signature with the presence of other symptoms of fire. If no other symptoms of fire exist, the detection system may delay setting off the fire alarm until another symptom is present or the smoke continues.

Manual Fire Alarms

The codes consider a manual fire alarm to be part of the detection system. In this case, however, it is the occupant who detects the fire. When a fire is detected, an occupant set off the manual alarm using a *pull station* or *alarm box*. If an automatic smoke detection system or sprinkler system is not provided in a building, the codes typically require a manual fire alarm. However, certain occupancies require a manual fire alarm even if a smoke detection system or sprinkler system is provided. It will depend on the number of occupants, the capabilities of the occupants, location above or below the level of discharge, and the height of the building, as well as other specific requirements. Common examples include Educational occupancies, large Assembly, Business, and Storage occupancies. These requirements are found in the building codes, fire codes and the *LSC*. A manual fire alarm will set off an alarm to notify the occupants of a problem, but it will not activate the extinguishing system.

◪ **Note**

The traditional manual fire alarm is a pull device. Accessible types of devices require pushing with minimal effort. Both types must be red.

◪ **Note**

Some building types may require the use of a protective cover over the pull box to deter vandalism. This is usually determined by a code official.

FIRE TECHNOLOGY

Technology, especially the use of computers, has created advances not only in the individual detectors but in the detection systems as well. Now systems can monitor and check each detector individually to see if it is working properly. In the event of a fire, a detection system can determine the exact location of the fire, not just the floor on which the fire originated, and notify certain areas or zones in the facility rather than the entire building. The sensitivity of a particular zone of detectors can also be modified to account for different levels of heat, or other symptoms, that might be present in normal conditions.

Newer tools, such as remote fire command stations and graphic annunciation panels, which indicate exact locations within a building using imported digital drawings, provide valuable information to local authorities responding to an emergency. Another technology currently being developed involves the use of video systems that can detect and analyze a fire. (See also the inset titled "Integrated Alarms".)

The codes consider a manual fire alarm to be part of the detection system. In this case, however, it is the occupant who detects the fire. When a fire is detected, an occupant detects the fire. They set off the manual alarm by the use of a *pull station* or *alarm box*. If an automatic smoke detection system or sprinkler system is not provided in a building, the codes typically require a manual fire alarm. However, certain occupancies require a manual fire alarm even if a smoke detection system or sprinkler system is provided. It will depend on the number of occupants, the capabilities of the occupants, and the height of the building, as well as other specific requirements. Common examples include Educational occupancies and large Assembly and Business occupancies. Although the alarm does not usually activate the extinguishing system, it will notify the occupants of a problem.

When manual fire alarms are provided, the codes typically require the box to be located adjacent to each exit doorway. The alarm box should be easily seen and located on the latch side of the door no farther than 5 feet (1524 mm) from the doorway as shown in Figure 7.2. Some occupancies may require a more unique location. For example, alarm boxes in hospitals are typically located at control rooms or nurses' stations for use by staff members. In addition, on any given floor, the travel distance to an alarm box must typically be within 200 feet (60 m), so additional boxes may be required. The codes also specify their color, signage, and power supply.

◪ Note

Instead of listing all the alarm requirements within its text, the 2010 *ADA Standards* reference the 1999 and 2002 editions of the *NFPA 72, National Fire Alarm and Signaling Code*.

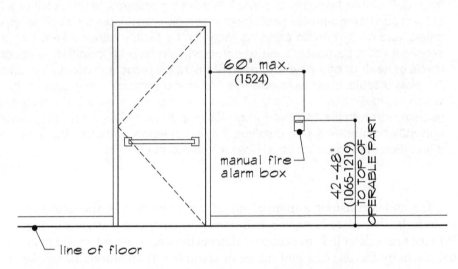

line of ceiling

60" max.
(1524)

manual fire
alarm box

42-48"
(1065-1219)
TO TOP OF
OPERABLE PART

line of floor

Figure 7.2 Typical manual fire alarm box mounting requirements.

Because the device is meant to be used by building occupants, accessibility requirements for the mounting of the alarm box will apply. The height of the box must be within the accessible reach range and typically have a clear floor space of 30 inches (760 mm) by 48 inches (1220 mm) in front of it. (*ICC A117.1* may require a deeper clear floor space.) In addition, new types of manual alarms have been developed to be more easily used by persons with disabilities. These include devices that are more easily grasped and do not require complex movement to activate.

Carbon Monoxide Detection

The detection systems that have been discussed so far have been to detect a fire. However, exposure to fire, heat, or smoke is not the only danger to occupants. Carbon monoxide is produced by incomplete combustion of organic materials. If inhaled, it accumulates in the body over time; prolonged exposure to carbon monoxide can be fatal. The first sign of a problem is often occupants' experiencing flu-like symptoms. Continued and prolonged exposure will cause drowsiness to the point of unconsciousness and ultimately death.

✎ **Note**

The codes now require carbon monoxide detectors in several occupancy classifications, including Residential, Institutional, and Educational. Check the codes for specifics.

Exposure to this gas is usually related to the use of appliances or engines powered by gas, such as automobiles, lawnmowers, stoves, and hot water heaters. Carbon monoxide detection systems include detectors and audible notification appliances. In 2009, the *International Residential Code* began requiring carbon monoxide detectors and alarms in one- and two-family dwellings if the home includes a fuel-fired appliance or an attached garage. Typically, a detector/alarm must be located outside of or adjacent to bedrooms. (See Appendix C.)

Beginning in 2012, the *IBC* began requiring carbon monoxide detection and alarm systems in other occupancies and locations. Currently, carbon monoxide detection can be required in Assembly, Institutional, Residential (with dwelling and sleeping units), and Educational occupancies that have a fuel-fired appliance or an attached garage. For each occupancy, the code specifies the device type, location, power source, maintenance, and so on.

Requirements for carbon monoxide systems are found in the same standard as for fire detection, *NFPA 72, National Fire Alarm and Signaling Code*. The detectors must comply with *UL 2075, Gas and Vapor Detectors and Sensors* and the alarms must comply with *UL 2034, Standard of Safety for Single and Multiple Station Carbon Monoxide Alarms*. These standards regulate the proper installation and maintenance requirements for carbon monoxide detection systems and may require additional alarm locations.

High levels of carbon monoxide will trigger the detector and cause it to alarm more quickly while lower levels must be present for a period of time before the alarm will trigger. In most cases, the alarm is integral with the detector device, but they can part of a detection system as well. Once sounded, the alarm relies on the occupants to report to authorities, usually the fire department, so that the problem can be resolved.

✐ **Note**

NFPA 72 National Fire Alarm and Signaling Code includes information on emergency voice/alarm communication systems (EVACSs) and mass notification systems (MNSs).

ALARM SYSTEMS

Alarm systems within a building or space make occupants aware that something unusual is occurring. In most cases, alarms are used to warn occupants that a fire has been detected and that they should evacuate. Alarm systems also can be used to notify occupants of other types of emergencies, such as toxic spills, severe weather conditions, or a bomb threat. The fire codes, the fire protection chapters of the building codes, and the *Life Safety Code* specify the type of alarm, its location, and the wiring required. For installation of the alarms and other details, the codes also refer to the standard *NFPA 72*. Certain accessibility requirements also apply. These requirements are found in the *ICC A117.1* standard and the *ADA Standards*.

The devices that make up the different types of alarm systems are sometimes referred to as *notification appliances*. An alarm system can be activated either manually using a pull device or automatically by a detection system (for example, a smoke detector.) The codes designate smoke alarms and fire alarm systems. The codes will specify which type of system is required for each occupancy classification. Some occupancies may require both types of activation.

A *smoke alarm* is essentially a smoke detector that detects smoke and sets off an integral alarm as a self-contained device. Smoke alarms can be single-station or multiple-station alarms. A single-station alarm will sound only at the device that has detected the fire and warns the occupants in the immediate area. A multiple-station alarm system is a set of devices that are interconnected. When smoke is detected by one device, it will alarm the limited series of connected devices.

A *fire alarm* is a notification appliance that is part of a fire alarm system. The fire alarm is initiated by a detector that can be any of the types discussed previously (smoke, fire, heat, combination, etc.) or a manual pull station. The type of notification signal and system may depend on the use and type of occupants within a specific zone of the building. The NFPA 72 and the LSC require low-frequency fire alarm notifications signals in new hotel, dormitories, and other sleeping rooms because they have proven to wake sleeping or hard-of-hearing occupants more effectively. In larger occupancies, the alarms may be interconnected to create specific zones so that evacuation can be controlled in stages or by floor. In other occupancies, such as hospitals or nursing homes, the signal will only annunciate at a controlled station, such as a nurses' station, so that only staff members are alerted. The alarm can also go to a control room where someone decides what action should be taken. Or the notification can sound throughout the building and trigger a total evacuation. In many cases, the fire alarm will notify the local fire department as well.

Similar to the detection system, an alarm system is tied to the electrical system of a building and may be tied to other similar systems as well. For example, a building may be required to have a control panel at the fire department entrance to the building so that firefighters can quickly determine the location of the problem. (See also the inset titled "Integrated Alarms" in this section.) An electrical engineer typically designs the alarm system and references the appropriate codes. Collaboration will be necessary to coordinate the location of devices with other design elements and confirm that the system meets the intent of the design. The various categories of alarm systems are described next.

⌔ Note

Fire alarms in R-1 and R-2 sleeping areas must provide a low-frequency signal complying with NFPA 72, which is more effective in waking sleeping occupants.

Visual and Audible Alarm Systems

Fire and emergency alarms are required to use audible and visual signals. This ensures that as many people as possible within a building will be notified. An *audible* alarm signals an emergency by a loud sound or series of sounds. A *visual alarm* emits a pulsing light that cannot easily be ignored or a rotating beacon. Alarm devices for audible and visual can be separate or in one unit.

Typically, the response to a fire alarm is to exit the building. In some cases, such as hospitals, occupants are not expected or capable of exiting on their own. Visual and audible alarms have two modes of notification: public and private. Public mode informs all occupants of the danger. Private mode alerts only occupants who are expected to respond to the emergency. In that case, the alarm notification may be limited to corridors and areas occupied by control staff members.

For *audible* alarms, the codes specify different patterns and levels of sound based on the location and emergency. The fire alarm may make a single loud blast, but the emergency alarm may be a pattern of short blasts. *NFPA 70* includes separate requirements for areas considered public, private, and sleeping areas. There are additional considerations for the sound level for various conditions including in toilets, when multiple rooms, doors, or curtains may be between the occupant and the alarm signal device, when there is noise being produced in the room, and in sleeping areas. For example, an audible alarm in a factory where machines are working may require a louder sound than one in an office building. In most cases, the alarm must be able to be heard throughout the building and must be located accordingly. The alarms must also be placed in a natural path of escape because the noise from the alarm helps occupants to locate the exits during a fire. Audible alarms must meet additional accessibility requirements that affect the location, type, sound level, and pulse rate.

Although visual fire alarms were first required by the ADA, they are now required by the building and fire codes whenever a fire alarm is required with few exceptions. A visual alarm is critical to notify occupants that are hearing impaired and/or to awaken occupants who are sleeping.

A *visual alarm* is typically white or clear flashing lights; they are sometimes referred to as *strobes*. The color, intensity, flash rate, and pulse duration of a visual alarm are regulated by the codes and standards. Where different types of warnings are required, each would have a different

✍ Note

Visual alarms can be referred to as visual alarm signals, visible signal devices, visual signaling appliances, or visual notification appliances.

✍ Note

Visual alarms must typically be installed in more locations than audible alarms, because a visual alarm can be observed only in the space in which it is installed.

☑ **Note**

Visible alarms are not required in exits such as stairwells because of the distraction and/ or tripping hazards they may create.

pattern or intensity. The codes also set mounting heights above the floor and spacing distances. (See the *ADA Standards* and the *ICC A117.1* standard for details.)

As part of a design, it may be necessary to coordinate placement of the audible and visual alarm systems with an engineer to ensure that the alarms can be seen and heard and be in appropriate locations in the design. The distances between alarms, intermediate walls, and closed doors could reduce the level of sound. The placement of the devices must be mounted not to create a protruding object as defined within the accessibility requirements.

Emergency Communication Systems

☑ **Note**

A *public mode* alarm notifies all occupants. A *private mode* alarm notifies only control staff.

Some occupancies and building types are required by the codes to have an emergency communication system (ECS) tied into the fire alarm. According to the *NFPA 72*, an ECS is defined as "a system for the protection of life by indicating the existence of an emergency situation and communicating information necessary to facilitate an appropriate response and actions." An ECS is like a fire alarm and public-address system which provides direction to the occupants during an emergency. Sometimes the ECS can also be integrated with other noncode-required building systems including security, card access control, video monitoring, background music, and building automation if the fire notification is not affected. However, *NFPA 72* will allow the audible fire alarm to be briefly disrupted while a verbal information is being given.

Typically activated by an automatic fire detector, a sprinkler water-flow device, or a manual fire alarm box, the ECS will sound an alert tone followed by voice instructions. The code requires the fire alarm must be distinctive: in some cases, there may be a unique sound for different levels of emergency. The emergency verbal message may vary based on the emergency. For example, occupants may be told to evacuate, relocate to another part of the building, or remain in place. Some systems may also indicate the location of the emergency. *NFPA 72* regulates the message as well as the location of speakers. It is important that the messages be "intelligible" (easily understood), not just audible (heard).

☑ **Note**

An emergency voice/ alarm communication system can use prerecorded or live announcements or both. A jurisdiction may require one over another and often requires approval of the message(s).

Types of buildings that are required by code to have an ECS include factories, some Institutional occupancies such as hospitals and assisted living facilities, Educational, large storage facilities, occupancies in high-rise buildings, and other Assembly and Hazardous occupancies. The codes specify speaker locations for each occupancy based on *paging zones* created within the building. At a minimum, paging zones are required at each floor, elevator group, exit stairway, and areas of refuge. An ECS is also required to be tied to an emergency power source (see Chapter 9). Because an ECS may integrate multiple systems, some not code regulated, it is important to work with the proper engineers, consultants, and AHJ to ensure that critical emergency notification is not affected.

The codes also regulate the use of a mass notification system (MNS). As part of an emergency communication system, an MNS not only lets people know that there is an emergency other than fire, but also can provide real-time information and instruction as to what to do in response to the emergency. These are common in large facilities with multiple buildings. Examples include schools, college campuses, and industrial complexes. Recognizing that there are other dangers (weather emergencies, terrorist threats, active shooter, etc.) that building occupants must be warned about, *NFPA 72* now allows mass notification events to take priority over fire alarm signals in some situations. They incorporate traditional alarm and voice-delivery systems as well as a wide variety of other technologies that can be used separately or in conjunction with each other, depending on the emergency. In addition, even if the LSC can require an assessment to be made for the need for a mass notification system based on the occupancy regardless if it is required by the fire protection system. The NFPA chapter "Emergency Communications Systems" provides prescriptive and performance criteria to provide the appropriate level of communication and response plan based on the emergency.

An MNS is unique because a wide array of technology is used to notify occupants of an emergency. Examples include scrolling electronic signs in more public areas, indoor paging systems, outdoor speaker systems, pop-up messages on computer networks, and distributed text messaging. A system is often integrated with other building systems and can consist of visible and tactile signals, video imaging, graphics, and text. (See the inset titled "Integrated Alarms" in this section.) MNSs are becoming common government and military buildings, college campuses, and other large multibuilding facilities. If working with an occupancy that requires an ECS and/or an MNS, check for specific code requirements and include the necessary accessibility requirements as well. Using the prescriptive and performance code requirements may be necessary to ensure the emergency messages are understood by the most people possible.

Accessible Warning Systems

As already mentioned, visual alarms were first required by the ADA for accessibility. Now, audible and visual alarms are required by the building

✎ Note

An emergency communications system can also be referred to as emergency voice/alarm communication system (EVAC).

✎ Note

For EVACs, intelligibility is as important as audibility. *Audibility* is the ability to hear the warning system. *Intelligibility* is the ability to understand the message being given.

✎ Note

NFPA 72 requires verification of the clarify of voice messages. It includes a definition of "intelligibility" as an "audible voice information that is distinguishable and understandable." Although it does not provide a quantifiable measurement method, Annex D of *NFPA 72* provides suggested practices.

✎ Note

Some jurisdictions may allow the use of directional sound devices in a building to assist occupants in locating exits. These devices provide intuitively audible cues for easier egress.

codes, the fire codes, and the *LSC*, as well as the *ADA Standards*. Although not currently required by the codes, additional accessible warning systems are available. The ADA does not specifically require these other types either; however, it does require that an appropriate system be provided for occupants with disabilities. The safety of the occupants using the space or building must be considered and a special type of system may be required. For example, tactile notification appliances that produce a vibrating sensation could be specified where many occupants are seeing impaired and/or hearing impaired, such as those in a special school or dormitory. A visible text messaging system could also be used to assist persons with other types of disabilities. In these cases, the *ADA Standards* would be referenced for the placement and visual characteristics of audible and visual alarms.

With the growing influence of the ADA on safety and accessibility concerns for the disabled, new types of accessible warning systems will continue to be developed. There can sometimes be conflicts within the technical requirements between the accessibility standards and the codes. However, the greatest degree of accessibility should be provided.

INTEGRATED ALARMS

Fire safety systems and alarms can be integrated with other building controls, such as mechanical and security systems. When alarm systems are connected to a mechanical system, they can shut down the air distribution system that would spread smoke to other parts of the building. When they are connected to the security system, they can signal the unlocking of doors that are normally required for security. When they are connected to the communication system, they can initiate audible direction to the building occupants. With the use of new technology, computers, motion detectors, and closed-circuit cameras can be used to tie multiple systems together to monitor and control evacuation and monitor a fire in a more comprehensive way.

As technology changes and improves, *NFPA 72, National Fire Alarm and Signaling Code,* also continues to evolve to allow alarm systems to become part of other building systems. (See the inset titled "Building Automation Systems" in Chapter 8 for more information.) However, it requires several safety measures for an integrated network including *NFPA 4, Standard for Integrated Fire Protection and Life Safety System Testing. NFPA 3, Recommended Practice for the Commissioning of Fire Protection and Life Safety Systems* is not required by NFPA 72, but it can be used as best practice if commissioning is desired. Some jurisdictions, however, may limit full integration if local fire departments are not equipped to work with the new technology.

The development of software and products to work within an integrated system is ongoing. However, this type of system is complex and most suitable for complex projects. In most cases coordination with a fire protection system designer and other engineers will be required.

EXTINGUISHING SYSTEMS

Extinguishing systems provide for the control and extinguishment of fires once they occur. (They were referred to as *suppression systems* in older editions of the codes.) Some are intended for use by occupants and some are designed to be used by professional firefighters. The design and installation of the extinguishing system will require coordination with other trades and design professionals. Whether they distribute water or other agents, a mechanical engineer usually needs to be involved. Although a fire protection designer or an engineer will typically design the system and reference the appropriate codes, coordination with other ceiling elements can be important for a good design.

The most common extinguishing systems include fire extinguishers, standpipes, fire hoses, and sprinkler systems. These are explained in more detail throughout this section.

Fire Extinguishers

Portable fire extinguishers are one means of fire suppression meant for use by the building occupant. Because they are movable and do not require access to plumbing lines, they are often specified by the designer on interior projects. They can be surface mounted where space allows or recessed within a wall using a special cabinet. The cabinet must either have a vision panel or be clearly marked with a sign because the fire extinguisher must always be visible. The fire extinguisher must also be tested and have an approved label.

Typically, it is the fire codes and the *LSC* that specify the occupancies and types of building uses that require fire extinguishers. They may also be required by OSHA for businesses and their location will be affected by *CFR 1910.157*. The information from the *IFC* is repeated in the *IBC*, as well. The codes also refer to *NFPA 10, Standard for Portable Fire Extinguishers*, which provides more detailed information, including specific numbers, sizes, and extinguisher types. Most occupancies require an extinguisher. Specific areas or rooms within a building require them as well. For example, most commercial kitchens, laboratories, computer rooms, as well as smaller kitchens and break rooms, require a fire extinguisher. (Other NFPA standards provide fire extinguisher requirements for special occupancies.) Some specific location requirements include the following:

❑ Within 30 feet (9145 mm) of commercial cooking equipment
❑ In areas where flammable or combustible liquids are stored, used, or dispensed

Note

The building codes and the fire codes should be referenced when determining extinguishing systems. The fire codes often include additional requirements.

Note

When surface-mounting a handheld fire extinguisher, consider code and accessibility heights and projection requirements.

❑ In buildings under construction

❑ Where open flames are present

❑ In laboratories, computer rooms, generator rooms, and other special hazard areas

The code official can require a fire extinguisher in areas that they feel it is necessary.

Fire extinguishers are available in various sizes and contain an array of substances including water, carbon dioxide, or other dry chemical agents. The type of extinguisher required will depend on the occupancy and the anticipated type of fire or burning substance. The fire codes classify potential fires as either a Class A, B, C, or K fire hazard. The extinguisher for each type of fire is identified by a specific shape, letter, and color as indicated in Figure 7.3. (if the shapes are in color, the triangle is green, the square is red, the circle is blue, the star is yellow, and the *K* is black.) Class A is the most common specified and can be used on the least hazardous of fire types. Typical locations would be office buildings, classrooms and assembly uses. Class B is specified for workshops, garages, storages areas, etc. for flammable liquid and gas fires, Class C for live electrical equipment, Class D for combustible metals, and K for fires involving cooking oils (fats, grease, and oils) in commercial kitchens. *NFPA 10* also requires a marking that shows the types of fire each can be used to extinguish and the efficiency of the device according to *UL 711, Rating and Fire Testing of Fire Extinguishers.*

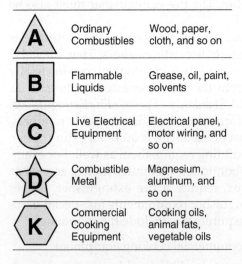

A	Ordinary Combustibles	Wood, paper, cloth, and so on
B	Flammable Liquids	Grease, oil, paint, solvents
C	Live Electrical Equipment	Electrical panel, motor wiring, and so on
D	Combustible Metal	Magnesium, aluminum, and so on
K	Commercial Cooking Equipment	Cooking oils, animal fats, vegetable oils

Figure 7.3 Fire Extinguisher types.

EXTINGUISHING SYSTEMS

The appropriate extinguishing system is assigned by the building codes, the fire codes, and the *LSC* by occupancy classification, building use, and to specific rooms based on the assumed fire loads and risk factors. Most extinguishing systems are defined by a specific NFPA standard. The most common are explained here:

> *NFPA 13, Standard for the Installation of Sprinkler Systems.* Buildings protected according to *NFPA 13* are considered 'fully sprinklered' by the codes. *NFPA 13* provides adequate coverage and management of the fire to allow occupants to leave the building and to control or extinguish the fire, protecting life and property. *NFPA 13* requires coverage throughout the building even in unoccupied spaces. The *NFPA 13* document includes separate chapters for the different types, applications, and sprinkler head orientations such as pendent, upright, sidewall, residential sprinklers, early suppression fast-response sprinklers, and so on. Most commercial buildings when required to be sprinklered must comply with *NFPA 13*. Some Residential occupancies and residential uses must comply with *NFPA 13* including hospitals (I-2) and nursing homes (I-1), dormitories, and some multistory residential buildings. A *NFPA 13* system is required to apply area and height increases as discussed in Chapter 4.

> *NFPA 13R, Standard for the Installation of Sprinkler Systems Low-Rise Residential Occupancies.* A building whose system complies with *NFPA 13R* is considered to be "partially sprinklered." This system provides adequate coverage for occupants to leave the building in the event of a fire and to prevent flashover in the room of origin only. *NFPA 13R* is typically specified for use in residential occupancies up to three to four stories (depending on the edition of the code). The *IBC* will allow this system to be used in some residential uses on a larger pedestal or podium buildings if the construction type of podium is Type I and is limited in overall height. *NFPA 13R* does not require coverage in unoccupied areas such as attics, closets, or bathrooms. Residential uses that typically can comply with *NFPA 13R* include hotels, apartment buildings, and large single-family dwellings. A *NFPA 13* system can be used where a *NFPA 13R* is required but it would increase the cost of the project.

> *NFPA 13D, Installation of Sprinkler Systems in One-and Two-Family Dwellings and Manufactured Homes.* Systems complying with *NFPA 13R* are considered to be "partially sprinklered." The objective of this system is to slow fire growth and prevent flashover to allow time for occupants to exit. *NFPA 13D* only requires sprinklers to be installed in living and sleeping areas, not including small bathrooms (55 square feet [5 sm] or less), closets (24 square feet [2.23 sm] or less), exterior balconies decks, garages, attics. This system is required by the *IRC* for most new homes and duplexes. However, many jurisdictions delete this requirement by amendment. (See Appendix C.)

Although life safety, not property protection, is the primary intent of an automatic sprinklering system, research indicates that property damage can be greatly reduced when sprinklers are present.

Each class of fire extinguisher is given an appropriate distance and size of container. For example, When Class A extinguishers are required, no occupant can be more than 75 feet (22,860 mm) from a fire extinguisher. This distance, as well as the overall size of the space or building, will determine the final quantity and size of the extinguishers selected. (Annex E of *NFPA 10* explains how to calculate this.) Ideally, extinguishers should be located along normal paths of travel. Other classes require shorter distances. Refer to *NFPA 10* for specifics.

The codes typically specify the maximum height of the extinguisher based on its weight; as shown in Figure 7.4. However, because a fire

☑ **Note**

Depending on the occupancy and types of hazards present, different types of fire extinguishers may be required. Five types are available: A, B, C, D, and K.

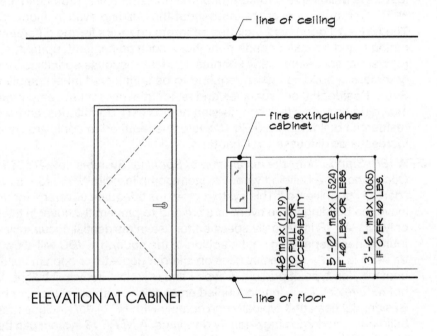

ELEVATION AT CABINET

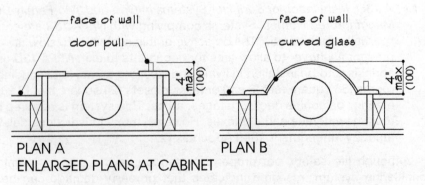

PLAN A
ENLARGED PLANS AT CABINET

PLAN B

Figure 7.4 Typical fire extinguisher and cabinet-mounting requirements.

extinguisher is meant to be used by an occupant, it must also be accessible. It must be mounted at height within an accessible reach from a front or side approach, as required by the *ADA Standards* and the *ICC A117.1*. The top of Figure 7.4 indicates the required code and accessibility heights in relation to the fire extinguisher cabinet. In addition, the extinguisher cannot protrude more than 4 inches (100 mm) into a path of travel. This may eliminate the use of bracket-mounted fire extinguishers in certain areas. Often a fire extinguisher cabinet is recessed either partially or fully into a wall. The bottom of Figure 7.4 shows two types of partially recessed cabinets. Even the pull on the cabinet must be within the required 4 inches (100 mm).

✒ Note

Newer technology allows fire extinguishers to be monitored electronically to ensure that they are properly mounted, properly charged, and remain unobstructed. Additional information can be found in the fire codes and the *LSC*.

Standpipes and Fire Hoses

Standpipes and fire hoses are typically installed during the initial construction of a building. However, they may also have to be upgraded when new work is done in an existing building. They are a manual, fixed fire system. The *IBC*, *IFC*, or *NFPA 1* will determine if a system is needed based on the height, number of stories, and whether sprinklered or unsprinklered. Some are easily recognized by the glass-enclosed cabinet and the folded fire hose. Others are simply large-diameter pipes that extend vertically through a building with connections for fire hose hookup. The system supplies water for extinguishing fires and can be used by firefighters or building occupants, depending on the class and type of system.

Classes of Standpipes

The codes establish three classes of standpipes. The classes are based on the purpose and intended use of the system.

- ❑ **Class I.** Class I standpipes consist of pipes with high-pressure 2½-inch (64-mm) outlets for hookup to fire department hoses. These are typically installed in buildings without sprinklers or high rise buildings. The assumption is that the fire will be fought by firefighters or by limited building personnel trained in its operation within the building.

- ❑ **Class II.** Class II standpipes have hoses attached that are usually limited to 1½ inches (38 mm) in diameter or less. They are designed for small-scale fire protection and are mostly used in buildings that do not have a sprinkler system. They are intended to be used by building occupants who have been trained to use the equipment until the fire department arrives.

☑ Note

A standpipe riser (e.g., pipe) may also serve as a sprinkler system riser if specific code require- ments are met.

❑ **Class III.** Class III is a combination of Class I and Class II stand- pipes. It is designed for use by trained building occupants or the fire department. It includes a 2½-inch (64-mm) outlet for fire depart- ment hookup and a 1½-inch (38-mm) outlet with a 1½-inch (38-mm) hose and nozzle.

Types of Standpipes

There are also five types of standpipe systems:

1. **Automatic wet system.** An automatic wet system has a water sup- ply within the piping system that is ready on demand. It is consid- ered the most effective and most reliable system.

2. **Automatic dry system.** An automatic dry system is normally filled with pressured air and is allowed where freezing may occur. The use of a hose valve is required to admit water into the system.

3. **Manual wet system.** A manual wet system does not have water in the pipes themselves but is connected to a water supply that must be pumped into the pipes by the fire department.

4. **Manual dry system.** A manual dry system does not have water within the pipes or in an attached supply. The water must be pumped in from a source from the fire department. It is commonly used in parking garages.

5. **Semiautomatic dry system.** A semiautomatic dry system is similar to an automatic dry system, but a remote control located at the hose connection is required to activate the valve to admit water into the system.

The type and class of a required standpipe depend on the code, the type of occupancy, the height of the building, and the presence of an automatic sprinkler system. The types of buildings that may require standpipes include multistory buildings with or without sprinklers, high-rise buildings (see the inset titled "High-Rise Buildings" in Chapter 4), storage buildings, and certain other spaces. Also, large stages within any building type must have a standpipe.

Each code sets slightly different requirements for standpipes. These requirements are included in the building codes and fire codes. The codes also refer to the standard *NFPA 14, Installation of Standpipes and Hose Systems,* which further specifies the number, type, and locations of standpipes. When required, a standpipe is typically located within an exit stair enclosure, on each side of a wall adjacent to the opening of a horizontal exit, and at the entrance of an exit passageway. Not only does this provide easy access but also it provides fire protection for 1 to 2 hours. Class II standpipes may require additional locations for accurate coverage with the fire hose. Because Class II and Class III standpipes are meant for use by building occupants, placing the fire hose cabinet so that it is accessible also becomes important. The pull to the cabinet and the operable parts in the cabinet should be at accessible heights and reach ranges.

Sprinkler Systems

Automatic sprinkler systems are vital to the containment of a fire. A sprinkler system controls fire spread by reducing the heat and wetting the unburned fuel load in the building. Research shows that the number of lives lost during a fire is greatly reduced when automatic sprinklers are present. As a result, although automatic sprinkler systems were once mostly optional, they are now required in almost all occupancies and use groups when certain conditions exist. In fact, the ICC codes and the NFPA codes now require sprinkler systems in one- and two-family homes. (See Appendix C.) Typical factors that determine if a sprinkler system is required include height and size of the building, size of fire areas, occupancy classification, and occupant load. In addition if a floor of a building is required to be sprinklered, all floors between that floor and the level of means of egress discharge may be required to be sprinklered as well. (The presence of hazardous materials may also require sprinklers.) However, when an automatic sprinkler system is installed, the codes allow trade-offs in other aspects of a design. For example, when an automatic sprinkler system is provided within an incidental use room, the 1-hour separation is often not required. (Refer to the section titled "Sprinkler Design Issues" later in this chapter for additional trade-offs.)

Sprinkler systems can be wet-pipe or dry-pipe systems, similar to standpipe systems. Sprinkler heads are the devices located within the spaces that will activate the sprinkler system. Both are discussed next. Most sprinkler systems are required to be tied into an alarm system as discussed previously so that the occupants, the appropriate building personnel, and the fire department are notified of the emergency when the sprinkler is activated. Although water damage may be caused by the

◀ Note

Automatic sprinklers have been in use since the beginning of the twentieth century. However, systems in older buildings may be considered antiquated. Ultimately, a code official must decide whether an old system must be replaced to meet current code requirements.

release of water by the sprinkler system (5 to 25 gallons or 19 to 95 liters/minute, depending on the type of sprinkler), it will be considerably less than the damage that would occur if the fire department had to extinguish the fire with a fire hose (200 to 250 gallons or 757 to 946 liters/minute).

The NFPA is the main source for sprinkler requirements. There are three basic systems referred to as *NFPA 13, NFPA 13R,* and *NFPA 13D.* Each standard provides detailed design and installation requirements and references several other NFPA standards. (See the inset of these systems.) However, it is the building codes, the fire codes, and the *LSC* that specify when an automatic sprinkler system is required. Each code specifies the types of occupancies, types of buildings, and special rooms that require sprinklers and which system(s) can be used.

Types of Sprinkler Systems

Using the codes and the NFPA standards, an engineer typically determines the type of system, size, and number of pipes and the spacing of the sprinkler heads. In many jurisdictions, separate drawings by a sprinkler engineer are required. Although *NFPA 13* recognizes seven types of automatic sprinkler systems, most systems are one of the following four types:

☑ Note

The typical wet-pipe sprinkler system is usually equipped with a fire department connection as a secondary water supply source when 20 or more sprinklers are present.

1. **Wet-pipe system.** A wet-pipe system is the most common system. It uses water to extinguish a fire and consists of pipes that are filled with water at all times. This type is typically considered the most effective and is used most often.

2. **Dr-pipe system.** A dry-pipe system is used in unheated building types such as storage facilities and parking garages, as well as other areas such as attics and freezers. They are used to prevent freezing. Instead of water, the pipes are filled with pressurized air or nitrogen. When activated by the heat of a fire, the air is released and water floods the pipes to extinguish the fire.

3. **Deluge system.** A deluge system is an open-head water system. It is usually activated by a separate detection system (sometimes a controlled system) and is used in hazardous situations. The deluge system discharges large quantities of water to control severe fires. In areas where large quantities of water are not desirable (e.g., electrical situations), it can be used in conjunction with other agents.

4. **Pre-action system.** A pre-action system is a combination of wet and dry systems that allows delayed reaction and requires additional fire detection signals. The delayed reaction allows the system to be manually intercepted and turned off if the sprinklers are not necessary. It is used primarily in areas where property is susceptible to water damage (e.g., museums, libraries, and data centers) or where sprinkler pipes are likely to get damaged.

5. **Water mist system:** A water mist system uses a very fine steam like spray of water. The small droplets cool the fire and reduce the oxygen available to the flames. It uses less water than other systems. It can be used in areas with equipment where alternative extinguishing systems using gases or foams would be dangerous to potential occupants. The delivery system can be either wet pipe, dry pipe, pre-action, or deluge.

Wet and dry systems require the same piping. The risers supply the water from the building's incoming water supply to the cross mains at each floor. The cross mains supply the branch lines. Sprinkler heads are located at the end of each branch line.

Types of Sprinkler Heads

A fire is detected by the sprinkler head in a sprinkler system. The typical sprinkler head is held closed by a fusible link or a glass bulb filled with heat-sensitive liquid. When a fire causes the temperature in a space to rise above a set temperature, the heat either melts the fusible link or causes the liquid to expand, breaking the glass. They are not activated by smoke. The temperature required to initiate the system varies based on the set level of sensitivity. Typically, water flows from only the affected sprinkler head. In a deluge or pre-action system, additional controls may be required to activate the release of water.

Sprinkler heads vary in how quickly they respond to a fire, the size of the orifice, and the distribution of water, as well as other special features. The orientation of the head also makes a difference in its effect. The most common orientations include pendant, upright, sidewall, recessed, and concealed. Figure 7.5 explains these orientation styles and their uses. The orientation of the head is typically determined by the design or construction requirements, the location of the head, and the area it is meant to cover. For example, a finished ceiling will require a sprinkler head with a

◄ Note

In some systems, fire and smoke detectors can be specified to detect carbon monoxide detection as well.

◄ Note

A water mist fire suppression system produces a fine spray and leaves little residual water.

◄ Note

Flexible sprinkler head connections that attach to the end of a cross main or branch pipe are designed for use in suspended ceilings. They are easier to relocate when the layout of a space changes.

different orientation than an exposed or open ceiling. In some cases, a wall-mounted head will provide better coverage. Following are the most common types of sprinkler heads. (New types of sprinklers are constantly being developed to address the specific needs of building uses and design ideas.)

❑ **Standard spray head.** This is the most common type of sprinkler head. It can be used in most occupancies and building uses. Each head can typically cover approximately 225 square feet (20.9 sm).

❑ **Fast-response sprinkler head.** The name is somewhat misleading. It does not mean that this system will actually respond more quickly than other systems. However, because it is activated by a low level of heat, it may activate earlier than alternative systems. Response time is affected by ceiling height, spacing, ambient room temperature, and distance below the ceiling. Sprinkler systems described as early-suppression and quick-response types typically use fast-response sprinkler heads.

❑ **Residential sprinkler head.** This type is not typically intended to extinguish the fire. Instead, it minimizes the heat buildup and the production of carbon monoxide, which reduces the toxicity of the space while the occupants are exiting. These heads have a unique spray pattern different from that of standard or quick-response sprinklers and are often recessed when used in Residential occupancies. Although designed for *NFPA 13D* systems, they can also be used in *NFPA 13R* and *NFPA 13* systems as allowed by code. (See Figure 7.1.)

❑ **Quick-response sprinkler head.** Sometimes residential and quick-response sprinklers are thought to be the same type; however, they have different uses, spray patterns, and designs. Quick-response heads can be used in Residential and Commercial occupancies as allowed by the codes.

❑ **Extended coverage sprinkler head.** These heads have a spray pattern that can cover up to 400 square feet (37.2 sm), requiring fewer heads but higher water pressure and water flow rate. These are often used in large open areas. Some can be considered quick response.

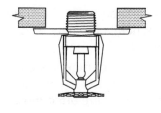

PENDANT
the head is surface mounted and extends below the finished ceiling, most commonly used in finished ceilings and suspended ceiling tiles

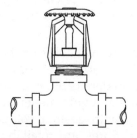

UPRIGHT
the head is fully exposed and sits above the branch 'feed lines' that supply the water, typically used in spaces with high or unfinished ceilings

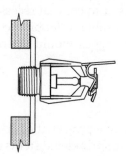

SIDEWALL
the head is surface mounted to a finished wall, commonly used in corridors and small rooms where one head or one row will adequately cover the area (also available to be mounted recessed)

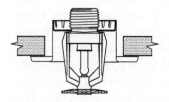

RECESSED
the head is partially recessed into the ceiling, the depth of the recess can vary but the lower portion of the head is always exposed, often used in residential occupancies

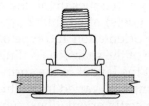

CONCEALED
the head is fully recessed and includes a cover that hides the fusible element so that you cannot see it, the cover falls off when a fire occurs to allow the head to activate and disperse water, often used in decorative ceilings

Figure 7.5 Orientation of sprinkler heads (Line drawings reprinted with permission from Viking Group. www.vikingcorp.com).

❑ **Large-drop sprinkler head.** These heads deliver water in large droplets and are often used in occupancies where a fire may be difficult to suppress, such as a large storage facility.

❑ **Open sprinkler head.** These heads are used in deluge systems. The heads remain open; they are not activated by their own heat detector, but by a separate detector. These systems are often monitored or controlled. When activated, the heads release large amounts of water. They are used in areas where a severe fire could occur.

❑ **Specialty sprinkler head.** Specialty sprinklers are available for other needs of a space, such as tamper-resistant or corrosion-resistant sprinklers. In addition, many new types of sprinkler heads are available for specific design criteria to meet functional requirements and aesthetic needs. Decorative sprinkler heads with custom colors, flush or low profiles, and other similar features are available. Different types of cover plates can also be used to conceal recessed sprinkler heads. These may be especially desirable in lobbies, conference rooms, and living areas where other types would distract from the design of the space.

Sprinkler Design Issues

Although adding a sprinkler system adds cost to a project, it has benefits to other areas of construction. When automatic sprinkler systems are included, the codes allow trade-offs for other code requirements. It may be a major trade-off, such as constructing a larger building, or a smaller trade-off, such as not having to add a rated wall. For example, in some occupancies, the corridor walls are not required to be rated if the building is sprinklered. Other common sprinkler trade-offs are listed in Figure 7.6. In most cases, the entire building must be sprinklered to use the benefits. Also, remember that an existing sprinkler system must typically meet the current code requirements for an automatic sprinkler system before any of the sprinkler trade-offs can be used.

For interior projects, the most significant design issues involving a sprinkler system include the selection of the type(s) of sprinkler system, the layout of the sprinkler heads, and the orientation and type of sprinkler heads. For instance, the configuration of the space, the ceiling height(s), and the required coverage will affect the layout of the sprinkler heads. If the ceiling is sloped, horizontal, smooth, varied in height, or coffered, additional sprinkler heads and specific orientations may be required. An exposed ceiling versus a finish ceiling also makes a

---

☑ **Note**

When ceiling finishes consist of combustible materials such as light-transmitting plastic or fabric panels, the codes typically require sprinkler heads to be installed in the ceiling as well as in the deck above the ceiling finish.

☑ **Note**

The sprinkler system must meet all the requirements of the codes to be considered an *approved* automatic sprinkler system as required by the codes for sprinkler trade-offs. In most cases, it must also be throughout the building.

Building Area
May allow some buildings to increase in size horizontally, resulting in more square feet per building.

Building Height
May allow one story to be added to the height of a building.

Construction Types
May allow a less fire resistant construction type.

Means of Egress
May allow an increase in the distance of travel from the most remote point to the exit; allow certain escalators not to be enclosed; allow certain exit stairs and accessible elevators not to have an area of refuge; allow longer dead-end corridors.

Fire and Smoke Separation
May allow up to three floor levels of stairways and other openings between floors not to be fully enclosed; eliminate separate means of venting smoke in elevators; omit fire dampers; reduce number of draft stops; allow larger areas of glazing, lower fire ratings of assemblies, and lower rating of opening protectives; allow less compartmentation in high-rise buildings.

Fire Protection
May reduce number of fire and/or smoke alarms; reduce number of fire extinguishers; eliminate or reduce number of standpipes.

Interior Finishes and Furnishing
May allow a lower class rating of a finish; eliminate fire-stops behind raised finishes; allow additional foam plastic insulation; allow additional decorative trim; allow lower furniture ratings.

Note: An existing sprinkler system must typically meet the most current code requirements of an automatic sprinkler system in order for you to use any of the sprinkler trade-offs listed previously. Be sure to consult with a code official when necessary.

Figure 7.6 Common sprinkler trade-offs.

difference. For most projects, these will be determined in conjunction with an engineer or fire protection (sprinkler) designer as part of the overall sprinkler system. Specialty sprinkler heads in certain areas, such as lobbies or conference rooms, may also be used for aesthetic reasons.

Familiarity with common sprinkler layout parameters is important so that other aspects of the design, such as lighting, ceiling grids, decorative ceiling elements, and furr downs can be coordinated. It is a good idea to coordinate these items with the sprinkler designer early in a project. For example, a sprinkler head typically requires a clearance of 18 inches (457 mm) below the deflector. The location of partial-height walls, tall furniture, shelving, or cabinetry can block the coverage of some sprinkler heads. In addition, any obstruction that exceeds 4 feet (1219 mm) in width may mean that an additional sprinkler head must be installed in or under the obstruction. This can include such things as a large air duct in an exposed ceiling, a decorative ceiling panel, or a kiosk or specialty display.

✍ **Note**

In a multistory building, it is possible to have a sprinkler system installed in one story and not another. However, some code requirements are based on the entire building being sprinklered, not just the immediate floor.

✍ **Note**

A project may have more than one type of sprinkler head, such as a concealed head in a decorative ceiling and an exposed pendant in less public areas.

☝ Note

In some locations, drapes and blinds on windows and glass walls may affect the performance of a sprinkler system.

The use of specialty sprinklers may require additional clearances. (See the codes and *NFPA 13* for more information.)

When making changes to an existing space or existing occupancy classification, updates to existing sprinkler system can be required. The addition or removal of walls may affect the required location and number of the sprinkler heads for proper coverage, or the addition of a suspended ceiling may require a change in the type of sprinkler head. Collaborate with a sprinkler system designer to coordinate these issues, or for small projects work closely with a licensed contractor.

Uses and Occupancies Requiring Sprinkler Systems

☝ Note

Depending on the occupancy, the number of hazards, and the type of system, most sprinkler systems require each sprinkler head to cover and protect 90 to 200 square feet (8.4 to 18.6 sm). The typical distance between the sprinkler heads ranges from 12 to 15 feet (3658 to 4572 mm). The sprinkler designer or engineer will determine the exact requirements.

Almost every occupancy can be required to have an automatic sprinkler system if certain conditions exist. In some cases, changes in the codes can require sprinklers to be installed in existing buildings and existing uses. The size of the space, the number of occupants, the mobility of the occupants, the location of the use within the building, the height and area of the overall building, the types of hazards present, and sometimes the capacity of the local fire department all factor into when the fire and building codes require sprinklers. The most common trigger is the size of the specific fire area. However, each occupancy also has exceptions for when an automatic sprinkler system is not required.

Sprinklers have been required in most commercial spaces for years. Their required use continues to expand. For example, with few exceptions Educational occupancies require sprinklers. For Assembly occupancies the thresholds are fairly low before sprinklers are required. And, most recently, the codes have made them required in many Residential occupancies, including one- and two-family dwelling residential structures, as well. (See Appendix C.) Certain building types regardless of size are also required to have sprinkler systems. These are shown in the following list. In addition, spaces considered incidental use, as discussed in Chapter 6 (see Figure 6.8), are often allowed to use an automatic sprinkler system in place of fire resistance–rated construction. Many of these are listed here as well. In each case, refer to the code for the specific requirements.

☝ Note

In recent years, certain existing building types have been required to add a sprinkler system. These include schools, hospitals, nursing homes, and high-rise buildings.

Building Types

- ❑ Aircraft hangars
- ❑ Amusement buildings
- ❑ Live/work units
- ❑ Parking garages
- ❑ Covered malls

❑ High-rise building
❑ Hospitals
❑ Underground structures
❑ Unlimited area buildings
❑ Windowless story

Special Rooms and Areas

❑ Atriums
❑ Commercial kitchen exhaust hood and duct systems
❑ Drying rooms
❑ Duct systems exhausting hazardous materials
❑ Furnace and boiler rooms
❑ Laboratories and vocational shops
❑ Laundry rooms over 100 square feet (9.29 sm)
❑ Incinerator rooms
❑ Rooms with hazardous materials
❑ Smoke protected assembly seating
❑ Spray-painting shops or booths
❑ Stages
❑ Tops of rubbish and linen chutes (additional if three or more floors)
❑ Unenclosed vertical openings
❑ Waste and linen collection rooms over 100 square feet (9.29 sm)

Unique situations often call for additional sprinkler locations. For example, if a continuous glass assembly is used as a rated wall, additional sprinkler heads may be required on both sides of the wall. Even using some finishes, such as light-transmitting plastic (see Chapter 10), may require the use of additional sprinkler heads.

Alternative Extinguishing Systems

Sprinklers may not be appropriate in every situation. Fires can begin in enclosed spaces or in locations where they are shielded from the sprinkler head. Other fires ignite and travel too quickly. In some cases, the fire should not be extinguished with water. For example, restaurant kitchens and other rooms with the potential for a grease fire should limit the use of water as an extinguisher. It is also best not to use sprinklers close to large electrical equipment, such as the computer and telephone

◀ Note

Sprinkler requirements for some occupancies may result in a partial system or a *limited-area* sprinkler system, where only a part of a building is covered by sprinklers to meet minimum code requirements. However, this is usually not recommended, and it must be approved by a code official.

equipment found in telecommunication rooms. Other buildings that contain extremely valuable items, such as libraries and museums, will want to limit water damage and may eliminate sprinklers, limit their use, or use an alternative extinguishing system.

When a sprinkler system does not use water, the system is often referred to as *alternative automatic fire extinguishing.* Alternate systems include wet-chemical, dry-chemical, foam, carbon dioxide, halon, and clean-agent extinguishing materials. Each agent may have a separate standard it must meet, many of which are listed in Figure 7.1. The codes generally allow the code official to approve the appropriate alternative agent. This allows the designer and the client to propose the best agent for the situation.

In the past, systems that discharged halon were widely used in situations where a water-based system was not desirable. But because halon has been determined to contribute to the erosion of the ozone layer, it is no longer produced. Halon systems that are properly maintained in existing buildings may remain in use. However, a space that undergoes significant changes is typically required to replace the halon with a clean-agent alternative such as halocarbon or inert gas.

SUSTAINABILITY CONSIDERATIONS

Fire detection and extinguishing or suppression systems are critical to life safety, and their requirements are comprehensively covered by the building and fire codes and the *LSC.* Thus, these systems are not typically part of the sustainability codes and standards. It could be argued, however, that an automatic sprinkler system benefits the environment. When used to suppress a fire, a sprinkler system minimizes toxic gases created by the fire, saves existing building materials so that less waste enters landfills, and uses much less water than conventional firefighting.

Currently, the *International Green Construction Code (IgCC)* offers a compliance elective that allows an automatic sprinkler system to be supplied with nonpotable water from an on-site rainwater collection system. A code jurisdiction can require this elective for certain types of projects in that jurisdiction, or, depending on the jurisdiction, a project designer may be able to select this elective for a specific project. If selected, the sprinkler system would also require emergency power for the pump and controls at the collection system, as well as a device that monitors the volume of water.

The fire protection industry is also beginning to incorporate sustainable practices. For example, many sprinkler manufacturers now indicate how much recycled content is used in their sprinklers, valves,

---

☑ Note

The code specifies *NFPA 13, 13R,* and *13D* sprinkler systems. Each system is appropriate for different scope of coverage and occupancy. Refer to the codes for the correct system.

☑ Note

If a building is required to be sprinklered, the local code official usually decides if an alternative extinguishing system can be used in special rooms such as electrical and communications rooms.

☑ Note

When testing a sprinkler system, sustainable practices can be put into place to recycle or reuse the water that is flushed through the system.

and fittings. Also, newer systems are being developed that use less water and more earth-friendly alternate agents (e.g., biodegradable foam).

RESEARCH: USING THE CODES

Although a complete fire protection system includes detectors, alarms, and suppression or extinguishing systems, not all of these will be required in all buildings or spaces. It is important to know at the beginning of your research project what level of fire detection and protection is existing or required. Whether existing, renovation, or new construction, the building codes, fire codes, and the *Life Safety Code (LSC)* determine the minimum requirements. Remember, for some buildings with a mixed occupancy or separate fire areas, a detection, a fire alarm, or suppression system may be required in only one area of the building.

The requirements for the active fire protection system can be found in the *IFC* and *IBC* in their Chapter 9, "Fire Protection and Life Safety Systems"; in Chapter 8, "Features of Fire Protection," in the *NFPA 5000*; and in Chapter 9, "Building Service and Fire Protection Equipment," in the *LSC*. Specific fire protection requirements are also found in the individual occupancy chapters of the *LSC*. For example each occupancy chapter, such as "Existing Educational Occupancies," has a section titled "Protection" where specific requirements for that occupancy are given. These code chapters and sections will provide the requirements for the various components of the fire protection systems including fire detection, alarm, communications, automatic sprinklers, portable fire extinguishers, standpipe systems, carbon monoxide detection, and so on.

Other protection-related systems and/or devices may be required as well, especially with the trend toward more building security and the importance of Homeland Security. A code jurisdiction or building owner may request additional items, such as multisensor detectors, an MNS, tactile notification appliances, or multicolored light strobes. If your project is part of a group of interrelated buildings such as a college campus, it may be necessary to know what systems are integrated among the various buildings. For example, as of the 2018 *IBC*, college and university campuses with a specific occupant threshold must perform a risk analysis to determine if an MNS is warranted for new construction. These will require additional research and coordination. In the building codes, fire codes, and the *LSC*, these systems are discussed in the same chapters with other parts of the active fire protection systems as detectors and alarms. Remember, the *LSC* will also have specific requirements in the individual occupancy chapters.

⬛ Note

The *International Build-ing Code (IBC)* includes several sections that are taken directly from the *International Fire Code (IFC)*. These sections include [*F*] in the title, indicating that the section comes from the *IFC*. If information from the *IBC* is duplicated in the *IFC*, the section carries a [*B*] designation.

Although some requirements overlap between the building codes and the fire codes, other chapters in the fire codes are unique and indicate special spaces that require fire protection. For example, the *IFC* has a section in Chapter 9 titled "Fire Protection Based on Special Detailed Requirements of Use and Occupancy." It may be necessary to determine if spaces within your project are included. The *IFC* also includes requirements for the proper installation and maintenance of detection, alarm, and automatic sprinkler systems.

When specific testing and installation methods are required for detection, alarm, and suppression components, the building codes, the fire codes, and the *LSC* refer to several the standards published by the National Fire Protection Association (NFPA). These standards specify locations, design details, and installation requirements, as well as testing standards that must be followed. The standards most often used for interior projects are listed in Figure 7.1. A mechanical or electrical engineer will typically specify the components and systems by referring to these standards such as *NFPA 72* and the *National Electrical Code* (NEC) for the design and installation of the system. (See Chapter 8.) It is important to understand that these standards affect the resulting design. For example, an automatic suppression system designed to NFPA 13 is a different system than one designed to NFPA 13R.

In the past, almost all fire protection systems were designed according to prescriptive code requirements. These technical requirements were based on criteria established by the industry (often in response to a devastating fire event) and were predetermined by typical engineering calculations. Now performance design is an increasingly acceptable way to design a fire protection system that can address the special needs of a design or building. You will find performance criteria as well as the prescriptive requirements in the fire protection chapters of each code as well as in chapters dedicated for performance-based options such as Chapter 5 in the *LSC*. Performance solutions to fire protection are most often used with multilevel atriums and one-of-a-kind facilities. It can also be helpful for buildings that do not meet the current codes, such as a historic building with an open stairwell, or a space with an unusual design, such as a unique ceiling pattern. In other cases, special needs of the occupants or unique kinds of fire hazards may need to be considered and accommodated.

With performance design, the design team defines the level of safety that must be provided. This can include how quickly a fire needs to be detected, how soon the suppression system activates, who will be notified of the fire, the safest egress patterns, and other criteria. The unique characteristics of the space or building are also considered. Then specific engineering calculations and computer fire modeling are used to analyze and create a system that responds best for that design. For example, one model determines the burn rate and heat-release rate of various construction materials to calculate potential fire sizes. Computer models can also calculate how fast a fire is likely to burn and the amount of smoke and carbon monoxide it may produce. In most cases, the design will use the performance criteria for selected parts of the building, but the rest of the fire protection system will be specified according to the prescriptive code requirements. This typically requires a team of designers, engineers, and fire protection specialists to develop. It will also require approval by the code official. (See Chapter 10.)

If your project has sustainability requirements or goals, you will need to research the rating system being used to see if there are credits or points awarded for automatic sprinkler systems. (See the section titled "Sustainability Considerations" in this chapter and Appendix A)

Accessibility standards such as the Americans with Disabilities Act (ADA) and the *ICC A117.1* do not play heavily in the development of fire protection systems. However, fire alarms and accessible warning systems must communicate appropriately to the disabled of an emergency. This may require information sent in various formats. Also, any device that is part of the fire protection system and meant for occupant use must be placed at accessible reach range heights and locations and cannot be located so that it becomes a projection into the accessible path. Signage, as well as the type and location of the operational mechanisms, is also important.

To help your research use the "Fire Protection Systems" section of the digital checklist provided with this book. You will be prompted to identify the types of detection, alarm, and extinguishing systems that will be required in the space or building. The checklist can be used to remind you of what to look for on site for an existing building, as well. If an emergency voice/alarm communication system or other integrated system is being planned, you can list the predominant components, such as loudspeakers or scrolling signs. You may want to attach a copy of a floor plan locating the systems and devices.

DOCUMENTATION

If an active fire protection system is part of your project, whether existing to be reused or new, it will need to be documented in drawings and/or specifications. This will typically require coordination with architects, mechanical engineers, and sprinkler designers depending on the size of the project. The engineers will typically document the location of these devices as part of their design. However, you should coordinate the location of detection devices, alarms, and sprinkler heads with other interior ceiling and wall components such as ceiling lights, pendants, wall sconces, ceiling features, and so on. Although the codes set required heights, distances, and locations, a comprehensive effort to coordinate these elements can prevent undesired conflicts or visual clutter.

Again, you can use the "Fire Protection Systems" section of the digital checklist provided with this book and to help document the existing conditions as well as the proposed components in your project. However, a plan with all the elements identified is the most effective way to confirm all components are located properly.

CHAPTER 8

PLUMBING AND MECHANICAL REQUIREMENTS

This chapter covers two separate code concerns: plumbing codes and mechanical codes. Unlike most of the codes already discussed in the previous chapters, the mechanical and plumbing codes address health and welfare concerns instead of life safety issues.

Interior projects that include major plumbing or mechanical work will usually require collaboration with an engineer. (The scope of the work and the rules of the code jurisdiction will determine if a licensed engineer is required.) On smaller projects such as adding a break room sink or moving a supply vent, a licensed plumbing or mechanical contractor will know the requirements that apply. However, it is important to be familiar with certain requirements in each code as part of the design process. Examples include knowing how to determine the quantity of plumbing fixtures required in a project, how to correctly locate them in a space, and being aware of how a design affects various components of a mechanical system.

The codes, standards, and federal requirements for plumbing and mechanical systems are discussed throughout this chapter. The first part of the chapter is dedicated to the plumbing codes required for interior projects. It covers the quantities and types of plumbing fixtures and plumbing facilities required by the codes and discusses the accessibility standards for each. It concludes with a discussion of plumbing-related sustainability requirements. The second part of the chapter discusses the main types of mechanical systems and the codes and standards that affect the various components, followed by a section that covers mechanical-related sustainability issues. The "Research and Documentation" sections at the end of the chapter will help you research, coordinate, and document the plumbing and mechanical requirements for your project.

◀ **Note**

Depending on the jurisdiction and the scope of the project, a licensed mechanical engineer may be required to design and specify the plumbing and mechanical system of a project. (See Chapter 11.)

◀ **Note**

Life safety can be an issue for plumbing and mechanical systems if chemical, biological, and radiological threats to a building need to be considered.

311

NUMBER OF PLUMBING FIXTURES

✎ Note

Remember that the plumbing fixture tables specify *minimum* requirements. Additional fixtures may be desired, especially in Assembly occupancies where it is normal for large groups of people to use the restrooms at the same time, such as during intermissions.

Almost every project will require plumbing fixtures. Determining the number of required plumbing fixtures is an important early task for a project. The number of required fixtures must be calculated for new construction, for a building addition, and when an occupancy classification changes in an existing space. In some cases, the owner may want additional fixtures. For example, in a small doctor's office, only one toilet may be required by code. However, additional toilets may be requested to provide separate toilets for staff and patients. In other cases, the owner may only want to provide the minimum number required by code. The number of water closets, urinals, lavatories, sinks, drinking fountains, bathtubs, showers, and other required plumbing fixtures will affect the types of toileting and/or bathing facilities to be provided in each project. Typically, the number of *fixtures* (toilets, lavatories, etc.) must be known before the type or number of *facilities* (fixtures located in separate or shared rooms) can be determined. These decisions will also affect how many are required to be accessible.

All these factors will affect the design. For example, the number of standard and accessible water closets will affect the size of a restroom or toilet facility. The plumbing code table is explained first, followed by a discussion of other code and accessibility requirements. Requirements for each fixture and how to use them together for the necessary toileting and bathing facilities are discussed in the next sections.

Calculating Required Fixtures

The number and type of plumbing fixtures required are determined by the plumbing code. The code indicates when water closets (toilets), lavatories, bathtubs or showers, drinking fountains, and other miscellaneous fixtures, such as service sinks and washing machines, are required by the codes. Typically, every floor in a building will require at least one toilet, but the actual number of fixtures depends on the type of occupancy and the occupant load. (See Chapter 3.) In addition to the required fixtures, some tenant spaces may want their own toilet facilities even if they are not required by the code. In addition, an executive might want a private bathroom adjacent to his or her office. Neither of these would count toward the required number of fixtures by the code. In most cases, each building must provide independent toilet or bathing facilities; only in

PLUMBING SYSTEMS

Most plumbing systems can be broken down into three main components:

1. **Drainage system.** This part of the plumbing system is usually referred to as the *drain-waste-vent* (*DWV*) system. It consists of a gravity-operated system of wide pipes that start at the plumbing fixture and end at the public sewage system. It consists of three parts. *Traps* are used at the discharge of each fixture to prevent odors, gases, and insects from entering the building. Branch and stack *pipes* are required to transport the used water from the trap to the sewer. (It is a *soil stack* if it carries solid human waste and a *waste stack* if it carries other wastes.) Vertical stack *vents* penetrate the roof of a building and allow harmful gases to escape, admit oxygen to the waste system to allow sewage breakdown, and equalize the pressure on both sides of a trap, allowing the trap to hold water and the system to work.

2. **Water supply system.** This system consists of small-diameter pipes that use pressure to convey hot and cold water. First is the *main water line,* which brings water into the building from the public water system. Once in the building, it splits into two *distribution lines.* One leads cold water directly to the plumbing fixtures, and the other leads to a water heating system before it is distributed to a fixture. The water supply system is controlled by valves located at the entry into the building and at each fixture.

3. **Plumbing fixtures.** The fixtures are the beginning of the drainage system and the end source for the water supply system. They consist of water closets, lavatories, urinals, sinks, drinking fountains, bathtubs, showers, dishwashers, clothes washers, and other miscellaneous fixtures.

rare cases are multiple buildings allowed to share plumbing facilities to meet the required number. And typically, this requires approval by the code official. For example, a guard station separate from the main building may need its own restroom.

The occupant load represents the number of people that are expected to be in the building or space during use. (See Chapter 3 for more information on calculating occupant loads.) The occupant load is used to determine the number and type of plumbing fixtures required. Each plumbing code has a table similar to the *IPC* Table 403.1, "Minimum Number of Required Plumbing Fixtures," shown in Figure 8.1. (The same table is also repeated in the *IBC* as Table 2902.1.) In most cases, the code directs you to separate the total occupant load equally by male/female

Note

Beginning in 2009, the *IPC* clarified that the total occupant load must be divided in half to represent half for female and half for male before the calculating the required number of plumbing fixtures.

users. Once the occupant load is divided in half, the fixture ratios in the table are used to do the calculations. If the calculated fixture total results in a fraction, *round up* to the nearest whole number.

For example, if designing a school that will have 680 occupants, the first step is to divide this total number in half to represent 340 males and 340 females. Then, refer to the Educational (E) occupancy section of the table in Figure 8.1. It requires one water closet for every 50 people. By dividing 340 by 50 and rounding up, the fixtures require include a minimum of 7 water closets for men and 7 water closets for women. Continuing across the *IPC* table, the school in this example would require the same number of lavatories for each sex, 7 drinking fountains, and 1 service sink. These numbers would then be used to design the appropriate plumbing facilities for the school.

Additional fixtures particularly lavatories and sinks may be required by other design guidelines or standards that are particular to a use or building type. For example, health care guidelines may require hand-washing sinks at various locations and sinks at other clinical locations. These are not counted in the overall requirements by the codes

The plumbing fixture table should be used in conjunction with the other plumbing and fixture requirements specified in the plumbing code chapter. For example, the table does not specify the use of urinals, but the code text will specify when urinals can be substituted for toilets. The table also has multiple footnotes that provide clarifications affecting the distribution of fixtures. Following are additional requirements that may affect the distribution and arrangement of plumbing fixtures within a project:

❏ **Male/female ratios.** When determining the required number of plumbing fixtures, the codes designate an assumption of 50/50 male/female split among occupants. However, if statistical data can show that the distribution of the actual occupants will differ adjustments may be approved by the local code official. The performance codes also allow for flexibility based on the intended use of the space or building. These modifications are typical for a large Assembly uses such as a sports stadium. However, it might be appropriate to request a different allocation of fixtures in facilities that are used predominantly by one gender, such as an all-female health club or an all-male high school. In each case, satisfactory data must be provided to the code official.

❏ **Fixture distribution per sex.** When designating the required number of fixtures per sex, the plumbing fixture table will typically require the same number of fixtures for male and female toilet facilities. However, under the Assembly occupancies, some of the

TABLE 403.1 MINIMUM NUMBER OF REQUIRED PLUMBING FIXTURES[a] (See Sections 403.1.1 and 403.2)

NO.	CLASSIFICATION	DESCRIPTION	WATER CLOSETS (URINALS: SEE SECTION 424.2) MALE	FEMALE	LAVATORIES MALE	FEMALE	BATH-TUBS/SHOWERS	DRINKING FOUNTAIN (SEE SECTION 410)	OTHER
1	Assembly	Theaters and other buildings for the performing arts and motion pictures[d]	1 per 125	1 per 65	1 per 200		—	1 per 500	1 service sink
		Nightclubs, bars, taverns, dance halls and buildings for similar purposes[d]	1 per 40	1 per 40	1 per 75		—	1 per 500	1 service sink
		Restaurants, banquet halls and food courts[d]	1 per 75	1 per 75	1 per 200		—	1 per 500	1 service sink
		Casino gaming areas	1 per 100 for the first 400 and 1 per 250 for the remainder exceeding 400	1 per 50 for the first 400 and 1 per 150 for the remainder exceeding 400	1 per 250 for the first 750 and 1 per 500 for the remainder exceeding 750		—	1 per 1,000	1 service sink
		Auditoriums without permanent seating, art galleries, exhibition halls, museums, lecture halls, libraries, arcades and gymnasiums[d]	1 per 125	1 per 65	1 per 200		—	1 per 500	1 service sink
		Passenger terminals and transportation facilities[d]	1 per 500	1 per 500	1 per 750		—	1 per 1,000	1 service sink
1	Assembly	Places of worship and other religious services[d]	1 per 150	1 per 75	1 per 200		—	1 per 1,000	1 service sink
		Coliseums, arenas, skating rinks, pools and tennis courts for indoor sporting events and activities	1 per 75 for the first 1,500 and 1 per 120 for the remainder exceeding 1,500	1 per 40 for the first 1,520 and 1 per 60 for the remainder exceeding 1,520	1 per 200	1 per 150	—	1 per 1,000	1 service sink
		Stadiums, amusement parks, bleachers and grandstands for outdoor sporting events and activities[f]	1 per 75 for the first 1,500 and 1 per 120 for the remainder exceeding 1,500	1 per 40 for the first 1,520 and 1 per 60 for the remainder exceeding 1,520	1 per 200	1 per 150	—	1 per 1,000	1 service sink

(Continued)

TABLE 403.1 (Continued)

NO.	CLASSIFICATION	DESCRIPTION	WATER CLOSETS (URINALS: SEE SECTION 424.2) MALE	WATER CLOSETS FEMALE	LAVATORIES MALE	LAVATORIES FEMALE	BATH-TUBS/ SHOWERS	DRINKING FOUNTAIN (SEE SECTION 410)	OTHER
2	Business	Buildings for the transaction of business, professional services, other services involving merchandise, office buildings, banks, ambulatory care, light industrial and similar uses	1 per 25 for the first 50 and 1 per 50 for the remainder exceeding 50		1 per 40 for the first 80 and 1 per 80 for the remainder exceeding 80		—	1 per 100	1 service sink[e]
3	Educational	Educational facilities	1 per 50		1 per 50		—	1 per 100	1 service sink
4	Factory and industrial	Structures in which occupants are engaged in work fabricating, assembly or processing of products or materials	1 per 100		1 per 100		—	1 per 400	1 service sink
5	Institutional	Custodial care facilities	1 per 10	1 per 10	1 per 10	1 per 10	1 per 8	1 per 100	1 service sink
		Medical care recipients in hospitals and nursing homes	1 per room[c]		1 per room[c]		1 per 15	1 per 100	1 service sink per floor
		Employees in hospitals and nursing homes[b]	1 per 25		1 per 35		—	1 per 100	—
		Visitors in hospitals and nursing homes	1 per 75		1 per 100		—	1 per 500	—
		Prisons[b]	1 per cell		1 per cell		1 per 15	1 per 100	1 service sink
		Reformatories, detention centers, and correctional centers[b]	1 per 15		1 per 15		1 per 15	1 per 100	1 service sink
		Employees in reformatories, detention centers and correctional centers[b]	1 per 25		1 per 35		—	1 per 100	—
6	Mercantile	Retail stores, service stations, shops, salesrooms, markets and shopping centers	1 per 500		1 per 750		—	1 per 1,000	1 service sink[e]

No.	Classification					
7	Residential					
	Hotels, motels, boarding houses (transient)	1 per sleeping unit	1 per sleeping unit	1 per sleeping unit	—	1 service sink
	Dormitories, fraternities, sororities and boarding houses (not transient)	1 per 10	1 per 10	1 per 8	1 per 100	1 service sink
	Apartment house	1 per dwelling unit	1 per dwelling unit	1 per dwelling unit	—	1 kitchen sink per dwelling unit; 1 automatic clothes washer connection per 20 dwelling units
	Congregate living facilities with 16 or fewer persons	1 per 10	1 per 10	1 per 8	1 per 100	1 service sink
	One- and two-family dwellings and lodging houses with five or fewer guestrooms	1 per dwelling unit	1 per dwelling unit	1 per dwelling unit	—	1 kitchen sink per dwelling unit; 1 automatic clothes washer connection per dwelling unit
	Congregate living facilities with 16 or fewer persons	1 per 10	1 per 10	1 per 8	1 per 100	1 service sink
8	Storage	Structures for the storage of goods, warehouses, storehouse and freight depots. Low and moderate hazard.	1 per 100	1 per 100	—	1 per 1,000	1 service sink

a The fixtures shown are based on one fixture being the minimum required for the number of persons indicated or any fraction of the number of persons indicated. The number of occupants shall be determined by the *International Building Code*.

b Toilet facilities for employees shall be separate from facilities for inmates or care recipients.

c A single-occupant toilet room with one water closet and one lavatory serving not more than two adjacent patient sleeping units shall be permitted provided that each patient sleeping unit has direct access to the toilet room and provision for privacy for the toilet room user is provided.

d The occupant load for seasonal outdoor seating and entertainment areas shall be included when determining the minimum number of facilities required.

e For business and mercantile classifications with an occupant load of 15 or fewer, service sinks shall not be required.

f The required number and type of plumbing fixtures for outdoor public swimming pools shall be in accordance with Section 609 of the *International Swimming Pool and Spa Code*.

Figure 8.1 International Plumbing Code® (IPC®) Table 403.1, "Minimum Number of Required Plumbing Fixtures" (2021 *International Plumbing Code*, copyright © 2021. Washington, DC: International Code Council. Reproduced with permission. All rights reserved. www.iccsafe.org).

provided ratios are different for male and female water closets. The code has considered the expected male/female ratio and the typical rate at which the facilities will be used. If plumbing fixtures must be calculated for multiple occupancies on the same floor, each would be calculated separately for male and female and then added together for the results for each sex before rounding up.

❑ **Public versus private.** The required number of plumbing fixtures must be "public" and available for all occupants. The code defines *public* as "unrestricted exposure to walk-in traffic." So, a single-user toilet located in a tenant space would not contribute to the required fixture count for the building floor because it is not public to all building occupants. A separate toilet facility provided for use by an individual cannot count toward the total common facilities either. For example, an executive suite might have a private toilet within the suite. Toilet facilities within a tenant space would have to meet accessibility requirements, but a toilet room for a private office is only required to be adaptable.

❑ **Grouping fixtures:** When multiple fixtures are required, they can be in a common toilet facility location if all occupants have access to them. For example, if five female water closets are required on a floor, they can be combined into one women's restroom. In a large building, maximum allowable travel distances might also require the total number of required fixtures to be separated into more than one location, each with several fixtures, to better serve the entire occupant load. In this case, not only would a certain percentage of the total fixtures be required to be accessible but also a percentage at each location must be accessible. These can be exemptions to this for some existing buildings.

❑ **Separate male, female, and non-gendered facilities.** In the past, the codes required single-user and multi-fixture toilet facilities to be designated for male or female users. The codes allowed unisex single-user toilet rooms in specific situations. However, in the recent codes, this has begun to change. For example, in the 2018 *IPC*, single-user toilets are *not required* to be labeled per gender. In the 2021 *IPC*, the code indicates that single-user toilet at bathing rooms, family or assisted-use toilet, and bathing rooms should be identified as being available for use by persons regardless of their sex. Also, in the 2021 *IPC*, multiple-user facilities that serve all genders are not required but can be provided instead of multiple-user facilities separated by gender. Urinals in these facilities must be provided in an area that is visually separated from the rest of the facility or each urinal must be in a separate stall, like a water closet. In this case, all fixture types must be accessible according to the *ICC A117.1* (not just a percentage.) Signage may indicate the use of the room as "Unisex" or simply "Toilet" or "Bathing Facility" (i.e., if gender is not indicated it is to be assumed to be used by all occupants regardless of identity).

❑ **Family, assisted-use single toilet/bathing rooms.** These terms typically apply to a single-user toilet or bathing room intended to allow someone who is elderly or disabled, or even a child, to be assisted by someone regardless of gender. Thus, they are considered unisex/non-gendered facilities. The codes *require* separate family/assisted-use toilet or bathing facility in some occupancies in addition to the main facilities. Family or assisted-use toilet facilities are often required when six or more water closets are provided. This includes many Assemblies and large Mercantile occupancies (e.g., malls). In addition, recreational facilities (e.g., gyms or health spas) that provide separate-sex bathing facilities will also require a family or assisted-use bathing room. These facilities are counted in the total number of required plumbing fixtures, not in addition to the required number. They are usually noted by a sign such as "Family" or sometimes as "Unisex." The space allowances, configuration, and placement of fixtures must allow independent use by someone with a disability and/or assistance by another individual. Beginning in the 2018 *IPC*, an accessible child height water closet and lavatory can be provided in addition to adult fixtures within the room as well. (See the section titled "Single-Toilet Facilities" later in this chapter.)

In some Institutional occupancies including assisted living, rehabilitation and nursing home facilities, another type of assisted-use toilet or bathing facility may be required. These facilities are designed for assisted use but not for independent accessible use. Although the configuration will allow maneuvering space for a wheelchair, the toilet location and grab bar configuration is different than a typical accessible room. For example, the toilet does not have to be adjacent to a wall. And, the grab bars are located on either side of the toilet and can swing up and out of the way to allow assistance by a health care worker or family member.

❑ **Public and employee facilities.** Typically, toilet facilities must be provided for the customers, patrons, and visitors of the space as well as the employees who work in the space. In most occupancies, public and employee facilities can be separate or combined. However, if the location is not accessible to the public, separate toilet facilities would be required. An example is a toilet facility located in a manufacturing area that might not be safe for a customer to walk through.

Note

The plumbing codes
limit the travel distance
to toilet facilities within
a building.

Note

Assembly occupan-
cies that have seasonal
outdoor seating and/or
entertainment must
include the occupant
load for these areas
when determining the
number of required
plumbing fixtures.

Toilet facilities in Mercantile and Assembly occupancies such as restaurants, nightclubs, retail stores, and malls can be shared as well. Some jurisdictions may require larger restaurants to have separate employee and customer facilities. In addition, Detentional/ Correctional and Health Care occupancies must typically keep their employee toilet facilities separate from those of the inmates and patients.

❑ **Access to facilities.** The codes limit the travel distances to public and employee toilet facilities. Typically, no path of travel to the toilet facility can be longer than 500 feet (152 m). (Travel distance in covered malls usually cannot exceed 300 feet (91.4 m.) In addition, public toilets cannot be accessed through kitchens, storage rooms, or closets. For example, public toilet facilities cannot be located within a restaurant kitchen or a retail store storage room. However, public facilities can be accessed from the exterior (e.g., gas service station) or the interior of a building. All routes should also meet the accessibility requirements of the *IBC* as well as the *ADA Standards*. (See Chapter 5.)

❑ **Unusual use group.** If a particular occupancy or use group is not covered by the plumbing fixture table, a local code official should be consulted for the specific requirements. (To get an estimate, use the type of occupancy most similar to the project; however, remember that the code official makes the final decision.)

Accessibility Percentages

Once the required types and number of plumbing fixtures are calculated, the quantity that are to be usable by persons with disabilities must be determined. The accessibility chapter of the building code and the *ADA Standards* provide the percentage of required fixtures that must be accessible. (The technical characteristics of the elements are described in the *ICC A117.1* standard and the *ADA Standards*.) Typically, all the components in a single-user toilet/bathing room must be accessible. However, the *IBC* and the *2010 ADA Standards* allow only half of single-user toilets (and bathing units) to be accessible if they are grouped together. Typically, at least 5 percent of each plumbing fixture type (if grouped together) must be accessible. But at least one of each type (with a few exceptions.) For some occupancies, the percentage of accessible fixtures and facilities will vary and are specified in the *IBC* and the *2010 ADA Standards*. For example, when a Residential and some Institutional occupancies have numerous individual dwelling or sleeping units, such as hotels, apartment buildings, or assisted living facilities, a varying percentage of the total units are required to be accessible. The percentage of accessible toilet facilities for Institutional occupancies varies with the condition and treatment level of the patients. For example, toilet rooms in ICU areas of the hospital are not required to be accessible but the toilet rooms in a mobility rehabilitation wing would all have to be accessible.

Toilet facilities that were designed before the ADA legislation or before the adoption of the current *2010 ADA Standards* or may have noncompliant conditions. (See the section titled "Existing Facilities" in Chapter 2.) Renovations to update or make them more accessible can be complicated. For example, it may not be possible to modify a multiple fixture toilet room to include a compliant accessible stall within the existing configuration. The need for more floor area at the accessible toilet may necessitate the removal of the adjacent toilet and partitions. This could in effect reduce the number of provided fixtures, which may make the room ADA compliant but not code compliant. One solution is to add a new accessible single-toilet (or single-bathing) facility instead of renovating the existing toilet facility. This can be an acceptable solution for an existing condition; however, providing an accessible single-user toilet instead of an accessible stall in a multiple fixture toilet room in new construction is not allowed by the ADA.

Also, as mentioned previously, the plumbing code requires some building types to have a separate family or assisted-use toilet facility, in addition to and separate from, the other required accessible facilities. In most cases, because the family or assisted-use toilets are intended for use by persons needing minor assistance including children, the elderly, or disabled individuals, they should be compliant with the *ADA Standards* (and the *ICC A117.1* when applicable) and provide the appropriate types of fixtures that are largely meant for independent use. For some occupancies such as assisted living and nursing homes, the typical occupants may need a different level of assistance. For these uses, the fixtures and layout slightly different than a typical assessable toilet. Although they allow space for the maneuvering of a wheelchair, the location of the toilet and the configuration of the grab bars is different. For these uses, parallel grab bars are provided at either side of the toilet. The grab bars at the toilet typically swing up and out of the way until seated. This also allows a second person to provide additional assistance. When renovating existing toilet facilities, improving the accessibility of the individual room, floor and building should be considered. (See the section titled "Toilet and Bathing Facilities" later in this chapter.)

> ✎ **Note**
>
> Previously, all single-toilet or single-bathing facilities were required to be accessible. However, starting in the 2006 *IBC* and the 2010 *ADA Standards*, single-user facilities that are clustered together only require 50 percent of them to be accessible.

> ✎ **Note**
>
> The *ICC A117.1* standard and 2010 *ADA Standards* provide alternate requirements and dimensions for plumbing fixtures used primarily by children. When designing a building or space for children 12 years of age or younger, consult these documents.

PLUMBING FIXTURE REQUIREMENTS

☑ Note

Additional plumbing fixtures that are less common include spas, hot tubs, whirlpools, baptisteries, ornamental and lily pools, aquariums, and fountains. They have specific code requirements as well and will require additional research.

☑ Note

The local health department may have additional requirements for plumbing fixtures in specific occupancies such as restaurants or day cares.

☑ Note

When determining clearances and dimension requirements for accessible toilet facilities, pay attention to whether they are minimum, maximum, or absolute dimensions.

The codes set the required total number of each type of plumbing fixture, the number of fixtures that must be accessible, and other aspects about the use, location, and characteristic of each fixture type. The most common plumbing fixtures are discussed in this chapter. These include water closets, urinals, lavatories, sinks, drinking fountains, bathtubs, and showers. Requirements for other types of fixtures are discussed in the plumbing code as well. Examples include bidets, food waste grinders, and laundry trays. In most cases, the codes simply reference industry standards for the installation of these fixtures, so they are not discussed in this chapter. However, if using more specialized fixtures, such as footbaths, baptisteries, aquariums, ornamental water features, or swimming pools, check for other code requirements. For these, accessibility must be considered as well. Fixtures in certain building types, such as restaurants and hospitals, may have to meet local health code requirements as well. A jurisdiction may have other special requirements. For example, certain jurisdictions now require the use of automatic faucets in public toilet facilities.

The code requirement that is common to all plumbing fixtures is that each fixture must be durable and finished with a smooth, impervious material to be cleanable and sanitary. For each typical material whether vitreous china, stainless steel, plastic, or other material, there is a standard to judge the quality of the product. For example, vitreous and nonvitreous china fixtures including toilets and urinals must meet the *ASME A112.19.2* standard. Although most fixtures are fabricated by the manufacturer to be compliant, meeting the appropriate standard might be a concern when specifying, retrofitting, or designing custom plumbing fixtures. (See the section titled "Finish Requirements" later in this chapter.)

Although the initial step is knowing how many fixtures are required in a space or building and how many must be accessible, knowing how to design for each fixture so that it usable by someone with a disability is more complex. Providing the appropriate clear floor space around the fixture and specifying the fixture and controls at the correct mounting height and location is essential to its usability. For these technical requirements, the codes refer to the *ICC A117.1* standard. However, the *ADA Standards* technical requirements typically apply as well. (See the inset titled "ADA-ABA Accessibility Guidelines Development.") The following sections discuss the various code and accessibility requirements for each fixture. Additional requirements that apply when these fixtures are used together in a toilet or bathing facility will also explained.

In addition to meeting the minimum code and sanitation requirements, there are several ways that the plumbing fixtures and the plumbing system can contribute to the sustainability of a project. These will be discussed in the section titled "Plumbing Sustainability Considerations" later in this chapter.

Water Closets

The codes typically require every floor in a building to have at least one water closet (i.e., toilet). The plumbing code requirements for water closets include the types allowed and the clearances for installation. The most common requirement is that all water closets specified for public or employee use must have an elongated bowl and a hinged seat with an open front. The codes also specify the maximum flow and water consumption allowed per flush. (See the section titled "Plumbing Sustainability Considerations" later in this chapter.) Clearances for installation include specific dimensions at each side and in front of the bowl. For example, the *IPC* requires a typical water closet to have a minimum of 15 inches (381 mm) from the center of the bowl to any side wall, partition, or vanity and at least 21 inches (533 mm) clear in front of the bowl. If enclosed, the compartment cannot be less than 30 inches (762 mm) wide by 56–60 inches (1422–1524 mm) deep for floor-mounted or wall-hung fixtures. Compartments must have a privacy lock.

Requirements for accessible water closets are found in the *ADA* and *ICC A117.1* standard. These are often different from standard fixtures. For example, instead of a 15-inch (381-mm) minimum to the centerline of the bowl, 16 to 18 inches (405 to 455 mm) is required. (The original *ADAAG* required 18 inches [455 mm].) The height of the toilet seat must be between 17 and 19 inches (430 to 485 mm), as shown in Figure 8.2. Required floor clearances around the toilet are also specified. The clearance dimensions will depend on whether the water closet is the only one in the room or located in a toilet compartment (i.e., stall). It can also matter if the stall partitions and/or water closet are wall hung or floor mounted. (See the section titled "Toilet and Bathing Facilities" for additional options.) The most common accessible clear floor space for a single water closet is 60 by 56 inches (1525 by 1420 mm). This extra clearance allows for the maneuverability of a wheelchair and access to grab bars.

Accessible water closets can have an automatic flushing mechanism or a manual control. If a manual flush control is used, it must be located on the open side of the toilet within the required reach range as defined by the guidelines (see Figure 8.2) and must meet certain conditions to be

◪ **Note**

The clear floor space required at an accessible water closet varies depending on whether the water closet is located in a room or stall, if the stall is wheelchair accessible or ambulatory accessible, and if the toilet is wall hung or floor mounted within the stall.

◪ **Note**

When required to be approached by a wheelchair, a minimum clear floor space is 30 by 48 inches (760 by 1220 mm) according to the *2010 ADA Standards*. There space required by the *ICC A117.1* beginning in 2018 is 30 by 52 inches (760 by 1320 mm). A larger space can be required in Assembly areas.

◪ **Note**

The *IBC* and *ICC A117.1* standard requires vertical grab bars at the side wall of water closets, showers, and bathtubs. The *ADA Standards* do not.

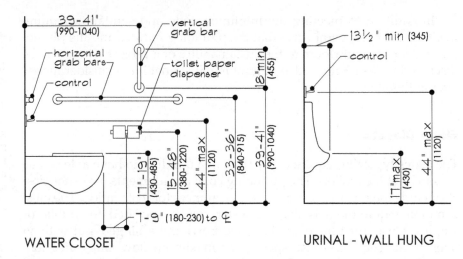

WATER CLOSET   URINAL - WALL HUNG

NOTE: The vertical grab bar is required by the ICC A117.1standard. Refer to the ICC A117.1 and ADA standards for additional grab bar and toilet paper dispenser information. A privacy panel may be required; refer to the codes and standards.

Figure 8.2 Typical accessible plumbing fixture dimensions: Water closets and urinals.

usable by someone with a disability. For example, it must be operable with one hand, and it cannot take more than 5 pounds (22.2 N) of force to operate. Additional requirements for accessories such as grab bars and toilet paper dispensers are described later in this chapter.

Urinals

✍ **Note**

The clear floor space specified in the 2010 *ADA Standards* and the *ICC A117.1* for wheelchair-accessible stalls and accessible single-toilet facilities is necessary to provide for a side transfer at the water closet.

Urinals are not required by the plumbing codes for most occupancies. If they are required or provided, they are usually substituted for one or more of the water closets, but only up to a certain quantity. *IPC* does not allow urinals to be substituted for more than 67 percent of the required number of male water closets in Assembly or Educational occupancies and 50 percent in all other occupancies. Urinals are typically specified for male restrooms of schools, restaurants, clubs, lounges, transportation terminals, auditoriums, theaters, and churches. However, in some cases, they may be provided in single toilet rooms in addition to a toilet. Similar to water closets, urinals must meet a maximum water consumption requirement when flushed. (Trough urinals are typically not allowed anymore.) Waterless urinals are an option as well. In addition, the codes specify the type and location of the finish material surrounding the urinal for ease of cleaning and sanitation. (See the section titled "Finish Requirements" later in this chapter.)

The codes and accessibility standards set minimum requirements for urinals, as well. However, if only one urinal is provided, neither the *IBC* nor the *2010 ADA Standards* require the urinal to be accessible. If two or more urinals are provided, then at least one is required to be accessible. (This is a change from the original *ADA Standards,* which required at least one accessible urinal for all toilet rooms.) To be accessible, a urinal must be either a stall-type or a wall-hung fixture with an elongated rim at a maximum height of 17 inches (430 mm) above the floor, as shown in Figure 8.2. The 2010 *ADA Standards* also require the rim to be a minimum depth of 13½ inches (345 mm). Clear floor space allowing a front approach must be provided as well. This is typically 30 by 48 inches (760 by 1220 mm) or 30 by 52 inches (760 by 1220 mm). Urinals used by the public or by employees require walls and/or partitions (i.e., privacy panels) to create privacy. When a privacy panel is used, it can be located either inside or outside the clear floor space. If it is located inside the required clear floor space, it cannot extend past the front edge of the urinal rim. The accessible flush control requirements are similar to those for water closets.

Note

Requirements for urinal privacy screen in the *IPC* and the accessibility publications can vary slightly.

Lavatories

Wherever a water closet or urinal is provided, a lavatory (i.e., handwashing sink) must also be provided. However, the required ratio of water closets to sinks is not always one to one. In other words, when multiple water closets are needed, the codes may allow fewer lavatories than water closets/urinals.

The plumbing codes set minimum clearances for installation of lavatories like they do for water closets and urinals. For example, when a lavatory is placed next to a water closet, the centerline of a lavatory and the centerline of the water closet are required to be a minimum of 30 inches (762 mm) apart. When multiple lavatories are provided in a continuous counter, there must be a minimum of 30 inches (762 mm) from centerline to centerline of each lavatory, as well. An accessible lavatory, however, must have a wider clear floor space between adjacent lavatories. The typical clear floor space required is 30 by 48 inches (760 by 1220 mm) or 30 by 52 inches (760 by 1320 mm) at the lavatory. This clear floor space must also extend between 17 to 25 inches (430 to 635 mm) underneath the lavatory to allow for a forward approach which provides for the knee space and toe space as shown in Figure 8.3.

Note

When plumbing pipes under an accessible sink are wrapped with insulation, the insulation must meet Class A requirements of the *Steiner Tunnel Test.* (See Chapter 10.)

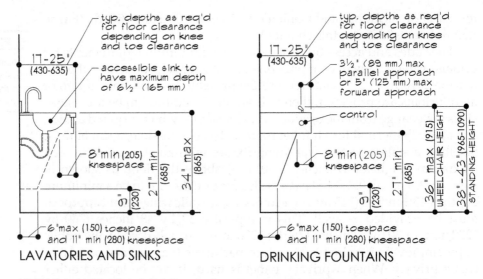

LAVATORIES AND SINKS   DRINKING FOUNTAINS

NOTE: If a drinking fountain is located on an accessible path, you may need to create an alcove so that the drinking fountain does not project into the corridor more than 4" (100 mm).

Figure 8.3 Typical accessible plumbing fixture dimensions: Lavatories, sinks, and drinking fountains.

◀ Note

Although not required by the 2010 *ADA Standards*, automatic water and flushing controls that activate on movement are also considered accessible. They may be required by the sustainability codes and/or some jurisdictions in certain occupancies.

When specifying a lavatory, you must confirm that when mounted within the allowable height, the shape and dimensions of the fixture also provides for the correct knee and toe clearances as shown in Figure 8.3. Although you can choose to mount all of the individual sinks or the entire continuous counter with sinks at the same height as the accessible fixture for consistency of design, it is not required. An option is a wash fountain with multiple spray heads which can accommodate multiple users. The total unit would have to be accessible or a separate accessible handwashing location would need to be provided. (Per the *IPC*, every 20 inches [508 mm] of rim space is considered one lavatory.) These are found in building types such as schools, athletic facilities, industrial plants, movie theaters, and large retail facilities. (See the section titled "Multiple-Toilet Facilities" later in this chapter for additional requirements.)

The *IPC* regulates several aspects of the faucet and pipes to prevent scalding from hot water. First, it limits the amount of hot water delivered by the faucet at the lavatory, especially in public facilities. And because a knee space is required at an accessible lavatory, hot water and drainpipes must be covered to prevent harmful direct contact. This is typically accomplished by insulated pipe wrappings or a counter design that creates a barrier, as shown in Figure 8.3. (Insulated covers must meet flammability finish requirements. See Chapter 10.) The cover must be removable to allow access to the pipes when necessary. In addition, the faucet at the lavatory must be within accessible reach ranges and have controls that are easy to operate. Lever handles, push types, and automatic faucets are often used. The energy codes and sustainability codes can require the faucets to conform to specific water consumption limits. This may require the faucet to be automatic (i.e., sensor-operated) or metered so that it will automatically shut off.

Sinks

A sink in the codes indicates a container to hold water for general washing opposed to a *lavatory*, which is for the washing of hands (typically in a bathroom). Sinks required by the codes are listed under the category of "Other" in the plumbing fixture table or required in the text. They can include service sinks, utility sinks, and laundry basins. For example, most occupancies require a "service sink" (i.e., janitor or mop sink). Similar to lavatories, sinks and their controls can also be required to limit water use and contribute to the sustainability of a project. Utility sinks are not generally required to be accessible.

Various kinds of sinks are often included in a project even when they are not required by the plumbing code. Examples include a wet bar in a break room or a handwashing sink at a nurse's station. When provided, you need to determine the required level of accessibility. First, in most cases, at least one sink in every unique location (and at least 5 percent when multiple sinks are used) is required to be accessible by the codes and accessibility standards. In some cases, there are conditions and exceptions that determine if a sink must be accessible and to what degree. A sink in a kitchen or break room is a good example. According to the ADA, if a breakroom has a sink but does not provide any permanent cooking appliances such as a cooktop or conventional oven, then the sink is not required to be accessible or provide for a front approach. However, an office break room, which includes a cooktop or conventional range, is actually considered a kitchen and provide for a front approach including appropriate knee and toe space. However, in either configuration, the faucet must control, mounting height at the sink or counter height for the preparation of food must meet the accessible requirements.

> **✔ Note**
>
> Although not required by the codes, the *LSC* does place restrictions on the location of waterless, antiseptic hand-sanitizer dispensers when installed because the alcohol-based liquid is considered flammable.

> **✔ Note**
>
> When determining the clear floor space at a fixture, the clearances are dictated by the clear knee space and toe space, not necessarily the location of the wall supporting the fixture.

> **✔ Note**
>
> There are at least three different ways to prevent contact with hot water and drain pipes under a lavatory or sink: (1) wrap them with insulated materials, (2) create an enclosure around the pipes, or (3) reconfigure the location of the pipes.

The mounting requirements for sinks are similar to those for lavatories, as shown in Figure 8.3. The height is especially important when designing food prep areas in a break room or kitchenettes in a hotel room for example. The counter height in these locations is typically 36 inches (915 mm) above the floor; however, an accessible counter has a maximum height of 34 inches (865 mm), which means that either a bilevel counter is needed or the entire counter is lowered to 34 inches (865 mm) above the floor. The depth of a kitchen counter should also be limited to 25 inches (635 mm) so that reach ranges for items installed above the sink are not exceeded. If a front approach is required at the work surface or sink, knee and toe space must be provided as well.

Most sinks or counters with sinks for general use must allow a front approach. Similar to a lavatory, the typical clear floor space is 30 by 48 inches (760 by 1220 mm). The knee clearance of 27 inches (665 mm) is required. And a knee and toe clearance that extends between 17 inches (430mm) at the top and 25 inches (635 mm) near the floor is also required. Clearances can be provided by leaving the counter open below the sink and covering the pipes accordingly or by installing specially designed doors that, when open, provide full clearance beneath. It is also best to use a sink that is not too deep. A common depth of an accessible sink is 6½ inches (165 mm).

Drinking Fountains

Drinking fountains are required in most occupancies and on each floor in a multistory building. However, there are some exceptions. Drinking fountains are not required in certain Residential occupancies, in restaurants that serve water, and individual tenant spaces if there is a shared drinking fountain within 300–500 feet (91,440–152,400 mm) and spaces with an occupant load of less than 15 occupants. In some cases, cooled water dispensers, water coolers, or bottle fillers can be substituted for a required drinking fountain. The 2015 *IPC* limited the substitution of bottled water dispensers or coolers to 50 percent (or less) of the required number of drinking fountains. Beginning with the 2021 *IPC*, the term *water dispenser* is used to indicate the various devices including bottle filling stations that can be used in lieu of a portion of the drinking fountains. If a space requires one drinking fountain, a drinking fountain must be installed. If multiple drinking fountains are required, the optional devices (including a bottle-filling station) can be included to the limits set by the plumbing code or local jurisdiction. If only one bottle-filler is provided, it must be accessible.

✇ Note

The *ICC A117.1* standard and the 2010 *ADA Standards* allow for some parallel approaches to lavatories, sinks, and drinking fountains. However, a clear floor space positioned for a forward approach is preferred.

The codes restrict the location of drinking fountains and water dispensers. They cannot be installed in public toilet rooms or the vestibules leading to the toilet room. One of the most common locations for a drinking fountain is the corridor outside the toilet room area. This typically provides a central location for the user and easy access to the plumbing pipes. If the drinking fountain is in a corridor or other accessible path of travel, it must be located so that it will not be considered a "protruding object" by the accessibility standards. In many cases, this will require an alcove or recessed area along the corridor. A *protruding object* is any object between 27 inches (685 mm) and 80 inches (2030 mm) above the floor that protrudes more than 4 inches (100 mm) into an accessible path of travel.

The *IBC*, the *IPC* and the accessibility standards require two types of drinking fountains: one that is wheelchair-accessible and one that is at standing height for people who find it difficult to bend low. The wheelchair-accessible drinking fountain, like the one shown in Figure 8.3, requires the spout to be no higher than 36 inches (915 mm) above the floor and to have a front or side control that is easy to operate. A standing-height drinking fountain should be mounted so that the spout is between 38 and 43 inches (965 and 1090 mm) above the floor. Therefore, even when the codes require only one drinking fountain, both types of drinking fountains must be provided. This can be accomplished either with two separate water fountains or with one "hi-low" drinking fountain that combines the two types. When more than one fixture is required, 50 percent must be standing height and 50 percent must be wheelchair-accessible. When providing other devices in place of drinking fountains, they must be accessible as well.

Wheelchair-accessible drinking fountains must have a clear floor space of 30 by 48 inches (760 by 1220 mm) or 30 by 52 inches (760 by 1320 mm) that allows a front approach. This will typically require a cantilever-type drinking fountain that is wall mounted. The position of the clear floor space in relation to the wall will depend on the knee space and toe space clearances provided, as shown in Figure 8.3. If the unit is built into an alcove, the alcove must be a minimum of 36 inches (915 mm) wide to allow the forward approach. (Parallel-approach drinking fountains were allowed in the original *ADAAG*. Some exceptions are still allowed in the new ADA and *ICC A117.1* standard.) Accessible floor clearances are not required at standing-height drinking fountains.

Bathtubs

For bathing, the codes typically allow either a bathtub or a shower to be provided. Bathtubs are most often provided in Residential occupancies

✎ Note

When locating a drinking fountain in a corridor or other path of travel, it must be located so that it does not project more than 4 inches (100 mm) into the path, according to the ADA and ICC *A117.1*.

such as hotels, dormitories, and apartment buildings, as well as single-family homes and showers are typically provided in more public bathing facilities. However, several Institutional occupancies require at least one tub to be available for occupant use.

Although the plumbing codes do not regulate the size or type of bathtub, they do have requirements for certain accessory components, including the faucet, enclosure, and mechanical equipment. The faucet must be able to regulate the mix of hot and cold water to prevent scalding and meet water consumption requirements. If the tub is enclosed by glass and/or glass doors, safety glass must be used, as specified in the building codes. In addition, if a whirlpool or spa-type bathtub that includes a motor is used, the codes require that access be provided to the pump. Often this requires preplanning in the arrangement of the room and/or how certain finishes, such as ceramic tile, are used.

If a bathtub is intended to be accessible it must meet additional requirements. All accessible tubs must have a seat. This can be either a removable in-tub seat that spans the width of the bathtub that is 15 to 16 inches (380 to 405 mm) deep or a permanent fixed seat at the head of the tub for a maximum of 15 inches (380 mm). Several other aspects of an accessible tub depend on which type of seat is provided.

Grab bars of differing number, height, and location are required on two or three sides of a tub based on the type of seat. For example, the back wall of a bathtub requires two horizontal grab bars. However, these grab bars must be longer when a fixed seat at the end of the tub is provided. A single grab bar is required at the control wall (at the same end as the drain) with either type of seat. Also, at the control wall, the *ICC A117.1* requires a vertical grab bar. (Because the *IBC* and *IPC* reference the *ICC A117.1* for technical requirements, it is a requirement of the ICC codes but not required by the ADA.) And in addition, if a permanent seat is provided, a grab bar is required at the head wall adjacent to the seat. (See Figure 8.4.)

The required clear floor space adjacent to a bathtub also depends on the type of seat provided. For a tub with a removable seat, the required clear floor space is 30 inches (760 mm) wide for the full length of the tub. When a fixed seat is used, the clear floor space should extend a minimum of 12 inches (305 mm) past the seat end of the tub.

The control device for the tub and shower must be located on the short wall opposite the seat toward the front edge of the tub. The shower spray unit must be able to convert from a fixed to a handheld unit and have a hose that is at least 59 inches (1500 mm) long. If there is a tub enclosure, it cannot encroach on any of the accessibility requirements and no tracks can be mounted to the top of the tub rim. (Glass doors are not recommended at accessible bathtubs.)

✎ Note

A bathtub seat that extends from outside the tub into the head of the tub allows a person to maneuver onto the seat while outside the tub and provides for the greatest level of use.

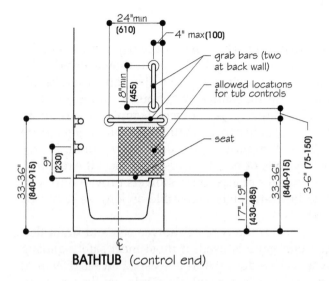

BATHTUB (control end)

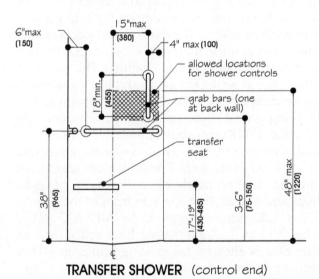

TRANSFER SHOWER (control end)

NOTE: An accessible shower head must be
able to convert from a handheld to a fixed type
with a hose at least 59" (1500 mm) long. Vertical
grab bars are required by ICC/ANSI standard.

Figure 8.4 Typical accessible plumbing fixture dimensions: Bathtubs
and showers.

Showers

☛ **Note**

When safety showers are required, refer to ANSI Z58.1, Emergency Eyewash and Shower Equipment.

☛ **Note**

Seats are required in transfer showers. They are optional in roll-in showers.

☛ **Note**

The *ICC A117.1* standard and the 2010 *ADA Standards* specify the clear floor space at roll-in showers to be 30 inches (760 mm) deep instead of the 36 inches (915 mm) deep required for transfer showers.

Showers can be provided to fulfill the bathing fixture requirements of the plumbing codes. Bathing fixtures are required in Institutional, Residential and some Assembly occupancies such as school locker rooms and health clubs. In addition, manufacturing plants, warehouses, foundries, and other similar establishments may require showers if employees are apt to be exposed to excessive heat or skin contamination. The plumbing fixture table shown in Figure 8.1 will indicate when they are required. If provided, whether required by code or not, showers must meet the required percentage of accessible units (or at least one. Showers provided for private use do not have to be completely accessible as long as it can be adapted later, if required.

The plumbing code specifies the type of shower pan and drain that must be used. If a glass enclosure is used, it must meet safety glazing requirements and have an access door that is at least 22 inches (559 mm) wide. The code also requires faucets to be within maximum flow rates for water consumption and maximum hot water temperatures to prevent scalding. When prefabricated showers and shower compartments are not used, the codes specify the types of finish materials allowed. (See the section titled "Finish Requirements" later in this chapter.) The size of a shower is regulated by the codes as well. Overall, the typical shower cannot be less than 900 square inches (0.58 sm), with the minimum size in either direction typically being at least 30 inches (762 mm). The minimum shower wall height is 70 inches (1778 mm) above the shower drain.

If a shower is required to be accessible, two basic types of showers are allowed: transfer showers and roll-in showers. *Transfer showers* are smaller and are typically required to have an inside clear dimension of 36 by 36 inches (915 by 915 mm) and a clear floor space in front of the shower of 36 by 48 inches (915 by 1220 mm). (However, the 2017 *ICC A117.1* requires a 36 by 52 inches [915 by 1320 mm] clear floor space for new construction. The smaller area is allowed for existing buildings.) They must also include a fixed or folding seat of a specific size and shape. *Roll-in showers* are more elongated and are typically 30 by 60 inches (by 1525 mm) with an adjacent clear floor space of 30 by 60 inches (760 by 1525 mm). A second type of roll-in shower is referred to as an alternate roll-in shower. It is elongated like a roll-in shower but allows for a transfer to a seat. Grab bar sizes and locations are different for each type of shower. (See Figure 8.9.) Neither the codes nor the accessibility guidelines indicate what type of accessible shower must be provided, just that at least one should be provide. The space available and the configuration of the space may determine which type can be achieved in the design.

Accessible controls and shower spray device requirements are like those for an accessible bathtub. Allowed locations are shown in Figure 8.4. If a curb or threshold is used, it can only be 0.5 inch (13 mm) high. (If it is more than 0.25 inch [6.4 mm], the edges must be beveled. See Figure 10.17 and the section titled "Accessible Finishes" in Chapter 10.) This is especially important in roll-in showers so that the curb does not hinder the wheelchair user. In addition, if an enclosure is used (i.e., a shower stall or door), it cannot obstruct the transfer of the person into the shower or any use of the controls in the shower.

Dishwashers and Clothes Washers

There are only a few code requirements for dishwashers and clothes washers. Dishwashers are not required in any occupancy (even commercial kitchens). Clothes washers are required only in certain Residential occupancies. For example, a clothes washer connection is required in a one- or two-family dwelling. In buildings with multiple residential units, one clothes washer is typically required for every 20 units. These can be combined in a shared laundry room. Most plumbing codes about dishwashers and clothes washers are installation standards and indicating when floor drains are required.

> ☞ **Note**
>
> Accessible requirements for washers and dryers are included in newer editions of the *ICC A117.1* standard and the 2010 *ADA Standards*.

When multiple clothes washers and/or clothes dryers are provided in a laundry facility, at least one of each must be accessible. If it is top loading, the top of the machine should be no higher than 36 inches (915 mm) above the floor. If it is a front-loading machine, the bottom of the opening must be between 15 and 36 inches (380 and 915 mm) above the floor. All operable parts should be within accessible reach ranges, accessible floor clearances positioned for a parallel approach, and turning space within the room should also be provided to allow approach to and use of the appliance.

TOILET AND BATHING FACILITIES

Once you have determined the required number and type of plumbing fixtures for a project and are familiar with the individual characteristic of those fixtures, you can decide how they will be distributed or grouped to create separate toilet bathing rooms or multi-fixture facilities. When fixtures are grouped together, additional code and accessibility requirements apply to the location and layout of these facilities.

The codes require that toilet and bathing rooms have privacy. This will affect the configuration at the entrance to the restroom and within

✎ Note

In occupancies where multiple single-toilet rooms or bathing rooms are clustered in a single location, at least 50 percent of them must be accessible.

✎ Note

Although not yet regulated by the codes, increased desire for privacy in toilet rooms including for gender-inclusive facilities have raised the interest in alternative partition types including gap-free partition systems and full wall dividers.

✎ Note

The ADA specifies a clear turning space of 60 inches (1525 mm) but the *ICC A117.1* standard specifies a turning space of 67 inches (1700 mm) for new construction. When a full circle is not possible, a *T*-shaped space is allowed. See the ADA and *ICC A117.1* standard for specific requirements.

the room when there are multiple water closets and bathing fixtures. Sightlines need to be considered. When a restroom or bathing facility is connected to a public area or passageway, it must be screened so that no one can look directly into the toilet or bathing facility. This is usually accomplished with either a vestibule leading into the room or a deliberate arrangement of walls in front of or beyond the doorway. When a door is used at the entrance, the codes typically require a closer on the door so that it self-closes with each use.

Toilet and bathing facilities should be directly available to the public from public corridors or spaces. This includes accessible corridors leading to the facility, minimum door clearance into the room, and an unobstructed turning space within the room. The *ADA Standard* and the accessibility chapter in the building codes will indicate when a toilet or bathing facility is required to be accessible or include accessible fixtures. The *ADA Standard* and *ICC A117*.1 will then specify the actual requirements for the stalls, clear floor space, grab bars, accessories, and other characteristic within the space. Some have been presented in the previous section. The requirements for various types of toilet and bathing facilities are described next, followed by a discussion of the appropriate use of finishes, grab bars, accessories, and signage.

Single-User Toilet Facilities

Single-user facilities typically consist of one lavatory and one water closet. They are provided in a building or space for several reasons. Most commonly, they are used in smaller spaces or occupancies where a limited number of toilets are required—for example, if only one or two male and female toilets were required. Single-toilet facilities may also be used as a family, assisted-use, or unisex facility. As described previously in this chapter, these may be required in certain Assembly and Mercantile occupancies in addition to group facilities. In some cases, a single user may be the solution during a renovation to provide an accessible toilet in an existing building. Also, a urinal can be provided in addition to a water closet in a single-user toilet. And most recently the codes have allowed a child height toilet and sink to be provided in addition to adult fixtures and still be considered a single-user facility.

Most single-toilet facilities must be accessible. However, there are exceptions. In Institutional (e.g., hospital) and Residential (e.g., hotel) building types where there are multiple dwelling units, only the toilets in the sleeping units or dwelling units designated to be accessible are required to be accessible. Also, the 2010 *ADA Standards* allows for 50 percent of single-toilet facilities to be accessible if there are several toilet rooms located near one another. Accessibility requirements do not apply to a toilet facility used for private use, such as an executive toilet room. Instead, the *IBC* requires that the private facility be adaptable so that it could easily be converted to an accessible room if it becomes necessary. For example, the room should be sized accordingly, and blocking should be included in the walls so that grab bars can be added and fixtures may be adjusted for later conversion.

In an accessible single-toilet facility, all fixtures, accessories, and grab bars must be mounted at accessible heights and specific floor clearances must be provided. Maintaining the clear floor areas at the fixtures and the door as required by the ADA, *ICC A117.1* and other local accessibility standards will drive the configuration of the toilet room. Figure 8.5 indicates the requirements of a an accessible single-toilet facility where the door swings out of the room. Figure 8.6 shows how the door swinging

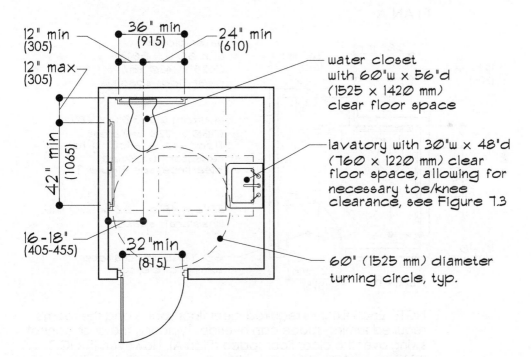

NOTE: Each fixture's required clear floor space and the room's required turning space can overlap.

Figure 8.5 Accessible single-toilet facility: Out-swinging door example. (See also Figures 8.2, 8.3, 8.8, 8.9, and 8.10 for accessible fixture and accessory heights and Figure 8.2 for vertical grab bar location.)

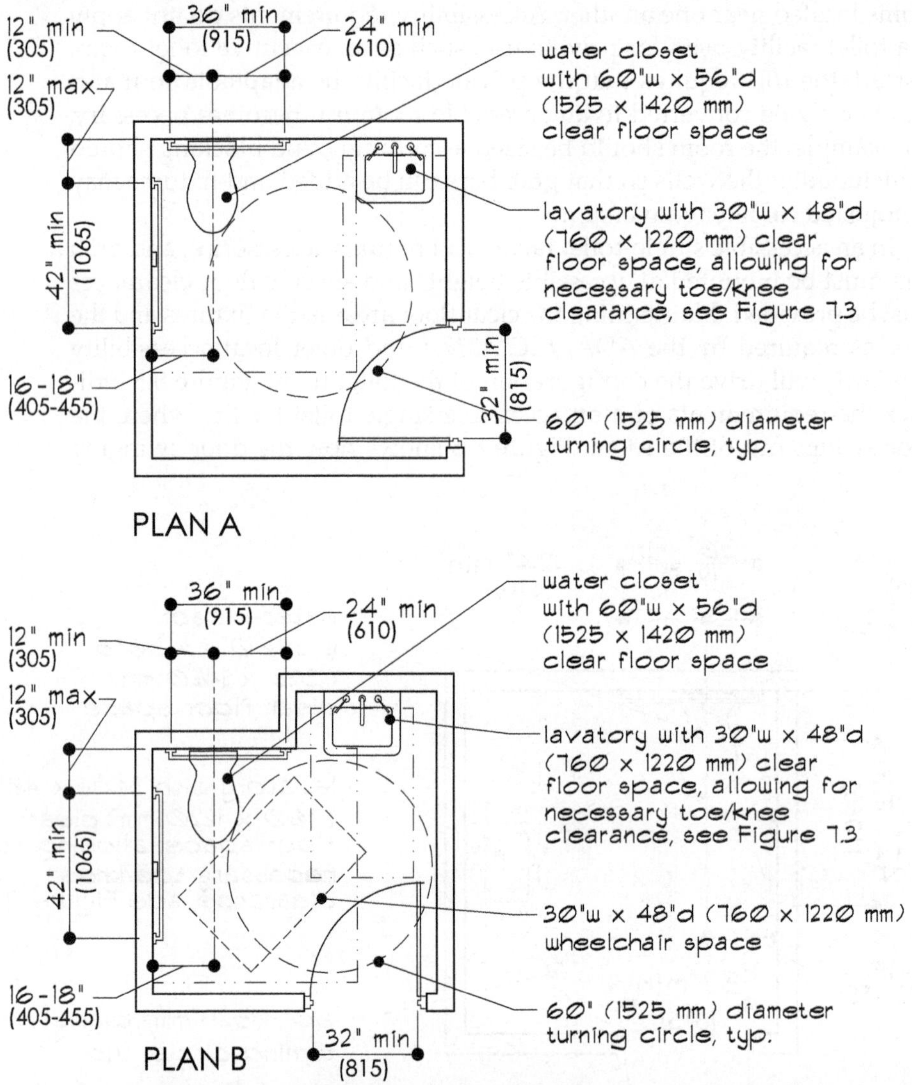

12" min (305)
36" min (915)
24" min (610)
12" max (305)
42" min (1065)
16-18" (405-455)
32" min (815)

water closet with 60"w x 56"d (1525 x 1420 mm) clear floor space

lavatory with 30"w x 48"d (760 x 1220 mm) clear floor space, allowing for necessary toe/knee clearance, see Figure 7.3

60" (1525 mm) diameter turning circle, typ.

PLAN A

36" min (915)
12" min (305)
24" min (610)
12" max (305)
42" min (1065)
16-18" (405-455)
32" min (815)

water closet with 60"w x 56"d (1525 x 1420 mm) clear floor space

lavatory with 30"w x 48"d (760 x 1220 mm) clear floor space, allowing for necessary toe/knee clearance, see Figure 7.3

30"w x 48"d (760 x 1220 mm) wheelchair space

60" (1525 mm) diameter turning circle, typ.

PLAN B

NOTE: Each fixture's required clear floor space and the room's required turning space can overlap. Typically, the door cannot swing over the clear floor space (Plan A). However, the ICC A117.1 and ADA standards allow the door and clear floor spaces to overlap if a 30" x 48" (760 x 1220 mm) wheelchair space is provided outside of the door swing (Plan B).

Figure 8.6 Accessible single-toilet facility: In-swinging door examples. (See also Figures 8.2, 8.3, 8.8, 8.9, and 8.10 for accessible fixture and accessory heights and Figure 8.2 for vertical grab bar location.)

into the toilet facility can change space needs. Also, if designing a family or assisted-use toilet room such as those required in certain Mercantile or Assembly occupancies, additional space may be needed so that someone can assist in the room or to allow for amenities not typically required by the codes, such as a fold-up changing table or a wall-mounted baby seat. (See Figure 8.10.) Alternative requirements for special uses including rooms designated for bariatric patients are not required to be follow the requirements of *ICC A117.1*, and rooms used primarily by children can follow the requirements for children in the *ICC A117.1* and the ADA.

The fixtures in single-toilet facilities must be arranged so that they do not overlap a required clear floor space for an adjacent fixture. However, as shown in Figure 8.5 and Figure 8.6, the clear floor spaces for different fixtures can overlap each other. In addition, accessible toilet facilities require an unobstructed turning space that is 60 inches (1525 mm) in diameter. (*ICC A117.1* requires 67 inches [1700 mm] for new construction but allows 60 inches [1525 mm] for existing buildings.) This turning area can overlap the clear floor space and the space under the fixtures where knee space and toe space are provided. (It is helpful for the clear floor spaces and the turning circle to be drawn directly on the floor plan in the construction drawings to indicate compliance.) Typically, the door into the room is not allowed to open over the clear floor space required at any fixture, as indicated in Figure 8.6A. However, if an unobstructed wheelchair space is provided beyond the swing path of the door, the door swing is allowed to overlap a fixture clear floor area by the 2010 *ADA Standards* and the *ICC A117.1*, as indicated in Figure 8.6B. (Note, this may not be allowed in some local accessibility standards and was not allowed in some past editions.)

Multiple-Fixture Facilities

When multiple plumbing fixtures are required for males and/or females in the same space or floor, a multiple-fixture facility is typically used (one for males and one for females). In a multiple-toilet facility, the water closets must be separated from one another and from the rest of the room by water closet compartments (i.e., toilet stalls). There are many ways to design the layout of a multi-toilet facility. Figure 8.7 shows one type of layout. The plumbing codes require minimum clearance dimensions to the side of each fixture and in front of each fixture, as well as a minimum water closet compartment size. These dimensions were explained for each fixture in the section titled "Plumbing Fixture Requirements" and are included in Figure 8.7. The figure also includes the minimum

> **✒ Note**
>
> Doors are permitted to swing into the 60-inch (1525-mm) turning space within a restroom or toilet stall in the *ICC A117.1* and the *2010 Standards*, but may not be allowed in local accessibility guidelines.

> **✒ Note**
>
> The clear floor spaces required at each plumbing fixture can overlap.

✎ Note

The 60-inch (1525-mm) turning circle can overlap the clear floor space for a fixture; it can overlap part of the fixture, too, but only if there is appropriate knee space and toe space.

✎ Note

If appropriate toe clearances of 9" (230 mm) height is provided under toilet partitions for a minimum of 30" (760 mm) wide, the required clear floor space can extend under toilet partitions. Dimensions for children differ.

✎ Note

A standard accessible stall and the "alternate" stall are shown in Figure 8.7. However, the use of the alternate stall is not typically required unless six or more stalls are provided.

✎ Note

The plumbing codes typically require a floor drain in multiple-toilet facilities.

dimensions required for a standard toilet stall, as shown by *C*. Urinals must be separated by a partition (i.e., privacy panel) as well, but no doors are required. (See the section titled "Urinals" earlier in this chapter for more information on privacy panels.)

The accessibility chapter of the *IBC* and the scoping chapter of the *ADA Standards* indicate how many accessible fixtures must be provided within a multiple fixture toilet room. At minimum, one of each type of fixture must be wheelchair accessible (exception for urinals). As the number of fixtures increase, additional requirements occur. For example, when the number of water closets is six or more, at least one of the remaining water closets must be "ambulatory accessible." (A wheelchair accessible and ambulatory accessible stall are different and are described next.) As the number of fixtures increases even more, the number of wheelchair accessible water closets increase (minimum 5 percent of the total number of fixtures provided) and the number of required ambulatory fixtures increase (5 percent of the remaining water closets.) This would be typical of toilet facilities in a stadium or where large numbers of people occur. In addition, when more than six lavatories are provided, at least one lavatory must include "enhanced reach ranges": where faucet and soap dispenser controls are a maximum of 11 inches (280 mm) from the front edge of the lavatory. (See the *ICC A117.1* standard for more information.)

There are two types of accessible stalls. When one accessible stall is required, it must allow for use by a person in a wheelchair, often called a *wheelchair-accessible* stall or compartment, as shown by *A* in Figure 8.7. If the door swings out, the typical size of this stall is 56 by 60 inches (1420 by 1525 mm) if it is a wall-hung water closet and 59 by 60 inches (1500 by 1525 mm) if it is a floor-mounted water closet. These dimensions assume that there are toe clearances at each side of the compartment. If the stall compartment walls are full height from the floor, additional width may be required. If the door swings in, it cannot overlap these clear floor spaces. Specific grab bar locations are important as well. When a second accessible stall is required, the "alternate stall" described in the ADA and *ICC A117.1* standard is required. This alternate stall is also called an *ambulatory-accessible* stall or compartment. Shown as stall *B* in Figure 8.7, it is not as wide and the arrangement of grab bars is different, requiring the water closet to be centered in the stall. The alternate stall configuration provides for use by a person who has a mobility disability but who does not necessarily use a wheelchair.

In addition to the clear floor space required in each accessible stall, a clear floor space must be provided at each accessible urinal, lavatory, and accessory in the facility. At least one area in the room must also allow a 60–67 inches inch (1525 mm–1700 mm) diameter turning space. (See the sections titled "Grab Bars" and "Accessories" later in this chapter.)

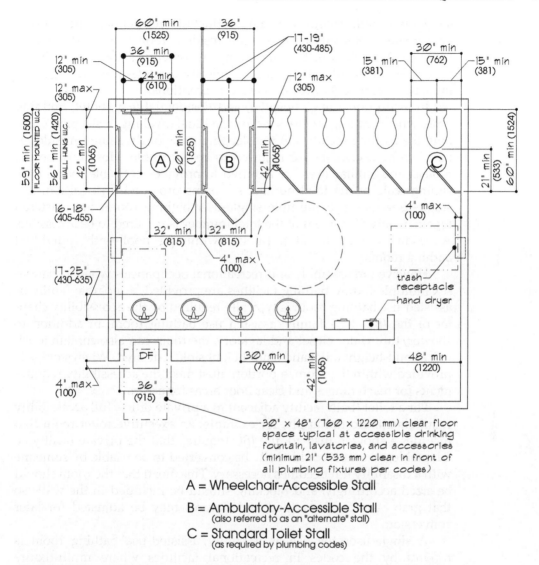

A = Wheelchair-Accessible Stall

B = Ambulatory-Accessible Stall
(also referred to as an "alternate" stall)

C = Standard Toilet Stall
(as required by plumbing codes)

Figure 8.7 Accessible multi-toilet facility example. (See also Figures 8.2, 8.3, and 8.10 for accessible fixture and accessory heights and Figure 8.2 for vertical grab bar location.)

Single-User Bath Facilities

Single-user bath facilities may be provided for convenience as part of the design or as required by the codes. Most single-user bathing rooms include a water closet, lavatory, and a bathtub or shower. Some Residential occupancies with dwelling or sleeping units will provide or require single-user bath facilities. Examples include residential care houses, apartments, hotel guest rooms, and resident rooms in assisted living facilities. A single-user bathing room can sometimes count as a single-user toilet for the plumbing count. Typically, a single-user bathing room must be accessible. However, there are exceptions.

In Institutional (e.g., hospital) and Residential (e.g., hotel) building types where bathing facilities serve individual dwelling or sleeping units, only the bathing facilities in the sleeping units or dwelling units designated to be accessible are required to be accessible. Hospitals, hotels, motels, and similar uses are required to provide accessible rooms on a sliding scale of the total number of rooms provided. In addition, like single-user toilets, if multiple single-user bathing rooms are clustered together, only 50 percent of the total number is required to be accessible. An example may be at a public swimming pool with individual bathing rooms.

However, in assembly and recreational occupancies where separate-sex multiple-fixture bathing facilities are provided, a separate family or assisted-use bathing room is typically required by the accessibility chapter of the *IBC*. In a family/assisted use bathing room, in addition to shower/tub, water closet and lavatory, the room can also contain a urinal, a child-height toilet and child-height sink, if desired. When storage is provided within the room, a portion must meet the accessibility requirements for reach ranges and clear floor areas for access.

For a toilet/bath facility adjacent to a private office, full accessibility requirements do not apply, for example, an executive toilet room that includes a shower. Instead, the *IBC* requires that the private facility be adaptable, so that it could easily be converted to be usable by someone with a disability if it becomes necessary. This mean that the room should be sized accordingly, and blocking should be included in the walls so that grab bars can be added and fixtures may be adjusted for later conversion.

A single-user for use as a family/assisted-use bathing room is *required* by the codes in recreational facilities where multi-fixture separate-sex bathing rooms are provided. This may be required even if the multi-fixture bathing facility includes accessible fixtures. A family/assisted-use bathing includes a lavatory and a water closet in addition to the bathtub or shower. The purpose of the separate family-assist accessible bathing room is to provide accessible fixtures but to also be assisted by another person regardless of gender. (A family/assisted-use bathing facility could also count as a family/assisted-use toilet facility if both are required.)

In an accessible single bathing facility, fixtures, accessories, and grab bars must be mounted at accessible heights and specific floor clearances must be provided. Figures 8.8 and 8.9 indicate the requirements of an accessible single-toilet/bath facility for tub and shower configurations. Remember that clear floor areas can overlap other clear floor areas, but fixtures cannot impede the required floor area of an adjacent fixture. A turning area within the room must be provided. And an in-swinging door versus an out swinging door can affect the configuration of the space and the overall area required. (See the section titled "Single-User Toilet Facilities" for additional requirements.)

Multiple-User Bathing Facilities

When multiple bathing fixtures are required by code or are part of a project, they are typically grouped into a single area to create a multiple-user bathing facility. Water closets and lavatories are typically provided within the same general space but may also be in connected areas. An example would be a locker room in a recreational facility. Other building types, such as schools, dormitories, health spas, and even prisons, are more likely to have group bathing facilities where there are multiple showers in one room.

> **✎ Note**
>
> In certain Institutional building types, such as rehabilitation centers, all toilet and bathing facilities are required to be accessible. Other Health Care facilities may only require a percentage of them to be accessible.

When a building has multiple bathing fixtures (i.e., shower stalls) located in the same room, at least one of them must be accessible. At each accessible plumbing fixture, the grab bars and controls must be mounted at accessible heights and specific floor clearances must be provided. Figures 8.8 and 8.9 give several examples of single bathing facilities but the clearances apply for an accessible tub or shower within a multiple fixture facility. Specific floor clearances are designated for each type of bathing fixture.

When planning a multiple fixture room, it is important to review the individual requirements to create the most efficient layout. For example, as shown in Figure 8.8, a bathtub with a removable seat in the tub will require less floor space than one with a fixed seat at the end of the tub. Figure 8.9 shows a roll-in shower that is larger and will require clearer floor spaces than a transfer shower. At least one area in the room must allow a 60–67 inch (1525–1700 mm) diameter turning space. A variety of layouts is possible. If it is a multi-fixture bathing facility, at least one of each type of accessory (soap dispenser, paper towel dispenser, storage, and so forth) in the space must be accessible as well. (See sections "Accessories" and "Grab Bars" later in this chapter.)

> **✎ Note**
>
> When the *International Green Construction Code (IgCC)* requires a building or tenant space to provide long-term bicycle parking and storage, it also typically requires at least one on-site changing room and shower facility.

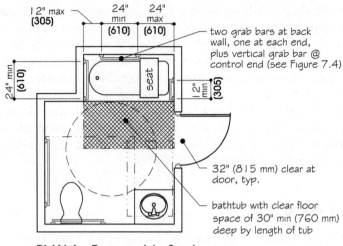

PLAN A - Removable Seat

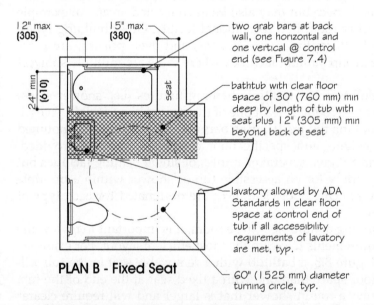

PLAN B - Fixed Seat

Figure 8.8 Accessible bathing facility examples: Bathtubs. (See also Figures 8.2–8.4, and 8.10 for accessible fixture and accessory heights and vertical grab bar locations. See Figure 8.5 for additional information on water closets and lavatories.)

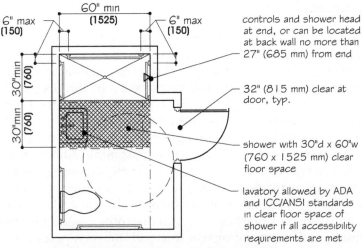

6" max (150) — **60" min (1525)** — **6" max (150)**

30"min (760) **30"min (760)** **30"min (760)**

controls and shower head at end, or can be located at back wall no more than 27" (685 mm) from end

32" (815 mm) clear at door, typ.

shower with 30"d x 60"w (760 x 1525 mm) clear floor space

lavatory allowed by ADA and ICC/ANSI standards in clear floor space of shower if all accessibility requirements are met

PLAN A - Roll-in Shower (without seat)

1. Alternate roll-in shower compartment with modified configuration also available in the ADA and ICC A117.1 standards.
2. If seat is provided, grab bar at back wall is to be within 6" max. of seat. Grab bar not to exceed 48" (1220mm)

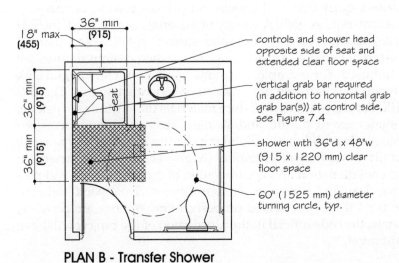

18" max (455) — **36" min (915)**

36" min (915) **36" min (915)**

controls and shower head opposite side of seat and extended clear floor space

vertical grab bar required (in addition to horizontal grab grab bar(s)) at control side, see Figure 7.4

shower with 36"d x 48"w (915 x 1220 mm) clear floor space

60" (1525 mm) diameter turning circle, typ.

PLAN B - Transfer Shower

Figure 8.9 Accessible bathing facility examples: Showers. (See also Figures 8.2–8.4, and 8.10 for accessible fixture and accessory heights and vertical grab bar locations. See Figure 8.5 for additional information on water closets and lavatories.)

Finish Requirements

Note

Finish requirements for toilet and bathing facilities are found in the plumbing codes and the building codes.

Both the plumbing codes and the "Interior Environment" chapter of the *IBC* specify that public toilet and bathing rooms must have smooth, hard, nonabsorbent surfaces. This limits the spread of germs and allows easy cleaning. It applies to floor finishes, the intersections of the floor and wall, and the wall base. For example, the *IBC* typically requires the floor finish throughout the room to extend upward onto the wall at least 4 inches (102 mm) to allow for wet mopping without damaging the wall. (Previous editions of the codes required 6 inches [152 mm].) Although in the past, ceramic tile was often used to meet these requirements, today other hard surfaces are available including resin, epoxy, luxury vinyl tile, sheet tile, and a growing number of products. Walls must also have smooth, hard, nonabsorbent finishes at certain distances around urinals and water closets and surrounding shower and tub compartments. Again, ceramic tile is often used but other materials such as vinyl, plastic wall coverings, phenolic panels, and other products can meet the code requirements for durability.

Note

Toilet and bathing facilities must also be mechanically ventilated. See the section titled "Exhaust Requirements" later in this chapter.

In addition, any accessories such as grab bars and soap dishes installed on or within the walls must be properly sealed to protect the wall beyond. (Also see the section titled "Accessible Finishes" in Chapter 10.)

The codes require that stall panels and privacy screens be made of impervious materials as well. A variety of materials can be used, including laminate, stainless steel, stone, solid surface, plastics, and painted metal. Finish requirements are also important when custom fixtures are designed and used. For example, a custom counter with an integral sink must be impervious and free of unnecessary concealed spaces. The *IPC* and the *UPC* list allow alternate fixture materials that include soapstone, chemical stoneware or plastic, and stainless steel and other corrosion-resistant metals. In addition, the plumbing chapter in the *ICC Performance Code* generally states that all plumbing fixtures shall be constructed "to avoid food contamination and accumulation of dirt or bacteria and permit effective cleaning." This may allow finishes such as wood and concrete to be used if they are sealed properly. Many options are possible, but ultimately, the code official in the jurisdiction of the project will have the final approval.

Note

The required height of horizontal grab bars at accessible fixtures such as water closets, bathtubs, and showers is measured to the top of the gripping surface.

Grab Bars

The *ADA Standards* and the *ICC A117.1* standard include requirements for grab bars. (The *IBC* refers to the *ICC A117.1*.) They are required at accessible water closets, showers, and tubs. They must be located beside and behind the water closet and on at least two to three sides of bathing fixtures. Grab bars must also be mounted at specific heights. Most commonly, a horizontal grab bar must be mounted at 33 to 36 inches (840 to 915 mm) above the finished floor at water closets, bathtubs, and showers. In the I-Codes, height is measured to the top of the gripping surface, as shown in Figures 8.2 and 8.4. In the NFPA codes, the height is measured to the centerline of the grab bar. (You need to detail their location so that the location is within the tolerances of both codes if applicable.) The *ICC A117.1* standard requires a vertical grab bar at certain water closet, bathtub, and shower locations as well.

The specific length, spacing, and orientation (horizontal or vertical) depend on the location of the grab bar in relation to the type of fixture. Locations have been shown in the various toilet and bathing facility floor plans used in this chapter. The size and strength requirements of the grab bar are also regulated. The typical diameter allowed is 1¼ to 2 inches (32 to 51 mm), which must be mounted with a clearance of 1½ inches (38 mm) between the grab bar and the wall. In addition, some jurisdictions or local agencies (e.g., health department) may require grab bars in locations other than those specified by the ADA or *ICC A117.1* standards. For example, a diagonal bar may be required over a tub to assist in getting in and out of the tub. A *swing-up* grab bar at certain toilet locations, as described in the *ICC A117.1* standard, is another option. It can be used as support by a disabled person when in position, or it can be moved out of the way to allow another person to assist. (Refer to the ADA and *ICC A117.1* standards for additional grab bar options.)

Accessories

Toilet room accessories are also regulated by the *ADA Standards* and the *ICC A117.1* standard. Accessories include, but are not limited to, mirrors, dispensers, receptacles, trash receptacles, air hand dryers, and vending machines. The type and number of accessories are not typically specified by the codes. In single-toilet and bathing facilities, where one of each type of accessory is used, all accessories must be accessible. In multi-fixture facilities, at least one of each type of accessory must be accessible.

A wide variety of accessory styles is available. For example, a hand dryer and a paper towel dispenser are available in accessible styles. However, the appropriate choice usually depends on the type of space, the traffic pattern of the occupants, and the client's preference. (In some cases, a jurisdiction will require specific accessories for certain building types.)

◀ Note

The height of a grab bar is measured to the top of the gripping surface, not the centerline.

◀ Note

When specifying and locating restroom accessories, a maximum 4-inch (100-mm) projection is allowed in circulation pathways.

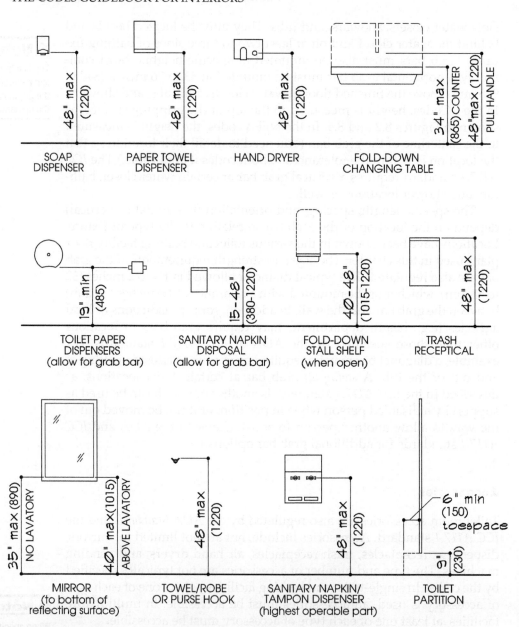

NOTE: Heights are measured to control part of accessory. If accessory is in path of travel, it cannot protrude from wall more than 4 inches (100 mm).

Figure 8.10 Typical accessible toilet accessory heights.

When selecting an accessible accessory, remember that the controls on the device must be easy to operate using one hand, with minimal turning and pressure. Devices that are automatic or use levers or push buttons are typical choices. In addition, it is important that the location of a device does not create a projection of more than 4 inches (100 mm) into the accessible circulation path. To accommodate this, many accessories are available that recess fully or partially into a wall. To avoid unnecessary projections and allow for required floor clearances within a toilet or bathing facility, it is a good idea to recess accessories whenever possible. When a recessed accessory cannot be used, walls can be built to create an alcove so that the device is not in the direct path. For example, in Figure 8.7, an alcove was created to allow the deeper hand dryers to be surface mounted on the wall. (The trash receptacles are shown partially recessed into the wall in the same figure.)

In addition, accessible toilet and bathing room accessories must be installed so that they are within reach ranges designated by the *2010 ADA Standards* and the *ICC A117.1*. The operating part of the device must be located between 15 inches (380 mm) and 48 inches (1220 mm) above the floor as indicated in Figure 8.10. The actual mounting height of the unit will vary as it will depend on the accessory shape, type, how it operates, and whether it is located over a counter. For example, a fold-down changing table, an amenity often supplied in public restrooms, must be installed so that when folded down, the top is no higher than 34 inches (865 mm) above the floor—similar to an accessible counter height. Other accessories, such as toilet paper holders, have minimum and maximum placement requirements; they must be located a certain distance from the front edge of the water closet while allowing for the adjacent grab bar. (See Figure 8.2 and the ADA and *ICC A117.1* standards for specific requirements.) Clear floor space in front of the accessory is also required. Typically, at each accessible accessory, a clearance of 30 by 48 inches (760 by 1220 mm) for 30 by 52 inches (760 by 1320 mm) should be allowed. This does not include the accessories located within a toilet stall.

Signage

Requirements for signage are found in the *IPC*, the *IBC*, and the accessibility documents. Most toilet and bathing facilities will require at least one sign. The type of sign will depend on the type of facility and the types of other facilities located in the same building. If all locations provide the accessible fixtures, then the International Symbol of Accessibility (the wheelchair symbol) is not required on facility signage. However, if a

✎ Note

Baby-changing tables should be installed to meet accessibility requirements. (See Figure 8.10.) The pull handle required to fold down the table should also be within the accessible reach range.

✎ Note

Although the original *ADAAG* allowed a reach range up to 54 inches (1370 mm), the 2010 *ADA Standards* and the *ICC A117.1* standard limit the maximum reach range of 48 inches (1220 mm).

☑ Note

Directional signage for public facilities is required by the *IPC*. Some jurisdictions may have additional signage requirements as well.

building contains both accessible and non-accessible facilities, the non-accessible facilities must have a sign directing occupants to the location of the accessible facilities and the International Symbol of Accessibility must indicate the location of rooms and facilities with accessible fixtures. In addition, each multi-toilet or multi-bathing facility must also indicate the location of the nearest family or assisted-use facility, if not adjacent. Likewise, if drinking fountains for standing and wheelchair users are in separate locations, signage is required to indicate the location of the other fountain type.

The signs shown in Figure 8.11 are examples of compliant signage for a women's toilet facility, a family toilet facility, and bathing facility. Each accessible stall in a multi-toilet or multi-bathing facility must also have the of the International Symbol of Accessibility on the door (see Figure 8.11). In addition, beginning in 2009, the *IPC* requires directional signage to be posted at the entrance of a building or space, which indicates

WOMEN'S TOILET FACILITY

FAMILY TOILET FACILITY

BATHING FACILITY

ACCESSIBLE STALL

Figure 8.11 Types of accessible signs for toilet and bathing facilities. (Illustrations by APCO Graphics, Inc. www.apcosigns.com).

the route to a public toilet facility (as required for customers, patrons, and visitors).

Additional accessibility requirements typical to room identification signs including location and mounting requirements are discussed in Chapter 10 in the section titled "Signage."

PLUMBING SUSTAINABILITY CONSIDERATIONS

The plumbing codes, *IECC*, *IgCC*, and other codes, standards, and federal laws continue to be revised to require buildings to be more sustainable and energy efficient. Voluntary or mandated participation in sustainable rating systems can increase performance as well. The individual plumbing fixtures and the overall design of the plumbing system can contribute to a reduction in water consumption and energy use of a project. When less water is used, less energy is used by the utility companies supplying the water and less energy is used inside the building to heat and distribute the water.

The plumbing and energy codes along with the sustainability guidelines require plumbing fixtures including water closet, showers, urinals, and some faucets to meet maximum water consumption limitations. Most plumbing fixtures and faucets currently made in the United States are built to meet or exceed the standards set by the plumbing codes. Other, more restrictive, low-flow and low-consumption requirements are found in the energy codes, such as the *IECC* with *ASHRAE/IESNA 90.1* as required by the Energy Policy Act (EPAct). The *IgCC* includes additional requirements for fixtures and faucets. Various tables in the *IgCC* provide a maximum flow rate for each type of fixture (or fitting), as well as the estimated daily use per occupant and the average duration of each use for each type of fixture. Using these numbers, along with the expected number of occupants, the total expected water consumption for the building can be calculated. This information can be used to help specify appropriate "low-flow" plumbing fixtures so that the building's overall water consumption falls within specified thresholds as required by the code. In some cases, the fixture must also meet the requirements of the Environmental Protection Agency's (EPA's) WaterSense® program, which certifies products that meet minimum water consumption standards set by the EPA. (See the inset titled "Federal Sustainability Certifications" in Appendix A.) Plumbing fixtures that are considered low flow include high-efficiency fixtures, dual-flush toilets (which provide a full flush mode for solids and light flush mode for liquids), and waterless urinals, among others. Both the *IgCC* and *ASHRAE 189.1* also include

☑ **Note**

Clear floor space for a wheelchair is required at accessible signs by the *ICC A117.1* and the 2010 *ADA Standards.*

☑ **Note**

The newest technology in efficient plumbing fixtures includes low-flow faucets, dual-flush toilets, water-free urinals, and solar-powered faucets. Some jurisdictions require certain types of fixtures in new construction. Others are required by the energy and sustainability codes.

Note

ASHRAE 189.1 includes requirements for special water features, such as ornamental fountains. When alternate on-site sources or reclaimed water cannot be used, the standard limits the size of the water feature.

Note

Some form of building automation system (BAS) is typically required when following sustainability codes and standards so that water and energy efficiencies can be measured and monitored. (See the inset titled "Building Automation Systems" in Chapter 9 for more information.)

Note

Even though promoted by the sustainability codes and standards, some jurisdictions may not allow the use of reclaimed or graywater systems inside a building.

performance criteria, so alternate sustainable fixtures may be allowed. For example, composting toilets (using foam-flush or no-flush) may be an option in certain facilities such as universities, offices, park visitor centers, and other recreational areas.

In addition to the individual plumbing fixtures, the design of the overall plumbing system can also be important for water conservation and consumption parameters. The *IPC* (starting in 2018) and *IgCC* provides parameters for the use of alternate on-site water sources. For example, a building may include a graywater system, which gathers waste flows from lavatories and handwashing sinks, bathtubs and showers, and clothes-washing machines. These systems use separate drainage pipes to collect this reclaimed water (and sometimes rainwater as well) for reuse in water closets, urinals, and subsurface irrigation; it will use fresh potable water for these functions only if additional water is needed. The *IgCC* includes water metering and measurement of building water sources (e.g., potable, reclaimed, on-site). Similar requirements are included in *ASHRAE/USGBC/IES 189.1*.

The energy codes also focus their requirements on the water heating system. The *IgCC* references the *IECC* for these requirements including wastewater heat recovery systems. These systems use the heat recaptured from warm outgoing drain water to preheat incoming main water on its way to the water heater. It is required in certain Assembly, Factory, Institutional, and Residential occupancies and building types. Other sustainable techniques include recirculating systems for centralized hot water distribution and point-of-use water heating systems to reduce the need to transport hot water over long distances.

Some of these water conservation and energy-efficiency items are incorporated into the plumbing system design by the mechanical engineer. However, others affect the selection of fixtures and appliances used in the space. Because older fixtures may not meet the most current water consumption standards, this may limit the reuse of existing fixtures in renovation projects. In addition, if specifying fixtures manufactured in other countries, confirm that they will meet the necessary requirements. These requirements must also be considered when custom fixtures are designed and used; research the specific requirements. (See Appendix A for more sustainability information.)

MECHANICAL REQUIREMENTS

Mechanical systems provide ventilation, regulate the interior temperatures, and improve air quality in a building so that occupants are comfortable and healthy while indoors. The heating, ventilation, and air conditioning system (HVAC) can be accomplished by a variety of system types, and each is made up of various parts. These systems and their parts are regulated mostly by the building and mechanical codes. Other provisions are found in energy codes. Some parts of the systems such as rated vertical (mechanical) shafts and fire/smoke dampers have been discussed in Chapters 6 and 7 of this book. The main mechanical-related requirements to be aware of as a designer are discussed in this section. Sustainability codes and standards are discussed in the following sections.

Mechanical Rooms

Mechanical rooms can include furnace or boiler rooms, fan rooms, and refrigeration rooms. (They are also sometimes called *appliance rooms*.) Depending on the size of the building and the type of mechanical system used, these rooms can be separate or combined into one. It is the size and location of the mechanical room(s) that are important. The size of the room will be driven by the size and number of components which make up the system. The codes specify that each room must have a minimum door width and an unobstructed passageway so that appliances and equipment can be easily replaced. In addition, minimum working space along the control side of each appliance is required. If a mechanical room needs to be located in the layout of an interior project, work closely with the mechanical engineer to size and locate the room effectively. In addition, these rooms often must have fire-rated walls. (See Chapter 6 for fire-rating requirements.) Mechanical rooms are not typically required to be disability accessible.

Heating and Cooling Loads

Heating and *cooling loads* refer to how much energy is required to heat or cool a space to maintain a comfortable interior environment. The heating/cooling loads and the required capacity of the system are typically calculated by a mechanical engineer. Cooling loads tend to be the primary factor in determining the size and type of a mechanical system. (Heating loads are also a determining factor.) There are human and spatial considerations. The size, volume, and configuration of the space and the number of people who will occupy the space are typically the initial determinants for the capacity (and thus the size) of the system. In addition, the types of human activities occurring in the space (such as a basketball game with cheering spectators in a gym) can contribute heat to

✇ **Note**

Many smaller buildings have their HVAC units either on the roof or on the ground adjacent to the building and may not require a mechanical room. If one is needed, discuss the size and location with the mechanical engineer.

the space and the actual amount and type of glazing used in the exterior windows that allow solar heat gain into the space (or heat loss) can affect the cooling loads, as well. As part of the interior design, certain window treatments can reduce solar heat gain and can reduce the total cooling load and should be part of the overall calculations, as well.

Another significant factor in determining the cooling load is the amount of heat-generating elements (beyond the occupants) that will be in the space, including lights and equipment. The location of equipment such as computers, printers, copiers, projectors, and various appliances may affect the necessary distribution of cooling. Location of large or unique equipment needs to particularly be considered. For example, if there is an x-ray machine in a doctor's office, separate calculations may be necessary for that room in addition to the calculations for the rest of the office layout. Therefore, it is important to work closely with the client, the engineers, and other consultants to accurately identify all elements that will affect the cooling load for the space or building.

Typically, the specification for each light fixture and piece of equipment should be provided to the mechanical engineer to determine how much heat they will generate within the space. This is measured in BTUs (British thermal units). The total expected number of electrical BTUs is factored in with the other loads of the space to determine the required load capacity of the HVAC system. The mechanical engineer uses these factors, in conjunction with the codes and standards, to determine the size of the main unit, the size of the ducts, and the number of supply diffusers and return grilles required. These loads are also critical to determine efficient energy use as required by the energy codes. The *IECC* sets the temperature used for heating and cooling load calculations to be maintained by the system to be maximum 72 degrees Fahrenheit (22 degrees Celsius) for heating and minimum of 75 degrees Fahrenheit (24 degrees Celsius) for cooling. The codes require submission of these calculations as part of the permit process for some uses. (See also the section titled "Electrical Sustainability Considerations" in Chapter 9.)

Zoning and Thermostat Locations

Separating the overall area of a building or space into unique *zones* allows the HVAC system to be designed to provide appropriate levels of comfort and to meet the heating and cooling needs of each particular area efficiently. For example, it may be desirable for some areas to be warmer than others (e.g., exam rooms versus offices). Typically, parts of a floor or building with similar temperature requirements are grouped into the same zone. In addition, perimeter rooms that have exterior windows are

---

✎ Note

Sustainability code requirements often give occupants more control over their "thermal comfort." Examples include providing access to thermostat controls and installing local diffusers or individual radiant panels.

typically zoned separately from interior spaces because of the difference in heat gain from exterior windows. Some unique spaces may even be a separate zone and have a supplemental system because of a special use, condition, or equipment. Examples include a kitchen in a restaurant, a locker room in a sports complex, an x-ray room in doctor's office, a computer room in a school, and a conference room in an office space. In some cases, the *IECC* may require areas to be zoned separately based on size or if they are not constantly in use to conserve energy.

Each mechanical zone has a separate sensor and thermostat to monitor the temperature within the zone and initiate the heating and cooling. The codes do not specify the location of the sensor or thermostat, but the location can affect the effectiveness of the overall system. Because energy and sustainability codes often require the system to provide different levels of heating and cooling based on the day of the week, time of day, actual amount of daylight, number of occupants, and other factors, the location of the sensor and thermostat is important. Sometimes the sustainability codes require occupants to have increased access to thermostat controls. This may require more sensors or thermostats located throughout a space. Ultimately, the number of zones and the general location of each thermostat are determined by the engineer, but they should be coordinated as part of the design of the space.

Programmable thermostats are increasingly required to meet the energy conservation requirements in the codes. For example, the *IECC* requires occupant sensors or card key controls to manage guestroom thermostat settings. In addition, thermostats in unrented rooms of a hotel, (thus not needing heating and cooling) must be prompted by a networked reservation system or after sensors indicate a prolonged continuous vacancy.

When a thermostat is located for occupant use, the *ADA Standards* and other accessibility standards require that the thermostat be within accessible reaching heights, similar to those of an electrical switch. (See Figure 9.4 in Chapter 9.) Clear floor space in front of the thermostat that allows either a side or front approach may also be required.

Exhaust Requirements

When air is removed from a building or space, the process is considered *exhaust*. The codes require an exhaust system in specific types of rooms and in certain occupancies. An exhaust system can remove air that contains smoke, germs, chemicals, odors, or other unhealthy or contaminated components. Although proper exhaust and indoor air quality is especially important in hazardous types of occupancies, the codes require

✐ Note

Codes often require that spaces adjacent to exterior walls and windows be zoned separately from interior spaces. Solar heat and outside temperatures typically cause different temperatures in perimeter rooms.

✐ Note

Every electrical fixture and piece of equipment has a BTU calculation. The total BTUs in a space are factored in when calculating cooling loads and the size of the cooling system.

✐ Note

The building codes, energy codes, and sustainability codes specify minimum and maximum temperature control ranges and other requirements for thermostats.

✐ Note

Makeup air is the air provided in a space to replace the air being exhausted.

a growing number of rooms and areas to be exhausted within several occupancies. These include toilet and bathing facilities, designated smoking areas, special use rooms in health care facilities, high occupant density spaces, and areas with cooking appliances. Clothes dryers are also required to be exhausted (see Appendix C). In some cases, such as clothes dryers, the codes set limits as to how close the exhaust terminals can occur to other air intake components. The rate at which air must be removed from an area is set by the codes and is generally based on the activity or type of air that is being exhausted. The rate is designated by requiring a specific number of total air exchanges per hour and/or create a specified air flow. In addition, gas detectors can be used to detect many harmful gases including carbon monoxide and carbon dioxide. Areas requiring special smoke control, such as atriums or malls, may also use an exhaust method.

To exhaust an area, an exhaust fan is connected to a pipe or duct, which draws the air out of the space is typically routed to the exterior of a building. Consideration must be given to its route and how it affects other elements in the building, such as floor/ceiling assemblies or vertical shafts. In multiple story buildings, its route needs to be considered through the adjacent spaces and floors. The mechanical codes also may limit the length of the exhaust pipe or duct, including the number of 45- or 90-degree bends it can make. In some cases, these limitations may require a room requiring exhaust to be located close to an exterior wall.

Ventilation Requirements

> **✎ Note**
>
> Good ventilation is critical for a building's indoor air quality and can help control carbon monoxide, carbon dioxide created by building occupants and appliances within the building, and naturally occurring gasses such as radon.

Whenever outside air is added to a building or space, the process is considered *ventilation*. Ventilation dilutes harmful elements or odors that are released into the indoor air by equipment, building materials (paint, carpet, wood, plastics), furnishings, products, and people. Ventilation can be brought in by natural air flow through operable windows, vents, or louvers (known as *natural ventilation*) or by a mechanical system (known as *mechanical ventilation*). The mechanical codes regulate both. They set the necessary amount of outside air based on the floor area of the space and the estimated maximum occupant load. If natural ventilation cannot meet the code requirements, the space is typically required to be ventilated mechanically. Ventilation rates are measured in cubic feet per minute (CFM) Using the parameters set by the codes, the mechanical engineer must calculate the amount of outside air required in all areas of the building. Some specialty rooms, such as a computer, beauty and barbershop, nail salons, print rooms, or x-ray rooms, may have more specific and higher ventilation and exhaust requirements. Other areas requiring special ventilation include atriums and vestibules.

To determine the required ventilation rate, each mechanical code (*IMC* and the *UMC*) has a table that lists various occupancy classifications, types of occupied rooms within each classification and assumed occupant density and provides the required minimum ventilation rates. (The required exhaust for some uses is also provided.) The code considers the concentration of people within the space as well as other building area contents such as building materials and furnishings whose offgassing can also affect the quality of air. The American National Standards Institute (ANSI) and the American Society of Heating, Refrigerating and Air-Conditioning Engineers, Inc. (ASHRAE) establish acceptable levels of indoor air quality. *ANSI/ASHRAE 62.1, Ventilation for Acceptable Indoor Air Quality*, for example, provides acceptable concentrations of contaminants and options for ventilation requirements.

The mechanical codes assume that ventilation is provided in a fixed rate. In other words, constantly. However, bringing outside air into a building by mechanical ventilation uses additional electricity and requires the HVAC system to condition (heat or cool) the new air. The energy and sustainability codes and standards provide alternative and more efficient ways to ventilate a building. Two common ways is the use of a dedicated outdoor air system or a demand control ventilation system. In some cases, the *IECC, ASHRAE 90.1, ANSI/ASHRAE 62.1*, and the *IgCC* may require their use to meet the ventilation and energy efficiency requirements. A dedicated outdoor air system (DOAS) separates the heating, cooling, and supply of outdoor air from the heating and cooling process of the building, which is a more efficient way to increase outside air without using more electricity. A demand control ventilation (DCV) system varies the amount of ventilation based on the actual need of the building and its occupants. For example, a DCV system modifies the ventilation based on when the space is in use and for the estimated number of occupants. These systems do this by sensing occupant movement or measuring CO_2 levels within the space by zoned sensors, following a programed schedule for when rooms should be occupied/vacant and similar methods. DCV systems are required by the *IECC* and *ASHRAE 62.1* for specific uses. This is especially efficient for spaces where the number of occupants varies greatly, such as conference rooms, schools, and media centers. The energy codes also include requirements for energy recovery systems, which use the ventilation air being expelled from the building to condition the air coming back in and air economizers, which monitor the outdoor air temperature and humidity levels to determine if outdoor air can be used to ventilate the building without the need for additional mechanical conditioning.

Efficient use of energy as promoted by the energy codes must be balanced with the need for indoor air quality as required by the mechanical codes. Some code authorities may require detailed calculations to verify that each area of a building receives a safe and healthy level of ventilation. Current standards and codes require a minimum level of ventilation to be provided at all times and in all areas of a building.

Plenum Requirements

Most HVAC systems use either a duct or a plenum for return air. (See the inset titled "Mechanical Systems" earlier in this chapter.) When ducts are not attached to the return grilles, the open space between the ceiling and the floor/roof above creates a ceiling plenum that acts as the duct and collects the return air. (If a raised floor system is used, the plenum space may be at the floor level.)

When a plenum system is used, it must be limited to a single fire area within the building. For example, a plenum cannot pass through a stairwell. In multi-tenant buildings, the plenum is typically limited to a particular tenant. This is accomplished by using a separate HVAC system for each tenant. In some cases, the plenum system may serve an entire floor of a building even if there are multiple tenants. However, if an opening is cut in a rated assembly to allow the return air to continue to another area (i.e., air transfer opening), a rated fire or smoke damper may be required.

The building codes prohibit the use of combustible materials in the plenum space. For example, only certain types of rated electrical and communication cables are allowed (see Chapter 9) and any foam plastic used as a ceiling or wall finish must meet certain standards (see Chapter 10). In existing buildings or renovations, code officials may require all materials that come in contact with the plenum air to be identified for health and safety issues. This can be difficult or expensive for some projects.

Duct Requirements

If the mechanical system uses ducts to supply the conditioned air to a space and/or retrieve the air as return air, the codes place fewer restrictions on the types of materials allowed in the space between the finished ceiling and the floor/roof structure. Instead, the codes place restrictions on the ducts themselves. The building codes set some requirements, such as the use of fire-stops and fire dampers when a duct passes through a

◀ Note

Designing for the use of exposed ceilings, exposed duct work, and limited dropped ceiling configurations can make the design of the mechanical system for air supply and return more complicated. Coordination with the mechanical engineer can be important.

fire resistance–rated wall and other assembly. Smoke stops and smoke dampers may also be required when a wall is considered a smoke barrier. (See Chapter 6.) Figure 8.12 shows the use of a fire damper on a duct that passes through a fire resistance–rated wall assembly. The fire-stop in this case is fire-rated caulk or sealant used continuously around the fire damper on each side where it passes through the wall. The building codes also specify when a damper or shaft enclosure is required around a duct that penetrates a floor/ceiling assembly.

Note

For some areas, stricter requirements for the bracing of piping and ductwork are required to provide seismic support.

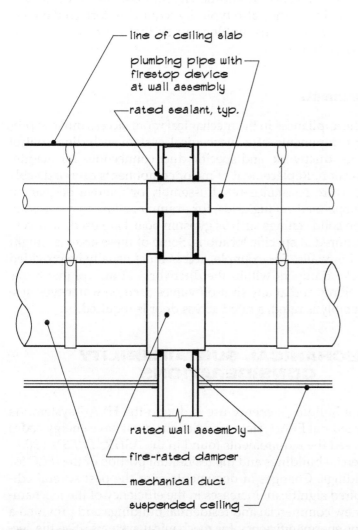

Figure 8.12 Mechanical/plumbing penetrations in a rated wall assembly.

Note

Building energy consumption accounts for approximately 40 percent of US energy use.

The mechanical codes specify such things as the size and length of the ducts, types of materials allowed, and mounting and clearance requirements. For example, flexible ducts are typically not allowed to penetrate a rated wall; only rigid ducts are allowed. The codes also prohibit the use of mechanical ducts in certain locations and specify when smoke detectors are required in a duct system. When activated, a duct smoke detector can interrupt the power to the fan distributing the air and close specific dampers. (See the section titled "Smoke Detection" in Chapter 7.) Energy codes include additional requirements for the insulation and sealing of ducts. They also typically require motorized dampers in ducts that supply or exhaust outdoor air so that they can be closed when a space is not in use.

Access Requirements

In addition to the appliances in the mechanical room, access must be provided to other components of a mechanical system including control devices, dampers, ductwork, and specific duct connections for maintenance and inspection. Replacement of major components cannot disable the function of a fire resistance–rated assembly or remove permanent construction. Suspended ceiling grids, for example, allow easy access to ductwork. When solid ceilings such as gypsum board are used, an access door may be required at specific locations. Some of these accesses might also be required in walls. For example, access must usually be provided at fire and smoke dampers within the ductwork, at air volume boxes located in the ceiling, and at any shut-off valves used on water-type systems. If the assembly is rated, a rated access door is required.

MECHANICAL SUSTAINABILITY CONSIDERATIONS

A large part of a building's energy use is due to the HVAC system. As required by the federal EPAct, state jurisdictions must have energy codes that meet or exceed the requirements found in the *ASHRAE/IESNA 90.1–2016* for commercial buildings and the residential portion of the *IECC* for residential buildings. Changes in documents over the past several editions have required significant increases in the efficiency of the mechanical systems of new commercial and residential buildings and provided a new baseline for energy efficiency for mechanical systems. (See the section titled "Energy Policy Act" in Chapter 1.)

These codes also require certified equipment that meets minimum efficiency requirements, effective sealing of ducts and building penetrations, specific insulation R-values around ductwork and pipes, types and location of temperature- and humidity-control devices (including thermostats), automatic shutdown requirements, and types of balancing devices. Requirements for water-heating systems, such as water heaters, storage tanks, boilers, and those used in swimming pools, are included as well. Although many of these items are covered in the mechanical codes, the energy codes provide additional efficiency parameters that must be followed.

By adopting the *IECC* document and/or other energy codes and standards, a local jurisdiction may set a higher level of sustainable performance for buildings in their area. For example, the *International Green Construction Code (IgCC)* and *ASHRAE/USGBC/IES 189.1, Standard for the Design of High-Performance Green Buildings Except Low-Rise Residential Buildings,* include many requirements for mechanical systems. In fact, the *IgCC* often references the *IECC.* In some cases, specific requirements within the *IgCC* and *ASHRAE 189.1* may supersede the requirements in *ASHRAE/IESNA 90.1* if both are applicable on a project. Examples include requirements for installing demand control ventilation in densely occupied spaces, air economizers that maximize the use of outside air for conditioning a building, nonpotable water (e.g., graywater, rainwater) piping in water-based HVAC systems, and methods for containing pollutants for better indoor air quality. In some cases, the HVAC system must be connected to a building automation system (BAS) so that energy and water consumption data can be collected on an hourly basis and monitored remotely. (See inset entitled "Building Automation Systems" in Chapter 9.) The *IgCC* chapter also includes requirements and the allowable levels of emissions and pollutants from the HVAC systems. There are also requirements for the acoustical qualities of a space. These requirements for acceptable levels of acoustic privacy and transfer of sound between rooms and adjoining occupancies can affect the wall and door assembly specifications.

Mechanical appliances and equipment that make up the HVAC system are usually required to meet minimum federal certifications for ENERGY STAR, as well as WaterSense when water-based systems are used. In some cases, these federal certifications are referenced by the codes, too. For example, the *IgCC* requires programmable thermostats to comply with the ENERGY STAR program. The sustainability codes and standards and the energy codes also include performance criteria that may allow the use of newer sustainable systems or products not yet allowed by the prescriptive codes. For example, the energy codes

☑ Note

Rigid ducts are typically made of metal (galvanized steel or aluminum), which can be lined with fiberglass for increased insulation and noise dampening. Other materials include fiberboard, polyurethane, and phenolic. Flexible ducts are a flexible plastic over a metallic wire and are bendable and relocatable.

☑ Note

Using efficient fixtures and minimizing heat leakage will improve the overall energy efficiency of a mechanical system. For example, properly sealed recessed light fixtures will eliminate leakage between conditioned and unconditioned spaces.

provide allowances for renewable energy sources such as solar radiation, wind, plant by-products, and geothermal sources.

Sustainability, however, is more than just the energy efficiency of the system. Sustainable goals consider initial cost and local sources of equipment, long-term operating costs, life cycle analysis, indoor air quality supported by the HVAC system, acoustical impact of noise from the system and other interior environmental factors. Because acoustic quality can contribute to the sustainability of a space, reduction in noise created by building systems is important as well. Many energy-efficient mechanical systems are quieter than previous models and thus add to the green and sustainable quality of the building by conserving energy and providing a quieter environment. To meet the green or sustainability goals required by the local jurisdictions or a client, additional influences may need to be considered that will affect the design and specification of the mechanical system, even if they are not required by the codes. You may have to refer to the specific green rating system for additional requirements. (See also Appendix A.)

RESEARCH: USING THE PLUMBING AND MECHANICAL CODES

Note

ASHRAE 189.1 requires the use of the mechanical system to "flush out" a building with outside air after construction is complete and before it is occupied to help improve the indoor air quality before occupancy.

Although the building codes have chapters on plumbing and mechanical, these chapters simply reference the separate plumbing and mechanical codes and other standards where most of the actual requirements are found. There are two main plumbing codes. The *International Plumbing Code (IPC)*, published by the International Code Council (ICC), and the *Uniform Plumbing Code (UPC)*, published by the International Association of Plumbing and Mechanical Officials (IAPMO). IAPMO also publishes another plumbing code, *National Standard Plumbing Code (NSPC)*, which may also be in use in some jurisdictions. The *IPC* is the most widely used plumbing code. Likewise, there are two main mechanical codes: the *International Mechanical Code (IMC)*, published by the ICC, and the *Uniform Mechanical Code (UMC)*, published by the IAPMO in partnership with the NFPA. The *IMC* is the most widely used.

First, you need to determine which plumbing and mechanical code applies to your project. Typically, the edition of the plumbing and mechanical codes is the same as the edition of the building code that is in effect. For example, if a jurisdiction uses the 2021 *IBC*, they will use the 2021 *IPC* and 2021 *IMC* as well. In rare cases, this may not be true. Check with the jurisdiction. Research in other codes and standards may be necessary as outlined here.

There are several energy and sustainability codes that will or might apply to the plumbing and mechanical systems. The most common energy code is the *International Energy Conservation Code (IECC)* with the *ASHRAE/IESNA 90.1, Energy Standard for Buildings Except Low-Rise Residential Buildings,* as required by the EPAct. Additional use of a sustainability code or standard will depend on the jurisdiction of the project or as part of the client's project goals. When required, sources for these requirements include the *International Green Construction Code (IgCC)* and *ASHRAE/USGBC/IES 189.1, Standard for the Design of High-Performance Green Buildings Except Low-Rise Residential Buildings.* In fact, the *IgCC* often references the *IECC.* In some cases, specific requirements within the *IgCC* and *ASHRAE 189.1* may supersede the requirements in *ASHRAE/ IESNA 90.1.* Coordination between these documents is important.

The *ICC Performance Code (ICCPC)* may be usable to direct innovative solutions for plumbing and mechanical systems using performance-based criteria if adopted and allowed by a jurisdiction. (See the section titled "Performance Codes" in Chapter 1 and the "Research" section of this chapter.)

For almost every project, the ADA *2010 Standards* (or *ABA*, if a federal project) will apply. The *ICC A117.1* is often adopted by a jurisdiction as its local accessibility code for technical requirements. Both have specific chapters for plumbing facilities, but many requirements within these documents are applicable to plumbing and mechanical systems as discussed in this chapter. Scoping parameters for the *ICC A117.1* is typically determined by the accessibility chapter of the building code.

▨ **Note**

The Department of Energy tracks the adoption of energy codes by individual states. See their website: energycodes.gov/ state-code-adoption-tracking-analysis for more information.

Researching Plumbing Requirements

The plumbing codes cover the plumbing system and the individual fixtures as discussed in this chapter. These codes also reference multiple industry standards. Most of these requirements will be incorporated into the plumbing design by the mechanical engineer or licensed mechanical/ plumbing contractor. So typically, the research process for a designer or architect begins in Chapter 4, "Fixtures, Faucets and Fixture Fittings" in the *IPC.* This chapter describes the types of fixtures and their requirements (including energy conservation requirements) and supplies Table 403.1, "Minimum Number of Required Plumbing Fixtures," shown in Figure 8.1. (The same table is also repeated in Chapter 29, "Plumbing Systems" of the *IBC* as Table 2902.1.) You will use this table to calculate the number and types of plumbing fixtures required for your project. Remember you must know the occupant load of your space or building to use the table. (See Chapter 3.) Likewise, the *UPC* has a similar Chapter 4, "Plumbing Fixtures

✎ Note

In 2007, Underwriters Laboratories (UL) introduced a new UL Plumbing Mark for plumbing fixtures. Products bearing this mark demonstrate compliance with the *IPC* and the *IBC*.

✎ Note

On projects that require minimal plumbing work, the mechanical contractor may be able to supply plumbing "shop" drawings instead of documentation within the construction drawings. In that case, separate mechanical engineering drawings may not be necessary.

✎ Note

If any discrepancies are found between the *ICC A117.1* and the *ADA Standards*, the most stringent requirements should be used.

and Fixture Fittings," that includes sections on each type of fixture, minimum number of required fixtures, requirements for specific occupancies and uses, and fixture requirements for persons with disabilities. Once you determine the number of required fixtures, you can begin to determine the number, size, and location of each toilet or bathing facility within your design.

When selecting materials and finishes for the toilet or bathing facilities, you may need to reference Chapter 12, "Interior Environment," of the *IBC*. This chapter includes a short section on the acceptable characteristics for materials used in toilet and bathing facilities. Examining the sections on the appropriate finish characteristics for plumbing fixtures can be particularly important if you are creating a sink or bathing element out of unusual materials or proposing nontypical materials for wet areas. Standard material and fixtures most likely have been designed to meet the code requirements. Fixtures sourced outside the US may also need to be reviewed.

If your project has specific sustainable goals (beyond what is required by the *IPC* or federal regulations.) you may have to do additional research in the appropriate energy code or sustainable rating system that is being used, such as LEED. (See Appendix A.)

If your project includes some challenging conditions or an approach inconsistent with the prescriptive codes, a performance-based solution may require looking in the *IPC* and potentially the *ICC Performance Code (ICCPC)* for performance based criteria. The *ICCPC* Chapter 12, "Plumbing," includes plumbing-related performance criteria. Sections in this chapter include personal hygiene, laundering, domestic water supplies, and wastewater. The *UPC*, by contrast, has some alternate materials and methods provisions within the code, but does not include a performance chapter. Instead, the performance chapter in other applicable NFPA codes should be referenced for related performance criteria.

Providing the appropriate number of accessible fixtures and specifying and locating plumbing fixtures correctly is critical to making the building or space usable by persons with disabilities. The scope (number or percentage of accessible fixtures or facilities) is defined in Chapter 11, "Accessibility," in the *IBC* (or Chapter 12 in the *NFPA 5000*) and in Chapter 2, "Scoping Requirements," of the ADA *2010 Standards* (or *ABA*, if a federal project). The technical requirements are then found in Chapter 6, "Plumbing Elements and Facilities," of the ADA *2010 Standards*, *ABA, or the ICC A117.1*. Reach ranges and maneuvering clearances as indicated in Chapter 3, "Building Blocks," in *ADA 2010 Standards* (or *ABA Standards*) and the *ICC A17.1* should be reviewed. Although there have been attempts to coordinate between these documents, differences can occur between the ADA/ABA technical requirements and the most current *ICC A117.1.* You may have to determine the most stringent requirement between the documents

While doing research, use the "Plumbing" section of the code documentation form provided with this book as a checklist to help you. The plumbing section will remind you what to research and the calculations that you need to do. You can document the types of existing fixtures and number and type of fixtures that need to be added.

The checklist will enabled you to note which type(s) of toilet facilities (single-user, family, assisted use, or multiple user) are required. You will be prompted to determine how many of those elements are required to be accessible, as well. A separate section under plumbing requirements is a checklist of the various fixtures and accessories that are included in a typical toilet and bathing facility to help you research and specify correctly.

Researching Mechanical Requirements

Although for most interior design projects the direct use of the mechanical codes by the designer or architect will be minimal, using your understanding of the components of the mechanical system and codes to collaborate with a mechanical engineer or mechanical contractor can be critical for a successful and efficient design. Many aspects of an interior project can affect the design of the mechanical system, such as the configuration of the space, types, and heights of ceilings; the selection of light fixtures; and the inclusion of other heat generating equipment. For the most economic or sustainable solutions, coordination at the preliminary design phase while still developing the plan layout, ceiling heights, and fixture selection can affect design decisions for the interior design and the mechanical system. In sensitive design areas, visual coordination of supply diffuser, return grill, and thermostat locations may be important as well.

Although the building codes, including the *IBC*, have a chapter on mechanical systems, they simply refer to the mechanical codes and other standards where most of the actual requirements are found. There are two main mechanical codes: the *International Mechanical Code* (*IMC*) published by the International Code Council (ICC) and the *Uniform Mechanical Code* (*UMC*), published by the International Association of Plumbing and Mechanical Officials (IAPMO) in partnership with the National Fire Protection Association. The *IMC* is the most widely used. In addition, Chapter 12, "Interior Environment," of the *IBC* includes mechanical-related sections including ventilation, temperature control, and sound transmission (often considered a sustainability concern.) The *IBC* also has a chapter titled "Energy Efficiency" that refers directly to the *IECC*.

The mechanical codes contain the requirements for the design, installation, and maintenance of heating, ventilation, cooling, and refrigeration systems. The mechanical codes include chapters on ventilation and exhaust systems, duct systems, chimneys and vents, boilers and water heaters, refrigeration, hydronic piping, and solar systems, among others. Numerous standards are referenced as well. These include those from the NFPA, ASME, ASTM, and the American Society of Heating, Refrigeration, and Air-Conditioning Engineers (ASHRAE).

Most commercial projects will have to comply with portions of the *IECC* and the *ASHRAE/IESNA 90.1* as part of the EPAct. Many jurisdictions require the use of the *IECC* as well. (In turn, the *IECC* references the *ASHRAE 90.1*.) The commercial and residential provision sections of the *IECC* include chapters on "Commercial Energy Efficiency" and "Existing Buildings." These chapters provide requirements for building mechanical systems and parameters of how the document applies to the different project scope within an existing building. (See the section titled "Energy Policy Act" in Chapter 1.)

In addition, the *IgCC* may need to be researched. In the *IgCC*, Chapter 6, "Energy Conservation, Efficiency and Atmospheric Quality," and Chapter 8, "Indoor Environmental Quality and Comfort" (including a section on HVAC systems, indoor air quality, sound transmission), address energy efficiency as well of other sustainability requirements for the HVAC system. *IgCC* gives provisions for the commissioning process which is an important part of the confirming and documenting energy and sustainable characteristics of a project. (See Chapter 11.) The *IgCC* also includes an appendix, "Sustainability Measures," which can be adopted as well.

In your project will require a mechanical system solution beyond the regulations of the *IMC*, it directs you to the mechanical chapter of the *ICC Performance Code* for the acceptable performance benchmarks. The *ICCPC* generally states that the installation of mechanical equipment must "safeguard maintenance personnel and building occupants from injury and deliver air at the appropriate temperature for health and comfort." This allows flexibility for the engineer if a building requires a more custom mechanical system design. Other performance requirements are given in the *ICCPC* for refrigeration and piped services. If using the *UMC*, the performance chapter in other NFPA codes would have to be referenced for performance criteria. The energy and sustainability codes have some performance-based criteria as well.

☑ Note

The ICC or NFPA fuel gas code and the fire code may apply to the mechanical scope of the project.

☑ Note

The controls used to adjust the mechanical system must be within accessible reach ranges if used by the general occupants.

MECHANICAL SYSTEMS

Mechanical systems include a variety of building systems that provide heat, ventilation, and air conditioning (cooling) to a building. Each system can be separate or combined into one system. The choice of each component and how it works customizes the system to meet the unique needs of the space or buildings. The factors that determine the right system include the size and use of the building, the number of occupants, the cost, and the maintenance. The three main types of mechanical systems are described here:

❑ **All-air systems.** This system uses centrally located fans to circulate hot and cold air to and from a space through long runs of ductwork. All-air systems are the most common mechanical systems in large buildings. They include the variable air volume system (VAV) and the constant air volume system (CAV). VAV systems manage the environmental temperature by providing conditioned air at a varying volume but at a constant temperature (separate temperatures for cooling or heating). VAV can be controlled by multiple thermostats. CAV provides a constant airflow at a varying temperature but it an only serve one zone and one thermostat.

❑ **All-water systems.** This system uses pipes to transport hot and cold water to and from each space where the air is locally circulated by a convector or fan to create the hot and cold air. All-water systems include fan-coil terminals, closed-loop heat pumps, and hydronic convectors (i.e., "chilled beams") These systems are typical in hospitals, motel, nursing homes, and other uses where a large number of controls for individual comfort are needed.

❑ **Air and water systems.** This is a combination system that uses a central fan to circulate fresh air to a space where it is heated or cooled by water before entering the space. The most common combination system is the air-water induction system.

Newer systems are continually being developed to meet the energy requirements in the codes and standards. One of these new systems combines heat and power. Also known as *cogeneration,* the system collects the heat generated from production of electricity and uses it to heat (or cool) the water or air for the HVAC system.

Most mechanical systems will require some type of ductwork to supply the air, registers to distribute the air, and/or grilles to retrieve the return air. Some buildings use a *duct system* for supply and return air. Other buildings use a *plenum system,* in which the open spaces above a suspended ceiling and/or enclosed vertical shafts are used to collect the return air. A raised floor system may also be used to create a floor plenum.

Very few accessibility issues affect mechanical code requirements. However, they do become important when locating devices, such as thermostats, are intended to be used by the occupants of the building. These accessibility-related items are mentioned in the sections that follow.

DOCUMENTATION

While doing research and throughout the design process, use the "Plumbing" and "Mechanical" sections of the digital code documentation form provided with this book to assist in the documentation of the research and coordination with the design engineer or contractor.

In the mechanical section, several questions will help you document the mechanical code issues that need to be coordinated on your project. You can document if a mechanical engineer is required on the project. It then lists the main mechanical items you should look for in an existing building or be aware of if a new building or space is being designed. You may also develop a schematic plan that indicates the location of rated walls and other assemblies so that the location of dampers and other items can be coordinated.

For most larger projects, a mechanical engineer will typically design and document most of the plumbing and mechanical requirements for a project; however, it is important to manage the integration of the interior design and engineering components. These forms will serve as a checklist for coordination among project team members and to confirm the appropriate systems, equipment, fixtures, and accessories are specified, detailed, and located properly throughout the design.

In many cases, meeting the requirements of the ADA will require additional details to indicate the appropriate clearances, location and mounting heights of plumbing fixtures, and plumbing and mechanical operating controls. Although some designers develop standard details, these should always be reviewed to make sure that they reflect the conditions of the actual project.

⬧ Note

Coordination of the mechanical and plumbing aspects of a project with the design team, including engineers, is important for the systems to work well and enhance the overall design.

CHAPTER 9

ELECTRICAL AND COMMUNICATION REQUIREMENTS

This chapter covers the codes, standards, and federal requirements for electrical systems and communication systems. When working on an interior project, knowledge of certain electrical codes and standards is necessary, especially when determining the types and location of outlets, fixtures, equipment, and appliances. To specify communication systems, you must also be familiar with their requirements. However, when a project involves substantial electrical work, an electrical engineer may be required to design the electrical system. Also, larger or complex communication systems may require an engineer or a special consultant. On smaller projects, such as changes to a tenant space, working with a licensed electrical contractor may be sufficient to address the electrical needs of the project.

The electrical codes pertain to the wiring of the electrical room/closets and the various types of cables, connections, and devices used to create the electrical systems in a space or building. The electrical codes also include information on types and locations of outlets, locations of light fixtures in wet areas, and other requirements specific to an interior project. The electrical codes apply to all types of occupancies and building types.

The electrical and communication requirements are discussed separately in this chapter. The first half of the chapter concentrates on electrical requirements. It begins with a discussion of the various codes and standards that affect electrical systems and then discusses the requirements for the various components of electrical systems. It also includes a section on sustainability, which highlights energy efficiency in relation to the codes and standards. The second half of the chapter discusses communication systems and how they are affected by the codes and standards.

✎ **Note**

There are several NFPA standards that address electrical systems including the *NFPA 70, National Electrical Code*, which is the most used electrical code in the United States. (See Figure 9.1.)

✎ **Note**

The NEC has requirements for the installation and removal of abandoned electrical and communication cables.

NFPA 70	National Electrical Code
NFPA 70A	National Electrical Code Requirements for One- and Two-Family Dwellings
NFPA 70B	Recommended Practice for Electrical Equipment Maintenance
NFPA 70E	Standard for Electrical Safety in the Workplace
NFPA 72	National Fire Alarm and Signaling Code
NFPA 75	Standard for the Protection of Information Technology Equipment
NFPA 76	Standard for the Fire Protection of Telecommunication Facilities
NFPA 77	Recommended Practice for Static Electricity
NFPA 110	Standard for Emergency and Standby Power Systems
NFPA 111	Standard on Stored Electrical Energy Emergency and Standby Power Systems
NFPA 262	Standard Method of Test for Flame Travel and Smoke of Wires and Cables for Use in Air-Handling Spaces
NFPA 269	Standard Test Method for Developing Toxic Potency Data for Use in Fire Hazard Modeling

Figure 9.1 Common NFPA standards for electrical and communication systems.

These systems include telephones, computers, security, background music, and audio/visual systems, among others. The sustainability of communication systems is discussed as well.

Throughout the chapter, accessibility-related requirements are also mentioned. These include relevant regulations in the Americans with Disabilities Act (ADA) standards and comparable *ICC A117.1* accessibility standard.

◂ Note

The electrical chapter of the *IBC* directly references the *NEC*.

ELECTRICAL COMPONENTS AND DEVICES

This section explains the various components and devices of an electrical system in relation to the codes and standards that apply to them. Components that make up the electrical system include the electrical panel and cabling, as well as the receptacles, switches, and other devices used by the occupants of the building. All parts and devices of an electrical system must be tested, approved for a specific use, and typically must be labeled. UL is the most common testing agency and recognized label. (See the inset titled "Testing Agencies and Certification" in Chapter 1.) Electrical equipment labels must indicate the voltage and branch use, for example, life safety, critical, or equipment specific. Light fixtures, as explained later, must also pass certain tests.

POWER AND ELECTRICAL SYSTEMS

A power system that provides electricity to buildings consists of three basic parts: the *generation* source, the *transmission* system, and the *distribution* system. In the United States, the common generation sources are hydroelectric power, nuclear, and fossil fuels. Interest in green power may lead to sun and wind power to be included in the future. The *transmission* (or *distribution*) system consists of high-voltage lines stretching hundreds of miles, which deliver power from the generation source to the local utility provider's substation. The *distribution* system then delivers power from the local distributor to the end user. Typically, the local utility delivers power to the end user in a voltage that is much higher than the end user can use. Thus, a transformer is used to step the voltage down to the desired voltage before entering the building. These can be pole mounted or pad mounted outside the building. The utility distribution system ends at the point of delivery to the building, referred to as a *service connection*. At this point, an electric meter measures the power consumption of the building.

The *premises wiring system* is the electrical system within the building. For smaller buildings, premises wiring begins where the utility service connection is made and extends to the building's main electrical panel and to the outlets used throughout the building for fixtures, appliances, and equipment. In larger buildings, where the utility company provides higher voltages, additional interior transformers may be used before or after the electricity reaches the panelboard. This panelboard is typically contained in an electrical room and may consist of a main disconnect switch, secondary switches, fuses, and circuit breakers. Sustainable buildings using renewable on-site energy may have additional electrical equipment.

Cables and wires run from this electrical panel to various locations throughout a building. In smaller buildings, these cables or branch circuits are directly connected to the electrical outlets. In larger buildings, feeder conductors are used to distribute the electricity horizontally and vertically to several smaller panelboards. These panelboards supply electricity to separate areas within the building. Branch circuits are then used to connect the smaller panelboards to the various electrical outlets.

The *National Electrical Code* regulates the design of the electrical system including the components, space needs, location of rated walls, and other aspects of the electrical system within a building.

Electrical Panels and Rooms

There are three typical categories of electrical panels in a building. The first and largest is the *service entrance*. The service entrance can be considered a switchboard or a panelboard depending on how much electrical service is being distributed from the utility service connection to the rest of the building. (This is measured in amperage.) Switchboards typically are used for larger service loads. As a rule, switchboards are two-sided and panelboards are one-sided. Switchboards are typically freestanding and panelboards are typically wall mounted. If a unit is the initial connection point of the electrical service from the utility company to the building, it is considered the service entrance whether it is classified by the code as a switchboard or a panelboard.

The *NEC* regulates the size of the room that contains a panel based on the equipment used in the room. For example, one of the most typical requirements is that there must be a clear working space at least 3 feet (914 mm) deep by 30 inches (762 mm) wide in front of the panel and clear space above the panel. (Larger panels or panels with higher voltages may require more clearance.) For a switchboard, the code requires enough working space on both sides of equipment. Other equipment in the room, including transformers, may require clearances as well. (See the inset titled "Power and Electrical Systems" earlier in this chapter.) Depending on the size of the room and the equipment in it, the room may be required to be fire rated. (See Chapter 6.) Also, depending on the size of the room and/or equipment, the door(s) must meet certain egress requirements for location, number of exits, direction of swing, and hardware used. The service entrance room must also be ventilated (see Chapter 8) to control heat buildup from the equipment. If the room is located on an outside wall, ventilation can be done directly to the outside. If not, ducts and fans must be used to provide outside air ventilation. Permanent signage indicating to maintain the required working spaces clear is required to be posted.

Once the electrical service is brought into the building, it is distributed by another series of panelboards to each floor and/or tenant or dwelling space throughout the building. (In very large buildings with high levels of electrical loads, these panels could be considered switchboards as well.) These panelboards are typically one-sided and are housed in smaller electrical rooms or in cabinets that are placed in or against a wall. In multistory buildings, the electrical rooms should be stacked directly above each other on each floor so that the electrical systems can be vertically distributed. Each floor may also have one or more smaller *branch panelboards* that supply electricity to a particular area or tenant. Typically, rooms that contain only panelboards do not have to be rated.

These requirements are important to consider, especially when creating a layout for a new building or space within a building in which one or more electrical rooms must be located. Work closely with an engineer to make sure that the rooms are located to optimize the efficiency of

☛ Note

There is often a conflict between sprinklers required in an electrical equipment room and/ or a communication room and the safety of the equipment with regard to water damage. Although *NFPA 13* allows sprinklers to be eliminated if certain requirements are met, a dry sprinkler system or an alternate extinguishing system may also have to be considered. (See Chapter 6.)

distribution and that the room sizes allow electrical panels and other equipment to have the correct clearances. In addition, these rooms typically require a visible sign clearly stating *Electrical Room* or similar approved wording.

Electrical Cabling and Conduit

To distribute electricity to all areas where it is needed, electrical wiring must pass through many building elements. When electrical wiring is installed, the diameter of any hole created for the passage of the cable cannot be more than ⅛ inch (3 mm) larger than the diameter of the cable, conduit, or other device passing through the hole. When these wires pass through a rated floor, ceiling, or wall assembly, the building codes require the use of a rated fire-stop and/or smoke stop. (See Chapter 6 for more information.)

In some cases, an electrical cable may be allowed to run on its own; in other instances, the codes will require the use of a protected enclosure such as a conduit or raceway. This typically depends on the type of cable and the construction type of the building (see Chapter 4), but it can also depend on the location of the cable within a building. For example, if a cable is run within a rated assembly, it typically must be within a conduit. Certain jurisdictions have special requirements or restrictions as well. Various cables, conduits, and raceways are explained next.

Cabling

The *NEC* specifies the types of electrical wiring or cables that can be used. Many different types of cables are available, and each cable must go through testing to be classified for its specific use. A variety of testing standards are used to determine performance and safety. Other tests are used to evaluate the flammability of the cable and determine its flame spread and smoke density (similar to the Steiner Tunnel Test described in Chapter 10). Because the protective sleeve of the cable can be highly toxic when exposed to a fire, certain cables must also undergo a toxicity test. (See the section titled "Toxicity Test" in Chapter 10.) Once tested, the cable is labeled with its appropriate classification.

The types of electrical cables used on a project are typically specified by the electrical engineer or contractor according to the requirements of the *NEC*. Although noncombustible cable is required in many occupancies, certain areas within a building may require other types of cables. For example, special rules apply for wiring in ducts, plenums, and other air-handling spaces, as well as shafts used for elevators, to limit the use of

---

✎ Note

If a cable is run continuously from the electrical panel to the device, without any intermediate connections, it is considered *a home run*.

✎ Note

Plenum spaces created by suspended ceilings or access (i.e., raised) floor systems require the use of specially rated electrical and low-voltage plenum cables.

materials that would contribute smoke and harmful products of combustion during a fire. The most common types of cables are listed here:

❑ **Romex.** Romex is a trade name that is commonly used to refer to *nonmetallic-sheathed cable* (Type NM, NMC, or NMS). It consists of two or more insulated conductors and should include a ground wire surrounded by a moisture-resistant plastic material. The *NEC* limits use of this cable mostly to Residential one- and two-family dwellings and multi-unit dwellings not exceeding three floors.

❑ **Armored cable.** Armored cable (Type AC), sometimes referred to as *BX* or *flex cable,* is a flexible cable that consists of two or more conductors wrapped in heavy paper or plastic and encased in a continuous spiral-wound metal jacket. It is commonly used in commercial applications. In new installations, the *NEC* requires AC to be secured in intervals, but in older installations the cable might have just been fished through walls, floors, and ceilings. In addition, AC is often used to connect light fixtures in suspended ceiling grids to allow relocation flexibility. In most instances, the *NEC* limits the length of an unsecured flex cable to 6 feet (1.8 m); however, other jurisdictions may be stricter. This cable type is not allowed in damp or wet locations, where it might be subject to physical damage or exposed to other corrosive conditions.

❑ **Metal-clad cable.** Metal-clad cable (Type MC) is often used when BX cable is restricted. It looks similar to BX cable, but MC cable has an additional green ground wire that provides extra grounding. As a result, it can be used in more applications than BX cable.

❑ **Flat wire.** Flat wire is the common name for *flat conductor cable* (Type FCC). It is a small cable in a flat housing that allows it to be used under carpet tiles without protruding. (The *NEC* specifies that carpet tiles covering flat wire cannot be larger than 36 inches [914 mm] square.) Flat wire can be used in many applications, and it is often used to rework obsolete wiring systems in existing buildings. The *NEC* prohibits the use of flat wire in wet and hazardous areas and in residential, hospital, and school buildings.

❑ **Fiber optic cable.** In the past, fiber optic cable was used mostly in low-voltage applications. However, it can also be used as a conductor for electrical components such as lighting. A fiber optic cable contains one or several hundred very thin strands of glass or plastics that carry light. In addition, an optical fiber can be run in a cable that

◄ Note

Some jurisdictions restrict the use of AC (flex) cable in buildings even if the *NEC* allows it.

contains an electrical wire. When this occurs, it is called a *composite cable* and is classified as an electrical cable based on the type of electrical conductor or wire used with it. (More information on fiber optic and composite cables can be found in the section titled "Low-Voltage Cabling" later in this chapter and in Figure 9.9.)

Conduit

Another option often used when wiring large residential and most commercial buildings is conduit. Also known as *tubing* in the *NEC, conduit* is hollow piping used to house and protect conductors or cables. More than one wire or cable can be fished through the conduit; however, the code may limit the types of cables that can be used together. For example, electrical cables often are not allowed to be used in the same conduit as communication cables. The conduit may also act as a system ground (see the section titled "Grounding and Circuit Interrupters" later in this chapter) and may protect surrounding building materials should a wire overheat.

There are several different types of conduit, including rigid and flexible metal conduit and rigid and flexible nonmetallic conduit. (Nonmetallic conduit can be made of plastic, PVC, resin, or fiberglass.) Conduits can also be referred to as *conduit bodies*. This term is used to describe larger raceways that have removable covers for access to the wires inside them. (See the following section titled "Raceways and Cable Trays.") The type of conduit required depends on where it will be used and the types of hazards present. For example, nonmetallic conduit is often used underground to bring the power into a building; however, its use inside a building is usually restricted, especially in fire-rated assemblies. Instead, rigid and flexible metal conduits are most often used in a building interior. The *NEC* allows rigid metal conduit in all occupancies and in almost any condition. Flexible metal conduit has some limitations. For example, it cannot be used in certain hazardous areas, and its length may be limited.

Other code requirements apply more to the installation of the conduit. This includes requirements for the diameter of the conduit allowed, as well as the types of connections and the number of bends allowed in each run. In addition, the building codes will require a fire-stop or smoke stop (see Chapter 6) when conduit is installed through a rated wall or ceiling assembly. This is shown as sealant in Figure 9.2. Additional restrictions might be enforced on a local level by a code jurisdiction.

☑ Note

Empty flexible metal conduit is also known as *green field*.

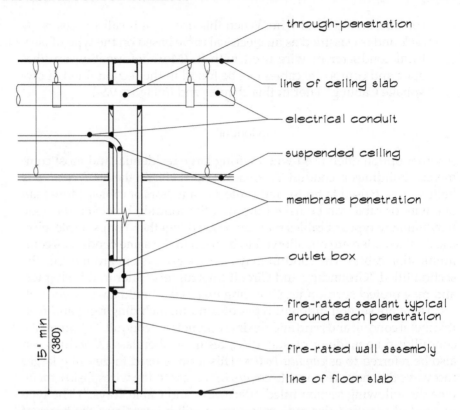

Figure 9.2 Electrical penetrations in a fire resistance–rated wall assembly.

Raceways and Cable Trays

Similar to conduits, *raceways* (or *wireways*) can also be used to house and protect electrical cables. Raceways may be used in place of a conduit or in conjunction with other conduits. For example, some types of buildings are constructed with concrete or metal floor raceways that are part of the structural floor system. Often referred to as *cells*, these raceways come in different shapes and sizes and are often laid out in a grid-type system, allowing cables to be run from one area of a building to another. The *NEC* may limit their use in some applications, but most of the code requirements affect the cable connections within the raceways. Raceways allow for flexibility so as the building occupants' needs change, the cabling can be changed and redirected. Other underfloor raceways may be added after the initial construction of a building as part of the finished floor assembly (e.g., a raised floor system).

Raceways may also be mounted on walls for easy access. For example, wireways that are enclosed with removable covers can be installed

☑ **Note**

Cable trays are an effective way to distribute cables in existing or historic buildings, especially in areas where the existing structure cannot be disturbed.

around the perimeter of a factory to allow access to the cables as equipment locations change. Openings (e.g., knockouts) in the wireways allow the cabling to be directed to different locations when needed. Other types of raceways can be used to cover a cable run on the surface of the wall. (Certain codes may restrict the use of raceways when used with fire-rated assemblies.)

A cable tray is another method of routing a large amount of wiring or cabling in a space. A cable tray is rigid support system used to run open wiring and cables and sometimes raceways. Historically, *cable trays* have been used in industrial building types, but now they are also commonly used in commercial occupancies with high communication or electrical requirements such as airports, banks, call centers, and health care facilities. They can be located exposed in an open ceiling or above a suspended ceiling. Types of cable trays allowed by the *NEC* include ladder, ventilated trough, ventilated channel, and solid bottom. They can be made of metallic or nonmetallic materials. The *NEC* specifies the width of the tray based on the number of cables, the allowed locations, and the type of cables allowed in the tray, among other things. Raceways and cable trays allow greater flexibility for the maintenance and modifications to the wiring or cabling in a space or building.

Circuitry

The distribution of electricity is managed and organized by creating different circuits. Separate circuits are created by wiring (or cable) that branches from the main electrical source to different areas of the building or space. Each circuit feeds electricity to a series of light fixtures, outlets, equipment, and/or appliances before it returns to the branch panel or power panelboard. Each circuit may be carrying a different voltage and amperage of power. For example, a washing machine will require a 220-volt circuit, which must be separate from the 120-volt circuit required general lighting.

The *NEC* limits the amperage that is allowed on a single circuit. Therefore, it is important to supply the electrical engineer with the correct number and types of lighting, equipment, and appliances that will be used in a space or building so that the circuitry can be designed correctly. The engineer uses the specifications of the items to determine the electrical loads of the space and how many circuits are needed to be within the code requirements. This will affect the number of light fixtures that can be switched together and the number of fixtures that can be controlled by dimmers. In addition, certain pieces of equipment that require more power may need a circuit that serves only a single outlet. This is called a

✇ Note

If an outlet has sensitive power requirements, a dedicated circuit can be specified so that it will be wired separately. This will prevent electrical disturbances from other nearby electrical equipment.

dedicated circuit. The outlet that it serves is referred to as a *dedicated outlet*. For example, dedicated circuits are often used for large equipment such as copiers and for many appliances such as refrigerators, electric ranges, and clothes dryers. Most mechanical equipment and the main equipment for many communication systems will require a dedicated outlet as well.

Electrical Boxes

There are three main types of electrical boxes: outlet boxes, switch boxes, and junction boxes. Unlike electrical conduit, which often penetrates the entire wall or ceiling assembly, electrical boxes usually penetrate only the outer membrane of the wall, as shown in Figure 9.2. (See Chapter 5 for more information on membrane penetrations.)

When electrical boxes are located in fire resistance–rated walls, floors, or floor/ceiling assemblies, the building codes set additional requirements, as noted in the following list. (If an electrical box is located in a smoke assembly, additional requirements must be met.)

❑ **Type.** The box must be metal. If not, it must be tested for use in fire resistance–rated assemblies. In addition, one box typically cannot exceed 16 square inches (0.0103 sm).

❑ **Quantity.** The total number of boxes in one wall or ceiling is limited. The total number of openings in a rated wall or ceiling surface measuring 100 square feet (9.29 sm) cannot exceed 100 square inches (0.0645 sm).

❑ **Location.** When boxes are used on opposite sides of the same wall, the boxes must be separated horizontally by 24 inches (610 mm) unless the boxes are listed for closer spacing or have some type of barrier or fireblocking between them. (See the section titled "Fireblocks and Draft Stops" in Chapter 6.)

❑ **Fire-stopping.** Fire-rated caulking or other type of fire-stop (or smoke stop) must be used around the box where it penetrates the membrane to seal the space between the box and the wall. (See Figure 9.2 and the section titled "Fire-Stops and Smoke Stops" in Chapter 6.)

This will apply to any type of electrical box (or communication box) that penetrates a rated assembly or membrane and might affect the design of a room or space. For example, if a break room is adjacent to a fire-rated wall, it may be best not to locate the counter with all its required electrical appliances along that wall, due to the number of outlets required. Also, be aware of accessibility requirements as they apply to electrical outlets.

◄ Note

If an existing electrical box is not being used, it must either (1) have a cover plate or (2) be totally removed (including the box and all wiring) and the wall opening properly patched.

◄ Note

Because the installation of electrical boxes creates a membrane penetration rather than a through penetration, as described in Chapter 5, fire-stopping is not always required.

Similar requirements are given in the *ADA Standards* and the *ICC A117.1* standard. The *NEC* and accessibility requirements are described here for each type of box. Issues related to energy efficiency are covered as well.

Outlet Boxes

Outlet boxes can be wall and/or floor mounted for electrical receptacles or wall and/or ceiling mounted for light fixtures. If the box allows the connection of a plug-in appliance or equipment, it is typically called a *receptacle outlet*. When used for a light fixture, the box is often referred to as a *fixture outlet* or a *lighting outlet*. Most outlet boxes are either 2 × 4 inches (50 × 100 mm), such as those used for duplex receptacle outlets or wall sconces, or 4 × 4 inches (100 × 100 mm) for a quadraplex receptacle outlet and certain ceiling fixture outlets. However, other sizes and different depths are available and will depend on the type or number of devices wired to the one box. For example, boxes used for hanging light fixtures are often octagonal.

> **◀ Note**
>
> A *pull box* is another type of electrical box that is used during installation as an intermediate box for pulling through long runs of cable.

Outlet boxes are usually mounted within a wall by fastening the box to a stud. For example, in a metal stud and gypsum board wall, the outlet box is mounted to the metal stud and a hole is cut around the gypsum board to allow access to the box. (Surface-mounted boxes are more common on masonry walls.) In the ceiling, the box can be mounted to a joist or directly to the underside of the ceiling slab. The *NEC* specifies that the opening in the wall or ceiling cannot exceed a ⅛-inch (3.1-mm) clearance between the box and the gypsum board. In a rated wall, this gap must be sealed to create a fire-stop or smoke stop. (See the section titled "Light Fixtures" later in this chapter for additional box requirements.)

Because the needs of residences are somewhat consistent, the codes provide more specific outlet requirements for Residential occupancies such as homes, apartments, dormitories, and even certain guest rooms in hotels. (They may also include some Institutional building types. See the inset titled "Rooms and Spaces" in Chapter 3.) If a building or space is considered a dwelling unit, the *NEC* specifies the minimum number of electrical boxes to be provided. In each room of the dwelling unit, receptacle outlet boxes must be installed so that no point measured horizontally along the floor line at any wall space is more than 6 feet (1.8 m) from an outlet. (A *wall space* is generally defined as any fixed wall that is at least 2 feet [600 mm] wide.) An example of how to place the outlets is shown in Figure 9.3. Hallways that connect the rooms within the dwelling unit and are more than 10 feet (3 m) in length also require at least one receptacle outlet. (This does not apply to common hallways or corridors that connect multiple dwelling units to each other.) Of course, more outlets can always be added based on the needs of the space, but the

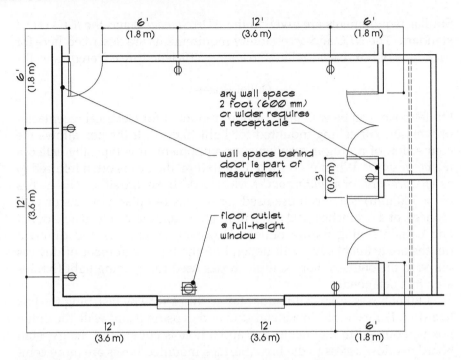

Figure 9.3 Dwelling unit receptacle outlet location example.

minimums must be met. In addition, the *NEC* and the *International Residential Code* require specific location of outlets in bathrooms, kitchens, laundry areas, basements, and garages.

The *NEC* also provides for special types of outlets in dwelling units in certain locations to protect against shock. This includes ground and circuit interrupters and tamper-resistant outlets. (See the section titled "Grounding and Circuit Interrupters" later in this chapter.) Tamper-resistant outlets require pressure on two or more of the prongs to open the outlet. This prevents someone (especially a child) from accidently sticking an object in one side and contacting the electrical current. First introduced in 2008 NEC, the requirements have expanded. As of 2017, all 15- and 20-ampere and 125 V and 250 V receptacle outlets in dwelling units including dormitories are required to be tamper resistant. Commercial uses that are now required to have tamper-resistant outlets include guest rooms and guest suites in lodging facilities (hotels, motels, etc.), child care facilities, preschool and education facilities (all areas), offices, corridors and waiting rooms within medical clinics and outpatient facilities, transportation stations, gymnasiums, skating rinks, and auditoriums, dormitories, and assisted living facilities. There are some exceptions if the outlet is located more than 5½ feet (1.676 m) above the floor, is part of a luminaire or appliance, or is located within dedicated space for an appliance that in normal use is not moved.

Because the needs and requirements in non-Residential facilities vary with the activities and equipment needs of a particular tenant or user, the codes do not set as many specific requirements as for dwelling units. The *NEC* does not typically specify number or locations of receptacle or lighting outlet boxes in these occupancies. Instead, their placement is determined by specific equipment requirements and convenience considerations. For example, the location of a copier or fax machine will determine the location of the receptacle; the typical length of a cord on a vacuum cleaner may be a good guideline for placement of receptacle outlets within a long corridor. However, starting in 2017, *NEC* specifies locations for outlets for meeting rooms. Outlets are required on the perimeter walls and within the room in the floor based on the size of the room. These are to accommodate the growing use of projectors and laptops by presenters and meeting attendees. There are also some building types, however, that will require special types of receptacle outlets; an example is hospital-grade receptacles at certain patient bed locations.

Certain outlet boxes are required to be accessible. This will depend on the location and use of the outlet, the type of equipment connected to it, and whether it is meant for use by employees and/or visitors. For example, an outlet in a janitor's closet or an outlet behind a permanent copier would not be required to be accessible. However, consider the possibility that the employee who will use the outlet will be disabled and need the outlet within the accessible reach ranges. Other outlets that are meant to be used by clients, visitors, or the general public should be accessible, such as an outlet meant for plugging in a laptop computer. (Certain locations may need to be reviewed with the building owner.) However, when specifying the typical location of wall outlets in a project, it is a good idea to use a height that meets accessibility requirements whenever possible. Should the function of a room or space change in the future, the outlets will already be accessible.

When the outlet box is mounted on a wall, it must be located within the accessibility reach ranges. It must be located at least 15 inches (380 mm) above the floor, as shown in Figures 9.2 and 9.4. In addition, when designing accessible work areas, such as study carrels in public libraries and workstations in offices, outlets must be located within the reach ranges allowed over objects that vary between 44 inches (1120 mm) and 48 inches (1220 mm) depending on the depth of the counter or surface. Whenever possible, locate the outlets directly above the work surface or counter. For example, many workstation panel systems now come

---

☑ Note

In Residential occupancies, when a wall is broken by a doorway, fireplace, or similar opening, each continuous wall space of 2 feet (600 mm) or more must be considered separately for the placement of a receptacle outlet.

☑ Note

For the placement of receptacle outlets, the *NEC* includes additional requirements specific to guest rooms, guest suites, dormitories, and similar spaces, which provide additional safety as well as convenience to the users.

☑ Note

The *NEC* includes requirements for freestanding panel systems or workstations. For example, when electrically connected, a panel run cannot exceed 30 feet (9.0 m), the power supply cannot be longer than 2 feet (600 mm), and the receptacle outlets must be on a separate circuit serving only the panels.

with electrical raceways at counter height rather than the traditional floor location. A special outlet could also be mounted toward the front edge under the work surface. (Floor outlets are not typically considered accessible, but if they are used, they should not be located within the clear floor space necessary at an accessible counter, table, or desk.)

Switch Boxes

Switch boxes are typically wall mounted and control the lighting (or fixture) outlet. The electrical connection between the light fixture and the switch device or control is made at the switch box. This control can be in the form of a toggle, dimmer, sensor, or remote. Many of the code requirements for switch boxes are similar to those for outlet boxes. For example, the switch box must be mounted to a stud or other blocking and the hole cut for the box cannot be larger than inch (3.1 mm) around the box.

The *NEC* has requirements specifically for dwelling units. The main requirement is that each habitable room, as well as hallways and stairs that lead up to these rooms, must have a switch outlet that controls the lighting in that room. In addition, a stairway must typically have lighting that is controlled at the top and bottom of the stair. The energy codes and standards impose additional requirements. For example, the *IECC* requires that sleeping units, such as hotel rooms, have at least one master switch at the room entrance that controls all light fixtures in the space (except the bathroom).

In occupancies and building types that do not include dwelling units, the *NEC* does not specify the frequency of switch outlets. It allows multiple switches to be ganged together and conveniently located in larger open areas. However, the energy codes and standards require at least one "manual control" (i.e., switch) for each area or room of a commercial building. (This does not include means of egress components.) These same areas must also typically include *dual switching*. Also known as *bi-level* or *split switching*, dual switching means that the light fixtures in a space are evenly distributed to two adjacent switches, allowing an occupant to use one of the switches to uniformly reduce the level of illumination by 50 percent. Typically required by the *IECC*, exceptions include sleeping units, storerooms, restrooms, and public lobbies. (Sleeping units have separate requirements.)

When multiple fixtures are ganged together, the *NEC* limits the number of light fixtures that can be circuited to one switch. This number is based on the wattage of the fixtures used. The total wattage is determined by the electrical engineer based on the cut sheets of the selected light fixtures and equipment. (See the section titled "Circuitry" earlier in this chapter.)

◪ Note

Receptacle and switch outlets located in bathrooms cannot be installed above bathtubs or within shower stalls. They can be installed adjacent to the plumbing fixtures. (Indoor spas and hot tubs have additional requirements.)

◪ Note

The energy codes and standards require automatic lighting shut-off devices in certain buildings. These types of systems must be coordinated with the light switches.

◪ Note

Lighting control technology can help meet code switching requirements. Examples include connecting to a building automation system (BAS) or using a wireless or digital addressable lighting interface (DALI) control system.

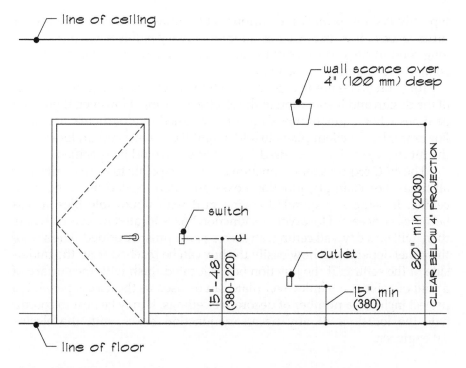

Figure 9.4 Typical accessible electrical device and fixture locations.

Switch boxes must be located within the accessible reaching height above the floor. They must be between 15 and 48 inches (380 and 1220 mm) above the floor, as shown in Figure 9.4, measured to the centerline of the box. If used by occupants, these controls need to be usable by someone with a disability—for example, a toggle switch. Switches that are not required to be accessible are those in areas used only by service or maintenance personnel, such as janitor closets and mechanical rooms. If there are multiple switches to the same fixture, not all of them are required to be accessible.

Junction Boxes

Unlike the other electrical boxes already explained, a junction box is not used to connect an outlet or fixture. Instead, it is used to tie (or splice) several wires together. For example, a main cable run that leaves the electrical panel will, at some point, have to branch off to electrify several light fixtures. At the point where these wires come together, a junction box is

☑ Note

Electrical junction boxes must be easily accessible, whether they are located in the floor, wall, or ceiling.

typically used to protect the various cable connections and to allow for future access. It is also used as an intermediary *pull box* when there are long conduit runs. The size of the box used will depend on the number of connections that have to be made.

Junction boxes are usually specified by an electrical engineer as part of the design and installation of the electrical wiring. However, there may be times when a junction box must be specified in a particular location. For example, if a client plans to add a light fixture in a certain location in the future, a junction box wired for future use would be specified.

The *NEC* requires that a junction box be accessible to the electrician at all times. For example, junction boxes are often located on or near the ceiling. If using a suspended ceiling grid with removable tiles, access becomes very easy. However, if a junction box is located in an area where there will be a drywall ceiling, an access panel must be added. The size of the panel depends on how easily the box can be reached from the underside of the ceiling. If the junction box is located flush with the surface of a wall or ceiling, a blank cover plate can be used as the access panel. If a project includes a number of decorative ceilings, it may be best to coordinate the locations of any necessary junction boxes with the electrical engineer.

GROUNDING AND CIRCUIT INTERRUPTERS

The electrical code requires that all electrical systems be *grounded*. This is accomplished by a third wire that typically accompanies an electrical cable. In general, this ground wire redirects live currents back to the source or to the earth to prevent a person from getting shocked when there is a short circuit. Because a grounding wire is not always 100 percent effective, in certain cases additional measures must be taken to protect the electrical outlet and the person using it. The *NEC* requires two types of *circuit interrupters*, depending on the location of a receptacle outlet. Both are described in this section.

Ground Fault Circuit Interrupters

The presence of water makes it easier for an electrical current to flow. If the circuit or outlet is wet, or if the person touching the outlet or adjacent appliance is wet or standing in water, there is a much higher chance of getting shocked despite the fact that the circuit is already grounded. As a result, the *NEC* requires special grounded circuits in rooms where water will be present.

These circuits are called *ground fault circuit interrupters,* also commonly known as *GFCI* (or sometimes *GFI*). The GFCI is a device that is able to detect small current leaks. If a current leak occurs, the GFCI disconnects the power to the circuit or appliance and thus prevents an electrical shock from occurring. The GFCI can be installed in the electrical panel as part of a circuit breaker, or it can be installed as a special type of receptacle at the electrical outlet.

The *NEC* requires that exterior receptacle outlets be GFCIs. On interior projects, typically all standard 125-volt, 15-amp, and 20-amp receptacle outlets located in areas where there is water should be specified as GFCIs. These areas include restrooms, bathrooms, kitchens, break rooms, bar areas, laundry rooms, and even pools or spas. The *NEC* divides these requirements into those for dwelling units (including guest rooms and dorm rooms with provisions for cooking) and those for more commercial applications. (See the inset titled "Rooms and Spaces" in Chapter 3.) Some of the more common *NEC* requirements for GFCIs in building interiors include the following:

❑ **Bathrooms in dwelling units.** The *NEC* requires a receptacle outlet to be located within 3 feet (900 mm) of each bathroom lavatory used in a dwelling unit such as private homes, assisted living facilities, apartments, and hotels. These outlets, as well as any other outlet in a dwelling unit bathroom, must be GFCI-protected. An example of a hotel bathroom with a GFCI outlet is shown in Plan A of Figure 9.5.

❑ **Kitchens in dwelling units,** All receptacle outlets that serve the countertop of a kitchen in a dwelling unit, no matter where the sink is located, must be GFCI-protected. This includes outlets in the walls above the counter, outlets in the side of a base cabinet, and outlets required at island and peninsular counters. It does not include standard-height wall outlets (e.g., 15 inches [380 mm] above the floor) adjacent to the counter or outlets installed for built-in appliances such as a garbage disposal, refrigerator, or range. However, the 2014 *NEC* requires a GFCI outlet for the dishwasher.

❑ **Laundry, utility, and wet bar sinks in dwelling units.** Any receptacle outlet within 6 feet (1.8 m) of the edge of a utility or wet bar sink or other water source located in a dwelling unit must be a GFCI-protected outlet. This is measured by the shortest distance, as shown in Plan B of Figure 9.5, not by the distance along the wall line. It affects all general outlets as well as those required for appliances. Typically, other outlets outside the 6-foot (1.8-m) perimeter of the sink are not required to be GFCIs. However, the 2014 *NEC* requires all outlets in a laundry room to be GFCIs.

⬥ Note

A GFCI outlet is not typically required at water coolers unless the water cooler is located in an area where GFCIs are already required.

⬥ Note

According to the *NEC,* when measuring the 6 feet (1.8-m) distance for location of GFCI, the measurement is taken as the shortest path a flexible cord would follow without piercing a wall, door, window, or similar object.

⬥ Note

Vending machines that dispense a product or merchandise and electrically powered drinking fountains have to be GFCI-protected. Water cooler dispensers do not.

❑ **Public and/or employee restrooms.** All receptacle outlets provided in public and/or employee restrooms found in non-dwelling building types must be GFCI-protected. This includes any outlet near the lavatory as well as any other outlet in the room. Examples include restrooms in commercial buildings, airports, and industrial facilities.

❑ **Commercial and institutional kitchens.** All receptacle outlets located in commercial and institutional kitchens used for food preparation and cooking (e.g., space that includes permanent cooking appliances) must be GFCI-protected. The GFCI requirement covers all receptacle outlets in the room or space, not just those that serve the countertop. Examples include kitchens in restaurants, hotels, schools, churches, and similar facilities.

❑ **Other food prep areas.** Kitchen or areas with a sink where food preparation or cooking occurs also must provide GFCI-protected outlets. This would include coffee shops, convenience stores, ice cream shops, and similar areas where food is offered. (This does not include a break room or kitchenette that includes only a plug-in microwave and/or coffee maker if no sink is provided.)

❑ **Sinks in other occupancies.** Receptacle outlets within 6 feet (1.8 m) of the edge of any sink in a non-dwelling situation must be GFCI-protected. (See Plan B of Figure 9.5.) Therefore, the typical break room or kitchenette (without permanent cooking appliances) now requires GFCIs in certain locations. This also applies to sinks in janitor closets, exam rooms, classrooms, and the like. (There are some exceptions for sinks in industrial laboratories facilities.)

❑ **Indoor wet locations in commercial facilities.** Wet areas such as car washes, food processing areas, and similar locations are required to provide the same protection as for similar outdoor locations. Also, areas adjacent to showers in commercial facilities such as locker rooms must provide GFCIs because of the proximity to water, potential wet travel path, and the use of electrical devices in the locker areas.

❑ **Garages.** The NEC requires electrical outlets in commercial and residential garages. To protect against wet conditions and the use of equipment, GFCI outlets are required.

❑ **Locations for reset buttons for GFCIs.** Once the GFCI is tripped, it must be reset for the outlet to work. The NEC requires that the reset button be easily located to make resetting possible. In addition, the codes also require that GFCIs be tested on a monthly basis, so it is important for the reset location be easily accessed to encourage testing. An example is outlets in soffits for holiday lighting.

✓ Note

Electrical outlets in kitchenettes and break rooms without permanent cooking appliances (e.g., stove or oven) are not required to be GFCI-protected; however, if the outlet is located within 6 feet (1.8 m) of the edge of a sink it must be GFCI-protected.

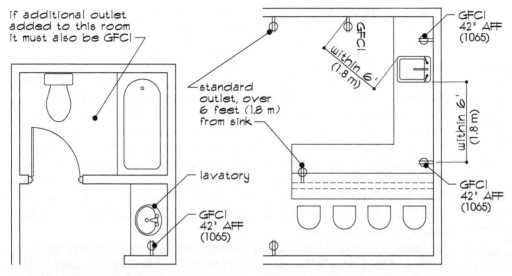

if additional outlet
added to this room
it must also be GFCI

standard
outlet, over
6 feet (1.8 m)
from sink

lavatory

GFCI
42" AFF
(1065)

GFCI
within 6'
(1.8 m)

GFCI
42" AFF
(1065)

within 6'
(1.8 m)

GFCI
42" AFF
(1065)

PLAN A - Dwelling Unit Lavatory

PLAN B - Dwelling Unit Wet Bar

Figure 9.5 Required GFCI outlet location examples.

Additional GFCIs may be required by the *NEC* or by a jurisdiction in certain building types. For example, additional GFCI outlets are required by the *NEC* in certain health care occupancies, and other GFCI requirements apply to hot tubs, Jacuzzis, pools, and so forth.

Arc Fault Circuit Interrupters

Sometimes an electrical wire will discharge an unexpected electrical current across the insulation meant to protect it, causing what is known as an *arc fault*. There are several reasons this can happen, but it is usually due to a defect in the cable that shows up after extended use or as a result of unseen damage during installation or renovation. An arc fault gets very hot. When it occurs, it creates pressure that will spread hot gases and molten metal to surrounding areas. It has the potential to ignite surrounding combustibles, such as wall insulation, and start a fire. As a safety precaution, the *NEC* requires protection of certain outlets and circuits.

☑ Note

Fire alarm systems should not be connected to GFCI or AFCI circuits. Single- or multiple-station smoke alarms that are not connected to a fire alarm system (with a control panel) should be connected to AFCI circuits.

☑ Note

Starting with the 2008 edition, the *NEC* continues to expand the use of AFCI protection in a dwelling unit beyond the sleeping room to cover most areas living areas. In 2017, the use was also expanded in commercial buildings.

Since 1999, the *NEC* has required the use of *arc fault circuit interrupters*, or *AFCIs*, in dwelling units. At first, they were only required in the sleeping rooms of a dwelling unit, residential home, or apartment building, and other building types such as hotels and nursing homes that are classified as dwelling units or are considered guest rooms or suites. (See the inset titled "Rooms and Spaces" in Chapter 3.) Between the 2014 and 2020 editions of the *NEC*, the requirement has expanded to include most areas in a dwelling unit, similar use rooms in dormitories, guestrooms and suites of hotels and motels and patient sleeping rooms in nursing homes and limited-care facilities. AFCIs are tested using the standard *UL 1699, Standard for Arc-Fault Circuit Interrupters*. This standard recognizes five types of AFCIs: branch/feeder, combination, cord, outlet, and portable. The combination type is what is typically required by the code. Check the electrical code for specifics.

Every 125-volt, 15-amp, and 20-amp outlet in these rooms must be connected to a circuit that is AFCI protected. This includes receptacles, light fixture and ceiling fan connections, switches, and even smoke detectors unless they are part of a fire alarm system. (Fire alarms should not be connected.) Unlike GFCIs, where a single device can be replaced to make a receptacle outlet GFCI protected, in most cases AFCI requirements do not allow this. Instead, the entire circuit within the room or space must have AFCI protection so that all devices attached to the circuit are AFCI protected. This is typically accomplished by installing an AFCI circuit breaker at the electrical panelboard. If an arc fault is detected anywhere along the circuit, the AFCI will essentially disconnect the power to (i.e., de-energize) the entire circuit, thereby making the arc harmless.

LIGHT FIXTURES

The choice of light fixtures in a design can have a significant effect on the overall quality of the design of the space. However, many codes and standards must be considered when specifying them. Light fixtures are referred to as *luminaires* by the *NEC*. The *NEC* requirements are based on the type of light fixture and where it is installed. The building codes refer to light fixtures as "artificial light" (as opposed to natural daylight) or "lighting" and typically specify minimum light levels allowed in various spaces. The energy codes and standards concentrate on the energy efficiency of the light fixture. In addition, the location of the fixture may be affected by accessibility requirements and the *ADA Standards* and the plumbing codes. Many of these requirements are discussed in this section.

Types of Light Fixtures

Only fire-tested and -labeled light fixtures should be used on interior projects. The most widely accepted standards are those created by Underwriters Laboratories. Each light fixture manufactured in the United States is tested to be used in a specific environment or location and is then assigned a UL rating or seal of approval. (See the inset titled "UL Labels" in Chapter 1.) For example, a fixture installed in a damp location, like the ceiling of an enclosed shower unit, must be marked "Suitable for Damp Locations." (Other bathroom fixtures typically do not require this rating.) Other light fixtures are specifically marked for wall mounting, under-cabinet mounting, ceiling mounting, and suspended ceiling mounting. Certain fixtures will also note when they are allowed in noncombustible, non-fire-rated, or fire- resistant construction. Selection of any fixture must ensure that it is appropriate to the location in which it will be used.

The codes and standards require only UL-approved fixtures on a project. However, not every light fixture is UL approved. When specifying fixtures supplied by countries outside the United States and fixtures made by custom fabricators, additional research may be required. Also, because of stricter federal requirements, older fixtures may have to be replaced (not reused) when renovating an existing space. Energy codes and standards limit the overall wattage of a space or building, which in turn affects the types of light fixtures selected for a project. This is explained in more detail in the section titled "Electrical Sustainability Considerations" later in this chapter.

In the past, the *NEC* allowed the light fixture to dictate the type of outlet box used to mount the fixture. The *NEC* requires all ceiling fixtures to be installed in a box rated for minimum of 50 pounds (23 kg). The only exception is for use equipment, such as smoke detectors, that do not weigh more than 6 pounds (3 kg). This is not required for wall sconces; instead, these boxes must be marked with the maximum weight permitted. Heavier fixtures, such as ceiling fans and larger pendants or chandeliers, must either be supported independently of the box or be attached to a box made specifically for heavier fixtures. UL standards for light fixtures also specify the maximum wattage of the lamp to be used in the fixture. Using a higher wattage can result in overheating and damage to the wiring, as well as affecting its efficiency.

Location of Light Fixtures

The *NEC* places strict requirements on the access to the various electrical components that are part of the light fixture. In addition to an accessible electrical box, all light fixtures must be placed so that both the lamp (i.e.,

> **✎ Note**
>
> UL standards for light fixtures also specify the maximum wattage of the lamp to be used in the fixture. Using a higher wattage can result in overheating and damage to the wiring.

> **✎ Note**
>
> A light fixture or other electronic device listed for a wet location can also typically be used in a damp location.

> **✎ Note**
>
> Light fixtures that include air handling as part of the mechanical system can typically be used if provisions are made to stop the movement of air through the fixtures at the start of a fire.

light bulb) and the fixture can be replaced when needed. This becomes especially important when light fixtures are used within architectural elements such as ceiling coves, custom light boxes, and specially designed millwork. The custom unit must be designed so that easy access is provided to the fixture. In addition, fixtures used in special applications must be carefully located so that they do not cause the fixture or other adjacent materials to overheat. The performance codes are also very clear on this. For example, the *ICCPC* specifically states that "building elements shall be protected from thermal damage due to heat transfer or electrical arc from electrical power installations." If the light fixture is used in an enclosed space, ventilation might be required to prevent heat buildup, especially when using low-voltage fixtures that tend to get very hot. In addition, if the fixture is used in conjunction with light-transmitting plastics, the "Plastics" chapter of the building codes imposes additional restrictions and may even require additional sprinkler heads to be provided. (Also see the inset titled "Plastic Finishes" in Chapter 10.)

In rated ceiling and wall assemblies, only certain types of light fixtures are allowed. For example, when light fixtures (i.e., recessed cans) are recessed into a ceiling that has a 1-hour fire rating, the mechanical part of the fixture must be rated. If not, a fully enclosed rated box must be built around the housing to maintain the 1-hour rating of the ceiling assembly. In other instances, noncombustible material must also be sandwiched between the fixture and the finished surface. In all cases, specify a fixture meant for the application so that the appropriate air circulation is maintained.

The *NEC* also places restrictions on certain light fixtures installed over bathtubs and shower areas (in any occupancy). It includes all light fixtures except surface-mounted and recessed fixtures. For example, no part of a hanging luminaire, pendant fixture, track fixture, or ceiling fan can be within 8 feet (2.5 m) above the top of the bathtub rim or within 8 feet (2.5 m) above a shower threshold up to 3 feet (900 mm) away from the plumbing fixture. (This is to make sure that they stay out of the reach of a person standing on the tub rim.) This is shown in Figure 9.6. (If the shower has no threshold, the measurement is taken from the floor.) This same requirement applies to hot tubs and similar types of bathing fixtures. The *NEC* gives other specific dimensions for light fixtures installed in clothes closets, in show windows, and over combustible materials. For example, a light fixture in a clothes closet must typically be installed so that there is a minimum clearance of 6 to 12 inches (150 to 300 mm) between the fixture and the nearest storage item (e.g., edge of shelf or hanging rod), depending on the type of light fixture. (LED fixtures are now allowed as well.) Similar clearances, although not specified, should be considered in other types of storage spaces where tall shelving may become an issue.

> ◢ **Note**
>
> Light fixtures placed over tubs and showers require luminaires listed for damp locations (or listed for wet locations when subject to shower spray). Other fixtures in a bathing facility typically do not require this rating.

> ◢ **Note**
>
> High-intensity discharge (HID) lighting, consisting of metal halide (MH), and high-pressure sodium (HPS), low-voltage lighting, and neon lighting have additional code requirements.

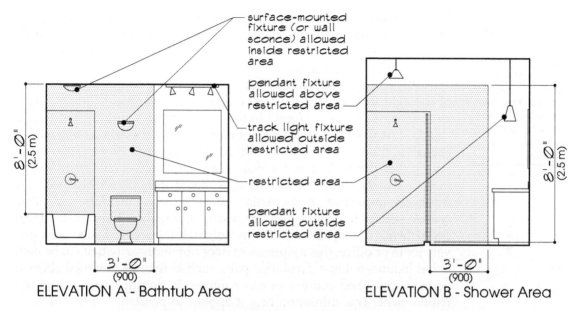

surface-mounted fixture (or wall sconce) allowed inside restricted area

pendant fixture allowed above restricted area

track light fixture allowed outside restricted area

restricted area

pendant fixture allowed outside restricted area

8'-0" (2.5 m)

8'-0" (2.5 m)

3'-0" (900)

3'-0" (900)

ELEVATION A - Bathtub Area

ELEVATION B - Shower Area

NOTE: Light fixtures inside the restricted area must be listed for damp locations (or wet locations if subject to shower spray)

Figure 9.6 Typical lighting restrictions at bathtubs and showers.

Previously in the chapter, it was mentioned that the *NEC* requires lighting outlets in certain locations within a dwelling unit. Although it does not restrict the number or location of light fixtures in most non-Residential occupancies, the building codes do set minimum light levels that must be met in all habitable spaces. (See the inset titled "Rooms and Spaces" in Chapter 3.) This is found in the "Interior Environment" chapter of the building code. That chapter specifies the amount of glazing that must be included in the exterior of the building to provide natural light into a habitable space. It also specifies the amount of artificial light that must be provided in a habitable space when enough natural light is not provided. This often applies to interior rooms and spaces that are not along the perimeter of the building and includes stairways in dwelling units. In these spaces, the lighting must typically provide an average illumination of 10 footcandles (107 lux) over the area of the room at a height of 30 inches (762 mm) above the floor. (Certain occupancies, such as Educational occupancies, may have additional requirements.) As long as these minimum light levels are met, the number, types, and locations of the light fixtures do not matter, according to the *NEC*. (See the next section

✍ Note

If only part of a wall sconce is more than 4 inches (100 mm) deep, only that part must be more than 80 inches (2030 mm) above the floor as required for accessibility.

for light levels in means of egress.) However, depending on the type of building or space, certain energy-efficiency requirements may also be required. This is explained in the section titled "Electrical Sustainability Considerations" later in this chapter.

If the space is required to meet accessibility regulations, then location of the light fixtures and their operating parts must meet certain height requirements. These are found in the *ADA Standards* and the *ICC A117.1* standard. Wall sconces cannot be mounted so that they are a "protruding object" so they must be mounted at least 80 inches (2030 mm) above the floor if they protrude from the wall more than 4 inches (100 mm). This is measured to the bottom of the fixture, as shown in Figure 9.4. This becomes especially important in circulation paths such as corridors and other spaces used by the public. If a light fixture is less than 4 inches (100 mm) deep, then it can be mounted at any height. If the sconce is used in a private room or office, this requirement does not necessarily have to be met. Other fixtures not in a circulation path, such as fixtures mounted above a permanently fixed counter or other millwork, do not have to meet the requirement. This minimum height applies to pendant fixtures as well. When hung from the ceiling, the fixture cannot hang below 80 inches (2030 mm) above the floor unless it is mounted directly over a piece of furniture. (The furniture will prevent anyone from knocking into the light fixture; if the furniture is moved, the height of the pendant can be changed more easily than that of a wall sconce.) In addition, the switch or mechanism that turns the light on and off must be located within the reach ranges and be usable by someone with a disability, as discussed previously.

REQUIRED ELECTRICAL SYSTEMS

In addition to the typical electrical system in a building, the building codes, the fire codes, and the *Life Safety Code (LSC)* have additional requirements for electrical systems. These include emergency power systems and standby power systems. When they are required and to what extent they are required typically depend on the type of occupancy and the building type. (A building owner may want to add these types of systems for other reasons as well.) The building codes and/or the *LSC* will specify when a system is required and refer to the *NEC* for the specifics of the system and how it is installed. The *NEC* also references the standards *NFPA 110, Standard for Emergency and Standby Power Systems,* and *NFPA 111, Standard on Stored Electrical Energy Emergency and Standby Power Systems.* Typically, an electrical engineer would design this type of system, but it is important to be aware of both systems because they affect the selection of fixtures and other interior elements.

Emergency Power Systems

Emergency power systems (EPSs) are required by the codes in most buildings to maintain all life safety systems in case of an emergency or loss of power. This includes means of egress lighting, exit signs, fire alarm systems, automatic door locks elevators, and other emergency equipment. They are also required in certain building types to provide power for essential equipment, such as life-support equipment in hospitals. EPS are especially important in high rises and buildings with sensitive activities or occupants. The goal is to allow the occupants of a building to stay safe or to evacuate safely.

The building codes and the *LSC* specify emergency lighting requirements. The requirements are found in the "Means of Egress" chapters of the codes. (See also the section titled "Emergency Lighting and Communication" in Chapter 5.) Each code specifically states the following basic requirements:

❑ **Illumination level.** Artificial lighting must be present in the means of egress when a building is in use. (There are exceptions for Residential occupancies.) The intensity of the emergency lighting must typically be 1 footcandle (11 lux) at the floor level on the path of egress. (These numbers can be reduced during performance times in some Assembly occupancies.) More recently, the NFPA codes added that new stairways be illuminated by at least 10 footcandles (108 lux).

❑ **Exit signs.** Exit signs must be located and illuminated in such a way that they can direct occupants safely out of the building. (See the section titled "Signage" in Chapter 5.) Exit signs can be externally illuminated, internally lit, or self-luminous. Typically, they must be illuminated by at least 5 footcandles (54 lux) at the illuminated surface and have a contrast level of not less than 0.5. (Some jurisdictions may require similar light levels for area of refuge signs and for signs at elevators used as a means of egress.)

❑ **Emergency power.** Provisions must be made so that in case of power loss, emergency or exit lighting will be available for a certain period of time. Most codes require that exit lighting be connected to an emergency power source that will ensure illumination for at least 1½ hours in case of power failure. For example, in Business occupancies, a battery pack can usually be used as the emergency source of power. In some occupancies, such as Assembly, Institutional, or Hazardous occupancies, a separate source of emergency power, or EPS, must be provided for the exit signs and illumination may be required for a longer time. In all cases, the codes specify how to periodically test emergency lighting equipment to make sure it will work in an emergency.

☜ **Note**

Important sources for emergency and standby power systems are *NFPA 110, Standard for Emergency and Standby Power Systems*, and *NFPA 111, Standard on Stored Electrical Energy Emergency and Standby Power Systems*.

☜ **Note**

Newer energy codes and standards also limit the power of an exit sign to 5 watts to provide additional energy efficiency in a building.

✍ Note

In some building types, such as hospitals and businesses with critical computer systems, the 10-second power delay may not be acceptable. It may be necessary to add an uninterrupted power supply (UPS) that keeps the electricity flowing during the 10-second transition time.

✍ Note

"Critical Operations Power Systems" were introduced in the 2008 *NEC.* These requirements enhance an emergency or standby power system to provide additional protection in buildings that are necessary for homeland security. Examples include certain government buildings, fire stations, and hospitals.

When allowed, the easiest method of creating emergency lighting in a design project is to add the typical twin-headed emergency light with a battery pack in the appropriate locations. An alternate solution is to include some of the general lighting fixtures on a separate circuit designated for emergency lighting. This allows the separate circuit to be connected to the main power source as well as the backup power source. Also, if one light fixture burns out, it will not leave an area in darkness. Some ways to ensure this are to use dual-lamp light fixtures or to design an overlapping light pattern. In addition, if there are switches connected to the emergency light fixtures, the *NEC* specifies that the switches be located so that it is convenient for authorized persons who will be responsible for their activation. Automatic, motion-sensor–type light switches may also be allowed.

The *NEC* establishes other requirements for EPSs as well. The main requirement is that when the power changes from the main power source to the emergency system, the delay while the changeover occurs cannot be longer than 10 seconds. It also gives the specifics for the types of backup systems that can be used. These usually include a generator, a storage battery system, or a totally separate (or redundant) electrical service into the building. UPS is also sometimes used. Which system to use is typically determined by the electrical engineer and the code official. The *NFPA 110, Standard for Emergency and Standby Power Systems*, also has requirements.

Standby Power Systems

Standby power systems are similar to emergency power systems. They are used to supply power when the normal power source fails in an emergency. However, instead of operating the emergency systems essential for life safety, standby power is used for other building systems, such as the fire pumps, mechanical system, general lighting, communication systems, elevators, and other essential equipment. The *NEC* divides these into two categories: legally required standby systems and optional standby systems.

Legally required standby systems are those that are required by the building codes, the fire codes, the *LSC*, or a code jurisdiction. For example, standby power systems are typically required in some building types, such as certain Assembly, Institutional, and Hazardous occupancies, as well as high-rise buildings. These systems are intended to provide electrical power to aid in firefighting, rescue operations, control of health hazards, and similar operations. They are also mandatory when a building has a smoke control system and may be required for other parts of a building's mechanical ventilation system. (See Chapters 6 and 8.) Many of the requirements for a legally required standby system are similar to those for an EPS. One difference is that the standby system has up to 60 seconds to begin operation after the failure of the normal power supply.

In other cases, the building owner or tenant may decide to include certain building systems on standby power. These would be considered *optional standby systems*. The decision to provide an optional standby system is usually based on the concern for physical discomfort, serious interruption to a business, or damage to certain equipment. Examples include telecommunication systems, refrigeration equipment, elevators not required on emergency systems, and building automation systems.

The specifics of both types of standby power systems are found in the *NEC* and the *NFPA 110*. Often the same system supplying the emergency electrical system will also be used for the standby power system, but it could be a totally separate system. More recently, the *NEC* includes "selective coordination" requirements for legally required standby systems as well as EPSs. Similar to the circuit interrupters described previously in this chapter, they are protective devices installed to detect overcurrent problems throughout an electrical system. These overcurrent protective devices are located by the engineer in a manner that causes the least interruption to the system. Should a power surge occur, the service interruption is limited to the circuit experiencing the problem, not the whole facility, which minimizes the extent of the power disruption.

ELECTRICAL SUSTAINABILITY CONSIDERATIONS

The electrical codes and standards concentrate on the safety of an electrical system. The energy codes as well as the newer sustainability codes and standards focus on making an electrical system more energy efficient so that a building is considered more sustainable. Although some of the requirements are similar between these various documents, there are differences. For example, in the energy codes, energy-efficiency requirements first concentrate on the exterior shell of the building. Several factors, including the number and types of windows, affect the amount of electricity needed to condition the interior air and to light the interior spaces over time. The sustainability codes and standards take a different approach. Their goal is to make a building self-sustainable so that ultimately all energy that is used is renewable on-site (i.e., net-zero energy). Although the technology to accomplish this is not yet commonly available and/or cost-effective, these codes concentrate on

◀ **Note**

Standby power must initiate within 60 seconds of a power failure. Emergency power must initiate within 10 seconds.

◀ **Note**

Depending on the edition of the *IECC* or ASHRAE standard required by a jurisdiction and that required by the federal government, energy-efficiency requirements will vary. Use the most restrictive requirements when necessary.

☑ Note

After considering the building envelope, the three largest components of a building's energy consumption are typically the HVAC system, the lighting system, and the appliances and devices plugged into the electrical system (i.e., plug load).

☑ Note

The *IECC* and *ASHRAE/IESNA 90.1* require lighting power density (LPD) calculations. Both include tables with LPD values for a whole-building method (based on building areas) and a space-by-space method (based on specific functions of the space).

setting up systems to monitor the building's electrical system. (This is also required by the 2005 Energy Policy Act; see Chapter 1.) As the requirements get more stringent, these monitoring systems should allow the building owner to analyze the existing conditions and make improvements accordingly.

Inside the building, the energy codes concentrate on efficiency of the equipment. Some of the energy requirements of mechanical and water heating systems were explained in Chapter 8. The goal of many of these requirements is to limit the amount of electricity required to run the systems. Because lighting accounts for between 20 to 30 percent of a building's electricity load, lighting energy efficiency continues to be a concern for a sustainable building. For example, *ASHRAE 90.1* has made changes to improve daylighting and daylighting controls and space-by-space power densities. The energy codes and required standards can affect the selection of light fixtures and their controls (e.g., switches). For example, where daylight is provided, the energy codes require switching to be zoned separate from the areas without daylight exposure. Equipment and appliances, such as copiers, dishwashers, and clothes dryers, are typically not regulated by the codes because they already must meet certain federal energy requirements in order to be sold in the United States. (See the discussion of the Energy Policy Act in Chapter 1.)

Although the energy codes and standards required for electrical systems will typically be incorporated into the design by an electrical engineer, the choice of light fixtures, appliances, and distribution of electrical outlets by the designer can affect the building's efficiency. For example, the *International Energy Conservation Code (IECC)* and the *ASHRAE/IESNA 90.1* standard include interior lighting power density (LPD) tables, such as *IECC* Table C405.3.2(1), "Interior Lighting Power Allowances, Building Area Method," as shown in Figure 9.7. Another table in the *IECC*,

TABLE C405.3.2(1) INTERIOR LIGHTING POWER ALLOWANCES: BUILDING AREA METHOD

BUILDING AREA TYPE	LPD (watts/ft²)
Automotive facility	0.75
Convention center	0.64
Courthouse	0.79
Dining: bar lounge/leisure	0.80
Dining: cafeteria/fast food	0.76
Dining: family	0.71

Figure 9.7 *(Continued)*

BUILDING AREA TYPE	LPD (watts/ft²)
Dormitory[a, b]	0.53
Exercise center	0.72
Fire station[a]	0.56
Gymnasium	0.76
Health care clinic	0.81
Hospital[a]	0.96
Hotel/Motel[a, b]	0.56
Library	0.83
Manufacturing facility	0.82
Motion picture theater	0.44
Multiple-family[c]	0.45
Museum	0.55
Office	0.64
Parking garage	0.18
Penitentiary	0.69
Performing arts theater	0.84
Police station	0.66
Post office	0.65
Religious building	0.67
Retail	0.84
School/university	0.72
Sports arena	0.76
Town hall	0.69
Transportation	0.50
Warehouse	0.45
Workshop	0.91

For SI: 1 watt per square foot = 10.76 w/m².

a. Where sleeping units are excluded from lighting power calculations by application of Section R404.1, neither the area of the sleeping units nor the wattage of lighting in the sleeping units is counted.

b. Where dwelling units are excluded from lighting power calculations by application of Section R404.1, neither the area of the dwelling units nor the wattage of lighting in the dwelling units is counted.

c. Dwelling units are excluded. Neither the area of the dwelling units nor the wattage of lighting in the dwelling units is counted.

Figure 9.7 International Energy Conservation Code® Table C405.3.2(1), "Interior Lighting Power Allowances: Building Area Method" (2021 *International Energy Conservation Code*, copyright © 2021. Washington, DC: International Code Council.) Reproduced with permission. All rights reserved. www.iccsafe.org).

Note

Newer editions of the *IECC* and *ASHRAE/IESNA 90.1* encourage the use of automatic shut-off task lights. When automatic shut-offs are used, these lights do not need to be calculated as part of the interior lighting allowance.

Note

The Green Seal standard, *GC-12, Environmental Criteria for Occupancy Sensors*, tests motion sensors and switching devices used in small, confined spaces as well as in large, open areas.

Note

The US Department of Energy's Building Energy Codes Program offers COMcheck software and other resources on its website to assist with energy code and standard compliance. (See www.energycodes.gov.)

Table C405.3.2(2), "Interior Lighting Power Allowances: Space-By-Space Method," gives similar density levels based on specific room use. These tables set the maximum wattage per square foot (square meter) allowed in building types or in specific spaces. The total wattage allowed is determined by multiplying the square footage of the conditioned spaces in the building by the LPD value on the table. Either the *whole-building method* based on assigning the building to certain "Building Area Types" such as a courthouse, exercise center, or museum as listed in Table C405.4.2(1) can be used, or a *space-by-space method* dividing the building into more specific functions such as office, locker room, reading area, and using LPD values for individual "Common Space Types" as listed in C405.4.2(2) can be used. (Table C405.4.2[2] is an extensive list and includes many specific room types and is not included in this book. See the *IECC* for the complete chart.) To meet the code, the sum of all interior lighting power cannot exceed the determined wattage allowance. This can affect the type and quantity of light fixtures included in the design. (Retail spaces require additional calculations, as shown in the table footnotes.)

When using the LPD table, remember that allowances are provided for special lighting needs, such as decorative, display, or accent lighting, as well as other safety-required lighting such as exit signs and emergency lights. Typically, these are not included in the calculation. For example, if calculating the total wattage allowed by the *IECC* for an educational facility with an adjacent office space, the square footage of the spaces for each building type would be determined separately. Then the LPD table in Figure 9.7 would be used to determine how many watts are allowed per square foot: The Office building type allows 1.0 watts per square foot and the School/University building type allows 1.2 watts per square foot. Multiply the square footage for each building type by the respective LPDs and add the results to determine the maximum wattage allowance for the facility. In this example, when adding up the total wattage of all the specified light fixtures, the following would not be included: emergency lighting, exit and directional signage, specialty lighting in a classroom, furniture-mounted task lighting, and maintenance task lighting. (See the code and/or standard for specifics.)

In addition, the energy codes and standards require automatic lighting controls devices in most buildings. These particularly focus on reducing the use of energy for lighting when the space does not require lighting for use by the occupants. This can be accomplished with occupant sensors, time-scheduling devices, daylight sensors, or other similar signals for open and enclosed spaces. The *IECC* requires occupant sensors in specific room types. See Figure 9.8. Time switch controls may also be required if occupant sensors are not provided. However, these are not required in sleeping units; continuous operation is required or where automatic shutoff would endanger occupant safety or security.

Spaces Requiring Occupant Sensor Controls
Classroom or lecture room
Training rooms
Copy/print rooms
Lounges
Employee lunch and break rooms
Private offices
Restrooms
Storage rooms
Janitorial closets
Locker rooms
Warehouses
Other enclosed spaces 300 square feet (28 m) or less

Figure 9.8 Spaces requiring occupant sensors.

For large open areas where interior lighting levels may be affected by changes in natural from skylights and vertical fenestrations (i.e., windows), the *IECC* may require that daylight-responsive controls be used. These requirements are affected by the natural light source, use of room, and location within the building. In any location, if an automatic switch sensor is used, the *NEC* requires that the lights be controlled by a manual switch as well. The overall goal is to reduce the electrical load required in a building by specifying more energy-efficient fixtures and equipment and/or reducing the number of fixtures. Examples of more energy-efficient light fixtures include high-performance T8 fluorescent fixtures, T5 fluorescent fixtures, or light-emitting diodes (LED). The type of lamp will make a difference as well. Some options include using high-output (HO) lamps, high-intensity discharge (HID) lamps, or compact fluorescent lamps in place of incandescent lamps. (See also the section titled "Types of Light Fixtures" earlier in this chapter.) The lighting layout also makes a difference. For example, using more indirect lighting combined with task lighting can often help to reduce the overall number of light fixtures.

The energy codes and standards will specify additional requirements including various types of lighting controls as explained in the section titled "Switch Boxes" earlier in this chapter. Specifying dimmers can also help to reduce the power used for a fixture and to lengthen the life of the lamp in the fixture.

Additional energy-efficiency requirements are included in the newer sustainability documents such as the *International Green Construction*

◀ **Note**

Some jurisdictions have passed benchmarking legislation, which requires certain building types to disclose their energy use. Many state and federal buildings require this as well. The EPA's Portfolio Manager, which is part of the ENERGY STAR program, is the software typically used to track energy and water consumption.

LOW-VOLTAGE CABLING SYSTEMS

The type of cabling system used within a building to support such things as voice, data, video, and security systems is called *structured cabling*. It is also known as integrated cabling or universal cabling. The system is made up of backbone cabling and horizontal cabling. *Backbone cabling* carries the signals to the main distribution areas of the building or space. It begins where the public utility enters the building. This location, where the utility wiring is connected to the building wiring, is called the *demark*. From there it goes to the main telecommunication room (referred to as the entrance room) and then to the distributed communication room(s). In large commercial projects, fiber cabling is often used for backbone cabling.

The cables that are pulled to each workstation or outlet are known as *horizontal cabling*. Connections to the individual desktops or outlets are typically made through the horizontal cabling system using fiber optic or copper cabling. Because copper is less expensive for individual connections, it is more widely used in horizontal cabling. However, where complex systems must be supported, fiber optics should be considered. A wireless system is another option, especially as technology continues to improve security and transmission rates (i.e., bandwidth). (See the section "Low-Voltage Cabling" later in this chapter.)

✐ Note

Energy and sustainability requirements may conflict with requirements in the *NEC*. You may need to consult with the local code official.

Code (IgCC) and *ASHRAE/USGBC/IES 189.1, Standard for the Design of High-Performance Green Buildings Except Low-Rise Residential Buildings*. For example, the *IgCC* requires the use of the *IECC* plus additional requirements and benchmarks that must be met. The *ASHRAE 189.1* references *ASHRAE/IESNA 90.1* in many cases but also includes additional and sometimes stricter requirements. Both documents include information on how to manage the energy consumption of a building, with details for data collection, data storage, and the like. In addition, *ASHRAE 189.1* requires calculations to determine how much space must be allocated for future on-site renewable energy systems. Space will be required on the exterior as well as the interior of a building to allow for equipment, pathways for installation, and associated infrastructure, and these considerations may affect the layout of an interior space. *ASHRAE 189.1* also includes more details for things such as occupancy sensor controls and ENERGY STAR equipment and appliances. (See the inset titled "Federal Sustainability Certifications" in Appendix A.)

Balancing the requirements of sustainability and energy efficiency with the occupants' safety and visual needs, as well as the aesthetics of the space, is one of the new challenges of design. Upfront and long-term costs need to be considered. For example, facility-wide dimming, although more costly on the front end, can save money over the long term because of the longer lamp life at each fixture. In some cases, the requirements in these additional codes and standards may not be easy to coordinate with those in the *NEC*. Work closely with an electrical engineer and the local code official when required. (Also refer to Appendix A for more information on sustainable design.)

☑ **Note**

Emerging lighting technology includes *hybrid lighting*, which uses sunlight-based solar energy to supplement the electrical energy to the fixture.

COMMUNICATION COMPONENTS AND DEVICES

This section explains the various components and devices of communication systems as they are affected by the codes and standards. Many projects now require one or more communication consultants to adequately plan the overall system. Consultants can include information technology (IT) specialists, sound engineers, certified low-voltage system designers, and vendor representatives, among others.

It is important to understand the current and future needs of the client and to coordinate the design of the space with the consultants doing the design and installation of the communication system(s). For example, if working on an auditorium project, interior aspects will need to be coordinated with the audiovisual system. Or, if specifying workstations for an open office, the power and voice/data needs will need to be coordinated. In addition, some projects and certain jurisdictions may require the involvement of an electrical engineer during the design of the system and/or a licensed electrician to install the system.

Communication Equipment and Rooms

Every building requires a central area where the incoming communication services are connected to the building's communication systems including internet, networking, telephone, security, and other data cabling. The initial location within the building is called the *entrance facility* or room. It typically contains racks for the cables and wiring as they enter the building before being distributed to the other areas and floors. It may also contain computer equipment (file and control servers) for the computer system for the building or space. The *NEC* and the industry standard, *ANSI/TIA 569 Telecommunications Pathways and Spaces*, are used to set many of the requirements of these spaces. *ANSI/TIA 569* gives parameters for the location, environmental conditions (including temperature, ceiling height, and size), finish treatments, lighting, door size, signage finishes, and various other characteristics. The main communication room is typically located in the basement or on the ground floor as close as possible to the entrance of communication services. (In small buildings, only a small panel located in the electrical room or a closet may be required.)

From the entrance communication room, the cabling is distributed to additional *telecommunication rooms* (sometime referred to as communication rooms or closets) on each floor and/or within separate tenants. There may be separate rooms: one for telecommunications and one for data/computer equipment, or one room that combines the equipment. The size of the building floor and number or tenants may also determine whether more than one telecommunication room is required. These rooms provide a central location from which to distribute cabling throughout the floor or space, either directly to equipment such as telephones and computers or to one or more satellite rooms. Similar to electrical rooms, it is preferred that these rooms be stacked vertically within the building, if possible. These intermediate rooms also help to limit the length of cabling; some cable runs are limited to maximum lengths.

When there are multiple tenants on the same floor, another room, known as a *satellite room,* is often used for each tenant space to allow the separation of utilities. When determining the final size of these rooms, the various consultants and vendors installing the communication systems (e.g., telephone, data, computer, security) should be consulted. In addition, these more remote rooms typically do not have to meet the requirements of the main communication room.

Telecommunication rooms are sometime confused with computer rooms, information technology equipment (IT or ITE) rooms, and/or data centers. These rooms may have similar equipment as a communication room. For example, some equipment may be considered IT and communications, such as voice over Internet (also referred to as voice over IP). However, the *NEC* defines IT equipment to be for the "creation and manipulation of data, voice, video, and similar signals that are *not* communications equipment." It is important to differentiate the purpose of the room because a computer room, IT, or data room have more stringent requirements within the *NEC* (*Article 645*) and *NFPA 75, Standard for the Protection of Information Technology Equipment,* than a communication room. For example, the IT room may be required to be separated from the rest of the building by fire-rated walls, floor, and ceiling assemblies, and fire-rated doors. The *NEC* also includes requirements on how to condition the space. This is especially important because of the heat generated by the equipment. If a raised floor is used, special cable and ventilation

◢ Note

In the past, all communication rooms were required to have sprinkler heads. Newer standards that provide alternate options for protection may be allowed by a jurisdiction.

requirements must be followed as well. You may have to consult with the engineer to determine the appropriate aspects of the *NEC* that will apply. (Also see the section titled "Telecommunication Systems" later in this chapter.)

Low-Voltage Cabling

Cables used for communication systems are different from electrical cables, because of the lower voltages required for communication systems. They are typically referred to as *low-voltage cabling*. Many are listed in the *NEC*; the more common types are shown in Figure 9.9. (There are many subcategories as well.) There are different cables for different applications. Each type of cable is divided into plenum, riser, general-purpose, and limited-use categories for use in different parts of a building. For example, if a cable is used horizontally in a mechanical plenum space (see Chapter 8), it must be marked as a plenum cable (unless it is in an approved conduit or raceway). A riser cable would be used in vertical shafts. General-purpose cables are typically used in commercial applications; limited-use cables are allowed in dwelling units. Similar to electrical

> **◀ Note**
>
> If a low-voltage cable is run continuously in conduit through a fire-rated area or assembly, the cable may not have to be rated.

COMMUNICATION CABLES		MULTIPURPOSE CABLES	
TYPE CMP	Communications plenum cable	**TYPE MPP**	Multipurpose plenum cable
TYPE CMR	Communications riser cable	**TYPE MPR**	Multipurpose riser cable
TYPE CM or CMG	Communications general-purpose cable	**TYPE MP or MPG**	Multipurpose general-purpose cable
TYPE CMX	Communications cable, limited use	**COAXIAL CABLE**	
TYPE CMUC	Undercarpet Communications Wire and Cable	**TYPE CATVP**	CATV plenum cable
FIBER OPTIC CABLES		**TYPE CATVR**	CATV riser cable
TYPE OFNP	Nonconductive optical fiber plenum cable	**TYPE CATV**	CATV cable
TYPE OFCP	Conductive optical fiber plenum cable	**TYPE CATVX**	CATV cable, limited use
TYPE OFNR	Nonconductive optical fiber riser cable	**FIRE ALARM CABLES**	
TYPE OFCR	Conductive optical fiber riser cable	**TYPE FPLP**	Power-limited fire alarm plenum cable
TYPE OFN or OFNG	Nonconductive optical fiber general-purpose cable	**TYPE FPLR**	Power-limited fire alarm riser cable
TYPE OFC or OFCG	Conductive optical fiber general-purpose cable	**TYPE FPL**	Power-limited fire alarm cable

Figure 9.9 Common types of communication cables.

wiring, each of these communication cables must go through various industry standard tests before it can be labeled for its appropriate use. These tests include the fire, smoke, and toxicity tests mentioned previously in the section titled "Electrical Cabling and Conduit." Because the speed at which information travels is a major factor, communication cables also go through additional performance testing to determine their bandwidth and capacity levels.

Typically, the communication consultants or vendors specify the type of communication cable. The following are the main types of cables and/or connections used most often.

✎ Note

When using copper cabling for telecommunication systems, industry standards often limit the length of the cable run to 300 feet (91 m).

❑ **Fiber optic cable.** A fiber optic cable transmits light along ultra-thin glass or plastic strands. Each strand is composed of layers of fibers protected by a cabling jacket and a plastic coating. Fiber optic cables provide higher bandwidth than other types of cable, which yields higher speed and capacity. Also, because they are smaller and lighter and can withstand greater pulling tension, they are easier to use than copper. In addition, because optical fibers use light waves instead of an electrical current to transmit information, they are not affected by electromagnetic and radio frequency interference. Fiber can also be used over much longer distances before the signal must be amplified, and additional fibers can easily be included in the initial installation for future expansion of a data or communication system. Multi-mode (OM1–OM4), single-mode (OS1 and OS2), and hybrid fiber optic cables are available. (See also the entry for composite cable further down in this list.)

❑ **Twisted-pair cable.** Twisted-pair cabling, sometimes referred to as *copper cabling*, uses a copper conductor to transmit data using an electrical current. It provides less capacity and speed than fiber optics, but it is still the most common type of low-voltage cabling used today. It is less expensive than fiber optics. The copper wire is twisted into pairs, encased in a protective sheathing, and available shielded and unshielded. The twisting helps reduce the amount of outside interference. Typically used for voice (i.e., telephone) and data (i.e., computer) connections, it is rated by *category*, which indicates its bandwidth performance. Manufacturers are continually developing copper cabling with more capacity. Most installations now use at least Category 5e (CAT 5e) or CAT 6, and in some cases CAT 7/Class F. One of the newest cable categories, released in 2009, is Category 6a (the *a* stands for "augmented"). It is defined for frequencies twice that of CAT 6 and can be used in longer lengths. Even as higher categories become available, any cable should be used only as appropriate for its rating.

❑ **Coaxial cable.** Coaxial cable (*coax* for short) is the standard cable used for video and cable-based transmissions. For example, it is used for cable TV and cable-based Internet connections, closed-circuit television connections, and TV antenna connections. Similar to twisted-pair cable, it uses conductive metal to transmit data using an electrical current, but instead it has a single central conductor. It has the capacity to carry great quantities of information. Different types include RG-6 cable for cable TV connections, RG-59 for video surveillance systems, and RG-60 for high-definition TV and high-speed Internet.

❑ **Composite cable.** Composite cabling, also known as *hybrid cabling*, bundles various types of cables into one jacket or sleeve. For example, one composite cable containing CAT 5, coaxial, and audio wiring could be run so that multiple communication connections to various systems can be made. This is often used in Residential-type occupancies to eliminate the need to run multiple cables to the same location. A multimedia conference room might also use a cable like this. A variety of composite cables are available, in a variety of qualities. If they consist strictly of communication cables, they are not typically regulated by the *NEC*. A composite cable can also consist of a combination of optical fibers and current-carrying electrical wires. The *NEC* calls this a "conductive" optical fiber because it can also carry electricity. The *NEC* has separate requirements for these types of composite cables, and they may not always be allowed. (Their use might also be limited by the manufacturer of the equipment being connected to the cable, for warranty reasons.)

❑ **Circuit integrity (CI) cable.** CI cables are a cable assembly that provides a 2-hour fire rating. Cables must pass additional testing requirements to obtain this rating and are labeled with the suffix –*CI*. They are used to wire building systems that are essential to the safety of the occupants. Examples include wiring to smoke dampers in ductwork (see Chapter 5) and fire alarm control stations (see Chapter 6).

❑ **Wireless.** Wireless systems use cable to connect the main transmitter to the communication service. Receivers are then used instead of cabling to allow individuals to connect to the system. They use infrared or radio transmission. Sometimes microwave and laser signals are used between facilities, similar to the microwave signals used to provide communication links to cell phones. Wireless systems are essential to many types of buildings and a wide variety of communication systems. Technology allows networks to be interconnected, in systems where each device can send/receive data from a number of other devices, so there is less down time and more security. Additional security is created because networks are

---

✎ Note

Because cables such as CAT 6 and composite cables have multiple pairs, one cable can be used to connect multiple devices (phone, computer, etc.).

✎ Note

Some buildings may require 2-hour rated cables for added protection of certain communication systems. These are called *circuit integrity (CI)* cables. (Type MI electrical cables would be an alternative.)

✎ Note

Certain building materials can be used to provide a radio frequency barrier to minimize signal leakage and electromagnetic interference with wireless systems. Examples include foil-backed drywall and certain window films.

constantly changing channels, making it more difficult to access information.

✎ Note

A building or space may use a raised floor system so cabling can be installed underneath. The outlet can then be installed flush with the floor.

❑ Certain communication cables, especially when used in conjunction with larger network-powered systems, are required by the *NEC* to be grounded. (See the section titled "Grounding and Circuit Interrupters" earlier in this chapter.) In addition, when communication cables are installed throughout a building, the codes typically require that they be kept separate from electrical cabling. In most cases, communication cables cannot be placed in any raceway, compartment, conduit, outlet box, or junction box used for electric light or power. (There are exceptions, depending on the type of cable used.) When communication cables are run horizontally across a ceiling, they can usually remain exposed. However, the codes specify that the cables must be run in a "neat and workmanlike manner," and they cannot block access when used above suspended ceiling systems. This is accomplished by using hangers, straps, and cable ties to keep the cables together. They are often secured at the ceiling using cable tray or *J*-hooks. (In some cases, a listed raceway will be required.) Because the *NEC* allows many types of communication cables to be run together, the various communication vendors will typically share this common path until they reach their respective outlet locations.

❑ When communication cables are run down a wall to a particular outlet, many jurisdictions (especially in certain occupancies) require the low-voltage cable(s) to be run in a conduit. (See the section titled "Conduit" earlier in this chapter.) Conduit is also required in rated walls. Because the cable must be separate from the electrical cable/conduit, it will require a separate conduit. For example, in a typical office, a computer and/or telephone outlet is often located next to an electrical outlet. Two conduits would be installed in the wall: one for the electrical wiring and one for the low-voltage wiring. In addition, if the conduit or box penetrates a rated assembly or membrane, it must meet the same rating requirements as electrical boxes. (See the section titled "Electrical Boxes" earlier in this chapter.)

✎ Note

The plastic sleeves covering communication cables can be very toxic if exposed to a fire. The *NEC* requires unused and abandoned cables that are accessible to be removed from a building.

❑ It is not uncommon for communication systems to be rewired as new types of cabling become available. This is especially true for computer systems, which may require a cable upgrade in order to increase the speed of the individual computers. Abandoned cables could increase fire loads and create toxic gases should a fire occur and could restrict the air flow in a plenum space. The *NEC* requires all accessible portions of abandoned low-voltage cables to be removed. (Some jurisdictions may require removal of all abandoned cables.)

BUILDING AUTOMATION SYSTEMS

A building automation system (BAS) is sometimes referred to as an *integrated building system,* a building information network, or an intelligent building system. It consists of various building systems connected into one automated system so that they can share data, affect another system's performance, and be managed through one source.

The building systems and the various components that can be supported by a BAS include the following:

❑ Mechanical systems: HVAC equipment, dampers, zone/thermostat controls, indoor air quality

❑ Electrical systems: Equipment, lighting systems, energy management, zone/switch controls

❑ Plumbing systems: Water usage, leak detection, sprinkler activation

❑ Security systems: Video, surveillance, access control devices, paging systems

❑ Voice/data systems: Local area networks, cable/satellite TV, telephone systems, wireless devices, audiovisual systems, sound masking systems

❑ Fire safety systems: Alarms, smoke detectors, voice communication systems, mass notification systems, sprinklers

❑ People transport systems: Elevators, escalators

There are several BAS systems, proprietary and custom, that can be used. Because each individual system becomes interconnected to the others, the key is to make sure that various components are correctly prioritized. For example, a fire detection system usually has a higher priority than a security program. The BAS can also be used to track performance criteria, such as energy use and reliability, and identify potential problems when they arise. The interconnected systems can also be used to help meet design criteria when using performance codes. For example, a BAS can be used to add life safety features to a building by programming office lights to flash when a fire alarm is activated. Other combined features can enhance energy efficiency, such as integrating lighting with access control systems.

Many new buildings are incorporating a BAS in the initial design, although adding one to an existing building is possible especially with the advances in wireless technology. Industry standards available to help integrate these systems include *TIA/EIA 776–5, TIA/EIA 862, and NFPA 731*. With a BAS, the facility manager can monitor the various systems from one source including a cell phone to operate the equipment and systems.

As a designer, it is important to be aware if a BAS system is planned, because it may affect the design of the space, choice of specific elements, and systems. Although connected, each of the individual systems must still meet the necessary code requirements. Note, however, that a code jurisdiction may restrict the connection of some fire safety systems to a BAS. (See also the inset titled "Integrated Alarms" in Chapter 7.)

TYPES OF COMMUNICATION SYSTEMS

A building's communication system can consist of several different systems. These include telephones, routers, computers, intercoms, audio and video systems such as surveillance equipment, cable services, and satellite hookups, as well as assistive listening systems. Often many of these systems are closely connected. In some cases, fire alarms are integrated into the building's communication system. (See the inset titled "Building Automation Systems" in this chapter.)

The low-voltage cabling used for most of these systems must meet the requirements found in the *NEC*, as discussed in the preceding section. Building codes will provide requirements when communications systems overlap life safety measures including emergency communication and locking of doors. Accessibility requirements will apply to all devices used by occupants. Other parts of the communication system should meet available industry standards. Communication systems are one of the fastest changing elements within a building. Continued integration of systems and updates to the infrastructure of systems continue to be required or expected.

Telecommunication Systems

The term *telecommunication* includes audio, visual, and data communication. (Radio communication is sometimes included as well.) As used here, it includes telephone and data/computer systems. As already discussed, the *NEC* has specific requirements for the main equipment room that houses a telecommunication system. It also includes specific requirements for the installation of cables, with separate sections for information technology (data) cabling and communication (voice) cabling. Most other requirements for telecommunication systems are found in standards developed by NFPA and the Telecommunications Industries Association (TIA) in conjunction with the Electronics Industries Alliance (EIA) or Building Industry Consulting Service International (BICSI). The standards cover everything from the testing and fabrication of components to the design and installation of an entire system. Some of the NFPA standards are specifically for large data facilities; however, for smaller telecommunication rooms, *NFPA 75, Standard for the Protection of Information Technology Equipment*, can be used. Industry standards not referenced by the codes include *TIA/EIA-568-B*,

Commercial Building Telecommunications Cabling Standard, which contains multiple sections that can be used depending on the type of cabling; and *TIA/EIA-569-A, Commercial Building Standard for Telecommunications Pathways and Spaces.* TIA offers other standards for residential and wireless systems as well.

These standards provide specifications and guidance for the installation and maintenance of the telecommunication system. Some of the requirements will affect the design and location of the communication room, as well as the overall design of a space or building. For example, the standards typically limit the length of a copper cable run going from the communication room to a data outlet to about 300 feet (91.4 m). In addition, the *TIA/EIA-589-B* standard incorporates the concept of *zone cabling* (also called *zone distribution*) for open office areas. This consists of dividing the ceiling into sections or zones and then running communication cables to the center of each zone. An intermediate multi-user outlet or terminal is installed in the ceiling within each zone so that separate cables can be run from the terminal to the outlets in a wall or in a run of workstations. (These are typically referred to as MUTOA.) Then, when the layout of an area changes, the cabling can be changed only in that particular zone up to the point in the ceiling, not all the way back to the main panel. This avoids having to abandon and remove old cables every time there is a change. (The terminals installed in the ceiling must have the same rating required for the ceiling cable.)

The *NEC* allows low-voltage cables for telephone (voice) outlets and computer (data) outlets to be "terminated" together so that they run through the same conduit to one box. The number of outlets or jacks will determine the size of the box. It is not unusual to have an outlet with four jacks, two for voice and two for data, or even more. Neither the *NEC* nor the standards specify the location of these voice and data outlets. Instead, they are located based on the layout and functional requirements of the space. However, voice and data outlet locations must stay within the reach ranges set by the *ADA Standards* and the *ICC A117.1* standard. This is shown in Figure 9.9. Outlets must be mounted on the wall at least 15 inches (380 mm) above the floor—similar to electrical outlets. Even if an area is not required to be accessible, this height is recommended in case the function of the space changes. (See the section titled "Outlet Boxes" earlier in this chapter for more accessibility requirements.) If locating an accessible wall-mounted telephone, it must be within 48 inches (1220 mm) above the floor, as shown in Figure 9.10.

> **◀ Note**
>
> Although codes do not require public telephones, some projects, such as hotels, may require phones for customer use. These would have to meet accessibility requirements including location on an accessible route, clear floor space, and within reach ranges. A text capable phone may also be required.

> **◀ Note**
>
> When specifying ceiling-mounted electronics, such as a television or projector, the accompanying receptacle outlet cannot be installed above a suspended ceiling. The *NEC* does not permit flexible cords in this space.

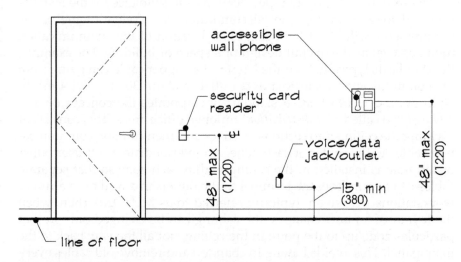

Figure 9.10 Typical accessible communication device locations.

Television and Radio Systems

The *NEC* includes some requirements for the installation of television and radio systems. Most of these requirements pertain to the exterior antennae that are usually located on top of the building to which the interior cabling is attached. Other requirements are geared to the interior coaxial cable that connects the devices to the radio and television receiving equipment, including the separation from certain other types of communication cables and the use of fire-rated cables. If raceways are used to run the cabling, these must be rated as well. (See the section titled "Low-Voltage Cabling" earlier in this chapter.) This equipment is used to operate such things as cable television, closed-circuit television, and security television cameras.

Alarm and Voice Communication Systems

Alarm and voice communication systems include fire and smoke alarms, emergency voice/alarm communication systems (EVACSs), intercom systems, and assistive listening systems. Some of these systems are used together or for multiple functions, and others are stand-alone systems. For example, a fire alarm system might also include an EVACS so that the occupants in the building can be given direction during an emergency. This is required by the codes in some occupancies such as Factories and high rises. In some cases, a jurisdiction may require a building or facility to use a mass notification system (MNS). (See Chapter 7.) These systems are more sophisticated than a typical public address system and require connection to an emergency power source. (See also the next section, "Audiovisual Systems.")

The requirements for fire and smoke alarm systems arc given in the fire codes and the building codes. The codes will indicate when they are required and reference standards for additional information. Certain accessibility requirements may also apply. (See the section titled "Alarm Systems" in Chapter 7.) These systems typically use low-voltage wiring that must meet additional requirements in the *NEC*. When the alarm system is connected to a BAS, the alarm system usually takes precedence over other connected systems because it is critical to the safety of the building occupants. That is why some jurisdictions do not allow its connection to a BAS. However, if it is connected to the other building systems, it can provide added features and often better response times. (See the inset titled "Building Automation Systems" earlier in this chapter.)

Another type of voice communication system that is required by the building codes and the *ADA Standards* is an assistive listening system. It is required in Assembly occupancies where audible communication is integral to the use of the space. Examples include a movie theater, a performing arts center, and a courtroom; however, it may be required in other building types as well. The assistive listening system is installed in conjunction with the main sound system and consists of accessible receivers. These receivers amplify the sound and are made available to those with hearing disabilities. The building codes specify the number and types of receivers required within a space or building based on the capacity of seating in the assembly area. The *ADA Standards* and the *ICC A117.1* standard provide additional requirements.

Audiovisual Systems

Audio and video systems include everything from a basic stereo system used in a small conference room to a highly complex audiovisual (AV) or multimedia room. The AV system can include a wide variety of components. The *NEC* covers equipment and wiring requirements for *audio*

Note

Unlike a standard public address system, an emergency voice/alarm communication system is required by the codes in certain occupancies and is tied to the fire alarm system.

Note

The *NEC* limits the types of low-voltage cables that can be installed with fire alarm circuits due to possible interference.

Note

The most current ABA and ADA standards and *ICC A117.1* include assistive listening requirements.

equipment and includes public address systems, intercommunication systems, and electronic instruments in this category. The code separates these requirements into permanent audio systems, portable/temporary audio systems, and audio systems near bodies of water (e.g., pools). For permanent audio systems, the *NEC* requirements cover the use of flexible cables, the grounding of equipment racks, the number of cables allowed in a conduit, and the installation of speakers in rated walls.

The *visual* part of an AV system could include the need to connect television, monitors, computers, projectors, DVD players, and so on to coaxial cable connections that require additional types of low-voltage cabling. Connection to other communication systems in the building may also be required. For example, a television or monitor in a conference center may include video conferencing capabilities, which requires connection to the telecommunication system. Coaxial cabling is typically required in conference rooms to be able to connect a projector, monitor, and a laptop for visual presentations. Although there are multiple standards for the components that make up an AV system, few if any are available for the overall design and installation. Instead, the industry has created multiple reference manuals to assist with this.

For more complicated AV systems, or where electrical interference may cause a problem, the *NEC* allows a separately derived electrical system called *technical power*. Previously permitted in motion picture and television studios, it is now allowed in any commercial or industrial building where there is concern that electrical noise may affect audio and video signals. Electrical noise is often caused by the grounds used with electrical wiring. (See the section titled "Grounding and Circuit Interrupters" earlier in this chapter.) Technical power systems allow alternate grounding options. However, additional precautions must be taken, which include using GFCI-protected receptacles and certain types of light fixtures if used as part of the system.

Security Systems

Security systems used inside a building typically concentrate on protecting the building from unauthorized entry. However, other systems may be used to contain the occupants. Examples of protecting against unauthorized entry include intrusion detection and alarms, access control systems such as card readers and biometric identifiers (e.g., fingerprint scanners and voice recognition), closed-circuit television (CCTV), digital video recording (DVR), and locking systems. These security components can be used individually and in unlimited combinations and typically

> **◀ Note**
>
> The *NEC* allows for a unique type of electrical system, called *technical power,* for commercial and industrial buildings where electrical noise may affect audio and video signals.

require space in a building's communication room. It is also more common for these systems to be monitored and controlled remotely through email and other electronic devices. In addition, a security system may be tied to other building systems such as a fire alarm system or a mass notification system. (See the inset titled "Building Automation Systems" earlier in this chapter.) In each case, the goal is to keep occupants safe.

Although the codes do not require security systems, some aspects of the use and installation of these systems are controlled by the codes. In fact, some security components can be in conflict with fire protection requirements, which require occupants to exit a building quickly during an emergency. Because it is an issue of life safety, the *LSC* and the building codes regulate security systems when they affect exiting. For example, the *IBC* includes requirements specific to access-controlled egress doors. The *NEC* covers cabling and installation requirements for certain security systems. The NFPA developed the standard *NFPA 731, Installation of Electronic Premises Security Systems,* to provide information on intrusion detection systems, electronic access control systems, and CCTV. Numerous other industry and manufacturing standards are available as well, including ones from Underwriters Laboratozries and the Security Industry Association (SIA). Most door hardware and locking-related standards are created by the Builders Hardware Manufacturers Association (BHMA), including newer standards geared to high-security doors.

One of the most significant code concerns is to prevent the locking of doors for security reasons from interfering with the required means of egress. However, as part of a security system (e.g., in psychiatric hospitals or prisons), certain doors within the means of egress may require locks. Various locking systems are available that will provide security while not endangering the occupants. Whether the lock should be fail safe or fail secure determines many of the other characteristics of the locking system. The lock is considered to be *fail safe* if the door automatically unlocks when power goes out, such as in the event of a fire. If the lock is *fail secure,* the door will remain locked even in the event of the loss of power. This type of lock may interfere with exiting if additional precautions are not provided, such as constant monitoring by personnel.

Three types of locks are typically used for security:

1. **Mechanical locks.** Mechanical locks are opened either with a key or by a code entered into a push-button mechanism. These types of locks are not usually allowed on an exit door unless there is constant supervision of the door. However, if it is an exterior door, a push bar or other type of panic hardware can be installed on the interior to allow exiting without a key.

✎ Note

UL has created three approval marks specifically for the security industry: security equipment, signaling equipment, and commercial security equipment. (See the inset titled "UL Labels" in Chapter 1.)

✎ Note

NFPA 72, National Fire Alarm and Signaling Code includes security-related requirements for emergency notification within a building.

✎ Note

A lock is said to be *fail safe* if the door automatically *unlocks* when power goes out. The lock is *fail secure,* if the door remains *locked* even in the event of the loss of power.

2. **Electrical locks.** Electrical locks can be electromechanical or electromagnetic. Two of the more common types of *electromechanical* locks include delayed egress or alarmed doors. Because they can be fail safe or fail secure, the proper action must be specified if the door is required for exiting. Standards that apply to electromechanical locks include *ANSI/BHMA 156.5, Auxiliary Locks and Associated Products,* and *ANSI/BHMA 156.25, Electrified Locking Devices,* as well as *ANSI/UL 1034, Burglary-Resistant Electric Locking Mechanisms.* *Electromagnetic* locks, often referred to as *maglocks,* use a magnetic field to hold the metal plate on the door or jamb in place. (These locks are similar to electromagnetic door holders, which are used to hold open fire-rated doors and release them to close when the fire alarm is activated. See the section titled "Rated Door Assemblies" in Chapter 6.) Because they have no mechanical parts and depend on electricity, they are considered fail safe and can be safely connected to the fire alarm system and the security system. Standards that apply to electromagnetic locks include *ANSI/BHMA A156.23, Electromagnetic Locks,* and *ANSI/BHMA A156.24, Delayed Egress Locks.* Because these doors do not rely on a mechanical latch for closure, additional hardware may be needed on a rated door to properly latch the door as required by the code.

3. **Pneumatic locks.** Pneumatic locks use electromechanical devices and pneumatic air pressure. They are used largely in Institutional occupancies such as hospital and prison facilities. These locks can be locked and released electronically and manually.

◀ **Note**

When deciding on hardware for egress doors, the appropriate combination of locks, latches, exit devices, and alarms must be determined.

The need for a security system should be considered when designing the means of egress. Each type of door should be reviewed separately and as part of the whole exiting plan. In some cases, the plan may need to be reviewed with a code official. In addition, when a security system is installed as part of a BAS, it cannot disrupt other systems that affect life safety. If the fire alarm is connected to the BAS, the BAS must be programmed to establish the proper priority of action. The fire alarm typically must take precedence over security issues. For instance, if a fire activates the fire alarm, certain security doors that are locked must be allowed to open for proper egress. If the power fails, the security doors should unlock as well. But that may not be the case depending on the occupancy or situation. It is also a good idea to include manual locks on security doors so that they can be locked after a building is evacuated.

If a space is required to be accessible, even in a high-security area, the security devices that are used by the occupants (or visitors) must be accessible. The requirements are found in the *ADA Standards* and the *ICC A117.1* standard. Not only must door handles be accessible (see Chapter 5) but also all security devices must be within accessible reach ranges and must have controls or buttons that are easy to use. The acceptable range is shown at the security card reader in Figure 9.9; however, the actual location will depend on the type of device and how it is used. For example, a card reader requires someone to pass a security card in front of it, whereas a key pad has to be viewed by the person punching in the numbers. Both a standing person and someone in a wheelchair need to be considered when determining the height. (In some cases, two devices may be needed—one high and one low.) In addition, the clear floor space in front of the device should be considered and might affect the location of the door. There should typically be at least a 30- by 48-inch (760- by 1220-mm) floor clearance in front of the device. If a turnstile is used, a means must be provided for a person in a wheelchair to get through. (Refer to the *ADA Standards* for specifics.)

COMMUNICATION SUSTAINABILITY CONSIDERATIONS

Communication systems are considered low-voltage and require less electricity to run than other electrical systems. However, when evaluating a building's energy efficiency, all systems should be considered. The key area of focus for sustainable communication systems is typically the main communication room. Not only does it contain large pieces of energy-consuming equipment but also this equipment must be kept cool as well.

Although current sustainability codes do not include provisions for communication systems, there are several things to consider. For example, the sustainability standard *ASHRAE 189.1* requires the energy-consumption management system to be monitored remotely. (See the section titled "Electrical Sustainability Considerations" earlier in this chapter.) This will require integration of the electrical system with the telecommunication system. Computers will be used to collect and compile the information, and also to send the information as required through email, text, or similar messaging. Using a building automation system to tie these systems together helps make this possible. (See the inset titled "Building Automation Systems" earlier in this chapter.)

Several sustainability standards are being developed by the communication industry. For example, in 2009, the Alliance for Telecommunication Industry Solutions (ATIS) published three standards used to determine telecommunication equipment's energy efficiency. These standards introduce a standard of measurement known as a Telecommunications Energy Efficiency Ratio (TEER), which can be used to measure and report energy

> **◢ Note**
>
> Information technology equipment (ITE) accounts for approximately 4 percent of electrical use in the world.

consumption of telecommunication equipment. Other standards using this system are being developed as well.

RESEARCH: USING THE ELECTRICAL CODES

Although for most interior design projects, the direct use of the electrical codes by the designer or architect will be minimal, using your understanding of the components of the electrical system and code requirements to collaborate with an electrical engineer or electrical contractor will be important.

But, to begin to understand where the information that we have discussed is located within the codes, we will review the primary resources. First, the building codes including the *IBC* and the *NFPA 5000* each have an electrical chapter: for example, the *IBC* Chapter 27 "Electrical" chapter. There are few requirements in these chapters; instead, they refer you to the *NEC* for most of the specific requirements. However, you should check electrical chapter in the building code for specific requirements that may apply. For example, the electrical chapter of the *IBC* and the *IFC* include a section on emergency and standby power systems that coordinates to other parts of the *IBC*. These requirements must be coordinated with the requirements in Chapter 10, "Means of Egress," for exit signs and egress illumination and Chapter 9, "Fire Protection Systems," for smoke control systems. In the *LSC* Chapter 9, "Building Service and Fire Protection Equipment," there is a section on electrical systems what works similarly.

In the *NEC*, however, many of the code requirements pertain to the wiring, types of cables, connections, and devices used to create the electrical systems. This information will be used primarily by the electrical engineer to specify elements within the system. However, there may be some requirements in Chapter 4, "Equipment for General Use," and Chapter 6, "Special Equipment," which may be helpful based on your project scope. These chapters include requirements we have discussed pertaining to electrical room/closets, types and locations of outlets, types and locations of light fixtures, and other typical components.

The *NEC* also references several standards throughout its text. Many of them are listed in Figure 9.1. In some cases, you may need to refer to them; however, most address conditions for the manufacture, testing, and proper installation for electrical and communication components. Although typical equipment developed for use in the US, should meet these requirements and licensed contractors should be aware of these requirements, you may need to confirm compliance for new to the market or imported fixtures or devices.

In addition, the NEC also has additional requirements for certain occupancies and building types such as Assembly occupancies, Health Care facilities and those with dwelling units, and certain facilities with high electrical needs, such as theaters and television studios. For these additional research may be required. For example, Health Care facilities must also comply with *NFPA 99, Standard for Health Care Facilities*. In addition the codes will also allow some Residential occupancies to follow the electrical requirements of the *International Residential Code* (*IRC*) instead of the *NEC*.

For energy efficiency requirements, most commercial projects will have to comply with portions of the *IECC* and the *ASHRAE/IESNA 90.1*, as part of the Energy Policy Act (EPAct). In turn, the *IECC* references the *ASHRAE 90.1*. Additional energy-efficient requirements are included in the newer sustainable documents, including *ASHRAE 189.1*.

Most commercial projects will have to comply with portions of the *IECC* and the *ASHRAE/IESNA 90.1*, as part of the Energy Policy Act (EPAct) and as required by a local jurisdiction. Many of these requirements will be integrated into the project by the electrical engineer; however, appropriate devices such as light fixtures for energy efficiency must be researched and selected. Within the commercial and residential provisions of the *IECC* is a chapter on "Commercial Energy Efficiency." Within this chapter is a section titled "Electrical Power and Lighting Systems" where many of the pertinent requirements can be found. The *IECC* also has a chapter on "Existing Buildings" that may apply. Additional energy-efficient requirements are included in the newer sustainable documents, including *ASHRAE 189.1*.

If your project calls for a unique electrical solution, researching allowable performance codes and criteria may be necessary. The *NEC* does not include performance requirements for electrical systems. If using other NFPA codes, their performance-related chapters can be referenced for performance criteria. However, if the *ICC Performance Code* (*ICCPC*) is allowed by the jurisdiction it does include electrical-related performance criteria. For example, *ICCPC* includes a chapter on electricity as well as a few electrical-related items are covered in the fire safety chapter. In addition, when using the *IBC*, the alternative materials and methods *IBC Section 104.11* is another option for unique solutions developed with performance criteria.

Accessibility issues related to electrical systems mostly apply to the mounting height of the outlets and fixtures. Therefore, there is not a dedicated chapter or section for electrical devices per se. However, many of the sections for reach ranges, operable parts, protruding objects, and clear floor area requirements, and so on found in "Chapter 3, Building Blocks," in the *ADA Standards* and the *ICC A117.1* will apply to the location and useability of devices within the electrical system.

> **✎ Note**
>
> The *NEC* includes special sections for hazardous areas. *Article 517*, for example, gives unique requirements for health care facilities where patients are examined or treated.

RESEARCH: USING THE COMMUNICATION CODES

Similar to electrical requirements, the primary code used by designers for communication requirements is the *NEC*. However, the *NEC* sets few requirements for communication systems compared to the number of requirements for electrical codes. This is partially because much of the wiring for communication systems is low voltage, which poses few safety problems. The *NEC* does not regulate the transmission of signals or the connection of communication services to the building. It regulates only the parts of these systems that are inside the building or controlled by the building. In addition, it is difficult to develop codes for systems that tend to change rapidly. As a result, the communication industry relies more on industry standards to meet certain performance and safety criteria— standards that can be modified quickly as technology evolves. The most current practices and standards are typically integrated into the available products or will be specified by the communication system provider or contractor. However, there are a few requirements in the *NEC*, for example, the need for cable trays or raceways, which may need to be researched. These requirements are found in Article 392 of the *NEC*.

The *IBC*, *IFC*, and the *LSC* may also affect certain communication systems. Most of the communication related requirements in the *IBC* will be found in Chapter 9, "Fire Protection Systems." The systems that address notification of and communication with occupants in the event of a fire are in this chapter. However, communication systems integrated into a building may require coordination with other requirements within the codes. For example, the means of egress chapters in the building codes and the *LSC* (and individual occupancy chapters) must be consulted when a security system is added because of the way the system affects the building's exits.

Accessibility requirements that affect communication systems mostly control the mounting height of the outlets and operable parts of equipment and devices like electrical devices. Other requirements may be more specific to an occupancy or building type. For example, in some Assembly occupancies, the building codes and the *ADA Standards* require the use of an assistive listening system if a microphone or sound projection is used. Emergency communications systems may be affected so that the same information is effectively provided for the hearing and hearing impaired. The sustainability codes and standards do not currently affect communication systems.

DOCUMENTATION

Whether an engineer or communication consultant (or other consultant) is required will depend on the size of the project, the amount of electrical or communication work, and the jurisdiction of the project. However, you will need to identify the electrical and communication devices in your design and coordinate with the project team. This is particularly important if you are renovating or doing a tenant build-out in an existing building.

Most of this will need to be documented on your drawings and specifications. However, it is especially helpful to research and coordinate the requirements before you get too far in the design development. You can use the "Electrical and Communication" sections of the digital code documentation form provided with this book to help you with this process. The first part of the documentation form concentrates on the electrical requirements, including systems and devices. To begin with, it prompts you to identify the main electrical items that will be incorporated or exist in your project. For example, you should know where the existing electrical panels are, the size of the proposed electrical room, and the number and capacity of the electrical panels, especially if you need to coordinate the size of a new electrical room with the engineer or are adding lighting and equipment to the space. You will also need to coordinate the location of electrical and communication outlets with the space plan and furniture and equipment locations. You might want to use a floor plan of the space to mark the locations as well. This will also make it easier to check in the field.

You may need to research and indicate the types of outlets for the project. In some cases, you may be reusing all existing receptacles and/or switches. However, in some projects, you may need to coordinate between existing outlets and new. Indicate any special or dedicated outlets as well. You will also want to indicate the types of light fixtures, equipment, appliances, or special systems that may be included in the project. It is also a good idea to attach the cut sheets of any items that are specified. For example, you may specify the light fixtures and appliances, the client might specify certain equipment being used in the space, and the electrical engineer will specify other electrical devices. The checklist can be used to remind you of the multiple devices that should be labeled or noted on your drawings.

The "Communication" section will help you identify the type of systems in your project and the various devices and components that need to be researched and coordinated with the design team. Many of these details are determined by a consultant, the communication vendor, or an engineer; however, this part of the checklist will help you keep these systems organized. For example, it may be important to indicate the companies installing the system for future reference. Similar to the electrical room, you may need to coordinate the location of the main communication room to optimize the system. Again, other communication systems, such as the surveillance monitors for the security system, special cabling, and special equipment, should be documented in your files and on the drawings.

CHAPTER 10

FINISH AND FURNITURE

Over the years, many fatal fires in the United States have been caused or escalated by flammable materials, finishes, and upholstery. One of the most noted incidents was the 1942 fire in Boston's Cocoanut Grove nightclub, which claimed the lives of 492 people. In response to that deadly fire, Boston established regulations dealing with interiors and interior finishes, known as the *Boston Fire Code*. Fatal fires continue to occur in which finishes and furniture are a contributing factor. In recent years, several nightclub and nursing home fires in the United States have claimed multiple lives. Whether or not the interior finishes and upholstered furniture are the initial *cause* of a fire, they are likely to contribute to its spread. For example, a wallcovering that is *not* flame resistant can spread a fire down the length of an entire corridor in a matter of seconds, setting other flammable items, such as draperies and upholstery, on fire and creating deadly smoke, heat, and toxic fumes.

Building codes and standards include strict directives for the selection and use of interior finishes, furnishings, and furniture. Chapter 6 discussed fire prevention through the use of rated interior building materials and assemblies (e.g., wall, floor, and ceiling systems). This chapter concentrates on the products that are either placed on top of the building materials (e.g., finishes) or set within the spaces created by the building materials and structural elements (e.g., furniture). The codes also regulate decorative materials and trim, some of which may be introduced to the space by the occupants rather than the designer. However, all of these items are considered part of the fuel load and can contribute to the ignition and spread of a fire. As a result, finishes and

> **✎ Note**
>
> *Interior finishes* are regulated differently than *decorative materials.* It is important to know in which category a material or product will be considered to know the requirements it must meet.

> **✎ Note**
>
> *Fire* resistance pertains to building materials and assemblies. *Flame* resistance focuses on the finishes applied to these materials and assemblies.

furniture (and some decorative materials) often must meet certain regulations.

The ratings given to finishes and furniture are different from those given to building materials and assemblies. Tested building materials are typically given hourly ratings, which represent the amount of time the material can resist a *fire*. The tests for finishes and furniture concentrate on the potential of a material to contribute to overall fire and smoke growth and spread. Typically, the fire source used is a *flame* (or lighted cigarette) or small fire. Some of the tests are considered small-scale and only use a small portion of the finish or furnishing being tested. Other finish and furniture tests are larger in scale, using either a larger sample of the finish but the full assembly consisting of the finish, substrate, adhesive, fasteners, and any other parts. In some cases, an entire room or piece of furniture is simulated.

This chapter begins by explaining the various types of finishes and furnishings as defined by the codes. After indicating the various codes and standard publications that will apply, the chapter describes the various finish and furniture standards and tests and their results. This information will be helpful when selecting products in conjunction with the requirements found in the codes. Other code requirements, as well as the sustainability and accessibility requirements related to finishes and furniture, are explained in this chapter. The chapter also discusses considerations not specified in the codes that should be applied for safety and liability reasons.

TYPES OF FINISHES AND FURNISHINGS

Interior finishes and furnishings covered by the codes and standards include a variety of materials and products and can be divided into seven categories. They are identified and defined in the following list and are discussed throughout this chapter.

❑ **Ceiling finishes.** Exposed interior surfaces of a building, including suspended ceiling systems and coverings that can be applied to fixed and movable ceilings, soffits, beams, space frames, and other similar elements.

❑ **Wall finishes.** Exposed interior surfaces of a building, including coverings that may be applied over fixed or movable walls and par-

> **✎ Note**
>
> The terminology used to describe products that are more resistant to fire has changed over the years. *Flameproof* is a common term that is used incorrectly, because very few products are totally unaffected by fire. The correct terms are *flame retardant* and *flame resistant.*

> **✎ Note**
>
> Most interior finishes and furnishings are considered combustible. The codes typically require that they restrict flame spread and smoke development to some degree if they are to be used in building interiors.

> **✎ Note**
>
> Works of art such as paintings and photographs are typically not regulated by the code if they do not exceed 20 percent of the wall area.

titions, toilet privacy partitions, columns, and other similar elements. Examples include vinyl and textile wallcovering, wood paneling or wainscoting, and applied acoustical finishes.

❑ **Floor finishes.** Exposed interior surfaces of a building, including coverings that may be applied over a finished or unfinished floor, stair (including risers), ramp, and other similar elements. Examples include hardwood, ceramic tile, vinyl, linoleum, carpets, and rugs. (Some types of wall base may also be included.)

❑ **Window treatments.** Decorative elements that control the amount of light and/or solar heat from a window area. These can include draperies, liners, blinds, and shutters as well plastic films applied to the glass. Curtains used in a space for privacy may also be included. These elements can be made of textiles, wood, vinyl, and other similar materials.

❑ **Decorative materials and trim.** Exposed decorative elements or protective materials attached to the interior wall or ceiling. These include decorative moldings, baseboards, chair rails, picture rails, handrails, and door and window moldings.

❑ **Furnishing finishes.** Exposed finishes found in case goods furniture, systems furniture, and soft seating, such as fabrics, wood veneers, and laminates. This category also includes nonexposed finishes, such as the foam in seating, liners in drapery, and other similar elements.

❑ **Furniture.** Whole pieces of furniture rather than separate parts and finishes. This category usually includes upholstered products, such as seating and movable panel systems. Also included are mattresses, which consist of the whole mattress composition, including fabric, padding, coils, and similar bedding assemblies.

The codes typically regulate only the first five categories. However, this situation is changing. Requirements are getting stricter and more standards are being developed. Sustainable requirements and considerations call for better ways to judge the sustainable characteristics of materials and assemblies that are used in the interiors and in furniture. As a result, new standards continue to be available. The codes are referencing more of these standards. Some states may also require the use of newer finish and/or furniture standards not yet mentioned in the codes.

☑ **Note**

NFPA 705 is a standard test that can be used in the field by a code official to assess finishes that have already been installed.

☑ **Note**

California has developed several finish and furniture standards through its California Bureau of Home Furnishings and Thermal Insulation Department. They are known as *technical bulletins*; several are discussed in this chapter as they relate to other required standards.

☑ **Note**

Finish and furniture testing is constantly changing. Older tests are being improved (or phased out) and new tests are being developed. It is critical to keep abreast of the changes so that the appropriate tests are referenced when specifying finishes and furniture.

FIRE DEVELOPMENT STAGES

To gain a better understanding of what makes a fire dangerous to the occupants of a building and why fire codes are necessary, it is important to review the four stages in the development of a fire.

Stage 1. Beginning with ignition, the initial phase is referred to as the *incipient* stage. Smoke produced during this stage can travel from the room of origin and pose a threat to occupants. At this stage, the fire could potentially be extinguished by a fire extinguisher.

Stage 2. In the *growth* stage, the fire begins to ignite material in the immediate area, including finishes and furniture. As a fire starts to consume more items, the temperature in the space increases dramatically. This heat can cause *flashover*. This occurs when the thermal radiation from the fire causes all the surfaces in an area or room to become heated to their ignition temperature, causing the materials to ignite spontaneously. This explosion usually occurs when a fire reaches the 1200-degree range and will cause the fire to spread rapidly. It also can greatly increase the rate of toxic smoke production. People are in danger of becoming trapped, exposed to toxic smoke or fumes, or burned during this stage of a fire.

Stage 3. When a fire is in the *fully developed* stage, it is at its hottest point and is consuming all available fuel. It is the most dangerous stage because smoke, heat, toxic gases, and possible structural collapse can harm occupants still within the space.

Stage 4. When the fire has used up the oxygen and the fuel sources in the space, it will begin the *decay* stage. Although this is the last phase before the fire is officially extinguished, non-flaming combustibles and harmful toxic fumes can still make it dangerous. In addition, the introduction of a new oxygen supply (like opening a door) can reignite the fire or cause a backdraft. This occurs when the superheated gasses in a room receive a new source of oxygen and causes them to explode.

The rate at which these stages of fire development progress varies tremendously with the construction materials of a building and fuel load within the building, including finishes and furniture. However, the first 5 to 10 minutes of a fire are the most critical. The materials and finishes selected can either contribute to the growth or prevent the spread of a fire—and can play a large role in the beginning stages of a fire. They can also contribute to the amount of toxic fumes generated. The goal of the code requirements is to lengthen the amount of time occupants have available to safely evacuate a building.

STANDARDS AND TESTING

Rather than listing specific requirements for finishes, furnishings, and furniture within their text, the codes reference several standards. They include standards from the National Fire Protection Association (NFPA), Underwriters Laboratories (UL), and ASTM International (ASTM). Figure 10.1 is an example of the finish- and furniture-related standards from the NFPA. Each standard sets performance expectations for the finish, materials, or furniture component. To verify this performance, a test is developed to assess the success or failure of the product under certain fire exposure conditions. These standards are referenced by the building codes, the fire codes, and the *Life Safety Code (LSC)*. These standards may also be required by certain jurisdictions or used voluntarily by designers to set industry standards for quality and safety.

Note

The codes do not necessarily mention or require every finish and furniture test discussed in this chapter. Some are required locally; others may be considered industry standards and used as best practices.

NFPA 253	Standard Method of Test for Critical Radiant Flux of Floor Covering Systems Using Radiant Heat Energy Source
NFPA 260	Standard Methods of Tests and Classification System for Cigarette Ignition Resistance of Components of Upholstered Furniture
NFPA 261	Standard Method of Test for Determining Resistance of Mock-Up Upholstered Furniture Material Assemblies to Ignition by Smoldering Cigarettes
NFPA 265	Standard Methods of Fire Tests for Evaluating Room Fire Growth Contribution of Textile Coverings on Full Height Panels and Walls
NFPA 269	Standard Test Method for Developing Toxic Potency Data for Use in Fire Hazard Modeling
NFPA 270	Standard Test Method for Measurement of Smoke Obscuration Using a Conical Radiant Source in a Single Closed Chamber
NFPA 286	Standard Methods of Fire Tests for Evaluating Contribution of Wall and Ceiling Interior Finish to Room Fire Growth
NFPA 701	Standard Methods of Fire Tests for Flame Propagation of Textiles and Films
NFPA 703	Standard for Fire-Retardant-Treated Wood and Fire-Retardant Coatings for Building Materials

Figure 10.1 Common NFPA standards for finishes and furniture.

FINISH CATEGORY	FINISH EXAMPLES	TYPICAL TEST REQUIRED
CEILING TREATMENTS[1]	Ceiling Tiles Fabric Coverings Vinyl Coverings Special Finishes	*Steiner Tunnel Test* *Room Corner Test*
WALLCOVERINGS[2]	Vinyl Wallcoverings Fabric Wallcoverings Expanded Vinyl Wallcoverings Wood Paneling Wood Veneers	*Steiner Tunnel Test* *Room Corner Test*
FLOOR COVERINGS[3]	Carpets Rugs Carpet Padding Hard Surface Flooring Resilient Flooring	*Pill Test Radiant Panel Test*
WALL BASE	All types 6 inches or less	*Radiant Panel Test*
WINDOW TREATMENTS AND VERTICAL HANGINGS[3]	Draperies and Liners Blinds Wood Shutters Wall Hangings Acoustical Fabrics Panel Fabrics	*Vertical Flame Test*
TRIM AND DECORATIVE MATERIALS[4]	Decorative Mouldings Wainscoting Chair Rails Picture Rails Baseboards	*Steiner Tunnel Test* *Room Corner Test*
UPHOLSTERIES	Fabrics Vinyls, Battings, Welt Cords Foams Interliners Fillings	*Steiner Tunnel Test* *Smolder Resistance Test* *Smoke Density Test*
FURNITURE	Seating Panel Systems Mattresses	*Smolder Resistance Test* *Upholstered Seating Test* *Mattress*

Notes:
1 If the wall or ceiling finish is a site-fabricated stretch fabric system, it may also have to pass *A STM E2573*.
2 Some finish applications may require an additional test as required by a jurisdiction.
3 If all or part of a finish consists of plastic, it might also have to pass *UL 1975* for foam plastics or *ASTM D2843* for light-transmitting plastics.
4 Any of the finish or furniture applications listed here may also have to undergo a toxicity test.

Figure 10.2 Typical regulated finishes/furniture and required tests.

Each finish and furniture standard and related test has a specific purpose. As shown in Figure 10.2, a finish will be subjected to a different test depending on whether it is used as a wallcovering, a drapery, an upholstery, or otherwise. The application of the finish (not just the finish type) determines the appropriate test. For example, the *Radiant Panel Test* is required for carpeting applied to floors. If the same carpet is used on a wall, a different test is required. In other situations, a certain test may better represent the proposed use of a finish. For example, the *Room Corner Test* is a more realistic test than the *Steiner Tunnel Test* because its testing apparatus more closely simulates an actual room. Furniture items are subject to specific tests. In some cases, where the piece will be used in a building or in what type of building may influence the required test. For example, a chair used in the lobby of a hotel may have to meet additional standards than that same chair used in the office of the hotel. In addition, a mattress used in a hotel must pass a more stringent test than the *16 CFR 1632* standard, which is required for all mattresses. For these reasons it is important to know the intent of the test and recognize the meaning of the test results.

In addition, each test or standard provides a specific result. Some of the tests are pass/fail, and others determine and assign a specific class or ranked rating. For example, the *CAL 133* and *NFPA 701* tests are pass/fail tests. If a finish passes, it is allowed; if it fails, it cannot be used. Other tests, such as the *Steiner Tunnel Test* and the *Radiant Panel Test,* assign class ratings to the tested finishes. Still others, such as *LC-50,* provide a ranked number rating. The manufacturer must supply the result from these tests. It is typically either a letter or number. For example, a tunnel test will result in an A, B, or C classification. The radiant panel test will result in a I or II classification. But the LC-50 test will result in a number. The codes will indicate the result that is required. (The type of result for each test is described in this section.)

Many additional industry standards that are not referenced by the codes are available. Remember, industry standards are ones not required by the codes but may be considered within "best practice" measures of a specific industry. These are described by the inset titled "Industry Standards" in this chapter and are not discussed in this book. Some standards that start as industry standards will eventually become an enforced standard. In addition, there are many newer sustainability standards, which are explained in the section titled "Sustainability Considerations" later in this chapter.

The standard tests described in this section have been grouped by the common test name. They are also summarized in Figure 10.3. Within each category, specific test names are listed, depending on the standards organization that provides the test. Often ASTM, NFPA, and UL have their own written standard for the same test. The federal government and the state of California have similar tests as well. In most cases, these tests are very similar; however, some differences do occur and are noted as well.

Remember, the codes set minimum requirements. In some cases, it may be wise to select finishes and furniture that exceed the standards required by the codes. (See the section titled "Documentation and Liability" in Chapter 11.)

☑ **Note**

Tests to support a specific standard can be developed by different agencies; they can be similar but may not be exactly the same. The building codes, fire codes, and *LSC* will reference the acceptable tests.

COMMON TEST NAMES	STANDARD NAME/NUMBER	TYPE OF RATING
STEINER TUNNEL TEST	ASTM E84 UL 723	Class Rating (A, B, or C)
RADIANT PANEL TEST	ASTM E648 NFPA 253	Class Rating (I or II)
PILL TEST	16 CFR 1630 (DOC FF1—70) 16 CFR 1631 (DOC FF2—70) ASTM D2859	Pass or Fail
VERTICAL FLAME TEST	NFPA 701 ASTM D6413	Pass or Fail
ROOM CORNER TEST		
(textile materials)	NFPA 265 UL 1715	Pass or Fail
(nontextile materials)	NFPA 286 ASTM E2257 (similar)	Pass or Fail
SMOLDER RESISTANCE TEST		
(component)	NFPA 260 ASTM E1353 CAL 117 (similar)	Class Rating (I or II)
(mock-up)	NFPA 261 ASTM E1352 CAL 116 (similar)	Pass or Fail
TOXICITY TEST LC-50 (or Pitts Test)	NFPA 269 ASTM E1678	Ranked
UPHOLSTERED SEATING TEST		
(full-scale)	ASTM E1537 CAL 133	Pass or Fail
(small-scale)	ASTM E1474	Ranked
MATTRESS TEST		
(commercial applications)	ASTM E1590 CAL 129	Pass or Fail
(all applications)	16 CFR 1632 (DOC FF4–72) 16 CFR 1633 CAL 603	Pass or Fail

Note: Several tests may be required by a jurisdiction depending on the occupancy and its location within a building. In addition, there may be other tests and/or test names not listed above that are more specific to a jurisdiction.

Figure 10.3 Summary of tests for finishes and furniture.

Steiner Tunnel Test

The *Steiner Tunnel Test* is the principal test used to determine the flame spread and smoke development ratings in the classification of interior finishes applied to walls, ceilings, and other structural elements, such as columns. As one of the first interior finish tests, its name comes from the fact that finishes are tested in a tunnel-like apparatus that is 25 feet (7.62 m) in length. Although the procedure of the test has been refined over the years, the overall test has not changed much since its inception. The *Steiner Tunnel Test* is particularly appropriate for typical building materials and for thicker materials. However, many new interior finish materials are more complex and testing by other methods may be preferred, but the codes do allow the Steiner Test in various applications. The same test is used under these names:

❑ *ASTM E84, Standard Test Method for Surface Burning Characteristics of Building Materials*
❑ *ANSI/UL 723, Standard for Test for Surface Burning Characteristics of Building Materials*

Using the tunnel apparatus, a finish is tested in a horizontal position attached to the entire length of the tunnel ceiling, as shown in Figure 10.4. The sample consists of the finish and any required substrate and/or adhesive (or other securing method) that would be used in the actual installation of the finish. For example, if a wallcovering is intended to be used on gypsum board, the sample will consist of the wallcovering applied to one layer of gypsum board using the adhesive recommended by the manufacturer. Once the sample is secured, a flame is started at one end and a regulated draft is applied through the tunnel. The test measures how quickly and how far the flame spreads during a specified time. Based on the markings along the tunnel and the progression of the flame on the material, a flame spread index (FSI) is assigned. The density of the smoke in relation to a light source is measured at the opposite end of the tunnel. This determines the smoke development index (SDI). These two indexes are used to assign a classification to the finish.

In the codes, these classifications are identified in three categories for interior wall and ceiling finishes, with Class A being the most restrictive and Class C being the least. (Floor finishes have a different test and rating system, as described next.) The classifications consist of the following:

❑ Class A: Flame spread index 0–25, smoke development index 0–450
❑ Class B: Flame spread index 26–75, smoke development index 0–450
❑ Class C: Flame spread index 76–200, smoke development index 0–450

☑ **Note**

The position of the finish sample in the *Steiner Tunnel Test* makes it difficult for some finishes (e.g., plastics) to be tested without a screen for support. Because of this, the codes sometimes recommend other standards.

☑ **Note**

Some woods that have been treated with a fire retardant can qualify as a Class A interior finish. Most untreated wood will either have a Class C flame spread rating or no rating at all.

☑ **Note**

The *Steiner Tunnel Test* is used for a wide range of materials in addition to wall and ceiling finishes. Examples include fire retardant–treated wood, fire-retardant coatings, and pipe and duct insulation (including pipe covers used under lavatories).

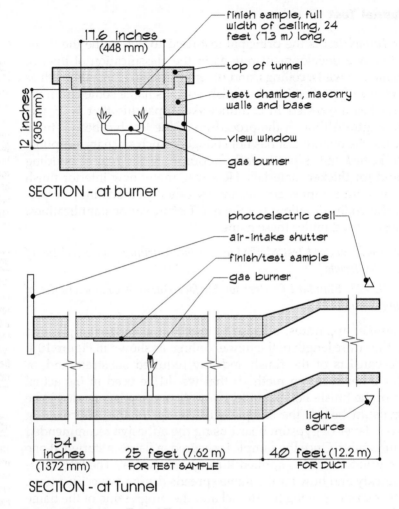

Figure 10.4 *Steiner Tunnel Test* apparatus.

The *FSI* indicates the speed at which a fire may spread across the surface of a material. The lower the number, the slower the fire will spread, which allows more time to evacuate the space or building. The index is determined by comparing the results of the test to the burning characteristics of two known materials: glass-reinforced cement board and red oak flooring. Arbitrarily, the cement board is given a flame spread of 0 and red oak flooring is assigned a flame spread of 100. All other materials are assigned FSI values based on their test results. Both interior finishes and building materials can be required by the codes to pass this test.

INDUSTRY STANDARDS

Not all standards that have been developed for finishes and furniture pertain to the flame resistance, smoke density, and toxicity of the materials and are referenced in the codes. Some standards address other health and welfare characteristics such as indoor area quality and may be referenced as sustainable criteria. Others are developed and are voluntarily used within the design industry to set standards for product characteristics, quality, and consistency in the manufacturing process. Some finish standards, for instance, address the colorfastness, lightfastness, breaking strength, and abrasion resistance of the material. This allows a valid comparison among various finishes and/or products so that the appropriate material can be chosen for the project requirements.

There are also industry standards that manufacturers follow when making their products so that consistency is maintained during production. For example, resilient flooring manufacturers might use standard *ASTM F1914, Standard Test Methods for Short-Term Indentation and Residual Indentation of Resilient Floor Covering*, which measures the amount of initial and residual indentation that can occur in the material; systems furniture manufacturers typically use *UL 1286, Standard for Office Furnishings*, to confirm the electrical and structural integrity of the components of the system, among other things. It may also be useful to include other standards in the project specifications for consistency of installation, such as *CRI 104, Standard for Installation of Commercial Carpet*.

New standards are continually being developed to address various objectives. For example, many new standards relate to sustainability. In general, standards can provide a consistency between products that helps when specifying for a project.

Figure 10.5 shows the flame spread ratings for a variety of materials. It provides a wide range of possible results, depending on the type of material.

The *smoke development index* (SDI) determines how much visibility is maintained when a material is on fire and creating smoke. A maximum acceptable SDI of 450 was defined by Underwriters Laboratories and is based solely on the level of visibility through the smoke created by the test. This would affect an occupant's ability to see exit signs while evacuating a building. The smoke development rating actually remains the same in each classification. Any finish with an SDI over 450 would create too much smoke and, therefore, would typically not be allowed by the codes.

Because the smoke development requirement does not change, it is the FSI number that distinguishes the difference in each class. Note, however, that there is no direct relationship between the FSI and the SDI. One finish can have low ratings on both, and another can have a low flame spread but a high smoke development rating. Any tested finish that results in an FSI or SDI above what is allowed by the codes would be considered a nonrated finish.

✓ Note

Site-fabricated stretch systems, often applied to walls and ceilings for acoustical purposes, consist of tracks/frames, fabric, and infill core material. The I-Codes require these systems to be tested by *ASTM E-84* with the *ASTM E2573* specimen mounting procedure.

Material	Flame Spread Rating
Glass-fiber sound-absorbing panels	15 to 30
Mineral-fiber sound-absorbing panels	10 to 25
Shredded wood fiberboard (treated)	20 to 25
Sprayed cellulose fibers (treated)	20
Aluminum (with baked enamel finish on one side)	5 to 10
Brick or concrete block	0
Cork	175
Gypsum board (with paper on both sides)	10 to 25
Wood—Northern pine (treated)	20
Wood—Southern pine (untreated)	130 to 190
Wood—Maple	104
Plywood paneling (untreated)	75 to 275
Plywood paneling (treated)	100 to 185
Carpeting	10 to 600
Concrete	0

Figure 10.5 Typical flame spread of common materials

Radiant Panel Test

The *Radiant Panel Test* is used to rate interior floor finishes such as carpet, resilient flooring, and hardwood floor assemblies, as well as wall base. Two standard tests are available:

- ❑ *NFPA 253, Standard Method of Test for Critical Radiant Flux of Floor Covering Systems Using a Radiant Heat Energy Source*
- ❑ *ASTM E648, Standard Test Method for Critical Radiant Flux of Floor Covering Systems Using a Radiant Heat Energy Source*

Originally developed to simulate the type of fire that develops in corridors and exit ways, the test measures the floor covering's tendency to spread a fire. Although flooring in general is not considered a major cause of fire spread, the flooring material in exit access corridors can be of concern because it can add to fire growth when flame and hot gases radiate through the walls from a fire in an adjacent room. (This test can also be used for cellulose insulation materials.)

The test determines the minimum energy required to sustain flame on a floor covering. In this test, a finish sample is secured to a substrate and then placed at the bottom of the test chamber, as shown in Figure 10.6. The finish sample consists of the entire floor covering system, which includes the floor covering, any required padding, adhesive (or other securing method), and the substrate. The sample is preheated by a radiant

☑ Note

The NFPA notes that most fire deaths due to smoke inhalation in the United States occur in areas other than the room of fire origin and are caused by fires that have spread beyond the room of origin.

heat source mounted at a 30-degree angle from the sample and then exposed to a gas burner. If the sample begins to burn, two things are measured as soon as the flame goes out: the length of the burn marks and the amount of radiant heat energy at the farthest part of the burned area. Both measurements are compared to existing data (e.g., a flux profile graph) to determine the *critical radiant flux* (CRF).

The CRF is measured in watts per square centimeter. The higher the value, the more heat energy it takes to ignite the finish, making it more resistant to flame spread. Test results determine whether a floor finish will be considered a Class I or a Class II. Class I is more flame resistant. (Floor coverings that do not fall within one of these two categories are considered non-rated or nonclassed.) The CRF for each is as follows:

❑ *Class I*: CRF, minimum of 0.45 watts per square centimeter
❑ *Class II*: CRF, minimum of 0.22 watts per square centimeter

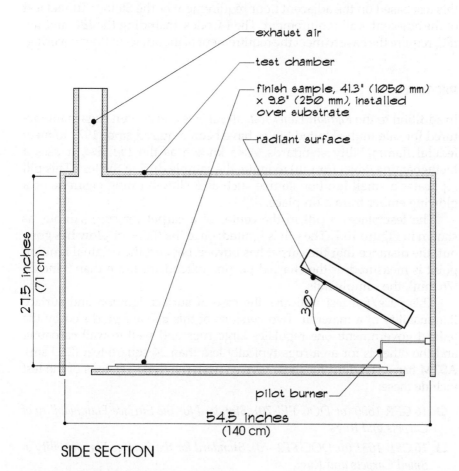

SIDE SECTION

Figure 10.6 *Radiant Panel Test* apparatus.

These two classes are referenced by the codes. Not all occupancies require a floor finish that has been tested by the *Radiant Panel Test*. If it is required, only exits and exit access corridors are typically regulated. The codes may also require it for lobbies in some health care occupancies such as hospitals and nursing homes. (See the section titled "Determining Finish Classifications" later in this chapter.) Although this test is often associated with the testing of carpet, these ratings also apply to other floor finishes. These include resilient floors such as VCT, as well as hardwood flooring installed over a combustible substrate such as plywood. (Hardwood floors applied directly to concrete are typically not required to be rated.) When furring strips are used under a floor covering, such as hardwood floors, other code restrictions may apply, as discussed later in this chapter. (See the section titled "Other Code Restrictions" toward the end of this chapter.)

The NFPA codes including the *UFC* and the *LSC* require a wall/floor base that is 6 inches (152 mm) or less to meet either the requirements of this test based on the adjacent floor requirement or the Steiner Tunnel test of the adjacent wall requirement. The I-Codes, including the *IBC* and the *IFC*, require the base to meet the requirement of the adjacent floor covering.

Pill Test

❏ Note

When carpet is used as other than on a floor finish, different tests may be required including the *Room Corner Test.*

In addition to the *Radiant Panel Test*, all carpets and certain rugs manufactured for sale in the United States have been required since 1971 to meet federal flammability standards. Also known as the *Pill Test*, it uses a methenamine tablet (or pill) to ignite the sample during the test. This pill replicates a small ignition source such as a slow-burning cigarette or a glowing ember from a fireplace.

The test places a pill in the center of a carpet (or rug) sample, as shown in Figure 10.7. The pill is ignited; once the flame or glow has gone out, the distance that the carpet has burned beyond the original ignition point is measured. If the charred portion extends to more than 3 inches (76 mm), the sample fails.

This pass/fail test indicates the ease of surface ignition and surface flammability of a material. Two versions of this test are produced by the federal government: one regulates large rugs and wall-to-wall carpeting and the other is for area rugs typically less than 24 square feet (2.23 sm). ASTM has a standard for these tests as well The three versions of the test include these:

❏ Note

A one-of-a-kind carpet or rug, such as an antique, an Oriental, or a hide, can be exempted from testing by the *Pill Test* for use in interiors, in some cases.

❑ *16 CFR 1630 (or DOC FFI-70), Standard for the Surface Flammability of Carpets and Rugs*

❑ *16 CFR 1631 (or DOC FF2–70), Standard for the Surface Flammability of Small Carpets and Rugs*

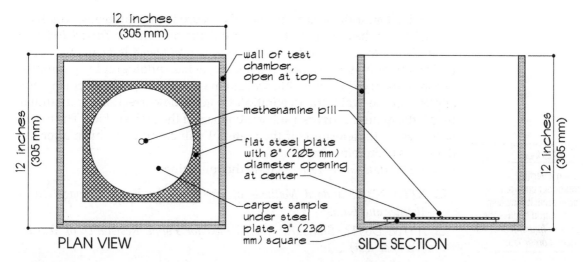

Figure 10.7 *Pill Test* apparatus.

❑ *ASTM D2859, Standard Test Method for Ignition Characteristics of Finishes Textile Floor Covering Materials (includes testing procedures for carpets and rugs)*

The federal government requires that all carpets and rugs sold in the United States be tested using *16 CFR 1630* and *16 CFR 1631*. Carpets must pass the test to be sold in the United States. All rugs, with few exceptions such as antiques or natural hides, must be tested and pass. If the rug does not pass, it must be labeled as flammable. The building codes typically require all carpets and large rugs (e.g., those tested by *16 CFR 1630* or *ASTM D2859*) to pass this *Pill Test* no matter what occupancy they are used in. Use of rugs that may be exempt from testing or do not pass the test may have to be approved by a code official. Although this test is considered standard protocol for carpets, and is referenced by the codes, additional flooring finish regulations may be required for occupancies that warrant more careful restrictions or where a codes official deems it necessary. (See the preceding section titled "Radiant Panel Test.")

Vertical Flame Tests

Vertical Flame Tests are generally required for vertical treatments such as curtains, draperies, window shades, large wall hangings or tapestries, and plastic films used for decorative purposes. Any vertical finish that is exposed to air on both sides is considered a *vertical treatment*. This includes wall hangings because air can get between the wall and the hanging.

However, if a fabric or tapestry is fully secured to a wall using adhesive, it will usually have to pass the requirements of a *Steiner Tunnel Test* or a *Room Corner Test*, as described next. The *Vertical Flame Test* can also apply to decorative materials used in a space, such as photographs, paintings, decorations, fixed or movable walls, paneling, wall pads, or crash pads applied to the walls for decoration or acoustic correction, and similar uses if the material covers a substantial part of the wall surface. The intent of the test is to determine if the material will continue to burn after the flame has been removed.

The *Vertical Flame Tests* include the following:

❑ *NFPA 701, Standard Methods of Fire Tests for Flame Propagation of Textiles and Films*

❑ *ASTM D6413, Standard Test Method for Flame Resistance of Textiles (Vertical Test)*

These tests are more representative of the actual use than the *Steiner Tunnel Test* because a flame source is used to create a vertical burning of the finish rather than the horizontal burning used in the tunnel test. *NFPA 701* is the oldest version of the test and the most commonly referenced by the building codes and the *LSC*. It is divided into two separate pass/fail tests known as *Test Method 1* and *Test Method 2*.

In both test methods, the sample must be exposed to conditions similar to those in which the fabric will be used. For example, fabrics for table linens must be laundered and drapery fabrics should be dry-cleaned. This gives the most realistic test results. It also indicates how important it is for clients to know how to clean and maintain the items specified and installed. If they do not follow the manufacturer's recommendations, the fabric's performance in a fire will be affected. The two test methods are described next.

✎ Note

When a vertical treatment covers a large area, it may also be required to pass the *Steiner Tunnel Test* or the *Room Corner Test.*

Test Method 1

Test Method 1 is a small-scale test and is required for lighter-weight fabrics that are either single-layered or multilayered. These include window curtains and drapes and other treatments such as swags, vertical folding shades, roll-type window shades, and fabric blinds (vertical and horizontal). These also include stage or theater curtains, hospital privacy curtains, display booth separators, table skirts, and linens, as well as textile wall hangings. (The maximum weight of the fabric is typically set at 700 grams per square meter, or approximately 20.5 ounces per square yard.)

The test consists of a fabric sample hung vertically on a bar in a test cabinet, as shown in Figure 10.8. A gas burner is applied to the lower edge

✎ Note

It is important to provide clients with manufacturer-recommended cleaning and maintenance information for the finishes and furniture specified. The way these items are maintained over the life of the product can affect their performance in a fire.

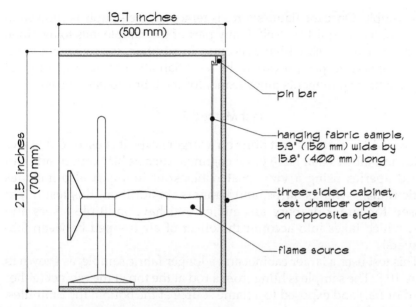

19.7 inches
(500 mm)

27.5 inches
(700 mm)

pin bar

hanging fabric sample,
5.9" (150 mm) wide by
15.8" (400 mm) long

three-sided cabinet,
test chamber open
on opposite side

flame source

TEST METHOD 1 - Side Section

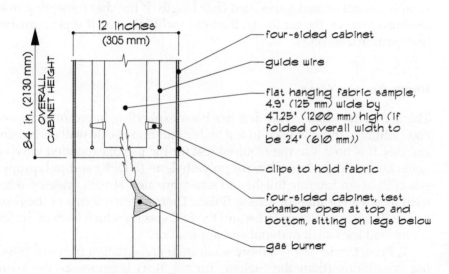

84 in. (2130 mm) OVERALL CABINET HEIGHT

12 inches
(305 mm)

four-sided cabinet

guide wire

flat hanging fabric sample,
4.9" (125 mm) wide by
47.25" (1200 mm) high (if
folded overall width to
be 24" (610 mm))

clips to hold fabric

four-sided cabinet, test
chamber open at top and
bottom, sitting on legs below

gas burner

TEST METHOD 2 - Side Section

Figure 10.8 *Vertical Flame Test* apparatus.

of the sample. Once the flame source is removed, the sample is allowed to burn until it extinguishes itself. If any part of the sample falls to the floor, it must self-extinguish within 2 seconds. In addition, the remaining sample is weighed; to pass, it cannot be less than 40 percent of its original weight. Both requirements must be met for the fabric to pass the test.

Test Method 2

Test Method 2 is a similar test done on a larger scale. It is used for heavier fabrics and fabrics that have vinyl coatings, such as blackout blinds and lined draperies using a vinyl-coated blackout lining. It also includes plastic films, awnings, tarps, and banners. In addition, this test might be used for larger drapery assemblies that have multiple layers and folds, which takes into account the effect of air trapped between fabric layers.

This test uses a larger cabinet and a longer fabric sample, as shown in Figure 10.8. The sample is hung from a rod at the top of the cabinet (either folded or flat) and exposed to a flame source at the bottom for 2 minutes. When the flame source is removed, the sample must self-extinguish within 2 seconds to pass the test. In addition, the burn marks left on the sample cannot exceed a specified char length. If the char remaining from the burn exceeds the set limits, the fabric will fail even if it extinguished itself within 2 seconds.

Room Corner Tests

The use of the *Room Corner Test* has been expanding in recent years and code editions. Initially used to test textile and non-textile wall and ceiling finishes, it is now also the required test for the use of expanded vinyl on walls and ceilings, high-density polyethylene (HDPE) and polypropylene (PP) as an interior finish, and site-fabricated stretch systems when used as a wall or interior ceiling finish. There are two forms of the *Room Corner Test*. The building codes and the *LSC* specify which form of the test is required for which material and application.

A *Room Corner Test* is a more accurate representation of actual building conditions (than the Steiner Tunnel Test) because, as the name implies, a complete room configuration is used for the test. The test determines how an interior finish material will add to fire growth (including heat and smoke) and if harmful combustion products such as gases are created. It also determines whether the finish will cause flashover or fire spread beyond the initial fire location. Although it is considered

> **✎ Note**
>
> If a backing is added to an approved textile during installation, it may make the original test invalid. However, the manufacturer may be able to provide a list of manufacturer-approved backings.

> **✎ Note**
>
> Expanded vinyl wallcoverings are high-density wall coverings that resist mold and mildew. They can also be resistant to fire.

a more rigorous test, the codes will, in some cases, allow the use of the Steiner Tunnel Test for textile and expanded vinyl wall or ceiling coverings (if the building is sprinklered) and site-fabricated stretch systems with additional conditions. The two versions of the tests are described here.

Textile and Expanded Vinyl Wall Coverings

The *Room Corner Test* standards for textile and expanded vinyl wallcovering. A textile wall covering would include, for example, when a napped, tufted, or looped textiles are applied to walls (i.e., carpets and carpet-like textiles.) Expanded vinyl wallcovering is a high density wall covering that is often used in commercial applications. It is resistant to mold and mildew and can be fire resistant. The two versions of the test are:

❑ *NFPA 265, Standard Methods of Fire Tests for Evaluating Room Fire Growth Contribution of Textile Coverings or Expanded Vinyl Wall Coverings on Full Height Panels and Walls*

❑ *UL 1715, Fire Test of Interior Finish Material*

These are pass/fail tests that simulate a fire within a full-size room, as shown in Figure 10.9. There were originally two testing methods: Method A and Method B. Although Method B is the only currently recognized protocol for the test, the codes still may refer to it by name. This testing method requires the finish sample to be mounted fully on the one rear wall and two long side walls using the adhesive intended for actual use. Note, Method A (which used a smaller sample) is now considered an alternative but not equal to Method B. In some codes or jurisdictions, it may be acceptable for finishes for existing buildings.

A fire source is started in the corner of the room. A square box located 2 inches (51 mm) from the back corner of the room is ignited. (See Figure 10.9.) It is first ignited at a heat level of approximately 40 kilowatts for 5 minutes and then increased to approximately 150 kilowatts for an additional 10 minutes. A duct system located outside the open doorway of the room collects the gases created by the fire and measures the gas velocity, temperature, and concentrations of gases. A finish passes the test if the criteria indicated by the standard and/or by the code are met. (If the acceptance criteria differ, the code requirements prevail.) For example, the flame cannot extend to the ceiling during the first heat exposure and flashover cannot occur during the second heat exposure. If the listed criteria are not met, the finish fails.

◪ Note

A significant difference between *NFPA 265* and *NFPA 286* is that the flame used in *NFPA 286* can reach the ceiling so can properly test ceiling finishes. The flame source per *NFPA 265* does not and should only be used for wall finishes.

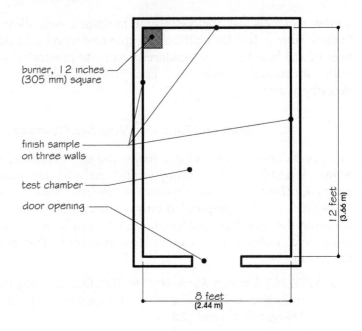

burner, 12 inches
(305 mm) square

finish sample
on three walls

test chamber

door opening

12 feet
(3.66 m)

8 feet
(2.44 m)

PLAN

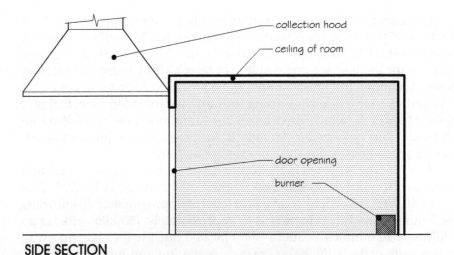

collection hood

ceiling of room

door opening

burner

SIDE SECTION

Figure 10.9 *Room Corner Test* apparatus—*Method B.*

Although the *Room Corner Test* is the preferred test for textile and expanded vinyl wall materials, the *IBC* and the *LSC* may allow the use of the *Steiner Tunnel Test* (*ASTM E84* or *UL 723*). The *Steiner Tunnel Test* can be used if the building is sprinklered, if the material does not cover the entire wall, or if the material is limited in height. The sample must also be mounted and prepared according to the *ASTM E2402* standard. Typically, to be accepted, the highest classification must be achieved under this test method. In addition, the Steiner Tunnel test must be used for textile or expanded vinyl ceiling coverings. (In this version of the Room Corner Test, the flame source does not reach the ceiling, so it does not adequately test the material applied to the ceiling.)

Nontextile Wall Coverings and Ceiling Coverings

There are two other standards that are also considered *Room Corner Tests*. These are intended to test nontextile materials used on walls or ceilings, textile walls or ceilings, expanded vinyl walls or ceilings, HDPE and PP used as an interior finish, and for site-fabricated stretch systems when used as an interior wall or ceiling finish. The standards for these tests are as follows:

❑ *NFPA 286, Standard Methods of Fire Tests for Evaluating Contribution of Wall and Ceiling Interior Finish to Room Fire Growth*

❑ *ASTM E2257, Standard Test Method for Room Fire Test of Wall and Ceiling Materials and Assemblies*

> **☞ Note**
>
> In addition to the *Room Corner Test*, the ICC codes allow expanded vinyl wall and textile and ceiling coverings to be tested using the *Steiner Tunnel Test* if additional criteria are met.

The basis for these tests and the *Room Corner Tests* described previously is similar. For example, the same simulated room shown in Figure 10.9 is used—same size, same instruments, same burning source, and so on. The finish samples are even applied to the room in the same way as in *Method B* described previously. However, for this test, the finish sample must also be secured to the ceiling of the room as well as the walls. (If it is exclusively a ceiling finish, then the finish sample can be applied only on the ceiling.) Additionally, the flame source is placed closer to the corner of the room so that it is in direct contact with the walls. The first ignition heat level and exposure length are also the same as in the test for the textile wallcovering, but the second exposure increases to approximately 160 kilowatts for 10 minutes. In addition to the criteria used for textile wallcoverings, tested finishes are given a smoke release value. If the nontextile finish does not pass all the required criteria, or if it exceeds the smoke release value (which is similar to the 450 SDI set by the *Steiner Tunnel Test*), it will fail. A textile finish must typically pass this test to be used on a ceiling.

The *ASTM E2257* test is similar to the NFPA test, except that different heat levels and time frames are used during the test. *NFPA 286* is the test most referenced by the codes.

The codes will require the use of Room Corner test for finishes PP and HDPE. Because these materials can drip or melt and fall to the floor, the Room Corner test is a more accurate evaluation of the impact of those materials in a fire.

Smolder Resistance Tests

The *Smolder Resistance Test* is also known as the *Cigarette Ignition Test*. It is a nonflame test that uses an actual smoldering cigarette as the ignition source to see how a product will smolder before either flaming or extinguishing. The test consists of placing a lighted cigarette on a sample and then covering it with a layer of sheeting material. The cigarette is allowed to burn its full length unless ignition occurs. (If ignition occurs, the sample automatically fails.) Once the cigarette burns its full length, the char length is measured in all directions. If the char is longer than allowed by the test, the sample does not pass.

This test is required by the *LSC* and the fire codes. It is required for most new upholstered furniture in board and care facilities, nursing homes, hospitals, detention and correctional facilities, and college and university dormitories. Although the methods used are virtually the same, there are two types of this test. One version of the test evaluates the individual *components* that make up a piece of furniture; the other version evaluates a combination of components or a partial *mock-up* of the piece of furniture. The codes will typically require one or the other, not both. Each is explained here.

Components

One type of *Smolder Resistance Test* is used to test an individual finish or textile. It is a pass/fail test and includes the following similar tests:

❑ *NFPA 260, Standard Methods of Tests and Classification System for Cigarette Ignition Resistance of Components of Upholstered Furniture*

❑ *ASTM E1353, Standard Test Methods for Cigarette Ignition Resistance of Components of Upholstered Furniture*

❑ *CAL 117, Requirements, Test Procedures and Apparatus for Testing the Flame Retardance of Resilient Filling Materials Used in Upholstered Furniture*

This test applies to a wide variety of furniture components and includes cover fabrics, interior fabrics, welt cords, decking materials, and barrier materials, as well as filling or padding materials. These filling/batting materials can be natural or manufactured fibers, foamed or cellular materials, resilient pads of natural or manufactured fibers, or loose particulate filling materials such as shredded polyurethane or feathers and down.

Depending on the component, the finish sample could be tested on one of two types of test apparatus: a "decking materials tester" or a "mini-mock-up tester." Both are shown in Figure 10.10. For example,

⬗ Note

The *Smolder Resistance Test* uses a smoldering cigarette. Because the test samples are not exposed to an open flame, the test is not a good indicator of flame spread or severe fire exposure.

⬗ Note

Standards are available that test the smoke density of an entire construction assembly. (See Chapter 6.)

⬗ Note

NFPA 270 can be used to test the smoke density of thinner interior finish assemblies.

⬗ Note

TB 117–2013 eliminated the open flame test and modified the smolder resistant test method. Although similar to NFPA 260, the TB 117–2013 is considered harder to pass for some materials.

samples that consist of decking material are typically tested horizontally using the decking material tester. Other components, such as fabrics, welt cords, filling or padding, and barrier materials, are assembled individually or in combination to fit on the standard base unit of the mini-mock-up tester. The mini-mock-up allows these materials to be tested with the cigarette in a crevice.

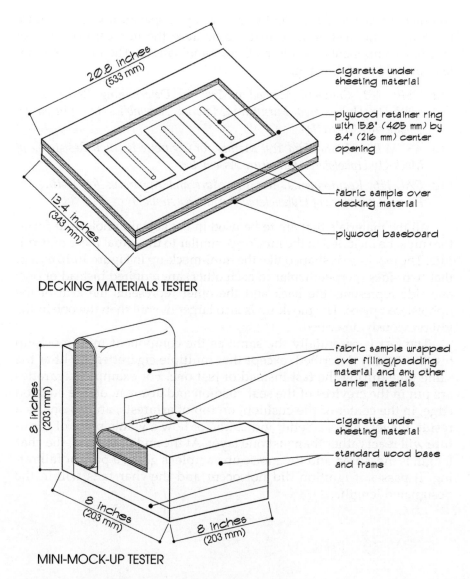

20.8 inches
(533 mm)

13.4 inches
(343 mm)

cigarette under
sheeting material

plywood retainer ring
with 15.8" (405 mm) by
8.4" (216 mm) center
opening

fabric sample over
decking material

plywood baseboard

DECKING MATERIALS TESTER

8 inches
(203 mm)

8 inches
(203 mm)

8 inches
(203 mm)

fabric sample wrapped
over filling/padding
material and any other
barrier materials

cigarette under
sheeting material

standard wood base
and frame

MINI-MOCK-UP TESTER

Figure 10.10 *Smolder Resistance Test*: Tester options.

Note

Every state in the United States and all of Canada now require the sale of "fire-safe" cigarettes. Designed to prevent the spread of fire, these cigarettes are made to self-extinguish if left unsmoked.

Note

Twenty-four states ban or limit the use of certain fire retardants and other additives used in plastics, foam, and upholstered furniture due to the toxins they emit. To see which states have bans or limits, go to https:// www.saferstates.com/ toxic-chemicals/ toxic-flame-retardants/.

Note

Not all upholstered furniture will require *CAL 133* testing. Some may only require a *Smolder Resistance Test*. The results of both tests can be improved with the use of certain fabric backcoatings, interliners, fire blockers, and special rated foams.

Although the test provides a cigarette resistance classification, Class I or Class II, it is essentially a pass/fail test. If the material resists ignition from the cigarette and does not exceed the maximum char length, it passes the test and is classified as Class I. Any material that does not pass the test is classified as Class II.

Mock-Ups

Another *Smolder Resistance Test* was developed specifically for furniture mock-ups. This test is more realistic because the mock-up consists of multiple components used in realistic combinations. The most common tests include the following:

❑ *NFPA 261, Standard Method of Test for Determining Resistance of Mock-Up Upholstered Furniture Material Assemblies to Ignition by Smoldering Cigarettes*

❑ *ASTM E1352, Standard Test Method for Cigarette Ignition Resistance of Mock-Up Upholstered Furniture Assemblies*

❑ *CAL 116, Requirements, Test Procedure and Apparatus for Testing the Flame Retardance of Upholstered Furniture (similar)*

All the materials that are to be used in the actual upholstered furniture must be included in the mock-up, similar to the actual piece of furniture. The mock-up is shaped like the mini-mock-up in Figure 10.10 except that two sides (perpendicular to each other) are required instead of one; one side represents the back and the other represents the arm of the upholstered piece. The mock-up is also larger overall than the one in the test previously described.

The test is essentially the same as the component mini-mock-up test previously described, except that multiple cigarettes are lit at the same time during the test instead of just one. For example, cigarettes are put in the crevices of the seat cushion and armrest, on the cushion edge, in the center of the cushion, on top of armrests, and so on. As a result, the test gives a better indication of how a whole piece of furniture will react rather than just one layer. At the end of the test, the char length is measured and the mock-up sample is given a pass or fail rating. It passes if ignition did not occur and the char falls within the designated length.

Toxicity Test

Toxicity testing applies to finishes and furnishings. The first *Toxicity Test* was developed by the University of Pittsburgh and was known as the *Pitts Test* or *LC-50*. More recent versions of the test are as follows:

❑ *NFPA 269, Standard Test Method for Developing Toxic Potency Data for Use in Fire Hazard Modeling*

❑ *ASTM E1678, Standard Test Method for Measuring Smoke Toxicity for Use in Fire Hazard Analysis*

These tests measure the amount of toxicity a material emits when it is burned. The testing covers a wide range of materials in addition to finishes and furniture. Included are wall, ceiling, and floor finishes, furniture upholstery, and mattresses and bed pads, as well as electrical wire and conduit, mechanical ductwork, thermal insulation, and plumbing pipes. The degree of toxicity is reported as an LC-50 (also called LC50) value.

The test consists of subjecting a small finish sample (or other material) to an ignition source and then exposing it to radiant heat lamps. (See Figure 10.11.) The concentration of gaseous toxicants is monitored. The data collected, along with the measured mass loss of the test sample, are used to predict the LC-50 rating of the test sample. The same procedure is then repeated using six live mice to confirm the predicted LC-50 rating, and adjustments are made as required based on the reaction of the mice.

Although it is a rated test, currently, there is no industry standard or code-established acceptable or unacceptable level of rating. However, an increasing number of manufacturers are testing their products and listing the LC-50 ratings on them. Therefore, when selecting a finish or furnishing with an LC-50 rating, two or more products can be compared. A higher test score indicates a less toxic product.

Although the tests are not currently required by the ICC or NFPA codes, this situation may change in the future. Some jurisdictions do require the test. For example, the state of New York was one of the first to enforce use of the test. And some jurisdictions may require a rating to remain within or above the natural ratings for wood of LC-16 through LC-25. Check with the local code jurisdiction for specific requirements.

◈ Note

In the *Pitts Test*, the LC stands for *lethal concentration*. LC-50 or LC50 represents the measure of lethal toxic potency. A higher number indicates a less toxic material or product.

◈ Note

The *Pitts Test* measures the toxicity of a material when it burns. Other standards are available that measure the toxicity of a product (i.e., volatile organic compounds [VOCs]) during normal offgassing as it affects indoor air quality.

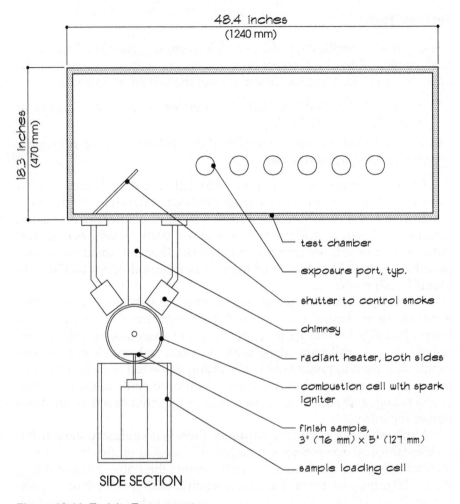

Figure 10.11 *Toxicity Test* apparatus.

Upholstered Seating Tests

Most of the standard tests described so far test individual finishes and components. However, other tests are available for upholstered seating and mattresses that test the full assembly. There are two basic types: full-scale tests and small-scale tests. A *full-scale test* can use an actual piece of furniture or a large mock-up of that piece of furniture, whereas a *small-scale test* uses smaller mock-ups that consist of multiple parts or components of a piece of furniture.

Full-Scale Tests

The full-scale test is a pass/fail test of a *whole* piece of furniture rather than of an individual finish or material. It was first developed by the state of California and titled *California Technical Bulletin 133*, also referred to as either *CAL 133* or *TB 133*. Since then, other standards organizations have developed similar tests. Full scale furniture tests include these:

❏ *ASTM E1537, Standard Test Method for Fire Testing of Upholstered Furniture*

❏ *CAL 133, Flammability Test Procedure for Seating Furniture for Use in Public Occupancies*

The aim of the test is to eliminate the flashover that occurs in the second phase of a fire. (See the inset titled "Fire Development Stages" in this chapter.) It is a flame-resistance test that measures the carbon monoxide generation, heat generation, smoke, temperature, and weight loss of an entire piece of furniture. The test sample is either an actual upholstered piece of furniture or a full-scale mock-up that simulates the construction of the furniture item. There are three versions of the test (A, B, or C), two of which are done with the test sample in the corner of an enclosed room. As in a *Room Corner Test*, the exhaust collection hood is located outside the room. In the third option (Option C), shown in Figure 10.12, the collection hood is directly above the test sample. In each case, a burner is held just above the upholstered seat, ignited, and then turned off. The exhaust hood collects all the products of combustion. The furniture sample passes the test if the peak heat release and the total energy release do not exceed a predetermined level.

The California test was originally developed for furniture used in public buildings in any area or room that contains 10 or more pieces of seating. This applies to prisons, health care facilities, nursing homes, day care facilities, stadiums, auditoriums, and public assembly areas in hotels and motels. Newer editions of the *LSC* and *IFC* require upholstered furniture that passes *CAL 133* and/or *ASTM E1537* in certain occupancies where sprinklers are not used, hospitals, ambulatory care facilities, and college and university dormitories. If it is not required by the local jurisdiction, products complying with *CAL 133* can still be specified to provide better protection to the occupants for appropriate uses. (See also the inset titled "*CAL 133*–Tested Products" in this chapter.)

✎ Note

Many furniture manufacturers offer *CAL 133*–compliant seating. Work closely with the manufacturer to specify correctly.

✎ Note

The *CAL 133* test is essentially the same as *ASTM E1537*, but it uses a different-size test room and has a few stricter requirements.

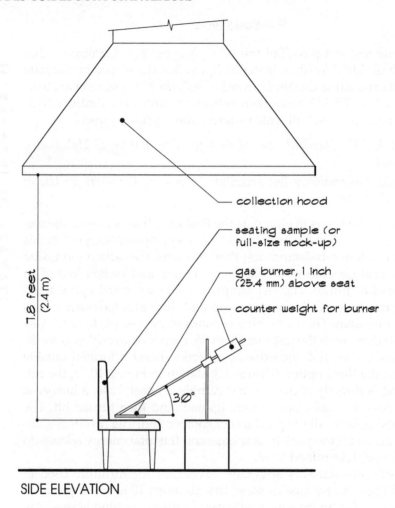

SIDE ELEVATION

Figure 10.12 Upholstered seating test apparatus: Full-scale.

Small-Scale Tests

The small-scale test listed here is often required for upholstered furniture and mattresses in commercial, institutional, and high-risk building types. However, this test is not referenced by current codes. This type of test measures how quickly upholstered furniture and mattresses will ignite. It also measures the rate of heat release.

❑ *ASTM E1474, Standard Test Method for Determining the Heat Release Rate of Upholstered Furniture and Mattress Components or Composites Using a Bench Scale Oxygen Consumption Calorimeter*

The sample used in this test consists of various components, including the fabric and padding material of the proposed upholstered item

☑ **Note**

The small-scale uphol-stered seating test, *ASTM E1474*, references *ASTM E1354* standard for its testing procedures.

plus any layers in between, such as liners, polyester fiber, and other fillers. The assembled finish sample is in the shape of a small block 2 inches (100 mm) square. Although it is small, the test results are still useful in predicting the performance of a full piece of furniture.

Mattress Tests

Although mattresses can be tested using the small-scale tests mentioned in the preceding section, there are other tests that apply only to mattresses, some of which are required by the federal government. The full-scale tests for mattresses include these:

❑ *ASTM E1590, Standard Test Method for Fire Testing of Mattresses*
❑ *CAL 129, Flammability Test Procedure for Mattresses Used in Public Buildings*
❑ *16 CFR 1632 (or DOC FF4–72), Standard for Flammability of Mattresses and Mattress Pads*
❑ *CAL 603, Requirements and Test Procedure for Resistance of a Mattress/ Box Spring Set to a Large Open Flame*
❑ *16 CFR 1633, Standard for the Flammability (Open Flame) of Mattresses and Mattress/Foundation Sets*

> **☑ Note**
>
> All mattresses sold and used in the United States must pass the federal tests in *16 CFR 1632* and *16 CFR 1633*. Mattresses used in certain commercial facilities must pass additional stricter tests.

The first two tests are the most stringent and are required by the fire codes and the *LSC* for new mattresses in certain occupancies such as board and care facilities, nursing homes, hospitals, detention and correctional facilities, and college and university dormitories. (They are not intended for use in the evaluation of residential mattresses.) These tests determine the heat release, smoke density, generation of toxic gases (carbon monoxide), and weight loss that occur when an individual mattress or a mattress with its foundation (i.e., box spring) is exposed to a flame.

To conduct the *ASTM E1590* test, the mattress or mattress set is placed on a frame with an exhaust hood above, similar to that shown in Figure 10.12. A T-shaped gas burner is positioned to the side of the test sample and the exhaust hood collects all the products of combustion for up to 30 minutes after the flame is removed. The result of the pass/fail test is based on the peak heat and energy release. (The *CAL 129* test has slightly different requirements.)

The third mattress test in the preceding list, *16 CFR 1632*, is required by the federal government and is applicable to mattresses used in single-family dwellings as well as commercial projects. It is a pass/fail test that measures the char size created when exposed to a lit cigarette, similar to the *Smolder Resistance Test* discussed previously in this chapter. It is required for most types of mattresses as well as mattress pads sold in the United States. The codes also require this test, requiring a maximum char length of 2 inches (51 mm) in certain occupancies. (California has a similar test, known as *CAL 106*.)

The *16 CFR 1633* is a federally required test based on California's mattress test, *CAL 603*. These tests use a dual-burning gas flame device to apply flames to the sides and top of a mattress or mattress set, simulating a fire caused by bed linens rather than a smoldering cigarette. Since July 2007, all mattresses sold in the United States must comply with federal mattress tests *16 CFR 1633* and *16 CFR 1632*.

DETERMINING FINISH REQUIREMENTS

For most of the finishes that will be specified for an interior project, the codes will indicate the minimum fire resistant characteristics using some of the tests discussed in the previous section. In the past, there were few requirements, but as new materials are developed that perform differently in a fire, new requirements are necessary. Most of these requirements will be in the finish chapter of the building and fire codes or in the various occupancy chapters of the *LSC*. Some material requirements will be in separate chapters. For example, the *IBC* has chapters on glazing and plastics that may need to be referenced if these products are included in your design. Generally, the requirements will apply to all uses, but, in some cases, stricter requirements may be required for certain occupancies or building types. If working in a jurisdiction that requires more than one of the code publications, compare the requirements to make sure that the most restrictive ones are being used, especially in the many jurisdictions that use a building code, fire code, and the *LSC*.

Finish Classifications

Most wall and ceiling finish materials must be tested and classified for their fire performance and smoke development using either the Room Corner Test or the Steiner Tunnel Test. If the material passes the Room Corner Test, it is assigned an A classification. The Steiner Tunnel Test can result in an A, B, or C classification. There are some materials that do not have to be tested or have other requirements. For example, finishes or materials that are less considered "thermally thin" and are applied directly to the surface do not have to be tested (i.e., paint.) Materials that are not allowable unless additional requirements are met include exposed heavy timber elements and foam plastics.

◄ Note

The *ICCPC* does not specifically discuss alternate options for finishes and furniture.

◄ Note

CAL 117 is the most common test required for furniture in public spaces. Products that meet CAL 117 are readily available from contract furniture manufacturers.

◄ Note

CAL 133 requires the testing of an assembled piece of furniture (not components). Furniture that meets this CAL 133 may be more limited than meeting CAL 117.

SPECIFYING TESTED FURNITURE

Even if *CAL 133* or one of the other related standards is not required by a jurisdiction, tested products can still be specified to provide additional safety to the building occupants. Seating that meets *CAL 133* is increasingly available and may be marketed as such. In addition, manufacturers can often indicate a combination of fabrics and components within their products that have already been tested to meet *CAL 133* requirements. As laws, codes and standards for furniture testing get stricter, more areas of responsibility and liability develop as related to the specification of upholstered furniture. Here are some other issues to consider:

❑ Selecting a special fabric or *COM* (customer's own material) may change the *CAL 133* test results for a piece of furniture if it has not been pretested by the manufacturer. Remember CAL 133 is a full-scale test, so the exact combination must be tested (burned.) If the combination has not been pretested, this will result in additional cost, lead time, or length of production.

❑ Specifying a fireblock liner may make a piece of furniture *CAL 133*–compliant. Fireblock liners are often used between the foam and upholstery instead of a flame-retardant foam. Other items such as fire-retardant thread might also need to be considered. Work with the manufacturer and within the requirements of the test standards.

❑ Buildings with sprinklers are not always required to have *CAL 133*–tested furniture. However, should a fire occur, the lack of tested furniture may contribute to the severity of the fire.

❑ Be aware that specifying custom furniture, as well as having furniture reupholstered, may not meet the standard. Unless a mock-up is built and tested, there is no way to verify that a one-of-a-kind piece of furniture complies with *CAL 133*. Remember, the testing process ruins the piece being tested.

❑ As with all other tested finishes and furniture, the way a piece of furniture is cleaned and maintained affects its rating. The appropriate maintenance information should be given to the client so that furniture is maintained in a way that does not defeat the fire resistant characteristics.

In some areas and uses, floor finishes also have classification requirements. (See the "Decorative Materials" section later in the chapter.) These minimum classifications are assigned by occupancy and location within the building. This information is presented in a table in the *IBC* and given in each individual occupancy chapter of the *LSC*. However, in the *LSC*, the information is also compiled into a table from the individual occupancy chapter (new and existing). This table is in the Appendix of the *LSC*. (See Figure 10.13.) The table is described in more detail in the next section and is followed by an example of how to use it.

The Code Table

◪ Note

If working on a building in one of the cities or states with its own code, check with that jurisdiction for additional or unique requirements.

The tables in the *IBC* and the *LSC* are similar. They provide the minimum allowable wall, ceiling, and floor finish classification for specific locations within the building per occupancy. Figure 10.13 shows *LSC* Table A.10.2.2, "Interior Finish Classification Limitations." The *IBC* table is Table 803.5, "Interior Wall and Ceiling Finish Requirements by Occupancy." (It is also repeated in the *IFC*.) Unlike the NFPA tables, the table in the *IBC* does not specify floor finishes; this information is included within its text. In addition, the *IBC* divides the table into sprinklered and nonsprinklered buildings, whereas the *LSC* table is based on nonsprinklered buildings and uses a footnote in the table to cover requirements for sprinklered buildings.

There are five different finish classes represented in the finish table. There are three classes for wall and ceiling finishes (Classes A, B, and C), which are obtained using *Steiner Tunnel Tests*, and two separate classes for interior floor finishes (Classes I and II), which are obtained using *Radiant Panel Tests*. (Refer to the section "Standards and Testing" earlier in this chapter.) These different classes recognize that all parts of the means of egress must be safe. However, because it is especially important for exitways to be free of fire and smoke for safety and visibility, you can notice that the more stringent classifications are required in these parts of a building.

Before using the *LSC* table shown in Figure 10.13, the occupancy classification of the building (or space) must be determined and whether it is considered new or existing. (This is described in Chapter 3.) Once the occupancy is known, the table lists the finish classes allowed in each area of the building. Each of the codes divides these areas similarly. They consist of exits, exit access corridors, and other rooms or spaces. (Refer to the section titled "Means of Egress Components" in Chapter 5 for a description of each.) For clarification, the *IBC* lists the exit category as "exit enclosures and exit passageways."

Reading across the table in Figure 10.13 for a particular occupancy indicates which class of finishes is allowed in each of these areas. Generally, the closer to the exterior of a building or exit discharge, the stricter the class rating and fire resistance requirements for the finish. Spaces that are not separated from a corridor, such as reception areas in Business occupancies and waiting areas in Health Care occupancies, would be considered part of the exit access corridor.

◪ Note

Decorative vegetation such as natural cut trees and artificial plants is also regulated by the codes. The *International Fire Code (IFC)* includes requirements for these in its "Interior Finish" chapter.

Some occupancies in the table have a symbol or footnote following the recorded class. This indicates that the occupancy has further finish restrictions or requirements. Further research will be required in the *LSC* or the building codes under the specified occupancy. The fire codes may also have requirements specific to a certain occupancy. Occupancies and

Table A.10.2.2 Interior Finish Classification Limitations

Occupancy	Exits	Exit Access Corridors	Other Spaces
Assembly — New			
>300 occupant load	A	A or B	A or B
	I or II	I or II	NA
≤300 occupant load	A	A or B	A, B, or C
	I or II	I or II	NA
Assembly — Existing			
>300 occupant load	A	A or B	A or B
≤300 occupant load	A	A or B	A, B, or C
Educational — New	A	A or B	A or B; C on low partitions†
	I or II	I or II	
Educational — Existing	A	A or B	A, B, or C
Day-Care Centers — New	A	A	A or B
	I or II	I or II	NA
Day-Care Centers — Existing	A or B	A or B	A or B
Day-Care Homes — New	A or B	A or B	A, B, or C
	I or II		NA
Day-Care Homes — Existing	A or B	A, B, or C	A, B, or C
Health Care — New	A	A	A
	NA	B on lower portion of corridor wall†	B in small individual rooms†
	I or II	I or II	NA
Health Care — Existing	A or B	A or B	A or B
Detention and Correctional — New (sprinklers mandatory)	A or B	A or B	A, B, or C
	I or II	I or II	NA
Detention and Correctional — Existing	A or B	A or B	A, B, or C
	I or II	I or II	NA
One- and Two-Family Dwellings and Lodging or Rooming Houses	A, B, or C	A, B, or C	A, B, or C
Hotels and Dormitories — New	A	A or B	A, B, or C
	I or II	I or II	NA
Hotels and Dormitories — Existing	A or B	A or B	A, B, or C
	I or II†	I or II†	NA
Apartment Buildings — New	A	A or B	A, B, or C
	I or II	I or II	NA
Apartment Buildings — Existing	A or B	A or B	A, B, or C
	I or II†	I or II†	NA
Residential Board and Care — (See Chapters 32 and 33.)			
Mercantile — New	A or B	A or B	A or B
	I or II		NA
Mercantile — Existing			
Class A or Class B stores	A or B	A or B	Ceilings — A or B; walls — A, B or C
Class C stores	A, B, or C	A, B, or C	A, B, or C
Business and Ambulatory Health Care — New	A or B	A or B	A, B, or C
	I or II		NA
Business and Ambulatory Health Care — Existing	A or B	A or B	A, B, or C
Industrial	A or B	A, B, or C	A, B, or C
	I or II	I or II	NA
Storage	A or B	A, B, or C	A, B, or C
	I or II		NA

NA: Not applicable.Notes:
(1) Class A interior wall and ceiling finish — flame spread index, 0–25 (new applications); smoke developed index, 0–450.
(2) Class B interior wall and ceiling finish — flame spread index, 26–75 (new applications); smoke developed index, 0–450.
(3) Class C interior wall and ceiling finish — flame spread index, 76–200 (new applications); smoke developed index, 0–450.
(4) Class I interior floor finish — critical radiant flux, not less than 0.45 W/cm².
(5) Class II interior floor finish — critical radiant flux, not more than 0.22 W/cm², but less than 0.45 W/cm².
(6) Automatic sprinklers — where a complete standard system of automatic sprinklers is installed, interior wall and ceiling finish with a flame spread rating not exceeding Class C is permitted to be used in any location where Class B is required, and Class B interior wall and ceiling finish is permitted to be used in any location where Class A is required; similarly, Class II interior floor finish is permitted to be used in any location where Class I is required, and no interior floor finish classification is required where Class II is required. These provisions do not apply to new detention and correctional occupancies.
(7) Exposed portions of structural members complying with the requirements for heavy timber construction are permitted.
†See corresponding chapters for details.

Figure 10.13 Life Safety Code Table A.10.2.2, "Interior Finish Classification Limitations" (Reprinted with permission from NFPA 101®, *Life Safety Code*®, Copyright © 2017, National Fire Protection Association, Quincy, MA. This reprinted material is not the complete and official position of the NFPA on the referenced subject, which is represented only by the standard in its entirety).

building types that most often have additional finish-related requirements follow, with examples of each.

❑ **Assembly.** Special allowances for religious uses, lobbies and limited occupant loads, fabric of stage curtains, motion picture screens, stage scenery, specifics for assembly seating, storage of personal effects and clothing versus metal lockers, exhibit booths

❑ **Educational (and Day Care).** Percentage of bulletin boards, posters, and/or artwork/teaching materials attached to walls, storage of personal effects and clothing versus metal lockers

❑ **Health Care.** Allowances for finishes below 48 inches (1.2 m) in corridors, fabrics for cubicle curtains, allowable wall decorations, upholstered furniture and mattresses, administrative versus patient care areas

❑ **Detention/Correctional.** Fabric of privacy curtains, allowable wall decorations, waste container specifications, upholstered furniture and mattresses (also with regard to vandalism)

❑ **Mercantile.** Plastic signage, temporary kiosks, ceiling-supported fabric partitions, display window allowances

❑ **Hotels and Dormitories.** Draperies, wall hangings, and mattresses

❑ **Board and Care/Nursing Homes.** Upholstered furniture and mattresses, allowable wall decorations

❑ **Unusual Structures.** Water-resistant finishes in buildings located in flood zones, finish restrictions in atriums

❑ **Hazardous.** Limited use of combustible finishes

The general rule of thumb is that stricter finishes are required in occupancies where the occupants are immobile, sleeping, or have security measures imposed on them that restrict freedom of movement. This includes Institutional occupancies in the *IBC* and *IFC* (Health Care and Detention/Correctional facilities in the NFPA codes) or where occupants are provided with overnight accommodations, such as hotels and dormitories. By contrast, more relaxed requirements are found in Industrial and Storage occupancies where occupants are assumed to be alert, mobile, and fewer in number. Certain buildings that have fewer stories and lower occupant loads may also be subject to fewer restrictions.

The bottom of the table also includes a note that automatic sprinklers used throughout a building can change the required finish class ratings. The *LSC* uses this note to allow a required finish class to be reduced by one rating if there is an approved automatic sprinkler system in a building. For example, if a space in a nonsprinklered building normally requires a *Steiner Tunnel Test* Class B finish, the same space in a sprinklered building would require a Class C finish. As noted previously, the

✎ Note

Finish and furniture standards for one- and two-family dwellings are typically less stringent than for other occupancies. Exceptions are the *Pill Test* for carpets and rugs and some mattress tests. (Refer to Appendix C.)

✎ Note

The building and plumbing codes specify certain finishes in toilet and bathing facilities.

✎ Note

The *LSC* places additional restrictions on textile and expanded vinyl wallcoverings used in nonsprinklered buildings. For example, some Class A wallcoverings can only extend a certain height above the floor.

IBC specifies this information more clearly within the table itself. Therefore, it is important to know if the building has an *approved* automatic sprinkler system before reducing a finish class. (Confirm with a local code official if necessary.)

Example

Figure 10.14 is a floor plan of a high school without a sprinkler system. To specify the finishes for this existing school, a code table such as the table in Figure 10.13 must be referenced. Under "Educational—Existing" in the occupancy column, this table indicates the following:

❑ Class A wall and ceiling finishes must be used in all exit areas, such as stairwells.

❑ Class A or B finishes are allowed in exit access areas, such as corridors.

❑ Any of the three classes (A, B, or C) is allowed in all the remaining spaces, such as classrooms, offices, and so on.

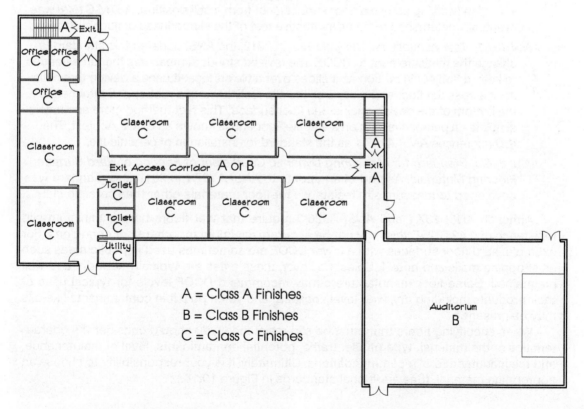

Figure 10.14 Finish selection example: High school, nonsprinklered building.

SLIP RESISTANT FOR ACCESSIBILITY AND CODES

Although neither the building codes nor the accessibility standards specify a test standard to measure or validate an acceptable slip resistance level of a product, there are several industry recognized measurements and standards that can be referred to by designers. Slip resistance is measured in three basic ways: Coefficient of friction (COF), Static Coefficient of Friction (SCOF), and Dynamic Coefficient of Friction (DCOF). COF is the basic gauge of the frictional resistance of a surface. A COF of 0 (zero) means that there is no friction between the two surfaces. They can categorized as measured as static (S) or dynamic (D). A higher number indicates a less slippery material. Most floor surfaces will have a COF that is less than 1. The most widely used test methods are explained here:

ASTM C1028, Standard Test Method for Determining the Static Coefficient of Friction of Ceramic Tile and Other Like Surfaces by the Horizontal Dynamometer Pull-Meter Method. One of the original standards, it was specifically developed for ceramic tile. In this test, a weighted plate with a sensor is placed on a wet floor. The sensor measures the force required to overcome the friction caused by the floor material to set the weighted plate in motion. The required force results in a Static Coefficient of Friction (SCOF). However, because slipping typically occurs when people are already in motion (walking across a floor surface), not from a still position, *ASTM C1028* was eventually determined to be an ineffective test of the slipperiness of floor surfaces.

ANSI 137.1, Specifications for Ceramic Tile. In 2012, the ANSI updated this standard to change the measurement to DCOF. The revised standard measures the force needed to keep an object in motion as it slides over a tile surface. It uses a device that pulls itself across the floor and measures the slip resistance of a rubber pad attached to the bottom of the device against the floor surface. This test method more accurately simulates a person walking on a wet tile floor and is known as DCOF Acutest. The *IBC* references *ANSI A137.1* as the standard for installation of ceramic tile.

ANSI 326.3, Standard for Measuring Dynamic Coefficient of Friction of Hard Surface Flooring Materials. As part of an update to *ANSI A137.1* in 2017, this standard was developed to measure slip resistance for floor materials other than ceramic tile.

Although *ANSI 137.1* and *ANSI A326.3* require that wet floors have a minimum slip resistance of 0.42 DCOF, this may not be accurate minimum for other floor conditions. For example, hard floor surfaces with a lower DCOF are sometimes used in public areas such as shopping malls and hotel lobbies; however, these areas are typically kept dry and well maintained. Some floor manufacturers may recommend DCOF levels for typical uses of their products including dry, wet, level, inclined, and when possible contaminants like oils may be present.

When specifying floors that must be slip resistance, you should consider the characteristics of the material, type of use, traffic, potential contaminants, level of maintenance, and the manufacturers' recommendations. Ultimately, it is your responsibility to choose an appropriate material. (See additional standards in Figure 10.18.)

Standards for Measurement of Slip Resistance of Floor Surfaces
ANSI 137.1, Specifications for Ceramic Tile:
ANSI 326.3, Standard for Measuring Dynamic Coefficient of Friction of Hard Surface Flooring Materials
ANSI B101.1, Test Method for Measuring Wet SCOF of Common Hard-Surface Floor materials.
ANSI B101.2, Test Method for Determining the Impact on Wet Dynamic Coefficient of Friction of Various Chemical or Physical Walkway Surface Treatments
ANSI B101.3, Test Method for Measuring Wet DCOF of Common Hard-Surface Floor Materials
ANSI B101.4, Test Method for Measuring the Wet Barefoot Condition of Flooring Materials or Products
ANSI B101.6, Standard Guide for Commercial Entrance Matting in Reducing Slips, Trips and Falls
ASTM D2047, Test Method for Static Coefficient of Friction of Polish-Coated Flooring Surfaces as Measured by the James Machine

Figure 10.18 Standards for Slip Resistance

However, many high schools are considered multiple occupancies by the codes because of the gymnasiums, auditoriums, and/or cafeterias typically built with them. If the auditorium in this high school, for example, was designed for 325 people, the finish requirements for this area would be found in the occupancy column of the table under "Assembly—Existing" in the subcategory ">300 occupant load." The required finish classes are almost the same except that, in this case, Class C finishes will not be allowed in the general areas of this assembly space.

In the previous example, the table did not specify a particular class of floor finish anywhere in the school. However, if designing the interior of a new day care center, the table indicates that a Type I or II floor finish is required in exits and exit access corridors. Therefore, a floor covering that passes a *Radiant Panel Test* must be used. (See Figure 10.3.) The code requirements also require that certain wall bases pass the same test. (See the section titled *"Radiant Panel Test"* for details.)

When specifying finishes, also consider if the building or space is used for multiple functions. For example, it is common for day care centers to be located in buildings that share other functions, such as churches or residential homes. The finishes must meet the requirements of the most restrictive use.

Other Finish Requirements

Although the Steiner Tunnel test is the most often used standard to assign a classification and to define how interior finishes can be used, other tests may be required or allowed. Some interior finishes and materials will have requirements in addition to or instead of a classification. This may require additional research based on your project needs. Often these separate requirements are because the material performs differently in the event of a fire, so different testing or limitations are needed. For example, a material may melt instead of burning when exposed to fire. These requirements continue to change. Following is a list of types of materials that have separate requirements and may require additional research.

Thickness exemption. Any wall or ceiling covering that is less than 0.036 inch (0.90 mm) thick is not required to be treated as an interior finish. Therefore, thermally thin finishes such as paint and most wallpapers (not vinyl wallcoverings), when applied to noncombustible building materials, do not have to be rated. Various tests have proven that thermally thin finishes do not significantly contribute to the fuel of a fire when they are applied to noncombustible building materials such as gypsum board, brick, or concrete. (This rule does not apply when finishes are continually applied on top of one another.)

Heavy timber exemption. Exposed elements of a heavy timber structure are not required to be tested as an interior finish unless they are in an exit stairway, exit ramp, or exit passageway.

Foam plastic. When used as an interior finish or to be a component of a textile or vinyl facing, cellular or foam plastic must pass the *Room Corner Test* and meet additional flame spread and smoke-developed index requirements of the *Steiner Tunnel Test*. In some cases, it may require approval by the code official. Depending on its use as a interior finish or trim, other standards may apply including: *UL 1975, Standard for Fire Test for Foamed Plastics Used for Decorative Purposes, NFPA 289, Standard Method of Fire Test for Individual Fuel Packages, NFPA 286, Standard Method of Fire Test for Evaluating Contribution of Wall and Ceiling Interior Finish to Room Fire Growth, UL 1715 Standard for Safety Fire Test of Interior Finish Material* or *FM 4880 Evaluating the Fire Performance of Insulated Building Panel Assemblies and Interior Finish Materials.* Foam plastics that do not pass a large-scale test are typically allowed only when the foam plastic is covered by a noncombustible material that acts as a thermal barrier. Foam plastics used within a plenum as interior wall or ceiling finish or interior trim have additional requirements. You may need to verify which standard applies based on the specific use of the material.

Textile wall and ceiling coverings. These finishes can be tested and pass the Room Corner Test to be used. Or they can be tested by the Steiner Tunnel Test, but they must achieve a Class A rating and be in a sprinklered space.

Expanded vinyl wall and ceiling coverings. These finishes can be tested and pass the Room Corner Test to be used. Or they can be tested by the Steiner Tunnel Test, but they must achieve a Class A rating and be in a sprinklered space.

PP or HDPE. Use of these plastics is rapidly increasing in interiors for furniture, toilet partitions, carpeting, and other uses. It is required to be tested by the Room Corner Test.

Light-diffusing plastics and systems. Use of this material and systems is limited or not allowed in some occupancies based on occupant load or location.

Laminated products factory produced with a wood substrate. These can be used if tested by the Room Corner Test with special testing conditions or the Steiner Tunnel Test and meet the required classification by occupancy.

Wood facings or veneers site applied to a wood substrate can be used if tested by the Room Corner Test with special testing conditions and meet the required classification by occupancy.

Site-fabricated stretch systems. Site-fabricated stretch systems typically consist of a track system (or frame), fabric (or vinyl), and infill core material. The systems can be used for acoustical, decorative, or tackable purposes. The codes require the *Room Corner Test* or the *Steiner Tunnel Test* in conjunction with *ASTM E2573, Standard Practice for Specimen Preparation and Mounting of Site-Fabricated Stretch Systems.*

OBTAINING TEST RESULTS

Some of the standards and tests described previously in this chapter are specifically referenced by the codes and are therefore required by specific jurisdictions. Others are industry standards that should be considered when appropriate. For each test standard used, it is important to understand the meaning of the test result and whether the outcome is a pass/fail grade, a specific class rating, or a ranking, as discussed previously. The test result can affect the ability to use a product in a specific application. In Figure 10.3, this information is shown for each type of test. For example, the *Radiant Panel Test* is a rated test that results in a Class I or a Class II rating. When a standard or test is referenced by the codes, the required result is indicated for the specific use of the product.

Manufacturers typically have their products tested before putting them on the market. Manufacturers realize that their finishes and furniture must meet code requirements for them to be readily specified for a project. The manufacturer has its products tested according to the standards to the

◀ Note

Manufacturers' representatives can be very helpful in supplying technical and code information on their products. Manufacturers need to comply with the industry standards to remain competitive.

anticipated use of their product and provides the applicable test results for each item. By comparing these ratings to what is required by the codes, the appropriate finish and/or furniture can be selected. (Request the information from the manufacturer if it is not provided.) How to find and obtain the required test results is explained in this section.

Pretested Finishes and Furniture

Many manufacturers either list the test results on their samples and products or provide the information on request. (See the inset titled "Testing Agencies and Certification" in Chapter 1.) For example, you may find the testing information on the back of carpet books and on cards attached to fabric samples. Similar labels and/or specifications can be found for most wallcoverings, floor coverings, ceiling coverings, and other finishes. Even upholstered furniture must be labeled with the required test results.

Figure 10.15 shows the finish specifications for a Maharam upholstery fabric. Along with other necessary information, the specification indicates the standard tests the fabric has passed under "Flammability." (Also notice the sustainable-related information listed; see the section titled "Sustainability Considerations" later in this chapter.) The flammability heading indicates that the fabric has passed *CAL 117* and *NFPA 260*

> **✎ Note**
>
> Some finishes will list multiple test results on their sample information. This indicates that the finish can be used in more than one type of application.

Coincide009 Caribbean

Design: Maharam Design Studio
Style: 465808
Application: Seating
Content: 100% Polyester
Finish: Stain Resistant
Backing: Acrylic
Width: 54" (137cm)
Repeat: 1 1/8" H / 2.9cm H
Abrasion: 100,000+ double rubs 🅰
Flammability: This textile meets all appropriate flammability requirements, including California Bulletin #117 and NFPA 260, and is compatible with California Bulletin #133. 🔥
Lightfastness: 60+ Hours ✳
Maintenance: W/S-Clean with water-based cleanser or mild, water-free dry cleaning solvent.
Reduced Environmental Impact: Environmentally Improved Manufacturing Process: heavy metal free dyes with high exhaustion rates
ISO 14001 Environmental Management System: Manufactured at an ISO 14001 certified facility.
Reduced Emissions: Greenguard and Greenguard for Children and Schools certified for indoor air quality.
US Contract Net: $26.00
Canadian Contract Net: C$27.50
© 2010 Maharam

Figure 10.15 Typical specifications for an upholstery finish sample.

and that it is compatible with *CAL 133*. There is also a flame symbol at the end of the flammability information. This symbol, or certification mark, indicates that the fabric has passed certain industry tests.

This symbol was created by the Association for Contract Textiles (ACT), which was founded in 1985 to provide the design industry with information to help designers choose the right products for their projects. Concentrating on the contract interiors market, ACT sets standards for upholstery, wallcoverings, panels and upholstered walls, and drapery. A total of five ACT certification marks are voluntarily used by many textile manufacturers on their products; each mark indicates the test(s) or standard(s) that the material must meet in order to bear the symbol.

Although there are five different marks, the main certification mark that relates directly to the codes is the flammability symbol. This symbol is shown in Figure 10.16, along with the type of application for the interior finish and the standards that it meets. Depending on the intended use of the finish, the flame symbol indicates that a fabric has achieved

☑ **Note**

The five ACT certification marks indicate a material's characteristics in terms of flammability, colorfastness, physical properties (such as pilling, breaking, and seam slippage), and abrasion. (See the inset titled "Industry Standards" in this chapter.)

Flammability	
	The measurement of a fabric's performance when it is exposed to specific sources of ignition.
	Note: ACT guidelines specify different flammability tests dictated by the intended end use for the fabric.
	ACT GUIDELINES
	Upholstery
	California Technical Bulletin 117-2013 Section 1 – Pass
	Direct Glue Wallcoverings and Adhered Panels
	ASTM E84 (Adhered Mounting Method) – Class A or Class 1
	Wrapped Wall Panels and Upholstered Walls
	ASTM E84 (Unadhered Mounting Method) – Class A or Class 1
	Panel System Furniture
	Any one or combination of the following: UL recognized component under Office
	Panel Fabrics category, UL 1286 Listed, ASTM E84 (Adhered or Unadhered
	Mounting Method) – Class A or Class 1
	Drapery
	NFPA 701 Method 1 or 2 as appropriate – Pass

Figure 10.16 Flammability portion of *ACT Textile Performance Guidelines* (Reprinted with permission from the Association for Contract Textiles, Inc. [ACT]. The flame mark is a Registered Certification Mark and is owned by ACT, Inc. See ACT website for the entire guidelines and the most current edition, www.contracttextiles.org).

✎ **Note**

The codes require that upholstered furniture that has passed either *a Smolder Resistance Test* or an *Upholstered Seating Test* be labeled by an approved agency to confirm compliance. Similar labels are required for mattresses.

✎ **Note**

The BIFMA International website (www .bifma.org) includes a comprehensive list of testing laboratories located throughout the world.

✎ **Note**

In addition to chemical treatments and applied coatings, some finishes, such as plastics and foam, can be impregnated with a flame retardant during fabrication.

Class A of the *Steiner Tunnel Test (ASTM E 84)*, has passed test *Method 2* of the *Vertical Flame Test (NFPA 701)*, or has passed the *Smolder Resistance Test (CAL TB 117* or *UL 1286)*. So, if a fabric's specification or tag carries the flame mark, it means that the material meets the requirements of at least one of the tests. For example, in Figure 10.15, if this fabric sample is intended for use as upholstery, the flame symbol indicates that the fabric passes *CAL 117*. (This information is also repeated in the text of the label.)

Upholstered furniture also have industry systems for flammability labeling. One voluntary standard was developed in 1978 by the Upholstered Furniture Action Council (UFAC) to increase the cigarette-ignition resistance of prefabricated furniture, typically residential furniture. A manufacturer can attach an approved UFAC hangtag if the upholstered furniture meets testing requirements similar to *NFPA 260*, the *Smolder Resistance Test* for components. In the contract furniture industry, BIFMA International recommends that its manufacturer members produce upholstered furniture that meets *TB 117–2013 Requirements, Test Procedure and Apparatus for Testing the Smolder Resistance of Materials Used in Upholstered Furniture.*

For most interior projects, upholstered furniture is manufactured specifically for the project. In these cases, the UFAC label will not apply. Instead, textiles and furniture will meet other code and industry standards as applicable for a specific project. If upholstered furniture (or mattress) is specified to meet certain testing requirements, the delivered piece should include a label by an approved agency confirming that it meets the appropriate requirements. This is required by the codes for certain occupancies.

Nontested Finishes and Furniture

There will be situations in which testing information is not available. For example, a smaller finish or furniture manufacturer that makes specialty items may not be able to afford to test its finishes and/or furniture. Or, a certain finish may be required to undergo additional testing before it can be used in a particular occupancy or jurisdiction. In these cases, the finish or component will either need to be tested or fire-resistant treatments or components added.

There are several third-party *testing agencies* throughout the country that will perform the tests necessary to classify a material or piece of furniture. The standards organizations such as UL, ASTM, and NFPA can help determine where to get a finish tested. (Some agencies also act as treatment companies as well.) However, these flame tests can be costly, because they must be performed under conditions simulating actual installations and within the precise requirements of the test standard.

For example, a wallcovering should be tested on the appropriate wall surface with the adhesive that will be used to secure it to the wall, or a carpet with the padding that will be used underneath it. And for furniture, the exact composition of materials and configuration is required.

The alternative is to have the finish treated. This is often much more cost-effective. Before doing so, though, it is suggested that you confirm that the local jurisdiction will allow an added fire retardant coating as a way to meet finish code requirements. There are several *treatment companies* that can add fire retardant coatings, also known as *flame-resistant finishes*, to materials that have not initially passed the required tests or untested. (The manufacturers can often be a good source for alternative companies who treat finishes and materials.) The retardant can be either a surface treatment or a fire-resistant coating applied as a backing. It will delay ignition of a material and slow flame spread, usually without changing the basic nature of the material. (See the inset titled "Flame Retardant Treatments" in this chapter.) It can also lower the smoke development value.

The typical procedure requires sending the fabric (or other finish) to the treatment company, indicating which test that the finish must meet and the required rating. For example, if a fabric wallcovering must have a Class B rating, you would indicate to the testing company that the finish must meet the *Steiner Tunnel Test* with a Class B rating. The treatment company will add the appropriate fire-retardant coating. In addition, if specifying sustainable finishes, request that low-emission treatments be used.

When wood is used as an interior finish, it may have to be treated as well. For example, if wood veneer is being used as a wall covering or a large area of wood paneling in a commercial space, it may have to meet the appropriate class rating of the *Steiner Tunnel Test* as required by the codes. Very few woods naturally qualify as Class A or B. Most are considered Class C or below. (Some wood species are shown in Figure 10.5.) It depends on the species of wood and the thickness of the wood being used. Typically, thinner woods and veneers have lower ratings than thicker ones. However, some new types of intumescent paints and coatings may be applied to the wood to improve its performance and obtain a better rating. These coatings expand and char when exposed to heat, which protects the wood underneath; typically, these materials must meet *NFPA 703, Standard for Fire-Retardant-Treated Wood and Fire-Retardant Coatings for Building Materials.* However, check with the local code official to confirm that this type of finish will be accepted.

Fire-retardant treatments and coatings can usually upgrade non-classed finishes and can even raise the performance of some rated materials to a higher class. On completion of the treatment, a finish treatment company should be able to provide a Certificate of Flame Resistance indicating which tests the finish will pass. If completed in the field, the appropriate information should be obtained from the manufacturer and the

◄ Note

Whenever concentrated amounts of furniture are introduced into a space, confirm with a structural engineer that they will not exceed the design load of the floor or structure. Some examples include library areas, file rooms, and assembly seating.

◄ Note

Movable partitions or panel systems are typically classified as furniture. However, if they exceed a certain height, a jurisdiction may consider them to be walls, in which case they would have to meet fire separation requirements. (See Chapter 5.)

◄ Note

When specifying office systems furniture using a customer's own material (COM), the UL Recognized Components directory can be used to find preapproved rated fabrics (www.ul.com).

company that applied the coating. In all cases, you will have provide sufficient information to the code official that it will perform similar to one that has been tested and meets the intent of the codes for it to be included in your project.

The fire resistance of a piece of furniture is affected by every material and component of the furniture piece. In some cases, treating the fabric can be sufficient. However, in some cases, the manufacturers can suggest how to add or substitute certain materials or components to improve the fire resistance and/or obtain the test results required. For example, a fire-block liner added to a sofa may allow it to comply with *CAL 133*.

Remember, many, but not all, finishes are required to meet a standard and thus be tested. And, not all furniture is required to be tested. When specifying either a finish or furniture, check to see compliance with testing is required because it may be too costly to have an item tested and/or treated. For example, having a piece of furniture tested may only make sense if a large quantity of the same item is being ordered. In addition, if the necessary test results for a finish or piece of furniture cannot be obtained from the manufacturer, you may have to consider it untested. In many cases, it will be more efficient to choose a different finish or furniture item that can be verified to meet the code requirements for its intended use.

FLAME RETARDANT TREATMENTS

A flame-retardant treatment may be necessary for certain items in a project; however, be aware that the treatment can sometimes alter the finish or piece of furniture. For example, for some treatments the finish or piece of furniture is immersed in a chemical bath. The following are several problems that can occur when a fire retardant is added to a fabric:

❏ The fabric may shrink.

❏ The hand or feel of the fabric may change, perhaps resulting in stiffening of the fabric.

❏ The strength of the fabric may decrease, causing it to tear more easily.

❏ If a fabric has a texture, the texture may flatten or become distorted.

❏ The treated fabric may give off toxic fumes, especially in the presence of fire.

❏ A wet treatment may cause the dye in the fabric to bleed or possibly change or fade in the future.

A treated fabric may no longer meet the low-emitting standards required for indoor air quality in sustainable buildings. If you are concerned about any of these issues, consult the company treating the fabric and, when necessary, submit a sample for testing before purchasing or treating the entire amount. The results are often based on the content of the fabric and the type of treatment used. It is also better to have a fabric treated before applying it to a surface or piece of furniture in case there are any negative consequences of the treatment.

ACCESSIBILITY REQUIREMENTS

The accessibility chapter of the building codes, the *ADA Standard*, and the *ICC A117.1* standard place very few accessibility restrictions on finishes and furniture. The pertinent regulations can be broken down into three main categories: floor finishes, seating, and surfaces. However, also consider any operable parts that are part of a furnishing system. Each of these is described in this section. Check the codes, the ADA regulations, and any other required accessibility standards for specifics and to determine the most stringent requirements. (Also see Chapter 2.)

Floor Finishes

Floor finishes are the primary finish that must meet accessibility requirements because they can affect an occupant's ability to walk or travel safely and independently. The ADA and the *ICC A117.1* require floor surfaces of the accessible route to be stable, firm, and slip resistant. A "stable" surface remains unchanged and/or returns to its original condition after being walked on (i.e., hard rubber flooring). A "firm" surface resists deformation by being walked on (i.e., hard wood floors). A "slip-resistant" surface provides sufficient frictional resistance to allow it to be walked on without slipping.

A primary concern for the accessible route being stable and firm is for exterior paths (i.e., unpaved paths, small stone paths, etc.) However, some interior floor finishes, such as loose rugs, carpet with padding, and soft rubber flooring can make using a wheelchair and walking difficult or a trip hazard. To prevent this, a floor surface such as carpet that is thick or loose must be securely fastened at the edges. Another method is to use carpet that is glued directly to the floor (without padding) or by using carpet tiles. Because abrupt changes in floor surface heights are prohibited by the accessibility standards, carpet pile cannot be more than 0.5 inch (13 mm) high; also, whether it is cut pile, loop, or a combination, the pile must be level. Any exposed edges must also have trim to make the transition from the adjacent surface. Rubber flooring or pads must be firm enough so that a wheelchair can maneuver without difficulty.

> ◀ **Note**
>
> The Access Board has a technical bulletin, *Ground and Floor Surfaces*, which explains the requirements for stable, firm, and slip resistance in greater detail.

Note

Directly gluing a carpet to the floor instead of using a pad will help to eliminate thickness problems, as well as future warping or binding of the carpet from wheelchair use.

Note

The Advisory information for the ADA says that "a slip-resistant surface provides sufficient frictional counterforce to the forces exerted in walking to permit safe ambulation." However, the guidelines do not give a specific coefficient of friction or standard to be met.

Note

Because floors in accessible paths of travel must be slip resistant, polished floor finishes such as marble and VCT can become a challenge. Special slip-resistant sealers may be needed.

Floor surfaces are required to be slip resistant by the building codes and accessibility guidelines along the accessible route. (Slip resistant can be considered a safety concern as well as an accessibility concern.) The natural characteristics and finish of the material along with the activities within the room can increase or decrease the slip resistance performance. For example, wet ceramic tile in bathrooms and greasy floors in a commercial kitchen. Materials typically have an inherent slip conducive or resistant quality, but the specified finish or applied texture can make a difference between polished marble, natural finish or polished concrete, or ceramic tile with an added rough finish. The slope of the surface and the wet/dry condition of the surface must also be considered (i.e., at ramps, steps, and bath areas.) In addition to specifying the correct finishes, providing instructions for correct cleaning or sealing methods may be necessary to maintain the slip resistance of the product over time.

Because of these various influences, it is hard to establish exact guidelines for the slip resistance for all conditions. The ADA guidelines, *ICC A117*.1, and the current *IBC* neither provides nor advocates a specific test standard or minimum measurement to indicate if a floor is sufficiently slip resistant. Because there are no specific measurements, you must apply your professional judgment relying on the information available within the industry. (See the Inset titled "Slip-Resistant Finishes" in this chapter.) So, specifying a flooring material that is required to be slip resistant may require additional research.

When two adjacent floor finishes occur, a transition may be necessary. For accessibility, a beveled transition strip or ramp is required between different floor surfaces for even slight changes in elevation. For example, as shown in Figure 10.17, there may be a change in floor level where stone or marble is adjacent to another type of flooring. Floor changes can also occur at the threshold of a door. The goal is to make sure that wheelchairs have easy access. Typically, the overall change in height cannot be more than 0.5 inch (13 mm), as shown in B of Figure 10.17. Only if the vertical distance is 0.25 inch (6.4 mm) or less can it be a straight vertical change, as shown in Section C. If the overall height is between 0.25 inch (6.4 mm) and 0.5 inch (13 mm), a bevel must be added with a slope not steeper than a ratio of 1 to 2. This is shown in Sections A and B of Figure 10.17. When a change in elevation is more than 0.5 inch (13 mm), as shown in Section D, the requirements for an accessible ramp

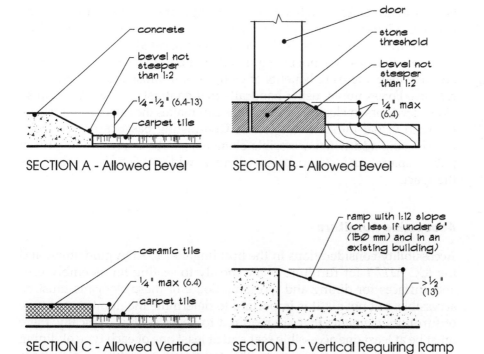

Figure 10.17 Accessible floor level change examples.

must be met. There are some exceptions for existing buildings. (See the section titled "Ramps" in Chapter 5.)

Flooring surfaces that create a detectable warning may be used in interiors to alert someone with poor vision of an approaching obstacle or change in level. Detectable warnings that meet the accessibility requirements must consist of a distinctive surface pattern of flattened domes. (Although not required, contrasting colors can also be beneficial.) They are mostly required by the ADA and the ABA at building exteriors and transportation platforms. However, they can used in interiors as well— for example, at an entrance to a hazardous area or at the top of an escalator or exposed stairway. (Refer to the *ICC A117.1* standard and the *2010 ADA Standards* for specifics.)

Accessible reach ranges must be considered for certain finish components or decorative elements when they are in spaces that are required to be accessible. For example, the controls to a window blind or drape must

◀ **Note**

When floor surfaces, such as entry mats and floor grills, are used, the ADA and *ICC A117.1* standards include specific requirements. The openings must be small enough so that a 0.5-inch (13-mm) sphere cannot pass through, and any elongated openings must be perpendicular to the path of travel.

◄ Note

Finishes and design elements that help someone with a disability better use a space are continuing to be developed but may not be required by the codes or standards. For example, darker baseboards may be helpful in corridors for those who are visually impaired.

be within accessible heights and easy to operate. They must be located between 15 and 48 inches (380 to 1220 mm) above the floor. (Clear floor space in front of the controls should also be provided.)

Some finishes may not be regulated by the ADA or *ICC A117.1* standard; however, there are benefits of using certain finishes for accessibility reasons. For example, using handrails that contrast with the wall finish along corridors in Health Care occupancies makes the rails easier for people with visual impairments to see. Contrasting baseboards also help. Considering additional accessible elements can be especially helpful in public spaces and occupancies where a wide variety of people use the space.

Accessible Furniture

Accessibility considerations in the building codes, ADA guidelines, and the *ICC A117.1* for furniture relate mostly to seating for assembly uses and surfaces for dining and working. Some of these elements must be accessible, but not all. It is important to determine the number and type of furniture elements that are required to be accessible. Typically, there must be at least one accessible seat and at least one of each type of dining or work surface. In some cases, the codes and accessibility standards make a distinction between similar elements that are freestanding (i.e., furniture) and elements that are built in. For example, the chapter that indicates the required height and clear floor areas for dining surfaces in the *ADA 2010 Standards* is in the chapter, "Built-in Elements." Similar information is in a chapter in the *ICC A117.1* titled "Furnishing and Equipment." In some cases, if the element such as a bench is not built in but an independent piece of furniture it may not have to be accessible. Once you know the furniture that must be accessible, you can apply the technical requirements of the *ADA 2010 Standards* and the *ICC A117.1*.

In most cases a percentage of furniture, built-in fixtures, and equipment for general use must be accessible. However, there are exceptions. For example, individual work areas are not required to be fully accessible. Work surfaces at individual employee offices or workstations can simply be adjustable and/or be replaced to meet individual or future needs. However, it may be effective to design or specify shared furniture components in an employee work area (e.g., break rooms and conference rooms) to be accessible to accommodate a variety of current and future employee needs.

One of the most significant impacts that furniture can have on accessibility is it placement within a room. When locating furniture within a space, make sure that minimum travel widths in spaces, corridors, aisles, and aisle accessways are maintained. Furniture and design elements cannot intrude on maneuvering clearances or wheelchair locations within the space. For example, a bookcase located in an office should not block the maneuvering clearance required at the door. (See Figure 5.4 in Chapter 5.). This is explained in more detail in Chapter 6. Seating and furniture requirements are discussed here.

Seating

The use of a particular type of seating is not regulated for accessibility. Instead, a clear floor area for a wheelchair must be provided in most places with seating. Typically, space for a wheelchair is required in public and common use areas such as a waiting area, lobby, and dining areas. The space required by the ADA guidelines for a wheelchair is 36 by 48 inches (915 by 1220 mm). The 2017 *ICC A117.1* requires a 36 by 52 inches (915 by 1320 mm) clear floor space for new construction but allows the smaller space for existing buildings.

In Assembly uses, when fixed seats are provided, spaces for wheelchairs are required to be included as part of the total seating capacity. The minimum number of wheelchair locations varies with the total seating capacity range. For example, a movie theater with fixed stadium seating with a total seating capacity between 151 and 300 must provide five dedicated wheelchair locations. These locations must be equally dispersed with the other seating and meet a variety of requirements depending on use. Companion seats are also required to be adjacent to each wheelchair space. In addition, 5 percent of the aisle seats must allow for transfer and/or use by persons with limited mobility. In almost all seating arrangements, at least one wheelchair location must be provided.

For restaurants, cafeterias, large breakrooms, and other dining uses, at least 5 percent of the dining surfaces must be provided with accessible seating spaces. If fixed seating is located at tables, such as in a fast food restaurant, wheelchair spaces must be dispersed among the various types of table configurations (e.g., tables for two or four). Providing the clear floor area at a dining surface will also require knee and toe clearance for a forward approach such as that required at a sink. (See Chapter 8.) Similar requirements apply to public workstations (i.e., study carrels in a library.)

A fixed seat which is meant to be accessible must be the appropriate height and location and provide wheelchair access. An example would be a fixed bench in a locker room. A bench must have the clear floor space at the end and parallel to the short side for transfer. The seat must be at least 42 inches (1065mm) long and 20–24 inches (510–610 mm) deep. The bench must either be attached to the wall or have a back. The height of

✒ Note

The *ICC A117.1* standard and *2010 ADA Standards* include requirements for accessible fixed benches. Specific dimensions and clearances ensure ease of transfer from a wheelchair to a bench.

the bench seat should be 17–19 inches (430–485 mm). See the standards for additional requirements and details.

The placement of the accessible seating and the surrounding furniture or elements must allow the required maneuvering space. Even furniture that may seem movable cannot impede the required clear floor areas or area needed to maneuver.

In nonpublic or employee work areas, the ADA requires that accessible seating be provided when required for special needs. For example, a person may need a desk chair with special features. In these cases, work closely with the client to determine what type of seating is required.

Counters, Tables, and Work Surfaces

☑ **Note**

The *ICC A117.1* standard and *2010 ADA Standards* include sections for accessible dining surfaces and work surfaces, sales and service counters, and checkout aisles. Refer to those documents for specifics.

Accessible counters, tables, and work surfaces are commonly a part of an interior project. Counters can be for the purchase of items or the exchange of information and include hotel reception desks, hospital check-in desks, security check desks, teller windows, ticketing counters, retail sales and service counters, and food service counters. The other types of surfaces that are required to be accessible include dining surfaces and work surfaces. Dining surfaces include bars, tables, lunch counters, and booths. Work surfaces include writing surfaces, study carrels, student laboratory stations, and baby-changing tables. The building codes and the *ADA Standards* will specify when counters, dining surfaces, and work surfaces in public spaces must be accessible. Typically, a sales counter in a retail store must be accessible. Similarly, reception desks in public areas must be accessible. If there is more than one, a percentage of the total must be accessible. In each case, the ADA and *ICC A117.1* standards specify that a portion of the counter at least 36 inches (915 mm) in length must be no higher than 36 inches (915 mm) above the floor, with clear floor space in front so that the public can access the desk. An example is shown at the top of Figure 10.19. If the transaction will require writing (such as signing documents), then the counter may need to be designed to accommodate a front approach with the proper knee and toe clearance.

Note, however, that the employee side of the desk does not necessarily have to meet all accessibility requirements, such as reach ranges, clear floor areas, and location of equipment. However, if someone with a disability were assigned that desk, then it would have to be modified to be accessible. In many cases, it is just as easy to design the desk to meet accessible requirements than to plan to modify it in the future. For example, if there is only one reception desk in a space, the entire desk is typically made accessible should an employee with special needs be hired. The desk could also be designed so that the employee side is adjustable. An example might be a work surface that raises and lowers. However, if

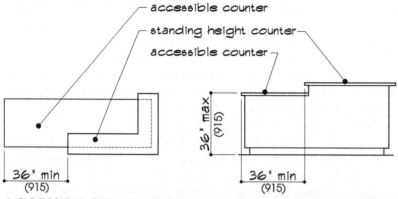

ACCESSIBLE SERVICE COUNTER - Plan View and Elevation

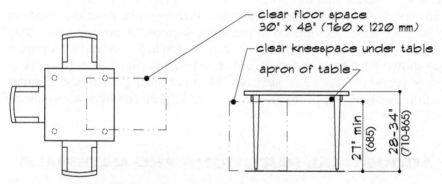

ACCESSIBLE DINING SURFACE (table) - Plan View and Section

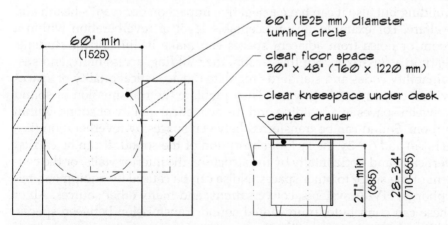

ACCESSIBLE WORKSURFACE (desk) - Plan View and Section

Figure 10.19 Accessible work surface and furniture examples.

there are multiple reception desks or counters in the same area, not all of them are required to be fully accessible. An example would be a row of bank teller stations. Although these elements must meet the minimum accessibility requirements in the ADA, when decisions must be made about how to accommodate potential employee accessible needs, discussion with the client is crucial. The client is ultimately responsible for providing a workable environment. (Document these decisions; see the section titled "Responsibility for Compliance" in Chapter 2.)

To make the employee side of the desk accessible, follow the additional requirements found in the ADA and *ICC A117.1* standards. The same requirements apply to other tables and work surfaces that are required to be accessible. Typically, the top of the surface must be between 28 and 34 inches (710 and 865 mm) above the floor. There must also be at least a 27 inches (685 mm) high by 30 inches (760 mm) wide knee space plus specific toe space below the work surface and a certain amount of clear floor space leading up to the work surface. (A turning space may also be required.) The requirements can be seen in Figure 10.19. Examples are shown for a table and desk, but similar requirements would apply to other types of accessible surfaces, as mentioned previously. (Similar requirements also apply to break room and kitchen counters, as explained in Chapter 8.)

ACOUSTICAL PARTITIONS AND MATERIALS

Unwanted noise can not only distract from the experiences within a building but also it can have a negative impact on occupant's health and welfare. For example, an unacceptable level of reverberation within a room or noise from adjacent spaces can make it difficult for students learn in a classroom. For this reason, the building, accessibility, and sustainability codes and standards regulate the acoustical quality of spaces within certain building types. They regulate the transmission of sound between spaces in a building and the acoustical quality of sound within a room. Sound can be transferred between spaces by reverberation (i.e., echoes) and/or by the lack of absorption of the sound. It can be carried vertically and horizontally by the structure, the interior walls, or the content of the space to other spaces. Noise can be caused by equipment, telephones, HVAC systems, conversations, and many other sources. All of these can contribute to unwanted sound transmission between spaces. Although not dangerous like the transfer of smoke or fire, it is regulated by the codes because it affects the indoor environmental quality (IEQ) of a building.

◀ **Note**

Noise can be caused by equipment, telephones, HVAC systems, conversations, and many other sources. All of these can contribute to the need to control sound transmission.

Sound traveling from one space to another can be a privacy issue as well as being considered "noise pollution" and can be disruptive to the use of the spaces. Requirements to control sound attenuation can affect many building components including structural elements, wall and door assemblies, finishes, and furnishings. There are many materials and products that can increase the sound attenuation qualities of floors/ceiling and wall assemblies. However, materials and components used in rated assemblies must not decrease the fire resistance of the assembly. (See Chapter 6.)

Many of the building codes and standards concentrate on the prevention of airborne sound transmission between specific types of spaces, such as hotel and dormitory rooms or apartment units. The most common measurements for sound transmission qualities are Sound Transmission Coefficient (STC) and Noise Reduction Coefficient (NRC). STC indicates approximately how much sound a wall, ceiling, floor, or window will stop from transferring through to the adjacent space. The NRC of a room rates the noise level of an interior space. Acoustical-type ceilings, carpet, sound attenuation panels, laminated gypsum board, upholstered furniture, and office panel systems can all contribute to the control of reverberation and decrease the noise level, thus reducing the potential sound transmission between spaces.

Specific STC levels for partitions and assemblies are required in most occupancies and particularly between areas where occupants may be sleeping. For example, separation between residences on multiple floors must maintain a minimum STC rating of 50. (Federal housing units may require a higher STC separation.) The *IBC* also requires walls, partitions, and floor/ceiling assemblies that separate dwelling units and dwelling units from public areas (e.g., corridors, stairs, service areas) to limit sound transmission. These elements must maintain an STC of not less than 45 to 50. This may affect the types of doors, sealants, and insulation used to close pipes, electrical outlets, recessed cabinets, bathtubs, and similar elements in the walls. ICC has published a more detailed guideline on sound, designated as *ICC G2 Guideline for Acoustics*.

The STC ratings assigned to a partition, assembly or component is based on the result when tested under the standard *ASTM E90, Standard Test Method for Laboratory Measurement of Airborne Sound Transmission Loss of Building Partitions and Elements*. Specifying components based on the STC ratings indicated by manufacturers is one way to design spaces with proper sound attenuation. However, another way is to field measure the sound attenuation of the actual construction. A field test performed according to *ASTM E336, Standard Test Method for Measurement of Airborne Sound Attenuation Between Rooms in Buildings* results in an Apparent Sound Transmission Class (ASTC). The *International Green Construction Code (IgCC)* provides separate STC and ASTC requirements for different occupancies. For example, wall and floor-ceiling assemblies separating Business, Institutional, Mercantile, and Residential occupancies are required to have an STC of 50 or an ASTC of 45. When unique conditions exist, other test standards may need to be referenced. For example, *ASTM E1414, Standard Test Method for Airborne Sound Attenuation Between Rooms Sharing a Common Ceiling Plenum,* may be appropriate for some spaces. Walls that separate mechanical and emergency generator equipment are also regulated. The *IgCC* may require a report to be generated by a third party and submitted to the jurisdiction to document compliance with the code. The *ANSI/ASHRAE USGBC/IES Standard 189.1* has similar requirements.

Another sound transmission measurement is the Impact Insulation Class (IIC). This is used to determine the sound being transmitted through the structure and building elements (not airborne sounds). The *IBC* and the *IgCC* requires floor/ceiling assemblies that separate sleeping and dwelling units from public or service areas to be acoustically separated as tested by *ASTM E492, Standard Test Method for Laboratory Measurement of Impact Sound Transmission Through Floor-Ceiling Assemblies Using the Tapping Machine.* For example, for most occupancies, the floor/ceiling assemblies between dwelling units and public areas must have an IIC that is not less than 45 to 50. The building codes also have performance criteria for meeting the required sound transmission class requirements in residential buildings.

The *IBC* requires that most standard size classrooms meet certain standards for enhanced acoustic consistent with the *ICC A117.1* standard. These requirements limit the maximum reverberation time within the room. The calculation is based on the size and materials on the floor, ceiling and walls. The ambient background noise is also limited. These sounds can include noises from outside or from adjacent spaces. Controlling the reverberation time is intended to increase the sound level and clarity of the voice communication within the room. *ASTM E2235, Standard Test Method for Determination of Decay Rates for Use in Sound Insulation Test Methods* is used to measure this affect. The calculation considers the NRC rating for every surface finish (floor, ceiling, walls, etc.)

The acoustical quality of a space can also affect the accessibility of a space and affect occupants with hearing impairments. Accessibility standards are mostly concerned that verbal communication is clear to the occupants. This can include voice communication that is part of the fire alarm or emergency warning system and the ability to hear instruction in a learning situation, for example, the *2010 ADA Standards* reference *ANSI S12.60, Acoustical Performance Criteria, Design Requirements and Guidelines for Schools*, which applies to classrooms, gymnasiums, conference rooms, and offices.

DECORATIVE MATERIALS

The codes make a distinction between interior finishes and decorative materials. Materials used as decorative elements or trim often do not have to meet the same level of fire resistance as interior finishes. However, because they can still add to or escalate a fire, the building and fire codes and the *LSC* have separate requirements and limitations for their use. In general, decorative materials must be considered noncombustible or meet the criteria set by the codes as tested by the *Vertical Flame Test*. A rule of thumb is that a material that is used in a small quantity (i.e., less than 10 percent of the wall area) be considered a decorative material; but if it is concentrated in a specific area, such as a paneled wall in a law office or a large banner in a college facility, it may have to meet the requirement as an interior finish as discussed previously in this chapter. However, a larger amount may be allowable with additional conditions. Certain materials will only be allowed to be used as a decorative material and will be limited in their overall use such as plastic trim.

The limits and requirements for decorative materials is often specific to an occupancy classification. Fabric partitions that are suspended from the ceiling in Business and Mercantile occupancies are not limited but would be in other occupancy types. For Assembly, Business, Educational, Institutional, Mercantile, and some Residential uses, including hotels and dormitories (R-1), the code limits the use of curtains, draperies, fabric hangings suspended from the wall or ceiling to not exceed 10 percent of the wall or ceiling area. (This does not include actual window coverings.) In some cases, if the building is sprinklered the requirements are different. For example, in auditoriums (Assembly), these same decorative elements can cover up to 75 percent of the aggregate wall/ceiling area if the building is sprinklered. And in R-2 dormitories, they can cover up to 50 percent of the aggregate wall/ceiling area if the building is sprinklered.

These limits between decorative materials and interior finishes apply to other elements as well including movable walls, paneling, wall pads, or crash pads that are used for decorative, acoustical, or safety reasons.

Trim is considered a decorative element by the code unless it exceeds the allowable area. Combustible trim must not exceed 10 percent of the wall area. (This does not include handrails or guardrails.) It must be tested by the *Steiner Tunnel Test* or the *Room Corner Test*. Trim can be a minimum of a Class C even if a higher interior wall or ceiling finish is required in the same area. When foam plastic is used as interior trim, additional density, thickness, area limitations, and test results apply. The codes will indicate the required flame spread index and classification for dense foam trim. Depending on its use as a interior finish or trim, other standards may apply including *UL 1975, Standard for Fire Test for Foamed*

◄ **Note**

When a building has an automatic sprinkler system, the codes may allow a lower rating for an interior finish and a larger area of decorative materials.

◄ **Note**

Interior wall base is considered separate from other trims and decorative materials. If it is 6 inches (152 mm) or less, it must be tested using the *Radiant Panel Test*. If it is larger, it may be required to be tested by the *Steiner Tunnel Test* or the *Room Corner Test*.

Plastics Used for Decorative Purposes, UL 1715 Standard for Safety Fire Test of Interior Finish Material or *FM 4880 Evaluating the Fire Performance of Insulated Building Panel Assemblies and Interior Finish Materials.* (See the discussion of foam plastics as an interior finish in the section titled "Other Finish Requirements" earlier in the chapter.)

Interior wall base is also considered trim. If it is 6 inches (15 mm) or less in height it is required to be tested by the *Radiant Panel Test*. In general, the classification for the floor base must be the same as required for the adjacent floor. Not all floors are required be classified. A minimum Class II is required in that case.

Often decorative elements are a temporary part of the interior design. These may not be part of the initial design and may be added by the occupants. However, these still may have to meet code requirements. Following are some items in this category:

Natural and artificial decorative vegetation (i.e., Christmas trees and wreaths). Natural cut trees used on the interior are typically not allowed in ambulatory care facilities, Assembly, Educational, Institutional, Mercantile, and some Residential occupancies unless the building is sprinklered. Wreaths and other decorative items on doors and walls are limited in the area that they can cover. They also cannot be located in a way the detracts from the means of egress. Artificial decorative vegetation must be tested by the *Vertical Flame Test* in most occupancies unless the building is sprinklered, as well.

Artwork and teaching materials. Typically found in educational facilities, artwork in corridors is limited to 20 percent of the wall area. And artwork in a classroom is limited to 50 percent of the wall area.

Decorations in Institutional occupancies. The amount of combustible decorative materials that is allowed on the walls of Institutional occupancies including assisted living facilities, hospitals, nursing homes, detention facilities varies between 10 to 50 percent of the wall area. The allowable percentage depends if it is in a sleeping unit, dwelling unit, corridor, classroom, or other area and if the building is sprinklered.

The key to determining the requirements for decorative elements is to first decide if they will be considered an interior finish or a decorative material. This is often based on what they are made of, how much of the wall they cover, and if they have been tested.

SIGNAGE

Signs are used in buildings to provide useful information to occupants for various reasons. Some signs help occupants to navigate within the building, define proper conduct within the space, or identify the use of the space. The codes may require their use, but most of these signs must also meet accessibility requirements. Typical signs that must meet accessibility requirements include directional and informational signs, means of egress signs, accessible entrances, elevators, toilet and bathing rooms, accessible check-out aisles, and room identification signs. Many of these signs have been discussed in the individual chapters of this book based on their purpose. However, typically, they share accessibility requirements that are found in the *ADA Standards* and the *ICC A117.1*. These documents include specifics concerning the mounting height and locations of the sign; specific details about the lettering font, height and visual contrast; and, in certain cases, the use of Braille.

Directional and informational signs that help occupants find their way within a building are required to be legible to as many people as possible. The *ADA Standards* and the *ICC A117.1* allow the use of visual letters and pictograms. It is important that the letters or characters contrast with their background so that the message is easily read at a distance. For example, the size of the actual characters is determined by their height above the floor. There are some signs such as building directories, company names and logos, and temporary signs that do not have to comply.

The ADA and the building codes require rooms or spaces whose use is considered permanent to be identified with a sign (for example, a conference room or a toilet room). Rooms such as offices whose occupant may change can identify the room generically (i.e., Office) or by room number but do not need to identify the occupant in Braille. To be compliant with the accessibility requirements, signs must be visual and tactile and allow for lettering, symbols, and Braille in a specified size and proportion. These requirements are found in the ADA Standards and the *ICC A117.1*.

It is important that signage be located in a standard location especially for the seeing impaired. As shown in Figure 10.20, the sign must be located on the latch side of the door entering the facility (not the hinged side). For a double door, the sign should be located on the inactive leaf or to the right of the double active doors. If there is no wall space on the correct side of the door, it should be located on the nearest adjacent wall. It must also be located so that the tactile lettering is between 48 and 60 inches (1220 to 1525 mm) above the floor, which is typically measured to the baseline of the lettering on the sign. (The original *ADAAG* measured this to the centerline of the sign.) Although the sign is not required to be a certain distance from the door frame or opening, it must be located far enough from the door so that the door swing does not overlap the required clear floor space of 18 by 18 inches (455 by 455 mm) below the sign. The overall goal is to allow a person to get close enough to the sign to read the raised letters or Braille without any obstructions.

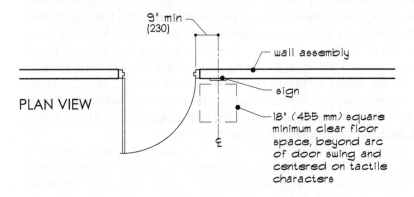

PLAN VIEW

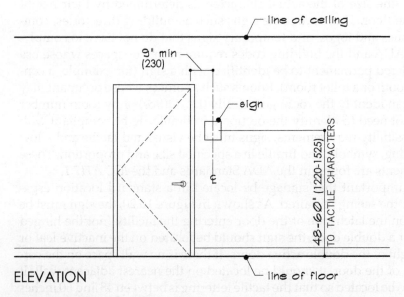

ELEVATION

NOTE: For an accessible sign that is visual only, mounting height may vary. See ICC A117.1 and ADA standards for additional requirements.

Figure 10.20 Typical accessible tactile sign locations

Specific requirements for signage for the means of egress, plumbing facilities, and other uses as required by the codes are discussed in the individual chapters.

OTHER CODE RESTRICTIONS

The building codes, fire codes, and the *Life Safety Code* set general requirements for interior finishes, decorative materials, and furniture. Some materials and applications require specific consideration. In addition, the development of new materials, products, and application systems used in interior design is ongoing. The codes continue to change to address these new and unique interior finish applications, decorative materials, and furniture products based on the way they may contribute to a fire or affect life safety. These updates may require specific research for each project. Some of the unique requirements are presented next.

1. **Pyroxylin plastic.** This product is used as imitation leather. It is not allowed to be used in Assembly occupancies because it is easily ignitable, emits high heat, and decomposes quickly in a fire.

2. **Furring strips.** When interior finishes are applied to furring strips instead of directly to fire-rated or noncombustible building materials, the furring strips cannot exceed a thickness of 1.75 inches (44 mm). In addition, the intervening spaces between the strips must be filled with a fire-rated material or fireblocked at specific intervals. Examples include wood flooring or wall paneling installed over furring strips. These code requirements reduce the chance of fire spread between the finish and the construction assembly behind it.

3. **Means of egress.** Exits and paths of travel to the exits must be clear of furnishings, decorations, or other objects. This includes no draperies obscuring exit doors and no mirrors on or adjacent to exit doors. In addition, attention must not be drawn away from the exit sign.

4. **Light-transmitting plastics.** Light-transmitting plastics include items such as Plexiglas and resin panels that can be used in a variety of applications, such as wall panels, light-diffusing panels, and signage. These are also available with fabrics sandwiched between two layers. Specific requirements for these plastics are found in the

☑ Note

Light-transmitting plastics used as interior finishes, for light fixture diffusers, or as interior signage must pass specific flame and/or fire tests and be labeled.

☑ Note

Lockers constructed of combustible materials (such as wood) are considered interior finishes and can be used only where a Class C finish is allowed. Using metal lockers is an alternative.

⬧ Note

Vinyl wallcovering is
regulated in all
thicknesses because
of its burning
characteristics.
It also has a high
smoke density.

⬧ Note

Expanded vinyl
wallcovering must
meet more testing
requirements than typical
vinyl wallcovering due to
its woven textile backing.

⬧ Note

Because of recent fires
involving flammable
plastics, the codes have
requirements for the use
of PP and HDPE. These
products are used in
various ways in interiors,
including toilet partitions
and lockers.

plastics chapter of the building codes and include large-scale test requirements as well as size, fastening, and sprinkler requirements. (Plastic veneers must comply with the finish chapter in each code. See also the inset titled "Plastic Finishes" in this section.)

5. **Wood use in placed of religious worship.** Wood used for ornamental purposes, trusses, and other decorative purposes are not limited.

6. **Insulation.** Various types of insulation can be used on an interior project. Those used within an assembly, such as a wall assembly, for sound insulation must meet the requirements of the assembly, especially as they apply to fire codes. Materials categorized as Class A by the *Steiner Tunnel Test* are often required. Similar requirements apply to the insulation materials used to wrap pipes and ducts, including those used to cover plumbing pipes under accessible sinks. (See Chapter 8.)

7. **Safety glass.** In addition to fire-rated glazing, glass can be used in several other interior applications. Examples include a glass panel in a stair railing, a shower enclosure, a decorative glass sign or feature, and as tabletop. Based on the location and the thickness and size of the glass, the codes will require the glazing to pass certain tests to meet safety glass requirements. For example, tempered glass is often required. (See the section titled "Rated Glazing and Frames" in Chapter 6.)

8. **Play areas or structures.** The codes continue to develop requirements for play areas, the allowable finish and materials used to make them and the applicable tests and results. Requirements includes the use of fire retardant wood, light-transmitting plastic, foam plastic, textiles, and other materials used to make the tubes, windows, panels, pipes, slides, and decks of the play areas. Depending on the size, specific test standards may apply to the finishes and materials.

Generally, occupancies where the occupants have mobility difficulties have stricter requirements than occupancies with fully mobile occupants. The occupancies that offer overnight provisions for multiple occupants are usually the strictest. These include Institutional occupancies, such as Health Care and Detention/Correctional facilities, and most Residential occupancies (except single-family homes). For example, hotels must use additionally rated finishes and furnishings such as bedding and draperies.

PLASTIC FINISHES

In the past, plastic-related codes were geared to plastics (e.g., insulation) used on the exterior of a building. However, it has become more common for plastics to be used as decorative elements in interior projects, and some code requirements apply to these as well. Essentially, there are two main types of plastics. The first is *thermosetting plastic*, which cannot be softened again after being cured. This group includes materials such as polyurethane, melamine, epoxy, and silicone. When exposed to fire, they typically decompose rather than burn and have the potential for creating toxic gases. The second type— the kind of plastic that can be recycled—is called *thermoplastic* and is capable of being repeatedly softened by heating and hardened by cooling. This group consists of polyvinyl chloride (PVC), acrylics (Lucite and Plexiglas), acetates, polycarbonate (Lexan), polyester (Mylar), polyethylene, polypropylene, and certain resins, as well as nylon. During a building fire, these typically melt.

The codes divide these various plastics into several different categories for the purpose of providing restrictions:

❏ Foam or cellular plastics—such as those used for trim and mouldings

❏ Pyroxylin plastics (consisting of imitation leather or other materials coated with pyroxylin)—such as those used as upholstery on furniture or wall panels

❏ Light-transmitting plastics—such as those attached to fluorescent light fixtures or used as decorative panels with backlighting

❏ Plastic veneers—such as those used on millwork or as decorative panels

❏ Fiber-reinforced polymers or fiberglass-reinforced polymers—such as those used as decorative trim and/or light-transmitting material

❏ PP and HDPE—such as that used for specialty finishes

❏ Plastic signage—larger signs such as those used in covered malls or possibly large rear-projection television screens

The building codes establish requirements for these plastics in the finish chapter and the plastics chapter. When using plastics, both chapters will have to be referenced—as well as the occupancy chapters and the fire codes in some cases. Depending on the application and the type of plastic, different tests will be required. Some are finish-related tests such as the *Room Corner Test*. Other tests are those used for building materials. The use of plastics may also affect the need for sprinklering the building or space.

SUSTAINABILITY CONSIDERATIONS

✎ **Note**

The VOCs typically found in many finishes and furniture vaporize at room temperature. This contributes to the creation of ozone and other toxins inside the building, which can lead to unhealthy indoor air quality.

✎ **Note**

A green rating system, such as LEED or Green Globes (as explained in Appendix A), can also require a product certification or the use of a sustainability standard.

Typical code and standards requirements for finishes and furniture are mostly concerned with how they could contribute to the ignition and/or spread of a fire. In other words, the impact on the life safety of the building occupants. Sustainable codes and standards focus on the effect of the finishes and furniture on the health and welfare of building occupants and the environment. This includes the materials used in the interior, how they are manufactured, and their effect on the environment when they are disposed of. However, sustainable and fire resistant qualities of a product do not have to be exclusive. For example, the *Toxicity Test*, as explained previously in the chapter, tests the toxicity of finishes and other building materials when they burn. It is easy to see that products that emit a toxic fume when burning can be detrimental to life safety and to the welfare of occupants. Other toxicity-based tests, as required by the sustainability codes and standards, determine the level of VOCs that can offgas and possibly affect IEQ of a space or building.

The state of California was one of the first jurisdictions to require sustainable finishes and furnishings by requiring low-emission finishes in schools. Although California was also the first to develop a sustainability code, there are now several documents that encourage sustainable and "green" selection of finishes and furniture. This includes the *International Green Construction Code (IgCC)*. The *IgCC* is partnered with the *ASHRAE/USGBC/IES 189.1, Standard for the Design of High-Performance Green Buildings Except Low-Rise Residential Buildings*, as part of its requirements. The *IgCC* also references *ICC 700 National Building Standard*. Together these documents include sustainability requirements for finishes and furniture. They provide requirements for materials, adhesives and sealants, paints and coatings, office furniture systems and seating, floor covering materials, interior wood products, ceiling and wall assemblies, carpet cushion, cabinets, work surfaces, wallcoverings, fabric, and other interior products. These requirements focus on the emissions and the VOC content. (Some VOC and emissions requirements are at the time of install and some are measured over a period of time.) In some cases, specific conditions must be met, or they reference a sustainable product standard or product certification program for compliance. Although a jurisdiction can choose to require the mandatory and/or optional levels of the *IgCC* to set sustainability levels for new buildings, designers can also use the information to inform their choices of materials and products to increase the sustainability of their project.

Sustainable Product Standards

Sustainable product standards (SPS) can be used to evaluate a single type of product or one or more aspects or "attributes" of a range of building products, including interior finishes and furniture. Recognizing if the standard focuses on "multi-attribute" or a "single attribute" can be important to evaluating the product's contribution to the sustainability requirements or goals of the project. These standards and testing guidelines appear to be one of the most actively growing components of interior regulations and standards. A few of the most prominent guidelines are discussed here.

The state of California's *Section 01350, Standard Practice for the Testing of Volatile Organic Emissions from Various Sources Using Small-Scale Environmental Chambers,* was initially developed as a specification section for procuring environmentally sensitive open-office systems furniture for a specific state project. It was later modified and expanded to become a benchmark specification for specifying and procuring other sustainable building products and elements for any project. There have been several modifications (including title changes) to the document to broaden the sustainability considerations to include energy, water efficiency, and indoor air quality, as well as product selection guidelines and measurement of the VOC emissions of building products and interior elements. The most current edition of the document also addresses the receiving and handling of materials, revises testing methods and reporting requirements, refers to comparable standards for some specific products, modifies acceptable levels of toxins for certain products, and includes instructions for evaluating total volatile organic compounds (TVOCs) and other harmful chemicals. In 2010, the title was changed to *Section 01350, Standard Method for the Testing and Evaluation of Volatile Organic Chemical Emissions from Indoor Sources Using Environmental Chambers (2010).* It is also referred to as the *CDPH/EHLB/Standard Method V1.1* and is one of the most widely used standards to evaluate building and interior products for low chemical emissions. It is referenced by rating systems such as LEED and Green Globes and codes and standards including *IgCC, CALGreen*, and *ASHRAE 189.1*.

SMaRT is a sustainable product standard and label controlled by the Institute for Market Transformation to Sustainability (MTS). SMaRT is used to evaluate individual products and finishes. It recognizes the use of multiple standards for various types of products. SMaRT can be used to evaluate architectural products, paints and coatings, flooring, furniture, lighting, carpet, and fabric manufacturers' and retailers' processes. For example, it is considered the standard for the Sustainable Furnishings Council. SMaRT is considered a multi-attribute standard because it eval-

> ☑ **Note**
>
> The SMaRT standards program by MTS tests and classifies building products in four categories based on the number of points received: Sustainable, Silver, Gold, or Platinum. All SMaRT standards also include the use of a life cycle assessment (LCA). (See Appendix A.)

> ☑ **Note**
>
> California Section 01350 is also known as CDPH/EHLB/Standard Method V1.1

☑ Note

Finishes that do not have a specific SPS are commonly tested using California's *Section 01350* standard. For example, wallcoverings and ceiling coverings can be tested using the *Section 01350* criteria to measure specific emission requirements and VOC content. Paints and coatings can also be tested using this standard.

☑ Note

BIFMA provides a searchable database of certified products on their website at levelcertified.org.

uates the effect of a product on the global supply chain, environment, and the multiple stages of product development and use from raw materials extraction to end of life/reuse, including LCA and SMaRT's Environmental+Health Product Declaration (EPD+HPD) is based on LCA. Credit is given particularly for reduction of pollutants in or produced by the material, use of renewable power, use of post-consumer recycled or organic materials, product reuse or reclamation, and social equality from manufacturers and suppliers. It uses a four-level rating system. SMaRT can be used in sustainable building certification systems in the United States, Canada, and other countries to verify product performance by third-party certification. For example, SMaRT was approved for LEED Credit in 2007. (See the section titled "Sustainability Considerations" in Chapter 7 for more information on sustainable building products and construction materials.)

Finish Standards

Some SPSs are more specific to a particular type of finish. NSF International has developed individual standards for several finish types. For example, the most common green standard for commercial carpeting is *NSF/ANSI 140, Sustainable Carpet Assessment*. Developed by NSF International in conjunction with the Carpet and Rug Institute (CRI), the standard is based on LCA principles and offers three levels of certification for reduced environmental impact: Silver, Gold, and Platinum. The standard uses a point system to evaluate carpet against established requirements and performance criteria in areas of health, the environment, energy efficiency, use of preferable materials and content, manufacturing process, recyclability, and innovation.

NSF International has a standard for hard surface and resilient floor coverings, titled *NSF/ANSI 332, Sustainability Assessment for Resilient Floor Coverings*. This standard measures the product through six categories, including product design, manufacturing, long-term values, end-of-life management, corporate governance, and innovation. Certification signifies a Conformant, Silver, Gold, or Platinum level. If certified by NSF, manufacturers can place a certified mark on their product. This standard is gaining use by manufacturers of resilient floor products.

NSF/ANSI 336, Sustainability Assessment for Commercial Furnishing Fabric, is used to evaluate commercial furnishing fabrics. This standard applies to woven, nonwoven, bonded, knitted, felted, and composite materials for furniture upholstery, window treatments, panel systems, wall treatments, and other decorative applications most commonly used in health care, hotels, and offices. Based on sustainability performance characteristics, different levels can be achieved, including Compliant,

Silver, Gold, or Platinum. If certified by NSF, manufacturers can place a certified mark on their product. The NSF also supports *NSF/ANSI 342. Sustainability Assessment for Wallcovering Products*, which evaluates wallcovering products. This includes textiles, vinyl, paper, polymers, paper, and other natural products. Points under this standard come from characteristics of the manufacturer and the distributors.

Furniture Standards

There are several furniture-related SPSs. Business and Institutional Furniture Manufacturers Association (BIFMA) is a trade association for the commercial furniture industry that develops safety and performance standards for business and institutional furniture. Two standards developed by BIFMA International concentrate for the measurement of VOCs: *ANSI/BIFMA M7.1, Standard Test Method for Determining VOC Emissions from Office Furniture Systems, Components and Seating*, and *ANSI/BIFMA X7.1, Standard for Formaldehyde and VOC Emissions of Low-Emitting Office Furniture Systems and Seating*. They can be used to measure VOC concentrations in built-in cabinets, shelves, and work surfaces (i.e., millwork) as well as office furniture systems and seating. BIFMA also collaborated with NSF to develop *BIFMA e3, Furniture Sustainability Standard*. This SPS addresses additional sustainability criteria including material selection and use, energy and atmosphere impacts, human and ecosystem health, and social responsibility; it is directly connected to BIFMA's product certification program called LEVEL™. It has three performance tiers: the higher the number the more sustainable criteria that has been met. There is also the *BIFMA Sustainability Guidelines for Office Furniture (2005)*.

Millwork Standards

In addition to the two BIFMA standards just mentioned, there are other SPSs that can be used to specify built-in millwork (i.e., cabinetry) components so that it meets sustainable criteria. For example, millwork should consist of products that do not contain added urea-formaldehyde. This includes composite wood and agrifiber products such as particleboard, medium-density fiberboard (MDF), wheatboard, and strawboard. These must typically meet the California standard *Section 93120, Airborne Toxic Control Measure to Reduce Formaldehyde Emissions from Composite Wood Products*. In addition, any adhesives and sealants used in the millwork, or for securing other finishes used in an interior space, must indicate reduced toxicity and use of hazardous ingredients and meet specific VOC levels. Examples include adhesives used to secure plastic laminate and veneers to the substrate (or to secure wallcovering or carpet to a surface).

◁ Note

Green Seal SPSs include *GS-11, Environmental Standard for Paints and Coatings*, and *GS-47, Environmental Standard for Stains and Finishes*.

One SPS that can be used is developed by Green Seal, *GS-36, Environmental Standard for Commercial Adhesives*. Others are specified in the codes and standards.

Product Certifications

There are a growing number of tests and standards that are used to develop or support product certification systems to quantify a sustainable product especially in fabrics and furnishing components. These are standards or certification systems may be directly referenced in the codes and sustainable programs or may be used as voluntary criteria. For example, two product certifications typically referenced by sustainability documents are Green Label and Green Label Plus. Developed by the Carpet and Rug Institute, both programs use *NSF/ANSI 140* to test carpet, cushions, and adhesives. The Green Label program identifies products with very low emissions of VOCs. The Green Label Plus program is similar but sets higher benchmarks for IAQ and identifies the lowest emitting products using *Section 01350* for reference. The updated *ASTM D5116, Standard Guide for Small-Scale Environmental Chamber Determinations of Organic Emissions from Indoor Materials/Products,* can also be used.

Another flooring product certification is called *FloorScore®*. Developed by the Resilient Floor Covering Institute (RFCI) in conjunction with Scientific Certification Systems (SCS), it certifies a wide variety of hard-surface flooring and flooring adhesives for compliance with indoor air quality emission requirements. Products tested include vinyl, linoleum, rubber, cork, ceramic, laminate flooring, and engineered hardwood flooring, as well as wall base and stair treads. The standard used to verify the VOC emissions is California's *Section 01350*.

These include OEKO-TEC®, which produces several measures including *Standard 100*, Leather *Standard*, the *STeP certification*, *DETOX TO XERO* analysis, and *ECO PASSPORT*. Each has a purpose to identify textiles free of specific harmful substances and are manufactured under sustainable conditions and certifies production facilities and their processes.

GREENGUARD Environmental Institute (GEI) has two certification programs. *GREENGUARD Certification Program*^SM is a program for low-emitting interior building materials, furnishings, and finish systems to protect indoor air quality and reduce exposure to chemicals and pollutants. GREENGUARD Certification criteria have been used to define compliance toward third-party building rating systems like LEED for low-emitting furniture. Office furniture products that are GREENGUARD Certified are also compliant with the BIFMA X7.1 standard and BIFMA e3 credit 7.6.1. The program *GREENGUARD Gold*^SM is similar, but the tested

◪ Note

GREENGUARD Building Construction^SM is a program, offered by the GREENGUARD Environmental Institute (GEI), which certifies the design, construction, and ongoing operations of newly constructed buildings specifically to minimize the risk of mold.

◪ Note

There are several product certifications for wood, including FSC Certified and SFI Certified.

◪ Note

GREENGUARD Certification Program was formerly referred to as GREENGUARD Indoor Air Quality Certification. GREENGUARD Gold Certification was formerly known as Children & Schools.

products must meet even more rigorous emissions criteria to further protect sensitive occupancies such as those found in schools and health care facilities. In addition to limiting VOCs and chemical exposure, products must comply with California's *Section 01350* (discussed previously). This latter program is specifically intended for use for facilities to protect individuals with chemical sensitivities such as in schools and health care facilities.

BIFMA's *Level* program is a certification program developed specifically for furniture. It is based on the *BIFMA e3* standard (see previous section). It is applicable to all types of furniture, components, and materials. The products are evaluated for conformance to the standard, which rates the material use, energy and atmosphere, human ecosystem health, and social responsibility of a product. The certification is modeled after LEED, with specific prerequisites, optional credits, and three conformance levels. Products that are certified receive a *level* conformance mark, with *level 3* being the highest level awarded.

The SCS *Indoor Advantage*™ certification program reviews furniture as well. It uses the standard *ANSI/BIFMA X7.1*, CA 01350, and other requirements to test products for VOCs. Developed by SCS, it is composed of two programs: *Indoor Advantage*, which certifies office furniture; and *Indoor Advantage Gold*, which certifies paints and coatings, adhesives and sealants, insulation, wall coverings, and furnishings.

There are other certification systems that can help identify environmentally friendly furniture or components. Certification programs each have specific areas of concerns regarding sustainability. The Forestry Stewardship Council (FSC) is a voluntary certification system that ensures that wood products are from responsibly harvested sources. These products can include building materials, cabinetry, furniture, and flooring. The UL Environmentally Sustainable Produce Certification and the McDonough Braungart Design Chemistry (MBDC) Cradle to Cradle Certification program are examples of other programs.

Whether selecting or designing new finishes, furniture, or built-ins for a project, there are many additional sustainability requirements, standards, and certification programs to consider. Although not all of them are required by a particular sustainable code or standard at this time, they will provide health benefits to the building occupants and possible cost savings to the client or building owner. Many manufacturers are listing these SPSs and/or certifications on the products they sell (see an example in Figure 10.15) or have it available on request. (For more about sustainability, see Appendix A.)

◥ **Note**

There is a growing number of websites to help identify green products. A couple of examples include www.sustainablesources.com and www.interiorsandsources.com. (See also Appendix A.)

RESEARCH: USING THE CODES

It is critical to determine the tests, classifications, ratings, or other characteristics required for each area or interior element before beginning to select finishes or furniture. The main sources for interior finish regulations are the building codes, the fire codes, and the *LSC*. The building codes each have chapter dedicated to interior finishes. For the *IBC*, it is Chapter 8, "Interior Finishes"; in the *NFPA 5000* it is Chapter 10, "Interior Finish." In the *IBC*, general and specific requirements by occupancy classification are found in this chapter. In the NFPA codes including the *LSC*, common requirements that apply to all occupancy types are in the interior finish chapter and specific requirements per occupancy are found in the individual occupancy chapters. For example, interior finish requirements that are specific to new movie theater (Assembly) will occur in the "New Assembly" chapter in the "Protection" section and the subsection on "Interior Finishes." (Remember, in the *LSC*, requirements can differ between existing and new occupancies.) The *International Fire Code* (*IFC*) also has a chapter: Chapter 8, "Interior Finish, Decorative Materials, and Furnishings." Some of this information is repeated in the *IBC*. If the jurisdiction is using *NFPA 1, Fire Code*, the interior finish requirements are in Chapter 20, "Occupancy Fire Safety." Although the chapters in each code are organized differently, much of the information is similar, but you will have to look for differences as part of your research.

Depending on the products and materials you are using in your project, other chapters and sections of the codes may need to be referenced. For example, the *IBC* has a chapter on glass and glazing and another on plastic. Finishes for plumbing fixtures and restrooms are found in the plumbing codes in Chapter 12, "Interior Environment" of the *IBC*. In addition, although interior finish requirements unique to a specific occupancy will be found in the specific occupancy chapters in the NFPA codes, in the *IBC* similar specific requirements would be found in the occupancy sections in Chapter 4, "Special Detailed requirements Based on Occupancy and Use." Occupancies and uses such as high-rises, Institutional (day cares, assisted living, hospitals, nursing homes, detention), Assembly, Residential (hotels, dormitories, group homes), and Educational often will often have special finish requirements and will require additional research.

Requirements for furniture, including mattresses will be found in the finish chapter of the *IFC* and the *LSC*. (The building codes do not include furniture requirements.) Within the interior finish chapter of the *IFC*, there are sections on "Upholstered Furniture and Mattresses in New and Existing Buildings" and "Furnishings Other Than Upholstered

Furniture and Mattresses or Decorative Materials in New and Existing Buildings." In the *LSC*, the requirements can be found in the section on "Contents and Furnishings" within the finish chapter. Similar to finishes, special requirements per occupancy for furnishing are found in the individual occupancy chapters. For example, furnishing requirements that are specific to a new school (Educational) will occur in the "New Educational" chapter in the "Operating Features" section and the subsection on "Furnishings and Decorations." (The subsection title can vary slightly in each occupancy chapter, for example, a similar section for Health care is titled, "Furnishings, Mattresses, and Decorations" and "Furnishing, Decoration, and Scenery" for Assembly.) The furniture requirements in the *IFC* are in Chapter 8, "Interior Finish, Decorative Materials, and Furnishings."

Requirements for decorative elements and materials as discussed in this chapter will be found in the interior finish chapters of the building codes, fire code, and the *LSC*. This includes the parameters of when a material must be considered an interior finish or a decorative material. If you determine a material will be considered an interior finish, then you will need to research the requirements based on its use as a wall, ceiling, or floor finish, for example. If the material is too combustible to be considered an interior finish, is temporary, and/or is used in a smaller amount, then the requirements for use as a decorative materials may be appropriate. In the *IFC*, there are also sections on "Decorative Materials and Artificial Decorative Vegetation in New and Existing Buildings" and a similar section for natural decorative vegetation.

Although the use of certain finishes and materials may be a part of a performance design, performance codes do not specifically mention finishes and furniture. But, if a performance code such as the *ICC Performance Code* (*ICCPC*) were to be used for another portion of a project, finish or furniture selection may need to be considered in the overall solution. For example, if performance criteria were used to design the fire protection system in a building, the fire loads of the selected finishes and/or furniture might have to be incorporated into the computer fire model or engineering calculations.

In some cases, your research may need to include reviewing the various standards that apply to interior finishes and furniture. Many of these have been discussed in this chapter. Some standards are developed and enforced on a local level (for example, California), some are developed and referenced by the codes, and some are required by the federal government. Although the code may dictate the compliance with a specific standard, the designer may also choose to use an industry standard to evaluate a material or product for a specific use. It is important that the standard is appropriate to your proposed use of the material. In addition,

◢ Note

If a jurisdiction requires the use of a sustainability code or standard or a green building program, be aware that these include requirements for finishes and/or furniture as well. The requirements must be coordinated with the building and life safety codes.

◢ Note

Some jurisdictions have their own finish and furniture regulations. Some of the most stringent ones include those of the city of Boston and the state of California.

the development of standards and testing in ongoing, especially for new materials and to measure sustainability. It is important to keep up-to-date. Checking for updates from the National Fire Protection Association (NFPA), Underwriters Laboratories (UL), and ASTM International (ASTM) or subscribing to their website can help.

As indicated in the accessibility section of this book, the Americans with Disabilities Act (ADA) and the *ICC A117.1* may affect the selection of finishes and how furniture is designed, specified, or arranged in a space. The first step in all research for the ADA is to determine if and how many of the spaces or elements must be compliant. This is affected initially if the project will be governed by Title I or Title II of the ADA. (See the discussion on ADA in Chapter 1 of this book.) Then, you will need to review the scope of elements that are required to be compliant as indicated in "Chapter 2, Scoping Requirements" of the *2010 Standards*. The individual elements and spaces each have a section which identifies the required accessible scope. For example, there is a scoping section for "Dining Surfaces and Work Surfaces" and a section on "Kitchens, Kitchenettes, and Sinks." Once you know what spaces and elements are required to be accessible, you can research the technical requirements for this scope. The requirements that drive the need for slip-resistant finishes and the allowable changes in level between floor surfaces can be found in "Chapter 3, Building Blocks." The specific dimensions for built-in, casework, and dining and work surfaces can be found in "Chapter 9, Built-In Elements." In some cases, other sections of the ADA Standards will have to be reviewed. For example, "Chapter 8, Special Rooms, Spaces, and Elements" will have additional requirements for those uses. Because of the efforts between the Access Board and the ICC to coordinate the 2010 Standards and the *ICC A117.1*, the organization of the documents are similar although the technical requirements may differ. Remember, the most stringent requirement should be applied.

IgCC does not have a specific finish or furniture chapter but "Chapter 8, Indoor Environmental Quality (IEQ)" contains most of the emission and VOC and other requirements that affect interior products and furniture. In addition, Chapter 9, "Materials and Resources" has prescriptive and performance criteria for the use of recycled and salvaged content, bio-based products, multiple-attribute products, and LCA for specified products.

DOCUMENTATION

The purpose of early documentation is not to have to do the work twice. This can be especially important with finishes and furniture because there are often many selections in a project. The "Finishes and Furniture" sections of the digital code checklist provided with this book can help you with your research and documentation. For example, the code checklist will prompt you to determine if specific test for finishes or furniture must be met, and then will provide a place for you to indicate the appropriate tests and mark when the selection of an appropriate material has been made. This process will help to avoid having to retrace your research or selections. Depending on the size of the project, the code checklist can be used for the whole project or separately for each space or room within a larger project.

Clear documentation is important if you are dealing with a variety of rooms or spaces, each with its own finishes and furniture. It is also important when some rooms or areas have stricter requirements than others. For example, requirements for public areas are often stricter and typically require finishes and furniture that are different from those of other areas within the project. The digital code checklist includes places to document code compliance, accessibility, and sustainability. Although this list does not take the place of checklists for specific sustainable programs, it will allow you to note what has been considered.

It is important to keep documentation simple. For example, as you choose finishes and furniture, you may want to keep digital scans of labels for finishes or furniture that must meet testing requirements that include the manufacturer, catalog number, and proof test results. The Checklist will help you identify the requirement that has to be met, and the scan will document that the selection complies. Or, if you chose to have a finish or component treated, this will remind you to keep a copy of the certificate verifying its compliance with the test.

When documenting the project for construction, it is important to indicate which code documents and specific requirements must be met. For finishes and furniture for a project, this can be important when being reviewed by the code official or during pricing. For example, if it is clearly indicated on the drawings that the appropriate classification of finishes has been provided in each area, the review by the code official is simpler. In addition, if furniture in certain areas must meet higher testing

> ◤ **Note**
>
> Although codes for interior finishes are much *stricter* in commercial projects, they should be considered *equally critical* in residential projects. Death from smoke and fire exposure occurs more often in residential fires.

standards than others, then making this clear in the documents (plan or specifications) may promote more accurate pricing. This also makes it easier for review by the required code officials. In many cases, meeting the requirements of the ADA will require additional details to indicate the appropriate clearances, heights, and configuration of built-in elements and arrangement of spaces and furniture. Although some designers develop standard details, these should always be reviewed to make sure that they reflect the conditions of the actual project.

CHAPTER 11

CODE OFFICIALS
AND THE CODE PROCESS

Each chapter in this book discusses a specific step in the code process, beginning in Chapter 1 and 2 with determining the publications required by local and federal jurisdictions, moving on to Chapter 3 with determining occupancy classifications, and ending in Chapter 10 with finish and furniture requirements. Throughout each chapter, references are made to code officials, jurisdictions, and determining which requirements apply to your project. This chapter concentrates on the *code process*: the interaction between the designer and the code official (or the authority having jurisdiction) during the development and implementation of a design project. It introduces the different types of code officials, outlines the various steps that should be taken during the development of the design, and proposes how and what to document as it relates to code requirements. How to integrate performance and sustainability criteria will also be discussed.

While reading this chapter, the important thing to remember is that the interior project must be designed to meet the codes, standards, and federal regulations required in *that jurisdiction*. The necessary research and inclusion of these regulations must be thorough and properly recorded in the project drawings and specifications. It is your responsibility to make sure the design meets the intent of the codes. It is the code official's job to review the project documents (drawings and specifications) and verify their code compliance. Although the code official is there to guide and clarify requirements, if needed, it is not the official's responsibility to design the space or to indicate which codes apply to a project. The overall intent of this book is to create a foundational understanding of the various code sources and requirements. From that initial understanding, appropriate research can identify the requirements for a particular project. And through good design, you can apply the various code requirements properly and work with the code official to produce a safe and effective project.

AUTHORITY HAVING JURISDICTION

☜ **Note**

There are various types of code consultants who can be used to provide added expertise during code research, especially on large or specialized projects.

The *authority having jurisdiction*, or *AHJ*, is used to indicate the entity that has the authority to decide whether the design and construction are compliant with the required codes and to enforce code compliance. In general, the term can apply to a legally defined area (such as a city or county), a specific code department, or an individual code official who has the right to review and approve construction. Collectively, these entities decide which codes are being enforced, manage the review and approval of the design and construction, and monitor construction within their area to ensure that buildings are safe. As the designer, it is important to understand the roles and responsibilities of the AHJ and know how and when to work with them to ensure that a project meets the code requirements. Each type of AHJ is described in more detail in this section.

Code Jurisdiction

☜ **Note**

The authority having jurisdiction, or AHJ, can be a legally defined area, a code department, or an individual code official.

☜ **Note**

Sometimes it is unclear whether a project will fall under the jurisdiction of the city, county, or state. You may have to contact each jurisdiction (AHJ) to confirm. This is important because it could affect which codes apply to the project.

The code jurisdiction of a project is determined by the location of the building. A *jurisdiction* is defined as a geographical or governmental area that uses the same codes, standards, and regulations. At the broadest level, a state typically mandates codes that must be followed by each jurisdiction within the state. In addition, a county or city municipality may also establish a set of codes to be used in their local jurisdiction. The relationship of the state code and the local code varies among states. Sometimes the state code must be followed in conjunction with other locally adopted codes, or it might apply only to buildings in areas that do not have a local enforceable code. Typically, the state will at least enforce regulations on state-owned buildings.

Just as each jurisdiction decides which code publications are to be enforced, it also decides when to change or update the codes. The newest edition of the code may not be the one being enforced. For example, the building code enforced by a state may be the 2012 *IBC* but the building code enforced by a particular city in that state may be the 2018 *IBC*. If both apply to your project, it can cause conflicts. You may have to be aware of the differences between the two editions. Also, each jurisdiction can make amendments to the codes that change the original code requirements. These modifications may remove a particular requirement, call for a more stringent requirement, and/or modify a requirement so that it is more relevant to that jurisdiction. (See the section titled "Code Publications" in Chapter 1 for more information.)

It is important to determine the correct jurisdiction of your project, the enforceable codes for that jurisdiction (including the edition of the codes), and if there are any addendums that have been made. All this is necessary at the beginning of a project so that proper code research can be done.

Code Department

The local government agency that administers and enforces the codes within a jurisdiction is typically referred to as the *code department* or *building department*. (The most recent edition of the *IBC* uses the term *code compliance agency*.) Some small jurisdictions may have a code agency or department that consists of only one person or code official; larger jurisdictions may support many different agencies and departments. The administration chapters in the building codes and the *Life Safety Code (LSC)* give basic requirements for the code review and administrative process. However, each code department can modify these requirements to suit its own organization and typical volume of projects. For example, a large code department may require multiple sets of drawings to be submitted or sets to be provided electronically, whereas a small code department may require only one hard-copy set. These modifications are often included in the local amendments to the enforced code. (See the inset titled "Administration Chapter" in this chapter.)

Most code departments use digital technology to simplify and expedite the code submission process. Examples include these:

❑ **Online permit applications and processing.** Allows permit applications to be filed online. Designers, contractors, and citizens can often check on the status and scope of submitted and active permits.

❑ **Electronic plan submission and review.** Maintains plans in electronic format from design to permit review, allowing markups to be done electronically.

❑ **Scheduling and conducting inspections.** Site inspections can be posted in the field using wireless devices, allowing for quicker turnaround times. (See the section titled "Inspections during Construction" later in this chapter.)

Because the code submittal process and roles and responsibilities of the code official can vary by jurisdiction, it is important to contact the code department that will be reviewing a project to understand their unique process. These variations can affect the best way to work with them during a project.

Code Official

A *code official*, also known as a *building official*, is someone who has the authority to administer, interpret, and enforce the provisions of the adopted and/or amended code within a particular jurisdiction. The code official is included when the codes refer to the AHJ. However, the term *code official* has been used throughout this book as a general term that may represent a variety of roles or functions and that may represent more than one person in a particular code department.

The role of code official can be filled by a variety of people, each with a different job title. Or several roles may be held by a single person. In smaller jurisdictions, one person may have several responsibilities. For example, there may be one person who does multiple types of inspections. In larger jurisdictions, several people with the same title may be grouped into a department, each with his or her area of expertise. Some jurisdictions may also hire a private agency to handle some of the responsibilities. The most common types of code officials are described in the following list.

❏ **Plans examiner.** A code official who checks the construction drawings (including floor plans), specifications, and other documents in the preliminary stages and in the final permit review stage of a project. The plans examiner checks for code and standards compliance. Designers typically work most closely with the plans examiner.

❏ **Building inspector.** A code official who visits the project job site after a permit is issued to make sure that construction complies with the codes as specified in the construction documents and in the code publications. (See the section titled "Inspections during Construction" later in this chapter.)

❏ **Special inspector.** A code official who is qualified to inspect a particular type of construction that requires special knowledge. This may include electrical, mechanical, and other specialties and systems.

❏ **Fire marshal.** A code official who typically represents the local fire department. A fire marshal checks the drawings in conjunction with the plans examiner during the preliminary stages and the final permit plan review, checking the construction documents for fire code and means of egress compliance. The fire marshal also typically reviews the project job site on completion of construction, and, depending on the type of project, may perform periodic reviews during the life of the building.

Similar to the growing complexity of the building industry, the role of the code official has become more complex. Although the administration chapter in each building code sets a level of experience and knowledge of the design, engineering, or the construction industry for a code official,

> **✎ Note**
>
> The International Accreditation Service (IAS), a subsidiary of the International Code Council (ICC), offers an accreditation process for code departments. It is used to evaluate a code department in multiple categories, including departmental policies and procedures including permitting, inspections and plan reviews, code interpretation, and enforcement. You can identify departments that have been accredited on the IAS website.

> **✎ Note**
>
> The role of the code official is defined in Chapter 1, "Administration," of the building codes for the ICC codes. For National Fire Protection Association (NFPA) codes, the revised *NFPA 1030, Standard for Professional Qualifications for Fire Prevention Program Positions*, can be used beginning in 2023. Local jurisdictions can also make amendments to both.

each jurisdiction can modify these requirements based on the qualifications considered important. (See the inset titled "Administration Chapter" in this chapter.) Most jurisdictions require code officials to have a comprehensive understanding of a how a building's structural system, means of egress, detection and suppression systems, and similar aspects work together to protect the occupants of the space or building. They must also understand the actual building process. In larger jurisdictions, some code officials have more specialized responsibilities. Similar to other design and construction industry professionals, code officials must keep up with changes in the codes and construction technology and methods.

The ICC and the NFPA each have a certification process for code officials. Certification indicates that the person has the necessary knowledge and experience to inspect, interpret, and enforce the codes. Certifications are available for specific areas of construction and code compliance and in some cases qualifies them for specific titles. In ICC programs, there are separate certification for inspectors and code specialists. There are separate certifications for building, electrical, fire, plumbing, mechanical, housing, accessibility, sustainability, and energy conservation. In some cases, they are divided by commercial or residential codes. Additional certificates are available for advanced levels of expertise. For example, "Certified Building Official" (CBO), "Certified Fire Marshal" (CFM), "Master Code Professional," "Master of Special Inspection," and "Certified Sustainability Professional" are the highest levels of designation. NFPA certifications typically focus on knowledge pertaining to the fire protection elements of a building including emergency power systems, means of egress, and sprinkler systems. The NFPA certification programs recognize different levels of expertise with designations that include "Certified Electrical Safety Compliance Professional" (CESCP), "Certified Fire Plan Examiner" (CFPE), and "Certified Fire Inspector I" (CFI). Also, beginning in 2023, the new voluntary standard *NFPA 1030, Standard for Professional Qualifications for Fire Prevention Program Positions,* will replace several standards that previously set the minimum requirements for fire inspectors, electrical inspectors, plan examiners, and fire marshals.

The code official's knowledge of the codes and the construction process makes them an important resource during design. For many projects it can be important for the code official to become involved early in the design process to develop the best design and without delays. This is true especially as more projects are designed using sustainable concepts, alternative methods and materials, and performance codes. Although the code official always must approve the design and/or the use of building materials and systems to move forward, it is an integral part of these types of projects. There will be situations in which neither the designer nor the code official will be able to rely on the straightforward approach of the prescriptive code for a particular design solution. In these cases, collaboration will be key.

ADMINISTRATION CHAPTER

The first chapter of each code publication describes the purpose of that particular code. It also provides basic requirements for the application and administration of that code. In the ICC codes this chapter is called "Scope and Administration," and in the NFPA it is called "Administration." Here is a list of typical information included in an administrative chapter based on the *IBC*:

❑ Scope of work requiring code compliance and permitting
❑ Permit requirements and related fees
❑ Submittal requirements for construction documents
❑ Types of required inspections
❑ Requirements for certificates of occupancy
❑ Connection of service utilities
❑ Means of appeals
❑ Types of violations
❑ Issuance of stop-work orders

The ICC chapter also describes the duties and powers of the code official and the code department. However, for the NFPA codes, this is determined by *NFPA 1030, Standard for Professional Qualifications for Fire Prevention Program Positions*. Local jurisdictions often have amendments or additions to these requirements to be consistent with how their department works.

Other codes, such as performance codes and sustainability codes, will have additional information pertinent to use of the code. The "Administration" chapter of the building codes is the one most often modified by local jurisdictions. Check for local amendments to confirm any revisions.

CODE REVIEW AND ENFORCEMENT

As discussed in the preceding section, each jurisdiction adopts its own set of codes and standards. Code officials review and inspect projects based on those requirements. However, an interior project may need to meet additional regulations and be reviewed by other representatives. These can include regulatory agencies within the state, sustainable programs, and laws mandated by the federal government. Each is enforced by a different group or entity.

Agency Review

In addition to the codes required by the jurisdiction, certain projects may also be under the authority of another agency that develops and enforces its own regulations. These are often specific to a use. These regulations may be developed and enforced on a state, county, or city level. For example, a state or local health department usually has specific requirements that restaurants, cafeterias, and day cares must meet for food prep and sanitation. Other agencies may have jurisdiction because of licensure or voluntary participation in a regulatory program. For example, many hospitals are accredited by the Joint Commission on Accreditation of Healthcare Organizations (JCAHO). Although JCAHO uses the *LSC* for its fire safety requirements, it also has uses a separate document *Guidelines for Design and Construction of Hospitals and Outpatient Facilities (FGI)* for detailed requirements for the spatial, mechanical, and interior finishes within the various parts of a hospital. These are reviewed by regularly by JCAHO agents, not by the local code officials. Some zoning and historical ordinances can also affect an interior project. Although these may also be controlled by a local governmental department, they often have separate review and approval processes from the code department. Other reviewing agencies may include the US Environmental Protection Agency and Occupational Safety and Health Administration for certain project types. The requirements of these agencies may have to be incorporated in the design along with the codes and standards. It may be helpful to have a review with a representative from the required agency(ies) before finalizing a design. In some cases, a site visit after construction is required for approval.

⬛ **Note**

Certain occupancy classifications and/or building types must meet additional regulations enforced by state or local agencies. Examples include hospitals, restaurants, day care centers, and schools.

Sustainability Programs

There are sustainable provisions in the existing codes, especially in the energy codes, plumbing codes, and mechanical codes. These requirements are enforced as part of the normal code review and inspection process. However, the adoption of more comprehensive sustainability codes and standards is becoming common. With the growing attention to sustainable design and green construction processes, many jurisdictions have instituted their own sustainability programs. Some programs use portions of the *IgCC*, which can be enforced similarly to other codes or through a third party. In some cases, certain criteria must be met to obtain permits or final approvals.

Other jurisdictions require the use of a green rating system, such as LEED or Green Globes for certain building projects, such as schools or city/state-funded buildings. A jurisdiction may also set a reduced energy use to be met by a certain date. In these cases, a variety of ways to review and enforce sustainable practices are used. Large codes departments may have staff members who can review and approve the compliance with a rating or certification program; in other cases, an independent review and approval by a third party may be required. (See Appendix A for more information on the use of sustainable codes.)

Federal Laws and Regulations

The enforcement of federal laws and regulations is a little more complicated. Each federal agency such as the DoD, HUD, GSA, and the USPS enforces its own regulations for their federally funded buildings under the ABA. (See Chapter 2.) However, for projects that are not federally owned or funded but must meet a federal regulation, such as the ADA, there is no clear enforcement procedure. Although compliance with these federal laws is mandatory, the DOJ, who enforces the ADA, does not have the manpower to enforce them in every jurisdiction. And the local AHJ is not technically responsible for enforcing a federal standard.

For that reason, many state and local jurisdictions formally adopt the ADA standard or create a standard that is at least equivalent to the federal requirements so that they can use the document to legally enforce them on a local level. To support local assessment, the DOJ will certify a document if it is equal or exceeds the current ADA guideline requirements. (This was discussed in Chapter 2.) In many cases, this may mean that there is a local accessibility code, which can be used for review by local code official, but it does not mean that the project is absolutely consistent with the federal ADA requirements. Thus, noncompliance with the ADA is typically discovered and subsequently enforced through lawsuits. (See Chapter 2 for more information on the ADA.)

> **✎ Note**
>
> Code officials review and inspect projects using the codes and standards required by that jurisdiction. However, they do not review or inspect projects to check for compliance with federal regulations such as the *ADA Standards*.

THE CODE PROCESS

Although the process for code approval may vary slightly, depending on the type of project and the code jurisdiction, the ultimate goal is for the design to meet all the code requirements so that a building permit can be obtained, construction can begin, and that the finished project will meet code. Most interior projects, unless they consist of minor repairs or minimal finish or furniture selection, cannot be constructed without a permit.

To obtain a permit with minimal delay or difficulty, it is important to understand the process endorsed by the code officials in the jurisdiction of the project. Although the building codes define the basic roles and process for obtaining a permit, each jurisdiction typically will modify it to fit their department resources. Learn to work with the code officials while moving through the code process explained in this section. Several steps are done directly by the designer, including the initial code research, preliminary review, and any appeals that may be necessary. The other steps in the process directly affect the construction contractor and include the permit approval, the inspection process, and the final approval that allows the space to be occupied. This process is diagrammed in Figure 11.1 and groups the steps into three subcategories: the design process, the permit process, and the inspection process. Refer to Figure 11.1 as the steps are described in more detail in the next sections. (Construction documents and liability are explained later in the chapter.)

Code Research and Design

Research should begin by determining the jurisdiction of the project. Remember, the jurisdiction may be a township, city, county, or state—and in some cases, state and local codes may both apply. (See the sections titled "Code Jurisdiction" and "Code Review and Enforcement" earlier in this chapter.) You can contact the local code department to request a list of codes and standards that are enforced but they are typically also listed on the code department's website. In addition, it is necessary to know which edition of the specific code publication is being used and if an update adoption is planned. As described in Chapter 1, most codes and standards go through major updates every three years and minor changes on a yearly basis. Jurisdictions are not required to automatically use the updates. And, because each jurisdiction adopts these changes on a different schedule, it is important to know when a new edition may be adopted. (Some jurisdictions will issue notices when updates are pending or occurs.) This is especially important if an adoption might occur during the design of a project because the construction documents must be compliant with the current adopted codes when they are submitted for permitting. (See also inset titled "Knowing What Is New in the Code" in this chapter.)

Also, because each jurisdiction can make amendments, deletions, and additions that alter the original code publication, you need to determine if there are amendments to the code publications as well. For

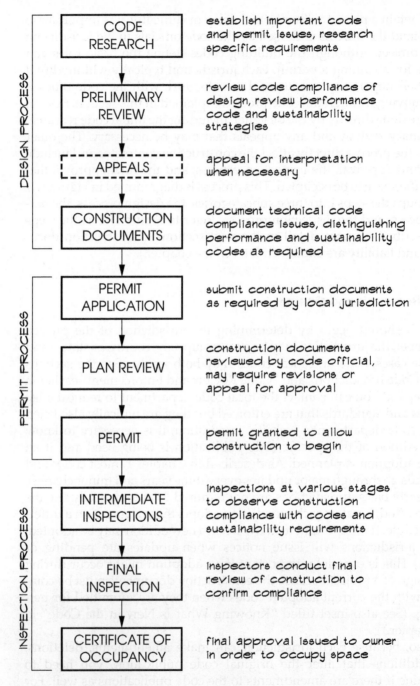

DESIGN PROCESS

| CODE RESEARCH | establish important code and permit issues, research specific requirements |

| PRELIMINARY REVIEW | review code compliance of design, review performance code and sustainability strategies |

| APPEALS | appeal for interpretation when necessary |

| CONSTRUCTION DOCUMENTS | document technical code compliance issues, distinguishing performance and sustainability codes as required |

PERMIT PROCESS

| PERMIT APPLICATION | submit construction documents as required by local jurisdiction |

| PLAN REVIEW | construction documents reviewed by code official, may require revisions or appeal for approval |

| PERMIT | permit granted to allow construction to begin |

INSPECTION PROCESS

| INTERMEDIATE INSPECTIONS | inspections at various stages to observe construction compliance with codes and sustainability requirements |

| FINAL INSPECTION | inspectors conduct final review of construction to confirm compliance |

| CERTIFICATE OF OCCUPANCY | final approval issued to owner in order to occupy space |

Figure 11.1 Typical steps in the code process.

example, a jurisdiction that adopts the *International Building Code* may have some local ordinances that override specific *IBC* requirements. These amendments are also typically available on their website, but hard copies may also be available. Based on the project type, you should ask if any other local agency regulations or ordinances will affect the project. (See the discussion in the section titled "Agency Review" earlier in the chapter.) You should also determine which federal regulations apply to the project. (See the section titled "Federal Regulations" in Chapter 1.)

Before you begin design, you should determine who can document and submit drawings for a building permit. Most jurisdictions have strict requirements about who can design an interior project based on the use or occupancy classification, size, and scope of the project. For example, the drawings for some projects or portions of a project must be stamped by the appropriate design professional. This may be an architect, interior designer, or engineer, depending on the state regulations and the purpose of the drawing. If a professional stamp is required, the design and documentation must be typically done by or under the direct supervision of the required registered professional. To meet these various requirements, many firms employ a variety of design professionals or establish contractual relationships with other professionals to address the project scope of work.

At the beginning of the project it is also important to determine what documentation and information must be submitted to obtain a permit for construction. Many code departments will have a list of required drawings, specifications, and information that must be provided based on the project type, size, and complexity. Although interior project documentation typically requires demolition plans, partition plans, reflected ceiling plans, and power and communication plans, other documentation including automatic sprinkler layout drawings, life safety plans, interior elevations, specific details, and schedules may also be required to fully document the design and to indicate code compliance. (See the section titled "Construction Documents" later in this chapter.)

After determining which codes and standards apply to a project, the specific requirements should be researched, beginning with the occupancy classification. For example, if renovating an existing college classroom facility, concentrate on the code requirements for Business occupancies. But if the project includes renovation of the cafeteria, the requirements for Assembly may have to be reviewed as well. To help you, the chapters of this book have been organized starting with Chapter 3, "Occupancy Classification and Loads," in the typical order of research.

This initial research is ideally done at the same time the client and project programming/scope information is being collected and before

☑ Note

A jurisdiction may allow some interior projects to be built without stamped or sealed drawings. The decision is usually based on the use of the space and the building's total square footage and number of stories.

☑ Note

Some projects may require the code official(s) to walk through the building at the beginning of a project to determine which codes will apply to a project. This is especially important in older buildings that require updating. (See Appendix B.)

starting the actual project design. The code requirements can then be incorporated into the design from the beginning, which avoids having to redesign to meet the code requirements later. It may be helpful to note important applicable sections of the code or copy them into the project files, either electronically or as hard copy. This is especially important if a code requirement will directly affect the design layout or will require specific systems be included. Noting them will help you remember the reason for certain decisions later in the design process. This documentation, along with the use of the checklists provided with this book, will help track the code issues that affect the design of the project. This, too, can be especially useful if questions arise later.

Once in the design process, additional specific research may be required. For example, when space planning an office furniture systems layout, you may need to determine the minimum allowable aisle widths. With experience, some code requirements will become part of your basic design knowledge and will not have to be checked every time you begin a project. However, keep in mind, that codes change and the requirements for different project types can be different. So, designing with codes from memory is not always the best or most accurate process. For example, the minimum corridor width is typically 44 inches (1118 mm), but for Educational uses it is 72 inches (1829 mm). And the minimum allowable aisle width for a Mercantile occupancy changed from 36 to 44 inches from the 2012 *IBC* to the 2015 *IBC*. In many cases a specific code requirement can be different for an unsprinklered project than one with a sprinkler system. So, knowing the basic codes that apply to a project and doing proper research prepares you to design a project efficiently and results in a design that will be approved by the code official.

Preliminary Review

Most code jurisdictions have some form of preliminary plan review procedure that can occur in the early stages of a project. Although a preliminary review may not be required on all projects, for some projects it may be crucial so that critical aspects can be finalized before taking the design to the next phase. It may be as informal as sending an email to that code official with a floor plan indicating the pertinent code issues or as formal as a meeting with several code officials. When arranging a preliminary review meeting, request the presence of the plans examiner, the fire marshal, and any other necessary official so that all code concerns can be addressed at once.

As shown in Figure 11.1, the preliminary review should occur in the early stages of the design process, typically during the schematic design phase. Most of the code research should have been completed by that time; be prepared to discuss and clarify specific code issues. The preliminary floor plans should have enough detail to enable discussion of the key code topics particularly means of egress. Whether presented electronically or hard copy, it may be helpful if drawings are measurable so distances can be checked. Certain information should be readily known or indicated on the drawing, such as the overall size of the building or space, the division of occupancies, and the arrangement of exits. If designing only a portion of a building, a location plan that indicates the layout of the remaining portions of the floor or building is helpful.

The purpose of the preliminary review meeting is to go over the major code issues and determine if the conclusions drawn from the research are valid. For example, discuss any code conflicts or unclear requirements that were found during the research.

This is also an opportunity to ask if the code officials have any concerns about the design and if they foresee any potential code issues. Their experience with multiple projects can often provide foresight into issues or requirements that have not yet come up. Likewise, if there is a situation that cannot easily meet the requirements of the code, be prepared to present an alternate solution. As a type of performance provision or equivalent means and methods, the code official has the power to approve your proposal as satisfactory to the intent of the code. However, it is not prudent to rely on code officials to solve a design problem, because they may come up with a solution that meets the intention of the code but does not fit with the design intentions.

It can be important to take accurate notes during any meeting with the code officials. Making note of requested changes, decisions made, and possible code concerns that need additional research or solutions can be helpful in the design progress. It can also be beneficial to prepare a summary of the meeting for the project records. After the meeting, send a copy of the summary to all attending code officials and ask them to indicate agreement or exceptions to the summary. On smaller projects, the necessary corrections and notations could be made directly on the drawings; then ask the code officials to sign their approval on it. In either case, it is important to get documentation of all approvals and permissions, because each code official can have a different interpretation of the same code, as discussed in the following section on the appeals process.

If a design requires the use of a performance code instead of certain prescriptive requirements, then a preliminary review with the code official is required rather than optional. In fact, a concept report may have to be submitted before beginning the design, because the code official must agree to the use of the performance criteria (and the extent of use) in the building or space. When using performance codes, the code official must

> ✎ **Note**
>
> If two required codes have conflicting requirements, usually the more restrictive requirement applies. However, the code official has the authority to make the final decision.

> ✎ **Note**
>
> Having an approval signature after a code review meeting may become important during the permit approval process as well as the inspection process if difference in interpretation occur.

also agree that the design satisfies the code intent before the completion of the construction documents. If this process is not done correctly and the code official rejects the final design, a lot of time, money, and energy will be wasted.

Formal reviews for compliance with federal regulations are not typical for most projects. For example, the DOJ will review projects for compliance with the ADA, but this is a lengthy process and is usually undertaken only for very large or public projects. Some federal agencies, such as the Access Board for the *ADA Standards* and the DOE for the EPAct, may provide an interpretation when requested. However, these interpretations are not an official approval. Some clients who have multiple buildings may hire outside reviewers for ADA compliance in their buildings and projects. But, in most cases, designers must use their professional judgment as to whether a design complies with the federal regulation.

It is the designer's responsibility to know the codes, standards, and federal regulations and to design accordingly. However, it is important to clarify potential code issues as soon as possible in the design process: a preliminary code review can help. In addition, it typically results in a smoother permit approval. Not only will the necessary requirements be incorporated into the drawings but also the code officials will be familiar with the project before the plans are brought in for review for the construction permit.

> **◀ Note**
>
> Most code officials will agree to meet with a designer to review a project. Request a meeting whenever it is needed to clarify a specific code issue, but only after doing the necessary code research.

Appeals Request

All codes, standards, and federal regulations are written for the safety and protection of the building's occupants. However, they are not always as detailed as needed to clearly apply to every situation. Often a code provision can seem to have more than one interpretation. Usually these discrepancies can be settled with the help of a code official. Code officials undergo training, attend code review programs, and, therefore, can usually provide additional insight into the intent of a specific code provision. They also have access to the expertise of other officials.

However, there can be situations when the designer may not agree with or be satisfied with the code official's interpretation. To begin with, no code can anticipate every design situation. At times it may be difficult to apply prescriptive codes to a specific situation. For example, you may be proposing the use of a new building or finish material that is not yet included in the code, a build-out in an older building may call for an alternative method of achieving code compliance to avoid excessive cost or work, or it may not be clear as whether the code requirement applies to the design. In most cases, it is beneficial to try to work out a solution with the code official. If a mutually acceptable solution cannot be reached, or an allowed performance criterion cannot be found, the appeals process may be necessary.

The *appeals process* is a formal request made in writing either through a code official or directly to a Board of Appeals. Generally, each of the codes provides specific reasons why an appeal can be made. (See the inset titled "Administration Chapter" in this chapter.) The codes also regulate who can make the appeal; usually this is the owner or a representative of the owner. A designer can typically represent the owner and make the appeal to the board. The Board of Appeals consists of a variety of professionals who meet to review conflicts about how a code is interpreted or applied to a specific situation. The board does not have the authority to waive a code requirement; it determines if the proposal meets the intent of the code. This process can occur in the early review process or when a project fails to be approved for a permit. (This is why an early review may be very important.)

Usually, separate appeal requests must be made for building, fire, plumbing, mechanical, and electrical codes. This will depend on the scope of the appeal. Once the Board of Appeals receives the petition, the designer (or owner) and the code official are scheduled to present their sides of the issue. As the designer, be prepared to explain the current code interpretation, your view of the resolution of the requirement, and how compliance with the code will be met within the design project. The board's responsibility is to review the appeal and listen to both sides. Ultimately they decide whether the appeal follows the intent of the code, an incorrect interpretation has been applied, the code requirement does not fully apply to the specific situation, or the proposed solution is equally good or better than the code requirement. If the board accepts the appeal, it applies only to the situation at hand. For other projects and even future projects in the same space, a similar process must occur. Sometimes, it is said that a *variance* has been granted, but this term more often is used with requests for a design to modify zoning requirements for a particular building location, not building codes.

Plan Review and Permit

A permit is typically required for any interior project that requires construction. This includes, but is not limited to, the following:

1. New construction or additions to an existing building (including tenant fit-out)
2. Alterations made to a building
3. Change in occupancy

> **⊿ Note**
>
> Often a good source for justifying an appeal is another code publication. For example, the *LSC* may have an alternative requirement or method not found in a local jurisdiction's building code that could be applicable.

> **⊿ Note**
>
> The words *variance* and *appeal* are sometimes used interchangeably. However, variances usually pertain to local zoning laws, whereas appeals are made regarding code questions.

4. Installation of regulated equipment

5. Certain types of repairs or building maintenance

In most cases, the licensed contractor submits the information required by the jurisdiction for a permit. This typically includes a permit application, a permit fee, and the documents for the project to the code department. These construction documents usually consist of drawings, specifications, and any other documentation that may be required (especially for performance code criteria). A growing number of jurisdictions have an online permit submittal process and may even require or allow drawings to be submitted digitally. However, some jurisdictions may still require at least one set of drawings in hard copy form to be provided. Some jurisdictions may have separate process for small projects such as a tenant fit-out and for large projects and new construction. The requirements might also be different for residential (single-family and duplexes) and commercial buildings. In some jurisdictions (especially in larger cities) an independent consultant, known as a *code expeditor,* is required, or can be used to obtain the permit. It is not typical for the building owner or a registered design professional to obtain the permit because that person will not be the one performing or managing the construction process. Most jurisdictions require separate permits for plumbing, electrical, and mechanical work. These are usually obtained by the appropriate subcontractors because these permits make each subcontractor legally responsible for the specified work.

Once the documents are submitted for permit, the review by the code department begins. Most of the time, a review is handled by the inhouse code officials or plan reviewers. It can be reviewed by one person or separated into the various aspects of a building and building systems and reviewed by several people depending on the scope of the work and the size of the code department. For example, there may be separate building, mechanical, plumbing, and electrical code examiners. In some cases, a jurisdiction may use the plan review services of a code organization for an especially large project or when workloads could cause a delay in the permitting process. For example, the ICC will review specific issues of a project, such as means of egress, fire protection, sprinklers, standpipes, lighting, ventilation, and other similar issues. There are also third-party code consultants who specialize in code review also. Therefore, it is important that you know what process will be used and that all relevant code correspondence generated during the preliminary review and any granted appeals be attached to the application or noted directly on the construction drawings. This is especially helpful if the preliminary review and the permit plan review are performed by different code officials even within the same department.

☑ Note

Due to complexity of the laws, ordinances, rules, and project schedule in some jurisdictions it may be imperative that an expeditor be used as a liaison between the contractor and the codes department in order to obtain a permit.

☑ Note

Although it is rarely done, a permit can be revoked after construction begins if it is discovered that the granting of the permit was based on incorrect information, even if the error was made by a code official.

☑ Note

Many jurisdictions have converted to an online permit process and electronic submittals of site inspections.

In addition to the review by code department and the plans examiners, many projects must be reviewed by the fire marshal, as well. This is particularly true for assembly uses, schools, and health care projects and when a fire sprinkler system is required. The fire marshal is typically associated with the fire department, not the codes department. But they have similar goals: the safety of the occupants in the building in the event of a fire. (The dominant documents used by the fire marshal is the *LSC* and the fire code.) Projects that require review by the local or state fire marshal can vary by jurisdiction. In some cases, they have a different process and require more specific information than required by the building code officials. For example, life safety plans and detailed documentation of the means of egress capacities may be required.

As discussed, for certain projects, documents may also need to be sent to another state or local agency, such as the health department, for review. You should check for their process and review times to coordinate with submittal for the building permit. In some cases, approval by the special agency may specifically be required before or after the approval of the local jurisdiction.

The process of being granted a building permit can take from one day to several weeks, depending on the size of the project, the number of code officials who must check the project, and the workload of the code department. Code-related discrepancies found in the documentation by the building official, fire marshal or agency review will require corrections and resubmittal of the updated documentation, extending the approval process. The permit is issued only after the code review has been completed and approved. In some jurisdictions, approval for permit is posted on the code department website, an email is sent or other communication indicates the review is final and approved. Typically, the code department keeps one set of drawings (electronic or hard copy) and at least one approved set must always be kept on the job site. Some jurisdictions issue a plans approval letter, which should be kept in the project files. In addition, the permit itself must be clearly posted at the job site during construction.

Inspections during Construction

The code review process does not stop with the issuance of a permit. (See Figure 11.1.) During the construction of a project, a code official must make intermediate inspections of the job site. This is done to guarantee that the work matches what is in the construction documents and that the work continues to comply with the codes. These site inspections are made at certain intervals during the construction, usually before the work is concealed or covered up by the next phase of construction.

Typically, the contractor is responsible for notifying the code department when it is time for an inspection. Depending on the type of interior project, these intervals usually include the following.

1. **Framing inspection.** The walls, ceilings, and floors are usually framed. Gypsum board may be attached to one side of the walls, but all framing must be exposed. The side that is open allows the inspector to check the construction materials and framing.

2. **Systems inspection.** Separate inspections are made for the plumbing, mechanical, and electrical installations. This includes automatic sprinkler systems. Certain jurisdictions may also require an inspection of some communication systems. These inspections can be made at the same time as the framing inspection if these systems are complete. There is usually a preliminary rough-in inspection before the walls are closed and then a final inspection at the end of construction.

3. **Gypsum board/lath inspection.** When all the gypsum board or lathing is in place, but before any taping or plastering is done, the inspector will check to make sure that all wall and ceiling assemblies are built to code. Rated assemblies such as fire- and smoke-rated assemblies typically require additional inspections.

4. **Fire and smoke resistant penetration inspection.** After the rated assemblies, including walls and floor/ceiling assemblies, are taped and plastered, they are inspected again to confirm that the joints, intersections, and penetrations in the rated assemblies are properly installed and sealed. Any fire resistant materials sprayed onto structural elements must also be inspected before, during, and after application.

5. **Energy-efficiency inspection.** Items such as the insulation of mechanical ducts, the water heating equipment, and the HVAC system are inspected for compliance with energy standards.

6. **Special inspection.** Certain inspections occur after the construction or installation of a specific design element is complete, such as an elevator, swimming pool, or other special element. In addition, the codes specify when certain products and systems require a separate inspection. These include special wall panels, sprayed fire resistant material, and smoke control systems. Special inspections may also be required when materials or systems are used in unusual or creative ways, especially as part of a performance approach to the code or when using alternative materials and methods as allowed by the

☑ **Note**

The *IBC* requires that an approved set of construction documents be approved as marked as "Reviewed for Code Compliance." A hard copy set is required to be kept at the construction site for review by code officials during construction.

☑ **Note**

While a project is under construction, the appropriate design professional(s) should periodically make site visits to ensure that the project design and code instructions are being followed. This should be part of every project's construction administration.

IBC. Sustainability-related inspections may also be required. The code official will indicate when a special inspection is required for an individual situation.

After each intermediate inspection, construction can continue only if the inspector grants an approval. If the inspector finds that the project is not acceptable, a correction notice is issued and another inspection is scheduled, allowing the contractor time to correct the problem. If the inspector feels that a condition is unsafe or that the construction is not being carried out in an acceptable manner, a stop-work order will be issued. This means that no other work on the site can occur until the specific problem is addressed and corrected to the satisfaction of the inspector or code official.

An inspection may not always be done by a code official. Some jurisdictions allow or even require the owner to have the construction process inspected by a separate inspection agency. This is sometimes referred to as a self-inspection. Typically, a third party performs the site inspections and documents the process. In some cases, if approved by the local code jurisdiction, the architect or engineer for the project can do the special inspection. The inspection information is submitted to the local code official to verify that inspections are being done. The code official often still performs the inspection necessary for the final approval and issuance of the Certificate of Occupancy.

Sometimes changes must be made to the construction documents after construction begins. For example, a change may be necessary because of a stop-work order or to clarify an item on the construction drawings. In other cases, the owner may request a design change. These changes should be submitted to the code department as well as to the construction site. In some cases, the code official will issue a plans approval letter or notification for each revision. The building inspectors review the project in the field according to the set they have approved. If there is a conflict between their approved set and what is being built, it can delay inspections and approvals.

> ◸ **Note**
>
> Unfortunately, there is no guarantee that work consistent with the approved plans will be approved in the field. An inspector may see a code issue in the field that was missed during review of the construction drawings. If this occurs, either the designer must work out the discrepancy with the appropriate code official or the contractor must make the changes necessary to comply with the code.

Final Inspection and Approval

The inspection process is the way the code officials verify that the project is being built according to the most current drawings and that the construction meets the applicable codes. Once the project is complete, the inspector will do a final walk-through to confirm final compliance with codes and to make sure that the space is ready to be occupied. In most jurisdictions, a separate inspection is also done by a fire marshal. When the final inspections are completed, the construction of the project is typically considered finished. However, before the occupants can move into the space or building, additional approvals are necessary. The various types are explained here.

Certificate of Completion

A Certificate of Completion is issued when the structure or systems within a space or building are complete and have been inspected. This certificate is usually necessary to connect to local utilities. It is often used for renovation and major repairs. However, it does not give the right to occupy the space or building. A Certificate of Occupancy must still be issued to allow the tenant to occupy the space or building.

Certificate of Occupancy

A Certificate of Occupancy (C of O) is issued after the final inspection has been completed. The person who obtained the building permit (usually the contractor) requests a final inspection by the code official to get a C of O. If during the final inspection the code inspector, including the fire marshal, is satisfied that the building or space complies with the code and that the construction is complete, a certificate is issued. In some jurisdictions, the Certificate of Occupancy is referred to as a Use and Occupancy (U and O) letter. This certificate is typically required before the tenant can occupy the building or space, and it must be posted in a conspicuous location in the building. Once the C of O is issued, the code process is complete.

Temporary Certificate of Occupancy

The client might not want to wait until all portions of the project are completed before occupying the facility. Perhaps a certain aspect of the project cannot be completed because of a delay in the arrival of material or equipment—for example, custom granite countertops or water fountains. In those cases, some jurisdictions will issue a Temporary Certificate of Occupancy. This will allow the project or portions of the project to be occupied if the code official feels that the occupants will not be in any danger because the entire project is not complete. The uncompleted work must eventually be inspected before a final Certificate of Occupancy is issued. The Temporary Certificate of Occupancy is also known as a Partial Certificate of Occupancy or a Partial Use and Occupancy Permit. It is usually issued with a time limit, such as 90 days, giving the contractor the time to complete the work.

Note

If changes are made to a set of construction documents after a building permit is issued, an amended set of documents must be resubmitted to the code official for approval.

Note

Most nonresidential building types (including apartment complex common areas) continue to undergo required periodic inspections by building inspectors, fire marshals, and/or the fire department after the building is occupied.

Note

A Temporary Certificate of Occupancy may be issued on projects when part of a building can be safely occupied before completion of the remainder of the project.

Some jurisdictions will not issue a temporary certificate because often owners or contractors never request final inspections once they have occupied the space. Not all code departments have a way to track temporary certificates; thus, if a final inspection is not requested, they may not know if the final work was done or whether it was done correctly.

Phased Certificate of Occupancy

For a larger project, construction may be done in phases but under a single permit. Usually, these phases are determined during the design process and are identified in the construction documents when permitted. A Phased Certificate of Occupancy allows the client to occupy the portions of the project that are complete. For example, in the renovation of several floors of a hospital, it may be important to allow the renovated emergency room to be occupied as soon as it is completed, without waiting for the renovation of the cafeteria on another floor to be completed. Phasing also allows code officials to do final inspections on the completed areas. Another way to accomplish the same thing is to permit parts of a large project separately, and then each part would have its own review and inspection process and receive a separate Certificate of Occupancy. The code official may decide which way this should be handled.

Commissioning

Although not technically the responsibility of the code official, the use of energy codes, sustainable standards, and rating programs and performance codes has made building commissioning of new construction more commonplace. Commissioning is used to verify that the building systems and components are installed and operate correctly. It is often required to gain points in the sustainability program or to confirm compliance with the performance criteria. Verification is made by a series of observations and diagnostic and functional tests of the building systems and components. This process is typically done by a *commissioning agent* or *commissioning authority* contracted directly to the building owner as a third-party representative. The commissioning agent can sometimes also be an employee of the building owner, architect, engineer, or subcontractor. ICC publishes a *Guideline for Commissioning* designated as *ICC G4*. It was specifically developed to support the use of the *International Green Construction Code* and the *ICC 700* but it can be used to validate other codes and goals.

✎ Note

If a green code such as the *International Green Construction Code (IgCC)* is used on a project, a Certificate of Conformance may also be required to confirm that the construction meets the requirements of that code.

OPTIONS IN CODES

Specific and thorough code research is imperative for the safety of a particular project. However, a well-rounded understanding of the codes will allow the most effective design to be developed. Options already included in the codes can allow innovative solutions and save costs if you know where they are and how they work together. In his book *Building and Safety Codes for Industrial Facilities*, Joseph N. Sabatini lists several reasons for overlooked options in industrial buildings. They can be generalized to include all design projects.

1. Options are not clear in the codes. Sometimes options, alternatives, or exceptions are scattered throughout the chapters, and finding them requires familiarity and expertise.

2. Unfamiliarity with and infrequent use of codes lead to poor enforcement. Many designers merely spot-check the codes on an intermittent basis, and therefore miss important details because they do not have or take the time to review them thoroughly.

3. Some trade-offs are interdisciplinary. Because sometimes designers are scheduled to participate in planning on a staggered basis, poor communication and coordination result.

4. Preliminary meetings do not involve all disciplines. Effective decisions can be made only if all disciplines are involved in the early planning stages.

5. Design time is too short. When there is a rush to get a facility in operation, design time is often abbreviated, and therefore comprehensive code reviews are often not done.

6. Overkill. Because of item 5, conscientious professionals commit overkill and include items in the design that are not always mandated by the building codes, regulations, and enforced standards.

DOCUMENTATION

In the "Documentation" section of each chapter there has been a discussion of how to document your code research for the topic presented in the chapter. You were also encouraged at each chapter to use the individual checklists provided with this book to guide your documentation throughout the design process. These checklists are provided digitally with the purchase of this book. They are also available in full-page hard copy format in the *Study Guide for the Codes Guidebook for Interiors*. Following are more suggestions as to how to document your research and your design in a way that clearly shows that it is compliant with the codes. This will help make review and approval by code officials easier because you will have the answers to questions that they might ask ready at hand. And, it will have prompted you to include the code requirements into the project design.

To bring it all together, Figure 11.2 provides concise summary check-list for your use, as well. You can expand or modify these checklists as necessary for your typical project scope. It is impossible to put every code requirement on a checklist because the requirements will be different on every project. Instead, the purpose of the checklist is to act as a reminder of the code and standard requirements that must be researched and documented on the drawings and specifications. When necessary, attach or save the appropriate backup as part of your documentation. Information that you may want to save includes the manufacturer's warranty or speci-fications, a product evaluation sheet, a product label listing the codes and standards with which the product complies, a copy of a certificate from a testing agency, and so on. You can scan this information provided on actual samples, if necessary. For performance criteria or sustainability requirements, also collect verification of performance tests results, prod-uct certifications, or product declarations from manufacturers or an out-side source.

As you do research in the various code documents that we have dis-cussed throughout this book, it is especially important to note the code publication, code sections, and standard numbers of the certain require-ments. This is particularly true for code conditions that vary from the standard requirements or will have a domino effect on other require-ments within the code. For example, you may need to remember that a note on Table 803.11 allows the use of a Class C finish (instead of Class B) in a small unsprinklered movie theater (A-1) if the occupancy load is 300 or less. So, in the checklist space for the interior wall finish for that space, you would note: "*IBC*-2015, Table 803.11, Note e." Or you would want to document the chapter and section if you found an exception that would allow your project not to be sprinklered. Because this will affect multiple other code requirements, it is important to remember where that exception was found in the code. Later, in the review of the project you can quickly reference your finding during your discussion with the code official.

Documentation for clients is a critical part of a project as well. They need to know how to operate systems or maintain finish and materials so that it continues to meet codes. For example, if finishes are not cleaned appropriately, they might not retain their fire retardancy or slip resistance. Improper maintenance might affect the indoor air quality of the building, energy efficiency of an electrical system, or water conservation of plumb-ing fixtures. Depending on the size and type of the project, the designer may supply this information to the client. On larger projects, the project

☑ Note

To accommodate tight construction schedules, some jurisdictions allow building permits to be issued in phases. This becomes especially important in new build-ings, where construc-tion can begin while designers complete the interior details.

☑ Note

Properly and consistently prepared code docu-mentation is imperative should any liability issues arise after a project is completed.

Summary Interior Project Checklist　　　　　　　　　　　　**Date:** _____

Project Name: _____　　Space: _____

1　DETERMINE WHICH CODES ARE REQUIRED (Chapter 1)
___ Building Code
___ Energy Code
___ Fire Code
___ Life Safety Code
　　Performance Code
___ Sustainability Code/Standard
___ Other Code Publications
___ Local Codes and Ordinances
___ Government Regulations
___ Standards and Tests

2　OCCUPANCY REQUIREMENTS (Chapter 2)
___ Determine Building Types(s)
___ Determine Occupancy Classification(s)
___ Calculate Occupant Load(s)
___ Adjustments to Occupant Load(s)
___ Review Specific Occupancy Requirements
___ Compare Code and Accessibility Requirements

3　MINIMUM TYPES OF CONSTRUCTION (Chapter 3)
___ Determine Construction Type
___ Determine Ratings of Building Elements
___ Calculate Maximum Floor Area (as required)
___ Calculate Building Height (as required)
___ Review Construction Type Limitations

4　MEANS OF EGRESS REQUIREMENTS (Chapter 4)
___ Determine Quantity and Types of Means of Egress
___ Calculate Minimum Widths
___ Determine Arrangement of Exits
___ Calculate Travel Distance
___ Determine Required Signage
___ Compare Code and Accessibility Requirements
___ Review Emergency Lighting Requirements

5　FIRE AND SMOKE RESISTANCE REQUIREMENTS (Chapter 5)
___ Determine Use of Fire Walls
___ Determine Fire Barriers/Partitions and Horizontal Assemblies
___ Determine Smoke Barriers and Partitions
___ Determine Location of Opening Protectives
___ Determine Location of Through-Penetration Protectives
___ Review Types of Fire Tests and Ratings Required
___ Determine Sustainability Requirements
___ Review Requirements During Assembly Specification
___ Review Required Standards

6　FIRE-PROTECTION REQUIREMENTS (Chapter 6)
___ Determine Fire and Smoke Detection Systems
___ Determine Required Alarm Systems
___ Determine Types of Extinguishing Systems and Possible Sprinkler Trade-Offs
___ Compare Code and Accessibility Requirements
___ Coordinate with Engineer (as required)

7　PLUMBING REQUIREMENTS (Chapter 7)
___ Determine Types of Fixtures Required
___ Calculate Number of Each Fixture Required
___ Determine Required Toilet/Bathing Facilities
___ Review for Finishes, Accessories, and Signage
___ Compare Code and Accessibility Requirements
___ Review Water Conservation Requirements
___ Coordinate with Engineer (as required)

8　MECHANICAL REQUIREMENTS (Chapter 7)
___ Determine Type of Air Distribution System(s)
___ Determine Items Affecting Cooling Loads
___ Determine Access and Clearance Requirements
___ Figure Zoning and Thermostat Locations
___ Compare Code and Accessibility Requirements
___ Review Energy and Water Efficiency Compliance
___ Coordinate with Engineer (as required)

Figure 11.2 *(Continued)*

9 ELECTRICAL REQUIREMENTS (Chapter 8) __ Determine Types/Locations of Outlets, Switches, Fixtures __ Determine Emergency Power and Lighting Requirements __ Compare Code and Accessibility Requirements __ Review Energy Efficiency Compliance __ Coordinate with Engineer (as required) **10 COMMUNICATION REQUIREMENTS (Chapter 8)** __ Determine Systems Required by Client __ Compare Needs versus Code/Standard Requirements	__ Check for Accessibility Compliance and Sustainability Requirements __ Coordinate with Engineer/Consultant (as required) **11 FINISH AND FURNITURE REQUIREMENTS (Chapter 9)** __ Review tests and types of Ratings Required __ Determine Special Finish Requirements __ Determine Special Furniture Requirements __ Compare Code and Accessibility Requirements __ Review Sustainability Requirements __ Compare Requirements During Selection/ Specification __ Review Required Standards

NOTE: Be sure to review all codes and standards required in the jurisdiction as well as required federal regulations. Consult a local code office/official at any step if questions arise.

Figure 11.2 Summary interior project checklist.

specifications should specify that the contractor will supply the client with record drawings (as-builts) of each system installed, as well as operation and maintenance (O & M) manuals that explain how to use and maintain each system and/or material. Client training may also be necessary.

An O & M manual is especially important in performance design and when using alternate materials. Some jurisdictions require them. In addition, an O & M manual is required when using sustainability codes and standards and must include an operations plan. The plan should include procedures for maintaining indoor air quality; instituting a green cleaning program; and measuring, verifying, and tracking both energy and water use.

The importance of documenting your research and decisions clearly in the construction drawings, specification manuals, and project files cannot be overstressed. Although it has been mentioned throughout this book that the use of performance codes and alternative means and methods provisions require additional research and documentation for approval, all projects must be well documented concerning codes. Even if proper research and inclusion of code requirements were done throughout the development of the entire project, if it cannot be proven when required, time and energy will be wasted. Keep documentation of your research, correspondence with the code officials, and other documentation with other project records.

Construction Documents

Although construction documents are initially intended to convey the design in a way that it can be built and meet the aesthetic and functional requirements, it also represents the way the project must be built or what must be included to meet codes. These documents include drawings, specifications, and additional documentation required by a code jurisdiction.

⬛ Note

Certain sections in each code indicate specific information that must be included in the construction documents prior to code review. A jurisdiction may have additional requirements.

The most fundamental code information is typically summarized on the cover sheet of the documents. Providing the list of codes, standards, and federal regulations that are applicable to the project confirms for the reviewer that you have considered these code requirements in your design. Other basic code information about the project is typically indicated here as well, including the occupancy classification, construction type, building height and area limits (if applicable), whether the building is sprinklered or not, and project or building area information. If the project is small or simple in scope, other general code requirements can be listed on the cover sheet as well, including finish classification information. Any unique code considerations, such as a granted appeal, use of performance criteria, or project phasing should be indicated as well. This information is the introduction to the project as a whole. Consider that in the future, if this space is renovated, another professional may rely on this information to understand the basis of this design.

It is equally important to have the rest of the documentation including space planning, furniture layout and specification, mechanical, electrical, plumbing, and other parts of the design organized to easily show proper research and the inclusion of the code requirements in the design. It is also especially important to use the proper terminology in all documentation. For example, a *corridor* is an enclosed passageway, but an *aisle* is not enclosed. The code requirements for these two are very different. In addition, *hallway* is not a term recognized by the codes and does not suggest any specific requirements: but *corridor* is recognized and does suggest potential code requirements.

The codes require certain information to be included in the construction documents. Other information is either common design practice or is required by the jurisdiction. This section lists the typical code information that should be included in the construction documents, either on the drawings or in the written specifications. Note, however, that this list is not all-inclusive. Other information specific to a project type, required by a jurisdiction, local or state agency, or specific to a green building program may also be required.

Cover Sheet

- ❑ Applicable code publication(s) and edition(s) (recognize local or state amendments)
- ❑ Applicable standards and regulations including federal
- ❑ Name of the design professional responsible for each aspect of the design (plan, electrical, mechanical, etc.)
- ❑ Construction type(s) of the building
- ❑ Area of space designed (square footages or square meters)
- ❑ Building area limitations
- ❑ Occupancy classification(s)
- ❑ Sprinkler status of building or space (i.e., sprinklered or nonsprinklered)
- ❑ Occupant load per floor (or area if necessary)
- ❑ Identification of any appeals or equivalencies granted

Drawings

- ❑ Location plan (when designing a portion of a floor or building)
- ❑ Identification of use of rooms and spaces
- ❑ Compartmentation of fire areas
- ❑ Location of rated walls and floor/ceiling assemblies
- ❑ Location of rated doors, windows, and other through penetrations
- ❑ Exit access and exit doors (size, location, swing, hardware, security, etc.)
- ❑ Egress routes (location, size, and components)
- ❑ Details of stairs and ramps that are part of the means of egress
- ❑ Location and heights of electrical devices
- ❑ Reflected ceiling plan, including lights, emergency lighting, smoke detectors, and exit signs
- ❑ Location of plumbing fixtures (drinking fountains, water closets, lavatories, etc.)

❑ Location and placement of furnishings and finishes
❑ Accessibility clearances and critical dimensions
❑ Sections of rated assemblies (walls, ceilings, etc.)
❑ Details for penetrations (electrical, plumbing, environmental and communication conduits, pipes, and systems)
❑ Elevations (indicating mounting heights and locations of fixtures, equipment, and accessories)

Specifications, Schedules, and Legends

❑ Types of rated doors, frames, and hardware
❑ Types of rated windows and through penetrations
❑ Types of electrical outlets, including GFCIs and AFCIs
❑ Types of light fixtures, including emergency lights and exit signs
❑ Types and locations of regulated finishes and furniture
❑ List of required standards and tests

Additional information may be required for review by the code official for approval of the design. This documentation, which is usually developed by an engineer or other consulting professional, may include the following:

❑ Sprinkler riser diagram
❑ Sprinkler coverage calculations
❑ Electrical system design and load calculations
❑ Lighting power density calculations
❑ Mechanical system design and load calculations
❑ Plumbing system design and fixture calculations

Performance Design Documentation

When a performance criterion has been used as part of the design, it should be clearly indicated in the construction documents. This documentation may need to be distinguished from the rest of the documentation, because often it will have to undergo a separate review process. The design and review of the performance portions of a project take more of a team effort than when prescriptive codes are used. The team should include design professionals (architects, engineers, and interior designers), special experts, and code officials who are qualified to evaluate the proposed design. In some cases, the code official may choose to have the design reviewed by another consultant who is more knowledgeable in the review of performance criteria and/or a specific area of design. In all cases, the documentation of the design must be acceptable to the code official having jurisdiction. (See also the inset titled "Performance Codes" in this section.)

The documentation of a performance design may include the information listed here:

❑ Performance criteria
❑ Technical references and resources
❑ Plans, specifications, and details of the building design
❑ Design assumptions, limitations, and factors of safety used
❑ Description of the design hazards
❑ Input information for calculations and computer modeling
❑ Calculations
❑ Computer modeling
❑ Scope of inspection and testing required to demonstrate compliance
❑ Prescriptive requirements used
❑ Maintenance requirements
❑ Reliability of the method of research and process

Depending on what aspect of the building has been designed using performance criteria, the documentation may include drawings, specifications, and additional reports. It might be clearly indicated in the main set of construction documents or be separately documented and cross-referenced to the main set. Additional media, such as computer modeling, may also be part of the documentation.

Once the plans have been approved, anyone involved in the ownership or management of the building must be made aware that the building was approved based on performance criteria (not standard prescriptive code requirements). A performance design option is designed for the actual situation. If any aspect of the building is changed during design or after the client occupies the space, it may require reapproval by the local code official. Even the maintenance done by the client after move-in can affect the safety of the building.

✔ Note

Even when performance-related codes are used on a project, typically only a certain aspect of the project will be designed using the performance criteria. The prescriptive codes will be used on the rest of the project.

✔ Note

When using performance codes or alternative methods such as those allowed by *IBC* Section 104.11, documentation is very important. All documentation must be clear and designated separately from prescriptive code requirements.

✔ Note

Special inspections might be required when performance codes or unusual construction materials are used. It may be necessary for an inspector to observe the actual installation.

PERFORMANCE CODES

Developing a unique design solution, specifying innovative materials, incorporating sustainable elements, or working in an existing building with unusual characteristics are a few of the many opportunities to use performance criteria. The flexibility that comes with performance codes may even make a project more cost-effective. It is the designer's responsibility, however, to prove to the client and the code official that the proposed design meets the performance criteria that have been developed by the project team including the design team, owner, and code official. Additional steps must be taken to prove that the design will provide safety equivalent to that yielded by the prescriptive requirements. Examples of additional steps that may be required include these:

❏ **Preparation of a concept report.** Work with the code official, design team including engineers, and necessary industry experts to set the performance criteria. The solution will be judged by these goals.

❏ **Acquiring data.** The design team works together to obtain specific data or develop new data using available design guides, calculation methods, and computer models. These are currently used in supporting fire, smoke, and structural-related scenarios, but they may have other applications as well.

❏ **Obtaining reports.** Research specific materials and assemblies by obtaining reports from product evaluation services (see the inset titled "ICC Evaluation Service" in Chapter 1) and working with the manufacturer of a particular product or system. Existing products often have already gone through the necessary testing and thus have available evaluation reports. But when developing something new, a manufacturer may be able to obtain the necessary tests and reports.

❏ **Finding comparables.** Look to other buildings and projects with similar situations or a similar use of a product. Contact the designers and contractors involved in those projects for information that could be useful. (This usually cannot be the only supportive documentation.)

New ways to analyze and support the use of performance codes and alternative methods continue to be developed. Part of the challenge of performance codes is to determine the best method to validate the proposed solution.

Sustainability Design Documentation

When documenting a project with sustainable requirements, additional information beyond what is required for a typical project may be necessary. The goals and methods of achieving the sustainable goals or requirements must be documented. These may affect the constructions methods, handling of construction waste, and selection of qualified building systems, materials and finishes, and so on. In addition to indicating the location, nature, and scope of the green building features, how the desired outcome will be validated or measured must be included in the drawings or specifications. Several of the green rating system, such as LEED or Green Globes, have guidelines and lists to identify the necessary information and documents that are required. For an interior project, this may include ventilation schedule, documentation of finishes and their VOC content with certifications, lighting power density calculations, power demand model, and similar information. If a local sustainable program is being used, then follow their requirements. In most cases, the relevant sustainability information must be distinguished from the rest of the documentation, because in some cases this information will be reviewed by a third party.

Achieving the desired level of sustainability and/or obtaining the expected sustainable program credits requires close coordination with the local code official/ program representative, project team, contractor, and owner from the very beginning of the project. If insufficient documentation results in a loss of sustainability, this could cause a client to refuse to occupy the space, jeopardize funding, or cause a building official to refuse to issue a permit or Certificate of Occupancy.

TECHNOLOGY AND PROCESS

Not so long ago, submission of construction documents, review, and communication between designers and the code officials was done by paper, phone, onsite meetings, and the occasional fax. Today, the process, similar to much of our personal communication, is almost totally digital. This has resulted in many changes in the resources, communication processes, and documentation methods associated with codes as well. For example, each code organization such as NFPA and ICC sells digital and hard copy versions of their code publications. Some digital formats have very useful search capabilities. In some cases, the organizations allow limited online access to their codes and standards as well. Downloaded or online formats can be viewed on multiple electronic device (including your phone) and make the code resources equally available in the office and on site. As mentioned previously, code departments are also incorporating more technology in their processes, including online permit applications, electronic plan review, and digital submittals of documents and site inspection reports.

The documentation process, once completely hand drawn is essentially been replaced by computer-aided design (CAD) software and by various programs that allow the designer to virtually draw and model the building and spaces in three dimensions. Especially growing in use are programs referred to as building information modeling (BIM)

◄ Note

Using alternate methods/materials and performance-based codes makes a building unique. It is important to educate the building owner so that the building can be properly maintained to provide optimum health, safety, and welfare to its occupants.

◄ Note

Commissioning is another part of the documentation process for sustainability projects. Among other things, this process verifies and documents that the selected building systems have been designed, installed, and function in accordance with the owner's prerequisites, the construction documents, and the minimum sustainability and other code requirements.

◄ Note

If a jurisdiction mandates sustainable requirements not yet included in the codes, such as the use of a green rating system, ask the code official how this information should be documented.

programs. As a design tool, three-dimensional programs allow designers to create and view the space from multiple perspectives which is helpful for them and their clients. From a code perspective, it also allows the designer to see and solve potential problems before construction. This can be especially useful to simulate the coexistence of mechanical, plumbing, walls, and ceilings to identify potential conflicts between building elements and building systems prior to construction. BIM programs also have the capacity to link data bases and specifications for each component of the building. There is even code validation software in development that may soon be used to automatically check if a building or space design is compliant with specific codes and accessibility requirements during design. Also, from a code perspective, these modeling programs allow designers to test how different aspects of a building will act in a fire, earthquake, and other emergency situations so that alternatives to existing code solutions can be developed and incorporated into buildings. This is especially critical for projects developed with performance criteria. For sustainability objectives, it is also used to predict how the building will operate throughout its life cycle. These digital systems can be used by everyone involved in the building over its lifetime: designers, code officials, contractors, facility managers, service technicians, and fire and police departments, among others.

The use of computer modeling will continue to enhance a building's performance and will continue to affect the specific way that design professionals document and share their information. It will be especially helpful as more performance-based options are used in the development of not only complicated building conditions but as it becomes a more common process in general. For example, computer models can be used to investigate possible fire scenarios or egress patterns so that the most effective way to address the fire in a specific building and configuration can be incorporated into the design. These new ways might make building even safer than the conditions created by the prescriptive codes. To be used this way, research and documentation become more critical.

The increasing integration and automation of building systems will continue to require changes in the codes. (See the insets titled "Integrated Alarms" in Chapter 7 and "Building Automation Systems" in Chapter 9.) As the building industry becomes more complex and the development of new products and building systems becomes even

◳ Note

Membership in a code organization, such as ICC or NFPA, often includes the ability to request an interpretation of a specific code requirement from the organization's technical department. However, it is not a guarantee that the local code official will agree with that interpretation.

more fast-paced, both designers and code officials must keep up with these innovative technologies. At times, these advances may outpace the code publications and the local jurisdictions ability to address these changes. This is where performance criteria and alternative means and methods allowed by the code can be useful. But as discussed throughout this book, integration of new technology, strategies, and systems will require discussion and approval by the local jurisdiction. This will often take research, data, and a good working relationship with the code official.

Remember that code officials have the same goal as designers: ensuring the health, safety, and welfare of the building occupants. Code officials are a valuable resource to you and your project success. As we have suggested, because not all jurisdictions work the same way, it is important to know the process of the jurisdiction of your specific project. With everyone working together, design solutions that comply with the required codes, standards, and federal regulations while meeting design objectives are achievable.

MINIMUM REQUIREMENTS AND BEST PRACTICES

This book has discussed the many requirements that are necessary to be integrated into a design so that a building or space provides for the health, safety, and welfare of the occupants as defined by the various codes, standards, and regulations. However, it is important to also remember that these are considered *minimum* requirements for our built environment. What is a considered a minimum requirement continues to be updated, especially those that pertain to interior projects. For some projects, it may be appropriate to be aware of and incorporate stricter codes, requirements, or standards into your design. For example, a fabric may not be required to be flame resistant, but it might be appropriate to treat the fabric for extra protection in a project inhabited primarily by older occupants. Not only do these decisions potentially put people's lives at stake but also a designer may be held liable should an incident occur. It may be important to be able to prove that the most advanced tests or strictest requirements available at the time were incorporated into the design.

In some cases, a client may require that a higher level of safety, sustainability, and/or energy efficiency be incorporated into the project.

☜ **Note**

The required length of time to keep project records and code documentation is highly debatable. However, many states have a statute of repose, which sets a time limitation on how long after a project is completed a lawsuit can be brought against a designer or design firm.

☜ **Note**

Several websites are available to help you keep up-to-date with the codes. These include www.iccsafe.org and www.nfpa.org, as well as many local code jurisdictions. Frequently asked questions (FAQs) are often posted, and chat rooms may be available.

When requested, it important to know the resources available to enhance the project to meet these expectations while meeting the minimum code requirements of the local jurisdiction. Some of these have been introduced in this book. In some cases, it may be necessary to add consultants with a specific expertise to the project team.

As a professional, it is important to keep informed not only about the current codes but also about the best practices in interior design. This may be accomplished by attending conferences, reading industry journals, subscribing to code, interior design, and sustainability dedicated resources, and focusing continuing education efforts on enhancing your knowledge and awareness of developments in these areas. Many of the code organizations offer different levels of memberships that often provide automatic updates to testing standards, code summary updates and other resources. There are a multitude of websites and blogsites indicating how sustainable attributes are included and measured in an interior project. As the design professional, you are expected to be knowledgeable about and interested in the continual improvement of the interior of buildings. To improve the outcome of your design, you must be dedicated to continuing to expand yourself as a design professional.

APPENDIX A

SUSTAINABILITY

Although the goal of the codes have always been to protect the health, safety, and overall welfare of the building occupants, the emphasis has largely been on safety. As a result, many of the code requirements primarily regulated the way being in the *building* would affect the *occupant* in the event of a fire, storm, earthquake, or similar emergency situation. As the concept of considering the effect that a *building* has on the *environment* gained interest, the concept of sustainability was established. Along with this concern, an associated concern about how the building environment and the materials used in its creation affect the occupants every day while in the building also developed. Although there are many different definitions of the term *sustainable*, the one developed for the Brundtland Commission's report in 1987 is generally considered the most widely acceptable. It defined sustainable development as "development that meets the needs of current generations without compromising the ability of future generations to meet their own needs." Sustainability and green practices are increasingly being incorporated into the code requirements and by local jurisdictions. Together they are broadening their scope of influence to include the welfare of both occupant and the environment. This ultimately makes the building a healthier and safer environment.

Compared to fire or means of egress codes, green and sustainability codes and standards are relatively new. It has been only a few decades since a noticeable number of designers began incorporating more "green" practices and products into their projects. At that point there were very few guidelines to encourage or help this effort. As the desire for sustainable buildings and interiors, from both designers and owners, increased in the market, the industry recognized a need to monitor, track, and verify sustainable projects. Green rating systems, such as Building Research Establishment's Environmental Assessment Method (BREEAM), Leadership in Energy and Environmental Design (LEED), and Green Globes, were developed to fill this void. (Green rating systems are explained more next.) They also set the foundation for the development of the more recent sustainability codes and standards.

⊴ Note

In the past, the codes and standards concentrated on regulating the ways in which the environment affects buildings. Green and sustainability codes and standards, however, address how buildings affect the environment.

⊴ Note

The use of sustainable practices and products must not overshadow the safety of the building occupants. For example, water conservation cannot hinder the effectiveness of fire sprinklers, and certain building materials may require fire/flame retardants to meet specific fire ratings.

Over time, certain green requirements were incorporated into the codes. For example, when the *International Plumbing Code* was first published in 1995, it included information on water-efficient fixtures and, more recently, waterless urinals. In 1998, the *International Energy Conservation Code* was developed. It was the first code document that addressed sustainability more comprehensively, covering energy efficiency throughout the building. Energy standards such as *ASHRAE/ IESNA 90.1, Energy Standard for Buildings Except Low-Rise Residential Buildings*, and *ASHRAE/IESNA 90.2, Energy-Efficient Design of New Low-Rise Residential Buildings*, help set and define new levels of energy efficiency.

Several green codes and standards are now available. For commercial projects, there is the *International Green Construction Code (IgCC)* as well as the standard *ASHRAE/USGBC/IES 189.1, Standard for the Design of High-Performance Green Buildings Except Low-Rise Residential Buildings*. Residential projects can use *ICC 700, National Green Building Standard (NGBS)* or LEED for Homes. (These documents and many of their requirements have been discussed throughout this book. See Chapter 1 and the "Sustainability Considerations" sections within each chapter.) As these sustainability documents are adopted by code jurisdictions, they will need to be used in conjunction with the many other codes and standards discussed throughout this book. If a jurisdiction requires the use of a green rating system, the requirements between the codes and the rating system would need to be coordinated within the design.

However, when using the various code documents and green rating systems, it is important to realize that green design and the sustainability industry continues to evolve. For example, the term *green* is often used by both designers and manufacturers to describe many different "sustainable" aspects of a building or product. These terms are often used interchangeably, yet they are very different. *Green* can describe one attribute or multiple characteristics, such as an "energy-efficient building" and a "low-emitting finish." If something is to be considered *sustainable*, it must meet three specific benchmarks: environmental responsibility, economic strength, and social responsibility.

As the industry works toward true sustainability, new concepts and new tools continue to be developed. The traditional standard that measures a single attribute (e.g., toxicity) does not provide a comprehensive picture of a sustainable product. Instead, more comprehensive multiple-attribute standards are required. (See the section "Sustainable Standards and Certification Programs" later in this appendix.) More detailed and standardized documentation to enable accurate comparison of various products is also necessary. Examples include life cycle analysis and environmental product declarations (as explained later in this appendix).

✒ Note

The sustainable-related catch phrase "triple bottom line" refers to achieving three key benchmarks: environmental responsibility, economic strength, and social responsibility. Together, these are considered the primary aspects of sustainability.

This appendix summarizes many of the interior-related green resources available. It begins with a discussion of green rating systems and goes on to explain sustainable product standards (SPSs), product certification programs, life cycle analysis, product declarations, and other sustainability tools.

GREEN RATING SYSTEMS

One of the first green rating systems developed was called the Building Research Establishment's Environmental Assessment Method (BREEAM). Although it was originally developed in the 1990 in the United Kingdom, it is used in other parts of the world. By 2000, the U.S. Green Building Council (USGB) had developed the Leadership in Energy and Environmental Design (LEED) and Canada had developed Green Globes for Existing Buildings. All of these rating systems continue to be expanded to address different building types, scopes of construction, and uses. Two rating systems specifically for residential homes that are used more regionally in the United States are GreenPoints Rated by Build It Green, an organization based in California, and EarthCraft House initiated by the Greater Atlanta Home Builders Association and Southface. (See Appendix C.)

Each rating or certification system varies in the way a project or building is evaluated. However, the typical rating systems consist of credits and/or points that must be obtained. Specific benchmarks must be met as the building is being designed and constructed. Some of these benchmarks are found within the specification of the rating system; others require the use of specific industry standards or programs. The selection of sustainable building and interior products that are efficient, durable, renewable, and/or recycled is also critical. There are various tools to assist with product selection. These include product certifications, life cycle analysis, and product declarations, as well as various industry directories and databases. (These tools are explained later in this appendix.)

There are multiple states, local jurisdictions, and federal agencies that require LEED or Green Globes certification for certain building projects or provide incentives when they are followed. For example, the city of Baltimore requires new city-owned buildings greater than 10,000 square feet, commercial building, and multifamily residential buildings greater than 10,000 square feet to achieve LEED Silver certification; the state of Washington requires all new state agencies, state colleges/universities, and K–12 school construction and major renovation projects over 25,000 square feet to achieve LEED Gold certification; and the US Department of

> **✎ Note**
>
> The "three Rs of sustainability" consist of reducing, reusing, and recycling.

> **✎ Note**
>
> Some jurisdictions require the use of a green rating system such as LEED or Green Globes for buildings of a certain type or size as part of the code process. Many jurisdictions also adopt a separate rating system for residential homes.

Veteran Affairs has been using Green Globes to certify its existing medical centers. Contact the local jurisdiction to determine what is required and how to document the information for code review. (See Chapter 11.)

LEED

Note

The NAHB/ICC *National Green Building Standard* (*NGBS* or *ICC 700*) for residential buildings also includes a point-based system with multiple thresholds and could be considered a green rating system. (See Chapter 1 and Appendix C.)

First launched in 2000, the Leadership in Energy and Environmental Design (LEED) is a green rating system developed by the U.S. Green Building Council (USGBC). It is currently the most widely used green building program in the world. LEED provides a framework for assessing and rating a building's performance and its overall environmental impact. The most interior-related items that are recognized and measured include energy use, water efficiency, CO_2 emissions reduction, and indoor environmental quality. Material choices both in the general construction and as interior finish materials play a critical part and are evaluated by their affect to the internal and external atmosphere, indoor environmental quality, the stewardship of those resources, and management of their impact to the environment.

Since its initial development to address newly constructed buildings, LEED has expanded to include individual programs to evaluate different types and scope of projects. Programs included in the current LEED v4 are:

❑ *LEED for Building Design and Construction (LEED-BD+C)*: Within this category there are separate rating systems for new construction, core and shell, schools, retail, data centers, warehouses and distribution centers, hospitality, and health care. For example, *LEED for Core and Shell (LEED-CS)* would provide certification for the building core and shell for commercial buildings, which would include the structure, envelope, and building systems but would not include the individual tenant build-outs.

❑ *LEED for Interior Design and Construction (LEED ID+C)*: Within this category there are separate rating systems for retail, hospitality, and commercial interiors.

❑ *LEED for Building Operations and Maintenance (LEED-O+M)*: This program is directed at assessing and identifying ways that existing buildings can improve their impact on the environment by changes in operation and management of existing systems and incremental improvements.

❑ *LEED for Neighborhood Development (LEED-ND)*: This program applies to land development projects with residential, nonresidential, and mixed use.

❑ *LEED for Homes (LEED-Homes)*: This program applies to single-family and multifamily projects.

There are also unique volume certifications for owners with multiple projects, which simplifies the documentation to concentrate on similar aspects among the projects and speeds up the process. These can apply to several building types, for example, a hotel chain. There is a similar program for campuses. There are also programs for LEED projects that include the objective to be net zero for carbon emissions, energy, water, and waste. The USGBC continues to update their programs and develop new ones. To keep up-to-date on changes and new programs, visit their website at www.usgbc.org.

Typically, buildings can be awarded different sets of credits for design and construction aspects of the project. For example, the interiors program *LEED ID+C* addresses the selection of sustainable material in tenant spaces, efficiency of water use, energy efficiency of lighting and lighting controls, resource use for interior building systems and furnishings, and indoor environmental quality. In some cases, an existing sustainability standard such as *ASHRAE/IESNA 90.1* or ENERGY STAR is used as the benchmark. Credits can be gained for the aspects of the building process like use of locally resourced materials and maintenance of construction waste. When the minimum standards in each category are surpassed, points are earned and the total is used to classify a building into one of four levels: Certified, Silver, Gold, and Platinum.

Although LEED process was first adopted by the USGBC in 1998, the latest significant update was LEED version 4 (v4) which was adopted in 2013. The most recent update, LEED v4.1, was issued in 2019 to improve the useability of the program. Ongoing changes to the LEED system are necessary to address the quickly evolving and expanding expectations for sustainability in buildings. For example, LEED v4 added specific credit lists for retail, data centers, warehouses, distribution centers, hospitality building, and health care facilities. Overall, LEED focuses more on material use and its impact on human health and the environment than previous editions. New credit categories and prerequisites were established as well. The new criteria encouraged the use of performance and alternative solution development to increase sustainable outcomes. There were also changes in the reference standards to be used. Ongoing interpretations, corrections, pilot programs, and resources for implementation are available on the USGBC website (https://www.usgbc.org/).

Another major part of the 2009 update was the introduction of a new building certification model. The USGBC created the Green Building Certification Institute (GBCI) specifically to take over the management of LEED building certification, providing third-party review and on-site verification of LEED projects. Although the GBCI began with a network of 10 certification bodies that included organizations such as Underwriters Laboratories, NSF International, and Intertek to assist in the certification of products, the GBCI now directly performs these reviews.

✎ Note

Even if sustainability codes are not required for your project by the local jurisdiction, the owner may want the project to meet certain sustainable requirements for marketability.

✎ Note

LEED certification can be granted for just the core and shell of a building. In that case, lease spaces that are built out after the initial construction may not be required to meet the same level. However compliance may be mandated by the lease.

Green Globes

The Green Globes™ rating system originated from the BREEAM system developed in 1996 for use in Canada called BREEAM Canada. From that, in 2000, the *Green Globes for Existing Buildings* was developed. In 2004, Green Building Initiative (GBI) acquired the rights to the Green Globes building assessment and certification program and adapted it for use in the United States The system can be used for new and existing buildings of all types and includes three programs:

❏ *Green Globes for New Construction (NC)*. This program address all new building types but includes a specific certification checklists for multifamily and health care projects.

❏ *Green Globes for Existing Buildings (EB)*. This program has specific checklists for existing multifamily facilities. New considerations for Green Globes-EB are also pilot evaluation.

❏ *Green Globes for Core & Shell (C&S)*. This program is similar to the criteria for new construction but does not include the interior fit out of spaces.

❏ *Green Globes for Sustainable Interiors (SI)*. This program is for use with commercial or institutional interior spaces. This program allows the use of life cycle assessment (LCA) or environmental product declarations (EPDs) for evaluation of energy efficiency, material choices and resource consumption and indoor air quality.

Green Globes is an online self-assessment and rating tool that can be done in-house including a project manager and information from the design team. There are separate versions for use in the US and in Canada. These programs are based on a 1000-point scale in multiple categories that include energy, indoor environment, site, water, resources, emissions, and project/environmental management. Using a questionnaire-driven assessment, project information is entered online and a rating system is customized to the project. The system is interactive, so that it provides direct feedback as information is entered with advice and resources for improvements where required. All data submitted online are verified by a third party. A preliminary verification is conducted using construction documents, energy and life cycle modeling, as well as other methods, and a final verification is made by a site inspection after construction is complete. An approved building can receive a final rating of one, two, three, or four globes.

◀ Note

Green Globes originated in Canada. When it came to the United States in 2004, the two green rating programs diverged (www.thegbi.org is the US website and www.greenglobes.com is the Canadian website).

Green Globes is recognized by many jurisdictions and in some cases may be required as part of the permitting process. In 2005, GBI became the first green building organization to be accredited as a standards developer by the American National Standards Institute (ANSI). To further support the development of Green Globe products, the GBI developed the standard *ANSI/GBI 01–2010, Green Building Assessment Protocol for Commercial Buildings*. This standard includes seven areas of assessment, minimum achievement levels, a water consumption calculator, and the use of LCAs, as described later in this appendix). In 2013, the US General Services Administration recommended Green Globes and LEED both as options for certification of federal projects.

> ☑ **Note**
>
> Some of the jurisdictions that have instituted green building programs have used the Green Globes rating system as a model.

Living Building Challenge

The Living Building Challenge™ is an international sustainable building rating and certification system developed in 2006 by the Living Future Institute. It is a system that measures and recognizes one of the highest level of sustainability among the green ratings systems. Projects must be identified by one of four typologies to determine which requirements will be measured. These include new building, existing building, interior, or landscape/infrastructure projects. To be certified under the Challenge, projects must meet a series of actual performance measures, including net zero energy, waste, and water, which is reviewed over a minimum of 12 months of continuous occupancy. Projects can achieve three types of certification: Full Certification, Petal Recognition, or Net Zero Energy Building Certification. This system comprises seven performance areas, or "Petals": Place, Water, Energy, Health, Materials, Equity, and Beauty. The Petals are subdivided further into a total of 20 Imperatives, each of which focuses on a specific aspect of sustainability. This system can be applied to almost every project type (renovation of a building or new construction), infrastructure, landscape, or community development. The most current changes to the program encourage greater buildings that are not only net-zero but in some cases are net-positive. For example, produce more energy or water than they need. The revised standards also set a higher standard for material transparency including expanding the Red List for the first time since 2006. (The Red List is explained in a following Note.) In addition, furniture is now included. The Living Future Institute also has a product rating program discussed later on in this appendix.

> ☑ **Note**
>
> NSF has developed the new *NSF/ANSI 391: General Sustainability Assessment Criteria for Professional Services* to identify maintenance services, installation professionals, and other service industries that use sustainable practices. They are evaluated on environmental impact, health and safety, employment practices, and contribution to the community.

SUSTAINABLE STANDARDS AND CERTIFICATION PROGRAMS

Sustainable product standards are similar in some ways to other standards used by the codes. SPSs, as discussed in this book, are used specifically to evaluate green and/or sustainable characteristics of building materials and products. Some SPSs set high-reach standards for the sustainable characteristic of a building (including social and environmental impact of a product or practice); others set minimal standards to eliminate unacceptable toxins, materials, or practices. Because of this range of measurement, the variety of SPSs is growing quickly. Many were discussed in Chapter 1 and within the various "Sustainability Considerations" sections included throughout this book.

Before reliable SPSs could be developed, however, guiding parameters needed to be created. Internationally, the International Organization for Standardization (ISO) has led the way in creating guiding standards. (See the inset titled "ISO Standards for Sustainability" previously in this appendix.) In the United States, ASTM International (see Chapter 1) has assumed a leadership role in developing standards related to sustainable development. For example, *ASTM E2432, Standard Guide for General Principles of Sustainability Relative to Buildings*, defines the three primary aspects of sustainability as environmental, social, and economic and emphasizes the continual improvement of standards.

Various standards organizations, trade associations, and other interested parties have used these guiding standards from ASTM and ISO as they develop new SPSs. These SPSs can be used in a number of ways. They can be:

❑ Referenced by the sustainability codes and standards. A common example is the standard *NSF/ANSI 140, Sustainable Carpet Assessment* (see Chapter 10).

❑ Used by the industry as common practice in the specification of green products, such as *SMaRT Sustainable Building Product Standard* (see Chapter 6).

❑ Included as part of a green rating system, as a way to benchmark a particular requirement for a LEED credit.

❑ Used as a benchmark for a specific product certification program.

Product certification programs are used to validate the information supplied by the manufacturer. Their development was necessary to counteract "greenwashing," that is, marketing or promoting a product

Note

Originally, many of the sustainability standards for finishes and furniture concentrated on emission requirements and VOC criteria. Newer standards are more comprehensive and measure multiple sustainable attributes.

Note

There are several websites to help keep you up-to-date on changes concerning sustainability and energy codes such as www.energycodes.gov.

Note

USGBC approves certain product certification programs as an alternative compliance path. For example, FloorScore® can be used to meet LEED credit EQ4.3 Low-Emitting Materials: Carpet Systems.

ISO STANDARDS FOR SUSTAINABILITY

The International Standards Association (ISO) is the world's largest developer of voluntary international standards for business, government, and society. ISO establishes procedures that are used by other standards-developing organizations. Although, ISO standards are not as widely used in the United States as other standard sources, a few are referenced in the model codes.

More recently, ISO has taken the lead in developing sustainability standards. As a result, more ISO standards have begun to be referenced in the United States. Most predominately, *14000 Standard Series* is a series of environmental management standards, guides and technical reports that are used in the US and internationally. By these standards, ISO identifies and defines three types of environmental labels, or eco-labels (seals of approval):

❑ Type I (*ISO 14024*) is the multi-criteria label that requires third-party verification but does not require an LCA. It has the widest applicability. SPSs and product certification programs fall in this category.

❑ Type II (*ISO 14021*) is when a manufacturer or business indicates that based on its own criteria, the product has sustainable or green characteristics. It is considered a "self-declared" claim. And, because it does not require verification or LCA, it is considered to be the least reliable.

❑ Type III (*ISO 14025*) is the strictest because it requires use of a more formalized set of environmental criteria with third-party verification, use of an LCA for environmental impacts, and other product performance data. Environment Product Declarations (EPD) are considered a Type III eco-label.

These standards set principles for how manufacturers can promote their product or service as being sustainable or green including the use of symbols, pictures, or logos, how they quantify or verify their claims, and provides guidance for developing programs to verify environmental attributes. Thus, providing some transparency to designers and customers when they are selecting a product.

For more information on ISO standards, go to www.iso.org.

as sustainable beyond its actual eco-friendly characteristics. Product certification programs are typically verified by an independent group (i.e., third-party certifiers), which creates more reliable authenticity. Product certification programs help to recognize appropriate levels of achievement or green qualities to support claims of being sustainable or "green." Otherwise, for example, a natural product like wood could be promoted as "green" even though it was treated with toxic chemicals.

📝 **Note**

Greenwashing is when a company markets or promotes a product as sustainable beyond its actual eco-friendly characteristics. Product certification programs can be used to validate the information supplied by the manufacturer.

📝 **Note**

UL Environments™, NSF International, ASTM International, and ICC Evaluation Service (ICC-ES) provide third-party certification for a variety of sustainability programs and sustainable product certifications.

📝 **Note**

The EPA website has several links to help you identify and select green products. See www.epa .gov/greenerproducts.

Product certification programs have been developed by private sector, industry-specific organizations, and the federal government. Examples of third-party certifiers include SCS Global Services (formerly, Scientific Certification Systems), UL Environments, ASTM International, and NSF International. The Federal Trade Commission has created the *Green Guides* program to establish guidelines to keep claims of sustainable or green attributes truthful and non-deceptive to the consumers. When creating a program, organizations develop their own criteria or use an established standard. Examples of product certification programs include the Forestry Stewardship Council (FSC) program for wood (see Chapter 4.) *FSC Certified*, for instance, uses the standard *FSC Principles and Criteria* to evaluate wood forests. The wood from an approved forest is tracked as it is shipped, manufactured, distributed, and sold. The Carpet and Rug Institute's *Green Label* and *Green Label Plus* certification programs for carpet, cushions, and adhesives (see Chapter 10). Both use the standard *NSF/ANSI 140* and California Section 01350. The federal government has two certification programs called ENERGY STAR and WaterSense, which use standards set by the US Environmental Protection Agency (EPA). (See the inset titled "Federal Sustainability Certification" in this appendix.) In 2012, The International Living Future Institute launched its "Declare" program. Declare provides manufacturers and specifiers of building materials a free online searchable database of building materials with a clear ingredients list to help identify sustainable products. A specific intent of this list it to identify product that do not contain any of the 14 worst in class chemicals listed on the program's Red List.

Manufacturers can test or have their products tested by third-party certifiers using these SPSs to verify that they meet a specific certification program. Often this information is labeled directly on the product. "FSC Certified," for instance, may be stamped directly on a piece of lumber. These types of labels are known as *eco-labels*. Other eco-label examples include the GreenSeal mark, SMaRT Certified, and *LEVEL* conformance mark. Products can also be identified with a Declare label. The manufacturer typically includes this information on finish samples and product literature as well. For example, the information for the upholstery sample in Figure 10.15 in Chapter 10 indicates that it is certified to meet *GREENGUARD* and *GREENGUARD Children & Schools*SM. Many of the third-party certifiers or the creators of the certification programs will also maintain a database of approved products, which can be accessed by the internet.

FEDERAL SUSTAINABILITY CERTIFICATIONS

Some of the first sustainable product certification programs originated with the federal government. ENERGY STAR® was developed by the EPA in 1992. It sets a benchmark for electrical equipment and appliances. Generally, a product will earn an ENERGY STAR label if it uses 15 to 50 percent less energy than the required federal standard. Depending on the type of product, other criteria are required as well and might include maximum power consumption when a unit is turned on, voltage tolerances, sleep mode options, and so forth. In the beginning, ENERGY STAR was a self-certifying specification where each manufacturer was responsible for testing its own products. However, beginning in 2010, the EPA started verifying all manufacturer reports and requiring independent laboratories to confirm the test results. Many countries outside the United States also use the ENERGY STAR program and label. Some are based on the EPA's criteria and other countries use additional benchmarks.

In 2007, the EPA introduced WaterSense℠, which is a program that emphasizes water-efficient products and services. Products are tested to ensure sustainable, efficient water use while maintaining a high level of user satisfaction based on several industry standards. WaterSense products are independently tested and certified to meet the criteria in the WaterSense specification as determined by the EPA. They are typically at least 20 percent more efficient than other appliances. The EPA has licensed certain testing laboratories, such as NSF International and Underwriters Laboratories (UL), to do the testing. (The ICC Evaluation Services is also approved to certify products.) If a product passes the specifications set by the EPA, it is considered certified and is allowed to use the WaterSense label. Example products include high-efficiency toilets and urinals, lavatory faucets and accessories, and showerheads. Product searches can be done at www.energystar.gov/products and www.epa.gov/watersense/.

More recently, the EPA expanded the ENERGY STAR and WaterSense programs to include certification of new single-family homes. The original certification required a 20 percent increase in efficiency from the requirements of 2009 *International Energy Conservation Code (IECC)*. Currently, to receive an ENERGY STAR home label, the energy efficiency of the home must exceed the 2012 *IECC* by 15 percent. A WaterSense home must follow certain EPA guidelines to receive a label. On completion, the home undergoes a certification process similar to that of a green rating system.

Be aware, however, that there are different levels of product certification programs. The scope of the program can range from identifying a single-product attribute, such as its recycled content or water conservation, to a multiple-attribute focus. Multiple-attribute examples might include toxicity of chemicals and materials, types of energy used, water

✎ Note

McDonough Braungart
Design Chemistry (MBDC)
was cofounded by
William McDonough and
Michael Braungart which
created a certification
program known as Cradle
to Cradle, or simply C2C.
It is one of the few certification programs that is
not third-party verified.

✎ Note

The EPA currently has
two sustainable certification programs: ENERGY
STAR and WaterSense^{SM.}
To learn about sustain-
ability programs and
partnerships, see www
.epa.gov/sustainability/.

✎ Note

The USGBC now
integrates LCAs into
their LEED green rating
systems. The recently
completed GBI standard,
which is used in Green
Globes system incorpo-
rates LCAs as well.

quality, conservation of natural resources, and recovery and recycling of materials. More comprehensive certification programs concentrate on the entire life cycle of the product and incorporate manufacturer responsibility as well. (LCAs are discussed next.) The transparency of information should also be considered. Some organizations are creating their own certification programs and self-testing products using these programs. This may not create as reliable of a process as those organizations that include input from multiple participants and third-party certification.

LIFE CYCLE ASSESSMENTS

Life cycle assessments (LCAs) were developed to provide a more comprehensive view of a sustainable product. It is the assessment of the environmental impact of a given product throughout its life span, from the earliest stages of raw material extraction to what happens to it at the end of its life—often coined "Cradle to Grave" or, if more comprehensive, "Cradle to Cradle." An LCA assessment typically includes information on the raw material production, manufacture, distribution, use, and disposal (including all intervening steps).

Most of the SPSs and product certification programs discussed previously measure one or more environmental claims. This may indicate the green characteristic of the product or building material. However, in most cases it does not cover a product's overall sustainability. This might provide a benchmark to compare similar products, but it does not take into consideration many other factors; the product may be environmentally harmful in other ways. For example, a product might be made from sustainably harvested wood, but requires shipment over a long distance to the facility; or products are typically tested for the emissions of VOCs, but other semi-volatile compounds, such as phthalates (found in PVC plastics) or halogenated flame retardants, are not taken into consideration. LCAs, however, measure a wide variety of information. The trend is to incorporate LCAs into more standards and certification programs as well as into green rating systems. In some cases, the LCA incorporates an SPS.

A full product LCA includes 12 environmental impacts as defined by the EPA: global warming, acid rain, water pollution, fossil fuel depletion, indoor air quality, habitat alteration, water use, ambient air pollution, ecological toxicity, human health, ozone depletion, and smog. Currently, the most widely used LCA-related standards are from International Organization for Standardization (ISO): *ISO 14040* and *ISO 14044*. (See the earlier inset titled "ISO Standards for Sustainability.")

LCAs can be used to analyze and optimize the environmental performance of a single product, a company or an entire building. LCAs for products are typically developed by the manufacturer. The LCA data can be used by the manufacturer internally as a tool to monitor and improve their processes and to market their sustainable practices and products. (LCAs are typically available on request from the manufacturer.) Because of the complex assessment that is required, software must be used to collect and capture the information. Manufacturers either use available LCA software or develop their own. Some LCA software or databases are available online. Two examples are BEES (Building for Environment and Economic Stability) for building products and BIRDS (Building Industry Reporting and Design for Sustainability) for buildings. These are developed by NIST. The BEES Online is their database for the sustainable performance of more than 230 products.

Some green rating systems incorporate LCAs as part of their evaluation. For example, certain LEED programs allow an additional point for conducting an LCA on structural, envelope assemblies, and interior-related materials. *Green Globes* programs encourage the use of LCAs by offering education credits and providing a software evaluation tool. LCAs are also typically required when using the performance option in the sustainability codes and standards. *ASHRAE 189.1*, for instance, requires a LCA report that must be reviewed by a third party and submitted to the code official as part of the construction documents. LCA requirements can be called for from a manufacturer and/or for a product in the specifications of an interior project if you want to make sure the product or material meets the requested level of sustainability.

> **✎ Note**
>
> LCAs emphasize the environmental impacts of a product and do not concentrate as much on human health and safety impacts. Environmental Product Declarations typically consider LCA and health and safety.

THE RED LIST

There are several ingredients in products that would make them harmful to the environment and to potentially to humans. These products can include interior finishes, treatments, and plastics, among others. As part of the *Living Building Challenge*, the Living Future Institute developed a list of elements that were considered unacceptable. They call this list the Red List. It identifies ingredients that would not contribute to the sustainability of a product and should be avoided. For their certification process, products cannot contain any of these products unless unavoidable in the current market place. The list includes chemicals and elements such as chlorofluorocarbons, cadmium, formaldehyde, phthalates, creosote, and many more. As of May 2014, the complete list included 815 chemicals. For the complete list go to www.living-future.org/declare/declare-about/red-list/.

ENVIRONMENTAL PRODUCT DECLARATIONS

An Environmental Product Declaration (EPD) takes LCA and product certification to another level. Although an LCA evaluates the environmental impact of a product, company, or building, an EPD includes all the data of an LCA as well as data pertinent to human health, mechanics, and safety. An EPD provides a much higher level of detail and product information with more analysis, transparency, and disclosure of information. More important, an EPD must be verified by a third party. Although typically required in a product certification, it is not required for an LCA.

The criteria typically used by manufacturers to develop EPDs are based on standard *ISO 14025* by the ISO. (See the previous inset titled "ISO Standards for Sustainability.") When they are evaluated by ISO 14025, they are often referred to as "Type III Environmental Declaration." For a particular product category (e.g., carpet, seating, textiles), Product Criteria Rules (PCRs) are created that all manufacturers must use so that there is consistent data, calculations, and methodologies between similar products. For example, ISO released a standard on EPDs titled *ISO 21930, Sustainability in Buildings and Civil Engineering Works: Core Rules for Environmental Products Declarations of Construction Products and Services.* This can set standard performance information to be evaluated including environmental impacts, life cycle costs, mechanical resistance, energy efficiency and heat resistance, safety in use, and protection against noise. The specific information required will vary based on the product category.

Typically an EPD will include the manufacturer's LCA information as well as any product certifications the item has passed. The goal of an EPD is to be able to review comparable information on the sustainability and environmental performance of similar products in order to judge which is the least burdensome to the environment. This is often referred to as an Environmentally Preferable Product (EPP). Manufacturers are beginning to make EPDs readily available for their products for customers and other businesses. In some cases, they may be available on request or found on the manufacturer's website. In addition, various organizations are developing programs and databases for EPDs. An example is the *International EPD System.*

Note

Eco-efficiency analysis (EEA) is another tool used to measure and evaluate products. Unlike LCAs, which concentrate on the environmental impacts, EEA also addresses the economic impacts. This tool was developed by NSF International.

Note

When researching the environmental claims of green materials and products, it is important to look at more than single attributes. Impacts to the environment, human health, and even the economy may cause equal or greater damage.

TOOLS AND RESOURCES

In addition to the various sources discussed in this appendix, there are other tools in the industry that can be helpful when trying to incorporate sustainable products and practices in interior projects. Some of these tools are referenced in the codes and include software that helps measure building-related benchmarks. Others are comprehensive lists developed by various sources to help locate and evaluate existing conditions, identify sustainable practices, and select green products. Each has their own system of gathering and/or presenting information and may include some or all the items discussed in this appendix. A few of these resources are briefly explained as follows:

Note

Another useful resource for sustainability and green building products is www.buildinggreen.com.

❑ *Building for Environment and Economic Sustainability (BEES)* and *Building Industry Reporting and Design for Sustainability (BIRDS)*: Developed by the National Institute of Standards and Technology (NIST) Building and Fire Research Laboratory (BFRL) is software that can be used to guide selection of building products that are cost-effective and environmentally preferable. All products listed are evaluated using the LCA approach. (The software is available online at nist.gov/service-resources/software/bees.)

❑ Healthy Building Network has developed several tools including the *Pharos Project* and *CompAIR. Pharos Project* is a database that presents product information in a graphic wheel format, allowing a quick evaluation of product data and benchmarks against key health, environmental, and social impacts. Also provided are product scores using a 10-point scale within four categories: Indoor Air Quality and Other Toxic User Exposure, Manufacturing and Community Toxics, Renewable Materials, and Renewable Energy. CompAIR is a tool that can calculate the volatile aspect of a product based on its application. (See www.pharosproject.net.)

Note

For a very comprehensive database of sustainable standards and other programs both in the United States and worldwide, check out the *ASTM Sustainability Standards Listing* at www.astm.org/Standards/sustainability-standards.html.

❑ *Green Guide EcoList (editor needs Trademark symbol)*: A database developed by the Green Standard and *Interiors & Resources* lists certified interior products, finishes, and furniture by manufacturer. Information includes product categories, brand names, third-party certifications, and LEED protocol credits. Green Guide EcoList can be accessed at www.interiorsandsources.com.

❑ *CHPS High Performance Products Database*: The Collaborative for High Performance Schools (CHPS) in conjunction with the EPA and the California Department of Resources Recycling and Recovery (CalRecycle) created a list of materials that are considered low-emitting; contain recycled content, certified wood products, rapidly renewable content, and organically grown content; and have been LCA, EPD or HPD (health products) evaluated. CHPS has also identified acceptable alternate programs such as FloorScore, Green Label Plus, and Indoor Advantage Gold with low-emitting materials. The information can be found at www.chps.net.

❑ *SAVE Program*: The Sustainable Attributes Verification and Evaluation (SAVE) program was developed by the ICC Evaluation Services to provide a list of third-party-verified sustainable building products as required by the *National Green Building Standard*, LEED, and Green Globes. Manufacturers can elect to have their products evaluated under the SAVE program so they can be included in the directory and use the SAVE mark. (Available at www.icc-es.org/save.)

❑ *EPA ENERGY STAR Portfolio Manager*: Developed by the EPA, it is an interactive energy management tool that can be used to track and assess energy and water consumption and benchmark a building's ENERGY STAR score. It can be found at www.energystar.gov.

❑ *DOE COMcheck and REScheck*: Software developed by the US Department of Energy for commercial and residential projects, respectively, to simplify compliance with the *International Energy Conservation Code* and *ASHRAE/IESNA 90.1*.

Additional tools are available as well. As the sustainable industry continues to grow, new terminology, methods, and systems will continue be developed. Some will improve on various items discussed throughout this appendix; others will replace them. Continued research is required to keep up-to-date on the latest information.

APPENDIX B

EXISTING AND HISTORIC BUILDINGS

Most of the time, the codes will apply to interior projects in existing buildings and historic buildings the same way that they do for a new building. However, in other cases it may be slightly different. In fact, a different code may even apply. A building can be considered an *existing* building if it falls into one of four categories:

1. A building or structure was erected and occupied prior to the adoption of the most current building code.
2. A permit has been pulled for the construction of the building.
3. A building is currently under construction.
4. The shell of the building is completed but unoccupied, and individual tenant spaces are being constructed.

Eventually every building is considered an existing building. Whether an existing building is *historic* depends on two additional conditions: It must either be listed (or eligible to be listed) in the *National Register of Historical Places or* designated as historic by a specific state or local authority. This appendix briefly describes how the codes apply to both types of buildings.

When working on interior projects in existing and historic buildings, many of the codes, standards, and federal regulations described throughout this book must still be referenced. In addition, some codes have a chapter specifically for existing buildings. For example, the *International Fire Code (IFC)* has a chapter called "Construction Requirements for Existing Buildings" and an adoptable appendix called "Construction Requirements for Existing Ambulatory Care Facilities." The NFPA codes, including the *Life Safety Code (LSC),* have a chapter called "Building Rehabilitation." The *LSC* also has separate requirements for existing occupancies within each its occupancy chapters. Each of these codes includes requirements and exceptions for historic structures.

The *International Existing Building Code* began as an appendix and then a chapter of the *IBC* and became a separate code in 2003. This code

☑ Note

The requirements found in the *International Existing Building Code (IEBC)* are sometimes less restrictive than those found in the *International Building Code.*

☑ Note

The *LSC* includes a chapter titled "Building Rehabilitation." When an existing building is being renovated, a jurisdiction may require that this chapter be referenced as well.

Note

The *International Existing Building Code* was developed by the ICC specifically to apply to existing buildings.

establishes regulations specifically for repairs, alterations, and work performed because of changes in occupancy in existing buildings and historic buildings. It also includes requirements for additions and relocated buildings. There are three methods recognized by the *IEBC* for compliance including "prescriptive compliance method," "work area compliance method," and "performance compliance method." The changes must comply with one method in its entirety. In general, the *IEBC* is meant to encourage the reuse of existing buildings by setting realistic standards while still providing for reasonable life safety within an existing building. In some cases, the requirements of the *IFC* chapter on retrofitting will apply to a project before the conditions of the *IEBC* can be used. When working in an existing or historic building, confirm with the local jurisdiction which of the existing building codes will apply.

The alternate means and methods requirements found in the building codes (such as *IBC Section 104.11*) and performance criteria found in the performance codes (*ICC Performance Code*) may also be useful when working in an existing building. These optional methods and criteria set *goals* instead of exact requirements so that alternative solutions can address the unique conditions found in older buildings. If the use of alternate means and methods or performance codes is allowed by the jurisdiction, and performance criteria are used, it is important to work closely with a code official. Starting in the 2015 edition, the *IBC* Chapter 34, "Existing Buildings," merely makes reference to the *IEBC*.

Depending on the jurisdiction, sustainability codes and standards may apply as well. In addition, meeting sustainability goals may be requested by the client. Sustainability requirements would apply similarly to new construction; however, there are exceptions. (See the section titled "Sustainability Considerations" later in this appendix.) In most cases, the reuse or renovation of an existing building is considered a valuable credit in sustainability codes and rating systems.

Although the *IEBC* includes accessibility requirements for existing buildings, other accessibility guidelines including the *ADA Standards* and the *ICC A117.1* may apply as well. Existing buildings are not exempt from compliance with the federal Americans with Disabilities Act (ADA) requirements. In some conditions, there are more lenient requirements such as allowable slopes, accessible route between floors, and so on. Research will be necessary for the specific condition. There are also some distinct exceptions for historic buildings. In addition, depending on the use of the project, other federal guidelines may apply, including the Department of Housing and Urban Development's (HUD) *Rehabilitation Guidelines* and the US Department of the Interior's (DOI) *Secretary of the Interior's Standards for Rehabilitation,* written specifically for historic buildings on the *National Register*. See Chapter 2 for more on accessibility in existing and historic buildings.

EXISTING BUILDINGS

Because codes change over time, there are almost always parts of any existing building that do not comply with the most current codes. When a repair, alteration, addition, or change of occupancy occurs the necessary modifications and new work typically must comply with the most current codes. However, the codes do not usually require the whole building to be brought into compliance with the most current building codes, only the area being modified. However, at times this can be up to the discretion of the code official. The *IEBC* or similar existing building requirements can help to define an appropriate scope of correction within the building, particularly if some work is required in other areas of the building. The *IEBC* provides three ways to deal with the rehabilitation of an existing building: a *prescriptive compliance method*, a *work area compliance method*, or a *performance compliance method*. One method must be used for the whole project scope. In unique situations, a building alteration can be allowed to comply with the code under which it was originally built, but this would have to be approved by the authority having jurisdiction (AHJ).

When using the *prescriptive compliance method* for changes to an existing building, the *IEBC* refers to the requirements in the *IBC*. The intent of this method is to use current code requirements to the greatest degree possible. Building materials used in any level of work should comply with the current prescriptive requirements. However, the modifications cannot make the condition less conforming than the existing condition. The levels of work are characterized as additions, alterations, repairs, change of occupancy with special conditions for fire escapes, historic buildings, and accessibility.

The *work area compliance method* relies significantly on the separate classifications of work scope as defined in the *IEBC*. These levels of work as defined in the chapter "Classification of Work" are repairs, alterations, changes in occupancy, and additions. Alterations are further divided into three separate levels. In general, the more work being done in an existing building, the more improvements the code will require. The NFPA codes use similar categories (repairs, renovations, modifications, reconstructions, and additions); however, some of the details may vary. If working in a jurisdiction that requires the *LSC* in addition to the *IEBC*, review each publication. Also, because the *IEBC* and requirements for existing

✒ Note

An initial walk-through of an existing or historic building with the local code official an offer a better understanding of available options before you start the design process.

✒ Note

When renovating a building that was originally designed using performance codes, it is important to review existing building documentation and the original operations and maintenance manual. This may prevent the conditions of the performance-based design from being compromised.

buildings are sometimes more lenient than new construction requirements, it could be very important to discuss and establish agreement with the code official for which parts of the projects must meet the requirements for new or existing.

The *performance compliance method* in the *IEBC* sets performance criteria (see the section titled "Performance Codes" in Chapter 1) to maintain or increase the level of safety within the building without strict compliance with the prescriptive requirements of the *IBC* or *IEBC*. The chapter in the *IEBC* addressing this method provides a series of values, scores, and objectives to help develop the appropriate design. However, additional documentation may be required, as with use of other performance criteria. Coordination and approval from the AHJ are also required.

Repairs

⚐ Note

When using the *IEBC*, work is designated as repairs, alterations, change in occupancy, or additions.

According to the *IEBC*, *repairs* include patching or restoration of materials, elements, components, equipment, or fixtures of a building. It is considered the lowest level of change within a building, because in most cases the work is done for maintenance reasons only.

Usually, when repairs are made to an existing building, the *IEBC* allows the current conditions to be maintained and does not require the area or materials to be brought up to current code. For example, fire protection, accessibility, and means of egress can be repaired so that the same level of safety is maintained. In addition, materials that would not typically be allowed in new buildings may be allowed to be used to repair existing conditions. However, there are exceptions. For example, hazardous conditions or materials such as asbestos and lead-based paint cannot be reused; glazing located in hazardous locations that is being replaced must meet the current requirements for safety glazing. In addition, some system requirements call for increased safety, but not to the level of what would be required for new construction. Repairs can include changes to the individual building elements and materials, fire protection, means of egress, structural, electrical, mechanical, and plumbing systems. Check the specific requirements for each type of system.

Alterations

Typically, work done to a building that is not a repair or an addition is considered an *alteration*. For alterations made to an existing building, the codes typically require only the new work to comply with current code requirements, as long as this does not cause other portions of the building to be in violation of the code. For example, the new work cannot demolish an existing fire-rated wall or block an existing exit. However, the *IEBC* creates three levels of alterations. Each represents a different amount of work that is being performed within the building. The more work that is done, the higher the level of compliance with the *IBC* or *IEBC* is required. The *IEBC* refers to the physical scope of the area being altered as the *work area*. Level 1 represents the least amount of work or smallest work area and Level 3 represents the most amount of work. For example, the significant difference between a Level 2 alteration and a Level 3 alteration is the proportion of the building being altered. A brief description of the three levels follows.

◄ Note

There are three levels of alterations according to the *IEBC*. Each requires a different level of code compliance with the *IEBC* and the *IBC*.

❏ **Level 1.** This level of alteration includes the removal and replacement or covering of existing materials, elements, or equipment, using new materials, elements, or equipment. This would include replacing tile in a restroom or a handrail on a stair.

❏ **Level 2.** This level of alteration includes modification to the layout of a space, the doors or windows, or a building system. It also includes the installation of new equipment. Alterations considered to be Level 2 typically are equal or less than 50 percent of the building area. An example could include the reconfiguration of a tenant space in a multi-tenant building. If modifications are for accessibility only, it can comply with Level 1.

❏ **Level 3.** This level of alteration applies when the work area exceeds 50 percent of the building area. At this level of alteration, additional work may be required to increase building safety in other parts of the building even if work in that area was not planned.

Even if the *IEBC* is being used in the jurisdiction of a project, if the design calls for a significant change, the code official can require that more of the building be brought up to the new construction code such as the *IBC* or *NEC*. For example, in the renovation of an older building where a significant amount of electrical work is being done, the code official can require that the entire electrical service and wiring be updated. A general rule of thumb is if more than 50 percent of the system is being affected by the renovation, then the entire system will be required to be updated. In all cases, when working on an extensive renovation or alteration, it is important to work closely with a code official to determine what level of compliance will be required for the project and building.

Change in Use or Occupancy

Note

When a change of occupancy occurs in an existing building, a new Certificate of Occupancy may be required to confirm that an acceptable level of code compliance has been achieved.

When the purpose or level of activity within a building changes, it is considered a *change in use* or *change in occupancy*. (NFPA makes a distinction between change in use and change of occupancy. An example of a change in use would be a restaurant changing to a nightclub, which is not technically a change in the occupancy classification under NFPA.) A change of occupancy may occur if a new tenant moves into the building or an existing tenant changes its use or classification. (See also the section "New versus Existing Occupancies" in Chapter 3.) The space must typically meet the most current code requirements for that occupancy. However, other spaces within the building can usually be left alone. The *IEBC* chapter "Change of Occupancy" indicates to what extent the codes must be met. In most cases, the requirements are based on whether the new occupancy is considered more or less hazardous than the original occupancy.

Additions

Note

According to the codes, an *addition* is an increase in the floor area, number of stories, or height of a building.

According to the codes, an *addition* is an increase in the floor area, number of stories, or height of a building. In most cases, new additions to an existing building must comply with the current building code. In the *IEBC*, most of the requirements focus on how the increase in area or height will affect the structural components of the existing building. Additions to Residential occupancies may trigger the need for fire protection in the new area and in some cases in the existing area as well.

Accessibility Requirements

In most cases, whether an existing building is being repaired or altered, accessibility must be maintained or increased as changes are made. The *IEBC* indicates the minimum accessibility requirements for each type of change. A repair must maintain the existing level of accessibility. An alteration must comply with the accessibility requirements of the *IBC* unless *technically infeasible* and at least to the *maximum extent technically feasible* (as explained in Chapter 2). When a change of occupancy occurs, the *IEBC* requires that (1) one accessible entrance, (2) one accessible route from the entrance to the primary function area, and (3) accessible signage be provided.

In addition, changes to an existing building must meet certain requirements in the *ADA Standards* that may be more stringent than the *IEBC*. The *Fair Housing Accessibility Guidelines (FHAG)* may also apply in certain residential occupancies. Although the ADA specifically states that existing buildings must fully comply with the accessibility requirements as stated in the *ADA Standards*, there are some alternate solutions for existing buildings and for alterations to existing buildings. For example, the ADA does allow exceptions where compliance is either structurally infeasible, too costly, or would cause an unsafe situation. These exceptions must be fully analyzed. Refer to the ADA and other experts when necessary. In most cases, additions are required by the codes and the federal laws to be fully compliant with the ADA requirements. (See Chapter 2 more information.)

📝 **Note**

The ADA includes some alternate solutions for existing buildings and for alterations to existing buildings.

HISTORIC BUILDINGS

When working on a project in a historic building, there is an obvious need to balance protection of the historic character of a building or interior space with provision of an acceptable level of life safety and accessibility. It is important to know the requirements that apply and the alternative solutions that may be acceptable. As previously mentioned, the *IBC*, the *IEBC*, and the NFPA codes all have special provisions for historic buildings. (The *IEBC* has a separate chapter titled "Historic Buildings.") In addition to codes, many jurisdictions have state or local regulations for historic buildings as well. It is important to check for local regulations before starting a project. For example, some regulations control only the preservation of the exterior of a historic building; however, this may include any interior work that is visible from the exterior of the building.

The key to historic projects is to determine which codes must be met and what approval procedures must be followed. According to the *IEBC*, when a historic building undergoes a repair, alteration, or change of occupancy, a written report may be required to evaluate the condition of the building as it relates to the current codes. It must also identify historic characteristics that may be damaged or destroyed by bringing the building or space up to current codes. Although the code official can allow alternative solutions or allow aspects of the existing building to remain, any conditions that potentially create a danger to life safety may be required to be modified. Communication with the code department and historic preservation organizations is imperative. Some historic organizations have the power to grant alternatives or waivers to code provisions. For example, some jurisdictions may allow safety equivalencies. In addition, many of the codes include alternative requirements that can be used if approved by the code official. It may also be necessary to apply to the appeals or variance boards in special circumstances. (See Chapter 11.)

📝 **Note**

Old or historic buildings for public use must still be safe and in most cases accessible.

Remember that an old or historic building must still be safe. In addition to the codes and documents already mentioned, there are some additional documents that may be mandatory or useful to develop alternatives for safety and accessibility:

❏ *NFPA 914, Code for Fire Protection of Historic Structures*
❏ *The Secretary of the Interior's Standards for Rehabilitation*
❏ State historic building codes including California, Washington, North Carolina, and others

For example, *NFPA 914* can be useful in providing increased life safety and an appropriate level of property protection for the historic structure itself while minimizing the intrusion of the fire protection system on the historic quality of the spaces. This standard designates ways to evaluate the potential threat of fire and damage to the building and contents. This can inform the design of an appropriate fire protection system for the actual building conditions, which may not be the same as if it were new. In conjunction with the fire protection plan, the design may include increasing safety features of other systems (such as electrical) to further reduce the chance of a fire starting as part of the overall protection plan. Because this standard requires evaluation and potentially alternate methods, approval by the local code official as well as working with representatives of the historic structure may be required.

In most cases, a historic structure will be required to be accessible if used by the public. In some cases, a limited level of accessibility or alternate solutions may be allowed by the building codes, accessibility standards, and even the ADA if meeting the most stringent requirements is not feasible or readily achievable. (See Chapter 2.)

For example, when a required modification or change would destroy a historic detail and/or potentially harm the historic significance of the building or space, the ADA allows exceptions or alternative solutions. Some of these alternative solutions are stated in the ADA. Others may need to be discussed with the state or local historic preservation official or directly with the Access Board. Remember, though, that approval of an alternative solution for one space or area does not exempt the whole building from meeting other requirements. Any variation from strict compliance with the regulations should be discussed and approved by the owner and local code official.

The ADA does establish minimum requirements that all historic buildings must meet. These include (1) at least one accessible route into the building, (2) at least one accessible toilet when toilet facilities are provided, (3) access to all public areas on the main floor, and (4) accessible displays and written information. There are several requirements in the

☑ Note

The ADA sets minimum accessibility requirements that existing and historic buildings must provide. However, all ADA requirements should be followed whenever possible.

ADA Standards that can typically be met without major disruption. Examples include installing compatible offset hinges to widen doorways, adding full-length mirrors and raised toilet seats in restrooms, and replacing door and faucet handles with lever controls.

Full compliance with the codes and ADA regulations must reached whenever possible. When existing conditions make meeting the codes and accessibility requirements difficult, the allowances and exemptions for existing and/or historic buildings should be considered. It may be necessary to discuss alternatives with local or federal officials. In other cases, a code variance may be required. However, whether the building is existing or historic, the overall goal when making interior changes is to make the building as safe as possible—and, in the process, as accessible as possible.

SUSTAINABILITY CONSIDERATIONS

Many of the sustainability requirements that apply to new buildings or spaces apply to repairs and alterations in an existing or historic building. However, there are also special provisions in many of the sustainable codes and standards for these types of projects. For example, the *International Green Construction Code (IgCC)* has a specific chapter on "Existing Buildings." It sets different levels of compliance for additions or an alterations. For additions, the requirements for new construction must be met in the new spaces. When alterations are being made to existing portions or components of a building, the *IgCC* sets minimum energy, HVAC, and water requirements for the building. For lighting issues, the *IgCC* refers to the *International Energy Conservation Code (IECC)*.

In most cases, there are exceptions to the requirements in the *IgCC* to address unique conditions within an existing building. Additional requirements for existing buildings include maintenance issues and planned phase-out of undesirable use of chemicals and systems that do not contribute to the sustainability of the building. In some cases, an energy audit and report must be submitted to the code official to evaluate the green status of the existing building to define what requirements must be met.

A local jurisdiction may require the use of *ASHRAE 189.1, Standard for the Design of High-Performance Green Buildings Except Low-Rise Residential Buildings*. However, this sustainability standard does not include specific requirements for existing and/or historic buildings. Instead, the sustainability requirements are typically applied as they would be to new construction.

> ◥ **Note**
>
> Both the *IgCC* and the *National Green Building Standard* provide alternate levels of sustainability compliance for existing building, which can be used in certain situations.

✎ Note

A jurisdiction may also require the use of a green rating system as part of its code process. Examples include LEED-EB and Green Globes. (See Appendix A.)

Certain Residential building types may also require the use of the *ICC 700, National Green Building Standard (NGBS)*. The NGBS has separate performance requirements for renovations and additions of a limited size. These requirements are different from those for new construction. If a larger addition is made, the requirements for new construction may apply to the whole project. The "Compliance Method" chapter of the *NGBS* specifies how the standard applies to a renovation or addition, how points are allocated, and how threshold environmental performance levels are obtained. Although the usual *NGBS* point allocation is used for existing buildings, there may be special criteria that affect whether specific green practices are mandatory. In addition, special points applicable only to renovations of existing buildings may be available. Both affect the ability to reach the desired performance levels for the building. Typical criteria include the efficient use and disposal of construction materials, durability of materials, maintenance, material choices, energy efficiency, water efficiency, and indoor air quality.

In addition, the *NGBS* has two levels of compliance depending on when the building was originally constructed. Buildings that were constructed during or after 1980 follow guidelines known as the *Green Building Path*. This path requires the incorporation of several green practices, similar to the process for new construction, although there are some adjustments. Points are given in six green building categories as well as an overall total for each certification level. Buildings constructed prior to 1980 can follow either the *Green Remodel Path* or the *Green Building Path*. However, the emphasis of the *Green Remodel Path* is on reduction in energy usage and water usage and indoor environmental quality practices. The *Green Remodel Path* allows a slightly lower level of achievement and may make it simpler for existing or historic buildings to reach sustainability goals. (Refer to the standard for specific requirements.)

APPENDIX C

FAMILY RESIDENCES

When multiple families reside together in a single building and have separate dwelling or sleeping units, it is considered a Residential occupancy by the codes. These include apartment buildings, hotels, dormitories, and some care facilities. Many of these have been discussed throughout this book. In other cases, one or two families may live within a single building in separate units. These single-family homes, duplexes (two-family dwellings), and townhouses that have their own means of egress are also considered Residential occupancies by the codes. However, the I-Codes have a separate publication for these uses. The *International Residential Code (IRC)* is the code used by most jurisdictions for family residences. If the building is sprinklered, additional Residential uses can follow this code instead of the *IBC*. These uses include townhouses with live/work units, owner-occupied-lodging houses with five or fewer guestrooms, and care facilities providing custodial, medical, or general care if the number receiving care is five or less. All other Residential uses must follow the *IBC*. If the *NFPA 5000* has been adopted, requirements for all Residential uses are included in that code publication.

The *IRC* is considered a comprehensive code. This means that all code requirements that pertain to these buildings are included in the single publication. This is different than projects that must comply with the *IBC*. As the building code, the *IBC* must be used in conjunction with other code publications, such as separate mechanical, plumbing, energy conservation, and electrical codes, to know all the requirements that apply. These separate codes were introduced in Chapter 1 and have been discussed throughout the book. In the *IRC*, mechanical, electrical, plumbing, structure, and other code requirements are included. However, like the *IBC*, the *IRC* also refers to a variety of standards as part of its requirements. Although family residences do not have as many interior-related regulations as other buildings, several interior codes and standards still

◪ **Note**

The National Fire Protection Association (NFPA) does not have a separate code for family residences. Instead, the *NFPA 5000* and the *Life Safety Code (LSC)* each contain a chapter specific to this building type.

◪ **Note**

Another ICC code that includes requirements for Residential buildings is the *International Energy Conservation Code (IECC)*. It can be adopted by a jurisdiction or used as a design guide to increase energy efficiency of a residence.

◪ **Note**

The *IRC* is used or adopted in 49 states of the US. If *NFPA 5000* is used, it contains requirements for single-family dwellings.

apply. Brief descriptions of the most common interior requirements are given in this appendix. (They are presented in the same order as in the rest of the book.)

CONSTRUCTION TYPES AND BUILDING SIZE

Although most family residences are constructed of wood, the *IRC* does not actually specify the use of a material or system for the construction of family residences. Instead, it sets up design performance criteria that the building structure "shall be constructed to safely support all loads, including dead loads, live loads, roof loads, flood loads, snow loads, wind loads and seismic loads." This allows for a variety of construction methods and materials, but there are no assigned construction types in the *IRC* as in the *IBC*. A single residence could be composed of more than one structural system as well. The intent of the *IRC* is to allow for new materials and innovative systems. For example, the appendix of the *IRC* includes requirements for light straw-clay and strawbale construction.

In most areas, wood framing is a quick and economical construction method for a small structure like a residence. In some areas, metal framing is frequently used or required, especially where seismic codes are critical. With either wood or metal stud construction, concrete or concrete block are typically used to create the foundation of the structure. Because there are fewer variations in the way a residence is typically built than commercial buildings, the *IRC* provides more detailed information for proper construction. In many cases, there are drawings that show the proper detailing and connection of structural elements. Information is provided for floors, walls, ceilings, and roof of a residence. Even requirements for exterior materials, such as brick, stucco, and wood siding that are used for aesthetic reasons, are included in the *IRC*. The *IRC* also establishes requirements for the construction of interior walls, which generally consist of wood studs with gypsum board or lath and plaster in older homes.

Requirements for the structure include performance provisions as well as prescriptive requirements. If the design of the structure varies from the typical framing conditions as indicated in the *IRC*, the use of alternative provisions or engineered design as allowed by the code or approval by the code official may be necessary. For example, because the structural components of a log house would not go together like a typical framed house, the code allows the *ICC 700 Standard on the Design and Construction of Log Structures* to be used. Likewise, unusual structural elements or conditions may need to be engineered for the unique condition

Note

The *IRC* includes an appendix containing provisions for home day care centers operating within a dwelling. It also has an appendix for tiny houses.

Note

In some projects, a code official may require the use of other codes and standards in addition to the *IRC*, especially for plumbing, mechanical, and electrical requirements, particularly in homes with larger square footages (sm).

Note

The *IRC* specifies many aspects of *habitable* Residential spaces, including minimum room sizes, proper lighting, ventilation, and heating requirements.

and approved by the code official as well. If the residence is to be constructed in areas of the country affected by high winds, seismic forces, and other unique conditions, additional requirements apply. This can mean that similar houses built in Florida and Texas will have different detailing and structural requirements.

These are several types of regulations that can determine the allowable height of a residence. However, to be under the jurisdiction of the *IRC*, the structure cannot be more than three stories high. (Basements and attics are not included in the number of stories, even if they are habitable.) If a structure has more than three stories, the building codes (i.e., *IBC*) will apply. The *IRC* limits the height of each story, as well. (See the definition of *story* in the Glossary.) The maximum allowable height of a story is determined by the structural material of the supporting wall. These limits along with the type and depth of the floor system will determine the allowable height of the interior. If a wall or story exceeds the allowable height set by the *IRC*, additional engineering or compliance with the *IBC* may be required. Apart from the codes, the allowable height and number of stories allowed for a residence is often regulated by the zoning ordinances of the jurisdiction or neighborhood. Zoning ordinances typically regulate what can be built on a specific property including the allowable height and size.

The *IRC* does not limit the size of a residence. However, the size is sometimes regulated by the zoning laws of the jurisdiction or neighborhood by establishing setbacks from the street and adjacent property lines and maximum allowable percentages of land that can be covered by a building on the site. When it comes to regulating size, the *IRC* sets minimum requirements to make sure habitable spaces are adequate for the health, safety and welfare of the occupants. To do this, it imposes minimum square footage (sm) and minimum ceiling height requirements on each habitable room within the residence. For example, the minimum area of a habitable room, except for a kitchen, is 70 square feet (6.5 sm). The ceiling height throughout most of the house must be a minimum of 7 feet (2134 mm) above the finished floor. Certain rooms, such as bathrooms, laundry rooms, and some areas of basements can have a ceiling height of 6 feet 8 inches (2032 mm).

MEANS OF EGRESS

Because the usual number of occupants in a residence is much less than that in a similarly sized nonresidential space, determining a safe level of means of egress is not as complicated for residences as it is for

■ **Note**

Most homes rely on exterior windows as a means of egress during an emergency. The codes set minimum requirements for the size, height, and operation of these windows.

nonresidential spaces. The *IRC* requires a minimum of one regulated exterior exit door in each residence. One of the few specifics about the location of the main door is that it cannot exit through a garage. It must have a minimum clear width of 32 inches (813 mm) and a clear height of 78 inches (1981 mm) with a specific type of landing on both sides. (See Figure 5.3 in Chapter 5.) Other doors to the exterior can have smaller widths. All exterior doors must be easily operable without the need for a key to exit. The width of interior doors is not regulated, but the code does set a minimum width for hallways and exit accesses. The minimum hallway width is typically 3 feet (914 mm). Wider doors and hallways may be necessary if it is required or desired that the residence is accessible.

In basements, habitable attics and sleeping areas (i.e., bedrooms) within a residence, the *IRC* requires an emergency means of egress. (See the description of the requirements in Chapter 5.)

Stairs and ramps within a residence are regulated similarly to those in commercial occupancies; however, there are some differences. For example, because tread depths can be smaller and riser heights can be greater than those of stairs in nonresidential spaces, a steeper stair ratio is allowed. Another difference is that a handrail is only required on one side of a stairway. Stairs to a habitable basement or attic must meet the codes as well; however, stairs to an uninhabitable crawlspace or attic may not. If a ramp is provided to a door that is required as part of the means of egress, it must meet the accessible requirements such as width and slope. Similar to other codes, the *IRC* specifies handrail requirements, such as the mounting height and the handrail grip size. However, handrails are only required at stairs that have at least four risers. The requirements for handrails are similar to the nonresidential spaces. (See Chapter 5.) Guards are also required at changes of elevation over a certain height in locations such as porches, balconies, and raised floor areas. However, the dimensions for guard components in the *IRC* may be different than in the *IBC*. For example, a guard in the *IBC* is typically required to be 42 inches high (1067 mm) but the required height in the *IRC* is 36 inches (914 mm). There may be other variations for use of materials, opening configurations, and locations, as well. Although special staircase types such as spiral and alternating treads are allowed in residences, not all are allowed as part of the means of egress or only with specific conditions.

FIRE AND SMOKE RESISTANCE

Fire and smoke separation is required to separate family units and certain spaces within a family dwelling. Depending on whether the units or spaces are side by side or above each other, they must be separated by either a fire resistance–rated wall or a horizontal assembly. Typically, the wall assembly must extend to the underside of the roof: Floor assemblies must be continuous to each exterior wall. The *IRC* shares the same methods and standards for validating the fire resistance rating as the *IBC* including *ASTM E119, Standard Test Method for Fire Tests of Building Construction*, and *UL 263, Standards for Fire Tests of Building Construction and Materials*. The requirements for the separation of townhouses and duplex units differ. For townhouses, the required rating is 2-hour unless the building is sprinklered, then a 1-hour separation may be allowed. For two-family dwellings (i.e., duplexes) the require separation is 1-hour rating and can be reduced to 1/2 hour if sprinklered. In addition, through penetrations must be firestopped, and draft stops in attic spaces may be required. (See Chapter 6.)

In single-family residences, exterior walls may require fire resistant construction to resist exposure to adjacent structures (i.e., the neighboring house). However, the most common separation requirement pertains to attached garages. A 1-hour assembly must separate any part of the garage that connects to the house, including walls and floor/ceilings. The door between the garage and the living space must be equivalent to a 20-minute fire-rated and be self-closing. Through, membrane and duct penetrations in the rated wall must be sealed and protected as well. Although not required to be rated, spaces under a stair accessed by a door or access panel have gypsum board on all interior wall surfaces and the under-stair surfaces for protection of the stair.

Throughout the family dwelling, fireblocking is required in concealed spaces to form an effective fire barrier between each story and the top story and attic space. Examples include concealed areas in stud walls, duct and wiring penetrations, and openings in the top and bottom of stair stringers. Fireblocking is also required when a clothes dryer exhaust duct penetrates a floor or ceiling membrane. (See Chapter 6 for more information on fireblocking.) The code the materials that can be used. Other fire code requirements are specified for items such as fireplaces and wood-burning stoves.

FIRE DETECTION AND PROTECTION

Previously, fire detection and suppression in family residences consisted primarily of independent smoke detectors and manual fire extinguishers. All new homes must have smoke alarms that consist of smoke detection and an alarm-sounding appliance. (Review the difference between alarms and detection in Chapter 7, if necessary.) They must be interconnected and tied into the electrical system with battery backup. Typically, smoke alarms are required in each sleeping room, outside each sleeping area, outside a bathroom with a shower or tub, on all inhabitable floors

> **◀ Note**
>
> Townhouses require stricter separation requirements than two-family dwellings. Some fire and smoke ratings can be reduced when an automatic sprinkler system is installed.

> **◀ Note**
>
> As more people turn to home health care, additional fire hazards are being created that may not be covered by the codes. Added precautions should be taken.

📝 Note

If the 2009 or later edition of the *IRC* is adopted, automatic fire sprinklers are required in new one-family and two-family homes and townhouses but not in additions where sprinklers do not already exist. Some jurisdictions may elect to amend the code and not require sprinklers in new homes. Check with the jurisdiction.

📝 Note

When a fire alarm monitoring system is installed as part of the smoke alarm system, the *IRC* now requires that the monitoring system become a permanent fixture of the residence. Homeowners can no longer remove the main panel when moving. Doing so disables the smoke alarm system.

📝 Note

Recent studies by the Fire Protection Research Foundation (FPRF) of the NFPA, NIST, and UL suggest that safe egress times during residential fires is being reduced. This may be attributed to significantly faster fire growth caused by the types of materials used in current furnishings.

(including attics), and in basements and garages. New in the IRC 2021, a smoke alarm is also required in areas that are open to a hallway when the ceiling height of the room and hall differ by 24 inches (610 mm) or more. The code also indicates that they should not be installed where a false alarm might occur, such as near a cooking appliance. These detectors are required to be interconnected so that if a detector indicates smoke in one area, all the detectors will sound. The *IRC* requires that smoke alarms be listed and labeled under *UL 217, Standard for Smoke Alarms,* and installed consistent with the household fire warning equipment provision of *NFPA 72, National Fire Alarm Code and Signaling Code.* If an alteration, repair or addition is being made to an existing residence that requires a permit, the code requires that an interconnected smoke-detecting and alarm system be added to the entire house.

A fire alarm system can be used instead of a smoke alarm system. In these systems, the fire alarm must comply with the fire warning equipment provision of *NFPA 72* and the smoke detectors must be listed with *UL 268.* For both smoke alarm and fire alarm systems, combination smoke and carbon monoxide detectors can be used in the place of smoke detectors. These must be listed by *UL 268* and *UL 2075.*

Automatic sprinkler systems are predominately associated commercial buildings. However, beginning with the 2009 edition of the *IRC,* an automatic sprinkler system is required in new townhomes and one- and two-family dwellings. (Similar requirements have been part of the NFPA codes for family residences since the 2006 edition of the codes.) The *IRC* references either the plumbing section of the code or the standard *NFPA 13D, Installation of Sprinkler Systems in One- and Two-Family Dwellings and Manufactured Homes.* Although the sprinkler system is required throughout the residence, certain areas, such as closets and pantries, are exempt. (See also the section "Sprinkler Systems" in Chapter 7.) If an addition is made to an existing residence that does not currently have an automatic sprinkler system, it is not required in the new construction.

Although not a component of fire protection, carbon monoxide alarms and detection systems may also be required by the *IRC.* An alarm or detection system is required when the residence includes a "fuel-fired" appliance (gas furnace, gas water heater, etc.) or has an attached garage. This includes both new construction or renovation to an existing residence unless the renovations only affect the exterior or mechanical or plumbing systems. When required, detectors must be installed directly outside each separate sleeping area. In addition, if a fuel-burning device, such as a gas fireplace, is in the bedroom or an adjacent bathroom, an alarm or detector must be located in the bedroom as well. Carbon monoxide alarms must be listed by *UL 2034, Standard of Safety for Single and Multiple Station Carbon Monoxide Alarms.* Combination carbon monoxide and smoke alarms can be used instead, but must comply with *UL 2034* and *UL 217, Standard for Smoke Alarms.* A carbon monoxide detection system can be used instead of individual carbon monoxide alarms. These systems must comply with *NFPA 720, Standard for the Installation of Carbon Monoxide Detection and Warning Equipment.* And the detectors within the system must be listed in accordance to *UL 2075, Standard for Gas and Vapor Detectors and Sensors.* (See the inset titled "Carbon Monoxide Detection" in Chapter 7.)

PLUMBING

The minimum requirements for plumbing fixtures in family residences typically include one kitchen sink, one water closet, one lavatory, one bathtub or shower unit, and one washing machine hookup. (In a duplex residence, one washing machine hookup may be adequate if it is available to both units.) In addition, each water closet and bathtub or shower must also be installed in a room with privacy. Some jurisdictions may require additional plumbing fixtures, based on the number of bedrooms.

The *IRC* specifies the size, clearances, installation requirements, and finishes for most fixture types. For example, a shower must have a minimum floor area of 900 square inches (0.581 sm), have a minimum dimension of 30 inches (762 mm) in one direction and a minimum height of 70 inches (1778 mm), and be surrounded by nonabsorbent materials. Sometimes these dimensions are less than those required by the *International Plumbing Code (IPC)* for other building types. Other dimensions, such as clearances for water closets, bidets, and lavatories, match those of the *IPC*.

For each type of plumbing fixture, additional standards are referenced as well. This includes faucets that regulate the maximum temperature of water. In most cases, the manufacturer will have produced the fixture to meet the applicable standards for its use, and/or the contractor will be aware of its proper installation. However, check the requirements for each type of fixture, especially for custom designs. If accessible plumbing facilities are required, the appropriate accessibility document must be referenced. (See the section "Accessibility Considerations" later in this appendix.)

MECHANICAL

The mechanical requirements for residences include ventilation, heating and the proper installation of these systems. The codes require that adequate ventilation be provided in all habitable spaces within a residence.

✎ Note

Most carbon monoxide poisoning in single- and multifamily homes occurs because of faulty fuel-fired appliances, such as a gas water heater or automobile exhaust.

✎ Note

Plastic (i.e., PVC) plumbing pipes are not allowed in some jurisdictions.

✎ Note

Beginning in 2006, the *IRC* no longer allows "green gypsum board" as the backer behind tiled bath and shower walls. Instead, cement, fiber-cement, or glass mat gypsum backers must be used.

◢ **Note**

Limits on the length of certain ventilation and exhaust pipes may dictate the location of an appliance, such as a clothes dryer or vented stove top. In some cases a ventless or ductless appliance may be used.

This ventilation can be provided by natural ventilation through windows, skylights, doors, louvers or other similar openings. If adequate natural ventilation is not provided, the codes require mechanical ventilation. To achieve the proper amount of natural ventilation, the codes prescribe the size of openings to allow air to come into each room. For example, the *IRC* specifies that a bathroom should have an operable window of a certain size. If it does not have a window, an exhaust fan with a duct leading directly to the exterior of the building is required. This is called *spot ventilation*. (A range hood exhaust fan is another example of spot ventilation.) If the minimum ventilation requirement for the residence is not met by natural ventilation, a mechanical *whole-house ventilation system* is required. This system includes the necessary supply and exhaust fans, ducts, and controls to provide the movement and change of air required by the code.

Room ventilation and exhaust removal is required from certain common appliances, such as clothes dryers, range hoods, gas fireplaces, fireplace stoves, and heating, ventilating, and air conditioning (HVAC) equipment. For example, a clothes dryer must typically be ducted to the outside. Because the *IRC* limits the maximum length of the duct, it may restrict the location of a laundry room within the house. Some jurisdictions may allow the use of a condensing (ductless) dryer or a dryer exhaust duct power ventilator—which may extend the allowable duct length.

The *IRC* will require a mechanical heating system in most residences. (Residences in locations where winter temperatures do not require heat to be habitable may be exempt.) The mechanical heating system must be able to maintain a specific room temperature in all habitable rooms within the residence. (Cooling is not required by the *IRC*.) Because the size of a house can vary greatly, a wide variety of systems can be used. Some examples include air units, heat pumps, radiant heat, and baseboard heating. The *IRC* and the *IECC* require that the system have an efficiency rating that is equal to or exceeds the minimum required by federal law for that location. Because the calculation is location specific, the *IRC* and the *IECC* also require the local jurisdiction to provide the design criteria specific for the load and capacity calculations. The mechanical engineer or contractor will use this information to determine the appropriate capacity of the system and design the size and layout of the duct system for an efficient system. In some cases, these calculations may have to be submitted to obtain a permit to confirm that the heating and cooling equipment has been properly sized and will operate efficiently. Equipment is required to have a factory-applied label, and they must be located where they are easy to access and maintain. Other requirements are specifically for the ducts and piping needed to run the HVAC systems.

Because the mechanical system is one of the largest uses of energy within a residence, additional mechanical requirements for efficiency of the HVAC system can be found in the *IRC* and the *IECC*. It provides detailed requirements for air sealing, duct lengths, and insulation within the residence and within the system. This in turn will affect the building's heating load and the type of HVAC equipment required. ENERGY STAR equipment and a programmable thermostat are typically required.

The IRC also indicates when separate systems are required for individual areas. For example, separate systems are required to heat or cool a garage and the residence living spaces.

ELECTRICAL AND COMMUNICATION

Although the *IRC* includes several chapters covering electrical, these requirements are actually the electrical provisions of the *National Electrical Code (NEC)* that apply to single family and two-family dwellings. (See Chapter 1.) These chapters cover the electrical service, circuits, wiring methods, distribution of outlets and lighting, switching and controls, and types of lighting. Some of the information is used mainly by the engineer or contractor, but other requirements may require coordination with the designer, owner, and contractor.

The codes set minimum requirements for the installation and distribution of electrical elements within a residence including light switches, receptacles for appliances, general use receptacles, and lighting. The codes indicate locations where outlets, receptacles, and switches can and cannot be located for safety (for example, in a bathroom.) In addition to the minimum code requirements, the design may call for and owners may request controls and outlets in specific locations for their convenience. The proposed layout of furniture, cabinets, and use of the space may also necessitate outlets in specific locations for wall-mounted lights, table lamps, floor lamps, exercise equipment, device charging locations, and other electrical needs. The coordination of code-required and design-specific electrical controls and components is important in the design of a residence. For example, the codes require outlets at a prescribed frequency based on the configuration and use of each room (see Figure 9.3); however, by understanding the codes it is possible to accommodate the code requirements and the design needs and minimize the need for additional receptacles in some cases.

Note

The *NEC* includes additional requirements for GFCI and AFCI outlets. (See Chapter 8.) For example, any appliance located within 6 feet (1.8 m) of the edge of a kitchen or laundry sink must have an outlet that is GFCI-protected.

Note

According to the *NEC*, all 15- and 20-ampere receptacle outlets installed in a dwelling unit, including a Residential home, must be tamper resistant. These allow the receptacle slots to remain closed until the correct type of plug is inserted. (Inserting an object into one side will not open the circuit.)

Note

Switching from an incandescent bulb to an LED lamp can reduce the electrical use by 80 percent.

For some locations, the codes will require additional safety measures. GFCI outlets are required in damp and wet areas, garages, bathing areas, laundry areas, outdoor outlets and receptacles, basements (inhabited and non-inhabited and in other areas within six feet of the outside edge of a sink). AFCI outlets are required in living areas, dining rooms, kitchen, laundry, bedrooms, sunrooms, hallways, and closets. (These were discussed in Chapter 9.) Tamper-resistant outlets are also required in most rooms of a residence. In some cases, the codes also restrict the placement and type of outlets for safety. For example, an outlet cannot be located within reach of or over a bathtub or shower. In the kitchen and similar areas, the location of electrical outlets along counters and work surfaces, islands, peninsular countertops are required in specific regularity and in specific locations. This may need coordination with the expected use and location of counter devices. Outlet locations and distributions are also indicated for bathrooms, laundry areas, basements, garages, hallways, and foyers.

Lighting is another electrical element that is regulated in residences by the *IRC*, the *NEC*, and the *IECC*. For example, all habitable rooms must have a wall switch to control lighting in the room. It can either control an outlet for a lamp or an overhead light fixture. Lighting must be provided at a stairway and have a wall switch at each floor level. Certain types of light fixtures are limited by the code in certain locations, as well. For example, special light fixtures must be used in damp locations such as over a tub and certain types of light fixtures may not be allowed in closets. The use of track lighting is limited by the codes as well.

Beginning with the 2012 *IRC*, Chapter 11, "Energy Efficiency," was revised and expanded to include new mandatory requirements and alternative performance criteria for energy efficiency from the *IECC Residential Provisions*. There continue to be updates to these requirements. For example, the required use of high-efficacy lamps in permanently installed light fixtures in a residence has increased from 50 to 90 percent between 2009 and 2021 *IRC*. These requirements will continue to be important to Residential construction, because the federal government uses the *IECC* as minimum requirements for many programs and for houses seeking qualifications for federal tax credits and federally funded mortgage assistance programs.

Several interior appliances must also meet certain electrical code requirements as well as federal energy standards, including ENERGY STAR® compliance. These include ranges and ovens, open-top gas broiler units, clothes washers and dryers, HVAC units, and water heaters. The

IECC includes specific appliance requirements as well. In addition, the ENERGY STAR program includes a home label that can be used to certify an entire residence. (See the inset titled "Federal Sustainability Certifications" in Appendix A.)

Communication systems in single-family homes are subject to few code-related requirements. However, the *NEC* does require that all cables be listed and that at least one telephone outlet be wired in each residence. The industry standard most used is *TIA/EIA-570, Residential Telecommunication Cabling Standards*. Others are available as well. (See also Chapter 10.)

FINISHES AND FURNITURE

Requirements for finishes and furniture in private residences are not as strict as those in other occupancies. However, there are some requirements. For example, as discussed in Chapter 10, all carpet and rugs used in commercial and residential spaces must meet the federally required *Pill Test*. The *IRC* does require that wall and ceiling finishes, except for materials that are less than 0.036 inch (0.91 mm) thick, have at least a Class C rating using the *Steiner Tunnel Test*. The *Room Corner Test* is also allowed as an alternate. (These tests are discussed more fully in Chapter 10.) Picture molds, chair rails, crown moulding, baseboards and handrails, doors and windows, and frames are typically exempt from this requirement. Because of their minimal thickness, the most popular residential finishes, paint and typical wallpapers, are also exempt from these requirements. However, if the trim is made of foam plastic, it cannot constitute more than 10 percent of the specific wall and ceiling area of a room or space. Other wood finishes, such as wood veneer and hardboard paneling, must conform to other standards.

Finishes in shower and bath areas are also regulated. These areas must have finishes with a smooth, hard, nonabsorbent surface (e.g., ceramic tile, marble, or vinyl tile). If glazing is used (e.g., shower walls), safety glass is typically required. (This applies to mirrors of a certain size as well.)

Although furniture for private residences is not currently regulated by the codes, the federal government does require all mattresses sold in the United States to meet certain standards. In addition, multiple industry standards are available that can be used to evaluate the flame resistance of specified upholstered furniture and mattresses. These are explained in detail in Chapter 10. Also, refer to the section "Pretested Finishes and Furniture" in Chapter 10.

◄ Note

The *IRC* requires that a "permanent energy certificate" be posted on the main electrical panel to provide energy conservation–related information, such as insulation used in construction assemblies and ducts, ratings of windows and doors, and equipment efficiency.

◄ Note

All states in the United States have enacted "fire-safe cigarette" laws, which require cigarettes to self-extinguish when not being actively smoked. These laws are intended to reduce fire-related deaths, especially in Residential occupancies. They apply nationwide in Canada as well. (See www.firesafecigarettes.org.)

◄ Note

Although the *IRC* does not regulate floor finishes, all carpets and certain rugs must still meet the requirements of the *Pill Test*. (See Chapter 10.)

ACCESSIBILITY CONSIDERATIONS

☑ **Note**

If part of a private residence is used for business, that part of the residence may have to meet the requirements of the *ADA Standards*.

The Americans with Disabilities Act (ADA) does not typically apply to private residences. In some cases, the Fair Housing Act (FHA) may set accessibility requirements for residences, however, these pertain mostly to multi-unit housing, not single or duplex residences. (See Chapter 1.) In addition, live/work units that combine dwelling and work-related spaces may have to provide accessibility to the work area and to plumbing fixtures located in the work area. In addition, the *IBC*, will also require a residential portion to meet the requirements of a Type B unit or adaptable. The ICC standard, *ICC A117.1*, also has a section dedicated to dwelling units, kitchens, toilet and bathing rooms, and other spaces common to a private residence. Even if not required, planning for future accessibility needs or as requested by the client may be a good design strategy.

☑ **Note**

The *2004 ADA–ABA Accessibility Guidelines* include requirements for dwelling units throughout the text. Although not typically required for private residences, they can be referenced when designing an accessible home.

Most private residences are not required by code or law to be accessible. However, the 2021 *LSC* requires that grab bars (including a vertical bar) be provided in bathtubs and showers in one- and two-family dwellings where the transition from the room floor to the shower floor exceeds ½ inch (13 mm) and/or all the surfaces are not slip resistant when wet. (See the inset titled "Slip Resistant for Accessibility and Codes" in Chapter 10.) In addition, housing built with government funds, even if eventually sold to private individuals, may require partial or full accessibility. Other interior projects may require a house to be "adaptable." This means that areas of the house could easily be converted to be accessible. An adaptable house may include such things as adjustable counters, movable cabinetry, structurally reinforced walls for future grab bars, and specific fixtures and equipment, such as wall-mounted water closets and a stove with front controls. The necessary additional maneuvering space would also have to be designed into the layout of the dwelling. When a private residence is *required* to be accessible, the requirements of the *FHA Accessibility Guidelines (FHAG)* must be met. These guidelines include information on doors, accessible route, electrical switches, outlets, thermostats and other controls, reinforced walls for grab bars, and kitchen and bathroom configurations. The *ICC A117.1* is also an acceptable guide for the FHA.

☑ **Note**

In addition to setting requirements for new home construction, the *NGBS* also addresses renovations and additions to existing homes.

SUSTAINABILITY CONSIDERATIONS

The ICC collaborated with the National Association of Home Builders (NAHB) to create the first sustainability-related standard specifically for single-family and multiple-family home and lodging. Known as

ICC 700, National Green Building Standard (NGBS or ICC 700), it was first published in 2008 by the NAHB. A state or local jurisdiction may adopt the *NGBS* to be used in conjunction with the *IRC*. A jurisdiction may also adopt *ASHRAE/IESNA 90.2, Energy-Efficient Design of Low-Rise Residential Buildings*, which is the energy-efficiency standard specifically for residential homes; or the *International Energy Conservation Code (IECC)*, which includes a chapter on Residential buildings. Since 2008, the *ICC 700* has been updated to include advancement in sustainability practices and add more options for compliance. In 2020, the *ICC 700* updated and expanded to include assisted living, residential care, and certain commercial uses within mixed-use buildings.

The *IRC* includes a chapter on energy efficiency. Many of the provisions of the *International Energy Conservation Code–Residential Provisions (IECCRE)* are now included in this chapter. It contains both mandatory and optional requirements that can be adopted by the jurisdiction. These mandatory provisions call for certain levels of energy efficiency to be achieved in residences without the jurisdiction enforcing the entire *IECC* requirements. These requirements particularly affect the design and construction of the building envelope and selection of mechanical, water heating, electrical, and lighting systems. They are applicable for new construction, additions, alterations, and repairs to different degrees. For example, a programmable thermostat that can control different temperature set points during the day for the HVAC systems. A jurisdiction may also require the use of *ASHRAE/IESNA 90.2* for energy efficiency. (See Chapter 1.)

If a jurisdiction requires compliance with *ICC 700, National Green Building Standard (NGBS)*, there are additional sustainability requirements to be considered. As discussed in Chapter 1, this standard is specifically for Residential occupancies, including single-family homes. It includes minimum requirements as well as performance thresholds similar to a green rating system.

For residences, the *NGBS* includes sections for resource efficiency, water and energy efficiency, and indoor environmental quality (IEQ). Resource efficiency includes using salvaged materials, recycled-content building materials, renewable materials, resource-efficient materials, and indigenous materials. For example, when installing hardwood floors, points could be earned by using salvaged hardwood or by using resource-efficient engineered wood. Water and energy efficiencies are accomplished as in other occupancies, as discussed in Chapters 7 and 8. For instance, occupancy sensors can be used and ENERGY STAR appliances are required. Points earned for IEQ cover everything from properly venting fireplaces and fuel-burning appliances to reducing emissions in wood materials (e.g., cabinetry) and finishes (e.g., carpet, paints, wallcoverings).

◢ Note

If a homeowner or builder wants to use the *NGBS* but the jurisdiction has not adopted it, an approved third-party verifier can be used to administer, rate, and certify the project. Go to www.nahbgreen.org for more information.

Note

A survey performed by Harris Insights & Analytics indicates 83 percent of homebuyers and 89 percent of builders are likely to consider a Zero Net Energy home for their next purchase or build.

Note

The EPA's WaterSense program also now has a certification program for new single-family homes.

Note

Additional sources for designing sustainable homes include the *Model Green Home Building Guidelines*, developed by the NAHB and ICC, and www.greenhome-guide.org, developed by the USGBC.

Another section of the *NGBS* requires both a building owner's manual to address the operation and maintenance of the residence and training for the building owner. For example, the manual must at least include a list of the residence's green building features and the manufacturer's product manuals. Training must include how to operate equipment and control systems. Ultimately, the code official will check a project for the compulsory minimum requirements and will confirm that the appropriate threshold level was achieved in each section of the code so that the home can receive one of four levels: Bronze, Silver, Gold, or Emerald.

Some jurisdictions may require the use of a green rating system to confirm sustainability goals for Residential homes. The U.S. Green Building Council's (USGBC's) LEED for Homes program is one of the newest additions to the LEED green rating system. (See the section on LEED in Appendix A.) It is for use for one- and two-family homes and multifamily buildings. Some jurisdictions may suggest or allow the use of a local or regional rating system as well. For example, many jurisdictions in and around California use the system GreenPoints Rated, which is maintained by Build It Green, an organization based in Berkeley, California. (It can be used for new and existing homes.) In the southeast United States, some jurisdictions require the use of the Home Energy Rating System (HERS) developed by Greater Atlanta Home Builders Association and Southface as part of their certification program, EarthCraft. There are other similar programs in Colorado and Washington. More are under development. For example, California's new home energy code provides a performance path that increases the zero net energy goal to be 50 percent tougher than previous requirements.

If a jurisdiction requires a rating system, it is important to determine the minimum certification level the project must attain as well as how to incorporate the information into the construction documents required for permitting. (See Chapter 11.)

GLOSSARY

ACCEPTABLE METHODS   When using performance codes, these are the design, analysis, and testing methods that have been approved for use in developing design solutions for compliance with a code requirement.

ACCESSIBLE   As it applies to accessibility, a building, room, or space that can be approached, entered, and used by persons with disabilities. Also, generally applies to equipment that is easy to approach without locked doors or change in elevation or to wiring that is exposed and capable of being removed.

ACCESSIBLE MEANS OF EGRESS   See Means of Egress, Accessible.

ACCESSIBLE ROUTE   A continuous and unobstructed path connecting all accessible elements and spaces of a building, including corridors, floors, ramps, elevators, lifts, and clear floor spaces at fixtures.

ACCESSIBLE UNIT   A dwelling unit or sleeping unit that meets all the requirements for accessibility.

ACCESSORY   When discussing plumbing requirements, refers to miscellaneous equipment and/or devices found within a typical toilet or bathing facility. (See also Occupancy, Accessory)

ADDITION   An expansion, extension, or increase in the gross floor area of a building, the number of stories, or the height of a building.

AISLE   An unenclosed path of travel that forms part of an exit access or the space between elements such as furniture and equipment that provides clearance to pass by and/or use the elements.

AISLE ACCESSWAY   The portion of an exit access that leads to an aisle.

ALARM NOTIFICATION APPLIANCE   A part of the fire alarm system that notifies occupants that a fire has been detected; can include audible, tactile, visible, and/or voice instruction.

ALARM SYSTEM   See Emergency Alarm System and Fire Alarm System.

ALARM VERIFICATION   A feature of a fire alarm system that delays notification of occupants in order to confirm the accuracy of the smoke or fire detection.

ALLEY   See Public Way.

ALTERATION   Any construction or modification to an existing building or facility other than a repair or addition.

ALTERNATE METHODS   Refers to methods, materials, and systems used other than those specifically mentioned in the codes; use of these alternates requires prior approval from the authority having jurisdiction. (See also Equivalency.)

ANNULAR SPACE   The opening around a penetrating item.

ANNUNCIATOR   A device with one or more types of indicators, such as lamps and alphanumeric displays, that provides status information about a circuit, condition, or location.

APPROVED Acceptable to the code official or Authority Having Jurisdiction (AHJ).

ARC-FAULT CIRCUIT INTERRUPTER A device that disconnects the electrical power to the circuit when it detects an unexpected electrical surge (or arc); typically required in sleeping rooms; commonly known as AFCI.

AREA, FIRE The aggregate floor area enclosed and bounded by fire walls, fire barriers, exterior walls, and/or fire-rated horizontal assemblies of a building.

AREA, GROSS FLOOR The area within the inside perimeter of a building's exterior walls, exclusive of vent shafts and interior courts, with no deduction for corridors, stairs, closets, thickness of interior walls, columns, toilet rooms, mechanical rooms, or other unoccupiable areas.

AREA, GROSS LEASABLE The total floor area designated for tenant occupancy and exclusive use measured from the centerlines of joint partitions to the outside of the tenant walls; includes all tenant areas as well as those used for storage.

AREA, NET FLOOR The area occupied within a building, *not* including accessory unoccupied areas such as corridors, stairs, closets, thickness of interior walls, columns, toilet rooms, and mechanical rooms.

AREA OF REFUGE A space or area where persons who are unable to use the stairways can remain temporarily to await instruction or assistance during an emergency evacuation; it may or may not include physical protection by rated enclosures and/or an approved fire protection system. (Code term.)

AREA OF RESCUE ASSISTANCE An area that has direct access to an exit where people who are unable to use stairs may remain temporarily in safety to await further instructions or assistance during emergency evacuations. (Accessibility term.)

AREA, WORK The portion of a building affected by renovation or modification based on work indicated on construction documents. In some jurisdictions, the work area may also include incidental areas not included in the permit but affected by the work.

AS-BUILT DRAWINGS See Record Drawings.

ASSEMBLY, CONSTRUCTION Building materials used together to create a structure or building element.

ASSEMBLY, FIRE DOOR Any combination of a door, frame, hardware, and other accessories that together provide a specific degree of fire protection to the opening in a rated wall.

ASSEMBLY, FIRE-RATED A combination of parts (including all required construction materials, hardware, anchorage, frames, sills, etc.) that, when used together, make up a structural or building element that has passed various fire tests and has been assigned a fire rating; includes fire resistant assemblies and fire protection assemblies. (See also Rating, Fire Resistance and Rating, Fire Protection.)

ASSEMBLY, FIRE WINDOW Any combination of glazing or glass block, frame, hardware, and other accessories that together provide protection against the passage of fire.

ASSEMBLY, FLOOR FIRE DOOR Any combination of a fire door, frame, hardware, and other accessories installed in a horizontal plane that together provide a specific degree of fire protection to a through-opening in a fire-rated floor.

ASSEMBLY, HORIZONTAL   A continuous fire resistance–rated assembly of materials designed to resist the spread of fire in which openings are protected; includes floor/ceiling assemblies and floor/roof assemblies. (See also Barrier, Fire.)

ATRIUM   A roofed, multistory open space contained within a building that is intended for occupancy.

ATTIC   The space between the ceiling joists of the top story and the roof rafters above.

AUTHORITY HAVING JURISDICTION (AHJ)   Used by the codes to indicate organizations, offices, or individuals that administer and enforce the codes. See also Code Department, Code Official, and Jurisdiction.

AUTOMATIC CLOSING   An opening protective (e.g., door, window) that has a closure activated by smoke or heat, causing it to close in an emergency to prevent the spread of fire and smoke.

BACKCOATING   The process of coating the underside of a fabric or finish to improve its durability and/or serve as a heat barrier.

BACKDRAFT   An explosive surge in a fire caused by a sudden mixture of air with other combustibles. (See also Flashover.)

BALLAST   A magnetic coil that adjusts current through a fluorescent tube, providing the current surge to start the lamp.

BANDWIDTH   Refers to the capacity for communication cabling to move information; for telephone cabling it is measured in cycles per second (Hz), and for data cabling it is measured in bits per second (bps).

BARRIER   Any building element, equipment, or object that restricts or prevents the intended use of a space and/or protects one building material or finish from another.

BARRIER, FIRE   A continuous fire resistance–rated vertical wall assembly consisting of materials designed to resist the spread of fire in which openings are protected. (See also Assembly, Horizontal and Partition, Fire.)

BARRIER, SMOKE   A continuous vertical or horizontal membrane, such as a wall, floor, or ceiling assembly (with or without protected openings), that is designed and constructed to restrict the movement and passage of smoke. (See also Partition, Smoke.)

BASEMENT   Any story of a building that is partially or completely below grade level, located so that the vertical distance from the grade to the floor below is greater than the grade to the floor above.

BATHING FACILITY   A room containing a bathtub, shower, spa, or similar bathing fixture either separately or in conjunction with a water closet and lavatory. Also sometimes called a bathroom.

BENCHMARKING   A term used when tracking a building's energy use and water consumption as well as other measurable building uses.

BIO-BASED MATERIAL   A commercial or industrial material or product that is composed of or derived from living matter such as plant, animal, and marine materials, or forestry materials.

BORROWED LIGHT   An interior stationary window that allows the passage of light from one area to the next.

BOX, ELECTRICAL   A wiring device that is used to contain wire terminations where they connect to other wires, switches, or outlets.

BOX, JUNCTION An electrical box where several wires are joined together.

BRANCH A horizontal pipe that leads from a main, riser, or stack pipe to the plumbing fixture or sprinkler head.

BUILDING Any structure usually enclosed by walls and a roof used or intended for supporting, sheltering, enclosing, or housing any use or occupancy, including persons, animals, and property of any kind. Any structure used or intended for supporting or sheltering any occupancy IBC 2015.

BUILDING CODE Regulations that stress the construction of a building and the hazardous materials or equipment used inside.

BUILDING CORE A building element that is vertically continuous through one or more floors of a building, consisting of shafts for the vertical distribution of building services. (See also Shaft.)

BUILDING ELEMENT Any building component that makes up a building, such as walls, columns, floors, and beams, and can include load-bearing and non-load-bearing elements; known as structure elements in some older codes. (See also Structural Element.)

BUILDING ENVELOPE Term used by energy codes to refer to the element of a building that encloses conditioned spaces through which thermal energy is capable of being transferred to or from the exterior or other spaces not inside the shell of the building envelope.

BUILDING, EXISTING Any structure erected and occupied prior to the adoption of the most current appropriate code, or a structure for which a construction permit has been issued.

BUILDING HEIGHT See Height, Building.

BUILDING, HISTORIC A building or facility that is either listed in or eligible for listing in the *National Register of Historic Places* or that is designated as historic under a state or local law.

BUILDING OFFICIAL See Code Official.

BUILDING TYPE A specific class or category within an occupancy classification.

CABLE A conductor, consisting of two or more wires combined in the same protective sheathing and insulated to keep the wires from touching.

CEILING HEIGHT See Height, Ceiling.

CEILING RADIATION DAMPER See Damper, Ceiling Radiation.

CHANGE IN USE or OCCUPANCY See Occupancy, Change in Use.

CHILDREN As defined by the codes, people 12 years old and younger (i.e., elementary school age and younger).

CIRCUIT The path of electrical current that circles from the electrical source to the electrical box or fixture and back to the source.

CIRCUIT, BRANCH A circuit that supplies electricity to a number of outlets or fixtures.

CIRCUIT INTERRUPTER A safety device that opens or disconnects a circuit to stop the flow of electricity when an overload or fault occurs.

CIRCULATION PATH An interior or exterior way of passage from one place to another such as walks, corridors, courtyards, stairways, and ramps.

CLEAN OUT An access opening in the drainage system used to remove obstructions.

CLEAR FLOOR SPACE The minimum unobstructed floor or ground space required to accommodate a single stationary wheelchair and its occupant.

CLOSED-CIRCUIT TELEPHONE A telephone with a dedicated line, such as a house phone, courtesy phone, or phone that must be used to gain entrance to a facility.

CODE DEPARTMENT A local government agency that administers and enforces the codes and standards within a jurisdiction; also sometimes referred to by the codes as Authority Having Jurisdiction, or AHJ.

CODE OFFICIAL An officer or other designated authority charged with the administration and enforcement of the codes, standards, and regulations within a jurisdiction; also known as a building official and sometimes referred to by the codes as Authority Having Jurisdiction, or AHJ.

CODE, PERFORMANCE A code that is generally described and gives you an objective but not the specifics of how to achieve it. The focus is on the desired outcome, not a single solution, and compliance is based on meeting the criteria established by the performance code; engineering tools, methodologies, and performance criteria must be used to substantiate the use of the code requirement.

CODE, PRESCRIPTIVE A code that provides a specific requirement that must be met for the design, construction, and maintenance of a building. The focus is on a specific solution to achieve an objective or outcome based on historic experience and established engineering.

CODE VIOLATION Not complying with a code as stated in a code book or required by a jurisdiction, whether the noncompliance is deliberate or unintentional.

C.O.M. An acronym for "customer's own material"; refers to fabrics that are ordered separately from the furniture that they will cover.

COMBINATION FIRE/SMOKE DAMPER See Damper, Combination Fire/Smoke.

COMBUSTIBLE Refers to materials, such as building materials or finishes, that are capable of being ignited or affected by excessive heat or gas in a relatively short amount of time.

COMMON PATH OF TRAVEL That portion of an exit access travel distance measured from the most remote point of each room, area, or space to that point where occupants have separate and distinct access to two exits or exit access doorways. Paths that merge can also be considered common paths of travel.

COMMON USE See Use, Common.

COMPARTMENTATION The process of creating confined spaces or areas within a building for the purpose of containing the spread of fire or smoke.

COMPARTMENT, FIRE A space within a building enclosed by fire barriers on all sides, including the top and bottom.

COMPARTMENT, SMOKE A space within a building enclosed by smoke barriers on all sides, including the top and bottom.

CONCEALED Items in a building rendered inaccessible by the structure or finish of the building.

CONDITIONED SPACE An area, room, or space being heated and/or cooled, containing uninsulated ducts, and/or with a fixed opening directly into an adjacent conditioned space.

CONDUCTOR A cable or wire that carries and distributes electricity.

CONDUIT, ELECTRICAL A raceway or pipe used to house and protect electrical wires and cables.

CONDUIT, PLUMBING A pipe or channel for transporting water.

CONSTRUCTION ASSEMBLY See Assembly, Construction.

CONSTRUCTION DOCUMENTS Written, graphic, electronic, and pictorial documents prepared or assembled for describing the design, location, and physical characteristics of the elements of the project necessary for obtaining a building permit; includes construction drawings, specifications, and any other required code information.

CONSTRUCTION DRAWINGS The floor plans, elevations, notes, schedules, legends, and other drawing details used to convey what is being built and included as part of the construction documents.

CONSTRUCTION TYPE The combination of materials and assemblies used in the construction of a building based on the varying degrees of fire resistance and combustibility.

CONSULTANT An individual who provides specialized services to an owner, designer, code official, or contractor.

CONTROL AREA A building or portion of a building where hazardous materials are allowed to be stored, dispensed, used, or handled in maximum allowable quantities.

CORRIDOR A passageway that creates a path of travel enclosed by walls, a ceiling, and doors that lead to other rooms or areas or provides a path of egress travel to an exit.

COURT See Egress Court.

CUSTODIAL CARE Requiring assistance with day-to-day living tasks but can respond to emergency situations and evacuate at a slower rate.

DAYLIGHT ZONE See Zone, Daylight.

DAMPER, CEILING RADIATION A listed device installed in a ceiling membrane of a fire resistance–rated floor/ceiling or roof/ceiling assembly to automatically limit the radiative heat transfer through an air inlet/outlet opening.

DAMPER, COMBINATION FIRE/SMOKE A listed device that meets the requirements of both a fire damper and a smoke damper.

DAMPER, FIRE A listed device installed in ducts or air transfer openings that automatically closes on detection of heat to interrupt migratory air flow and restrict the passage of flame.

DAMPER, SMOKE A listed device installed in ducts and air transfer openings that is designed to resist the passage of air and smoke during an emergency.

DEAD-END CORRIDOR A hallway in which a person is able to travel in only one direction to reach an exit.

DEAD LOAD The weight of permanent construction such as walls, partitions, framing, floors, ceilings, roofs, and all other stationary building elements and the fixed service equipment of a building. (See also Live Load.)

DECORATIVE MATERIAL Any material applied over an interior finish for decorative, acoustical, or other effect. Does not typically include wall coverings, ceiling coverings, floor coverings, ordinary window shades, interior finish and materials of a minimal thickness applied directly to and adhering tightly to a substrate. (See also Interior Finish.)

DEFEND IN PLACE A method of emergency response that relies on physical barriers and assistance from trained staff to protect occupants in the event of an emergency. Typically, assumes that occupants will remain in place or be relocated within the building but will not evacuate the building.

DELUGE SYSTEM An automatic sprinkler system connected to a water source that delivers a large amount of water to an area on detection of fire by a separate automatic detection system.

DEMAND CONTROL VENTILATION A ventilation system that is programmed to reduce the outdoor air intake when the number of people in the space is less than the design occupancy concentration.

DEMARK The point in a communication room or other location in a building where the wiring from the utility company enters the building and is connected to the building wiring.

DESIGN DOCUMENTS See Construction Documents.

DETECTABLE WARNING A standardized surface texture applied to or built into a walking surface to warn visually impaired people of hazards in the path of travel.

DETECTOR, FIRE A device that detects one of the signatures of a fire and initiates action.

DETECTOR, HEAT A fire detector that initiates action when it senses heat due to abnormally high temperature and/or a specific rate of rise.

DETECTOR, SMOKE A device that detects the visible or invisible particles of combustion and initiates action.

DEVICE A unit of an electrical system that is intended to carry but not use electric energy.

DISABLED A person who has a condition that limits a major life activity. This can include physical impairment (mobility, reaching and manipulation disabilities, lack of stamina, coordination, etc.), sensory impairment (hearing, seeing, reacting to sensory information, etc.), cognitive impairment (difficulty in interpreting, reading, or comprehension, etc.), mental illness, and various types of chronic disease.

DRAFT STOP A continuous membrane used to subdivide a concealed space within a building (such as an attic space) to restrict the passage of smoke, heat, and flames.

DRAIN PIPE Any pipe that carries wastewater in a building. (See also Soil Pipe.)

DUCT An enclosed rectangular or circular tube used to transfer hot and cold air to different parts of a building; can be rigid or flexible.

DWELLING Any building that contains one or two dwelling units to be built, used, rented, leased, or hired out and intended for living purposes. (See also Living Space.)

DWELLING UNIT A single unit providing complete independent living facilities for one or more persons, including permanent provisions for living, sleeping, eating, cooking, and sanitation.

EGRESS A way out or exit.

EGRESS COURT An outside space with building walls on at least three sides and open to the sky that provides access to a public way.

ELEVATOR A hoistway and lowering mechanism equipped with a car or platform that moves on glides in a vertical direction through successive floors or levels. (See also Hoistway.)

ELEVATOR LOBBY A space directly connected to the doors of an elevator.

EMERGENCY ALARM SYSTEM A system that provides indication and warning of emergency situations involving hazardous materials and summons appropriate aid. A signal may be audible, visual, or voice instruction.

EMPLOYEE WORK AREA As used for accessibility purposes, any or all portions of a space used only by employees and only for work; excludes corridors, toilet facilities, breakrooms, and so forth.

ENERGIZED   Electrically connected to a source of voltage.

ENERGY   The capacity for doing work in various forms that is capable of being transformed from one into another, such as thermal, mechanical, electrical, and chemical.

ENERGY ANALYSIS   A method for determining the annual (8760 hours) energy use of the proposed design and standard design based on hour-by-hour estimates of energy use.

ENERGY EFFICIENCY   Refers to products or methods designed to reduce energy or demand requirements without reducing the end-use benefits.

ENERGY, RENEWABLE   Includes energy derived from natural daylighting and photosynthetic processes and other solar radiation sources such as wind, waves, tides, and lake or pond thermal differences, as well as from the internal heat of the earth, such as nocturnal thermal exchanges.

ENERGY, SOLAR   Source of natural daylighting and thermal, chemical, or electrical energy derived directly from the conversion of solar radiation.

ENTRANCE   Any access point into a building or portions of a building used for the purpose of entering.

ENTRANCE, PUBLIC   An entrance that is not a service entrance or a restricted entrance.

ENTRANCE, RESTRICTED   An entrance that is made available for common use on a controlled basis, but not public use, and that is not a service entrance.

ENTRANCE, SERVICE   An entrance intended primarily for the delivery of goods and services.

ENVIRONMENTAL MANAGEMENT SYSTEM (EMS)   a set of practices that helps an organization achieve set environmental goals.

EQUIVALENCY   Term used by the codes to indicate alternate systems, methods, and/or devices that are allowed because they have been determined by a code official to meet or exceed a specific code requirement.

ESSENTIAL FACILITIES   See Facilities, Essential.

EXHAUST AIR   Air removed from a conditioned space through openings, ducts, plenums, or concealed spaces to the exterior of the building and not reused.

EXISTING BUILDING or STRUCTURE   See Building, Existing.

EXIT   The portion of a means of egress that leads from an exit access to an exit discharge and is separated from other interior spaces by fire-rated construction and assemblies as required to provide a protected path of travel.

EXIT ACCESS   The portion of a means of egress that leads from an occupied portion of a building to an exit.

EXIT DISCHARGE   The portion of a means of egress between the termination of an exit and the public way.

EXIT ENCLOSURE   Similar to an exit passageway but can be in a vertical or horizontal direction.

EXIT, HORIZONTAL   A fire-rated passage that leads to an area of refuge on the same floor within a building or on the same level of an adjacent building.

EXIT PASSAGEWAY   A fire-rated portion of a means of egress that provides a protected path of egress in a horizontal direction to the exit discharge or public way.

EXIT, SECONDARY   An alternative exit, not necessarily required by codes.

EXPANDED VINYL WALLCOVERING   A wallcovering that consists of a woven textile backing, an expanded vinyl base coat layer, and a nonexpanded vinyl skin coat distinguishing it from standard vinyl wallcovering; typically requires a more stringent finish test.

FACILITIES, ESSENTIAL Buildings or other structures that are intended to remain operational in the event of extreme environmental loading from flood, wind, snow, or earthquake.

FACILITY All or any portions of buildings, structures, site improvements, elements, and pedestrian or vehicular routes located on a site.

FAMILY TOILET FACILITY A single-toilet facility that provides additional space to allow for someone to assist in the room.

FAUCET A fitting that controls the flow of water at the end of a water supply line.

FEEDER A conductor that supplies electricity between the service equipment and the branch circuits.

FENESTRATION Term used by energy codes to include skylights, roof windows, vertical windows (fixed and operable), opaque doors, glazed doors, glass block, and combination opaque/glazed doors. (See also Opaque Area.)

FIRE ALARM SYSTEM A system that is activated by the detection of fire or smoke or by a manual pull station that sends a signal to the occupants of a controlled area that a fire has been detected; it may also be activated by an extinguishing system.

FIRE AREA See Area, Fire.

FIRE BARRIER See Barrier, Fire.

FIRE BLOCKER Fire-rated material used to protect materials that are not fire-rated.

FIREBLOCKING A building material (such as caulk or expandable foam) installed to resist the free passage of flame to other areas of the building through concealed spaces.

FIRE COMMAND CENTER The principal location where the status of various detection, alarm, and other control systems is displayed and can be manually controlled.

FIRE COMPARTMENT A space within a building enclosed by fire barriers on all sides, including the top and bottom.

FIRE DAMPER See Damper, Fire.

FIRE DEPARTMENT CONNECTION A hose connection at grade or street level for use by the fire department for the purpose of supplying water to a building's standpipe and/or sprinkler system.

FIRE DOOR ASSEMBLY See Assembly, Fire Door.

FIRE EXIT HARDWARE Similar to panic hardware but additionally provides fire protection, because it is tested with and included as part of a fire door assembly.

FIRE EXTINGUISHING SYSTEM, AUTOMATIC An approved system that is designed and installed to automatically detect a fire and discharge an extinguishing agent without human intervention to suppress and/or extinguish a fire; can consist of carbon dioxide, foam, wet or dry chemicals, a halogenated extinguishing agent, or an automatic sprinkler system.

FIRE LOAD See Fuel Load.

FIRE MODEL A structured approach using engineering analysis and quantitative assessments to predict one or more effects of a fire.

FIRE PARTITION See Partition, Fire. (See also Fire Wall.)

FIRE PROTECTION Refers to assemblies and opening protectives that have been chemically treated, covered, or protected so that they prevent or retard the spread of fire and smoke.

FIRE PROTECTION RATING See Rating, Fire Protection.

FIRE PROTECTION SYSTEM Approved devices, equipment, and systems or combinations of systems that are intended to protect the life safety of the occupants and the structural integrity of the building in the event of a fire; includes fire and smoke detectors, fire alarms, and extinguishing systems.

FIRE-RATED GLAZING Glazing with either a fire protection rating or a fire resistance rating.

FIRE RATING The time in minutes or hours that materials or assemblies have withstood a fire exposure, as established by a standard testing procedure; includes fire resistance and fire protection ratings.

FIRE RESISTANCE RATING See Rating, Fire Resistance.

FIRE RESISTANT Refers to construction materials, assemblies, and textiles that prevent or retard the passage of excessive heat, hot gases, or flame.

FIRE RETARDANT–TREATED WOOD Pressure-treated lumber and plywood that exhibit reduced surface burning characteristics and resist fire development.

FIRE RISK The probability that a fire will occur, with the accompanying potential for harm to human life and property damage.

FIRE-STOP An assembly or material used to prevent the spread of fire and smoke through openings in fire resistive assemblies.

FIRE SUPPRESSION SYSTEM See Fire Extinguishing System.

FIRE WALL A fire-rated wall having protected openings, which restricts the spread of fire and extends continuously from the foundation to or through the roof with sufficient structural stability under fire conditions to allow collapse of construction on either side without collapse of the wall.

FIRE WINDOW ASSEMBLY See Assembly, Fire Window.

FLAME RESISTANT Refers to finishes or furniture that prevent, terminate, or inhibit the spread of a flame on application of a flame or nonflaming ignition source with or without removal of the ignition source.

FLAME RETARDANT A chemical or other treatment used to render a material flame resistant.

FLAME-RETARDANT TREATMENT A process for incorporating or adding flame retardants to a finish or other material.

FLAME SPREAD The propagation of flame over a surface or the rate at which flame travels along the surface of a finish.

FLAMMABILITY The relative ease with which an item ignites and burns.

FLAMMABLE Capable of being ignited.

FLASHOVER A stage in the development of a contained fire in which all exposed surfaces reach ignition temperatures simultaneously and fire spreads rapidly throughout the space.

FLIGHT A continuous run of rectangular treads, winders, or combination thereof, from one landing to another.

FLOOR AREA The amount of floor surface included within the exterior walls. (See also Area, Net Floor and Area, Gross Floor.)

FLOOR FIRE DOOR ASSEMBLY See Assembly, Floor Fire Door.

FLUE A passageway within a chimney or vent through which gaseous combustion products pass.

FUEL LOAD Amount of combustible material present in a building or space that can feed a fire, such as combustible construction materials, paper, books, computers, and furniture.

FULL-SCALE TEST The simulation of an actual fire condition, such as for a full-size room or a full-size piece of furniture with all its contents.

FUSE A safety device that contains metal that will melt or break when the electrical current exceeds a specific value for a specific time period, causing the flow of electricity to stop.

FUSIBLE LINK A connecting link of a low-melting alloy that melts at a predetermined temperature, causing separation.

GLAZING The process of installing glass into frames; sometimes refers to the glass itself.

GRADE The average of the finished ground level where it adjoins the building at the exterior wall.

GRAYWATER Any nonindustrial wastewater generated from domestic processes such as dishwashing, laundering, or bathing.

GREEN DESIGN Design of products, environments, and buildings that treats environmental attributes as an important design objective. It aims to minimize the potential harmful effects on human health and the environment by choosing eco-friendly building materials and construction practices. It also can include systems that increase the efficiency of a building so that it uses less materials, energy, and water. (See also Sustainable Design.)

GROUNDED As it relates to electrical work, connected to the earth.

GROUND-FAULT CIRCUIT INTERRUPTER A device that detects small current leaks and disconnects the electrical power to the circuit or appliance, should a current leak occur, for the protection of the user; commonly known as GFCI or GFI.

GUARD A system of rails or other building components located near open sides of elevated walking surfaces that minimizes the possibility of a fall. (Previously known as a guardrail.)

GUEST ROOM or SUITE An accommodation that combines living, sleeping, sanitation, and storage facilities within a compartment or a contiguous group of rooms.

HABITABLE SPACE A room or enclosed space in a building used for living, sleeping, eating, or cooking but excluding bathrooms, toilet rooms, closets, halls, storage or utility spaces, and similar areas.

HANDICAPPED See Disabled.

HANDRAIL A horizontal or sloping rail intended for grasping by the hand for guidance or support.

HAZARDOUS MATERIAL A chemical or other substance that is a physical or health hazard, whether the material is in usable or waste condition; includes combustible or flammable materials, toxic, noxious, or corrosive items, or heat-producing appliances. (See also Toxic Material.)

HEAT BARRIER A liner or backcoating used between upholstery and the filling underneath to prevent the spread of flame or smoldering heat.

HEIGHT, BUILDING The vertical distance from the grade plane to the average height of the highest roof surface.

HEIGHT, CEILING The clear vertical distance from finished floor to finished ceiling directly above.

HEIGHT, STORY The clear vertical distance from finished floor to the finished floor above or finished floor to the top of the joists supporting the roof structure above.

HIGH-EFFICACY LAMPS Compact fluorescent lamps, T-8 or smaller-diameter linear fluorescent lamps, or other types of lamps with specific lumens per watt.

HIGH-RISE BUILDING A structure with a floor used for human occupancy more than 75 feet (22,860 mm) above the lowest level of fire department vehicle access.

HISTORIC BUILDING See Building, Historic.

HOISTWAY A vertical shaft for an elevator or dumbwaiter.

HOME RUN Refers to wiring that is continuous from a device directly back to a main electrical panel or communication equipment without any interruptions or intermediate connections.

HORIZONTAL ASSEMBLY See Assembly, Horizontal.

HORIZONTAL EXIT See Exit, Horizontal.

HORIZONTAL PASSAGE Allows movement between rooms or areas on the same floor or story—for example, a door, archway, or cased opening.

INCIDENTAL USE A small area, space, or room that exists within another larger occupancy or building type that is considered more hazardous than the rest of the occupancy or building.

INDIGENOUS MATERIAL Material that is originated, produced, or grows/occurs naturally in a region, typically within 500 miles (804.7 km) of a construction site.

INDOOR AIR QUALITY (IAQ) A general term used to describe the relative health of the air in an indoor environment that can be negatively impacted by volatile organic compounds (VOCs), such as those that offgas from building materials, finish, furniture, cleaning products, and other pollutants.

INDOOR ENVIRONMENTAL QUALITY (IEQ) Includes indoor air quality as well as other interior elements that affect a building occupant's well-being such as daylighting, thermal comfort, and acoustics.

INGRESS An entrance or the act of entering.

INITIATING DEVICE A component of the fire protection system that is the initial notification of fire, such as a smoke detector or a manual fire alarm box.

INSANITARY A condition that is contrary to sanitary principles or unclean enough to endanger health.

INSPECTION When a code official visits a job site to confirm that the work complies with the project's construction documents and required codes.

INTERIOR FINISH Any exposed interior surface of a building, including finished ceilings, floors, walls, window treatments, and decorative trim, as well as other furniture and furnishings.

JURISDICTION A governmental unit, such as a state, city, or municipality, that adopts the same codes, standards, and regulations; often referred to by the codes as Authority Having Jurisdiction, or AHJ.

LABELED Refers to any equipment or building material and assemblies that include a label, seal, symbol, or other identification mark of a nationally recognized testing laboratory, inspection agency, or other organization acceptable to the jurisdiction concerned with product evaluation, which attests to the compliance with applicable nationally recognized standards. (See also Listed.)

LANDING, DOOR A level floor surface immediately adjacent to a doorway or threshold.

LANDING, INTERMEDIATE A level floor surface between two flights of stairs or ramps.

LIFE CYCLE ASSESSMENT (LCA) A technique to evaluate the relevant energy and material consumed and environmental emissions associated with the entire life of a building, product, process, activity, or service. It considers raw material acquisition through manufacturing, construction use, operation, demolition, and disposal.

LIGHT-DIFFUSING SYSTEM System in which light-transmitting plastic is positioned below independently mounted electrical light sources (or natural light sources) to create a light feature, not including similar plastic lenses, panels, grids, or baffles used as part of the electrical or light fixture.

LIGHT FIXTURE A complete lighting unit consisting of at least one lamp (and ballast when applicable) and the parts required to distribute the light, to position and protect the lamp, and to connect the lamp to the power supply (with a ballast when required). Also referred to as a luminaire.

LIMITED COMBUSTIBLE Refers to material that is not considered noncombustible, yet still has some fire resistive qualities; a term used by the National Fire Protection Association.

LINTEL The member that is placed over an opening in a wall to support the wall construction above.

LISTED Refers to equipment or building materials and assemblies included in a list published by a nationally recognized testing laboratory, inspection agency, or other organization acceptable to the jurisdiction concerned with product evaluation that periodically tests the items to confirm that they meet nationally recognized standards and/or have been found suitable to be used in a specified manner. (See also Labeled.)

LIVE LOAD Any dynamic weight within a building, including the people, furniture, and equipment, and not including dead load, earthquake load, snow load, or wind load. (See also Dead Load.)

LIVING AREA See Dwelling Unit.

LIVING SPACE A normally occupied space within a dwelling unit other than sleeping rooms used for things such as living, eating, cooking, bathing, washing, and sanitation purposes.

LOAD-BEARING ELEMENT Any column, girder, beam, joist, truss, rafter, wall, floor, or roof that supports any vertical structural element in addition to its own weight.

LOW-VOC (PRODUCTS) Products or materials with volatile organic compound (VOC) emissions equal to or below the established thresholds established by a code or industry standard.

LOW-VOLTAGE LIGHTING Lighting equipment that is powered through a transformer such as a cable conductor, rail conductor, or track lighting.

LUMINAIRE See Light Fixture.

MAKEUP WATER The water temporarily supplied by a municipality (either reclaimed or potable) when onsite nonpotable water supply systems, such as graywater and rainwater systems, are not available.

MAIN, WATER The principal artery of any continuous piping or duct system to which branch pipes or ducts may be connected.

MAKEUP AIR Air that is provided to replace air being exhausted.

MANUAL FIRE ALARM A manual device used to signal a fire; usually used by an occupant.

MARK An identification applied to a product by a manufacturer indicating the name of the manufacturer and the function of the product or material. (See also Labeled.)

MASONRY The form of construction composed of stone, brick, concrete block, hollow clay tile, glass block, or other similar building units that are laid up unit by unit and set in mortar.

MASS NOTIFICATION SYSTEM A system that integrates fire, security, and communication systems to provide emergency notification to occupants in a building, in multiple buildings, or in a much larger area.

MEANS OF EGRESS A continuous and unobstructed way of egress travel, both horizontally and vertically, from any point in a building to a public way; it consists of the exit access, the exit, and the exit discharge.

MEANS OF EGRESS, ACCESSIBLE A continuous and unobstructed way of egress travel from any accessible point in a building to a public way.

MEANS OF ESCAPE A way out of a building that does not conform to the strict definition of a means of egress but does provide an alternate way out.

MEMBRANE PENETRATION An opening created in a portion of a construction assembly that pierces only one side (or membrane) of the assembly.

MEZZANINE An intermediate floor level placed between a floor and the ceiling above in which the floor area is not more than one-third of the room in which it is located.

MOCK-UP, FURNITURE A full or partial representation of a finished piece of furniture that uses the same frame, filling, and upholstery as the finished piece.

NATURAL PATH OF TRAVEL The most direct route a person can take while following an imaginary line on the floor, avoiding obstacles such as walls, equipment, and furniture to arrive at the final destination.

NET-ZERO ENERGY Refers to a building that produces at least as much energy as it consumes and derives such energy from renewable on-site sources, not outside sources.

NOMINAL DIMENSION Not the actual size, it is the commercial size by which an item is known. For example, the nominal size of a stud is 2 × 4 inches and the actual size is 1½ × 3½ inches.

NONCOMBUSTIBLE Refers to material, such as building materials and finishes, that will not ignite, burn, support combustion, or release flammable vapors when subject to fire or heat.

NON-LOAD-BEARING ELEMENT Any column, girder, beam, joist, truss, rafter, wall, floor, or roof that supports only its own weight.

NONPOTABLE WATER Water that is not safe for drinking, cooking, or personal use.

NOSING The leading edge of the tread on a stair and of the landing within a stairwell.

NUISANCE ALARM An alarm indicating a problem with a building system due to mechanical failure, malfunction, improper installation, or lack of proper maintenance; an alarm activated by an unknown cause.

OCCUPANCY The use or intended use of a building, floor, or other part of a building.

OCCUPANCY, ACCESSORY An occupancy that exists with another occupancy in the same space or building but is much smaller than the main occupancy. (See also Incidental Use.)

OCCUPANCY, CHANGE IN USE A change in the use, purpose or level of activity within a building, or portion of a building what requires a change in application of code requirements.

OCCUPANCY, MIXED A building or space that contains more than one occupancy; in some cases, parts of the common egress paths are shared by the occupancies.

OCCUPANCY, MULTIPLE A more general term that includes any building used for two or more occupancy classifications.

OCCUPANCY SEPARATION When more than one occupancy exists in a building and they are separated by fire resistance–rated assemblies.

OCCUPANT The person or persons using a space, whether they are tenants, employees, customers, or other.

OCCUPANT LOAD Refers to the number of people or occupants for which the means of egress of a building or space is designed; total number of persons who may occupy a building or space at any one time. Referred to as Occupant Content in older code publications.

OCCUPIABLE SPACE Refers to a room or enclosed space designed for human occupancy that is equipped with means of egress, light, and ventilation as required by the codes.

OPAQUE AREA Term used by energy codes to refer to all exposed areas of a building envelope that enclose conditioned space except openings for windows, skylights, doors, and building service systems. (See also Fenestration.)

OPENING PROTECTIVE Refers to a rated assembly placed in an opening in a rated wall assembly or rated ceiling assembly designed to maintain the fire resistance of the assembly. Can include a fire door assembly, a fire shutter assembly, a fire window assembly, or glass-block assembly.

OUTLET, FIXTURE An electrical box in which electrical wiring is connected to a light or the light switch; can also be called a lighting outlet.

OUTLET, RECEPTACLE An electrical box in which electrical wiring allows the connection of a plug-in appliance or other equipment.

OWNER Any person, agent, firm, or corporation having a legal or equitable interest in the property.

PANIC HARDWARE A door latching assembly that has a device to release the latch when force is applied in the direction of exit travel. (See also Fire Exit Hardware.)

PARAPET The part of a wall entirely above the roof line of a building.

PARTITION A nonstructural interior space divider that can span horizontally or vertically, such as a wall or suspended ceiling.

PARTITION, FIRE A continuous fire resistance–rated vertical assembly of materials designed to restrict the spread of fire, in which openings are protected; typically used to separate areas on the same floor of a building but not between floors; usually less restrictive than a fire barrier. (See also Barrier, Fire.)

PARTITION, PARTIAL A wall that does not extend fully to the ceiling and is usually limited by the codes to a maximum height of 72 inches (1830 mm).

PARTITION, SMOKE A wall assembly that is designed to form a barrier to limit the transfer of smoke; usually less restrictive than a smoke barrier. (See also Barrier, Smoke.)

PASSAGEWAY An enclosed path or corridor.

PATH OF TRAVEL A continuous, unobstructed route that connects the primary area of a building with the entrance and other parts of the facility.

PERFORMANCE CODE See Code, Performance.

PERFORMANCE TEST The check of a component for conformity to a performance criterion or standard, performed during manufacturing, at the site during or after installation, or at a certified testing agency.

PERMANENT SEATING Any multiple seating that remains at a location for more than 90 days.

PERMIT   An official document issued by code jurisdiction (or AHJ) that authorizes performance of a specified activity.

PHOTOLUMINESCENT   Having the property of emitting light that continues for a length of time after the normal light source has been removed.

PICTOGRAM   As it relates to accessibility, a pictorial symbol that represents activities, facilities, or concepts.

PLAN REVIEW   The review of construction documents by code official(s) to verify conformance to applicable prescriptive and performance code requirements.

PLASTIC   See Thermoplastic and Thermoset Plastic.

PLATFORM   A raised area within a building used for worship or the presentation of music, plays, or other entertainment; considered temporary if installed for not more than 30 days.

PLATFORM LIFT   A type of elevator, typically used when a ramp is not possible, to transport people short vertical distances.

PLENUM SPACE   A chamber that forms part of an air circulation system other than the occupied space being conditioned; includes the open space above the ceiling, below the floor, or in a vertical shaft.

PLUMBING CHASE   An extra-thick wall consisting of studs with a space between them to create a wall cavity allowing for wide plumbing pipes.

PLUMBING FIXTURE   Any receptacle, device, or appliance that is connected to a water distribution system to receive water and discharge water or waste.

POST-CONSUMER RECYCLED CONTENT   Waste material generated by consumers or facilities after it is used and that would otherwise be discarded.

POST-INDUSTRIAL RECYCLED CONTENT   See Pre-consumer Recycled Content.

POTABLE WATER   Water that is satisfactory for drinking, cooking, and cleaning and that meets the requirements of the local health authority.

PRESCRIPTIVE CODE   See Code, Prescriptive.

PRE-CONSUMER (POST-INDUSTRIAL) RECYCLED CONTENT   Proportion of recycled material in a product diverted from the waste created during the manufacturing process.

PROTECTED   Refers to a building or structural element that has been covered (or protected) by a noncombustible material so that it obtains a fire resistance rating.

PUBLIC ENTRANCE   See Entrance, Public.

PUBLIC USE   See Use, Public.

PUBLIC WAY   Any street, alley, or other parcel of land open to the outside air leading to a street, permanently appropriated to the public for public use, and having a clear and unobstructed width and height of no less than 10 feet (3048 mm).

RACEWAY   An enclosed channel designed to hold wires and cables.

RADIANT HEAT   The heat that is transmitted through an object to the other side.

RAMP   A walking surface that has a continuous slope steeper than 1 in 20 (5 percent slope).

RAMP, CURB   A short ramp cutting through a curb or built up to it, usually used on the exterior of a building.

RATING, FIRE PROTECTION   The period of time a fire opening protective assembly (fire door, fire damper, etc.) will maintain the ability to confine a fire when exposed to a fire as determined by a test method.

RATING, FIRE RESISTANCE   The period of time that a building element, component, or assembly (wall, floor, ceiling, etc.) will withstand exposure to fire in order to confine a fire or maintain its structural function as determined by a test method.

READILY ACHIEVABLE A term used by the Americans with Disabilities Act (ADA) to indicate a change or modification that can be done without difficulty or extreme expense.

RECEPTACLE As it applies to electrical work, a contact device installed at the outlet for the connection of an attachment plug.

RECLAIMED WATER Water that, as a result of treatment of waste, is suitable for a direct beneficial use or a controlled use that would not otherwise occur, but does not meet the definition of potable water and, therefore, is not suitable for drinking purposes. Also known as recycled water.

RECORD DRAWINGS Drawings that document the location of all devices, appliances, wiring, ducts, or other parts of various building systems; often referred to as as-built drawings.

REFRIGERANT A substance used to produce refrigeration by its expansion or vaporization.

REGULARLY OCCUPIED SPACE A room or enclosed space that is regularly occupied for at least 1000 daytime hours per year. Restrooms, corridors, stairwells, and mechanical and electrical equipment rooms are not considered to be regularly occupied. Dwelling units and sleeping units are considered to be regularly occupied.

REHABILITATION Any work undertaken to modify an existing building.

RENEWABLE ENERGY See Energy, Renewable.

REPAIR The reconstruction or renewal of any part of an existing building to good and sound condition for the purpose of its maintenance.

RESTRICTED ENTRANCE See Entrance, Restricted.

RETURN AIR The air removed from a conditioned space through openings, ducts, plenums, or concealed spaces to the heat exchanger of a heating, cooling, or ventilation system; either recirculated or exhausted.

RISER, PLUMBING A water pipe that runs vertically one full story or more within a building to supply water to branch pipes or fixtures.

RISER, STAIR The vertical portion of a stair system that connects each tread.

RISK FACTORS Conditions of the building occupants or space that can potentially cause a hazardous situation.

ROUGH-IN The installation of all parts of a system that can be completed before the installation of fixtures such as running pipes, ducts, conduit, cables, and the like.

SALLY PORT See Security Vestibule.

SECURITY BOLLARD Any device used to prevent the removal of products and/or shopping carts from store premises.

SECURITY GRILLE A metal grating or gate that slides open and closed, either vertically or horizontally, for security and protection.

SECURITY VESTIBULE An enclosed compartment with two or more doors where only one door is released at a time to prevent continuous passage for security reasons.

SEISMIC Refers to that which is a result of an earthquake.

SELF-CLOSING As applied to a fire door or other opening, equipped with an approved device (e.g., closer) that will ensure closing after having been opened. (See also Automatic Closing.)

SELF-LUMINOUS A fixture illuminated by a self-contained power source and operating independently of an external power source.

SERVICE ENTRANCE See Entrance, Service.

SEVERE MOBILITY IMPAIRMENT The ability to move to stairs without the ability to use the stairs.

SHAFT An enclosed vertical opening or space extending through one or more stories of a building connecting vertical openings in successive floors or floors and the roof. (See also Building Core.)

SIDE LIGHT A frame filled with glass or a solid panel that is attached to the side of a door frame.

SIGN or SIGNAGE A displayed element consisting of text or numbers or verbal, symbolic, tactile, and pictorial information.

SILL The horizontal member forming the base of a window or the foot of a door.

SITE A parcel of land bounded by a property line or a designated portion of a public right-of-way.

SLEEPING UNIT A room or space used primarily for sleeping that can include provisions for living, eating, and either sanitation or kitchen facilities but not both. A sleeping room or space that is part of a dwelling unit is not a sleeping unit.

SMOKE ALARM An alarm that responds to smoke and is not connected to another system; can be a single-station or multiple-station alarm.

SMOKE BARRIER See Barrier, Smoke.

SMOKE COMPARTMENT A space within a building enclosed by smoke barriers on all sides, including the top and bottom.

SMOKE DAMPER See Damper, Smoke.

SMOKE DETECTION SYSTEM, AUTOMATIC A fire alarm system that has initiation devices that use smoke detectors that provide early warning for protection of a room or space from fire.

SMOKE PARTITION See Partition, Smoke.

SMOKEPROOF ENCLOSURE. An exit consisting of a vestibule and/or continuous stairway that is fully enclosed and ventilated to limit the presence of smoke and/or other products of combustion during a fire.

SMOKE STOP An assembly or material used to prevent the passage of air, smoke, or gases through an opening in a smoke barrier.

SMOLDERING Combustion that occurs without a flame but that results in smoke, toxic gases, and heat, usually resulting in a charred area.

SOIL PIPE A pipe that carries sewage containing solids. (See also Drain Pipe.)

SOLAR ENERGY See Energy, Solar.

SPACE A definable area such as a room, corridor, entrance, assembly area, lobby, or alcove.

SPECIFICATIONS Written information that is a part of or an addition to construction drawings that logically communicates the requirements of the construction and installation as part of the overall construction documents.

SPRINKLERED Refers to an area or building that is equipped with an automatic sprinkler system.

SPRINKLER HEAD The part of a sprinkler system that controls the release of the water and breaks the water into a spray or mist.

SPRINKLER SYSTEM, AUTOMATIC A system using water to suppress or extinguish a fire when its heat-activated element is heated to a specific temperature or above.

STACK PIPE A vertical main that can be used as a soil, waste, or venting pipe.

STAIR A change in elevation consisting of one or more risers.

STAIRWAY One or more flights of stairs with the required landings and platforms necessary to form a continuous and uninterrupted vertical passage from one level to another.

STANDPIPE SYSTEM A fixed, manual extinguishing system, including wet and dry systems, with outlets to allow water to be discharged through hoses and nozzles for the purpose of extinguishing a fire.

STORIES, NUMBER OF   Typically counted starting with the primary level of exit discharge and ending with the highest occupiable level.

STORY   See Height, Story.

STRUCTURAL ELEMENT   Any building component such as columns, beams, joists, walls, and other framing members that are considered load-bearing and are essential to the stability of the building or structure.

STRUCTURE   See Building.

STRUCTURE ELEMENT   See Building Element.

SUPPLY AIR   The air delivered to a conditioned space through openings, ducts, plenums, or concealed spaces by the air distribution system, which is provided for ventilation, heating, cooling, humidification, dehumidification, and other similar purposes.

SUSTAINABLE DESIGN   More encompassing than green design, sustainability typically includes three main tenets: environmental responsibility, economic strength, and social responsibility. Buildings and spaces that incorporate sustainable design are designed to lessen their impact on the environment, stimulate the economy, and provide improvements to those involved in the development and the community.

TACTILE   Describes an object that can be perceived by the sense of touch.

TECHNICALLY INFEASIBLE   A change or alteration to a building that has little likelihood of being accomplished due to existing structural conditions that would affect an essential load-bearing element or because other existing physical constraints prohibit modification or addition of items that are in full and strict compliance with applicable codes and/or accessibility requirements.

TELEPHONE BANK   Two or more adjacent public telephones, often installed as one unit.

TENANT   A person or group of persons that uses or occupies a portion of a building through a lease and/or payment of rent.

TENANT SEPARATION   See Occupancy Separation.

TEXT TELEPHONE   Similar to computers with modems, a type of keyboard input and visual display output that provides telephone communications for persons with hearing or speech impairments, also known as a TDD or TTY.

THERMOPLASTIC   Plastic material that is capable of being repeatedly softened by heating and hardened by cooling and in the softened state can be repeatedly shaped for molding and forming.

THERMOSET PLASTIC   Plastic material that, after having been cured, cannot be softened again.

THERMOSTAT   An automatic control device triggered by temperature and designed to be responsive to temperature.

THROUGH PENETRATION   An opening created in a portion of a horizontal or vertical construction assembly that fully passes through both sides of the assembly.

THROUGH-PENETRATION PROTECTIVE   A system or assembly installed in or around a through penetration to resist the passage of flame, heat, and hot gases for a specified period of time; includes fire-stops, draft stops, and dampers.

TOILET FACILITY   A room containing a water closet and usually a lavatory but not a bathtub, shower, spa, or similar bathing fixture. Also known as a single-toilet facility. A room with multiple water closets is known as a multiple-toilet facility.

TOWNHOUSE A single-family dwelling constructed in attached groups of three or more units in which each unit extends from foundation to roof and is open to space on at least two sides.

TOXIC MATERIAL A material that produces a lethal dose or lethal concentration as defined by the codes and standards.

TRANSIENT LODGING Facilities other than medical care and long-term care facilities that provide sleeping accommodations.

TRANSOM An opening above a door that is filled with glass or solid material.

TRAP A fitting or device that creates a liquid seal at a plumbing fixture to prevent the passage of odors, gases, and insects back into the fixture.

TREAD, STAIR The horizontal portion of a stair system that connects each riser.

TRIM Picture molds, chair rails, baseboard, handrails, door and window frames, and similar decorative or protective materials used in fixed applications.

TURNSTILE A device used to control passage from one area to another, consisting of revolving arms projecting from a central post.

UNDUE HARDSHIP A term used by the Americans with Disabilities Act (ADA) to mean "significantly difficult or expensive"; also known as undue burden.

UNISEX TOILET FACILITY A single-toilet facility that is intended for use by both males and females.

UNPROTECTED Refers to materials in their natural state that have not been specially treated.

UNSANITARY See Insanitary.

USE, COMMON As it refers to accessibility, the interior or exterior circulation paths, rooms, spaces, or elements that are not for public use but are instead made available for use by a restricted group of people.

USE GROUP or TYPE Sometimes referred to as building type, use group usually gets more specific and can be a subclassification within a building type. (See also Building Type.)

USE, PUBLIC Interior or exterior rooms, spaces, or elements that are made available to the general public.

VALVE A device used to start, stop, or regulate the flow of liquid or gas into piping, through piping, or from piping.

VARIANCE A grant of relief from certain requirements of the code that permits construction in a manner otherwise prohibited by the code where strict enforcement would require hardship.

VENEER A facing attached to a wall or other structural element for the purpose of providing ornamentation, protection, or insulation, but not for the purpose of adding strength to the element.

VENTILATION The process of supplying or removing conditioned or unconditioned air by natural or mechanical means to or from a space.

VENTILATION AIR The portion of supply air that comes from outside the building plus any recirculated air that has been treated to maintain the desired quality of air within a space.

VENT, MECHANICAL The part of the air distribution system that dispenses and collects the air in a space, including supply diffusers and return grilles.

VENT PIPE A pipe that provides a flow of air to the drainage system and allows the discharge of harmful gases to prevent siphonage or backpressure. (Also called a flue.)

VERTICAL OPENING An opening through a floor or roof.

VERTICAL PASSAGE   Allows movement from floor to floor—for example, a stairway or an elevator.

VOLATILE ORGANIC COMPOUND (VOC)   A class of carbon-based substances and organic compounds that readily release gaseous vapors at room temperature, causing indoor pollutants and sometimes ground-level ozone when in contact with certain exterior pollutants. (See also Low-VOC.)

WALL, CAVITY   A wall, typically built of masonry or concrete, arranged to provide a continuous air space within the wall. (See also Plumbing Chase.)

WALL, DEMISING   A wall that separates two tenant spaces in the same building, typically requiring a fire rating or smoke resistance. (See also Occupancy Separation.)

WALL, EXTERIOR   A bearing or nonbearing wall that is used as an enclosing wall for a building other than a party wall or fire wall.

WALL, FIRE   A fire-rated wall that extends continuously from the foundation of a building to or through the roof with sufficient structural stability to allow collapse of one side while leaving the other side intact, typically requiring a 3-hour to 4-hour fire rating.

WALL, PARAPET   The part of any wall that extends above the roof line.

WALL, PARTY   See Fire Wall.

WASTE   The discharge from any plumbing fixture that does not contain solids.

WHEELCHAIR LIFT   See Platform Lift.

WHEELCHAIR SPACE   A space for a single wheelchair and its occupant. (See also Area of Refuge.)

WIRELESS SYSTEM   A system or part of a system that can transmit and receive signals without the aid of a wire.

WORK AREA   See Area, Work.

WORKSTATION   An individual work area created by the arrangement of furniture and/or equipment for use by occupants or employees.

ZONE CABLING   A ceiling distribution method for communication cables in which ceiling spaces are divided into sections or zones so that cables can be run to the center of each zone, allowing for flexible, changeable cabling of open office areas; also called zone distribution.

ZONE, DAYLIGHT   In general, an area below a skylight or adjacent to a vertical fenestration that receives daylight through the fenestration.

ZONE, FIRE   A protected enclosure within a building created by rated walls or a contained fire suppression system that can be controlled separately from other areas of the same building.

ZONE, HVAC   A space or group of spaces within a building with heating or cooling requirements that are similar and are regulated by one heating or cooling device/system.

ZONE, NOTIFICATION   An area within a building or facility covered by notification appliances that activate simultaneously.

INDEX